WhiteB
2

MW01233592

A Complete Appalachian Trail Guidebook

Rick "Attroll" Towle

A Complete Appalachian Trail Guidebook — WhiteBlaze Pages

Copyright © 2019 Rick Towle. All rights reserved.

web site

email

WhiteBlaze Pages
www.whiteblazepages.com
whiteblazepages@gmail.com

Contents

Trail Updates from the Appalachian Trail Conservancy (ATC)
Keep an eye out here for the most up to date trail information or changes.
www.appalachiantrail.org/home/explore-the-trail/trail-updates

Preface

WhiteBlaze Pages is designed for thru hikers, long distance hikers, and section hikers on the Appalachian Trail. Its aim is to assist you in determining your location and surrounding features, and to locate nearby re-supply options and other needed services.

With help from the Appalachian Trail Conservancy (ATC), I have made every effort to make this as up to date as possible; however the trail and its surroundings are constantly changing. If you find any inaccurate or wrong information in this book, I would greatly appreciate it if you would write through the web site or the email listed in this book.

This book was done by hands-on research and data collection. The establishments in this book do not pay to be listed. I receive no funding to produce this book. I currently do not pay anyone for furnishing information.

HELP ME KEEP THIS GUIDE UP TO DATE

I am constantly trying to find ways to improve this guidebook.
If you have any comments, suggestions, corrections or any other information to help me improve the next edition of this guidebook, please contact me at:

WhiteBlaze Pages
www.whiteblazepages.com
whiteblazepages@gmail.com

Printed in the United States of America
First Printing, 2017
978-0-9984562-2-5
WhiteBlaze Publishing
Denmark, ME 04022

Updates and Correction Information

Trail re-routes and other changes often occur after the guidebook has been sent to the printers. You can find the latest corrections at the following web address:
www.whiteblazepages.com/updates/2019/

Acknowledgments

Credits for data collection and inputs to WhiteBlaze Pages are as follows, by name or trail name:
Appalachian Trail Conservancy (ATC)
Alpha-Gal
Richard Anderson
Ed "atraildreamer" Brown
Vic Hasler
Stewart Holt
Michael "Ratjumper" Kinese
LittleRock
Margaret Mills
Mouser999
Jeff Taussig
Will Wright

I would also like to thank the members of the WhiteBlaze hiking community website for their many contributions to this guidebook.

Artwork done by: Geolyn Carvin of Boots Mcfarland. www.bootsmcfarland.com
Geolyn is an avid hiker who enjoys the outdoors. She first handedly captures the joys and frustrations that hikers experience and puts them in her drawings. These drawings are just a sample of what she has done. Visit her web site at www.bootsmcfarland.com

Common reoccurring Appalachian Trail questions

What is the Appalachian Trail?
The Appalachian Trail also known as the "AT" is a National Scenic Trail extending from Springer Mountain, Georgia, to Mount Katahdin, Maine.

How long is the Appalachian Trail?
The trail measured 2,192.0 miles in 2019. The total length of the trail varies slightly each year due to necessary trail re-routes.

How long does it take to thru-hike the entire trail?
If trying to complete the entire trail in one calendar year, it takes between five to seven months to complete. Only about 20 percent of hikers who begin the trail will complete it.

What is a thru hiker?
A thru hiker is someone who is attempting to complete the entire Trail in one calendar year. It does not have to be in one continuous direction, just complete the whole trail.

How much does a thru-hike cost?
The average cost to hike the entire Appalachian Trail as a thru-hike is approximately $3,000, which is about $1.50 per mile. This is just the spending money for hiking the trail. This does not include your gear.

What direction should you hike for a thru-hike, from GA to ME or ME to GA?
You can pick any direction you want.

The direction depends on the hiker and the start date. If you can start in early spring it is better to start in Georgia because the mountains in New England are still very cold and snowy. Most hike northbound, beginning in Georgia anytime from March to April. Southbound hikers generally start in Maine from late May to July.

Some hikers start down south and then realize they will not make it to Mount Katahdin before Baxter State Park closes on mid-Oct. Once they realize this they often jump ahead to Mount Katahdin, and then hike south to where they got off the trail. This is called Flip-Flopping.

Where do thru-hikers stay at night?
Most hikers stay at the many shelters and tent sites along the trail. There is always a shelter or a tent site within a day's walk.

How easy it is to get to a town?
The trail usually crosses a road about every five miles but this does not mean a trail town is close by. In this guidebook, the access points to get to the trail towns are marked at road crossings, along with the distance to them.

Where do thru-hikers get food and other supplies?
They obtain them from trail town grocery stores and other suppliers. Another option is to send pre-prepared packages as a series of mail drops to trail town post offices on, or near the trail. This is having packages sent to you in trail towns along the trail. Some hikers do this to make sure they have food and supplies to last until the next town. See "Mail drop information" in this guide.

They say there are bears, wild boars and poisonous snakes?
There is no need to fear bears, snakes and wild boars as long as you keep your eyes open and stay clear if you should happen to encounter any of them. The best thing a hiker can do is protect their food by hanging it, or using bear bags, or securing it in bear boxes when they are available. http://theultimatehang.com/2013/03/19/hanging-a-bear-bag-the-pct-method/

The following information was provided courtesy of the Appalachian Trail Conservancy

www.ATCamp.org - All thru-hikers and overnight hikers are encouraged to register their plans at ATCamp.org to help alleviate overcrowding. This system allows them to see how many people are already registered and adjust their plans to choose a less crowded date or location, and help preserve the Trail.

Northbound thru-hikers - are strongly advised to start at Amicalola Falls and walk the approach Trail instead of driving to Springer Mountain. This will help alleviate crowding on Springer Mountain (eliminating two-way traffic to and from the Springer parking lot, especially when family accompanies the hiker) and eliminate the possibility of encountering hazardous conditions on muddy, snow or ice-covered forest service roads.

Hikers should allow approximately an hour at the state park visitor center to register, weigh their packs, and attend a brief thru-hiker orientation.

INCIDENTS/EMERGENCIES

In an emergency requiring immediate medical or law-enforcement response - call 9-1-1.

Report the emergency, and then ask the dispatcher to contact National Park Service dispatch 24-hour communications center at 1-866-677-6677. More information about reporting incidents can be found at www.appalachiantrail.org/incidents

If you have an incident with a bear on the A.T. use a Bear Incident Report form available at www.appalachiantrail.org/bears

PLANNING

- Register thru-hikes, and any overnight, or section-hike, at www.ATcamp.org Registering will help you avoid crowded areas and will help preserve the Appalachian Trail.
- Avoid starting on peak days as shown on ATCamp registration charts, e.g., March 1 for Georgia start.
- Monitor the Appalachian Trail Conservancy's Trail's Updates page at www.appalachiantrail.org/updates for trail closures and alerts.
- Carry map and/or guidebooks and compass; while mobile apps can be extremely useful, they are useless when phone batteries run out, when it's cold, or raining
- Stop in at the Appalachian Trail Conservancy (ATC) HQ in Harpers Ferry, WV., to get your photo taken for the official hiker album, (If your goal is to complete hiking the entire A.T.).
- Stop in Monson Visitor Center in Maine for essential info about the 100 Mile Wilderness and Baxter State Park.
- Avoid climbing Katahdin (in Baxter State Park, Maine) on Saturdays if possible. Absolutely avoid climbing on Labor Day Weekend, the busiest weekend of the entire year. Be aware that second half of August is usually the most crowded time when it can be difficult to find a spot.
- If family is visiting you at the end of a northbound thru-hike, consider encouraging them to meet you at Abol Bridge before entering Baxter State Park, where they will get the best view of Katahdin, instead of in the park itself. Parking or camping spots in the park are limited and can be very challenging to obtain, especially during summer months, Labor Day weekend, and on nice fall Saturdays. Also advise them that Katahdin is the most difficult mountain on the entire A.T. and recommended only for those in superior hiking condition. Otherwise, having them tag along will slow you down so you won't be able to summit with your friends, or may even end in a rescue.

REGULATIONS

CAMPING

General

Camping and fire regulations can be found at www.appalachiantrail.org/camping

Site specific (not comprehensive, but highlights the most significant areas)

- You must stay in designated sites only in the following areas (no dispersed or "stealth" camping is allowed). These areas are either high-use or sensitive areas.
  ◇ Great Smoky Mountains National Park, NC/TN
  ◇ Grayson Highlands, VA
  ◇ Va. 624 to US 220, VA (Dragon's Tooth/McAfee Knob/Tinker Cliffs area)
  ◇ Maryland
  ◇ Cumberland Valley, PA
  ◇ Portions of Delaware Water Gap NRA, NJ
  ◇ New Jersey
  ◇ New York
  ◇ Connecticut
  ◇ Massachusetts

Above tree line in White Mountains, NH and other Forest Protection Areas.

Stealth camping is strongly discouraged anywhere in Maine, and is strictly prohibited in Baxter State Park.

Dispersed or "stealth" camping

Dispersed or "stealth" camping is not allowed in the following areas (and others) where there are no designated sites.

◇ Grassy Ridge, NC
◇ Deep Gap, VA
◇ Most valley crossings in Virginia
◇ Cold Mountain
◇ Harpers Ferry National Historical Park
◇ C&O Towpath National Historical Park

- When selecting a dispersed camping site where legal, camp 200' from trails and water
- No stealth camping in towns
- No stealth camping on farmland

CAMPFIRES

- Wherever camping is prohibited, campfires are also prohibited.
- Campfires should be avoided if possible; if constructed, wood pieces should be small enough to break by hand
- Burn only wood; carry out all trash. Burn all wood to ash and do not leave fire pit until completely cold to the touch. Douse with water, if necessary!

Site specific

- Campfires are prohibited in these areas where camping is allowed in designated areas
◇ Annapolis Rock, MD
◇ New Jersey
◇ Connecticut

DOGS

Dogs are not allowed in the following areas:

- Great Smoky Mountains National Park in TN/NC (must be kenneled outside the park)
- Baxter State Park, ME (must be kenneled outside the park)
- Bear Mountain Zoo, NY (a very short alternate road walk is available)

MISCELLANEOUS.

Specific sites:

- No jumping off James River Foot Bridge in central Virginia (it's illegal and people have drowned when trapped by underwater snags)

TRAIL ETHICS & SUSTAINABLE CAMPING PRACTICES

All A.T. hikers should become familiar with the in-depth Leave No Trace (LNT) information available at www.apalachiantrail,org/lnt . Here are some of the specific guidelines found at the LNT site:

FOOD STORAGE & BEARS

- Do not leave food in shelters or along the Trail for other hikers. This leads to trash or problems with animals.
- Always store food and smellables in a bear-resistant container, or hang using PCT method, on a branch at least 18 feet high, 12 feet from the ground, and 6 feet from the trunk. http://theultimatehang.com/2013/03/19/hanging-a-bear-bag-the-pct-method/
- Filter food scraps from your dishwater and pack them out with you, or drink the "grey water."

MISCELLANEOUS

- No cutting switchbacks (this leads to erosion, creates more work for volunteers and creates an eyesore)
- Don't step on vegetation on edge of trails when allowing a person to pass (step onto rock, log, leaves, etc. instead); in muddy areas, avoid widening the path.
- No foraging (eating berries and nuts is fine)
- Do not «tag» shelters, signs or trees with graffiti or carvings. You are encouraged to get creative in shelter trail register

Ethics for Dog Owners

- Dogs should be on a leash at all times and kept away from water sources. Avoid taking dogs into crowded shelters, and always ask permission of other hikers. It is strongly recommended that hikers with dogs always tent.
- Dog should be kept away from springs and other drinking water sources.
- Dispose of your dogs waste as you would your own.
- More info at www.appalachiantrail.org/dogs

Electronics

- If listening to music, wear ear buds/headphones.
- When using cell phones or other electronics, do so out of sight and sound of other people (potentially excluding members of your own party who are comfortable with your use)

RECOMMENDED GEAR for sustainable hiking (in addition to all items that enable hikers to be prepared for all weather conditions they will encounter)

- **-Digging implement** such as a trowel or snow stake to dig a cathole, 200 feet away from trails, campsites, and water.
- **-Bear-resistant canister OR 50' of paracord, waterproof stuff sack, and carabiner** for the PCT-method of hanging food, 6 feet from trunk, hanging 6 feet below an 18' limb. An Ursack in combination with an odor-barrier bag and/or aluminum liner may be acceptable.
- **-Rubber tips for trekking poles** to avoid scarring rocks, disturbing/digging soil which can hasten the spread of invasive species, and eroding the treadway. Tips also reduce noise level.
- **-Tree saver straps for hammocks** – if hammocks are used, straps at least 1" in width should be used to protect trees.
- **-A piece of screening** to filter food scraps from your dishwater and pack them out with you, unless you are eating cold or willing to drink "gray water".

HEALTH & HYGIENE

- Treat all water with chemical, filtration, or UV method.
- Wash bodies, dishes, and clothing 200 feet away from water sources. Use biodegradable soap sparingly.
- When swimming, avoid polluting the water by rinsing off at a distance to remove your excess sunscreen, bug repellent, etc.
- Disperse dishwater and toothpaste, and urinate well-away (at least 100 feet) from shelters and popular campsites.
- Educate yourself on norovirus and how to prevent it at www.appalachiantrail.org/health; if you do suspect you have contracted it, email stomachbug@appalachian-trail.org as soon as possible.

AT THE END OF YOUR HIKE

Report your completion of the entire A.T. to the Appalachian Trail Conservancy to be added to the official registry of 2,000-milers. You'll receive a patch and certificate, and your name will be listed in the ATJourneys magazine and on the ATC website. The is available at www.appalachiantrail.org/ATcompletion.

One day you will wake up and there won't be any more time to do the things you've always wanted. Do it now.
~Paulo Coelho~

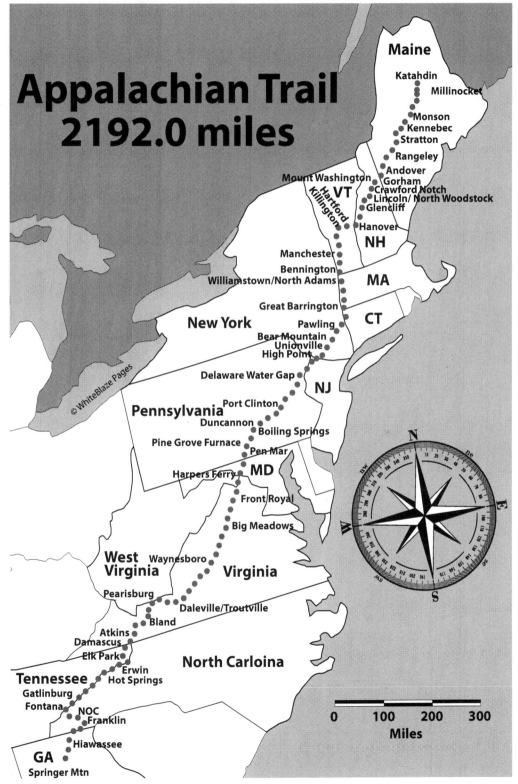

Appalachian Trail
2192.0 miles

Maine

Katahdin
Millinocket
Monson
Kennebec
Stratton
Rangeley
Andover
Mount Washington
Gorham
VT
Hartford
Killington
Crawford Notch
Lincoln/ North Woodstock
Glencliff
Hanover
NH
Manchester
Bennington
Williamstown/North Adams
MA
Great Barrington
New York
Pawling
CT
Bear Mountain
Unionville
High Point
Delaware Water Gap
NJ
Port Clinton
Pennsylvania
Duncannon
Boiling Springs
Pine Grove Furnace
Pen Mar
Harpers Ferry
MD
Front Royal
Big Meadows
West Virginia
Waynesboro
Virginia
Pearisburg
Daleville/Troutville
Bland
Atkins
Damascus
Elk Park
Erwin
North Caroina
Tennessee
Hot Springs
Gatlinburg
Fontana
NOC
Franklin
Hiawassee
GA
Springer Mtn

N
S
E
W

0   100   200   300
Miles

Ellijay

Big Creek Rd

Doublehead Rd

Hawk Mtn Shelter

USFS 42

Mtn Crossings

Blood Mtn Shelter

Suches

P

P

P

P

348

19

75A

Springer Mtn

Gooch Mtn Shelter

52

Winding Stair Rd

60

19

Whitley Gap Shelter

Amicalola Falls State Park

52

52

Dahlonega

515

53

Jasper

Dawsonville

136

53

60

129

53

Gainesville

140

575

19

975

20

Canton

Cumming

Lake Lanier

53

20

140

19

85

92

75

575

19

85

29

75

78

285

Atlanta

78

285

124

20

285

20

N

W   E

S

0   10.0 Mile

Atlanta Airport ✈

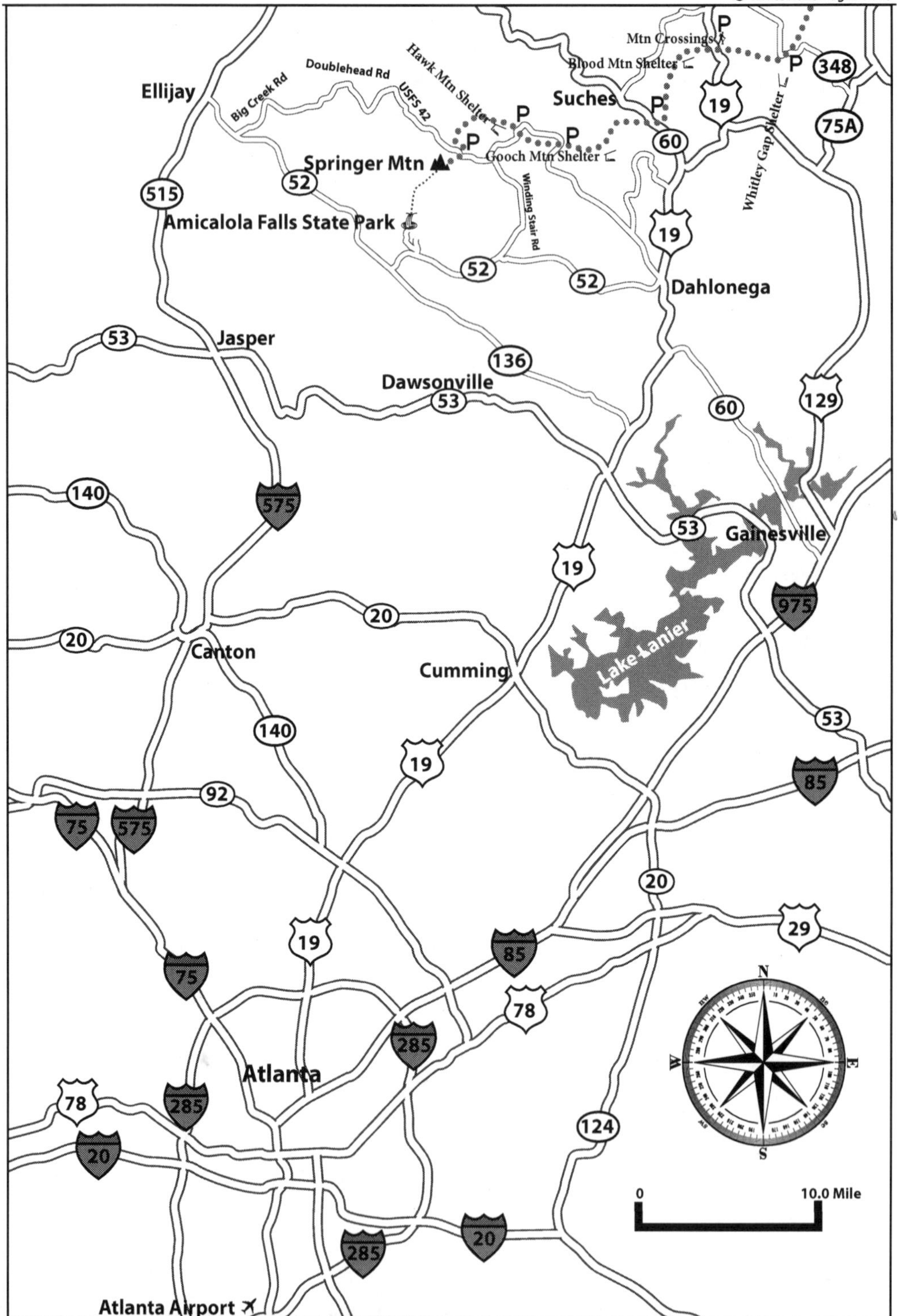

Getting to Springer Mountain

Getting to the Southern Terminus, Springer Mtn

This section provides suggested instructions for getting to Springer Mountain and Mount Katahdin. There are numerous shuttle services mentioned below that will help get you to these locations and other trail heads.

Getting to Springer Mountain

The southern terminus of the Appalachian Trail is on top of Springer Mountain, and is accessible only by foot.

Starting at Amicalola Falls or Big Stamp Gap

There are two factors to consider as to whether you want to start your hike at Big Stamp Gap/USFS 42 or at Amicalola Falls State Park.

1. If starting at Amicalola Falls State Park, you have to hike the Approach Trail that leads to the AT. The Approach Trail is 8.8 miles. The start of the Approach Trail is a staircase of 604 steps. Do you want to add another 8.8 miles onto your already planned 2,000 plus mile hike?

2. If you start at Big Stamp Gap, you are 1.0 miles north on the AT already. If you want to get to Springer Mountain (the actual beginning of the AT) you will have to hike south on the AT for 1.0 miles and then retrace your steps back. This is a very easy hike in and back out. Cost comparisons and time are the factors to consider here. Spending a day traveling from Atlanta to Amicalola Falls and another day to hike up the approach trail, vs. going direct to the AT from the airport and hiking northbound on the AT in about 4 hours after your plane lands.

Springer Mountain, Amicalola Falls State Park, Georgia

The closest major city to the southern terminus of the AT is Atlanta, GA, 103 miles from Big Stamp Gap and the nearest point to get on the AT. It is 82 miles from Amicalola Falls State Park, if you want to hike the Approach Trail. Some shuttle services will pick you up in Atlanta, but it is more economical to take Greyhound or AMTRAK to Gainesville to go 42 miles to Big Stamp Gap or 38 miles from the Amicalola Falls State Park.
Greyhound, https://www.greyhound.com/north
AMTRAK, https://www.amtrak.com/

Suggestions:

Hikers will likely find information directing them from the Atlanta airport to take public transportation (MARTA) from the airport to North Springs Marta station and find a ride to the AT from there. Some have found an Uber ride to Amicalola Falls Park where they climb the 8 mile approach trail to the AT.
MARTA train schedules, https://martaguide.com/train-schedules/

However, shuttle drivers like to avoid the very heavy traffic around North Springs, where snarled traffic often adds 2-3 hours to a trip leaving other hikers waiting. It is much faster to ride directly from the Atlanta airport to the top of Springer Mountain by a route that avoids the GA Hwy 400 traffic. By doing this, you will avoid a long, expensive ride around Atlanta to North Springs, finding transportation to Amicalola, paying for a campsite or a room at the lodge, and spending a day on the Approach Trail.

Going directly to Springer Mountain can save a hiker at least one and a half days by avoiding the Approach Trail out of Amicalola Falls State Park, but costing perhaps $30 more than the North Springs route.

Driving directions to Springer Mountain from Amicalola Falls State Park
Turn right when leaving Highway 52 for 7.8 miles.
Follow Southern Road for 7.8 miles.
Turn right onto Roy Road for 5.0 miles.
Turn right onto Doublehead Road for 2.1 miles until you see Mt. Pleasant Church on your left.
Turn right onto dirt road (Forest Service Road 42 is unsigned).
You should see a large sign indicating that this is the entrance to the Blue Ridge Wildlife Management Area. There should also be a small brown sign saying : "Springer Mt. 6.5 miles".

Driving directions from points in GA
Getting to Springer from points in northern GA
Get on US 76 in northern GA
Follow US 76 east until you get to Ellijay.
Once in Ellijay, follow the direction I mentioned below for Ellijay.

Getting to Springer from Elligay, GA (from western GA)
From Ellijay get on GA 52 East for about 5.3 miles.
Turn left onto Big Creek Road, which will turn into Doublehead Road. Stay on these roads for 12.6 miles.
Turn right onto dirt road (Forest Service Road 42 is unsigned).
You should see a large sign indicating that this is the entrance to the Blue Ridge Wildlife Management Area. There should also be a small brown sign saying : "Springer Mt. 6.5 miles".
Getting to Springer from Dahlonega, GA (from eastern GA)
Follow GA-52 West about 8.9 miles.
Turn right onto Nimblewill Church Road for 2.3 miles.
Turn right onto Forest Service 28-1/FS 28-1 Rd for 2.0 miles.
Turn left on Winding Stair Gap road/FS-77 for 5.0 miles.
Turn left on Forest Service Road for 2.6 miles to Springer Mountain parking lot.

Getting to Springer from southern GA
The best bet for doing this is the find your way to either Ellijay or Dahlonega and follow those drirections as mentioned above.

Shuttles to Springer Mountain/Amicalola Falls State Park:
Richard Anderson 706-276-2520(home) 404-408-2524(cell) richardjanderson@etcmail.com. Based in Ellijay. Hiker Rides from Atlanta Airport or bus station, from Gainesville Amtrak or Greyhound station, to Springer and all points on the AT in Georgia, NC, up to Fontana. Section hiker rides from any trailhead to another, prompt "rescue" rides if your plans change. 10+ years' Experience, reliable, friendly, and on time.
Ron Brown 706-669-0919(cell) 706-636-2825(home) hikershuttles@outlook.com Please leave a message with your phone number if you get voice mail.
Flat rate for shuttles to or from any part of the AT from Atlanta to Fontana and nearby towns, as well as Amicalola Falls S.P., Atlanta airport, and Gainesville, GA.
Dogs welcome; extra stops OK. Fuel on request.
Sam Duke 706-994-6633. Shuttles from Atlanta to Fontana. Based out of Blairsville.
Marty Rogers 678-576-6315(cell) mr814kw@hotmail.com, Based in Atlanta. Shuttles range Atlanta airport, train and bus stations to Amicalola or Springer. Can stop at REI outfitters in-route.
Roadrunner Driving Services 828-524-3265, 706-201-7719 or email where2@mac.com. Based in Franklin, NC. Shuttles range Atlanta to Damascus.
Adam & Christina's Airport Shuttle 479-250-5249, listoe-christina@outlook.com. Texts, call, or emails will be responded to within 24 hours for scheduling. Shuttles from Atlanta airport to trail head. Could also provide hikers with fuel canisters for a fee or be willing to take them by REI or the post office for an additional fee. Would be willing to do more than one shuttle in a day but would like to schedule our trips with a full back seat.

Getting to Northern Terminus, Mount Katahdin

The northern terminus of the Appalachian Trail is on top of Mount Katahdin, and is accessible only by foot.

Mount Katahdin, Baxter State Park, Maine:

Most routes to Mount Katahdin lead through Bangor, Maine, a town with an airport, bus terminal and train station. Bangor is approximately 91 miles from Baxter State Park. Some shuttle services will pick you up in Bangor, but it is more economical to take Cyr Bus Lines (www.johntcyrandsons.com) to Medway, 31 miles from Baxter State Park.

Driving direction to Baxter State Park/Mount Katahdin

From I-95, take exit 244 onto ME 157 heading to Millinocket.
Stay on ME 157 for 11.1 miles, will change into Central Street at the end.
Turn right onto Katahdin Ave for 0.2 miles.
Turn left onto Bates Street/Millinocket Road for 8.4 miles.
You will reach the North Woods Trading Post on your right.
Stay to the right on Baxter Park Road for 8.8 miles.
You will reach Baxter State Park gate.
After going through the gate, you will go left for 7.8 miles to the Katahdin Stream Campground, and the Birches Lean-to and campground. Follow the signs.

Getting to Medway and Millinocket area:

🚌Cyr Bus Lines Station, 153 Gilman Falls Ave, Old Town, ME 04468
800-244-2335, 207-827-2335, 207-827-2010 (www.johntcyrandsons.com)
Depart Bangor 6pm - arrive Medway 7:40pm, fare $10.50
Depart Medway 9:30am - arrive Bangor 11:10am
🚌Shaw's Hiker Hostel 207-997-7069, Monson, ME, shuttles covering all of Maine.

Shuttles and Taxis to Baxter State Park from the Medway Millinocket area:

🚌Town Taxi 207-723-2000, 207-447-3474 Rides from Medway to Millinocket $12, from Millinocket to Abol Bridge $45, Millinocket to Katahdin Stream/The Birches $55.
🚌Maine Quest Adventures 207-746-9615, 207-746-9615 (www.mainequestadventures.com) Medway, ME, will pick up at Medway bus station and drop off at Katahdin Stream or Abol Bridge $50, if late in the afternoon, stay at base camp and tent on lawn for free, access to bathroom (no shower), shuttles to Monson and parts of 100 Mile Wilderness, phone off late fall until spring.
🚌The Appalachian Trail Lodge 207-723-4321 (www.appalachiantraillodge.com) Millinocket, ME, shuttles within 150 miles.

Friends and family joining you in Baxter State Park

If friends and family are planning on meeting up and hiking with you in Baxter State Park, you should contact Park Headquarters, at 207-723-5140, well in advance. This will allow you to check on current park rules and regulations, visitor and day use fees, availability of park campsites and reservations. Reservations availability usually improve after the Labor Day weekend.

Profiles and their icons

The profiles are in 30 mile increments.
The icons on the profiles are placed in reference to their location on the trail as if you are hiking in the northward direction on the Appalachian Trail.
- If the icon is above the profile image, this means it is to the west side of the trail.
- If the icon is below the profile image, this means it is to the east side of the trail.

For off-trail locations, the icons in the profiles are oriented in the following manner:
- Icons above the profile line depict items located on the west side of the trail.
- Icons beneath the profile line depict items located on the east side of the trail.

Directions and mileages as mentioned in this book
When referring to North on the Appalachian Trail, it will always be the direction that leads to Mount Katahdin.

When physically on the Appalachian Trail
For North bound hikers: West is Left and East is Right.
For South bound hikers: West is Right and East is Left.

When stepping off the Appalachian Trail
When off the AT on a side trail or anything other than being on the AT, all directions will be either left or right. This applies the same to North bound and Soutbound hikers.

Mileages
Mileages are in miles and tenths. If you see something like (1.3), this means 1.3 miles. If you see something like (1.3W), this means 1.3 to the west. (1.3E) would mean 1.3 to the east.

Description of maps in this book
The maps in this guidebook will display what is of greatest interest to hikers. Priority is given to short and long-term re-supply options, (convenience & full-service grocery stores), post offices, pharmacies, laundry, showers, hostels and other lodgings. Other services will be listed on the maps, as space permits..

The maps are drawn to scale with a north is up direction and has a scale-mile legend on each map. Shows the direction on how to get back to the Appalachian Trail and the mileage. If the Appalachian Trail is on the map it will be noted.

Shuttle providers and their locations in this guidebook
Shuttle providers are listed in this guidebook by the location of their base of operations. This means where they reside and their proximity to the Appalachian Trail.

Always read a little ahead in the guidebook, or check a little behind, and read the description of local shuttle providers to determine if they cover your section of the AT, and the destination you wish to reach.

Understanding the white and blue blazes

White blazes
These blazes are normally 2"x6" in size. The single white blaze is most common, but a double white blaze (two blazes stacked on top of one another) indicate a sharp turn in the trail. On a double blaze the top blaze indicates the direction the trail is turning. If the blaze is to the right of the lower blaze, the trail is turning right. If the blaze is to the left of the lower blaze, the trail is turning left. The white blazes are usually within eyesight of each other but this is not always the case. Over time, the white blazes, and blazes of any color, can fade away and completely disappear.

Blue blazes
These blazes are normally 2"x6" in size. The single blue blaze is most common. A blue blaze is the indication of a spur trail branching off of the Appalachian Trail. Blue blazed trails could lead to a vista, water source, shelter or campground, or some unusual natural feature. The blue blazed trails may be dead ends but not always. This means that it would be an out-and-back walk to something like a vista. A blue-blazed trail can be an alternate route that allow you to bypass sections of the trail for various reasons. Blue-blazed trails generally rejoin the AT in a mile or two.

AT Passports

For centuries hikers of the Camino de Santiago Trail in Spain required a "passport" to stay in some municipal and parish Albergues. The passport has spaces for stamps, this proved that you have walked that day and are entitled to stay in an Albergue, (pilgrims only hostels), if there is space, they are valid for walkers and cyclist.

The AT Passport is a little different, as a passport is not a requirement to stay at hostels. There are a lot more than just hostels on the AT Passport. The intention of the passport is to document your journey, at designated locations along the trail and in trail towns. These are establishments with stamps that hikers can collect.

The passport often ends up being a treasured possession as it is a great reminder of all the places you have stopped at or stayed overnight. The stamps are all different, no two stamps are alike.

We have provided extra pages in the back of this guidebook for your personal notes, contact information for other AT hikers you may have met, and AT passport stamps that you can collect as keepsakes.

Trail Names and how they are derived

A trail name is a name that you can either give to yourself or someone will give you. Often times you are given a name from another hiker for an event or something that you did.

An example of this is a person named "Giggles". They received there trail name because they giggled a lot. There was another person that I know with the trail name of Nature's Own. They received the trail name because they used the plastic bags from the bread Nature's Own for boot liners when hiking in snow.

Beware... if someone gives you a trail name, and you answer to it, even once, there is a very strong possibility that you will get stuck with it.

Bear Safety and Canisters

- Cook and eat your meals 200 feet away from your tent or shelter, so food odors do not linger.

- The ATC recommends carrying a bear resistant canister—constructed with solid, non-pliable material and designed to resist bears—to store your food and "smellables." Although canisters do add bulk and weight, there are a number of benefits to carrying a bear canister.

- Where bear boxes, poles, or cable systems are provided, use them. Never leave trash in bear boxes, feed bears, or leave food for them. Do not burn food wrappers, or leftovers, or leave them in fire pits. This may attract bears.

- Where food storage devices are not provided, and if you are not carrying a canister, hang your food, cookware, toothpaste, personal hygiene items, and even water bottles (if you use drink mixes in them) 12 feet from the ground, 6 feet from the trunk, and 6 feet from the limb from which it hangs. The PCT Method of hanging is considered more effective than tying off a rope to a tree trunk.

- Avoid becoming complacent when storing your food. Just because there have been no reports of bear activity in the area does not mean that bears are not present. All it takes is one food bag that is not hung properly to change a bear's habits.

- Improperly stored food may lead to a bear becoming habituated to human food. Whether a bear is fed intentionally or unintentionally, a fed bear is a dead bear.

Prices in this book

The prices in this book are subject to change. When I call around, I called at the end of the previous year. The establishments gave me what they thought their prices would be for this year. They are not committed to stick to their prices.

Stealth Camping

What is stealth camping?

Stealth camping is camping at a non-designated camp site.

Most of the time hiker's stealth camp not on purpose but when they are at the end of the hiking day and realize they are too far to make it to the next designated campsite or shelter.

Is stealth camping illegal?

It is allowed in some areas, especially along portions of the southern third of the A.T., which means you can legally choose your own campsite. However, hikers are always encouraged to use designated sites, as you will have fewer impacts on vegetation and wildlife habitat and will keep the Trail corridor looking natural and pristine.

Stealth camping means leaving no impact on the environment — this means no camp-fires.

Notes, information, and warnings

Springs and water sources - The purity of springs and water along the Appalachian Trail from natural sources cannot be guaranteed. All water should be treated before use.

Pet owners - Carry an up-to-date vaccination certificate for your pet(s) with you at all times, a lot of localities are pretty strict about that. Keep your pet(s) on a monthly regimen of heartworm and flea & tick medications for the health of you and your pet(s).

Heartworm can be transmitted through mosquitoes. Fleas can carry and transmit typhus, plague, "cat scratch disease", and tapeworms that may infect your pet(s). Ticks transmit Lyme disease, Rocky Mountain spotted fever, relapsing fever, ehrlichiosis, tularemia and tick paralysis.

Most of these diseases can be transmitted from pets to humans.

http://www.petsandparasites.org/resources/fleas-ticks-your-pet/

Parking coordinates - The parking coordinates are not always 100% accurate but should get you within eyesight of the parking area. Always do your research ahead of time on the parking area to make sure there are no issues with using the parking area.

Hammocks and hammock camping - When the hammock icon is displayed it means that there are possibilities for hammocks in that area. In some cases you may have to branch out up to 100 feet or so beyond the area to find good trees. Hanging also varies from season to season due to the growth of the underbrush.

When using a hammock, please use Leave No Trace (LNT) procedures.

White Mountains - The AMC maintains campsites on the Appalachian Trail in the White Mountains from Eliza Brook south of South Kinsman in Franconia Notch to Speck Pond in Maine, including Hermit Lakes shelter in Tuckerman Ravine and 4 sites along the Grafton loop trail in Grafton Notch in Maine. Every one of these sites has space for hammocks. The caretakers usually have a place in mind not over platforms (need that space for tents) somewhere within the site, usually 3 or 4 sites known for hammocks.

There is no camping of any kind within the Forest Protection Area (FPA) at every hut in the White Mountain, this includes hammocks. The FPA is a quarter mile circle around the hut. Every hut has an FPA. This is a U.S. Forest Service law, not an AMC rule.

Establishment prices - The data and prices for establishments were collected by calling around, usually in the winter before this book went to the printers. This means the establishment owners or proprietors gave the prices for the upcoming year. Sometimes these prices were estimates. They are not obligated to maintain these prices. Not all prices listed in this book include tax. Keep in mind that listed prices may not include state and local taxes that are added to the listed price.

GPS formatting

I am in the process of changing the GPS formatting form DD MM.MMM to DDD.DDDD. I was not able to complete the process before I sent the book to the printers. You will find both formats in the book this year. I am sorry for the inconvenience.

Trail Tidbits

Dryer use for laundry - The dryers you will use on the trail are mostly gas. They can get very hot. Synthetics (poly/plastic things) will usually do OK for one cycle. Keep an eye out regardless. The second cycle will definitely melt some sock liners, stiffeners in certain hats, sleeping bags (yikes) etc.

Pictures - Start early. Take lots of pics of people. Lots of pics of shelter life, the woods, etc. but be sure and start early on people and write their names down. You will be very thankful of this later. It's better to take too many pictures, then a few more.

Chaffing - Many have this problem early.
All the creams and ointments in the world are great for AFTER the fact.
Even not wearing underwear under your shorts or pants does not work all the time as the salt builds up on your pants and chafes you anyway. With Spandex there is no rubbing, and it is light, durable, offers good support, and dries well, (overnight, in the sleeping bag), when damp. Others wear a kilt with nothing underneath.

Do your business before you head into a town - In town you can't just relieve yourself anywhere, like you are used to doing on the trail. Before you go to town, especially if you are hitching a ride, take your money holder, wallet, or whatever you use to hold your cash, credit/debit cards and Ids, and keep it on your person, in case you should get separated from your pack.

Trail and shelter registers - Read them, many tidbits of info can sometimes be found here. Write in them, if anyone is trying to get hold of you this will help a lot. It is a good security measure as it narrows down the search area significantly.

Caffeine - Be careful. Your body is not used to high doses (daily coffee drinkers ignore) of caffeine and drinking a lot in town WILL keep you up all night.
Be advised that iced-tea in the south is real tea and has caffeine.

The Four W's - Water, Weather, Weight and Where is the next blaze. Order varies with mood of hiker.

~ Walking Home ~

It's yours for the taking.
All you have to do is put one foot in front of the other.
Your the only one that can make it happen.
Hike Your Own Hike

`Attroll`

Abbreviations

AT or A.T. - Appalachian Trail
ATC – Appalachian Trail Conservancy
AMC – Appalachian Mountain Club
AYCE – All You Can Eat
AYH - American Youth Hostels
BMT - Benton MacKaye Trail
BRP - Blue Ridge Parkway
BSP - Baxter State Park
B/L/D - Breakfast/lunch/dinner
DOC – Dartmouth Outing Club
EAP – Each addition person
ETA - Estimated Date of Arrival
FedEx - Federal Express
GMC – Green Mountain Club
HYOH - Hike Your Own Hike
KSC - Katahdin Stream Campground
LT – Long Trail
LNT – Leave No Trace
MATC - Maine Appalachian Trail Club
MP - Mile Point or Mile Post
NHP - National Historical Park
NOC - Nantahala Outdoor Center
NPS – National Park Service
PATC - Potomac Appalachian Trail Club
PP – Per Person
SDMP - Skyline Drive Milepost
SMNP - Smoky Mountain National Park
SNP - Shenandoah National Park
USFS - United States Forest Service
USGS - United States Geological Survey
UPS - United Parcel Service
USPS - U.S. Postal Service
WFS - Work For Stay

It all begins and
ends in your mind.
What you give power to,
has power over you,
if you allow it.
~Leon Brown~

Mail drop information

When sending mail drops, whether to a Post Office or to business it should include the following information.

- Real name, don't use trail names.
- The "C/O" is important when sending a mail drop to any business. If you do not include this information you may not be able to pick-up your mail.
- ETA, estimated date of your arrival.
- ID's are required at Post Offices and some establishments to pick up mail.
- Don't send anything other than General Delivery mail to the Post Offices.
- Common courtesy, don't send mail drops to a lodgings or facilities if you don't plan on staying with them.

Post Office mail drops:

Joe Smith
C/O General Delivery
Town Name, VA 56789
Please hold for AT hiker
ETA March 19, 2019

Business mail drops:

Joe Smith
C/O Business Name
1920 Springer Ave
Town Name, VA 56789
Please hold for AT hiker
ETA March 19, 2019

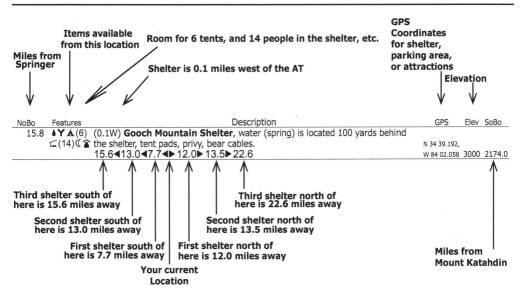

Icons in this book

The icons are intended for quick reference to help you see what is available at that specific location. Read to the left in the description column for that location to see a better explanation of that particular item or icon. Icons may have a different meaning depending on the location they reference.

Icons   Descriptions

Icons	Descriptions
★ ★ ★ ★ ★	See notes and establishments listed below this entry.
♦	Source of drinking water. Water is always listed first
◊	Seasonal water source, not always reliable (unreliable)
Y	Intersection, junction, side trail, connecting trail or adjoining trail.
⌒	Footbridge or any other bridge
⟑	Power line or electrical wires
⌣	Possibilities for hammocks available. In some cases you may have to expand up to 100 feet beyond the area to find trees but you can hang. Availability of hanging also depends on the growth of the underbrush. When using a hammock, please use LNT procedures.
⋀	(x) Tent sites, may sometimes be listed with (capacity) or tent platforms
⌂	(x) AT Shelter and (capacity)
ℭ	Privy
î	Bear cables or bear box available for food bags
◐	●●● Cell phone signal strength, based on a nice clear day.
$	Overnight/caretaker fee. On town maps it represents a bank.
▲	Summit or crest
◀▶	Direction and miles to next shelter South or North. This does not include the mileage distance the shelter is off the trail.
📷	Views, overlooks or photo opportunities
🗼	Lookout, fire tower or observation tower
⚑	Water falls
●	Attractions, important or historical features, other photo opportunities
🛣	Road, gravel road, logging road, woods road, or any other road
P	(x) Parking. Vehicle capacity, and fee inside parenthesis. If there is a fee there will be a "$". Coordinates should get you within eyesight of parking area. Always check ahead for parking safety.
♀	GPS coordinates are listed in the GPS column or in the description
✕	Railroad crossing, tracks
⚓	Swimming possibilities
⛱	Picnic Table or picnic area
🗑	Trash can usually available
⛵	Boating or boats available for use
✉	Post Office
⌂	Hostel
⛺	Lodging. Do not depend on the prices to include tax.
◈	AT Passport location. Get your book stamp here. (www.atpassport.com). When icon is on maps, it referres to the Appalachian Trail.
⊗	No Pets
⛏	Work For Stay (WFS)
⚒	Fuel for stove
△	Laundry
💻	Computer available for use
📶	WiFi available
🚿	Shower available to use with out stay
🎒	Slackpacking may be available
🚌	Shuttle, Bus or Taxi
✉	Mail drop location
🏧	Bank/ATM
🛒	Long term resupply
🏪	Short term resupply
🍴	Anywhere that serves food for a f
☎	Pay phone or public phone
🏃	Outfitter
✖	Hardware store
🚻	Public Restroom
⚕	Pharmacy
✚	First Aid, doctor, hospital or urgent care
🐕	Vet or Kennel. When listed in descriptions, it refers to dogs
✂	Barber
①	Information Area
🍸	Purchase or serves alcohol
🎬	Movie Theater
■	Not categorized
✈	Airport or airfield
🚏	Bus or bus station
🚆	Train or train station

Elevation profile with labeled features (NoBo, miles 0–30):
Springer Mtn/AT Southern Terminus, Springer Mtn Shelter, Big Stamp Gap/USFS Rd 42, Benton Mackaye Tr, Davis Creek, Rich Mtn, Stover Creek Shelter, Stover Creek, Three Forks Creek/USFS Rd 58, Long Creek Falls, Hickory Flats/USFS Rd 251, Hawk Mtn Campsite, Hawk Mtn Shelter, Hightower Gap/USFS Rd 42/69, Horse Gap/USFS Rd 42, Sassafras Mtn, Cooper Gap/USFS Rd 42/80, Justus Creek, Blackwell Creek, Gooch Mtn Shelter, Gooch Gap/USFS Rd 42, Ramrock Mtn, Woody Gap/GA Hwy 60, Big Cedar Mtn, Augerhole Gap, Dan Gap, Miller Gap, Lance Creek, Burnett Field Mtn, Jarrard Gap, Gaddis Mtn, Woods Hole Shelter, Slaughter Creek Gap, Blood Mtn Shelter

NoBo	Features	Description	GPS	Elev	SoBo
0	Y▲O♀	**Springer Mountain**, rock overlook at summit. AT bronze plaque located here and register located in rock. Blue blaze trail is the Approach Trail from Amicalola Falls. **Don't forget your starting photo and to sign the register**	N 34 37.603, W 84 11.633	3782	2192.0
0.2	◊Y▲(18) ⊑(12) ⌣((🐻(2) ♀	(0.2E) **Springer Mountain Shelter**, water (spring) 80 yards on a blue blazed trail in front of the shelter but is known to go dry, tenting, privy, 2 bear boxes. Benton MacKaye Trail (southern terminus) is located 50 yards north on the AT. ▶2.6▶7.9▶15.5	N 34 37.760, W 84 11.565	3730	2191.8
1.0	▲P(25)♀	Cross **USFS 42**, Big Stamp Gap. Information board. P Parking fee.	N 34 38.240, W 84 11.709	3350	2191.0
1.3	Y	Junction with Benton MacKaye Trail.		3430	2190.7
1.6	◊	Cross Davis Creek and small tributary		3235	2190.4
1.9	Y	Rich Mountain ridge crest. Benton MacKaye trail junction east.		3303	2190.1
2.6	◊	Cross Stover Creek		2993	2189.4
2.8	◊Y▲(3) ⊑(16) ⌣((🐻♀	(0.1E) **Stover Creek Shelter**, water behind shelter is often dry but good water can be found where trail crosses Stover Creek 100 yards north of shelter, tent pads, privy, bear cables. 2.6◀▶5.3▶12.9▶24.9	N 34 39.017, W 84 11.832	2954	2189.2
2.9	◊	Cross Stover Creek			2189.1
3.8	◊	Cross Stover Creek		2660	2188.2
4.2	Y	Junction with Benton MacKaye to the east, Duncan Ridge Trail to west		2580	2187.8
4.3	◊▲⌣▲ P(5-6)♀	Cross **USFS 58**, Three Forks. Stover Creek, Chester Creek, and Long Creek all converge here. Parking.	N 34 39.809, W 84 11.037	2530	2187.7
5.2	◊Y⚒	Trail junctions to Long Creek Falls, Benton MacKaye and Duncan Ridge Trails. BMT is marked with white diamonds, Duncan Ridge is marked with blue blazes to the west, Long Creek is also blue blazed.		2800	2186.8
6.2	▲🏠 P(6-8)	Cross **USFS 251**, Hickory Flats, picnic pavilion, Hickory Flats cemetery is located (0.1) west		3000	2185.8
7.4	◊▲(30)	Ridgecrest below Hawk Mountain, campsite, tent pads.		3250	2184.6
8.0	◊	Cross Stream, skirts the side of Hawk Mountain		3191	2184.0
8.1	◊Y▲ ⊑(12) ⌣((🐻♀	(0.2W) **Hawk Mountain Shelter**, water is located 400 yards on a blue blazed trail behind the shelter, tent pads, privy, bear cables. 7.9◀5.3◀▶7.6▶19.6▶20.8	N 34 39.965, W 84 08.183	3194	2183.9
8.6	▲P(8)♀	Cross **USFS 42/69**, Hightower Gap, parking.	N 34 39.818, W 84 07.786	2854	2183.4
10.5	▲P(6-8) ♀	Cross Horse Gap. USFS 42 is visible to the west.	N 34 39.344, W 84 06.348	2673	2181.5
11.5	▲	Sassafras Mountain, summit		3336	2180.5
12.2	▲P(6)♀	Cross **USFS 42/80**, Cooper Gap, parking	N 34 39.183, W 84 05.070	2800	2179.8
13.5	▲	Cross logging road		3024	2178.5
14.2	◊	Cross Justus Creek		2564	2177.8
14.4	Y◊▲	Trail to the west to tent pads. Water source is Justus Creek		2626	2177.6
14.9	◊	Cross Small stream		2605	2177.1

NoBo	Features	Description	GPS	Elev	SoBo
15.3	♦	Cross Blackwell Creek		2601	2176.7
15.7	♦Υ▲(12) ◁(14) ⏃ ⦅☎⚲	(0.1W) **Gooch Mountain Shelter**, water (spring) is located 100 yards behind the shelter, tent pads that can accommodate two tents each, privy, bear box. 15.5◀12.9◀7.6◀▶ 12.0▶ 13.2▶22.3	N 34 39.344, W 84 02.999	3000	2176.3
16.9	♦▲P⚲	Cross **USFS 42**. Gooch Gap, Water is located north 100 yards north and east 200 yards on a blue blazed trail.	N 34 39.126, W 84 01.938	2821	2175.1
17.0	♦	Marked trail to water 230 yards east on old road.		2804	2175.0
17.9	▲	Cross abandoned road.		2955	2174.1
18.2		Liss Gap		3032	2173.8
18.8		Jacks Gap		3045	2173.2
19.0	📷	Follow crest of Ramrock Mountain, rock outcropping, views to south.		3260	2173.0
19.3		Tritt Gap		3031	2172.7
20.5	♦▲⌷⁋ ⇌P(40)⚲ ★★★★★	Cross **GA. 60**, Woody Gap, picnic area, water (spring) is located (0.1) west of the AT on northern side of the gap.	N 34 40.659, W 83 59.987	3198	2171.5

⌂⇌ ◈ ⚱⇟ ⬤⇌⌧ ⚲	(6.0E) **The Hiker Hostel @ Barefoot Hills Hotel** 770-312-7342 reservations@barefoothills.com (www.barefoothills.com) ◈ AT Passport Location. Open year round. ⌂ Single bunk accommodations in hostel priced from $25+ per night, depending upon day of week, seasonality and general availability. ⇌ Private rooms and cabins begin at $95+ for up to two guests. Group rates and specials available. Discount for active and retired military personnel during direct reservation call. All stays include free continental breakfast, new bed linens and towels, and shower. ✗ Hot breakfast, lunch and dinner available for purchase. Beer, wine, bottled water and Coca-Cola products available for purchase in cans or bottles. ⌂ Limited retail supplies available for purchase onsite including ⚱ canister fuel, hiking gear, supplies, and dried food. P Overnight parking, △ laundry service and ⚓ kayak rentals also available (for registered guests only). ⬤ Free WiFi is available, and all accommodations are equipped with smart televisions for use with personal NetFlix, Hulu and other streaming services. ⬤ Ask about shuttles to and from select trail heads and gaps, local wineries, and downtown Dahlonega for an extra fee. ⚲ N 34 36.791, W 83 57.907 ⌧ Mail drops: (USPS/FedEx/UPS) 7693 US Highway 19N, Dahlonega, GA 30533.		

Thru Hiker Special: (Feb. 1, 2019 - April 30, 2019): Shuttle pickup, at a cost, based upon availability and pre-existing reservation payment and confirmation, from Atlanta North Springs MARTA Station (Sunday, Monday, Tuesday & Thursday) and Gainesville bus station (Wednesday only) with confirmed overnight stay in bunk (or upgrade to rooms & cabins, as available). Free continental breakfast, and group shuttle to Amicalola Falls or Springer Mountain the next morning.
A portion of the all proceeds from our Thru Hiking Special is donated to the Appalachian Trail Conservancy.

Suches, GA (2.0W)

⌂ ◈⌂ △⚱⬤⌧ ⚲	**Wolfpen Gap Country Store** 706-747-2271. ◈ AT Passport location. ⌂ Store: M–Th 8am–8pm, F 8am-9pm, Sa 9am–9pm, Su 9am–7pm. ⚱ Coleman fuel by the ounce & canisters. Full menu, with hamburgers, chicken, philly cheese steaks, etc served Thursday - Sunday. **Hostel:** ⌂ Bunks $32 for a bunk with an $18 deposit. ⚱ Non-guest shower $5. Pickup at Woody or Gooch Gap $5 to $10 each way. Accepts all major credit cards. ⬤ Shuttles for a fee to all Georgia Trail heads. Also a designated Post Office. N 34 41.363, W 84 01.322. ⌧ Mail drops: 41 Wolf Pen Gap Rd, Suches, GA 30572.		
⇌⌂▲✗ ⌂⚲	(7W) **Wildcat Lodge and Campground** 706-973-0321. Open year round. ⌂ $15 bunkroom, ▲ $15 camping. ⇌ Lodge room sleeps 8 $100, $25EAP. ⌂⚱ Camp store has Coleman and canister fuel. ✗ Diner serves Breakfast and lunch. ⚲ N 34 43.171, W 84 04.030		
■	**Jim and Ruth Ann Miner** 706-747-5434. Lives in town and are available if you need help.		
⬤	**Suches Hiker Shuttles** 678-967-9510, texting works best in the mountains. Murris Miller, ask for Murris. 24/7 emergency service. To and from any location in GA or Western NC, Dogs OK. Based out of Suches, GA.		

NoBo	Features	Description	GPS	Elev	SoBo
21.9	📷⚲	Rocky face of Big Cedar Mountain, Preaching Rock, rock outcrop just south of summit.	N 34 41.231, W 83 59.644	3737	2170.1
22.3	♦	Small spring to west in Augerhole Gap		3624	2169.7
22.8	♦	Cross small stream on east slop of ridge.		3310	2169.2
22.9		Dan Gap		3261	2169.1
23.6	♦ΥP	Miller Gap. Cross Dockery Lake Trail. Spring about 100 yards east on Dockery Lake Trail. Dockery Lake Trail leads (3.5) east top Dockery Lake Recreation area.		3050	2168.4
24.0	♦▲(4)⏝	Lance Creek, tent pads are located 100 yards north on the creek.		2880	2168.0
25.7		Flat area known as Burnett Field Mountain		3480	2166.3
26.1	◊	Water (spring) unreliable		3330	2165.9
26.3	♦Υ▲ ★★★★★	Jarrard Gap, USFS, water (stream) is located (0.3) west. Jarrard Gap Trail (1.0) west to Lake Winfield Scott.		3250	2165.7

🏕🚿🍴🚰 (1.0W) on the Jarrad Gap Trail (blue blazed) to **Lake Winfield Scott Recreation Area** (www.cfaia.org/lake-winfield-scott-recreation-area-campgrounds-in-georgia) 🏕 $18 Tent sites for 5 persons and two vehicles, 🚿🍴 showers and bathrooms. Parking coordinates. 🚰 N 34 44.420, W 83 53.520.

"Bear canisters seasonally required for camping between Jarrard Gap and Neel Gap"
A new U.S. Forest Service rule requires approved bear-resistant storage containers for overnight camping on a 5-mile stretch of the A.T. in the Chattahoochee National Forest between Jarrard Gap and Neel Gap, between March 1 and June 1 each year. This stretch is located between points **26.7 and 31.7** miles north of the southern terminus of the A.T. at Springer Moutain, Georgia, and includes Woods Hole Shelter, Slaughter Creek Campsite, and Blood Mountain Shelter. **Bear canisters should be used to store food, food containers, garbage and toiletries.**

NoBo	Features	Description	GPS	Elev	SoBo
26.7	📷	Reach shoulder of Gaddis Mountain.		3536	2165.3
27.7	🚰🍴🏕 ⛺(7) ☾🍴🐻 🚰	Bird Gap (0.4W) **Woods Hole Shelter**, water (stream) on trail to shelter is unreliable in dry months, privy, tenting, bear cables. 24.9◀19.6◀12.0◀▶ 1.2▶ 10.3▶15.1 Bird Gap, Freeman Trail just east bypasses Blood Mtn. and rejoins AT at Flatrock Gap	N 34 44.228, W 83 57.300	3650	2164.3
28.0	🚰🍴🏕🚰	Slaughter Creek Trail at Slaughter Creek Gap, water is unreliable.	N 34 44.239, W 83 58.416	3790	2164.0
28.1	🏕(8)	Slaughter Creek campsite to the west, tent pads. **Fires are not permitted**.		3800	2163.9
28.9	⛺(8) ☾🏕📷🚰	Blood Mountain, open rocky summit. **Blood Mountain Shelter**, is located south of summit, no water at shelter, privy, view. **Fires are not permitted**. 20.8◀13.2◀1.2◀▶ 9.1▶13.9▶21.2	N 34 44.399, W 83 56.243	4461	2163.1
29.5	📷	Trail follows steep rock slope with views		4334	2162.5

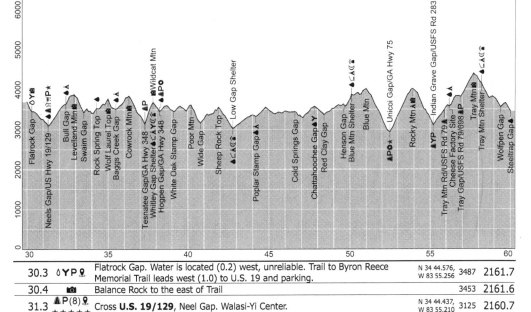

NoBo	Features	Description	GPS	Elev	SoBo
30.3	🚰🍴🏕🅿🚰	Flatrock Gap. Water is located (0.2) west, unreliable. Trail to Byron Reece Memorial Trail leads west (1.0) to U.S. 19 and parking.	N 34 44.576, W 83 55.256	3487	2161.7
30.4	📷	Balance Rock to the east of Trail		3453	2161.6
31.3	🏕🅿(8)🚰 ★★★★★	Cross **U.S. 19/129**, Neel Gap. Walasi-Yi Center.	N 34 44.437, W 83 55.210	3125	2160.7

🍴🏠⬨🅂 **Mountain Crossings** 706-745-6095. (www.mountaincrossings.com)
🛒🚿⛺🚗 ⬨ AT Passport location.
📧🚰 Open year round. 🛒🍴 Store hours change seasonally, closed Christmas. Full service outfitter. Store hours: M-Th 8am-5pm and F-Su 8:30am-6pm. Will do a gear shakedown for you, if you would like, just ask. Long term resupply. 🍶 Alcohol by the ounce.
Hostel: Hostel is open year round.
🅂 Absolutely NO PETS in hostel, leaving your animal outside while you stay in the hostel is NOT an option. No reservations. First come, first in. 🏠 Bunkroom $20 includes shower with towel. 🏕 Free camping out back. 🚿 Shower without stay $5, includes towel and soap. ⛛ Laundry $5. Ask about shuttles. Outgoing shipping is available. 🚰 N 34 44.110, W 83 55.073
📧 Mail drops (USPS/UPS/FedEx) held for 2 weeks, $1 donation fee upon pickup, 12471 Gainesville Hwy, Blairsville, GA 30512.

🛏 ◈ (0.3E) **Blood Mountain Cabins** 706-745-9454. (www.bloodmountain.com)
⛺🏪🏕🔧 ◈ AT Passportlocation.
🛏 Cabin includes full kitchen and bath, satellite TV, holds 4 adults and 2 children. 2 Pet friendly cabins. All linens, toiletries and paper products provided. Thru-hiker rate $72 is a walk in rate only. ⛺ Free laundry with stay. 🛒 Free WiFi in the store.
🏪 **Country store** on-site that offers Hunt Brothers Pizza and wings. Also sells sandwiches, ice cream, soft drinks, snacks and candy. 🧭 N 34 43.970, W 83 55.262

🛏⛺🛒🍴 (10.4) **Misty Mountain Inn & Cottages** 706-745-4786. (www.mistymountainproperties.com)
🍴🧭 New owners in 2016, Craig Griffiths.
🛏 B&B rooms without breakfast $108, additional $10 includes breakfast. 6 Cottages available in sizes range for 1 to 6 people, price range from $105 to $125. Full kitchen and bath. ⛺ Laundry, 🛒 free WiFi.
🚗 Shuttles: Free pickup and return from Neel Gap, Tesnatee and Hogpen Gap. 🔧 Slackpacking included with multi night stay. 🧭 N 34 49.918, W 83 52.853
Shuttle Services: Year round

🍴🧭 (7.5W) **Jim's Smokin' Que (BBQ)** 706-835-7427 (jimssmokinque.com) M-W closed, Th-Sa 11am-8pm, Sun closed. Mini golf available. 🧭 N 34 49.313, W 83 54.238

🚶♿🧭 (13.1) **Blairsville Bikes and Hikes** 706-745-8141.
M-F 10am-5:30pm, Sat 10am-3pm, Sun closed. 🔧Fuel and 🥾hiker food available "Hiking essentials". 🧭 N 34 52.547, W 83 57.555

🚗P **Neels Gap AT Shuttle** Devison Kuhlmann: 720-318-4800 Text/call, NeelsGapShuttle@gmail.com. 7 miles from Neels Gap. Up to 3 Passengers (ask if more). Shuttles from the Approach Trail/Springer Mtn. to Dicks Creek Gap, US 76, all points in between; Shuttles to/from Atlanta airport & Gainesville GA Greyhound

🚗 P **The Further Shuttle Appalachian** 772-321-0905, 706-400-9105.
(www.thefurthershuttleappalachian.com)
24/7 service year round. Based out of Blairsville, GA. Donald Ballard.
Shuttles from Atlanta, GA to Davenport Gap, TN, will discuss anything further. P Parking available at house for section hikers. Pets are welcome.

Blairsville, GA 30514 (14W) All major services.
Dahlonega, GA 30597(17E) All major services.

NoBo	Features	Description	GPS	Elev	SoBo
32.4	🛠🅰	Bull Gap, water (spring) on blue blazed trail to the west downhill 200 yards.		3644	2159.6
32.8	▲	Levelland Mountain, wooded summit		3942	2159.2
33.0	📷	Crest of Levelland Mountain, open rocky area, view.		3668	2159.0
33.5		Swaim Gap		3450	2158.5
34.3	🛠	Pass west of Rock Spring Top, water (spring) is located to the west of the trail.		3520	2157.7
35.0	📷	Wolf Laurel Top, open rock face east of the trail offers views.		3766	2157.0
35.5	🛠🅰⤵	Baggs Creek Gap, not an obvious gap. Water (spring) is located down an overgrown road to the west, not an ATC approved camping spot.		3591	2156.5
36.3	▲📷 🅰	Cowrock Mountain, summit offers good views of the valley below.		3842	2155.7
37.3	P(10-12) 🧭	Cross **GA. 348**, Tesnatee Gap and Russell Scenic Highway.	N 34 43.576, W 83 50.862	3138	2154.7
37.8	📷	Rock cliff with views of Cowrock Mountain and gorge of Town Creek.		3614	2154.2
38.0	🛠Y▲ 🅰(3)⊏(7) ⤵🌙 📷🧭 🍴🛠	Crest Wildcat Mountain. (1.2E) **Whitley Gap Shelter**, water (spring) located (0.2) beyond shelter, privy, (0.1E) beyond shelter to tent sites, 22.3◀10.3◀9.1◀▶ 4.8▶ 12.1▶20.2	N 34 42.743, W 83 50.064	3370	2154.0
38.2	P(10-12) 🧭 ★★★★★	Cross **GA. 348**, Hogpen Gap, water (spring) south side of road on a blue blazed trail. **AT plaque on rock**.	N 34 43.554, W 83 50.393	3450	2153.8

Blairsville, GA 30514 (14.0W) All major services. See Notes at mile 31.3

NoBo	Features	Description	GPS	Elev	SoBo
39.1		White Oak Stamp, ridge crest.		3470	2152.9
40.2	▲	Poor Mountain, summit.		3650	2151.8
40.8		Wide Gap.		3169	2151.2
42.0	▲	Sheep Rock Top, rocky summit.		3600	2150.0
42.8	🛠🅰(4) ⊏(7) ⤵🌙📷🧭	Blue blaze 190 yards east to **Low Gap Shelter**, water located 30 yards in front of shelter, tenting, privy, bear cables. 15.1◀13.9◀4.8◀▶ 7.3▶ 15.4▶22.8	N 34 46.576, W 83 49.470	3050	2149.2
44.2	🛠🅰	Poplar Stamp Gap, water (stream) is located several feet east down an old road bed.		3330	2147.8
46.6		Cold Springs Gap, pay no attention to the name you will not find a spring.		3300	2145.4
47.8	🛠YP(7)🧭	Chattahoochee Gap, Jack's Gap Trail west (2.4) to GA. 180 and parking. Water (spring) is located 200 yards east on a steep blue blazed trail.	N 34 50.872, W 83 47.924	3500	2144.2
48.5	Y	Red Clay Gap		3485	2143.5
49.2	🅰	Campsites to west of tail.		3600	2142.8
49.4	🛠Y	Spring is located several yards to the west on a trail down a rocky slope.		3500	2142.6

NoBo	Features	Description	GPS	Elev	SoBo
49.6	♦	Flat area known as Rocky Knob. Water is about 150 yards west down rocky slope.		3629	2142.4
49.7		Henson Gap		3580	2142.3
50.0	♦	Spring on west side trail. This is the water for Blue Mountain Shelter.		3890	2142.0
50.1	♦▲(4) ⊑(7) ↩(☾☎♀	**Blue Mountain Shelter** (no potable water) at shelter, water (spring) located (0.1) south of shelter on AT, tenting, privy, bear cables. 21.2◄12.1◄7.3◄► 8.1►15.5►23.6	N 34 49.033, W 83 46.004	3900	2141.9
51.0	▲	Blue Mountain, summit		4025	2141.0
52.5	▲○ P(14)♀ ★★★★★	Cross **GA. 75**, Unicoi Gap, **AT plaque placed in a rock on north side of road**.	N 34 48.107, W 83 44.569	2949	2139.5

Helen, GA 30545 (9.0E) See map of Helen, GA.

✉♀	**PO** M–F 9am–12:30pm and 1:30pm-4pm, Sa 9am-12pm. 706-878-2422. 7976 S Main St. Helen, GA 30545. ♀ N 34 41.881, W 83 43.181.
🛏☕♀	**Baymont Inn & Suits** 706-725-8764. Rate, $125 and up. Includes breakfast buffet during festivals. Microwave, fridge, pool outside, 📶 free WiFi. ♀ 34.70039, -83.72313
🛏⛺🖥☕ ♀	**Helendorf River Inn** 800-445-2271. (www.helendorf.com) Rates range from $45-$85, $10EAP depending on season. Weekend rates are higher. Pets $20. Includes continental breakfast, ⛺ Laundry, 🖥 Computer available for use, 📶 free WiFi. Visa/MC/Disc accepted. ♀ N 34 42.072, W 83 43.693
🛏⊛☕♀	**SureStay Hotel by Best Western** 706-878-2191. Open year round. ⊛ No Pets. Offers a hiker room with two bed for two people $50, EAP $5 with a maximum of 4 people, offer is good for M-Th, microwave, fridge. Indoor pool. 📶 Free WiFi. ♀ N 34 42.043, W 83 43.597
🛏☕♀	**Econo Lodge** 706-878-8000. Open year round. Weekday rates $68, weekend rates are higher, includes continental breakfast, microwave, fridge, 📶 free WiFi. Accepts only pets under 20 pounds with pet fee $20. ♀ N 34 41.827, W 83 42.808
🛏⛺- 🖥☕⚲♀	**Country Inn and Suites** 706-878-9000. Open year round. Call for rates, stay includes hot breakfast, indoor pool and whirl pool, ⛺ laundry, 🖥 Computer available to use, 📶 free WiFi. ♀ N 34 42.071, W 83 43.467
🛒♀	**Betty's Country Store** (IGA) 706-878-2943. (bettysinhelen.com) M-Th 7am-8pm, F-Sa 7am-9pm Su 7am-8pm. ♀ N 34 42.108, W 83 44.054
⛺♀	**Laundromat** 706-779-2066. ♀ N 34 42.100, W 83 43.545
✗♀	**Rib Country BBQ** 706-878-8008. (www.ribcountrybbq.com) M-Th 11am-7pm, F-Sa 11am-9pm, Su 11am-7pm. ♀ N 34 42.048, W 83 43.782
🖥♀	**White County Library** 706-878-2438. M-F 9am-6pm, Sa-Su closed. ♀ N 34 42.190, W 83 43.883

Hiawassee, GA 30546 (12E) See Hiawassee and map at mile 69.2

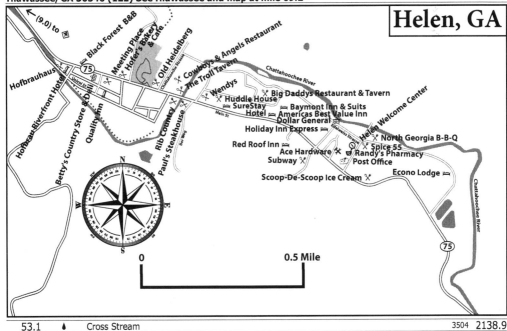

Helen, GA

53.1	♦	Cross Stream		3504	2138.9
53.4	Y	Rocky Mountain Trail leads (0.1) west to USFS 283.		3702	2138.6

NoBo	Features	Description	GPS	Elev	SoBo
53.9	🛆🔺📷	Rocky Mountain, summit		4017	2138.1
54.1	📷	Rock ledges with good views.		3965	2137.9
55.2	❤🛆🅿♀	Cross **USFS 283**, Indian Grave Gap. Blue blaze trail leads (1.9) east to Andrews Cove Campground.	N 34 47.562, W 83 42.858	3113	2136.8
55.9	🛆	Cross **USFS 79**, Tray Mountain Road		3580	2136.1
56.2	♦🛆〰	Cheese Factory Site, water (spring) is located 50 yards west. There is no cheese factory here. There is nothing here now that would make you even think there was one located here. However in the 1800's there was once one here. Now it is a good flat area for a picnic or camping.		3590	2135.8
56.7	📷	Rocky cliff with small overlook.		3853	2135.3
56.9	🅿(6)♀	Cross **USFS 79/698**, Tray Mountain Road, Tray Gap	N 34 47.963, W 83 41.460	3847	2135.1
57.7	🔺📷	Tray Mountain, small rocky summit, views in all directions.		4430	2134.3
58.2	♦❤🛆(3) ⊏(7) 〰☾🛜♀	Blue blaze trail 150 yards to **Tray Mountain Shelter**, water (spring) located 250 yards behind shelter, tenting, privy, bear cables. 20.2◀15.4◀8.1◀▶7.4▶15.5▶22.8	N 34 48.238, W 83 40.614	4200	2133.8
59.4		Wolfpen Gap		3600	2132.6

NoBo	Features	Description	GPS	Elev	SoBo
60.0	♦❤	Steeltrap Gap, water (spring) is located 280 yards east down blue blaze trail.		3490	2132.0
60.5		West side of Young Lick Knob.		3800	2131.5
61.8		Cross Swag of the Blue Ridge		3400	2130.2
62.9	♦🛆〰	Sassafras Gap, camp sites, water (spring) is located 150 yards downhill to the east.		3500	2129.1
63.8	♦🛆〰 🅿🅿	Addis Gap, old fire road leads (0.5) east to campsite and water and eventually to **USFS 26-2**. During Turkey hunting season the locals like to use this camp-site because they can drive into it. Old fire road leads (8.0) east to GA. 197.		3304	2128.2
64.8	❤	Trail to Kelly Knob (0.2) west		4276	2127.2
65.6	♦❤🛆(4) ⊏(12) 〰☾🛜♀	(0.3E) **Deep Gap Shelter**, water (spring) is located (0.1) south on the trail to the shelter, tenting, privy, bear cables. 22.8◀15.5◀7.4◀▶8.1▶15.4▶20.3	N 34 52.941, W 83 38.772	3550	2126.4
66.6	❤🛆📷	Blue blaze trail east leads several yards to campsites and view, **no water**.		3827	2125.4
66.8	🛆	McClure Gap		2121	2125.2
67.0	🔺	Powell Mountain, summit		3850	2125.0
68.0		Moreland Gap. An old overgrown roadbed leads west.		3050	2124.0
68.6	♦	Several streams in this area.		2650	2123.4

69.2	▲▲♨ P(12)♀ ★★★★★	Cross **U.S. 76**, Dicks Creek Gap, picnic area, water is located (0.5W). **See Map** of Dicks Creek Gap.	N 34 54.739, W 83 37.131	2675	2122.8

⛺♦◈ (0.5W) **Top of Georgia Hiking Center** 706-982-3252 (www.topofgeorgiahikingcenter.org)
△🛏☎⌨⚡ ◈ AT Passport location.
🏍🚗P🖥 ⊗ No pets please. No alcohol or drugs. Open year-round 7-7.
♀ Street sign with arrow marks the easy half mile downhill road walk to TOG from gap (NoBo hikers head left, SoBo hikers head right). ⛺ Bunk and shower $35 and private 2 bed 🛏 cabins $70. Both include free continental breakfast and use of full hostel kitchen with your stay. Advance reservations available but not required. △ Laundry $5/load (we do it for you) with free hospital scrubs provided. ⌨ Computer, ☎ free Wi-Fi. Pizza & snacks available. 🛒 Full resupply. 🏍 Ask about slackpacking. ♪ Discount outfitter on site specializes in limited thru-hiker gear. B&B rooms $125 and up, breakfast included. △ Free shuttles year-round to Hiawassee, Dicks Creek Gap and Unicoi Gap daily for overnight guests. TOG shuttles travel as far south as Atlanta Marta North Springs Station and north to Fontana for a fee. Offers slackpacking options (whole state of GA and up to NOC). Print your Smoky Mtn Permits here. Fun morning seminar "10 Keys for a Successful Thru-Hike". Pack shakedowns available. P Parking available. ♀ N 34 55.220, W 83 37.498
🖂 Mail drops: ($2 fee) held for 21 days. ID required to pick up packages: 7675 US Hwy 76 E., Hiawassee GA 30546.

🛏△🖥☎ (5.0W) **Henson Cove B&B** 706-896-6195. (www.hensoncoveplace.com).
🏍P🖥♀ 🛏 Cove Cabin (breakfast an additional $8.00 per per person per day, 2 guests ($100.00), 2 Guests and one dog ($120.00), 3 guests ($120.00) 3 guest and a dog ($135), 4 guests (135), 4 guests and a dog($150) 🐕 Only small well behaved pets. B&B rooms $125 and up, breakfast included. △ Free laundry and ☎ free WIFI at B&B. ⌨ Computer available for use. Stay includes free ride to and from Dick's Creek Gap or Unicoi Gap ($20.00) and for resupplying in town. 🏍P Shuttles and parking available for section hikers. Accepts Credit Cards. In town shuttles $10.00 per hour. ♀ N 34 55.852, W 83 41.381
🖂 Mail drops for guest only: 1137 Car Miles Rd, Hiawassee, GA 30546.

Hiawassee, GA 30546 (11.0W). See map of Hiawassee, GA.

🖂♀ **PO** M-F 8:30am-5pm, Sa 8:30am-12pm. 706-896-4173. 118 N Main St. Hiawassee, GA 30546. ♀ N 34 56.993, W 83 45.478.

🛏♦△🖥 **Hiawassee Budget Inn** 706-896-4121. (www.hiawasseebudgetinn.com)
☎🚗🖥♪ ◈ AT Passport location.
♀ Open year round. 🛏 $39.99 per person, limited to four per room, $5 for each additional person. $50 pet deposit. Rooms include cable TV, refrigerators, microwaves. △ Coin laundry. ⌨ Computer available for use. ☎ Free Wifi. 🏍 Free Shuttles for guests to and from Dick's Creek Gap and Unicoi Gap, leaves at 9 and 11 am for the months of March thru April. There is a fee for Non guest. ♀ N 34 56.677, W 83 45.212
🖂 Mail drops for guests: 193 S Main Street - Hiawassee, Georgia. 30546
♪ **Three Eagles Outfitters**, Located at the Budget Inn.
Open from March to the first week of May. Hours are 8:15 am to 2 pm, 7 days during season. Located at the Budget Inn. Stocks all that a hiker may neeed. 🔥 Fuel by the ounce. Offers free bumps to our main store in Franklin. If they are out of an item, it can be sent here by the next day.

🛏⊗☎🏍 **Mull's Inn** 706-896-4195.
🖥♀ ⊗ No pets. 🛏 Call for pricing, ☎ free WiFi. 🏍 Shuttles by arrangement
🖂 Mail drops for guests: 213 N Main St, Hiawassee, GA 30546. ♀ N 34 57.062, W 83 45.544

🛏⊗△♨ **Holiday Inn Express** 706-896-8884.
⌨☎🖥 ⊗ No pets. 🛏 $79 and up, includes continental breakfast, △ laundry. Indoor pool and hot tub. ⌨ Computer available for use, ☎ free WiFi. Accepts Credit Cards. ♀ N 34 57.157, W 83 45.441
🖂 Mail drops for guests: 300 Big Sky Drive, Hiawassee, GA 30546.

🛏△🖥☎ **Lake Chatuge Lodge** 706-896-5253. (www.lakechatugelodge.com)
♀ 🛏 Rates stating at $90 but can be more depending on month and higher on weekends, includes continental breakfast, △ laundry, ⌨ computer available for use, ☎ free WiFi. ♀ N 34 57.893, W 83 46.204

🛒✗✅♀ **Ingles** 706-896-8312. (www.ingles-markets.com) 🛒 ✗ Deli, bakery, salad bar. M-Su 7am-10pm. ✅ Pharmacy; M-F 9am-9pm, Sa-Su 9am-6pm. ♀ N 34 57.025, W 83 45.419

🛒✅♀ **Freds** 706-896-4302. 🛒 M-Sa 8am-9pm, Su 9am-8pm; ✅ Pharmacy 706-896-1774. M-F 9am-7pm, Sa 9am-4pm, Su closed. N 34 57.100, W 83 45.383

✗♀ **Bear Meadows Grill** 706-896-0520. (www.bearmeadowsgrill.net) M - closed, Tu 11 am-8 pm, W 11 am-2:30 pm, Th-F 11 am-8:30 pm, Sa closed. ♀ N 34 57.819, W 83 47.008

✗♀ **Georgia Mountain Restaurant** 706-896-3430. Serves breakfast, lunch and dinner. M-Su 6am-7:30pm. ♀ N 34 57.233, W 83 45.565

✗♀ **Daniels Steak House** 706-896-8008. All you can eat lunch and dinner. M-Su 11am-8:30pm. ♀ N 34 57.236, W 83 45.497

✗♀ **Big Al's Pizza** 706-896-1970. They also deliver. M-Sa 11:30am-8pm, Su 12pm-7pm. ♀ N 34 57.506, W 83 45.017

➕♀ **Chatuge Regional Hospital** 706-896-2222. M-Su 24 hours. ♀ N 34 56.789, W 83 45.229

✅ **The Medicine Shoppe** 706-896-4686. M-F 9am-5pm, Sa-Su closed.

△♀ **Wash Tub Coin Laundry** 706-896-4441. ♀ N 34 57.359, W 83 45.616

🐾♀ **Hiawassee Animal Hospital** 706-896-4173. (www.hiawasseeanimalhospital.com) M-F 8:30am-5:30pm, Sa 8:30am-1pm, Su closed. ♀ N 34 57.733, W 83 44.762

■ ⚲ **Goin' Postal** 706-896-1844. (www.goinpostalhiawassee.com)
M-F 10am-5pm Sa-Su closed. FedEx and UPS shipping, also offer DHL and USPS services. ⚲ N 34
56.770, W 83 45.302

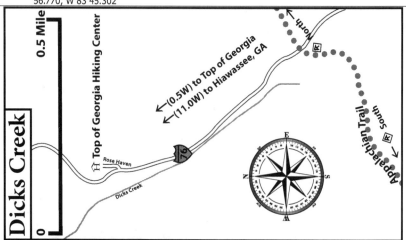

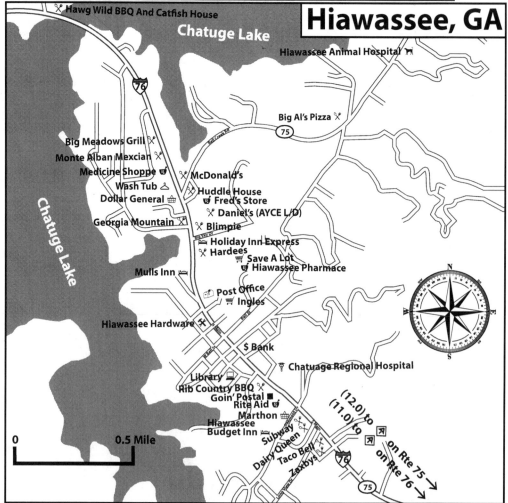

NoBo	Features	Description	GPS	Elev	SoBo
70.3	◊▲	Campsite east of trail, water.		3150	2121.7
71.0		Cowart Gap, tall pines.		2900	2121.0
72.1	📷	Good views from Buzzard Knob when the leaves are not on trees.		3675	2119.9
72.5		Bull Gap		3550	2119.5
73.7	♦Υ▲(6) ⊏(14) ⌣☾🐻♀	Plumarchard Gap. (0.2E) **Plumarchard Gap Shelter**, water located 200 yards west on AT beyond shelter, tenting, privy, bear cables. Caution the stump in front of the shelter has been home to copperhead snakes. Creek on trail to shelter and spring (0.1W) of AT. 23.6◀15.5◀8.1◀▶7.3▶12.2▶19.8	N 34 56.762, W 83 35.298	3050	2118.3
74.4		As Knob, crosses high point below summit.		3460	2117.6
75.0	⏣	Blue Ridge Gap, cross dirt road **USFS 72**.		3020	2117.0
76.0	♦▲	Campsite, water		3500	2116.0
76.2		Rich Cove Gap		3390	2115.8
77.6	📷	Small knob west of trail with good views.		3695	2114.4
78.1	State Line	Georgia–North Carolina State Line, register in tree.		3825	2113.9
78.2	♦▲⌣O	Bly Gap, water (spring) is located east of the trail and 250 feet south of the gap. Gnarly twisted oak tree located here. **Often photographed tree**.		3840	2113.8
78.9	📷	Sharp Top, skirts the summit, vista.		4300	2113.1
79.3	📷	View of Shooting Creek Valley.		4521	2112.7
80.1		Sassafras Gap		4300	2111.9
80.7	♦	Cross stream		4549	2111.3
80.9	📷	Viewpoint to the west.		4627	2111.1
81.0	♦Υ▲ ⊏(8) ⌣☾♀	Blue blaze 100 feet east to **Muskrat Creek Shelter**, water (spring) is located behind shelter, tenting, privy. 22.8◀15.4◀7.3◀▶4.9▶12.5▶21.2	N 35 01.232, W 83 34.896	4600	2111.0
81.8	♦Υ▲	Edge of White Oak Stamp, water (spring) is located to the east. Tent sites to west and east. Camp out of sight of the trail to the west or east.		4620	2110.2
82.0	Υ	Chunky Gal Trail to the west (5.5) to U.S. 64.		4700	2110.0
82.9		Water Oak Gap, small clearing.		4490	2109.1
83.9	📷	View.		4737	2108.1
85.0	♦Υ▲ P(8-10)♀ ★★★★★	Cross **USFS 71**, Deep Gap, Kimsey Creek Trail leads (3.7W) to USFS **Standing Indian Campground. See notes at NOBO mile 105.7.**	N 35 02.376, W 83 33.150	4341	2107.0
85.9	♦▲⊏(8) ⌣☾♀	Blue blaze 250 feet east to **Standing Indian Shelter**, water (creek) located 70 yards downhill from shelter, tenting, privy. 20.3◀12.2◀4.9◀▶7.6▶16.3▶19.7	N 35 02.520, W 83 32.884	4760	2106.1
87.4	Υ▲📷	Lower Ridge Trail junction, east leads 600 feet to Standing Indian Mountain summit. West leads (4.2) to Standing Indian Campground.		5498	2104.6

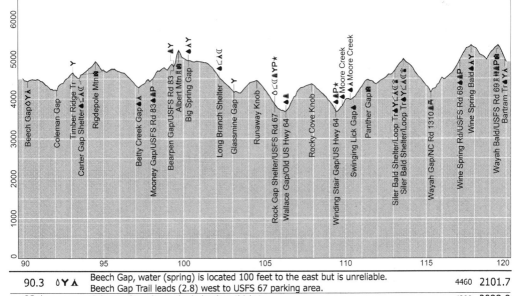

| 90.3 | ◊Υ▲ | Beech Gap, water (spring) is located 100 feet to the east but is unreliable. Beech Gap Trail leads (2.8) west to USFS 67 parking area. | | 4460 | 2101.7 |
| 92.1 | | Coleman Gap, dense rhododendron thicket. | | 4200 | 2099.9 |

NoBo	Features	Description	GPS	Elev	SoBo
93.1	⛟P(3)⛾	Timber Ridge Trail leads (2.3) west to USFS 67 parking area.	N 35 1.323, W 83 30.218	4700	2098.9
93.5	⬥🛏◻(8) ◖(⛾	Blue blaze 100 feet east to **Carter Gap Shelter**, water (spring) is located 200 yards west on blue blaze trail, tenting, privy. 19.8◀12.5◀7.6◀▶ 8.7▶ 12.1▶ 19.6	N 34 59.939, W 83 29.648	4540	2098.5
94.9	📷	North side of Ridgepole Mountain		4990	2097.1
95.2	⛟📷	Unmarked trail leads 25 feet east to Little Ridgepole vista of Pickens Nose.		4749	2096.8
97.2	⬥🛏 ᠵ	Betty Creek Gap, water (spring) is located to the east.		4300	2094.8
98.1	⬥P(1-2) ⛾	Cross **USFS 83**, Mooney Gap. Road closed mid-Dec thru first of Apr.	N 35 02.129, W 83 28.211	4400	2093.9
98.4	⬥	Log steps, spring		4500	2093.6
99.0	🛏	Bearpen Gap		4700	2093.0
99.4	⛟	Two blue blazed trails intersect here. Bearpen Trail (2.6) west to USFS 67, gravel. The other blue blaze trail is the Albert Mountain bypass trail that reconnects with the AT at mile 100.		4790	2092.6
99.7	🛏📷▮ P(7)⛾	Albert Mountain summit, fire tower	N 35 03.154, W 83 28.651	5250	2092.3
99.9		Albert Mountain bypass trail leads west (0.8) to reconnect with the AT at mile 99.2 northbound.		5035	2092.1
100.3		Big Spring Gap.		4954	2091.7
102.2	⬥⛟🛏(5) ◻(16) ᠵ◖(⛾	(0.1W) **Long Branch Shelter**, water, tent sites, privy. 21.2◀16.3◀8.7◀▶ 3.4▶ 10.9▶ 18.2	N 35 04.198, W 83 29.889	4932	2089.8
102.3	⬥	Cross stream		4930	2089.7
103.1	⛟	Glassmine Gap, Long Branch Trail (2.0) west to USFS 67		4130	2088.9
104.1	◊	Unreliable spring below trail. Several seasonal water sources are one mile in either direction.		4363	2087.9
105.6	◊⛟◻(8) ᠵ◖(⛾	Blue blaze 300 feet west to **Rock Gap Shelter**, water (spring) is known to go dry, privy. 19.7◀12.1◀3.4◀▶ 7.5▶ 14.8▶ 19.6	N 35 05.486, W 83 31.386	3760	2086.4
105.7	⬥⛟🛏 P(6-7)⛾ ★★★★★	Rock Gap, (0.7E) to water. (1.5W) **Standing Indian Campground**.	N 35 05.644, W 83 31.350	3750	2086.3
	🛏⌂👭 ⚸📱P	(1.5W) **Standing Indian Campground** 828-524-6441. Campsites $16, open Apr 1 - Nov 30. Showers, camp store, pay phone. Pets must be leashed. Parking is permitted year round.			
106.3	🛏	Cross **Old U.S. 64**, Wallace Gap		3738	2085.7
106.4	⬥	Cross stream.		3745	2085.6
108.7	⬥	Cross Stream.		3797	2083.3
109.4	⬥🛏 P(15-20) ⛾ ★★★★★	Cross **U.S. 64**, Winding Stair Gap, piped spring.	N 35 07.185, W 83 32.891	3770	2082.6

Franklin, NC 28734 (10E) (all major services) See map of Franklin north side and south side.

⌂⛾ **PO** M-F 8:30am-5pm, Sa 9am-12pm. 828-524-3219. 250 Depot St. Franklin, NC 28734. ⛾ N 35 10.731, W 83 22.460.

🛏◈ **Budget Inn** 828-524-4403. (www.budgetinnoffranklin.com)
△🖥◉🛏 ◈ AT Passport location. Open year round. 🛏 $39.99 per person, limited to four per room, $5 for each
✉⛾ additional person. $50 pet deposit. Rooms include cable TV, refrigerators and microwaves, 🖥 computer for use, ◉ free WiFi. △ Coin laundry. P ask about shuttles. N 35 10.937, W 83 22.639
✉ Mail drops for guest: 433 East Palmer Street, Franklin, NC 28734.

👭🍴△⚸ **Jack Tarlin Hostel** 828-524-2064. (www.baltimorejacksplace.com)
🖥◉🛏🚗✉ 🍴 On site outfitter - Satellite of Three Eagles Outfitter. 🏠 Bunk room $20 per person, 10 bunks on hand.
⛾ Private rooms single $49.99 plus $5 for each extra person per room. ⚸ Shower without stay $5. △ Coin laundry. 🖥 computer available for use, ◉ free WiFi. Smoky Mountain permits for free here. 🚐 Shuttle runs at 9 and 11 am for the months of March thru April to and from Rock Gap, Wallace Gap and Winding Stair Gap. Motel guests may call for free pickup. 4 pm shuttle around town for errands for guests. ⛾ N 35 10.945, W 83 22.682
✉ Mail drops: 7 Derby Street Franklin, NC 28734

🛏🏠ᠵ **Gooder Grove Hostel** 828-332-0228.
◈△◉🐕 Located in the heart of downtown Franklin, a short walk from Main Street breweries, restaurants and
✕P✉⛾ shops. 🚐 Daily shuttles to local outfitters stores.
◈ AT Passport location. Open Year Round. May be closed September 10 — October 1, please call ahead. Call for a shuttle or reservations. 🏠 Bunk: $23 per person, includes fresh linens Private room: $43. 🛏 Tent or ᠵ hammock: $13 per person. △ Laundry is $5. ◉ Free Wifi. 🚐 Shuttle from Winding Stair Gap or Rock Gap at 9:30, 12:30, and 3:30 daily, end of February through April. Pet friendly, with fenced dog lot and kennel. P Parking for section hikers. Shuttles for 🚐 slackpacking and guided hikes available. ⛾ N 35 10.686, W 83 22.679
✉ Mail drops: 130 Hayes Circle, Franklin, NC 28734

Sapphire Inn 828-524-4406. (www.sapphireinnfranklin.com)
◈ AT Passport location.
Our Hiker's Special starts at only $49.00 & up. Pet fee charges are based on pet size ☎ free WiFi. 📍 N 35 11.257, W 83 22.202
✉ Mail drops for guests: 761 East Main Street, Business 441, Franklin, NC 28734.

Microtel Inn & Suites by Wyndham Franklin 828-349-9000.
🛏 Call for prices, pet fee $25, microwave, fridge, stay includes continental breakfast. 🖥 Computer available for use, ☎ free WiFi. 📍 N 35 09.698, W 83 23.407
✉ Mail drops for guests: 81 Allman Dr, Franklin, NC 28734

Comfort Inn 828-369-9200.
🛏 Hiker Discount. Hot Breakfast, 🏊 Indoor Pool. ⛺ Guest Laundry. Dog Friendly rooms available. ☎ Free WiFi. Hotel has access to best hiker shuttle services in area. N 35 11.065, W 83 21.405
✉ Mail address: 313 Cunningham Rd Franklin NC 28734

1st Baptist Church Free Breakfast
◈ AT Passport location. Serves a pancake breakfast for Hikers starting the middle of March and ending the middle of April. Picks hikers up at the motels and hostels and take them back. 🍴 "We serve the breakfast!" M-Sun 7:30am. 📍 N 35 10.981, W 83 22.867

Lazy Hiker Brewing Company 828-349-2337. (www.lazyhikerbrewing.com)
◈ AT Passport location. 🍺 Spring and Summer hours, M-Thu 12pm-9pm, F-Sa 12pm-11pm, Su 12pm-6pm. 🍴 Food Truck onsite M-Th 12pm-8pm, F-Sa 12pm-9pm, Su 12pm-8pm. 🖥 Computer and printer available for use, ☎ free WiFi. Pet friendly. 📍 N 35 10.849, W 83 23.054

Outdoor 76 828-349-7676. (www.outdoor76.com)
◈ AT Passport location. M–Sa 10 am-7 pm, Su closed. 🥾 Specialty AT hiking store with lightweight gear, food & draft beer, right in center of town. ⛽ Fuels available. Footwear experts with Pedorthic trained staff to deal with injuries and various foot issues. 10% off total purchase for thru-hikers. 🖥 Computer available for use, ☎ free WiFi. Shipping services, in town shuttles. 📍 N 35 10.925, W 83 22.846
✉ No charge for Mail drops: 35 East Main Street, Franklin, NC 28734.
🍺 **Rock House Lodge taproom/restaurant:** Inside Outdoor 76
M-Sa 10 am-9 pm. 18 beers on tap, wine and food. Darts, indoor shuffleboard, community instruments for hikers, along with big screen T.V and occasional live music. Weekly food specials. ☎ Free WiFi.

Three Eagles Outfitters 828-524-9061. (www.threeeaglesoutfitters.net)
◈ AT Passport location. Open year round. M–Sa 9am–6pm, Su 12am–5pm.
🥾 Full service outfitter. 10% AT thru hiker discount. ⛽ Denatured alcohol and Coleman fuel by the ounce, fuel canisters. 🖥 Computer available for use, ☎ free Wifi. Coffee and espresso bar and offers free beer for shoppers. Listing of shuttle providers available. 📍 N 35 09.856, W 83 23.461
✉ Mail drops: Three Eagles Outfitters 78 Siler Rd. Franklin, NC 28734.

Ruby City Gems and Minerals 828-524-3967. (www.rubycity.com) gems@rubycity.com
◈ AT Passport location. M-Closed, Tu-Sa 10am-5pm, Su-Closed. 📍 N 35 10.936, W 83 22.730

Currahee Brewing Co. 828-634-0078. (www.curraheebrew.com)
◈ AT Passport location. 🍺 Hours: M-Th 12am-9pm, F-Sa 12am-10pm, SU 2pm-7pm. 📍 N 35 11.248, W 83 22.378

Lenzo Animal Hospital 828-369-2635 (www.lenzoanimalhospital.tripod.com) M-F 8:30 am-5 pm, Sa 8:30 am-12pm, Su sometimes open. Emergency clinic 828-665-4399. 📍 N 35 08.954, W 83 23.660

Jim Granato 828-342-1571. Atlanta to Davenport Gap. Speaks Italian, German, and Spanish. Please call a week in advance if wanting to get shuttled into the mountains for availability. Based in Franklin.

Zen Shuttles 828-332-0228. Slackpacking/section hiking shuttles, long and short distance from GA to VA. Will also shuttle from Atlanta to the Smokies. Call for availability. Based in Franklin.

Chuck Allen 828-371-6460. hometownshuttle@gmail.com. Call or text after 1pm. Shuttles from Springer to Fontana. Based in Franklin.

Beverly Carini 850-572-7352. Not available Su 9-noon. Shuttles from Amicalola to Davenport Gap. Based in Franklin.

Franklin, NC (north)

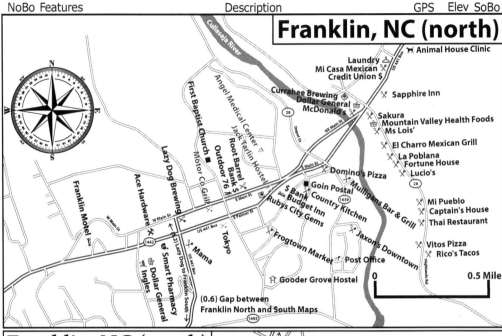

Franklin, NC (south)

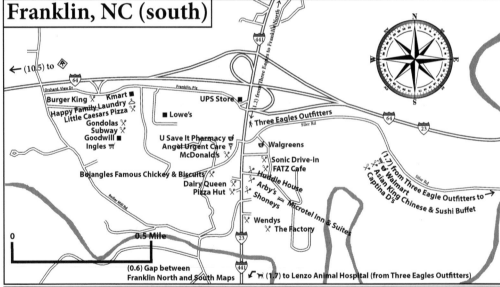

109.7	⬩	Cross east fork of Moore Creek, stone steps.		3676	2082.3
109.9	⬩⌒	Cross east fork of Moore Creek, bridge.		3803	2082.1
110.3	⬩△	Cross west fork of Moore Creek. Campsite to west.		3970	2081.7
110.5	⬩	Swinging Lick Gap, water		4100	2081.5
111.4	📷	Panther Gap, view		4480	2080.6
113.1	⬩Y△ ⌐(8) ☾☂⛺♀	Northern end of blue blaze of Siler Bald Loop(0.5E) **Siler Bald Shelter**, water (spring) is located 300 feet south of shelter on loop trail, tenting, privy, bear cable, south end of loop trail to shelter. 19.6◀10.9◀7.5◀▶ 7.3▶12.1▶17.9	N 35 08.648, W 83 34.350	4600	2078.9
113.6	⬩Y△ ⌐(8) ⌣☾☂⛺♀	Southern end of blue blaze of Siler Bald Loop Trail (0.6E) to **Siler Bald Shelter.**	N 35 08.648, W 83 34.350	4178	2078.4
115.3	△🚻♀	**NC. 1310**, Wayah Gap, picnic area	N 35 09.240, W 83 34.842	4180	2076.7

NoBo	Features	Description	GPS	Elev	SoBo
116.6	Y	Wilson Lick Ranger Station is located to the west.		4650	2075.4
117.1	♦▲P(4-5)	Cross **USFS 69**, water (piped spring) is located a few yards to the east		4900	2074.9
117.6	♦Y▲〜	Wine Spring, Bartram Trail is yellow blazed, tents sites and water (pipe spring) is located a few yards to the east.		5290	2074.4
117.8	▲	Woods road intersects.		5008	2074.2
119.2	▲	Cross woods road.		5158	2072.8
119.4	♦♦▲P	USFS Road termination, restrooms and parking to the east.		5302	2072.6
119.5	📷🏛️O P(20)🚻	**Wayah Bald**, stone observation tower. Has a parking lot and a paved footpath.	Tower N 35 10.816, W 83 33.643 Parking N 35 10.723, W 83 33.739	5342	2072.5
119.7	▲	Cross dirt road.		5178	2072.3
119.8	♦	Spring to the west of Trail.		5035	2072.2
119.9	♦▲Y	Yellow blazed Bartram Trail comes in from the east and joins the AT for (2.4). Reliable stream 200 yards east on the Bartram Trail. Not an ATC approved camping spot		5200	2072.1

120.4	♦▲(5) ⊏(8) 〜☾🚻	**Wayah Shelter**, shelter on AT. Water (Little Laurel Creek) is located 600 feet west of AT on blue blazed trail, tent sites, privy. 18.2◀14.8◀7.3◀▶4.8▶10.6▶15.5	N 35 11.367, W 83 33.864	4480	2071.6
121.7	♦▲	Licklog Gap, logging road, water is located (0.5) west.		4440	2070.3
124.0	▲P(7)🚻	Cross **NC. 1397**, Burningtown Gap, large clearing with apple trees.	N 35 13.338, W 83 33.732	4236	2068.0
125.2	♦▲⊏(6) 〜☾🛖🚻	**Cold Spring Shelter**, water located 5 yards in front of the shelter, privy, tent sites located (0.1) north on AT, bear cables. 19.6◀12.1◀4.8◀▶5.8▶10.7▶18.6	N 35 13.854, W 83 33.594	4920	2066.8
125.3	▲〜	Cold Spring Shelter tent sites. Water, privy and bear cables are located near the shelter.		4958	2066.7
125.9	📷	Vista to east near Copper Ridge Bald.		5080	2066.1
127.1	Y▲📷	Trail to Rocky Bald summit (0.2) east to view.		5030	2064.9
127.4	♦	Good spring.		4900	2064.6

Be someone that makes you happy

NoBo	Features	Description	GPS	Elev	SoBo
128.8	▲P(10)♀ ★★★★★	Cross **NC. 1365**, Tellico Gap	N 35 16.092, W 83 34.339	3850	2063.2

⚑🛏️◈⑧ (4.3W) **Nantahala Mountain Lodge** 828-321-2340. Out of hours (After 7pm 828-321-9949).
⛺🏠✗☕ ◈ AT Passport location.
🍴🚍P✉️ Run by 2010 thru hiker Wiggy.
Open 1st March - 1st June
⑧ No Pets. ALL NIGHTLY RATES INCLUDE BREAKFAST. ⚑ 2 x Bunks $35 per person (bedding provided). 🛏️ 2 x Private rooms with 2 twin beds $75. Private room with king bed, private bathroom $85. ⛺ Laundry $5.00. 🏠 Short term resupply available. ☕ Free wiFi. 🚍 Shuttle pickup and return to or from: Wayah Gap (115.1) $5PP per trip, Burningtown Gap (123.8) $5PP per trip, Telico Gap (128.6) $5PP per trip. 🍴 Slackpacking options Rock Gap to Fontana with reservations. P Parking for section hikers $4 day shuttles to start point available. Cash payment only if stay is under $50. There is a $3 surcharge for use of Credit Cards if stay is over $50. RESERVATIONS HIGHLY RECOMMENDED.
✉️ Mail drops for guests who are staying at Lodge: 63 Britannia Drive, Topton. NC 28781

130.2	Y📷ℹ️♀	Wesser Bald summit. Observation tower is located east 40 yards on side trail. Formerly a fire tower, the structure atop Wesser Bald is now an observation deck offering panoramic views. The Great Smoky Mountains and Fontana Lake dominate the view to the north.	N 35 16.623, W 83 34.641	4627	2061.8
130.9	💧	Water (spring) on blue blazed trail 125 feet to the east.		4100	2061.1
131.0	Y🛏️ ⊏(8) ⌇《⚑♀	(0.1W) **Wesser Bald Shelter**, water (spring) located (0.1) south on AT then 75 yards on a blue blazed trail, tenting, privy, bear cables. Blue blazed Wesser Bald Trail (2.0) east to Wesser Creek Road. 17.9◄10.6◄5.8◄▶4.9▶12.8▶21.9	N 35 16.941, W 83 34.932	4115	2061.0
132.6	📷	Vista to the west.		4162	2059.4
132.8	📷	Jump-up, rocky outcrop with outstanding views, not the same as the other jump-up within the next 10 miles north.		4000	2059.2
135.9	💧Y🛏️ ⊏(6) ⌇《♀	200 feet east to **A. Rufus Morgan Shelter**, water (stream) located west of shelter AT, tenting, privy. 15.5◄10.7◄4.9◄▶7.9▶17.0▶23.3	N 35 19.451, W 83 35.412	2300	2056.1
136.7	▲P(10)♀ ★★★★★	Cross **US 19/74**, Nantahala Gorge, Nantahala Outdoor Center. **See map of NOC**	N 35 19.872, W 83 35.532	1723	2055.3

⚑🛏️◈🔥 **Nantahala Outdoor Center** 828-785-5082. (www.noc.com) media@noc.com
⛺🍴✗☕ ◈ AT Passport location.
🛒👤🚍✉️ Walk in's with and without out reservation must check in at General Store between 10am and 7pm. Credit Cards accepted.
🛏️ **Motel rooms:** $79.99 and up, ☕ free WiFi.
⚑ **Base Camp Bunkhouse:** 828-785-5082, reservations are recommended, $39.99 for 2 people, $79.99 for 4 people, $109.99 for 6 people, $139.99 for 8 people, ⛺ all include shower, common area and community kitchen, ☕ free WiFi.
✗ **River's End Restaurant:** Serves breakfast, lunch and dinner. Opens mid-March. M-Thu 8am-7pm. No breakfast in the fall. F-Sa 8am-8pm, Sun 8am-7pm. ☕ Free WiFi.
👤 **NOC Outfitters:** Open daily. Lots of gear, trail food, 🔥 fuel by the ounce, ☕ free WiFi. They will do gear shakedowns if you would like them to, just ask. You can print Smoky Mountain permits from here. 🚍 Ask about shuttles.
✉️ Mail drops: dated and marked "Hold for AT Hiker", 13077 Hwy 19W, Bryson City, NC 28713.

	🏪	**Wesser General Store** Open Mar thru Oct
	🚍	**Jude Julius** 828-736-0086. Based in Bryson City, NC. Shuttle ranges from Hiawassee, GA to Newfound Gap, NC.
	🐕	**Crabtree Retrievers and Kennels** (www.crabtreeretrievers.com) Dog Transportation and Kenneling for thru hiker in the GSMNP. Pickup and Drop off in Hot Springs and NOC. Vet Services available upon request. Mild Grooming available. AC and Heated Kennels. Please visit for more information.

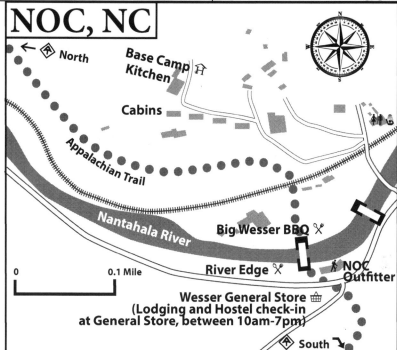

NOC, NC

← 🏠 **North**

Base Camp 🏠
Kitchen

Cabins

Appalachian Trail

Nantahala River

Big Wesser BBQ ✕

River Edge ✕ 🏃 **NOC Outfitter**

Wesser General Store 🏪
(Lodging and Hostel check-in
at General Store, between 10am-7pm)

🏠 **South** ↘

0 ——— 0.1 Mile

NoBo		Description	GPS	Elev	SoBo
136.8	✕	Cross railroad tracks.		1725	2055.2
138.0	⊤	Power line.		2428	2054.0
138.3	▲	Wright Gap, dirt road		2390	2053.7
139.8	♦	Grassy Gap, water		3050	2052.2
140.2	▲	Reach crest of Grassy Top.		3317	2051.8
142.2	📷	The Jump-up, views to Nantahala Gorge		3814	2049.8
142.9	♦▲	Swim Bald, summit, water (spring) is located 50 yards east of summit but is unreliable.		4710	2049.1
143.8	♦Y⋏ ⌂(14) ⌣☾♿	(0.1W) **Sassafras Gap Shelter**, water (spring) is reliable and located in front of shelter, tenting, privy. 18.6◄12.8◄7.9◄►9.1►15.4►22.1	N 35 19.841, W 83 40.020	4330	2048.2
145.0	♦▲Y⋏ ⌣📷	Cheoah Bald summit, vistas, good camping spot to see the sunrise, not an ATC approved camping spot. The terminus of the Bartram Trail.		5062	2047.0
145.4	Y	Bartram Trail to the west, yellow blazed.		3692	2046.6
147.4	♦⋏⌣	Locust Cove Gap, water (spring) is located 150 yards to the west and is somewhat reliable, not an ATC approved camping spot.		3690	2044.6
148.4		Simp Gap		3700	2043.6
149.8	♦	Good spring (0.1) west on logging road.		3292	2042.2

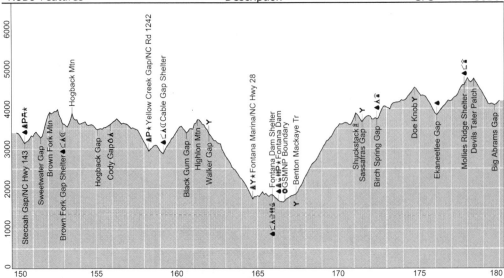

🌊🏔🅿 150.5 P(6-8)🍴 ★★★★★	Cross **NC. 143**, Sweetwater Road, Stecoah Gap, picnic table. Water (spring) is located 200 feet on blue blaze west on NC 143 then left 250 feet on abandoned overgrown logging road. **See Map of Stecoah Gap and Robbinsville, NC.**	N 35 21.497, W 83 43.074 3165 2041.5

🛏⛺🍴📶 **(1.2E) Appalachian Inn Bed & Breakfast** 828-735-1792. (www.appalachianinn.com). Located at Stecoah Gap
🛏 Room rates $145-$165. Breakfast is included, dinner can be added upon request. 📶 Free WiFi. 🚗 Shuttle services are available. Cash, check and credit cards are accepted.

⛺🛏🍴⛺ **(3.2E) Cabin in the Woods** Craig 980-406-6446 or Eileen 224-420-0273. (www.thecabinsinthewoods. 📶🚗✉ com)
⛺ $25 pp Hiker Lodging includes ride to/from Stecoah Gap, indoor shower, bathroom, satellite TV and 📶 Wifi. 🛏 Private cabins also available, but are often booked - reserve early. 🛒 Resupply to Robbinsville available. 🚗 For fee shuttle range from Amicalola to Hot Springs and Knoxville to Asheville. 🍴 Family style breakfast and laundry W/D available for hikers. Free Shuttle to Stecoah Valley Diners. Call for availability.
✉ Mail drops for only guest or for those using shuttle services. Mail drops: 386 W. Stecoah Hts., Robbinsville, NC 28771.

Robbinsville, NC (7.0W) from Stecoah Gap, see map

📪🍴	**PO** M-F 9am-4:30pm, Sa-Su Closed. 828-479-3397. 74 Sweetwater Rd. Robbinsville, NC 28771. N 35 19.438, W 83 48.060
🛏Ⓢ📶	**San Ran Motel** 828-479-3256. (www.sanranmotel.com) 🛏 Open Apr - Nov. Ⓢ No pets, no smoking. Fridge and microwave, 📶 free WiFi.
🛏📶	**Microtel Inn & Suites** 828-479-6772. 🛏 Nov-Mar $69.95D and up, breakfast, 📶 free WiFi. 🐾 $50 pet fee.
🛏	**Phillips Motel** 828-479-3370. (www.phillipsmotelonline.com)
🛏	**Mountain Manor Hotel** 828-479-4555. (www.mountainmanorhotel.com)
🛏	**River's Edge Treehouse Resort** 828-735-2228. (www.riversedgetreehouses.com)
🛏⛺	**Simple Life Campground and Cabins** 828-788-1099. (www.thesimplelifecampground.com)
🛒	**Dollar General** 828-479-6221. M-Su 8am-10pm.
🍴	**The Hub of WNC** 828-479-0478. M-F 9am-4pm, Sa-Su closed.
🍴	**The Pizza Man** 828-735-9405. M-Su 11am-10pm.
🍴	**Papa's Pizza To Go Inc** 828-479-2431. (www.papaspizzatogo.com) pies, wings and subs.
🍴	**El Pacifico Mexican Restaurant** 828-479-8448. M-Su 11am-9pm.
🍴	**Wendys** 828-479-4755.
🍴	**McDonalds** 828-479-6776.
🍴	**Lynn's Place** 828-479-9777. (www.grahamcounty.net) M-Sa 11am-9pm, Su 11am-2:30pm.
🍴	**Huddle House** 828-479-9695. M-Th 6am-10pm, F-Sa 24 hours, Su 6am-10pm.
💊	**Walgreens** 828-479-8791. M-Su 8am-9pm.
💊	**Robbinsville Pharmacy** 828-479-2273. (www.stores.healthmart.com) M-F 8am-6:30pm, Sa 9am-3pm, Su closed.

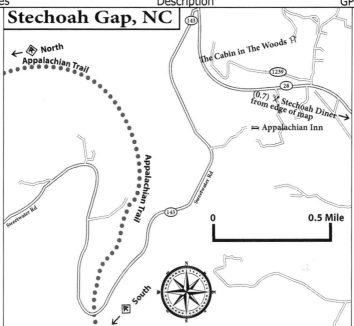

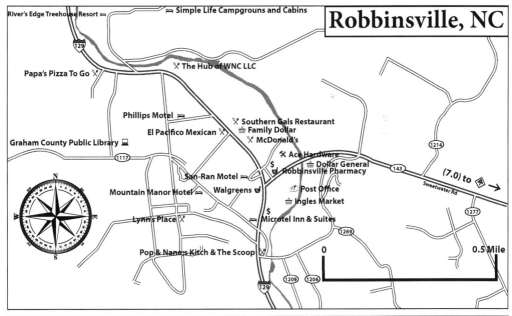

NoBo	Features	Description	GPS	Elev	SoBo
151.5		Sweetwater Gap	3220		2040.5
152.9	♦ Y ▲ ⊑(8) ⌣ (♀	Trail leads 70 yards east to **Brown Fork Gap Shelter**, water (spring) is reliable located on the right of shelter, tenting, privy. 21.9◄17.0◄9.1◄► 6.3► 13.0►24.9	N 35 22.454, W 83 44.034	3800	2039.1
153.3	♦	Brown Fork Gap, water is located south on the gap and 35 yeast east of the trail.		3600	2038.7
155.1		Hogback Gap		3500	2036.9
155.9	◊ ▲ ⌣	Cody Gap, water from spring, known to go dry up in hot weather.		3600	2036.1
156.7		Cross knob.		4000	2035.3
157.9	♦	Cross stream above Yellow Creek Gap.		3374	2034.1

NoBo	Features	Description	GPS	Elev	SoBo
158.3	⚑P(3)⚲ ★★★★★	Cross **NC. 1242**, Yellow Creek Mountain Road, Yellow Creek Gap. **See map.**	N 35 24.630, W 83 45.942	2980	2033.7

⌂▲⛺☕ **(2.0W) Creekside Paradise Bed and Breakfast** 828-346-1076 (No texting available). Cynthia and Jeff.

☏ Room rates: $60 per person, $45PP- 2 per room, $38PP-3 or more per room. ▲ Camping $10. Stays include pickup and return from Yellow Creek Gap, ⛺ laundry, hot tub. Breakfast and resupply trip to Robbinsville included with room rental, $10 for campers. ✗ Dinner $15 per person. ☎ Free WiFi. 🚗 Pickup and return from Stecoah Gap and Fontana $5 each way, NOC $15 each way. ⚑ Slackpacking available. Pets welcome.

✉ Mail drops: 259 Upper Cove Rd, Robbinsville, NC, 28771.

⌂⛺⚑☏ **(3.0E) The Hike Inn** 828-479-3677. (www.thehikeinn.com) (hikeinn@graham.main.nc.us).
☏ Open Mar thru Oct. A hikers-only motel and shuttle service run by Nancy Hoch since 1993, now joined by 2014 thru hiker Tom "High Loon" Barrett. ☏ Private room with bath, TV WiFi & coffee maker: $50 (2 person max). ⛺ Laundry $5. Thru & long distance hiker package (includes laundry, dinner/resupply trip to Robbinsville & pickup & drop off at Stecoah Gap, Yellow Creek Gap or Fontana Dam): $75PP, $50PP if 2 in room. ⚑ Free slackpacking between Stecoah Gap, Yellow Creek Gap & Fontana Dam with 2 night stay. Free parking for section hikers with stay and shuttle. Free printing of Smokies permit for guests. 🚗 Shuttles between Atlanta & Damascus.

✉ Free mail drop for guests: 3204 Fontana Rd, Fontana Dam, NC 28733.

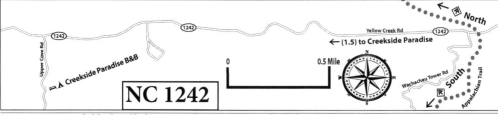

159.2	◆▲⛺(6) ☾☕⚲	**Cable Gap Shelter**, water (spring) located in front of shelter, tenting privy. 23.3◄15.4◄6.3◄►6.7►18.6►21.7	N 35 24.913, W 83 46.416	2880	2032.8
160.6		Black Gum Gap		3490	2031.4
162.0	Y	Walker Gap.		3450	2030.0
162.3	◆	Cross small stream		3629	2029.7
162.4	◆▲⛺	Campsite is not an ATC approved camping spot, water		3200	2029.6
164.7	Y▲⚲ ★★★★★	Cross **NC. 28**, Benton Mackaye Trail **Fontana Dam Village (2.0W)**	N 35 26.484, W 83 47.808	1810	2027.3
	🚻🚗	Phone available to call for shuttle service to Lodge.			

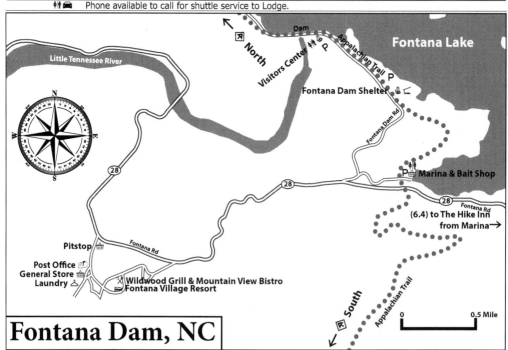

NoBo	Features	Description	GPS	Elev	SoBo
164.9	▲P(10)🚰 ★★★★★	Cross **SR 1245** at parking lot. **See map of Fontana area.**	N 35 26.496 W 83 47.743	1802	2027.1
	🚻🚮	Fontana 28 AT Crossing. Bathrooms, free phone, vending machines.			
	🚍	**Fontana Shuttle** 828-498-2211. Shuttles for $3 per person each way between AT Crossing, Visitor Center and Fontana Village. 8:30-6 daily Feb 15 thru May 15. Call for rides outside these dates.			

Fontana Village, NC (2W from NC 28) **See map.**

	📪🚰	**PO** M-F: 11:45am-3:45pm. 828-498-2315. 50 Fontana Rd. Fontana, NC 28733. N 35 26.104, W 83 49.531			
	🛏⑧ 📪🖥📠📠	**Fontana Lodge** 800-849-2258, 828-498-2211. ⑧ No pets. 🛏 Offers thru hiker rate $79 Sunday-Thursday and $99.00 for weekends for up to 4 people. Cabins $100 and up. 🖥 Computer available for use with printer in lobby, 📶 free WiFi, 📠 ATM. 📧 Mail drops: free for guests, $5 for non-guest. Fontana Village Resort, ATTN: Front Desk, 300 Woods Rd., Fontana Dam, NC 28733.			
	🛒🖥🛢	**General Store Grocery** 🛒 Mar 10-Thanksgiving. Open M-Th 9am-7pm, F-Sa 9am-9pm, Su 9am-7pm. Offers freeze-dried food, 🛢 Canister fuel, Coleman and alcohol by the ounce. 🖥 Computer available for use.			
	🏪🍴🛢	**Fontana Pit Stop** 🏪 M-Thu 8am-7pm, F-Saturday 8am-8pm, Su 8am-7pm. 🍴 Pizza, hot dogs and other light food, soda and coffee. Stocks some hiker food and 🛢 fuel when the General Store is closed.			
	🍴	**Mountview Restaurant** 828-498-2115, **Wildwood Grill,** Apr-Sept.			
	🧺	**Laundromat** Open year round, 7 days a week, detergent available in General Store.			
	🚐🛵	**Steve Claxton "Mustard Seed"** (2016 thru hiker) 828-736-7501, 828-479-9608. steve@steveclaxton.com (www.steveclaxton.com) Shuttle range from Hiawasee to Hot Springs and some area airports. Also offers slackpacking.			
165.9	▲Υ🛖 ⊏(24) 🚾🚻🛢📧 🚰	(0.1E) on paved sidewalk to **Fontana Dam Shelter "Fontana Hilton"**, water, tenting, shower, restroom. 22.1◀13.0◀6.7◀▶11.9▶15.0▶17.9	N 35 26.912, W 83 47.638	1775	2026.1
166.2	Υ	Fontana Dam bypass trail to the west.		1773	2025.8
166.3	▲🛢▲ P(10)🚰 ★★★★★	Fontana Dam Visitor Center, water. Southern end of dam.	N 35 27.113, W 83 48.137	1700	2025.7
	①◈ 🚻🛢📶	**Fontana Dam Visitor Center** 828-498-2234. ◈ AT Pasport loaction. Open daily April 2 - Sept 30: 9am-7 pm; October 9 am-6 pm. Soda machine outside. 🚻 Restrooms, 🛁 showers, 📶 free WiFi.			
166.7	◆▲P ★★★★★	Cross **Fontana Dam**, Little Tennessee River. Southern boundary of **Great Smoky Mountains National Park. North bounders must have a back-country permit before entering Great Smoky Mountains National Park. Dogs are not permitted inside the Great Smoky Mountains National Park.**		1740	2025.3
	🐕📧	**Loving Care Kennels** 865-453-2028 (www.LovingCareKennels.com) Will pickup your dog at Fontana Dam and return him/her to Davenport Gap. $400 for one dog, $575 for two. Will deliver maildrops upon pickup and return. Call at least 2 days in advance if you are heading north bound. 📧 3779 Tinker Hollow Rd, Pigeon Forge, TN 37863.			
	🐕	**Standing Bear Farm** 423-487-0014. Listed under Green Corner Road in Davenport Gap at the north end of the Smoky Mountinas.			
	🐕	**Barks and Recreation** 865-325-8245 (www.barksandrecgatlinburg.com) Does not offer rides, but you can drop off and pickups. Located at 2159 East Pkwy Gatlinburg, TN. M-Sa 8am-8pm, Su 10am-6pm.			

PERMITS

Great Smoky Mountains National Park (Tennessee/North Carolina)

-Thru-Hiker Permit: Hikers who meet the definition of an A.T. thru-hiker (those who begin and end their hike at least 50 miles outside the park and only travel on the A.T. in the park) are eligible for a thru-hiker permit of $20 (valid for 38 days from the date issued for an up to 8 day hike through the Park). Permits are available here. A permit may also be obtained in person at the park's Backcountry Office (at the Sugarlands Visitor Center near Gatlinburg) or over the phone; with permits issued by fax, mail or email. Permits are available at (https://smok-iespermits.nps.gov/). Hikers staying overnight in the backcountry are required to have a printed copy of the permit. For more information, call 865-436-1297.

No dogs or other pets are allowed on any park trails. No dogs or other pets may be carried into the backcountry. See mile 166.7 for kennel providers.

-Shelter Policy: Great Smoky Mountains National Park regulations require that you stay in a shelter. While other backpackers must make reservations to use backcountry shelters, thru-hikers are exempt. From March 15 to June 15, four spaces at each A.T. shelter are reserved for thru-hikers. If the shelter is full, thru-hikers can tent close by. Only thru-hikers are allowed to tent next to shelters, so they are responsible for making room for those who have reservations in the shelters.

Although the ATC recommends the use of bear canisters along the southern portion of the Appalachian Trail the National Park Service does not require them within the boundaries of Great Smoky Mountains National Park. Each campsite/shelter along the AT within our boundaries has a food storage cable system available. The NPS recommends hanging your entire pack in a plastic bag to protect it from wildlife and rain.

NoBo	Features	Description	GPS	Elev	SoBo
166.8	Y	Fontana Dam bypass trail to the west.		1725	2025.2
167.5	Y ▲ P(7) ⚲	**Lakeview Drive West**, Benton MacKaye Trail and Lakeshore Trail and Benton MacKaye Trail lead east. Roadside parking.	N 35 26.485, W 83 47.729	1800	2024.5
169.7	◊	Unreliable water source a few yards east at bend in trail.		3621	2022.3
171.1	⌂ ⚲	Old road leads (0.1) east to Shuckstack Fire Tower. Coordinates are for fire tower.	N 35 29.128, W 83 48.909	3800	2020.9
171.5	⚲ Y	Sassafras Gap. Intersection of Lost Cove Trail east and Twentymile Trail to west.	N 35 33.757, W 83 50.748	3648	2020.5
172.4	◊ ▲ ⌒ ☎	Birch Spring Gap, Tent pads are located 100 yards to west down slope, **camping not permitted along AT**, spring, bear cables.		3680	2019.6
174.5	Y ▲	Doe Knob summit, intersects with Gregory Bald Trail to the west.		4520	2017.5
175.0		Mud Gap.		4331	2017.0
176.1	◊	Ekaneetlee Gap, spring 300 feet west		3842	2015.9
177.8	◊ ⌐(12) ☎ ⚲	**Mollies Ridge Shelter**, water (spring) located 200 yards to the right of the shelter, bear cables. 24.9◄18.6◄11.9◄►3.1►6.0►12.1	N 35 32.753, W 83 47.618	4570	2014.2
178.3		Devil's Tater Patch		4775	2013.7
179.4		Little Abrams Gap		4120	2012.6
179.7		Big Abrams Gap.		4121	2012.3

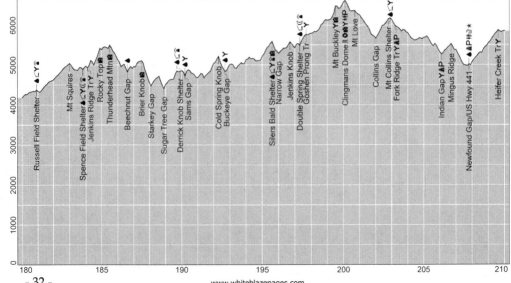

NoBo	Features	Description	GPS	Elev	SoBo
180.9	♦ Y ⊏(14) ☎ ♀	**Russell Field Shelter**, water (spring) located 150 yards down the Russell Field Trail toward Cades Cove, bear cables. 21.7◀15.0◀3.1◀▶2.9▶9.0▶14.7	N 35 33.704, W 83 45.996	4360	2011.1
181.2		MacCampbell Gap.		4329	2010.8
183.8	♦ Y ⊏(12) ☾ ☎ ♀	(0.15) east down Eagle Creek Trail to **Spence Field Shelter**, water (spring) 150 yards down the Eagle Creek Trail, privy, bear cables. Bote Mountain Trail to the west. 17.9◀6.0◀2.9◀▶6.1▶11.8▶13.5	N 35 33.708, W 83 43.962	4915	2008.2
184.2	Y	Jenkins Ridge Trail leads east.		4936	2007.8
184.9	📷	Rocky Top, views of Fontana Lake.		5440	2007.1
185.5	▲ 📷	Thunderhead summit, east peak, views of Fontana Lake and southwest.		5527	2006.5
186.6	♦	Beechnut Gap, water (spring) is located 75 yards west		4920	2005.4
187.2		Mineral Gap		5030	2004.8
187.6	📷	Eastern shoulder of Brier Knob, vista		5210	2004.4
188.9		Sugar Tree Gap, sugar maple trees.		4435	2003.1
189.9	♦ ⊏(12) ☎ ♀	**Derrick Knob Shelter**, water (spring), bear cables. 12.1◀9.0◀6.1◀▶5.7▶7.4▶13.0	N 35 33.991, W 83 38.514	4880	2002.1
190.2	♦ Y P(15-20)	Sams Gap, water (spring) is located 300 feet west, junction with Greenbrier Ridge Trail to the west (4.2) to Tremont Road and parking.		4995	2001.8
190.5	♦ Y	Miry Ridge Trail, water (spring) is located 600 feet west on Miry Ridge Trail.			2001.5
192.6	♦	Buckeye Gap		4817	1999.4
195.6	♦ ⊏(12) ☎ ♀	**Silers Bald Shelter**, water (spring) located to the right on a trail 75 yards, bear cables. 14.7◀11.8◀5.7◀▶1.7▶7.3▶15.3	N 35 33.857, W 83 34.099	5460	1996.4
195.8	📷	Silers Bald, partially wooded summit, view		5607	1996.2
196.0	Y	Welch Ridge Trail to east.		5432	1996.0
197.3	♦ ⊏(12) ☾ ☎ ♀	**Double Spring Gap Shelter**, water that is reliable is located on the North Carolina side, 15 yards from the crest. A second source is on the Tennessee side, 35 yards from the crest. Privy, bear cables. Gap is named for two springs that are unreliable in late summer. 13.5◀7.4◀1.7◀▶5.6▶13.6▶21.0	N 35 33.915, W 83 32.558	5505	1994.7
199.6	📷	Mt. Buckley, vista		6582	1992.4
200.1	♦ Y ◈ 📷 ⅋ O ♙ ▲ P(20) ♀	**Clingmans Dome** AT Passport location, in visitors center. Highest point on the AT. Observation tower provides 360-degree views. Trail east (0.5) to Clingman's parking area with restroom.	N 35 33.775, W 83 29.900	6643	1991.9
200.6	▲	Mt. Love, summit		6446	1991.4
202.9	♦ Y ⊏(12) ☾ ☎ ♀	Sugarland Mountain Trail leads (0.5W) **Mt. Collins Shelter**, water (spring) located 200 yards beyond shelter on Sugarland Mountain Trail, privy, bear cables. 13.0◀7.3◀5.6◀▶8.0▶15.4▶20.6	N 35 35.645, W 83 28.263	5900	1989.1
203.1	Y ▲ P(4-5) ♀	Side trail leads east 35 yards to **Clingmans Dome Access Road** and Fork Ridge Trail.	N 35 36.418, W 83 28.175	5269	1988.9
206.1	Y ▲ P(8-10) ♀	Indian Gap, intersection of Road Prong Trail. Parking 19 yards east off **Clingmans Dome Access Road**.	N 35 36.572, W 83 26.793	5286	1985.9
207.8	♦ ▲ ♙ 📷 P(20) ♀	Cross **U.S. 441**, Newfound Gap. Rockefeller Memorial. Restrooms. The only road crossing along the Trail in the Smokies. ★ ★ ★ ★ ★	N 35 36.665, W 83 25.519	5045	1984.2

Gatlinburg, TN (15.0W) see map of Gatlinburg.

✉ ♀	**PO** M-F 9am-5pm, Sa 9am-11am. 865-436-3229. 1216 East Pkwy 37738. 1216 East Pkwy. Gatlinburg, TN 37738. N 35 43.534, W 83 28.890	
🛏 ⊕ ☑	**Microtel Gatlinburg** 865-436-0107. 🛏 $69.99 to 89.99, includes continental breakfast. Pets fee $10. ⊕ Free WiFi. ☑ Mail drops for guests and advance reservations: 211 Historic Nature Trail, Gatlinburg, TN 37738	
🛏 ♨ ⊕ ☑	**Motel 6** 865-436-7813. 🛏 Reaonable rates, call for pricing. Pets under 25 lbs are free, There is a pet fee of over 25 lbs. Microwave, fridge, ♨ outdoor pool, ⊕ free WiFi. Accepts Credit Cards. ☑ Mail drops for guests: 309 Ownby St, Gatlinburg, TN 37738.	
🛏 ⊕	**Days Inn & Suites** 865-436-5811. 🛏 Call for pricing, ⊕ free WiFi.	
🥾 ♿ ☑	**NOC Great Outpost** 865-277-8209. (noc.com/retail-locations/noc-gatlinburg) 🥾 M-Th 10am-6pm, F-Sa 10am-8pm, Su 10m-6pm. ⚗ Coleman and alcohol by the ounce. △ Free showers and pack storage. ☑ Mail drops: 1138 Parkway, Gatlinburg, TN 37738.	
🥾	**The Day Hiker** 865-430-0970. (www.thedayhiker.com)	

NoBo Features	Description	GPS Elev SoBo

🚕 **Highlands Shuttle Service** (Ron McGaha) 423-625-0739 (home), 865-322-2752 (cell). (highlandsshuttleservice.com)
Shuttle area is from Wesser, North Carolina (NOC), to Damascus Virginia.
Shuttles anywhere in the Great Smoky Mountains National Park and the McGhee/Tyson Airport in Knoxville, Tennessee, as well as the Asheville, NC airport (AVL).

🚕 **A Walk in the Woods** 865-436-8283. (www.awalkinthewoods.com)
M-Su 9am-5pm, except holidays. Resupply and shuttling hikers. Shuttles range from Springer Mtn, GA to Damascus, VA. Ask about thru hiker rates.

🛒 **Old Dad's General Store & Deli** 865-430-1644. (www.olddadsgeneralstore.com) Deli, Grill, Grocery.
Also serves hot foods. M-Su 7am-11pm.

✗ Other restaurants intown include.
Bennett's BBQ, (bennetts-bbq.com) AYCE Breakfast bar include 50 items. AYCE Soup and Salad bar for lunch.
Smoky Mountain Brewery (www.smoky-mtn-brewery.com)
Park Grill Steakhouse (www.parkgrillgatlinburg.com)
Pizza Hut, TGI Friday's, Five Guys, Shoney's, Loco Burro fresh mex cantina

Cherokee, NC. (18.0E) (all major services)
💊 **Walgreens** M-Su 8 am-10 pm; **Pharmacy** M-F 11am-7pm, Sa-Su closed.

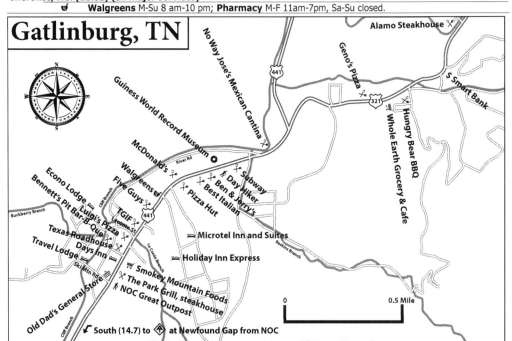

Gatlinburg, TN

209.6	Y P(10-15)	Sweat Heifer Trail leads (5.8E) to U.S. 441 via Sweetheart Creek and Kephart Prong.	N 35 35.148, W 83 21.498	5842	1982.4

NoBo	Features	Description	GPS	Elev	SoBo
210.2	📷	View.		6034	1981.8
210.6	Y📷	Boulevard Trail leads (5.5W) to Mt. LeConte.		5695	1981.4
210.9	♦Y ⊑(12) ☾ ☎ ♀	East 75 feet to **Icewater Spring Shelter**, water (spring) located 50 yards north of AT, privy, bear cables. 15.3◀13.6◀8.0◀▶7.4▶12.6▶20.3	N 35 37.789, W 83 23.179	5920	1981.1
211.5	♦	Spring on the west.		5884	1980.5
211.8	Y📷◑♀	**Charlies Bunion** (0.1) on loop trail west around Fodder Stack. From here to Porters Gap there are some spectacular views.	N 35 38.246, E 83 22.604	5500	1980.2
212.2		Dry Sluice Gap.		5314	1979.8
212.3	Y	Dry Sluice Gap Trail leads (8.7) east to Smokemont Campground.		5443	1979.7
213.2		Porters Gap, the Sawteeth. From here to Charlies Bunion there are some spectacular views.		5577	1978.8
213.9		False Gap.		5500	1978.1
215.1	▲	Cross Woolly Top Lead.		5880	1976.9
216.3	📷	Bradley's View, views east into deep-cut gorge of Bradley Fork.		5200	1975.7
218.1	📷	Cross Hughes Ridge.		5571	1973.9
218.3	♦Y ⊑(12) ☾ ☎ ♀	Hughes Ridge Trail leads east, continue (0.4E) **Peck's Corner Shelter**, water (spring) located 50 yards in front of shelter, privy, bear cables. From the shelter Hughes Ridge Trail leads to Smokemont Campground. 21.0◀15.4◀7.4◀▶5.2▶12.9▶19.8	N 35 39.049, W 83 18.511	5280	1973.7
219.2	📷	Good view of slopes and gorges.		5884	1972.8
220.7	▲	Mt. Sequoyah, summit		6069	1971.3
222.4		Reach high point on Mt. Chapman.		6417	1969.6
223.5	♦Y ⊑(12) ☾ ☎ ♀	Trail leads 100 yards east to **Tri-Corner Knob Shelter**, water (spring) located 10 yards in front of shelter, privy, bear cables. 20.6◀12.6◀5.2◀▶7.7▶14.6▶25.3	N 35 41.630, W 83 15.399	5920	1968.5
223.8	Y	Balsam Mountain Trail leads (10.1) along ridge of Balsam Mountains to Pin Oak Gap at Balsam Mountain Road, closed in winter.		5970	1968.2
224.9	♦Y	Cross Guyot Spur, AT skirts around Mt Guyot		6360	1967.1
225.5	♦	Guyot Spring, located on AT		6150	1966.5
226.2	📷	Good view.		6271	1965.8
227.5	Y	Snake Den Ridge Trail leads (5.3) west to Crosby Campground		5600	1964.5
230.8		Ridgecrest on west side of ridge near Cosby Knob.		5150	1961.2
231.2	♦Y ⊑(12) ☾ ☎ ♀	Trail leads 150 feet east to **Cosby Knob Shelter**, water (spring) is located 35 yards downhill in front of shelter, privy, bear cables. 20.3◀12.9◀7.7◀▶6.9▶17.6▶25.9	N 35 43.697, W 83 10.924	4700	1960.8
231.9	Y⚑	Low Gap Trail leads (2.5) west to Crosby Campground		4240	1960.1
234.0	Y▮	Side trail leads (0.6) west to Mt. Cammerer fire tower. Historic stone and timber structure rebuilt in 1994 that provides panoramic views from its platform. Not your run of the mill fire lookout, it's an octagonal rock tower.		5000	1958.0
234.4	♦	Water (spring) is located on AT west side.		4300	1957.6
234.6	📷	Large rock provides good views east.		4387	1957.4

© WhiteBlaze Pages 2019

NoBo	Features	Description	GPS	Elev	SoBo
235.9	♦Y	Water (spring) is located 80 feet to the east		3700	1956.1
236.1	Y	Lower Mt. Cammerer Trail leads west (7.8) public road at NPS Cosby Campground.		3469	1955.9
237.1	YP(10)	Chestnut Branch Trail, leads (2.0) east to parking at Big Creek Ranger Station and to the north end of BMT	N 35 45.592, W 83 06.333	2900	1954.9
238.1	♦Y⌐(12)⚲	Trail leads 200 yards west to **Davenport Gap Shelter**, water (spring) located to left of shelter. 19.8◀14.6◀6.9◀▶10.7▶19.0▶23.8	N 35 46.153, W 83 07.422	2600	1953.9
239.2	▲P(5-6)⚲	**Cross TN. 32, Davenport Gap, Cove Creek Road.** (Old NC. 284), eastern boundary, Great Smoky Mountain National Park. Parking is not recommend here, location has a history of vandalism with car thefts. **See Notes about Great Smoky Mountains National Park, Backcountry Permit Fees at NOBO mile 166.3.**	N 35 46.466, W 83 06.729	1975	1952.8

Advance notice for South Bounders:
See Notes about Great Smoky Mountains National Park, Backcountry Permit Fees at NOBO mile 166.7.

	🏪🛁	(1.2E) **Big Creek Country Store** 828-476-4492 December-February: Closed. April-November: Open daily 10 AM – 6 PM. March: hours vary weather permitting. Hours may vary. 🛁 Hot showers available April-November. **See Map of Davenport Gap, TN.**			
239.6	▲	Cross woods road.		1799	1952.4
239.9	⊤	Power line.		1822	1952.1

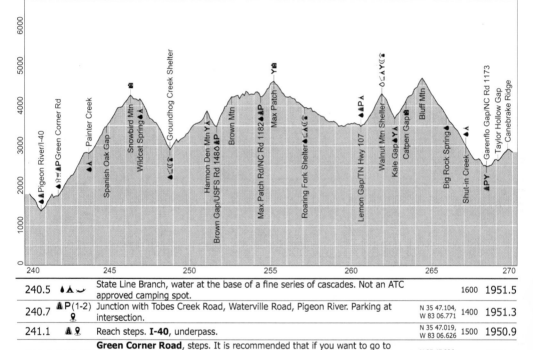

240.5	♦▲〰	State Line Branch, water at the base of a fine series of cascades. Not an ATC approved camping spot.		1600	1951.5
240.7	▲P(1-2)	Junction with Tobes Creek Road, Waterville Road, Pigeon River. Parking at intersection.	N 35 47.104, W 83 06.771	1400	1951.3
241.1	▲⚲	Reach steps. **I-40,** underpass.	N 35 47.019, W 83 06.626	1500	1950.9
241.6	▲P(2)⚲	**Green Corner Road,** steps. It is recommended that if you want to go to Standing Bear Hostle that you continue on another (0.4) miles to the next road crossing. Roadside parking.	N 35 47.006, W 83 06.558	1525	1950.4
242.0	▲P⚲ ★★★★★	**Green Corner Road. See map of Davenport Gap.**	N 35 47.169, W 83 06.108	1800	1950.0

	⌂⊨▲◈ 🛁⛺🏪⊕ 🚍P🐕▣	(0.1W) **Standing Bear Farm** 423-487-0014. ◈ AT Passport location. Open year round. ⌂ Bunk $20, ▲ tenting $15 per person. ⊨ Cabin or treehouse $50 per couple. 🏪 Resupply items available. Also has meals for purchase to cook. 🛁 Canister, Coleman and alcohol fuels. ⛺ Can hand wash laundry, electric dryer. ⊕ Free Wifi. 🚍 Shuttles anywhere. 🐕 Kennel service, dog shuttles around Smokies $250. P Parking. ▣ Mail drops for guests free (non guest $3 per package): 4255 Green Corner Rd, Hartford, TN 37753.

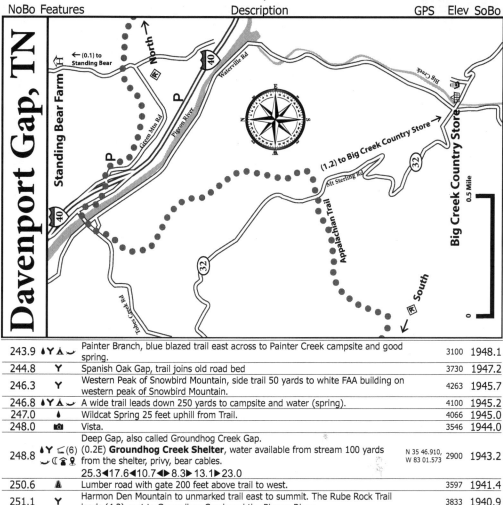

Davenport Gap, TN

NoBo	Features	Description	GPS	Elev	SoBo
243.9	♦Y⚑⌣	Painter Branch, blue blazed trail east across to Painter Creek campsite and good spring.		3100	1948.1
244.8	Y	Spanish Oak Gap, trail joins old road bed		3730	1947.2
246.3	Y	Western Peak of Snowbird Mountain, side trail 50 yards to white FAA building on western peak of Snowbird Mountain.		4263	1945.7
246.8	♦Y⚑⌣	A wide trail leads down 250 yards to campsite and water (spring).		4100	1945.2
247.0	♦	Wildcat Spring 25 feet uphill from Trail.		4066	1945.0
248.0	📷	Vista.		3546	1944.0
248.8	♦Y ⌐(6) ⌣(☾⚐⚑	Deep Gap, also called Groundhog Creek Gap. (0.2E) **Groundhog Creek Shelter**, water available from stream 100 yards from the shelter, privy, bear cables. 25.3◄17.6◄10.7◄▶ 8.3▶13.1▶23.0	N 35 46.910, W 83 01.573	2900	1943.2
250.6	▲	Lumber road with gate 200 feet above trail to west.		3597	1941.4
251.1	Y	Harmon Den Mountain to unmarked trail east to summit. The Rube Rock Trail leads (4.2) east to Groundhog Creek and the Pigeon River.		3833	1940.9
251.2	Y	Spur trail leads west 350 feet to formation known as Hawk's Roost.		4300	1940.8
251.7	♦▲P(2)⚐	Cross **USFS 148A**, Brown Gap, occasional spring is 100 yards down dirt road. Roadside parking.	N 35 46.389, W 82 59.753	3500	1940.3
252.1	▲	Cross Old road.		4393	1939.9
252.3	♦	Spring 100 yards west in steep ravine.		4562	1939.7
254.2	Y	Intersection of Cherry Creek Trail, yellow blazed.		4346	1937.8
254.4	▲P(3-4) ⚐	**Max Patch Road, SR 1182**	N 35 47.778, W 82 57.762	4380	1937.6
254.5	♦	Cross small stream.		4273	1937.5
254.8	▲	Cross gravel road leading west to SR 1182		4406	1937.2
255.2	▲ Y P(15-20)	Max Patch Summit, open summit, NO FIRES. Side trail leads west (0.2) to parking lot.		4629	1936.8
255.4	Y	Pass side trail that leads to old road, which leads to SR 1182		4487	1936.6
256.5	▲	Cross road with stiles on both sides.		4235	1935.5
256.6	♦	Cross stream.		4237	1935.4
257.1	♦Y⚑(8) ⌐(10) ⌣(☾⚐⚑	50 yards east to **Roaring Fork Shelter**, water located 800 feet north and south on the AT from the shelter, tent pads, privy, bear cables. 25.9◄19.0◄8.3◄▶ 4.8▶14.7▶28.9	N 35 49.340, W 82 56.316	3950	1934.9
257.2	♦	Cross stream.		4080	1934.8
257.4	⌒	Cross footbridge.		4020	1934.6
258.0	⚒	Nice cascades below the trail to the east.		3861	1934.0
258.1	♦⌒	Cross creek on footbridge.		3863	1933.9
258.9	▲	Cross old woods road.		3612	1933.1

© WhiteBlaze Pages 2019

NoBo	Features	Description	GPS	Elev	SoBo
260.4	♦▲	Cross stream with nice camping spot nearby.		3488	1931.6
260.6	▲ P(4-6) ♀	Cross **SR 1182**, TN. 107, Lemon Gap. Small clearing with three way road junction.	N 35 49.522, W 82 56.250	3550	1931.4
261.3	♦	Cross two branches of stream 150 feet apart.		3937	1930.7
261.9	◊▲ ⊑(5) ⌣ℂ☎♀	**Walnut Mountain Shelter**, water is located down a blue blazed trail to the left of Rattlesnake Trail and is difficult to locate, tenting, privy, bear cables. Walnut Mountain Trail to west 23.8◄13.1◄4.8◄►9.9►24.1►32.7	N 35 50.187, W 82 56.202	4260	1930.1
263.4	📷	Catpen Gap, views.		4146	1928.6
263.6	♦	Cross brooks.		4251	1928.4
264.3	▲	Bluff Mountain, large boulders on summit.		4686	1927.7
265.1	♦	Spring west on blue blazed trail 50 yards.		4036	1926.9
265.9	♦	Big Rock Spring, water (spring) is located 50 yards east at base of log steps.		3730	1926.1
266.2	▲	Cross old road.		3466	1925.8
266.6	▲	Cross woods road.		3366	1925.4
267.0	♦	Cross brook.		3081	1925.0
267.1	♦	Cross brook with cascades below trail.		3022	1924.9
267.6	▲	Cross old road that is now grassed over.		2679	1924.4
267.9	Y📷	Blue blaze leads (0.1) east to vista.		2649	1924.1
268.2	▲	Cross old road.		2499	1923.8
268.4	Y▲ P(6-8)♀	**Garenflo Gap Road**, Garenflo Gap. Shut-In Trail yellow blazed trail leads (2.0) west to Upper Shut-in Road/SR 1183.	N 35 51.204, W 82 52.554	2500	1923.6

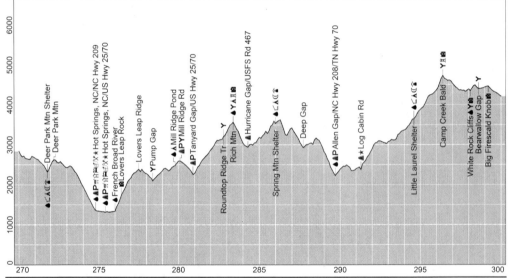

271.8	♦Y▲ ⊑(5) ⌣ℂ☎♀	Gragg Gap. (0.2E) **Deer Park Mountain Shelter**, water (spring) is located on the trail about half way to the shelter, tenting, privy, bear cables. Gravestones west of trail. 23.0◄14.7◄9.9◄► 14.2►22.8►30.1	N 35 52.550, W 82 51.684	2330	1920.2
274.5	📷	View of Spring Creek at switchback.		1593	1917.5
274.6	▲	Cross Serpentine Street near parking area.		1404	1917.4
275.0	●▲ P(15-20) ♀	**U.S. 25/70, N.C. 209, Hot Springs, NC. See Map of Hot Spings. Notice the AT logos in the sidewalks** **South bounders must have a backcountry permit before entering** ★★★★★ **Great Smoky Mountains National Park.**	N 35 53.370, W 82 49.938	1326	1917.0

Advance notice for South Bounders:
See Notes about Great Smoky Mountains National Park, Backcountry Permit Fees at NOBO mile 166.7.
Hot Springs, NC see map of Hot Springs, NC.

	⌂♀	**PO** M-F 9am-11:30am & 1pm-4pm, Sa 9am-10:30am 828-622-3242. 11 Bridge St. Hot Springs, NC 28743. N 35 53.568, W 82 49.661

Elmers Sunnybank Inn 828-622-7206. (www.sunnybankretreatassociation.org)
◈ AT Passport location.
Open year round. ⑧ No Pets. No Smoking. Located across from Dollar General. ⇐ Traditional thru-hikers $25 per person for private room, includes linens, towel and shower. ✗ Breakfast for guests only $6 dinner $12; gourmet organic vegetarian meals. Inn offers an extensive library and a well-equipped music room. ⊕ WiFi available. ♦ Work exchange possible. Does not take Credit Cards.
✉ Mail drops for guests: PO Box 233, Hot Springs, NC 28743. FEDX drops: 26 Walnut St. , Hot Springs, NC 28743.

Hostel at Laughing Heart Lodge
828-206-8487. (www.laughingheartlodge.com)
◈ AT Passport location.
Open year round. Pets welcome. ⌂ $20 bunks, $25 per person for ⇐ semi private, $35 per person for single private, $45 double occupancy in a private room. Pets fee $5, few pet rooms. All rooms include morning coffee, shower, towel, movies, use of hiker kitchen. Lodge rooms $100 and up, includes continental breakfast, must call to reserve at 828-622-0165. ▲ Tenting with shower $10 per person $15 for 2 (in one tent). Quiet time at night from 10 pm to 7 am. ⌂ Laundry $5 includes soap. ⌂ Shower only $5. ⊕ Free WiFi. Karoake and outdoor movie theater with 10 foot screen. Massage available, please call Glenda at 603-204-7893
✉ Mail drops for guests: 289 NW US Hwy 25/70, Hot Springs, NC 28743.

Iron Horse Station 866-402-9377. (www.theironhorsestation.com)
✗ Restaurant, tavern and coffee shop. Serves lunch and dinner, offers few vegetarian options, ⊕ free WiFi. ⇐ Hiker room rate $70D.

Little Bird Cabins
828-206-1487. natalie@littlebirdcabinrentals.com (www.littlebirdcabinrentals.com)
Open year round.
Located 500 feet east from the southern AT trail head in town. Cabin sleeps 7, includes kitchenette. ⇐ 10% Hiker's Discount. Use code WHITEBLAZE (online) or mention this guidebook's discount when booking by phone. Pet fee $15. ⊕ Free Wifi. Credit Cards accepted

Mountain Magnolia Inn 800-914-9306. (www.mountainmagnoliainn.com)
⇐ Discount hiker rates $80S, $105D, includes country breakfast, ⊕ free WiFi. ✗ Dinner Th-M.
✉ Mail drops for guests: 204 Lawson St, Hot Springs, NC 28743.

Creekside Court 828-215-1261. Call or text for availability 828-206-5473. (www.lodginghotspringsnc.com)
⇐ $79 and up, ask for hiker discount, pets allowed, pet fee $25. ⊕ Free WiFi.

Hot Springs Resort & Spa 828-622-7676. (www.nchotsprings.com)
▲ Tenting $24 up to 4 people. ⇐ Camping cabins $50 and up. Pets $10. Mineral water spa $20 per person before 6pm; 3-person rate $38 before 6pm, $43 after 6pm. ➹ Camp store carries snacks and supplies. ✗ Take Out Grill inside the campstore. ⊕ Free WiFi. Also offers massage therapy. Accepts Credit Cards.

Spring Creek Tavern 828-622-0187. (www.thespringcreektavern.com)
◈ AT Passport location.
⇐ Limited rooms to rent, call ahead.
✗ M-Th 11am-10pm, F-Sa 11:30am-11pm, Su 11am-10pm. special AT burger. Limited amount of rooms to rent, call for availability and pricing. ⊕ Free WiFi.

Alpine Court Motel 828-622-3590 (www.alpinecourtmotel.com/) Tax-included prices; Starting at $65, $10 EAP. Fee for Credit Cards.

Smoky Mountain Diner 828-622-7571
◈ AT Passport location.
✗ M-W 6am-8pm, Th-Sa 6:30-8pm, Su 6:30am-2pm.

Visitor Center 828-622-9932 Free WiFi, signal still accessible outside after closed.

Hiker's Ridge Ministries Resource Center
828-691-0503 godswayeen@gmail.com (www.hikersridge.com)
◈ AT Passport location.
Open M-Sa 9am-3pm, Mar 21 - May. Place to relax, coffee, drinks, snacks, ♦♦ restroom. ⌨ Computer available for use, ⊕ free WiFi.
⇐ Overnight stays, ask for pricing.

Bluff Mountain Outfitters 828-622-7162. (www.bluffmountain.com)
◈ AT Passport location.
⚡ M-Thu 9am-5pm, F-Sa 9am-6pm, Su 9am-5pm. Full service outfitter, ⌂ fuel by the ounce. ➹ Long term resupply. ⌨ Computer available for use. ☎ ATM. Hikers can print GSMNP permits here.
✉ Mail drops: (USPS) PO Box 114 Hot Springs, NC 28743 or (FedEx/UPS) 152 Bridge St.

Hot Springs Library 828-622-3584. M-F 10 am-6 pm, Sa 10 am-2 pm, Su closed.

Teresa Ramsay 828-707-2468
Facebook facebook.com/bootleggerteas

Hot Springs, NC

276.4	Y 📷	Lovers Leap Rock, Pump Gap Trail leads to the west	1820	1915.6
276.7	📷	Viewpoint overlooking the French Broad River 600 feet below.	1980	1915.3
278.3	Y	Pump Gap, another blue blaze trail crosses here	2130	1913.7
279.9	♦ ⚐	Reach saddle then turn right downhill to pond and campsite, not an ATC approved camping spot.	2490	1912.1
280.9 ★★★★★	⚑ P ♀	Cross **U.S. 25 & 70** overpass, Tanyard Gap. Trail follow fire road 70 feet.	N 35 54.622, W 82 47.467	2278	1911.1
282.3	♦	Cross foot log below good spring.	3097	1909.7
282.7	⚐	Trail is on road for about 50 feet.	3283	1909.3
282.8	Y	Roundtop Ridge Trail, yellow blazed leads (8.2) west back to Hot Springs.	3257	1909.2
283.2 ♦ Y ⚐ 📷		Rich Mountain. Side trail (0.1) west to Fire Tower and views, water (piped spring) is located north on AT. Campsite is located (0.1) west on side trail.	3600	1908.8
283.3	♦ ⚐	Head of ravine with camp site and spring to the west.	3030	1908.7
283.8	♦	Spring west on trail.	3321	1908.2
284.1	⚐	Cross road, **USFA 3514** leads east.	3019	1907.9
284.3	⚐	Junction with **USFS 467**, Hurricane Gap. Trail follows fire road 70 feet.	2900	1907.7
286.0	♦ ⚐ ⊏(5) ◖ ☂ ♀	**Spring Mountain Shelter**, water is located 75 yards down a blue blazed trail on the east side of the AT, tenting, privy, bear cables. 28.9◄24.1◄14.2◄►8.6►15.9►22.6	N 35 57.089, W 82 47.412	3300	1906.0
287.5	♦ Y	Water (spring) 10 feet west on trail in ravine.	3190	1904.5
289.6	⚐	Cross logging road.	2466	1902.4
289.7	♦ ⚑ P ♀	Cross **NC. 208, TN. 70**, Allen Gap, Paint Creek, water to the west 350 yards	N 35 59.216, W 82 47.232	2234	1902.3
290.7	⚐	Cross old dirt road.	2494	1901.3
291.3 ★★★★★	⚐	Log Cabin Drive. Private home in view to 100 yards east, please do not trespass. **See map of Log Cabin Rd.**	2560	1900.7

⌂ ⇔ ⚐ (0.7W) **Hemlock Hollow Inn** 423-787-1736(www.hemlockhollowinn.com) Owners Russ and Dianna ⊛ ✕ ☰ ⚲ Rosa.
P ⇔ ⇨ ⚲ ⊛ AT Passport location.
Closed during the winter (October 25th-March 25th). West on Log Cabin Dr. to paved Viking Mountain Rd. ⌂ Bunkroom $27PP with linens, $22 without. ⇔ Cabin for couples with linens $60. All rooms heated. ⚐ Tent site $15 per person. ☰ Pets fee $5. All stays include shower. ⚲ Non guest shower and towel for $5. ☰ Camp store stocked with long term resupply, some gear, cold drinks, foods, fruit, stove fuels. ⇔ Ask about shuttles. P Parking free for guests, fee for non-guests. Credit cards accepted.
☑ Mail drops free if you stay, $5 without staying.
Mail drops (ETA mandatory): 645 Chandler Circle, Greeneville, TN 37743.

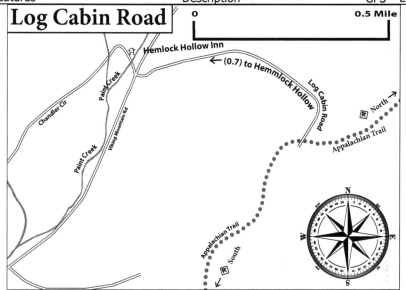

Log Cabin Road

Hemlock Hollow Inn

← (0.7) to Hemmlock Hollow

Log Cabin Road

Chandler Cir

Paint Creek

Viking Mountain Rd

Paint Creek

North

Appalachian Trail

Appalachian Trail

South

NoBo	Features	Description	GPS	Elev	SoBo
294.6	♦▲⊑(5) ⌣☾☏♀	**Little Laurel Shelter**, water (boxed spring) is located 100 yards down blue blazed trail behind shelter to west, tent sites are south of shelter, privy, bear cables. 32.7◀22.8◀8.6◀▶7.3▶14.0▶22.8	N 36 00.899, W 82 44.154	3300	1897.4
296.4	Y ▮🛶▲	Camp Creek Bald Trail leads (0.2) west to Camp Creek Bald Lookout Tower, catwalk is often locked. Trail least (6.2) east to Shelton Laurel Road.		4750	1895.6
298.1	♦Y	Water (spring), creek, blue blaze trails on both sides of the AT		4390	1893.9
298.2	Y🛶	White Rock Cliffs are located 50 feet east with views.		4450	1893.8
298.3	Y	Wide side trail to west.		4494	1893.7
298.4	Y🛶	Blackstack Cliffs are located 200 feet west with views.		4420	1893.6
298.6	Y	Trail to west is a bad weather route.		4434	1893.4
299.4	♦🛶	Big Firescald Knob		4360	1892.6
299.6	Y	Pass blue blaze trail.		4410	1892.4

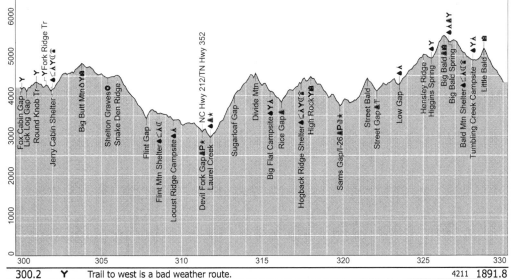

NoBo	Features	Description	GPS	Elev	SoBo
300.2	Y	Trail to west is a bad weather route.		4211	1891.8
300.8	Y	Round Knob Trail leads (3.0) to picnic area and Round Knob Spring and into Round Knob Campground Road.		4260	1891.2
301.7	Y	USFS Fork Ridge Trail leads (2.0) east to parking area at Big Creek Road.		4272	1890.3

NoBo	Features	Description	GPS	Elev	SoBo
301.9	♦▲⊏(6) ((🛏♀	**Jerry Cabin Shelter**, water is located 100 yards down a blue blazed trail behind the shelter, tenting, privy, bear cables. 30.1◀15.9◀7.3◀▶ 6.7▶ 15.5▶ 25.6	N 36 03.392, W 82 39.431	4150	1890.1
303.5	▲	Cross dirt road.		4477	1888.5
303.8	Y▲	Big Butt, summit to west, short bypass trail. Trail turns abruptly here.		4750	1888.2
304.9	♦	Water (spring) is seasonal and known to go dry.		4480	1887.1
305.4	○	**Shelton Graves,** William and David Shelton, uncle and nephew. When returning to a family gathering during the war, they were ambushed near here and killed by Confederate troops.		4490	1886.6
306.5	▲	Cross old logging road on Snake Den Ridge crest.		4577	1885.5
307.0	◊	Seasonal water.		4067	1885.0
307.8	▲	Flint Gap, cross old logging road.		3616	1884.2
308.6	♦⊏(8) ⌣((🛏♀	**Flint Mountain Shelter**, water (spring) located 100 feet north of shelter on the AT, there are two streams between the shelter and the spring, privy. 22.6◀14.0◀6.7◀▶ 8.8▶ 18.9▶ 29.5	N 36 02.087, W 82 35.814	3570	1883.4
309.5	♦▲	Campsite, water		3400	1882.5
311.3	▲P♀	Cross **NC. 212**, Devil Fork Gap, hostel and resupply (2.5E)	N 36 00.631, W 82 36.506	3100	1880.7
	🛏▲🏠 🛍⌂🚗	(2.5E) **Laurel Trading Post** 828-656-2016 Open year round. M-Su days 7am-7pm. 🛏 Bunkroom $25, ▲ tenting $10, 🛍 includes shower, ⌂ laundry $5, full kitchen. 🛁 Shower and towel without stay $5. 🛒 Lots of resupply items. 🚗 Free shuttle to store and return to trail. Credit cards accepted.			
311.8	♦▲	Cross **Rector Laurel Road**, spring north on AT, several stream crossings on the AT north of road.		2960	1880.2
312.1	♦	Small cemetery, water (stream).		3060	1879.9
312.4	♦	Cross stream and woods road.		3258	1879.6
312.7	♦🛆	Cross stream at waterfall.		3589	1879.3
313.1		Sugarloaf Gap. Sugarloaf Knob to the east.		4000	1878.9
313.5	♦	Pass spring and big rocks.		4203	1878.5
314.5		Pass apples trees from remnants of farm.		4477	1877.5
314.6	▲	Frozen Knob/Lick Rock, summit.		4579	1877.4
315.2	♦Y▲	Big Flat is located east of rock formation, water, campsite to east		4160	1876.8
316.2	▲	Rice Gap, dirt road		3800	1875.8
317.4	♦Y⊏(6) ⌣((🛏♀	(0.1E) **Hogback Ridge Shelter**, water (spring) (0.3) on a side trail near the shelter, privy, bear cables. 22.8◀15.5◀8.8◀▶ 10.1▶ 20.7▶ 31.2	N 35 57.837, W 82 35.232	4255	1874.6
318.0	Y📷	High Rock, blue blazed trail leads 150 feet to the west for view		4460	1874.0
319.8	♦▲P♀ ★★★★★	Cross Flag Pond Road, US. 23, I-26, Sams Gap.	N 35 57.149, W 82 33.655	3800	1872.2
	🛏🛌▲ ⌣(4)◈✗ 🏠🛁⌂🚗 🛍🍴🚗P 🖂	(2.8W) **Natures Inn Hostel** 828-216-1611 (www.naturesinnhostel.com) ◈ AT Passport location. Pets allowed but they must be leashed when on property. 🛏 Two bunkhouses, both have electricity, twin mattress, bed linens for extra fee, heaters available for rent for extra fee, covered outdoor space between the two buildings. 🛌 Cabins, 2 People, EAP for a fee up to a total of 4, electricity, queen and twin bed with mattress, bed linens for extra fee, heaters are available for rent for extra fee, fire ring (firewood for sale), 🪑 picnic table, charcoal grill (charcoal for sale). 🛁 Bath house; bath towels, soap and shampoo included with stay. 🛌 Private rooms available in house ask for prices, 2 queen beds, 1 king beds. ▲ Tenting, includes shower for a price. ⌣ 4 hammock spots (in ground spots) for a price, includes shower. ◈ Free WiFi. ⌂ Laundry facilities on site, for a fee, includes laundry powder. 🛁 Showers; with out stay for a fee, if shuttle to and from trail head needed there is a fee. 🏠 Small resupply store for Hiker food stuffs and we offer ✗ pizza, soft drinks, hamburgers, hot dogs, some fuels etc. 🚗 Shuttle: to and from trail head at Sams Gap, free with stay. To and from Devil's Fork trail head, ask for pricing. 🎒 Slackpacking: available, negotiated pricing dependent upon, where, when, etc. P Parking: No charge with stay, priced per day with out stay. We accept CC and cash. Reservations recommended. All reservations must provide CC to reserve or pay in advance. Full refund if cancelled 7 days prior to reservation, 50% refund if cancelled during 6 days up to check in date. 🖂 Mail Drops: 4871 Old Asheville Highway, Flag Pond, TN 37657			
	✗	(2.8E) **Little Laurel Cafe** 828-689-2307. M-Th 6am-2pm, F 6am-7:30pm, Sa 7am-2pm, Su closed.			
	✗🏠☎	(3.5E) **Wolf Creek Market** 828-689-5943. Open M-F 6am-10pm, Sa 8am-9pm, Su closed. **Hunts Bros. Pizza**, M-Sa 6am-10pm, Su 8am-9pm. **Convenience Store**, M-Sa 6am-10 pm, Su 8am-9 pm.			

© WhiteBlaze Pages 2019

NoBo Features

North Carolina/Tennessee

Description

NC/TN

GPS   Elev SoBo

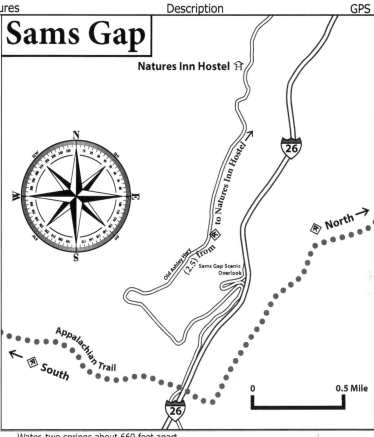

Sams Gap

Natures Inn Hostel ♫

to Natures Inn Hostel →

Old Ashley Hwy (2.5) from

Sams Gap Scenic Overlook

North →

Appalachian Trail

← South

0   0.5 Mile

NoBo	Features	Description	GPS	Elev	SoBo
320.5	♦	Water, two springs about 660 feet apart.		4000	1871.5
321.2		Pass around the east edge of an old abandoned talc mine, woods road to the west.		4357	1870.8
322.1	▲P ⚲	Cross Street Gap, gravel road.	N 35 58.133, W 82 32.429	4100	1869.9
322.2	夲	Power line.		4219	1869.8
323.3	♦Y	Blue blaze trail to east leads 20 yards to spring.		4342	1868.7
323.5	♦▲	Low Gap, water (piped spring) is located by campsite that are located downhill and to the west		4300	1868.5
324.1	♦	Pass spring.		4533	1867.9
325.0		Reach crest of ridge extending northwest.		4908	1867.0
325.5	♦	Blue blaze trail leads west 100 yards down slope to spring.		4850	1866.5
325.6	Y	Junction of blue blaze bypass trail east.		4959	1866.4
325.8	♦	Cross small streams in the area.		4965	1866.2
326.0		Slipper Spur, southern end of grassy bald.		5461	1866.0
326.3	▲▲	Big Bald, open summit.		5516	1865.7
326.6	♦Y▲▲	Big Stamp is a treeless saddle at the base of Big Bald, bypass trail to east. Water is located near campsite that is (0.3) west. Blue blaze bypass trail and road from Wolf Laurel ski resort.		5300	1865.4
327.5	♦Y▲ ⊏(10) ⌣ℭ☎⚲	(0.1W) **Bald Mountain Shelter**, water (spring) is located on the side trail to the shelter, tenting, privy, bear cables. 25.6◄18.9◄10.1◄► 10.6►21.1►33.9	N 36 00.011, W 82 28.692	5100	1864.5
327.7	♦	Spring beside trail. Stream crosses path.		4993	1864.3
327.9	♦Y▲	Blue blazed side trail leading west to a good campsite and continuing down (0.2) to Tumbling Creek and a reliable spring. This campsite is a good place to tent if the shelter is crowded.		4890	1864.1
328.9	▲	Little Bald, wooded summit		5185	1863.1

© WhiteBlaze Pages 2019

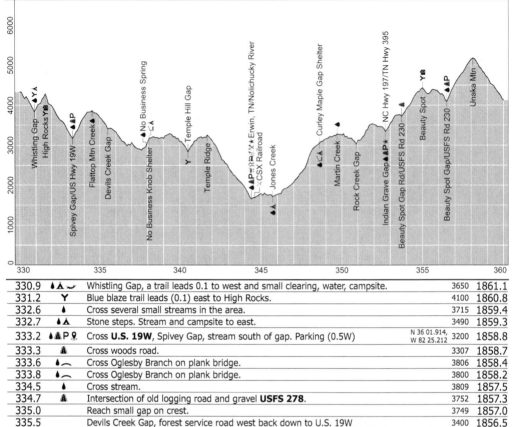

			GPS	Elev	SoBo
330.9	▲▲↙	Whistling Gap, a trail leads 0.1 to west and small clearing, water, campsite.		3650	1861.1
331.2	Y	Blue blaze trail leads (0.1) east to High Rocks.		4100	1860.8
332.6	↓	Cross several small streams in the area.		3715	1859.4
332.7	▲▲	Stone steps. Stream and campsite to east.		3490	1859.3
333.2	▲▲P♀	Cross **U.S. 19W**, Spivey Gap, stream south of gap. Parking (0.5W)	N 36 01.914, W 82 25.212	3200	1858.8
333.3	▲	Cross woods road.		3307	1858.7
333.6	↓⌒	Cross Oglesby Branch on plank bridge.		3806	1858.4
333.8	↓⌒	Cross Oglesby Branch on plank bridge.		3800	1858.2
334.5	↓	Cross stream.		3809	1857.5
334.7	▲	Intersection of old logging road and gravel **USFS 278**.		3752	1857.3
335.0		Reach small gap on crest.		3749	1857.0
335.5		Devils Creek Gap, forest service road west back down to U.S. 19W		3400	1856.5
337.9	↓	Spring to west in hemlock grove, water for No Business Knob Shelter		3300	1854.1
338.1	▲⌐(6)↙ ♀	**No Business Knob Shelter**, water is located (0.2) south of the shelter on the AT, tenting. 29.5◀20.7◀10.6◀▶ 10.5▶23.3▶32.4	N 36 04.006, W 82 26.016	3180	1853.9
340.5	Y	Temple Hill Gap, Side trails east and west from here.		2850	1851.5
341.2	▲	Access road to former fire tower.		2930	1850.8
342.6	📷	View of railroad and Unaka Springs below.		2671	1849.4
344.4	▲⌐P♀ ★★★★★	Cross **River Road**, Chestoa Bridge, Nolichucky River **Erwin, TN. (3.8W) (all major services). See maps of Erwin.**	N 36 06.312, W 82 26.794	1700	1847.6

⌂🛏▲◈ **Uncle Johnny's Nolichucky Hostel and Outfitters** 423-735-0548. (www.unclejohnnys.net)
🔥♨⛺🍴 ◈ AT Passport location.
🛏🍴🍺🛁 ◈ Open year round. ⌂ $20 per person per bunk. 🏠 Private cabins range from $30-$95, includes fridge,
🚲🛁🖥P microwave, and linens. ▲ Camping $10 per person. Included with stay are showers, shampoo, condi-
🚗🖂 tioner, and soap. 🔥 Work for Stay possible, just ask. ♨ Coleman and alcohol by the ounce. △ Laundry
$5. 🍴 Full resupply. 🖥 Computer available for use, 📶 free Wifi. 🔱 Outfitters store carries water filtration
systems and filters, headlamps and lots more hiker gear. Bike, 🛶 kayak and raft rentals. 🛁 Shower
without stay $5, includes soap and towel. 📞 Pay phone available. Accepts Mastercard, Visa. P Parking
available for guest. $2/day. P Parking fees for non-guests - $3.00 per vehicle per day. Free town shuttles
for guests, shuttle runs for breakfast, lunch and dinner. 🚐 Longer shuttles for a fee.
🖂 Mail drops: 151 River Rd, Erwin, TN 37650.

Erwin, TN 37650 see map of Erwin, TN.
📬♀ **PO** M-F 8:30-4:45, Sa 10-12, 423-743-9422. 201 N Main Ave, Erwin TN 37650. N 36 08.804, W 82 24.933

NoBo Features	Description	GPS	Elev	SoBo

🛏 ◈⊛ ⛺ **(0.9W) Cantarroso Farm & Apiary** 423-833-7514 or 423-360-1697. cantarrosofarm@gmail.com
◈🏠🛏P (www.cantarrosofarm.com)
◈ AT Passport location.
Located (0.9W) from Chestoa/Nolichucky River Bridge.
Open year-round. ⊛ No pets. CLEAN & QUIET setting with personal service. Free beverage and candy bar at pick up. 🛏 Two cabins: $40PP (2-7) or $60 private, Cabins offer ☎ free wifi, heat/AC, coffee/tea, full size beds, linens, shower, toiletries, towel, refrigerator, microwave, toaster oven, cooking gear, grill and fire pit. Stay includes pickup & return to Chestoa trail head, access to river and fishing gear ⛺ Additional charge for laundry, town shuttles, bikes and P parking. 🏠 Offer slack packing options..
✉ Mail drops: 777 Bailey Lane, Erwin TN 37650.

🛏⊛⛺💻 **Mountain Inn & Suites** 423-743-4100. (www.erwinmountaininn.com)
◈☎💻 ⊛ No pets. 🛏 Hiker rate $79.99 single, $10 each additional person up to four people, includes breakfast buffet. ⛺ Coin laundry, 💻 Computer in lobby for guest. ☎ Free WiFi. Hot tub & 🏊 swimming pool open (Memorial Day to Labor Day).
✉ Mail drops for registered guests only: 2002 Temple Hill Rd, Erwin TN 37650.

🛏☎💻 **Best Southern** 423-743-6438. 🛏 $50 and up. Pet fee $10, ☎ free WiFi.
✉ Mail drops for guests only: 1315 Jackson Love Hwy, Erwin, TN 37650.

🛏⊛⛺💻 **Super 8** 423-743-0200.
☎💻 ⊛ No pets. 🛏 $49.99 single, $59.99 double for two persons, $10 each additional person, max 4, includes breakfast. Microwaves, fridge, ⛺ coin operated laundry for guest, ☎ WiFi.
✉ Mail drops for guests only: 1101 N Buffalo St, Erwin TN 37650.

🛒 **Price Less Foods** M-Su 7am-9pm.

🍴 **Pizza Plus**, 423-743-7121. M-Su 11am-11pm. (AYCE 11am-2pm)

🚗P **Shuttles by Tom** 423-330-7416, 910-409-2509. hikersshuttles@gmail.com (www.hikershuttles.com) Owners Tom "10-K" Bradford and Marie "J-Walker" Bradford. Licensed and insured, permitted to shuttle in Pisgah and Cherokee National Forests. Based out of Erwin, TN. Shuttles to all area trail heads, bus stations, airports, outfitters, etc. Shuttle ranges from Springer to Harpers Ferry. P Free parking.

■ **Baker's Shoe Repair** 423-743-5421. Full service repair shop for shoes, leather, backpacks, etc. M 10am-5pm, Tu-Thurs 10am-3:30 pm. F 10am-5pm. Sa-Su closed. Sat--sometimes open but do not advertise any hours. Located across the street from the courthouse.

Erwin, TN

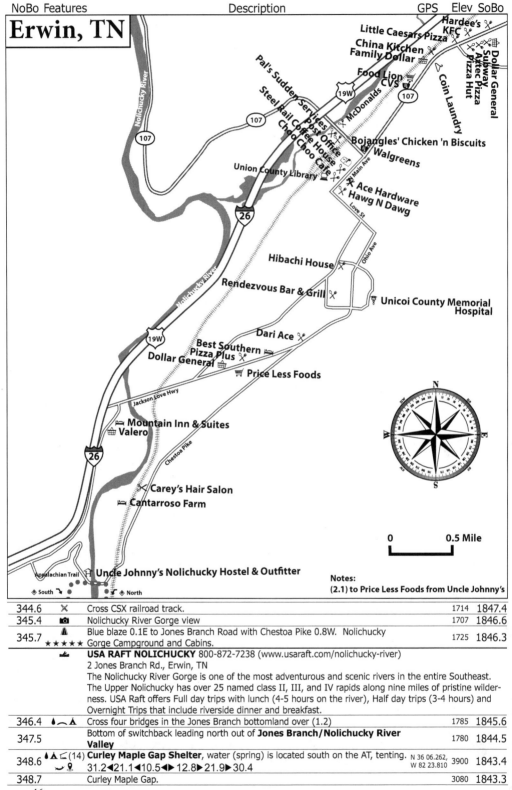

Nolichucky River

107

107

19W

107

Pal's Sudden Services
Steel Rail Coffee House
Choo Choo Cafe
Post Office
Union County Library

Little Caesars Pizza
China Kitchen
Family Dollar
Food Lion
CVS
McDonalds
Bojangles' Chicken 'n Biscuits
Walgreens
Ace Hardware
Hawg N Dawg

Hardee's
KFC
Subway
Aztec Pizza
Pizza Hut
Dollar General
Coin Laundry

Main Ave
Love St

26

Nolichucky River

Hibachi House
Rendezvous Bar & Grill

Ohio Ave

Unicoi County Memorial Hospital

19W

Dari Ace
Best Southern Pizza Plus
Dollar General
Price Less Foods

Jackson Love Hwy

Mountain Inn & Suites
Valero

Chestoa Pike

26

Carey's Hair Salon
Cantarroso Farm

0   0.5 Mile

Appalachian Trail   Uncle Johnny's Nolichucky Hostel & Outfitter

↘ South   North ↖

Notes:
(2.1) to Price Less Foods from Uncle Johnny's

344.6	✕	Cross CSX railroad track.	1714	1847.4
345.4	📷	Nolichucky River Gorge view	1707	1846.6
345.7	★★★★★	Blue blaze 0.1E to Jones Branch Road with Chestoa Pike 0.8W. Nolichucky Gorge Campground and Cabins.	1725	1846.3
		USA RAFT NOLICHUCKY 800-872-7238 (www.usaraft.com/nolichucky-river) 2 Jones Branch Rd., Erwin, TN The Nolichucky River Gorge is one of the most adventurous and scenic rivers in the entire Southeast. The Upper Nolichucky has over 25 named class II, III, and IV rapids along nine miles of pristine wilderness. USA Raft offers Full day trips with lunch (4-5 hours on the river), Half day trips (3-4 hours) and Overnight Trips that include riverside dinner and breakfast.		
346.4	💧⌒▲	Cross four bridges in the Jones Branch bottomland over (1.2)	1785	1845.6
347.5		Bottom of switchback leading north out of **Jones Branch/Nolichucky River Valley**	1780	1844.5
348.6	💧▲⌂(14)	**Curley Maple Gap Shelter**, water (spring) is located south on the AT, tenting. 31.2◀21.1◀10.5◀▶12.8▶21.9▶30.4	N 36 06.262, W 82 23.810 3900	1843.4
348.7		Curley Maple Gap.	3080	1843.3

NoBo	Features	Description	GPS	Elev	SoBo
349.7	♦	Cross small stream		3288	1842.3
349.9	♦	Spring		3271	1842.1
351.2		Cross through a gap.		3432	1840.8
352.7	▲P♀ ★★★★★	Cross **TN. 395, NC. 197**, Indian Grave Gap, water is located (0.1) east on outside of curve in road. **Erwin, TN (7.0W) See NOBO mile 344.4.**	N 36 06.646, W 82 21.665	3360	1839.3
	▲	(3.3W) **Rock Creek Recreation Area** (USFS) 423-638-4109 Tent site $12, Open mid-May to mid-Nov.			
353.4	⊤	Power line.		3749	1838.6
353.8	▲	Cross **USFS 230**, Beauty Spot Gap Road, gravel road		3980	1838.2
355.0		Beauty Spot, summit.		4437	1837.0
355.5	♦▲P	**USFS 230**, Beauty Spot Gap (northern end), water (spring) is located across from gated road. Parking is located to the west.		4120	1836.5
355.7	▲▲	Cross summit.		4358	1836.3
356.5	♦▲	Deep Gap, field		4100	1835.5
357.1	▲	USFS 230, Unaka Mountain Road is a few feet to the east.		4660	1834.9
358.1		Unaka Mountain, large stand of red spruce atop its summit.		5180	1833.9

[Elevation profile chart showing trail from mile 360 to 390, with elevation from 0 to 6000 feet. Labeled features include: Low Gap, Iron Mtn, Cherry Gap Shelter, Cherry Gap, Bald Knob, NC Hwy 226/TN Hwy 107, Beans Creek Rd, Iron Mtn Gap, Apple Orchard, Rock Pillar, Greasy Creek Gap, Clyde Smith Shelter, Little Rock Knob, Hughes Gap/NC Rd 1330, Beartown Mtn, Ash Gap, Roan Mtn, Roan High Knob Shelter, Roan High Knob, Carvers Gap/NC Hwy 261/TN Hwy 143, Round Bald, Jane Bald, Grassy Bald Trail, Stan Murray Shelter, Buckeye Gap, Overmountain Shelter, Little Hump Mtn, Bradley Gap, Hump Mtn]

360.3	♦	Low Gap, water (stream) is located (0.1) west		3900	1831.7
361.2	⌒	Cross bog bridge.		3902	1830.8
361.4	♦⌐(6) ⚲♀	**Cherry Gap Shelter**, water (spring) is located 80 yards on a blue blazed trail from the shelter. 33.9◄23.3◄12.8◄►9.1►17.6►22.8	N 36 07.754, W 82 15.852	3900	1830.6
361.8		Cherry Gap.		4016	1830.2
362.1		Reach several gaps within the next mile heading north.		3833	1829.9
363.9	▲	Trail intersects with road several time in this area.		3807	1828.1
364.5	▲P♀ ★★★★★	Cross **TN 107, NC 226**, Iron Mountain Gap **Unicoi, TN.**	N 36 08.589, W 82 13.998	3723	1827.5
	✕	(4.0E) **Mountain Grill** 828-688-9061. M-Sa 11am-8pm, Su closed. Cash only.			
365.0	Y🔲	Trail west provides good views across Stone Mountain.		3942	1827.0
365.3	🔲	Open field to the west provide good view of Unaka Mountain.		4096	1826.7
365.7	♦▲	Campsite at north edge of orchard and blue blaze down to water		3950	1826.3
365.9		Weedy Gap		3913	1826.1
366.8		Pass a large rock formation.		4426	1825.2
367.3		Pass through Gap		4390	1824.7
367.9		High point near summit of knob.		4332	1824.1
368.6	Y ★★★★★	Greasy Creek Gap, blue blaze trail leads west 300 yards to good campsite and water (spring) , campsite is located at the at gap. Old road bed to Greasy Creek Road To the east a trail leads (0.6) **Greasy Creek Hostel. See map of Greasy Creek Gap, NC.**		4034	1823.4

⌂ ▲ ◈ (0.6E) **Greasy Creek Friendly** 828-688-9948. greasycreekfriendly@gmail.com (www.greasycreek-
✕ 🛒 ⛁ friendly.com)
⛃ 📧 🚌 ◈ AT Passport location.
💻P 📷 Open year round, except during Trail Days. Call ahead during Dec-Feb, self serve during the Sabbath
(sundown Friday to sundown Saturday).
Directions; from Greasy Creek Gap; take old woods road Trail east, follow flags on branches and
painted arrows downhill. You should be going downhill all the way. Hostel is first house to your right with
gravel path, follow gravel path past bunk house to main house back door to check in.
🐾 Pets okay outside. There is a shed where guests can stay with their pets called the Pup Shed for $15,
includes dog. ⌂ Bunk house or bed on porch $15 per person (8 bunks available). Indoor beds $20 per
person (3 single beds available). ▲ Tenting $7.50 per person, stay includes shower. ⛃ Shower without
stay $3. ⛁ Laundry done by owner in the evening for staying guests only, $2 to $6 depending on the
load size. Limited kitchen privileges. 📧 Free WiFi. ✕ Home cooked meals. 🛒 Resupply options include
multi-day resupply including snacks, meals, and microwaveable entrees. ⛽ Coleman and alcohol fuel
by the ounce. 🚌 There is a free shuttle every evening (except Sunday) to Mountain Grill (made-to-or-
der food) and Dollar General that is outside of the dinner run for $5. There are shuttles available from
Hot Springs, NC to Damascus, VA and all trailheads and trail towns in between. Call or email to inquire
about availability and pricing. 📞 Free long distance calls within US. P Parking $2 per night. Credit cards
accepted.
✉ Mail drops: 1827 Greasy Creek Rd, Bakersville, NC 28705.

NoBo	Features	Description	GPS	Elev	SoBo
369.4	⬥▲	Campsite, water (spring) is located (0.1) west		4110	1822.6
370.2		Reach shallow Gap.		4335	1821.8
370.5	⬥Υ▲ ⊏(10) ⌣⛏	(0.1W) **Clyde Smith Shelter**, water is located 100 yards behind the shelter on a blue blazed trail, tent sites. 32.4◀21.9◀9.1◀▶8.5▶13.7▶15.6	N 36 08.906, W 82 09.678	4400	1821.5
370.9	⬥	Reach gap, spring (0.1) west in a hollow.		4460	1821.1
371.6	📷	Pass many overlooks with good views		4646	1820.4
371.7	📷	Little Rock Knob, high point near summit.		4918	1820.3
373.1		Series of rock steps.		4224	1818.9
373.3		Pass through Gap.		4120	1818.7
373.9	▲⌣⛏P ⛏	**Hughes Gap Road**, Hughes Gap	N 36 08.208, W 82 08.460	4040	1818.1
374.3	Υ	Blue blaze trail leads 65 yards west to small pipe spring.		4524	1817.7
376.4	▲	Summit of Beartown Mountain.		5481	1815.6
376.9	⬥▲⌣	Ash Gap, campsite at gap, water (spring) is located (0.1) east.		5350	1815.1
378.2		Trail gets steep with many switchbacks		6151	1813.8
378.3	⬥Υ⛺⛿ ⛺P⛏	Trail to Roan High Bluff leads (0.1) east to parking, picnic area. Open Memorial Day thru the first of October.	N 36 06.238, W 82 07.990	6200	1813.7
378.5	▲	Southern end of **old Hack Line Road** in small open gap. Pass old chimney.		6085	1813.5
379.0	⬥Υ▲ ⊏(15) ⌣⛏	(0.1E) **Roan High Knob Shelter**, piped spring, tenting. This is the highest shelter on AT. 30.4◀17.6◀8.5◀▶5.2▶7.1▶25.1	N 36 06.298, W 82 07.362	6285	1813.0
380.1	▲	Old Hack Line Road.		5574	1811.9

NoBo	Features	Description	GPS	Elev	SoBo
380.2		Cross several board bridges.		5756	1811.8
380.5		Cross **TN. 143, NC. 261**, Carvers Gap, water (spring), restroom, picnic area.	N 36 06.372, W 82 06.631	5512	1811.5
380.7		Southern end of wooded path.		5742	1811.3
380.9		Northern end of wooded path.		5836	1811.1
381.2		Trail skirts the side of Round Bald summit on gravel trail.		5801	1810.8
381.5		Engine Gap		5620	1810.5
381.8		Passes a rock formation with several locations for good views between Jane Bald and Round Bald.		5708	1810.2
381.9		Summit of Jane Bald.		5785	1810.1
382.4		Side trail to Grassy Ridge and views, AT to west		5770	1809.6
382.5		Spring east of trail.		5770	1809.5
384.2		Low Gap. **Stan Murray Shelter**, water (spring) is located east on a blue blazed trail opposite the shelter. 22.8◀13.7◀5.2◀▶1.9▶19.9▶29.5	N 36 06.736, W 82 03.954	5050	1807.8
384.6		Crest of Elk Hollow Ridge, view a short distance on trail.		5180	1807.4
385.3		Buckeye Gap.		4730	1806.7
386.1		Yellow Mountain Gap. (0.25E) **Overmountain Shelter**, water is located on way to the shelter, tenting, privy. 15.6◀7.1◀1.9◀▶18.0▶27.6▶35.8	N 36 07.411, W 82 03.260	4682	1805.9
387.3		Saddle in open field. Spring is about 100 yards east.		5272	1804.7
387.7		Little Hump Mountain, grassy summit with outstanding views.		5459	1804.3
387.9		Reach small gap, be careful of side trails.		5196	1804.1
389.0		Bradley Gap, grassy, water (spring) is located 100 yards east		4950	1803.0
389.9		Hump Mountain, Stan Murray plaque		5587	1802.1

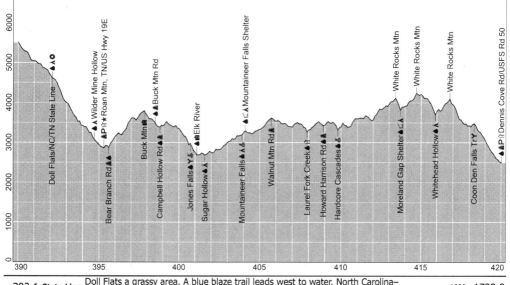

392.1	**State Line**	Doll Flats a grassy area. A blue blaze trail leads west to water. North Carolina–Tennessee State Line		4600	1799.9
392.7		Crest of rocky spur, overlook 50 feet east with views of Elk River Valley pastures.		4400	1799.3
392.8		Cliff with overhanging rock over trail.		4153	1799.2
394.3		Power line.		3420	1797.7
394.7		Campsite and water west of trail in Wilder Mine Hollow, water is located 100 yards north on AT		3200	1797.3
395.1		Northern end of old road in Wilder Mine Hollow.		3008	1796.9
395.3		Cross **U.S. 19E**. ★★★★★ **Elk Park, NC. (2.5E), Roan Mountain, TN (3.5W) SEE MAPS.**	N 36 10.647, W 82 00.707	2895	1796.7
		(2.3W) **PO** M-F 9am-12:30am & 1:30pm-4pm, Sa 8am-11:30am. 828-733-5711. 153 Main St. W, Elk Park, NC 28622. N 36 12.013, N 36 09.467, W 81 58.803			

🛏️🏠🛖 ◈ (0.3W) **Mountain Harbour B&B and Hiker Hostel** 866-772-9494. welcome@mountainharbour.net
🛒🍴🧺🛁 (www.mountainharbour.net)
🚗🏍🚐 ◈ AT Passport location.
P 🖥 Open year round.
🍴 Food Truck open during NOBO Season. 🏠 Hostel located over barn, $25 per person, king bed $55. Treehouse $75, 🛖 Tenting with shower $10. Stay includes linens, shower, towel, full kitchen, wood burning stove, video library. 🛁 Non guest shower with towel $5. 🧺 Coin operated laundry, Breakfast $12 when available. 🛏️ B&B rooms $125-$165 includes breakfast, A/C, refrigerator, cable TV, 🌐 WiFi. 🛒 General Store on site with hiker supplies, full resupply. 🚐 🏍 Shuttles can be arranged for slackpacking. P Parking $10 per day or $2 per day with shuttle.
🖥 Mail drops of non-guests $5. Mail drops for guests, 9151 Hwy 19E, Roan Mountain, TN 37687.

🏠 ◈ 🛒 🍴 (0.5E) **The Station at 19E** 575-694-0734.
🏍🚐P🖥 (www.thestationat19e.com)
◈ AT Passport location.
Open year round.
🏠 $30pp (flat rate), Includes bunk, shower, laundry, soaps, fresh linens, boot dryer. CRAFT BEER PUB, 🍺 food available & resupply on site. 🚐 Free shuttles to town with or without stay. 🌐 Free fast WiFi. Pets OK. 🏍 Slack pack & slack dog available. P Secure parking $10/day or $2/day with shuttle.
🖥 Mail drops to 9367 HWY 19E Roan Mountain, TN 37687. Mail drop free. NOBO blue blaze (brew blaze) to front door.

🏠🛒🍴🚐 (6.0W) **Doe River Hiker Rest** 575-694-0734.
🏍🚐P🖥 Open year round.
Free shuttle with stay. 🏠 $30pp (flat rate), includes private room, shower, laundry, and fresh linens. 🚐 Shuttles to town. 🏍 Slack pack available. 🌐 Fast wifi. Send
🖥 Mail drops to The Station at 19E hostel and they will be forwarded here.

Roan Mountain, TN 37687 (3.5W) See Map

🏤🍴 **PO** M-F 8am-12pm & 1pm-4pm, Sa 7:30am-9:30am 423-772-3014. 8060 US-19E, Roan Mtn, TN 37687. N 36 12.013, W 82 04.469

🛏️ ◈ (4.8W) **Roan Mountain B&B** 423-772-3207. campbell79@comcast.net (www.roanmtbb.com)
🍺🛖🌐 ◈ AT Passport location.
🏍🚐P🖥 Open year round. Pets considered, no alcohol, no smoking inside. 🛏️ Hiker rate $75 single, $95 double includes full hot breakfast. Free pickup and return at Hwy 19E and 5pm town shuttle. 🛖 Do it yourself laundry $5. 🍺 Some resupply items on site. 🌐 Free WiFi. Free 5pm shuttle into town for restaurants and restock for guests. 🚐 🏍 Shuttles and slackpacking Sam's Gap to Watauga Lake. P Parking for section hikers. Credit Cards accepted.
🖥 Mail drops; must have both the PO and physical address both on the mailing label. P.O. Box 227, 132 W. B. Mitchell Rd. Roan Mountain, Tennessee 37687

🍴🌐 **Puerto Nuevo Fresh Mex & Seafood** 423-481-1412 Mon-Su 11am-10pm. 🌐 WiFi. Ask for ride availability after eating if going back to 19E trail head.

🍴 ◈🌐 **Bob's Dairyland** 423-772-3641. (www.bobsdairyland.com)
◈ AT Passport location. M-Su 6am-9pm. 🌐 WiFi.

🍴🌐 **Smoky Mountain Bakers** 423-957-1202. M closed, Tu-Sa 8 am-8 pm, Su closed. Wood fired pizza. 🌐 WiFi.

🍴🌐 **Frank & Marty's Pizza** 423-772-3083. M closed, Tu-Sa 4 am-9 pm, Su closed. 🌐 WiFi.

🛒🏧 **Redi Mart** 423-772-3032. M-Sa 8am-10pm, Sun 10am-8pm. 🏧 ATM.

🛒 **Cloudland Market** 423-772-3201. M-Sa 8am-7pm.

Elk Park, NC

Roan Mountain, TN

NoBo	Features	Description	GPS	Elev	SoBo
395.4		High point on ridge.		2911	1796.6
395.5	♦▲P ⚲	Cross **Bear Branch Road**, water (streams) are located north of road	N 36 10.764, W 82 00.768	2900	1796.5
396.4		Lower end of Bishop Hollow.		3344	1795.6
396.8		High end of Bishop Hollow.		3623	1795.2
397.8	📷	Reach summit and stile. Many views in this area.		3820	1794.2
398.2		Circle around Isaacs Cemetery.		3602	1793.8
398.6	♦▲	Cross **Buck Mountain Road**, water (spigot) is located (0.1) east at church.		3340	1793.4
398.8	♦	Cross small stream.		3461	1793.2
398.9	♦▲	Cross **Campbell Hollow Road**, water (streams) are located south of road.		3330	1793.1
399.2	⌒	Cross small bridge.		4335	1792.8
399.6	♦	Pass by spring.		3422	1792.4
400.7	Y⚒	Side trail (0.1) east to Jones Falls.		3148	1791.3
401.7	♦▲	Campsite, water		3590	1790.3
402.9	♦	Cross creek.		2925	1789.1
403.5	⌒	Cross small log bridge.		2935	1788.5
403.9	♦▲⚒	Cross small stream below waterfall, blue blaze west to campsite.		3130	1788.1

NoBo	Features	Description	GPS	Elev	SoBo
404.1	♦Y▲ ⊏(17) ↵♀	**Mountaineer Falls Shelter**, water is located 200 feet on blue blaze in front of shelter, tenting. 25.1◄19.9◄18.0◄►9.6►17.8►33.6	N 36 12.212, W 81 59.141	3470	1787.9
404.9	♦▲	Blue blaze trail east leads to campsite, water		3260	1787.1
405.4	♦	Cross small stream.		3531	1786.6
405.5	▲	Cross worn Forest Service Road.		3572	1786.5
405.7	▲P♀	Cross **Walnut Mountain Road**	N 36 13.327, W 82 00.258	3550	1786.3
406.9	♦▲P	Stream, **Howard Harrison Road**		3400	1785.1
407.4	Y⊡	Viewpoint, memorial bench.		3350	1784.6
407.9	Y↵♀ ★★★★★	Upper Laurel Fork, footbridge, side trail (0.25W) to **Scotty's Back Porch Piano Bar & Hostel** .		3290	1784.1

Y⛺◈▲ Side trail (0.25W) along utility line from 406 miles sign just north of bench view spot.

⊂♨☂☎ **Scotty's Back Porch Piano Bar & Hostel** 423-772-3450. Hikerscotty@gmail.com.

🐾🖂 ◈ AT Passport location.

CLOSED from mid Nov thru mid Feb UNLESS called first.

Call for availability off season 15 Feb - 15 Nov. Overnights must sign registration form. ⛺ Bunk room with heat $10, without heat $5 night. Private room and deck, queen bed with linens, heat, $25 single/$35 double. 🐾 Pets okay if picked up after. No toilet, ☾ but privy, shovel, TP, hand sanitizer provided. ♨ Shower $2, if also using provided towel $3. Hot tub $5, pool table, ping pong, piano, guitar and fiddle. Live entertainment daily 7:30-9pm. Cash or paypal only. 🐾 Offers slackpacking from 19E, ask about rates. ☎ Short term resupply available daily 4-8pm: beverages, pizza, Ben & Jerry's ice cream and 🔥 stove fuels. P Limited parking $2.50/night.

☎ Limited WiFi on satellite: 8-11 pm, 2-8 am daily

🖂 Mail drops free if sent well in advance. Otherwise $10 round trip to PO in Roan Mountain. PO Box 185, Roan Mountain, TN 37687-0185

NoBo	Features	Description	GPS	Elev	SoBo
408.9	▲	Cross **USFS 293**		3442	1783.1
409.7	♦	Cross stream.		3410	1782.3
410.6	♦▲	Cross small stream, campsite.		3378	1781.4
413.0		Cross high point on White Rocks Mountain.		4121	1779.0
413.7	♦▲⊏(6) ↵♀	**Moreland Gap Shelter**, ♦ water is located (0.2) across from the shelter and down the hollow, ▲ tenting. 29.5◄27.6◄9.6◄►8.2►24.0►30.8	N 36 13.207, W 82 05.310	3815	1778.3
414.9	▲	Cross **Tower Road**, White Rocks Mountain		4206	1777.1
415.8	♦▲	Campsite on southern end of field, blue blaze trail leads to water.		3700	1776.2
416.1	Y▲	Cross forest road. Lacy Trapp Trail.		3810	1775.9
416.2	⌇	Power line.		3825	1775.8
416.8	⊡	Vista with views to the west.		4102	1775.2
418.3	Y🔥	Trail to Coon Den Falls is located to the east (0.8)		2660	1773.7
418.4	⊡	Cliffs with views.		3450	1773.6
418.8	⊡	Cliffs with views.		3442	1773.2
419.8	♦▲	Follow farm road by pond and field.		2606	1772.2

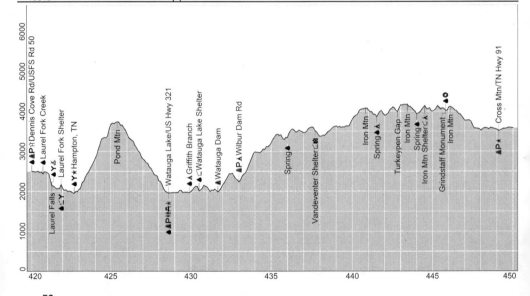

			GPS	Elev	SoBo
420.0	▲▲P♀ ★★★★★	Cross **USFS 50**, Dennis Cove.	N 36 15.854, W 82 07.389	2550	1772.0

    ⛺▲◈⑧ (0.3W) **Kincora Hiking Hostel** 423-725-4409.
    ⚒△▣▤ ◈ AT Passport location.
    🚗 ⑧ No dogs. ⛺ Bunks $5 a night recommended donation, 3 night limit. Cooking facilities, △ laundry. ⚒ Coleman and alcohol by the ounce. 🚐 Shuttles by arrangement.
    🖃 Mail drops free for guests, non-guest $5. 1278 Dennis Cove Rd, Hampton, TN 37658.

    ⛺🛏▲ (0.4E) **Black Bear Resort** 423-725-5988 (www.blackbearresorttn.com)
    ◈🍴△ ◈ AT Passport location.
    🖥🚐P🖃 Open Mar 1 - Oct 31.
    In the process of changing owners, pricing and amenities may vary. New owners, Travis and Linda Culp. Pet friendly. ⛺ Hostel bunks $20, upper bunkhouse $25 per person, ▲ tenting $15 per person. 🛏 Cabins available $50-$65 up to 4 people per cabin, $20 EAP with a max of 6 people. △ Laundry $5. 🖥 Computer available for use. 🍴 Camp store with long-term resupply items, snacks, sodas, pizza, beer, ice cream and food that can be bought and cooked on-site with microwave and stove. ⚒ Fuel by the ounce and canister fuel. Credit Cards accepted. 🚐 Shuttles available. P Parking free for guest who stay one night, $3 per day for non guests.
    🖃 Mail drops free for guests, non-guest $5. 1511 Dennis Cove Rd, Hampton, TN 37658.

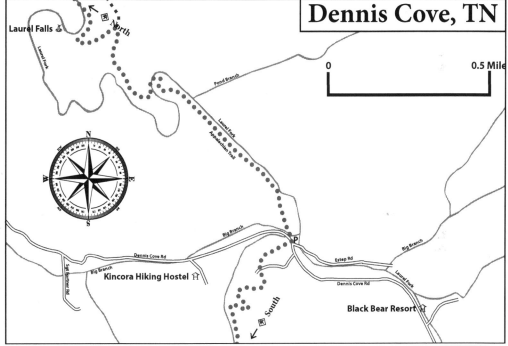

Dennis Cove, TN

420.1	▲〰	Pass two small bridges and a campsite that is near the area used for the old railroad.		2499	1771.9
420.8	▲〰	Cross Koonford Bridge over Laurel Falls.		2118	1771.2
420.9	Y	Unmarked trail junction to Potato Top		2450	1771.1
421.1	Y	High water bypass to Laurel Fork Shelter, reconnects again at Laurel Fork Shelter		2200	1770.9
421.2	▲⚓	Laurel Fork Falls, Laurel Fork Gorge. **Do not swim near or close to the falls. Hikers have been pulled in and drowned here.**		2120	1770.8
421.4		Skirt edge of cliff on walkway. If the walkway is flooded or icy, use high water bypass trail.		2211	1770.6
421.9	▲Y⊑(8)	Blue blaze trail 300 feet to **Laurel Fork Shelter**, water (stream) is located 50 yards behind the shelter. Also high water bypass trail. 35.8◄17.8◄8.2◄► 15.8► 22.6► 30.2		2450	1770.1
422.2	▲〰♀	Waycaster Spring, there are a few footbridges that go over Laurel Fork in this area	N 36 16.714, W 82 08.184	1900	1769.8
422.3	▲〰	Cross stream on footbridge.		2082	1769.7
422.5	▲〰	Cross stream on footbridge.		2137	1769.5
422.7	▲Y	Water, blue blaze side trail to leads west (0.8) to US. 321, Hampton TN is west on 321. **See Notes Below 428.6.**		1900	1769.3

NoBo	Features	Description	GPS	Elev	SoBo
425.1	💧	Pond Flats (south end).		2682	1766.9
425.2	💧	Spring located in rocky bottom of drainage.		3304	1766.8
425.5	💧🏕⌣	Pond Flats (north end), water (spring) is located (0.1) north on AT, campsite		3780	1766.5
428.1	Ⓨ🏕	Campsite to the east		2200	1763.9
428.5	Ⓨ🏕	Trail and **Shook Brach Road** intersect with gravel road to the east.		2023	1763.5
428.6	💧🍴🚐🏕P ⭐⭐⭐⭐⭐	Cross **US. 321**, Shook Branch Picnic Area. **See map of Hampton.**	N 36 18.112, W 82 07.735	1990	1763.4

🏠🏕⌣ **Boots Off Hostel & Campground** Owner Jim Gregory: 239-218-3904
◈🏧⛺ "Top-10 AT Hostel" - The Trek
🛁🍴🔌◐ AT Passport location.
�car P✉ PET- FRIENDLY! Please call ahead if you have dogs!. Just steps from the A.T. and 5 minute walk to Watauga Lake beach area. Shaded campground with semi-private sites with picnic tables: 🏕⌣ $12/pp (Tent or Hammock). 🏠 Air-conditioned/Heated bunkhouse (each bed has privacy curtains, individual light, & charging station): $25/pp+tax. 🏠 Private tiny cabins (full bed with twin bunk, mini fridge, coffee maker with supplies) sleeps up to 3 people: $60+tax for one person + $10/pp thereafter. All stays include: light continental breakfast, clean linens, towels, scheduled evening town shuttle ($5 without stay), 📶 Wi-Fi, and access to common area, kitchen, communal fire ring (regular fires during peak season), clean bathrooms and unique showers ($5 without stay). ⛺ Full-service Laundry is $5 pp (we do it for you!). ◐ Excellent cell phone signal! 🏪 Short term resupply and General Store available. 🏊 Swimming available at Watauga Lake. 🛶 Kayak/Canoe/Paddleboard rentals available at hostel. P Parking available $5/day. 🎒 Slackpacking available for a fee. 🚐 Shuttles available - range Sam's Gap to Damascus for a fee (Extended shuttles available out of season).
✉ Mail drops free with stay $5 without stay. Mail drops: 142 Shook Branch Rd., Hampton, TN 37658.

🏕🛁🚐📶 (0.8E) **Dividing Ridge Campground** 424-957-0821
Open until July. Donation based. 🛁 Hot showers, charging stations, wash tub and 🚐 local shuttles. 📶 WiFi. Call for pickup.

Hampton, TN 37658 (2.6W) See map.
📮🏣 **PO** m-f 7:30am - 11:30am, 12:30pm - 1:00pm. Sat-Sun Closed. 423-725-2177. 153 Main St. W. Hampton, TN 28622. N 36 17.173, W 82 09.916
🏠🛒◈ **Brown's Grocery & Braemar Castle Hostel** 423-725-2411, 423-725-2262.
🚐📶 ◈ AT Passport location.
Open year round. Operated by Sutton Brown; check-in at grocery to stay at the 🏠 hostel or for 🚐 shuttles. Pets okay. 📶 WiFi at hostel only. **Store:** 🛒 Open M-Sa 8am-6pm, Su closed. Store accepts Credit Cards; hostel is cash only.
⚕ **Medical Care** 423-929-2584
Family practice clinic
🚐 **Hampton Trails Bicycle Shop** 423-725-5000. (www.hamptontrails.com)
Offers shuttles and has few supplies in shop. M, T, Th, F 11am-6pm, Sat 10am-3pm, closed Wed & Sun.

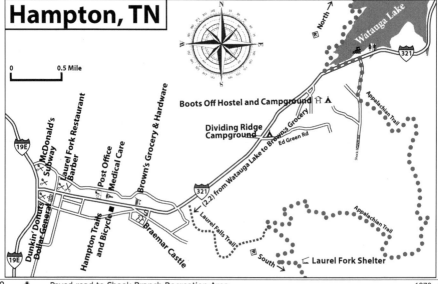

428.8	🏕	Paved road to Shook Branch Recreation Area.		1970	1763.2
428.9	💧⌣	Footbridge across stream.		1964	1763.1
429.3	🏕	Go through gate in old road.		2046	1762.7
430.1	💧🏕	Griffith Branch		2100	1761.9

NoBo	Features	Description	GPS	Elev	SoBo
430.5	♦♀	**Watauga Lake Shelter is closed and partially demolished.**	N 36 18.833, W 82 07.770	2130	1761.5
431.5	▲	**Lookout Road**, Watauga Dam, AT travels along this road for (0.4) miles, keep an eye out for the blazes		1915	1760.5
432.5	▲ 📷	Reach summit, views of Watauga Lake.		2480	1759.5
433.0	▲P♀	**Wilbur Dam Road**	N 36 19.728, W 82 06.690	2250	1759.0
435.4	▲	Cross summit		3420	1756.6
435.6	▲	Cross summit		3400	1756.4
436.0	♦	Water (spring)		3360	1756.0
437.0		Large rock formation to the east.		3482	1755.0
437.7	⊏(6)📷♀	**Vandeventer Shelter**, water is located is (0.3) down a steep, blue blazed trail south of the shelter (0.1) south of shelter. Views from shelter. 33.6◄24.0◄15.8◄►6.8►14.4►22.7	N 36 22.026, W 82 03.525	3620	1754.3
438.7	📷	Lookout to the east.		3632	1753.3
439.7	📷	Lookout to the east.		3947	1752.3
441.2	Y	Side trail leading west to private property.		3993	1750.8
441.5	♦▲	Water (spring) is located about 40 yards east beyond bog. There are good tent sites 175 yards north.		3900	1750.5
442.9		Turkeypen Gap		3840	1749.1
443.5	▲	Reach high point of Iron Mountain.		4190	1748.5
443.8	⊤	Power line. Views of fields around Doeville, TN.		4138	1748.2
444.3	♦Y	Water (spring) is also water for Iron Mountain Shelter, a more reliable spring is located 100 yards compass-south on blue blaze trail.		4000	1747.7
444.5	▲⊏(6) ⌣♀	**Iron Mountain Shelter**, water (spring) 500 yards south on AT, tenting. 30.8◄22.6◄6.8◄►7.6►15.9►35.6	N 36 26.132, W 81 59.460	4125	1747.5
445.8	○	Nick Grindstaff Monument, person was a hermit living here before the trail came through.		4090	1746.2
445.9	♦Y	Water (spring) on blue blazed trail west 100 yards to spring.		4090	1746.1
446.3		Cross over high point.		4113	1745.7
447.3		Reach top of ridge.		3750	1744.7
448.3	♦	Water (stream), or piped collection at short blue.		3500	1743.7
448.5	⌒	Cross several bog bridges.		3625	1743.5
448.6	▲	Cross USFS logging road.		3620	1743.4
449.1	▲P♀ ★★★★★	Cross **TN 91**.	N 36 28.882, W 81 57.622	3450	1742.9

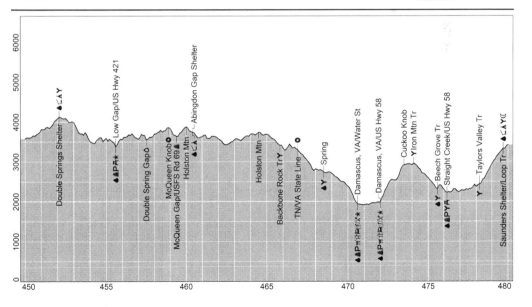

⌂ 𝗔 ⌣ ẟ **(1.9E) The Rabbit Hole** 423-739-3391
△ ♨ ⊚ ⊛ ◈ AT Passport location.
🚗 ⌂ $20 Bunkhouse, 𝗔 $10 tenting/hammocks, ẟ showers, $3 for △ laundry.
$5 Day pass available for ẟ showers and △ laundry without stay.
Batteries, frozen pizza and ice cream available.
Fresh made milk shakes available. Netflix and ☎ Wi-Fi. ⌘ Work for stay options. Possible, private room this season definitely private rooms in the future. ⊛🚗 Slackpacking and shuttle within a distance if 200 miles.
Free trail head pick up and drop off. No stay required, no day-pass required.
✉ Mail drops free without stay: 391 Hopper Rd. Shady Valley, TN 37688.

⌂ 𝗔 △ ☎ **(2.6E) Switchback Creek Campground** 407-484-3388. (www.switchbackcreek.com)
Open Apr 1 - Oct 31.
Location; (1.8) miles east to Sluder Rd, turn right for (0.2) miles, then right on Wallace Rd. (0.6) miles to 570 Wallace Rd, Shady Valley, TN 37688. ⌂ Cabin for two $40 3 people $50.00, 𝗔 campsite $10, cash or credit cards. Pets allowed except in cabins. ẟ Showers, △ laundry, ☎ free wifi. Call for ride at TN. 91 or Low Gap.

Shady Valley, TN (3.5E) See NOBO mile 455.6

NoBo		Features / Description	GPS	Elev	SoBo
451.2	◊𝗔	Campsite, water		3990	1740.8
451.8		High point on crest of Cross Mountain.		4135	1740.2
452.1	◊𝖸𝗔 ⌐(6)⌣ ⚲	**Double Springs Shelter**, water (spring) is located 100 yards in the draw beyond the shelter, tenting. Rich Knob to south, Holston Mountain Trail to north 30.2◄14.4◄7.6◄► 8.3► 28.0► 34.5	N 36 30.538, W 81 59.172	4060	1739.9
452.6		Locus Knob		4020	1739.4
454.2	𝗔	Cross old woods road.		3885	1737.8
454.3	📷	Views in the open field.		3712	1737.7
455.5	𝗔	Pass campsite on ridge crest.		3495	1736.5
455.6	◊🚗𝗔P⚲ ★★★★★	Cross **U.S. 421**, Low Gap, picnic table, spring.	N 36 32.331, W 81 56.893	3384	1736.4

Shady Valley, TN.(2.7E)

⊡⚲ **PO** M–F 8am-12pm, Sa 8am-10am, 423-739-2073. 136 Hwy 133. Shady Valley, TN 37688. N 36 31.177, W 81 55.682

🏪✗ẟ **Shady Valley Country Store & Deli**
423-739-2325. (www.shadyvalleycountrystore.com)
🏪 Open in the Spring until Thanksgiving: M-F 7 am-8 pm, Sa 8 am-8 pm, Su 9 am-6 pm. ✗ Deli serves burgers and sandwiches. ⚱ Coleman fuel.

✗ **Raceway Restaurant** 423-739-2499. M-Tu 7am-8pm, W 7am-2pm, Th-Sa 7am-8pm, Su 8am-2pm.

NoBo		Features / Description	GPS	Elev	SoBo
456.6		Cross a summit.		3643	1735.4
457.5	◊	Double Spring Gap, water is known to be unreliable at times		3650	1734.5
457.9		Gap, evidence of old farmstead.		3642	1734.1
458.9		McQueens Knob, little remains of old fire tower.		3900	1733.1
459.0		Old unused shelter, emergency use only shelter		3816	1733.0
459.3	𝗔P⚲	**USFS 69**, McQueens Gap	N 36 34.443, W 81 55.927	3680	1732.7
460.4	𝖸𝗔⌐(5)⌣⚲	**Abingdon Gap Shelter**, water (spring) is located spring (0.2) east on a steep, blue blazed side trail, downhill behind the shelter, tenting. Maple Spring Gap. 22.7◄15.9◄8.3◄► 19.7► 26.2► 38.6	N 36 34.861, W 81 54.132	3785	1731.6
465.8	𝖸	Junction of Backbone Rock Trail, heading (3.0) downhill and east to TN 133.		3466	1726.2
466.9	**State Line**	Tennessee–Virginia State Line, Mt. Rogers NRA sign		3302	1725.1
468.5	◊	Spring on blue blaze trail (0.1) east at and abandon homestead.		2600	1723.5
469.7	𝖸⚲	Wooded path intersects with old woods road.		1984	1722.3
469.8	⚲	Entering Damascus Park. Walk under "Welcome to Damascus" sign.	N 36 37.896, W 81 47.484	1946	1722.2
470.6	𝗔P(25)⚲ ★★★★★	Junction with **U.S. 58**. **Damascus, VA.** 24236. **See map of Damascus**.	N 36 38.160, W 81 47.376	1928	1721.4

⊡⚲ **PO** M-F 8:30-1 & 2-4:30, Sa 9-11, 276-475-3411. 211 N Renolds St. Damascus, VA 24236. N 36 38.165, W 81 47.393

🛒🍞 **Food City** (0.5W on US 58) 276-475-3653, M-Sa 6am-12am, Su 8am-12pm. Pharmcy, M-F 9am-7pm, Sa 9a,-3pm, Su closed.

⌂🛏𝗔 ◈ **The Broken Fiddle Hostel** 275-608-6220
△ẟ ◈ AT Passport location.
Pets OK outside.
Located on the AT. ⌂ 4 single beds in shared space, $25PP. 🛏 Two private rooms, $45/2. 𝗔 Tent or ⌣ hammock $10PP. △ Laundry $5. Stay includes continental breakfast. ẟ Shower without stay $3. Credit cards accepted with a processing fee.

Virginia

NoBo	Features	Description	GPS	Elev	SoBo

Hikers Inn 276-475-3788. hikersinn@gmail.com (www.hikersinndamascus.com)
◈ AT Passport location.
Closed in winter. ⌂ $25 bunks, hostel private room $50. ⇔ Rooms in house and Airstream $75 or $65/ night for multi-night stays. ⊿ Guest laundry $5. A/C everywhere. Smoking outside, dogs allowed in hostel and Airstream, ⊛ free WiFi, cash/check/credit/debit.

The Place Hostel (276-608-7283).
◈ AT Passport location.
⊗ No pets, alcohol, profanity or tobacco use anywhere on the church property. Methodist Church run ⌂ bunkrooms, ⌣ hammock polls, pavilion, ⊾ guest only showers with towel and soap. Suggested dona-tion $8. Please help Caretaker keep the hostel clean. Two night max, unless sick/injured. Check-in from 2-9 pm. Open mid-Mar (depending on weather)until mid-June, closed Summer, reopen weekend after Labor Day until mid-Nov(depending on whether). No vehicle-assisted hikers (except during Trail Days).

Crazy Larry's 276-475-7130.
◈ AT Passport location.
⌂ Hostel $35+tax, includes laundry, breakfast and morning coffee. Hostel has A/C and heat. ⊛ Free WiFi. ⊿ tenting only during Trail Daze for $35. Nightly rental that sleeps 12 or more, WiFi , satellite TV , 3 bathrooms laundry room fully stocked kitchen HVAC, $300 plus. Can call ahead for reservations. ⇔ Shuttles 276-206-1245 or 276-274-0907.
⌧ Mail drops: 209 Douglas Drive, Damascus, VA 24236.

Woodchuck Hostel 406 407 1272. chuckbissonnette@gmail,com (woodchuck hostel.com.)
Open year around. ⌂ Bed with linens $28 including tax. Private cabin $45S $55D. ⊿ ⌣ Tent/Hammock $15. Hot breakfast with stay. ⊾ Showers $5 without stay. ⊿ Laundry $5 ($8 without stay) kitchen privileges. Common area.large yard. Pavilion with gas grill. ⊛ Free Wi-Fi. Dogs welcome. ⚗ Alcohol fuel. Cold drinks and snacks. Free shuttle to Food City. ⌧ Other shuttles by arrangement. No drugs or alcohol. Credit card with $2 fee. Physical address 533 Docie St.
⌧ Mail drops to: PO 752, Damascus VA. 24236

Dancing Bear B&B 423-571-1830. (www.dancingbearrentals.com)
⊗ No pets, no smoking. ⇔ $70-$150. Breakfast for $5PP, ⊛ free WiFi. Credit cards accepted.
⌧ Mail for guest only: PO Box 252, 203 E Laurel Ave, Damascus, VA 24236.

Lazy Fox B&B 276-475-5838.
Open year round.
⊗ No pets, no smoking. ⇔ $75 and up includes tax and breakfast. Check or cash only.
⌧ Mail for guests only: PO Box 757, 133 Imboden St, Damascus, VA 24236.

Mountain Laurel Inn 276-475-8822.
(www.mountainlaurelinn.com)
⇔ $85-$145, includes breakfast. Discounts for extended stay. Optional dinners, ⊿ Laundry for regis-tered guests, saltwater pool, ⊛ free wifi. Located across from Food City and Family Dollar store.

Virginia Creeper Lodge 276-492-1143. (www.virginiacreeperlodge.com)
$125 and up, ⊛ free WiFi. ⊿ Coin laundry.

Appalachian Folk School 423-341-1843. (www.warrendoyle.com)
Open from mid-March to the end of October (except for 9 April-9 May 9; 20 May-20 June; 20 Aug-15 Sept). Nonprofit, run by Warren Doyle (18 AT traverses) ⊜ offers work for stay weeknights (M-Th) only (2-3 hrs/night) for all hikers who are conscientiously following the white blazes. Kitchen privileges, ⊾ shower, ⊛ free WiFi, ⊿ laundry and ⇔ rides to and from the AT between Route 321 (Hampton, TN) and VA 603 (Fox Creek).

Mt. Rogers Outfitters 276-475-5416 (www.mtrogersoutfitters.com)
◈ AT Passport location.
⊗ No Dogs, No alcohol.
⌂ Private rooms $21. ⚹ Full service outfitter, ⚗ fuel by the ounce, ⊞ short term resupply. P Parking $5 per day. ⇔ Shuttles to many area in TN and VA. ⊾ Shower with towel $3.
⌧ Mail drops: PO Box 546, 110 W Laurel Ave, Damascus, VA 24236.

Adventure Damascus 888-595-2453 or 276-475-6262 (www.adventuredamascus.com)
◈ AT Passport location.
Open year round, 7 days a week. ⚹ Catering to thru hikers with backpacking gear. ⊞ Offers hiker foods, ⚗ alcohol and Coleman by the ounce, other fuels available, bike rentals. ⊾ Showers $3. ⇔ Shuttles to area trail heads by arrangement
⌧ USPS and UPS Mail drops: PO Box 1113, 128 W. Laurel Ave. Damascus, VA 24236.

Sundog Outfitter 276-475-6252. (www.sundogoutfitter.com)
◈ AT Passport location.
Open year round, 7 days a week. ⚹ Backpacking gear and clothing, repairs, ⊞ hiker food, ⚗ Coleman and alcohol by the ounce, other fuels available. ⇔ Shuttles to area trail heads by arrangement,
⌧ Mail drops: PO Box 1113 or 331 Douglas Dr, Damascus, VA 24236.

Damascus Library 276-475-3820
M 9am-5pm, Tu 11am-7pm, W 9am-5pm, Th 11am-7pm, F 9am-5pm, Sa 9am-1pm, Sun closed.
⌨ Computers available for use, one hour internet limit. ⊛ Free WiFi. Charging stations are set up for hikers to charge their phones, IPads, tablets, etc.

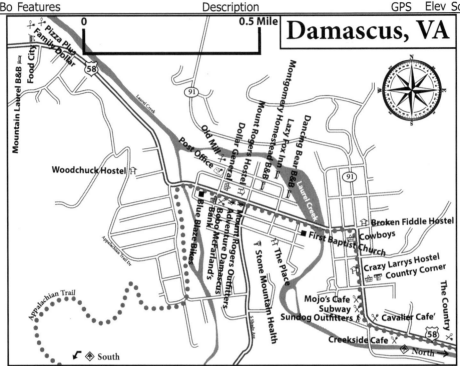

Damascus, VA

Virginia

NoBo	Features	Description	GPS	Elev	SoBo
471.6	▲	Junction with **US. 58 VA. 91**, Virginia Creeper Trail, steps		1928	1720.4
473.5	📷	Cuckoo Knob		2990	1718.5
474.1	Y	Iron Mountain Trail is blue blazed to the west, Feathercamp Ridge		2850	1717.9
475.6	Y	Beech Grove Trail is yellow blazed to the east.		2490	1716.4
476.1	Y	Juntion with Feathercamp Trail.		2300	1715.9
476.2	♦Y🚻▲ P(20)☕	Cross **US. 58**, picnic area, Straight Branch Feathercamp Branch, Feathercamp Trail.	N 36 38.694, W 81 44.196	2310	1715.8
477.6	♦⌒	Stream, footbridge		2490	1714.4
478.2	Y	Blue blazed Taylors Valley Side Trail leading 300 yards down Virginia Creeper Trail to the community of Taylor Valley, Virginia Creeper Trail		2850	1713.8
479.6	Y	Blue blaze trail is a loop trail that leads (0.3) Saunders Shelter		3439	1712.4
479.8	▲	Straight Mountain, crest		3440	1712.2

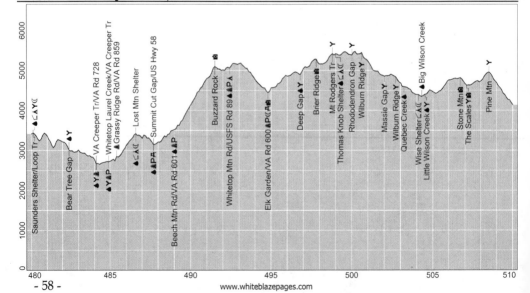

NoBo	Features	Description	GPS	Elev	SoBo
480.1	♦Y⩕ ⊏(8) ⌣℄♀	300 yards west to **Saunders Shelter**, water (spring) is located behind the shelter on the right and down an old road, tenting, privy. 35.6◀28.0◀19.7◀▶6.5▶18.9▶24.0	N 36 38.262, W 81 42.792	3310	1711.9
482.4	Y	Bear Tree Gap Trail, (3.0) west to Bear Tree Recreation Area		3050	1709.6
482.6	♦⩕	Campsite with man-made pond.		3020	1709.6
484.1	⩕	Cross **VA. 728**, Creek Junction Station, old railroad bed		2720	1707.9
484.2	Y⩕P♀	Virginia Creeper Trail, Whitetop Laurel Creek	N 36 38.964, W 81 40.344	2690	1707.8
484.8	⩕	Cross **VA. 859**, Grassy Ridge Road		2900	1707.2
485.4	♦	Streams		3040	1706.6
486.2		Lost Mountain		3400	1705.8
486.6	♦⩕⊏(8) ⌣℄♀	**Lost Mountain Shelter**, water is located on a trail to the left of the shelter, tenting, privy. 34.5◀26.2◀6.5◀▶12.4▶17.5▶23.5	N 36 38.644, W 81 39.378	3360	1705.4
487.7	♦⇌⩕P♀	Cross **US. 58**. Summit Cut, VA.	N 36 38.393, W 81 39.921	3160	1704.3
488.1	♦⩕	Campsites located near water (stream)		3300	1703.9
489.0	♦⩕P(5)♀	Cross **VA. 601**, Beech Mountain Road	N 36 38.237, W 81 38.422	3600	1703.0
491.5	◙	Buzzard Rock on the south slope of Whitetop Mountain		5080	1700.5
492.3	♦	Water (spring) on east side of trail, pipes		5100	1699.7
492.4	♦⩕⇌⩕ P(15)♀	Cross **USFS 89**, Whitetop Mountain Road to summit, parking 100 feet to the east.	N 36 37.908, W 81 36.076	5150	1699.6
494.2	♦	Small creek at log steps.		4763	1697.8
494.8	℄⇌◙⩕ P(12)♀	Cross **VA. 600**, Elk Garden, Whitetop, VA.	N 36 38.781, W 81 34.979	4463	1697.2
495.3		Boundary Lewis Fork Wilderness, fence		4640	1696.7
496.7	Y⩕	Campsites are uphill to the east on blue blaze trail		4850	1695.3
496.8	♦	Deep Gap, **No camping permitted here**, water is located (0.2) east		4900	1695.2
496.9	Y	Virginia Highlands Horse Trail, Mt. Rogers Trail, (4.0) west to USFS Grindstone campground, tenting		5200	1695.1
497.9	◙	Brier Ridge Saddle, views in meadows		5125	1694.1
498.8	Y	Spur Trail to summit of Mt. Rogers (0.5W)		5490	1693.2
499.0	♦⊏(16) ℄◙♀	**Thomas Knob Shelter**, ♦ water is located in an enclosed area in a pasture behind the shelter and please lock the gate after getting water as this will keep the ponies in the area from polluting the water. ℄ Privy, ◙ views. **No camping or open fires permitted around the shelter**. 38.6◀18.9◀12.4◀▶5.1▶11.1▶16.0	N 36 39.396, W 81 32.114	5400	1693.0
500.0	Y⩕	Rhododendron Gap, Pine Mountain Trail is a blue blaze trail to the west. Many large, established campsites between Thomas Knob and Rhododendron Gap		5440	1692.0
500.5	Y	Wilburn Ridge Trail is a blue blazed trail to the east.		5440	1691.5
500.6	O	**Fatman Squeeze**, a narrow rock passage in the rocks.		5300	1691.4
501.2	Y	Wilburn Ridge Trail is a blue blazed trail to the east.		4900	1690.8
502.0	⩕P♀	**Park service road** descending (0.5) west to Grayson Highlands State Park with parking at to Massie Gap	N 36 38.009, W 81 30.312	4800	1690.0
502.7	YP♀	Blue blaze AT Spur Trail leads (0.8) east to backpackers parking lot.	N 36 38.009, W 81 30.312	4882	1689.3
503.2	♦	Cross Quebec Branch		4629	1688.8
504.1	♦⊏(8)℄♀	Grayson Highlands State Park. **Wise Shelter**, water (spring) is located south of the shelter on a trail east of the AT, **no tenting around the shelter**; tent sites are located in the Mt. Rogers NRA, across Wilson Creek (0.3) north. Privy. 24.0◀17.5◀5.1◀▶6.0▶10.9▶20.1	N 36 39.242, W 81 29.906	4460	1687.9
504.2	♦⌣	Big Wilson Creek, footbridge		4300	1687.8
504.4	Y	Wilson Creek Trail		4300	1687.6
504.5	Y	Junction with Scales Trail, open to horses and hikers.		4650	1687.5
505.5	♦	Water (spring)		4610	1686.5
506.7	◙	Stone Mountain		4820	1685.3
507.1	℄OP(8)♀	**The Scales**, livestock corral, a grassy fenced in area used by campers and horse riders.	N 36 40.194, W 81 29.245	4620	1684.9
507.8	♦	Cross small stream.		4797	1684.2
508.5	Y	Pine Mountain Trail is a blue blazed trail to the west,		4960	1683.5

Elevation profile with labeled features (left to right): Old Orchard Shelter, Fox Creek/VA Rd 603, Hurricane Mtn, Hurricane Mtn Shelter, Hurricane Creek Tr, Hurricane Creek, Dickey Gap Tr, Corners Creek, Dickey Gap/VA Rd 650, VA Highlands Tr, Bobbys Tr, Dickey Ridge, Trimpi Shelter, Slabtown Rd/VA 672, South Fork Holston River/VA Rd 670, Slabtown Hollow, Brushy Mtn, Pugh Mtn Rd/VA Rd 601, Brushy Mtn, Georges Creek, Partnership Shelter, Mt Rogers NRA HQ/VA Hwy 16, Nicks Creek Rd/VA Rd 622, Brushy Mtn, Brushy Mtn, Locust Mtn, Chestnut Gap, Glade Mtn Rd/USFS Rd 86, Glade Mtn

NoBo	Features	Description	GPS	Elev	SoBo
510.1	♦((⊑(6) ~⚲	**Old Orchard Shelter**, water is located 100 yards west on blue blazed trail to right of shelter, privy. 23.5◄11.1◄6.0◄►4.9►14.1►23.9	N 36 40.993, W 81 30.672	4050	1681.9
510.2	Y	Upper Old Orchard Trail.		4020	1681.8
510.9	Y	Old Orchard Trail.		3750	1681.1
511.8	♦▲((▲ P(10)⚲	Cross VA. 603, Fox Creek Horse camp, (2.5) west leads to USFS Grindstone campground. 100 yards east to parking and port-a-potty.	N 36 41.796, W 81 30.381	3480	1680.2
511.9	♦~	Cross Fox Creek on long footbridge.		3450	1680.1
513.8	♦	Ridge crest on Hurricane Mountain on the Tennessee New River Divide.		4360	1678.2
514.1	Y	Iron Mountain Trail, Chestnut Flats		4240	1677.9
515.0	♦Y▲ ⊑(8) ~((⚲	Side trail across from stream leads 160 yards west to **Hurricane Mountain Shelter**, water (creek), tenting, privy. 16.0◄10.9◄4.9◄►9.2►19.0►26.0	N 36 42.921, W 81 30.570	3850	1677.0
515.6	Y	Hurricane Creek Trail, old logging road		3300	1676.4
516.4	♦	Water (stream)		3000	1675.6
516.7	⚡	Power line.		3013	1675.3
518.1	Y ★★★★★	Dickey Gap Trail, USFS Hurricane campground (0.5W) **USFS Hurricane Creek Campground.**		3090	1673.9
	♦▲~ ⚱♦♣⚶	**USFS Hurricane Creek Campground** 276-783-5196 Tent site $16, shower $2. Open mid Apr-Oct. Restroom and shower. N 36 43 21, W 81 29 26			
518.8	Y	Comers Creek Falls Trail		3120	1673.2
518.9	♦~♨	Comers Creek, footbridge, waterfalls		3100	1673.1
520.1	▲P⚲ ★★★★★	Cross **VA. 650**, Dickey Gap. 100 yards to VA. 16 **Troutdale, VA.(2.6E). See map of Troutdale.**	N 36 43.218, W 81 27.677	3300	1671.9

Troutedale, VA 24378 (2.6E)

	☏⚲	**PO** M 8am-12pm, Sa 8am-11am, Su Closed. 93 Ripshin Rd. Troutedale, VA . 24378. N 36 42.156, W 81 26.346			
	⌂▲◈⚶	(2.6E) **Troutdale Church Hostel** 276-677-4092. ◈ AT Passport location. Open Mar 15 thru Nov 15. 62 Sapphire Lane, Troutdale. Donations are appreciated. ⌂ Bunkhouse with microwave, ▲ tenting, ⚶ shower available. Pets stay outside, no alcohol. Hikers welcome to services in hiker attire. Pastor Ken Riggins. **No mail drops to here.**			

⛺ ⛏ ◈ 🏧 (3.2E) **Sufi Lodge** 276-677-0195. SufiLodgeVA@gmail.com (www.sufilodge.org)
🍽 🍴 🚗 ◈ AT Passport location.

🚗 Shuttle from Gap when available. NOBO's call at (Hurricane Shelter) to arrange pick-up. SOBO's call near (Trimpi Shelter).

Happy Family Friendly Environment, No Alcohol or Tobacco Products on the Property.

⛺ $25.00 Single Beds in the SUFI BUNGALOW, clean linen, towels, hot shower, toiletries and continental breakfast. Full Mediterranean breakfast, lunch and dinner served for an additional fee. Request VEGAN or VEG in advance. 🛏 Several private rooms are available in the Main SUFI LODGE starting at $45.00. 🏧 resuppling options. ☎ Free high speed WIFI. Free Epsom Salt Foot Bath for all Guests. Hiker Recover Room - Massage and other hiker wellness services, including expert Cupping Therapy and Dry Carbon Sauna. Hiker 🛒 Restocking Store - COSCO and other popular Hiker Favorites at shuttle rates. HIKER HEALING KITS sent anywhere on the AT (see website for details).

US Post Office 1000 yards away open till 12 Noon. Skyline Bank - ATM Machine. General Store, Restaurants and Dollar General within TEN MILES - Shuttle Fees Apply. 🍴 Slackpacking options available.

✉ Mail drops are free for all guests, non guests $10: Please include your full legal name on the package. Send to: 67 High Country Lane, Troutdale, ViA 24378 Attn: Mail Drop Service.

🏧 ◈ ✗ ⚓ (6.2E) **Fox Creek General Store**
◈ AT Passport location.
276-579-6033. M-F 7 am-7 pm, Sa 7 am-6 pm, Su closed.
Located 4 miles south on route 16. 🏧 Resupply food, ✗ short order grill, burgers, pizza, and deli items. ⚓ Fuel, denatured alcohol and canister fuel. Beer and wine available on and off premises.

🚗 **Shuttle Service @ Sufi Lodge** 276-677-0195(home), 276-759-1672(cell). Average $2.00 per mile. Based out of Troutdale VA

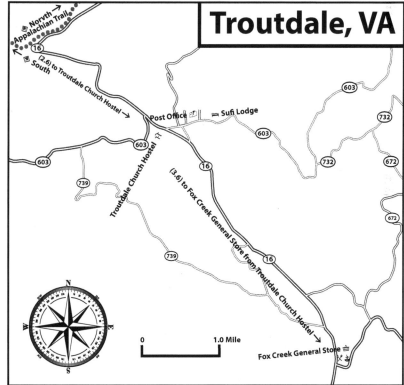

			GPS	Elev	SoBo
520.9	Y	Virginia Highlands Horse Trail		3450	1671.1
521.6	Y ⚑	Bobby's Trail leads (2.0) east to Raccoon Branch campground.		3570	1670.4
522.1	📷	High Point 200 yards on blue blazed trail.		4040	1669.9
524.2	◖Y⚑ ⌒(8) ⚓🏠🍴♨	(1.0E) **Trimpi Shelter**, water (spring), tent sites in front of shelter, tenting, privy. 20.1◀14.1◀9.2◀▶9.8▶16.8▶36.1	N 36 44.955, W 81 28.824	2900	1667.8
525.4	⛺(4)	Cross **VA. 672**, Slabtown Road, gravel		2700	1666.6
526.1	Y	Blue blaze Slabtown Trail to the east.		2645	1665.9
526.3	⛺ ⌒P(4) ♨	Cross **VA. 670, Teas Road**, South Fork Holston River, bridge	N 36 45.789, W 81 29.588	2450	1665.7

NoBo	Features	Description	GPS	Elev	SoBo
527.8	▲ ⌣	Campsite located in the pines in small hollow west.		2933	1664.2
527.9	◊	Stream, unreliable.		2674	1664.1
530.1	▲P(3)♀	Cross **VA. 601, Pugh Mountain Road**, gravel. A parking pull-off.	N 36 47.202, W 81 28.299	3250	1661.9
531.7	☛	Power line.		3316	1660.3
532.6	◖⌒	Cross creek on bridge.		3052	1659.4
533.3	▲	Junction of two roads.		3227	1658.7
534.0	◖⌂(16) ☾⌂♀	**Partnership Shelter**, water from faucet, bathroom, warm shower, no tenting around shelter, **No tenting permitted here.** Can call for pizza delivery at Visitor Center. 23.9◀19.0◀9.8◀▶ 7.0▶26.3▶35.7	N 36 48.564, W 81 25.356	3360	1658.0
534.2	◖☖▲P♀ ★★★★★	Cross **VA. 16**, Mount Rogers NRA Headquarters. Parking is not recommend here, location has a history of vandalism with car thefts.	N 36 48.695, W 81 25.279	3220	1657.8
	⊕⊛⊟P	**Mount Rogers National Recreation Area HQ** 276-783-5196. AT Passport location. Permit required for overnight parking (or park outside of gate).			
	⌂	(5.0W) **Boudicca's Legacy Hostel** Located in Marion, VA. 1502 Hwy 16, Marion, Virginia 24354			

Sugar Grove, VA 24375 (3.2E)

| | ✉♀ | **PO** M-F 8:30-12:30 & 1:30-3:30, Sa 8:15-10:30, 276-677-3200. 5444 Sugar Grove Hwy. Sugar Grove, VA 24375. N 36 46.521, W 81 24.785 | | | |

Marion, VA 24354 (6.0W). See map of Marion.

	✉♀	**PO** M-F 9am-5pm, Sa 9:30am-12pm, 276-783-5051. 200 Pearl Ave. Marion, VA 24354. N 36 49.934, W 81 31.052			
	🛏⛺⊛⊟	**Travel Inn** 276-783-5112 (www.travelinnmarion.com) 🛏 $43 and up. Includes microwave, fridge, free coffee in the morning. ⊛ Free WiFi. ⊟ Mail drops for guests: 1419 N Main St, Marion VA 24354.			
	🛏⊛⊛⊟	**Econo Lodge** 276-783-6031. ⊛ AT Passport location. 🛏 Special Hiker Rate: $54 - $64. Pet fee. Includes Free Hot Breakfast, microwave, fridge, ⊛ free WiFi. ⊟ Mail drops: 1420 N. Main St, Marion, VA 24354.			
	🛏⊛	**America's Best Value Inn** 276-378-0481. Continental breakfast, coffee, microware, fridge, pool. ⊛ Free WiFi.			
	✗🍴⊛⊟	**Kohi Cafe** 276-613-7385. (www.mkt.com/store/kohi-cafe) M-F 8am-4pm, Sa 10am-2pm, Su closed. ✗ Coffee, breakfast , lunch, and deli. 💻 Computer with printer, ⊛ free WiFi. ⊟ Mail drops: 201 E Main St Suite 102, Marion, VA 24354			
	🎪	**Park Place Drive-In** 276-781-2222. More than welcome to walk in. Offers mini golf, arcade, and ice cream shop.			

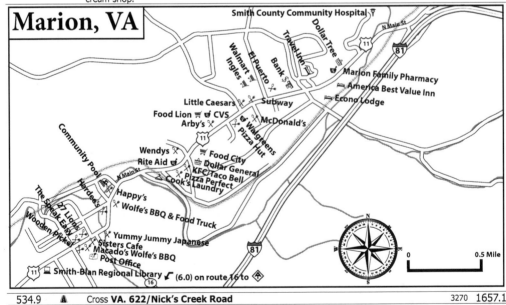

Marion, VA

534.9	▲	Cross **VA. 622/Nick's Creek Road**		3270	1657.1
536.8		Brushy Mountain		3600	1655.2
537.8	▲	Locust Mountain, wooded knoll.		3900	1654.2

NoBo	Features	Description	GPS	Elev	SoBo
538.2	▲▲▲ P(15)🍴	Cross **USFS 86, Glade Mountain Road**, Water (spring). Private road, permission required, may not be passable for vehicles.	N 36 50.089, W 81 22.232	3650	1653.8
539.5	▲	Glade Mountain		4093	1652.5

541.0	▲⌐(6)☽🍴	**Chatfield Shelter**, water (creek) is located in front of shelter, privy. 26.0◄16.8◄7.0◄► 19.3►28.7►39.4	N 36 50.995, W 81 21.798	3150	1651.0
541.3	▲	Cross **USFS 644**, stile.		3100	1650.7
542.5	Y	Trail intersects with old farm road. Farm road is part of Settlers Museum.		2731	1649.5
542.8	○◈▲ P(15)🍴	Cross **VA. 615, Rocky Hollow Road**. (0.1E) **Settlers Museum, Lindamood Schoolhouse** 276-686-4401. (www.settlersmuseum.com) Parking available at farm. (Apr 1-Nov 15) ◈ AT Passport location.	N 36 52.248, W 81 21.462	2600	1649.2
543.3	▲P(3)🍴	Cross **VA. 729**, Kegley Lane, gravel	N 36 52.507, W 81 21.589	2540	1648.7
543.7	Y▲	Junction with Kegley Trail, old road		2540	1648.3
544.4	📷	Good view at top of meadow of Brushy Mountain and Great Valley.		2560	1647.6
544.7	⌐✕	Cross Middle Fork of Holston River, railroad tracks		2420	1647.3
545.6	▲P(30)🍴 ★★★★★	Cross **U.S. 11, I–81, VA. 683. Atkins, VA. SEE ATKINS, VA Map**	N 36 53.171, W 81 22.408	2420	1646.4
	⌂🍴	(3.0W) **PO** M-F 8:30am-12pm & 12:30pm-3:15pm, Sa 9am-10:45am, 276-783-5551. 5864 Lee Hwy. Atklins, VA 24311. N 36 42.156, W 81 25.232			
	🛏⛺☕🍴 P🖃	**Relax Inn** 276-783-5811. 🛏 $50S $55D, $5EAP (max 4), pets $10. ⛺ Laundromat, ☕ free WiFi for guests. P Parking $3 per day. 🚐 Call for shuttle availability. 🖃 Free mail drops for guests, $5 for non-guests. Government issued ID require to pick up mail drops and for room registration. Relax Inn, 7253 Lee Hwy, Rural Retreat, VA 24368.			
	✕◈P🖃	**The Barn Restaurant** 276-686-6222. ◈ AT Passport location. ✕ M-Sa 7am-8pm, Su 7am-3pm. Sunday buffet from 11am-2pm. P Parking for section hikers $5 per day, $25 a week. 🖃 Mail drops: 7412 Lee Highway, Rural Retreat, VA 24368.			
	🏪🕾	**Shell Convenience Store** M-Su 24 hours, 🕾 ATM inside.			
	■	**Rambunny and Aqua** 276-783-3754 Shuttles and referrals for other help.			
	🚗	**Skip & Linda** 276-783-3604 by appointment only. Will know of accesses to trail from the 2016 fire damage, water levels and weather. Covers From Damascus to Pearisburg.			
	🛏🖥☕🖃	(3.7W) **Comfort Inn** 276-783-2144 🛏 Hiker rate, $79 double bed for two people. $10 EAP up to 4. $89 for Queen. Sometimes there is a discount book coupon at Exxon or ask for hiker rate. 🖃 Mail drops for guest only, call for mailing address.			

Atkins, VA

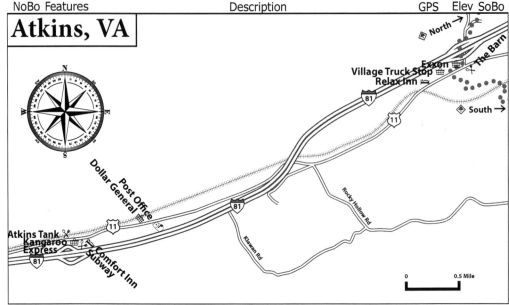

546.6	▲⌒	**VA 683**, pass under **I-81** over pass.		2431	1645.4
547.0	⌒	Cross puncheon, (a rough-hewn boardwalk), and bridge over Dry Run.		2433	1645.0
547.3	○	**Davis Fancy** historical marker. Path to east leads 100 yards to Davis cemetery.		2451	1644.7
547.4	▲P(3)♀	Cross **VA. 617**, Davis Valley Road	N 36 53.842, W 81 22.152	2580	1644.6
548.1	♦Y	Water, year round spring is located 300 yards east, blue blaze		2610	1643.9
549.3	▲☾	Davis Path campsite, no water		2840	1642.7
551.0	▲	South Ridgecrest of Little Brushy Mountain, limited views.		3300	1641.0
552.1	♦▲	Reed Creek in Crawfish Valley on east side of trail. Good campsites.		2600	1639.9
552.4	Y	Intersection with Crawfish Trail (Channel Rock), marked with orange diamonds.		2622	1639.6
554.2	▲	Tilson Gap, Big Walker Mountain, wooded crest.		3500	1637.8
555.7	▲P ★★★★★	Cross **VA. 610**, Old Rich Valley Road.		2700	1636.3

⌂▲◈⌂ (0.3W) **Quarter Way Inn** 276-522-4603. tina@quarterwayinn.com (www.quarterwayinn.com)
🛒🍴P @ AT Passport location.
⊛ No dogs. Open Apr 1–Jun 30. Renovated 1910 farmhouse run by '09 thru-hiker Tina (Chunky) & husband, Brett. ⌂ $30PP for indoor bunkroom with comfy mattress, pillow, shower, towel, laundry, loaner clothes, & a.m. coffee. $45S, $75D private room; or, ▲ $18PP tenting, both include the same. Gourmet breakfast $12 including their own honey, apple butter, and jam. 🛒 Full resupply (⛽ gas canisters, Mountain House, tuna, oatmeal, etc.), pizza, pop & ice cream. Extensive VHS collection, 📱 free phone calls, and hammock chairs in a majestic Sycamore tree. 🍴 Slackpacking often available, call in advance. Can ship outgoing packages. P Parking $3/day. Accepts Credit Cards, ID required.
✉ Mail for guests accepted: 4083 Old Rich Valley Rd, Ceres, VA 24318.

557.2	♦⌒▲	**VA. 742**, Shady Grove Road, North Fork of Holston River, bridge		2460	1634.8
557.6	♦	Blue blaze trail 25 yards downhill to reliable spring.		2550	1634.4
558.2	▲P(10)♀ ★★★★★	Cross **VA. 42**. O'Lystery Pavilion **(private, do not use). See map of VA 42.**	N 36 58.998, W 81 24.384	2650	1633.8

⌂🛏◈☾ (0.1E) **Bear Garden Hiker Hostel** 248-249-1951, 276-682-3769 beargardenhikerhostel@gmail.com
🍴⌂🍽🛒 Bob and Bertie Lingham owners.
⛽🍴�car✉ ◈ AT Passport location.
♀ 🐕 No dogs in the buildings. Hikers with dogs, dogs must sleep in the hikers tent. ⌂ Bunkhouse $20 sleeps 10, overflow can sleep 6, includes shower, cold breakfast with cereal, bread for toast and homemade jellies, coffee-tea-hot chocolate included. ☾ Privy, ⛺ washer/dryer are an additional charge. Chapel available for hikers. 🛏 Stay in house $80, sleeps 6 with full kitchen and laundry. ⛽ Usually have fuel. We have food, drinks and some resupply at fair prices and 📶 free WiFi at the bunkhouse. 🚗 Some shuttle service are available. ♀ 36.98495, -81.40314
✉ Mail drop: 306 W. Blue Grass Trail Ceres VA. 24318

NoBo Features   Description   GPS   Elev SoBo

⛺ ◈ ⊗ ⚲ (2.5W) **Appalachian Dreamer Hiker Hostel** 276-970-2834 (www.appalachiandreamerhikerhostel.
🏠 ⊕ 🍴 🚐 com)
P 🖥️   ◈ AT Passport location.
⊗ No pets or animals of any kind allowed. Open April thru October.
Accepts reservations only, call for availability. ⛺ $25.00 donation requested for stay, accepts credit
cards. Space for 8 hikers, 2 full baths for hikers, large screened in porch, full kitchen for hikers where
meals are served and hikers can prepare meals. ⚲ Laundry facilities, 📶 WiFi, land line phone, towels,
bath cloths and pillow case furnished. Photo I.D. required, max. 2 night stay must sign hold harmless
hiker agreement and accept rules which we have in place. Visit web site for rules and more info. We are
Christians and promote Christian Values. Complimentary meals, short term resupply, fuel, 🚐 🍴 (shuttle
service when availably for slack packing). No cell service from trail crossing of Hwy. 42 or Va. 610. Call
for pickup from top of Walker Mt. if heading north or from Chestnut Ridge if heading south. Will pick up
from either Hwy 42 or Va. 610. Photo I.D. required, max. P Ask about parking. **Located:** at, 502 Dot-
son Ridge Rd. Ceres, VA. 24318. It is located west of where trail crosses VA 42 and also west of where
trail crosses Old Rich Valley Rd.
    🖃 Mail drops: 502 Dotson Ridge Rd. Ceres, VA. 24318.

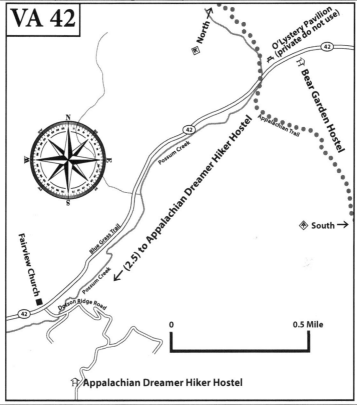

559.1		Brushy Mountain		3200	1632.9
560.3	♦⌐(8) ⌣(🚐♨	**Knot Maul Branch Shelter**, water is located (0.2) north on the AT, privy. 36.1◄26.3◄19.3◄► 9.4► 20.1► 33.6	N 37 00.040, W 81 24.276	2880	1631.7
560.8	♦🛈⌐	Cross bridge over creek. Campsite and water for Knot Maul Shelter.		2910	1631.2
561.4	♦⌐	Lynn Camp Creek, footbridge		2400	1630.6
562.5		Lynn Camp Mountain		3000	1629.5
563.7	♦⌐🛈⌣	Lick Creek, footbridge. Good campsites in the area.		2300	1628.3
564.9	♦	Cross creek.		2311	1627.1
565.1	🛈P(4)♨	Cross **USFS 222, VA. 625**, gravel	N 37 01.372, W 81 25.559	2300	1626.9
567.9	♦	Spring-fed pond, water for Chestnut Knob Shelter.		3800	1624.1
569.0		Chestnut Ridge		3700	1623.0
569.7	⌐(8) ⌣🛈♨	**Chestnut Knob Shelter**, no water at shelter but is sometimes found (0.2) south on the AT and then 50 yards east on an old Jeep road, privy. 35.7◄28.7◄9.4◄► 10.7► 24.2► 33.9 Burkes Garden Overlook	N 37 03.468, W 81 23.969	4409	1622.3

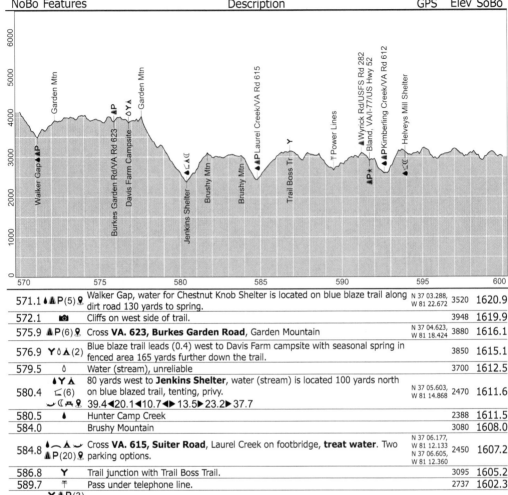

NoBo	Features	Description	GPS	Elev	SoBo
571.1	♦▲P(5)♀	Walker Gap, water for Chestnut Knob Shelter is located on blue blaze trail along dirt road 130 yards to spring.	N 37 03.288, W 81 22.672	3520	1620.9
572.1	📷	Cliffs on west side of trail.		3948	1619.9
575.9	▲P(6)♀	Cross **VA. 623, Burkes Garden Road**, Garden Mountain	N 37 04.623, W 81 18.424	3880	1616.1
576.9	Y◊▲(2)	Blue blaze trail leads (0.4) west to Davis Farm campsite with seasonal spring in fenced area 165 yards further down the trail.		3850	1615.1
579.5	◊	Water (stream), unreliable		3700	1612.5
580.4	♦Y▲ ⊏(6) ⌒℄⛺♀	80 yards west to **Jenkins Shelter**, water (stream) is located 100 yards north on blue blazed trail, tenting, privy. 39.4◄20.1◄10.7◄►13.5►23.2►37.7	N 37 05.603, W 81 14.868	2470	1611.6
580.5	♦	Hunter Camp Creek		2388	1611.5
584.0		Brushy Mountain		3080	1608.0
584.8	♦⌒▲⌣ ▲P(20)♀	Cross **VA. 615, Suiter Road**, Laurel Creek on footbridge, **treat water**. Two parking options.	N 37 06.177, W 81 12.133 N 37 06.605, W 81 12.360	2450	1607.2
586.8	Y	Trail junction with Trail Boss Trail.		3095	1605.2
589.7	☂	Pass under telephone line.		2737	1602.3
591.2	Y▲P(3) ♀ ★★★★★	Trail intersects with **USFS 282**.	N 37 08.308, W 81 08.141	3086	1600.8
591.4	☂	Power line.		3028	1600.6
591.7	▲ P(10) ★★★★★	Intersects with **U.S. 52**.		2920	1600.3

Bland, VA (2.5E). See map of Bland.

✉♀	**PO** M-F 8:30am-11:30am & 12pm-4pm, Sa 9am-11am, 276-688-3751. 207 Jackson St. Bland, VA 24315. N 37 06.016, W 81 06.966
🛏☕🖥	**Big Walker Motel** 276-688-3331
	🛏 $64.33(1-2), $69(3-4), pets okay. Fridge and microwave. ☕ WiFi.
	🖥 Mail drops for guests only: (UPS) 70 Skyview Lane, Bland VA 24315, (USPS) PO Box 155, Bland VA 24315.
✗	**Subway, Dairy Queen**
🛒	**Grants Supermarket** 276-688-0314 (www.shopatgrants.com) M-Sa8am-8pm, Su 10am-7pm.
🏪✗⚒🍴	**Citgo, Bland Square Grill** 276-688-3851.
☎	Open year round, M-Su 6:30am-7pm. 🏪 Groceries, ⚒ Canister fuel and Heet, ✗ Grill serves Breakfast, lunch and dinner, 🍴 payphone, ☎ ATM.
🏪	**Dollar General** Open M-Su 8am-10pm.
⚕	**Bland Family Clinic** 276-688-0500. M 10am-6pm, Tu 11am-7pm, W closed, Th 9am-5pm, F 10am-2pm, Sa-Su closed. Call ahead because they sometimes close early.
💻☕	**Bland County Library** 276-688-3737. M 10am-4:30pm, 10am-7:30pm, W 10am-4:30pm, Th 10am-7:30pm, F-Sa 10am-7:30pm, Su closed. Located at 697 Main Street. Computers available for use, ☕ free WiFi.

Virginia

VA

NoBo	Features	Description	GPS	Elev	SoBo

	🚗	**Bubba's Shuttles** 276-730-5869. barnes.james43@yahoo.com Shuttles from Damascus to Pearisburg and Roanoke Airport.			
Bastian, VA 24314 (3.0W)					
	🏤🪖	**PO** M-F 8am-12pm, Sa 9:15am-11:15am, 276-688-4631. 178 Walnut St. Bastian, VA 24314. N 37 09.134, W 81 09.126			
	✗	**Pizza Plus** 276-688-3332. M-Th 11am-10pm, F 11am-11pm, Su 11am-10pm.			
	🩹	**Bland Pharmacy** 276-688-4204. M-F 9am-5pm, Sa-Su closed.			
	⚕	**Bland County Medical Clinic** 276-688-4331. (www.blandclinic.com) M 8am-6pm, Tu-Th 8am-8pm, F 8am-5pm, Sa-Su closed. Located at 12301 Grapfield Rd.			

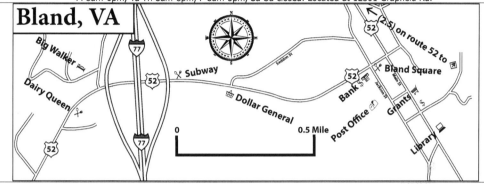

Bland, VA

592.1	⚲P(8)🪖	Intersects with **VA. 612, I–77 overpass**	N 37 08.391, W 81 07.386	2750	1599.9
592.5	◊⚲P(8)🪖	**VA. 612**, Kimberling Creek. **Do not drink water from creek, it is drainage off I-77.**	N 37 08.382, W 81 07.196	2700	1599.5
593.9	◖⊏(8) ⌣⊑🚗🪖	(0.3E) **Helveys Mill Shelter**, water is located (0.3) down a blue blazed switch backed trail in front of the shelter, privy. 33.6◄24.2◄13.5◄► 9.7►24.2►33.7	N 37 07.957, W 81 06.264	3090	1598.1
594.8	Y	Junction with wood road.		3102	1597.2
596.0	Y	Woods road intersects at double blaze.		3006	1596.0

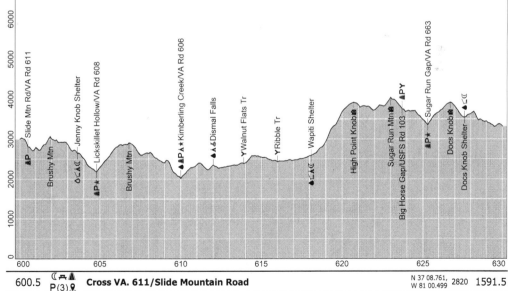

600.5	⊏🚗⚲ P(3)🪖	**Cross VA. 611/Slide Mountain Road**	N 37 08.761, W 81 00.499	2820	1591.5
601.9	⚲	Brushy Mountain summit, wooded.		3101	1590.1
603.6	◊Y⊑ ⊏(8) ⌣🚗🪖	130 yards east to **Jenny Knob Shelter**, ◊ two separate springs, each on blue blaze trail near shelter are unreliable, ⊏ privy. 33.9◄23.2◄9.7◄► 14.5►24.0►40.1	N 37 09.299, W 80 58.818	2800	1588.4
604.8	⊏🚗⚲ P(3)🪖 ★★★★★	Cross **VA. 608**, Lickskillet Hollow. **See map of VA 608.**	N 37 09.429, W 80 57.671	2200	1587.2

🏠 🐕 ⊞ ☑ **(0.8E) Lickskillet Hostel** 276-779-5447.
Open 01 March. 🏠 Donations accepted, � laundry, TV with dvd collection, pool table, 🐕 slackpacking available. Limited kitchen, fridge, microwave, hotplate. Pets OK. 🛜 Free WiFi.
☑ Mail drops for guest only: 35 Price Ridge Rd Bland, VA 24315

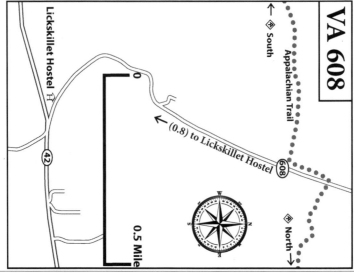

605.0	◊	Stream, unreliable.		2733	1587.0
606.0	🕆	Power line.		2739	1586.0
608.2	▲	Brushy Mountain, crest.		2800	1583.8
610.0	◊⌒▲	Kimberling Creek, suspension bridge		2090	1582.0
610.1	▲P(4)♀ ★★★★★	Cross **VA. 606**	N 37 10.542, W 80 54.498	2040	1581.9

▲🏠✕◈ **(0.5W) Trent's Grocery** 276-928-1349.
🍴🚿⚓⚓ ◈ AT Passport location.
🚗☑ Open year round. M-Sa 7am-8pm, Sun 9am-8pm. 🍴 ✕ Deli with pizza, hamburgers, hot dogs and more. ▲ Camping $6, 🚿 shower $3, ⚓ laundry $3. ⚓ Coleman and alcohol by the ounce, canisters. Soda machines outside. Accepts Credit Cards. 🚗 Shuttles. 🏧 ATM.
☑ Mail drops: 900 Wilderness Rd, Bland, VA 24315.

	🚗	**Larry Richardson** 540-921-4724. Shuttle range Bland to Pearisburg.			
612.0	◊Y🚿	Dismal Creek Falls Trail, waterfalls located (0.3) west, camping on side trail		2320	1580.0
613.1	⌒	Cross bridge over deep gully.		2387	1578.9
613.9	Y⌒▲	Side trail leads (0.4) west to Walnut Flats campground.		2400	1578.1
615.9	▲P(4)♀	Cross **Lion's Den Road**, gated forest service road.	N 37 12.774, W 80 51.389	2519	1576.1
616.0	Y▲	Ribble Trail south junction, trail leads (0.5) west to USFS White Cedar Horse campground		2400	1576.0
616.3	◊⌒	Water (stream), bridge.		2500	1575.7
617.3	▲	Intersects with woods road.		2493	1574.7
618.1	◊Y⌐(6) ⌐℃♀	100 yards east to **Wapiti Shelter**, water (Dismal Creek) just south of the turn off to the shelter, privy. 37.7◄24.2◄14.5◄►9.5►25.6►38.2	N 37 13.436, W 80 49.446	2600	1573.9
618.2	Y	Unmarked trail leads (0.1) to Wapiti Shelter		2662	1573.8
618.7	◊	Upper branch of Dismal Creek.		2656	1573.3
619.5	Y	Intersects with woods road.		3417	1572.5
620.7	▲📷	Sugar Run Mountain, rocky outcropping		3800	1571.3
623.6	◊Y	Junction with blue blazed Ribble Trail north junction		3800	1568.4
623.7	▲P(4)♀	Cross **USFS 103**, Big Horse Gap	N 37 14.521, W 80 51.835	3752	1568.3
624.9	▲	Cross **Nobusiness Creek Road**.		3711	1567.1
625.3	▲P(6)♀ ★★★★★	Cross **VA. 663, Sugar Run Gap Road**, Sugar Run Gap. **See map of VA 663/ Sugar Run Gap Rd.**	N 37 15.353, W 80 51.328	3450	1566.7

Seek what sets your soul on fire.

🛏🏠⚑⦿ (0.5E) **Woods Hole Hostel & Mountain B&B**
🍴🏪🐾⛺ 540-921-3444. woodsholehostel@gmail.com (www.woodsholehostel.com)
🖥📱🚐▣ ⦿ AT Passport location.
"A slice of heaven not to be missed."
An isolated 1880's Chestnut Log Cabin opened to hikers in 1986 by Roy & Tillie Wood. Granddaughter, Neville, continues their legacy with organic gardening, pottery, yoga (free), & massage therapy. **Directions:** Turn East at Sugar Run Gap/Dirt Road. Take a left at fork on gravel road to Hostel. Open Seasonal. Pet friendly. 🏠 Bunkhouse $20/person: Wood Stove, mattresses, electricity, and hot shower. ⛺ Camping $12/person. 🛏 Indoor rooms: $30/person shared/$60private (thru-hiker rate). Guests often invited to share local organic communal meals. 🍴 Dinner $14, breakfast $8. 🖥 Computer access, ⛺ laundry, smoothies, cheese, home roast coffee, baked goods . 🏪 Short term resupply. 🔥 Coleman fuel and alcohol by the ounce, fuel canisters. 🚐📱 Shuttles and Slack Pack for fee. ▣ Mail drops for guests only/or $5 fee: Woods Hole Hostel, 3696 Sugar Run Rd, Pearisburg, VA 24134.

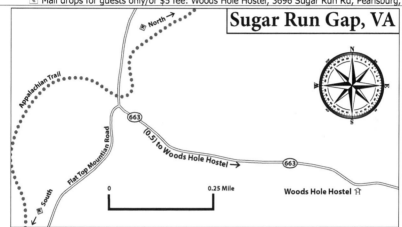

Sugar Run Gap, VA

626.7	📷	Blue blaze trail leads to Rock Cliff Overlook and views.		3850	1565.3
627.6	♦⌂(8) ☾☽⚑	100 feet west to **Doc's Knob Shelter**, water (spring) is located to left of shelter, privy. 33.7◀24.0◀9.5◀▶ 16.1▶28.7▶32.6	N 37 16.213, W 80 50.184	3555	1564.4

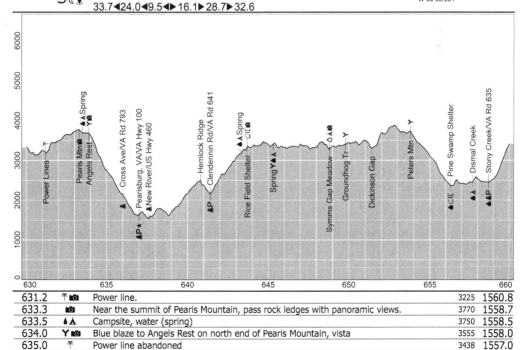

631.2	⚑📷	Power line.		3225	1560.8
633.3	📷	Near the summit of Pearis Mountain, pass rock ledges with panoramic views.		3770	1558.7
633.5	♦⛺	Campsite, water (spring)		3750	1558.5
634.0	Y📷	Blue blaze to Angels Rest on north end of Pearis Mountain, vista		3555	1558.0
635.0	⚑	Power line abandoned		3438	1557.0
635.4	♦	Water, spring 300 yards west.		2300	1556.6

NoBo Features	Description	GPS	Elev	SoBo
636.0 ▲	Cross **VA. 634**, Cross Ave.		2200	1556.0
636.4 ▲ ★★★★★	Intersects with **Lane Street to US. 460**.		1650	1555.6

Pearisburg, VA (0.9E) (all major services). See map of Pearisburg.

⌖☎ **PO** M-F 9am-4:30pm, Sa 10am-12pm, 540-921-1100. 206 N Main St. Pearisburg, VA 24134. N 37 19.689, W 80 44.139

🏠🛏▲〜 (0.9E) **Angels Rest Hiker's Haven** 540-787-4076, Cell: 540-922-2178. Your host Doc Peppa et al
◈⚠📶 (www.angelsresthikershaven.com)
◈ AT Passport location.
$12-$65 pp a night. ▲ Tenting, 🏠 Hammocking, 🏠 Bunks and 🛏 Private Rooms available. ⚠ Laundry $4, Day Passes $7 (includes laundry, shower, and use of the many amenities until 6pm, then upgrade to a stay if you can't tear yourself away). Courtesy shuttle to and from local trail heads. 🚐 Local Shuttles $2-$4. Shuttles between Damascus and Daleville, Va. (call for pricing) 🚐 Slack Packing. Chiropractic and Acupuncture Services Available by appt. 🐕 Well behaved canines $5 for entire stay. WiFi available.
🛏 **New for 2019:** "ChillaxInn", three bedroom ranch. Consists of two rooms with queen beds, a small single with a work station for bloggers, writers, and remote workers.
Mail drops: 204 Douglas Ln. Pearisburg, VA 24134.

🛏◈⚠🏊 **Holiday Motor Lodge** 540-921-1552.
📶📺 ◈ AT Passport location.
Open year round.
🛏 Lodging; Standard rooms $55, $10 for each addition person after 2, $10 pet fee, microwave, fridge, TV. ⚠ Coin laundry.
🐕 Pet friendly. Coffee in office. 🏊 Pool. 📶 Free WiFi. 🏧 ATM.
✉ Mail drops: 401 N Main St, Pearisburg, VA 24134.

🛏◈⚠ **Plaza Motel** 540-921-2591
💻📶 🛏 $44S $55D includes tax, ⊗ no pets, accepts credit cards. ⚠ Laundry, 💻 computer available to use, 📶 free WiFi.
✉ Mail drops: 415 N. Main St, Pearisburg, VA 24134.

🏠⊗▲ **Holy Family Hostel** Pat Muldoon 540-626-3337.
Open Mar-Nov. ⊗ No Pets, drugs or alcohol allowed. Volunteer caretaker on hand please don't call for a ride, no pickup. 🏠 Donations are requested, suggested $10PP, 2 night max. 🚿 Hot shower, bath room, electric stove, micro-wave, fridge, pots ,pans & dishes. Clean Towels provided. Bed mats, tables & benches, library, ▲ tents allowed on grounds. Wood Stove for heating. Keep hostel clean and neat. Co-ed sleeping area.

🛒 **Food Lion** M-Su 7am-11pm. **Walmart** M-Su 24 hours. **Grant's** M-Su 8am-9pm.

🛒◈🚗 **Pearis Mercantile** 540-921-2260.
◈ AT Passport location.
M-Sa 10am-5:30pm. 🛒 Has a small selection of hiker food, small gear items, ⛽ fuel.

⚠ **EZ Way Laundr**y M-Sa 6am-9pm, Su 6am-8pm.

🍴 **Dairy Queen, Pizza Hut, Wendys, La Barranca Mex. Grill, Lucky Star Chinese** (AYCE).

🍴⛽ **The Hardware Store** 540-921-1456. (www.harveystreethardwareandelectronics.com)
M-F 9am-5pm, Sa 9am-4pm, Su closed. ⛽ Canister fuel, alcohol by the ounce, tent repair kits.

💻 **Pearisburg Library** 540-921-2556. M 12pm-8pm, T 12pm-5pm, W 9am-5pm, TH 9am-8pm, F 9am-5pm, Sa 9am-1pm, Su closed.

⚕ **Community Health Center** 540-921-3502. M-F 8am-4:30pm, Sa-Su closed. Located at 219 South Buchanan Street Quick, low cost healthcare, hikers welcome.

🚐🚐 **Don Raines** 540-921-7433 ratface20724@aol.com Anytime, anywhere. 🚐 Slackpacking available.

🚐 **Tom Hoffman** 540-921-1184. gopullman@aol.com. Mid-range shuttles centered in Pearisburg area.

Narrows, VA (3.6W on VA 100)

⌖☎ **PO** MF 9:30am-1:15pm & 2pm-4: 15pm, Sa 9am-11am , 540-726-3272. 305 Main St. Narrows, VA 24124. N 37 19.861, W 80 48.611

🛏◈🍴🛒 **MacArthur Inn** 540-726-7510. (www.macarthur-inn.com)
🚿📶🚐 ◈ AT Passport location.
✉ 🛏 Hiker room $45 includes one double bed with half bath. Guest shower in our laundry area. Other rooms will receive a discounted price. 📞 Free long distance phone, cable TV, 📶 WiFi and use of guest kitchen. 🚿 Shower without stay $8. 🍴 Breakfast served by request Saturday and Sunday only; dinner is served Thurs. 5-8 p.m. with Old Time Mountain Music Jam. Located in center of town with all major services, grocery store, post office, restaurants, laundry all within close walking distance. Call for ride from Pearisburg area trail heads, ride $5 round trip. 🚐 Longer shuttles and 🚐 slack-packing can be arranged.
✉ Mail drops: 117 MacArthur Lane, Narrows, VA 24124.

▲🚻⌖ **Camp Success Camping** (www.townofnarrows.org) Primitive ▲ camping- tents or 〜 hammocks only. $5 tenting per night, no showers. Checkin at Town Office 540-726-3020 M-F 9 am-5 pm. Discount of $20 for 5 days (1 tent). They do have an outhouse and a slop-sink. Call ahead for after-hours arrivals or print permit form . N 37 20.081, W 80 48.711

🛒 **Grants Supermarket** 540-726-2303 M—Sa 8am—8pm, Sun 9am—8pm.

Virginia

Description

GPS Elev SoBo

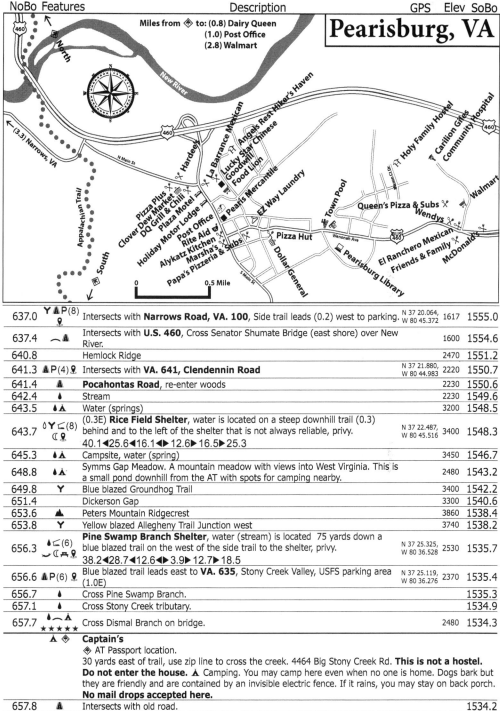

Pearisburg, VA

Miles from ◈ to: (0.8) Dairy Queen
(1.0) Post Office
(2.8) Walmart

NoBo	Features	Description	GPS	Elev	SoBo
637.0	Y▲P(8) ⚲	Intersects with **Narrows Road, VA. 100**, Side trail leads (0.2) west to parking.	N 37 20.064, W 80 45.372	1617	1555.0
637.4	⌒▲	Intersects with **U.S. 460**, Cross Senator Shumate Bridge (east shore) over New River.		1600	1554.6
640.8		Hemlock Ridge		2470	1551.2
641.3	▲P(4)⚲	Intersects with **VA. 641, Clendennin Road**	N 37 21.880, W 80 44.983	2220	1550.7
641.4	▲	**Pocahontas Road**, re-enter woods		2230	1550.6
642.4	♦	Stream		2230	1549.6
643.5	♦▲	Water (springs)		3200	1548.5
643.7	◊Y⊑(8) ☾⚲	(0.3E) **Rice Field Shelter**, water is located on a steep downhill trail (0.3) behind and to the left of the shelter that is not always reliable, privy. 40.1◀25.6◀16.1◀▶ 12.6▶16.5▶25.3	N 37 22.487, W 80 45.516	3400	1548.3
645.3	♦▲	Campsite, water (spring)		3450	1546.7
648.8	♦▲	Symms Gap Meadow. A mountain meadow with views into West Virginia. This is a small pond downhill from the AT with spots for camping nearby.		2480	1543.2
649.8	Y	Blue blazed Groundhog Trail		3400	1542.2
651.4		Dickerson Gap		3300	1540.6
653.6	▲	Peters Mountain Ridgecrest		3860	1538.4
653.8	Y	Yellow blazed Allegheny Trail Junction west		3740	1538.2
656.3	♦⊑(6) ☾⇋⚲	**Pine Swamp Branch Shelter**, water (stream) is located 75 yards down a blue blazed trail on the west of the side trail to the shelter, privy. 38.2◀28.7◀12.6◀▶ 3.9▶12.7▶18.5	N 37 25.325, W 80 36.528	2530	1535.7
656.6	▲P(6)⚲	Blue blazed trail leads east to **VA. 635**, Stony Creek Valley, USFS parking area (1.0E)	N 37 25.119, W 80 36.276	2370	1535.4
656.7	♦	Cross Pine Swamp Branch.			1535.3
657.1	♦	Cross Stony Creek tributary.			1534.9
657.7	♦⌒▲ ★★★★★	Cross Dismal Branch on bridge.		2480	1534.3
	▲◈	**Captain's** ◈ AT Passport location. 30 yards east of trail, use zip line to cross the creek. 4464 Big Stony Creek Rd. **This is not a hostel. Do not enter the house.** ▲ Camping. You may camp here even when no one is home. Dogs bark but they are friendly and are contained by an invisible electric fence. If it rains, you may stay on back porch. **No mail drops accepted here.**			
657.8	▲	Intersects with old road.			1534.2
658.7	▲P(15)⚲	Cross **VA. 635** (paved), Stony Creek	N 37 24.860, W 80 35.000	2450	1533.3
658.8	▲	Cross woods road.			1533.3
659.8	▲	Cross **VA 734**, gravel fire road.			1532.2

NoBo	Features	Description	GPS	Elev	SoBo
660.0	♦	Blue blazed side trail leads 125 yards east to water (spring)		3490	1532.0
660.2	♦⊑(6) ⌣《🚻♀	**Bailey Gap Shelter**, water is located (0.2) south on the AT and then east down a blue blazed trail, privy. 32.6◀16.5◀3.9◀▶ 8.8▶ 14.6▶20.9	N 37 24.052, W 80 34.632	3525	1531.8
662.8		Rock ledge west of trail.			1529.2
663.9	⚠P(14)♀	Cross **VA. 613** (gravel), Mountain Lake Road, Salt Sulphur Turnpike	N 37 24.719, W 80 31.360	3950	1528.1
664.1	Y📷	Wind Rock is located 100 feet west on side trail, vista		4121	1527.9
665.0	⚠Y	Cross old woods road, Side trail Potts Mountain Trail is 100 feet north on trail.			1527.0
665.3	♦⚠	Campsite, water (spring) located north of open area.		4000	1526.7
665.8	Y	Junction of old trail leading 150 yards west to Potts Mountain Trail.			1526.2
666.5		West side of Pine Peak.		4054	1525.5
667.0	Y	Junction with connector trail that leads to War Spur Trail to the east.			1525.0
667.3	♦	Water on east side of trail, rock field on west side.			1524.7
667.5	◊	Seasonal spring west on trail.			1524.5
669.0	♦⊑(6) ⌣《🚻♀	**War Spur Shelter**, water (stream) is located 80 yards north of the shelter on the AT, privy. 25.3◀12.7◀8.8◀▶ 5.8▶ 12.1▶18.1	N 37 23.852, W 80 28.440	2340	1523.0
669.8	♦⚠P(6)♀	Cross **USFS 156**, Johns Creek Valley	N 37 23.280, W 80 28.135	2102	1522.2
670.8	◊	Water (stream), seasonal		2700	1521.2
671.8	⚠P(3)	Cross **VA. 601**, gravel road, Rocky Gap		3250	1520.2
672.3	Y	Intersection with Johns Creel Mountain Trail east side.		3757	1519.7
672.4	Y	Unmarked trail west.		3779	1519.6
673.6	Y	Blue blaze trail leads 100 yards east to White Rock.		3809	1518.4
673.9		Kelly Knob.		3735	1518.1
674.8	♦Y⊑(6) 《🚻♀	Blue blaze trail 100 feet to **Laurel Creek Shelter**, water is located to the west on the AT and 45 yards south of the shelter trail junction, privy. 18.5◀14.6◀5.8◀▶ 6.3▶ 12.3▶22.4	N 37 21.535, W 80 25.272	2720	1517.2
675.8	♦	Water (spring), seasonal		2400	1516.2
677.2	⚠ ★★★★★	Cross **VA. 42**, Sinking Creek Valley		2200	1514.8

Newport, VA 24128 (8E) Not much located here.

	📫♀	**PO** M-F 8:15am-11:30am & 12:30pm-3:15pm, Sa 9am-11pm, 540-544-7415. 119 Blue Grass Trl. Newport, VA 24128. N 37 17.433, W 80 29.895			
	🛒	**Super Val-U** 540-544-7702. M-Th 6am-10pm, F-Sa 6am-10:30pm, Su 6am-10pm.			
677.8	📷	Top of hill with views.		2354	1514.2
678.1	♦⚠P (5)♀	Cross **VA. 630**, Sinking Creek	N 37 21.093, W 80 22.752	2100	1513.9
678.2	♦〜	Cross stream over footbridge.		2183	1513.8
678.6	⊙	**Keffer Oak**, this is the largest oak tree on the AT in the south		2240	1513.4
678.9	🗲	Power line.		3232	1513.1

Virginia

NoBo	Features	Description	GPS	Elev	SoBo
679.6	▲	Sinking Creek Mountain (south)		3200	1512.4
681.1	♦ Y ⊏(6) ((🍴♀	(0.4E) **Sarver Hollow Shelter**, water (spring) is located on a blue blazed trail near the shelter, privy.	N 37 21.286, W 80 20.245	3000	1510.9
		20.9◄12.1◄6.3◄►6.0►16.1►29.7			
683.5	📷	Walk along rock ledge with views east.		3364	1508.5
684.7	▲📷	Sinking Creek Mountain (north)		3490	1507.3
686.4	♦▲	Cross Cabin Branch		2490	1505.6
687.1	♦▲⊏(6) ⌣((🍴	**Niday Shelter**, water is located 75 yards down a blue blazed trail west of the AT, tenting, privy.	N 37 23.249, W 80 15.864	1800	1504.9
		18.1◄12.3◄6.0◄►10.1►23.7►24.7			
687.7	♦	Cross small stream.		1689	1504.3
688.4	▲P(10)♀	Cross **VA. 621**, Craig Creek Valley	N 37 22.755, W 80 15.004	1560	1503.6
688.5	🕇	Power line.		1539	1503.5
688.7	♦	High bridge over Craig Creek.		1571	1503.3

NoBo	Features	Description	GPS	Elev	SoBo
691.8	Y▲ P(10)♀	Intersection with grassy wood road at top of Brushy Mountain. Follow grassy wood road to Audie Murphy Monument Parking (0.1E)	N 37 21.462, W 80 14.250	3100	1500.2
692.2	Y〇	At intersection of woods road a Blue blaze trail leads 50 yards to **Audie Murphy Monument**, Murphy was the most-decorated American soldier of World War II. After the war, he starred in many Hollywood war movies and westerns. He died in a 1971 plane crash near this site. Monument on blue blazed trail to west.	N 37 21.871, W 80 13.544	3100	1499.8
693.0	Y	Intersects old road at ridge crest of Brushy Mountain.		1810	1499.0
694.3	📷	Pass vista as trail turns west.		1809	1497.7
694.4	📷	Brushy Mountain, vista on east side of trail.		2600	1497.6
696.0	♦▲P(5)♀	Cross **VA. 620**, Trout Creek, Miller Cove Road	N 37 23.393, W 80 11.780	1525	1496.0
696.4	🕇	Power line.		1738	1495.6
697.2	♦Y▲ ⊏(6) ⌣((🍴♀	(0.3E) **Pickle Branch Shelter**, water (stream) is located below the shelter, tenting along trail to shelter, privy.	N 37 23.286, W 80 11.466		1494.8
		22.4◄16.1◄10.1◄►13.6►14.6►17.0		1845	
699.8	📷	Pass Hemlock Point, a rocky outcrop with views 100 feet west.		2134	1492.2
701.3	▲	Cove Mountain Summit.		3005	1490.7

Be kind and kindness will find you.

NoBo	Features	Description	GPS	Elev	SoBo
701.4	⛰📷🔴♀	Crest of Cove Mountain, **Dragons Tooth**. Coordinates are to Dragons Tooth.	N 37 21.654, W 80 10.407	3020	1490.6
702.4	Y	Lost Spectacles Gap, Blue blazed trail to the west.		2550	1489.6
702.5	📷	Pass Devils Seat to east.		2346	1489.5
702.6	📷	Viewpoint Rock on the west side of trail.		2376	1489.4
702.9	📷	Rawies Rest, ridge narrows to knife-edge.		2350	1489.1
703.5	Y	Blue blazed Scout Trail with access to North Mountain Trail.		2102	1488.5
703.9	Y⛰P(3) ♀ ★★★★★	Cross **VA. 624**, Newport Road, North Mountain Trail. Parking at Dragons Tooth Trail head on VA 311. **See map of Catawba, VA.**	N 37 22.778, W 80 09.355	1810	1488.1
	⛺ ◈ ⛺🚿🖥🚐 🖥	(0.3E) **Four Pines Hostel** Owner Joe Mitchell, cell: 540-309-8615. ◈ AT Passport location. Open year round. ⛺ Hostel is a 3-bay garage with 🚿 shower. Please leave a donation. ⛺ Laundry $3 wash and $3 to dry. Pet friendly. 🖥 Computer available, 📶 free Wifi. Shuttles to and from The Homeplace Restaurant (Th-Su) and to Catawba Grocery. 🚐 Longer shuttles for a fee. 🖂 Mail drops: 6164 Newport Rd. Catawba VA 24070.			
	🛒✗	(0.4W) **Catawba Grocery** 540-384-8050. (0.3) west to VA 311 and then left (0.1) mile to store. Open M-Su 6am-10pm. Grill serves breakfast, pizza, burgers, ice cream.			

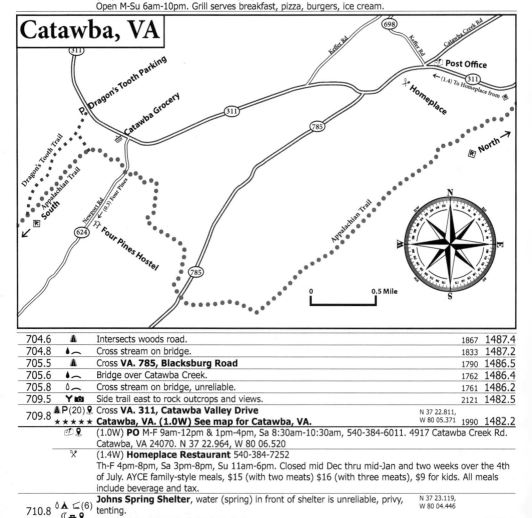

704.6	⛰	Intersects woods road.		1867	1487.4
704.8	💧	Cross stream on bridge.		1833	1487.2
705.5	⛰	Cross **VA. 785, Blacksburg Road**		1790	1486.5
705.6	💧	Bridge over Catawba Creek.		1762	1486.4
705.8	💧	Cross stream on bridge, unreliable.		1761	1486.2
709.5	Y📷	Side trail east to rock outcrops and views.		2121	1482.5
709.8	⛰P(20)♀ ★★★★★	Cross **VA. 311, Catawba Valley Drive** **Catawba, VA. (1.0W) See map for Catawba, VA.**	N 37 22.811, W 80 05.371	1990	1482.2
	⌂♀	(1.0W) **PO** M-F 9am-12pm & 1pm-4pm, Sa 8:30am-10:30am, 540-384-6011. 4917 Catawba Creek Rd. Catawba, VA 24070. N 37 22.964, W 80 06.520			
	✗	(1.4W) **Homeplace Restaurant** 540-384-7252 Th-F 4pm-8pm, Sa 3pm-8pm, Su 11am-6pm. Closed mid Dec thru mid-Jan and two weeks over the 4th of July. AYCE family-style meals, $15 (with two meats) $16 (with three meats), $9 for kids. All meals include beverage and tax.			
710.8	💧⛺⌂(6) (⛺🚐♀	**Johns Spring Shelter**, water (spring) in front of shelter is unreliable, privy, tenting. 29.7◄23.7◄13.6◄► 1.0►3.4►9.4	N 37 23.119, W 80 04.446	1980	1481.2
711.7	Y	Intersects old road.		2306	1480.3

NoBo	Features	Description	GPS	Elev	SoBo
711.8	◊ Y Å ⊏(6) ⌇ ⦅ 🚻 ⚲	Blue blaze trail leads to **Catawba Mountain Shelter**, water (piped spring) is located 50 yards south on the AT, tenting to the north, privy. 24.7◀14.6◀1.0◀▶2.4▶8.4▶22.8	N 37 23.292, W 80 03.444	2580	1480.2
711.9	Å	Primitive campsite at turn in trail.		2261	1480.1
712.2	Å	Dirt fire road.		2347	1479.8
712.7	⟟	Power line.		2448	1479.3
713.1	📷	Rock outcrop on west side of trail with views.		3192	1478.9
713.2	Y	Intersects old woods road.		2698	1478.8
713.4	Y 📷	Side trail west leads to cliffs.		3171	1478.6
713.5	📷 ⚲	Side trails lead to **McAfee Knob**, NO CAMPING. Coordinates are to McAfee Knob.	N 37 23.549, W 80 02.175	3199	1478.5
714.1	◊ Å ⌇ 🚻	Pig Farm campsite, picnic tables. Blue blaze trail a few yards south on AT leads (0.1) east to large spring.		3000	1477.9
714.2	◊ Y Å ⊏(6) ⌇ ⦅ 🚻 ⚲	100 feet east to **Campbell Shelter**, water (spring) is located on a blue blazed trail to the left and behind the shelter and follow the trail through meadow, tenting, privy. 17.0◀3.4◀2.4◀▶6.0▶20.4▶26.6	N 37 23.447, W 80 01.770	2580	1477.8
715.6	Å	Intersects old road.		2372	1476.4
717.3	Y	Brickey's Gap and a blue blazed trail.		2250	1474.7
719.1	📷	Tinker Cliffs, 1/2 mile cliff walk		3000	1472.9
719.6	Y	Scorched Earth Gap, Yellow blazed west to Andy Layne Trail.		2600	1472.4

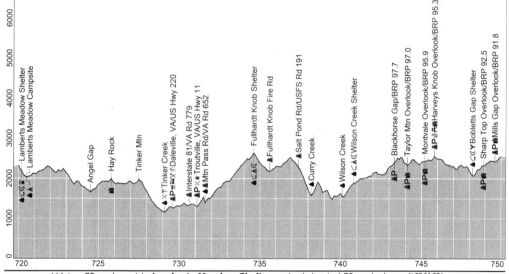

NoBo	Features	Description	GPS	Elev	SoBo
720.2	◊ Y Å ⊏(6) ⦅ 🚻 ⚲	50 yards east to **Lamberts Meadow Shelter**, water is located 50 yards down the trail in front of the shelter, tenting, privy. 9.4◀8.4◀6.0◀▶14.4▶20.6▶28.0	N 37 26.074, W 79 59.268	2080	1471.8
720.3	◊ ⌇	Cross bridge over stream.		2077	1471.7
720.5	◊ Å ⌇	Lamberts Meadow campsite, Sawmill Run, 100 yards north is a blue blazed trail.		2000	1471.5
724.5		Angels Gap		1800	1467.5
725.6	📷 ⚲	Hay Rock, Tinker Ridge. A climb to the top of Hay Rock provides some good views.	N 37 24.144, W 79 55.980	1900	1466.4
727.5	📷	Pass rock outcrop on east side of trail with view.		1951	1464.5
728.5	ⓘ	Trail kiosk.		1207	1463.5
729.0	✕	RR Crossing		1172	1463.0
729.1	◊ ⌇	Cross Tinker Creek, Trail crosses gated concrete bridge.		1165	1462.9
729.6	Å P(25) ⚲ ★★★★★	Cross **U.S. 220**	N 37 23.461, W 79 54.380	1350	1462.4

Trouteville, VA 24175

🏤 ⚲	(0.7W) from AT on Hwy 11 to PO M-F 9am-12pm & 1pm-5pm, Sa 9am-11am, 540-992-1472. 4952 Lee Hwy. Trouteville, VA 24175. N 37 24.757, W 79 52.855	
Å ⊗ 🚻 ♨ ⛺ ⚡	**Troutville Park and Fire Station**. Å Free camping at town park. ⊗ No pets. ⛺ Free laundry and ♨ showers at fire station. 🚻 Restrooms. ⚡ Free WiFi.	

Howard Johnson Express 540-992-1234.
◈ AT Passport location.
🛏 $49.95 hiker rate, continental breakfast microwave, fridge. 🛆 Coin laundry. Pets $10. Game room and pool. 🖥 Computer available, 🛜 free WiFi. 🕾 ATM in lobby.
🖃 Mail drops for guest: 437 Roanoke Road, Daleville, VA 24083.

Super 8 540-992-3000.
⊛ No pets. 🛏 $67.95 and up, includes continental breakfast, microwave, fridge. 🛆 Laundry. 🏊 Outdoor pool. 🖥 Computer available for use, 🛜 free WiFi. Accepts Credit Cards.

Comfort Inn 540-992-5600.
No smoking. 🛏 Hiker rate 52.99 +tax = 59.51 for 1-2 people, an additional 10 per person up to 4 people in a room, pets $25. 25.00 + tax = 26.33, the smoking fee is now $250.00 if you smoke in a room. Includes continental breakfast. Microwave, fridge, 🖥 computer available, 🛜 free WiFi. There is a $150 fine if caught smoking in the room. 🏊 Outdoor pool is open Memorial Day thru Labor day. Credit card is required even if you pay in cash.

Quality Inn 540-992-5335.
🛏 $72 and up, king or 2 doubles (hikers rate). $25.00 pet fee nonrefundable. Includes free Full Hot Breakfast. 🏊 Seasonal Pool
Microwaves/refrigerators/coffee makers in each room, 🖥 computer available for use, 🛜 free WiFi. Free WiFi/HD TV/Fitness Center.

Holiday Inn Express 540-966-4444
⊛ No pets. 🛏 $109-129, includes continental breakfast. 🛆 Coin laundry. 🖥 Computer available for use, 🛜 free WiFi.
🖃 Mail drops for guests: 3200 Lee Hwy, Troutville, VA 24175.

Red Roof Inn 540-992-5055.
🛏 Hiker special Su-Th $49.99. For special occasion weekends will charge $10.00 extra. Includes continental breakfast 6-9am every day, coffee in lobby, microwave, fridge, 🛆 coin laundry, 🛜 free WiFi, 🐾 pets stay for free.
🖃 Mail drops: 3231 Lee Highway South, Troutville, VA 24175

Motel 6 540-992-6700. $59.99 and up $6EAP, microwave, fridge, pets stay for free. 🛆 Laundry, 🛜 WiFi.

Three Li'l Pigs Barbeque 540-966-0165. (www.threelilpigsbbq.com)
◈ AT Passport location.
Open year-round, extended summer hours. M-W 7 am-9 pm, Th 7 am-9:30 pm, F-Sa 7 am-10:30 pm, Su 7 am-9 pm.
Hiker friendly, "hand-chopped BBQ, ribs, wings, fresh-ground burgers and a good selection of beer, much of it locally-brewed." In addition, during peak season (mid-April-June), we offer free Banana Pudding to thru-hikers with a meal purchase.

Kroger Grocery Store and Pharmacy 540-992-4920. 🛒 M-Su 24 hours, ✚ pharmacy M-F 8am-9pm, Sa 9am-6pm, Su 12pm-6pm.

Outdoor Trails 540-992-5850 (www.outdoortrails.com)
◈ AT Passport location.
🚶 Full service outdoor specialty shop. Open Mon-Fri 10am-8pm, Saturday 10am-6 pm. Footwear, equipment and clothing, freeze dried & dehydrated food, ⛽ fuel by the ounce. 🛜 Wifi & charging stations. 🚗 Shuttle service.
🖃 Mail drops: Address to: Outdoor Trails, Hold for AT Hiker: Your Real name, 28 Kingston Dr, Daleville, VA 24083.

Homer & Therese Witcher 540-266-4849. Shuttles from Daleville to Waynesboro or south to Damascus. Based in Daleville.

Daleville, VA 24083
(1.1W) from AT on route 220 to **PO** M-F 8am-5pm, Sa 8am-12pm, 540-992-4422. 1492 Roanoke Rd. Daleville, VA 24083. N 37 24.376, W 79 54.775

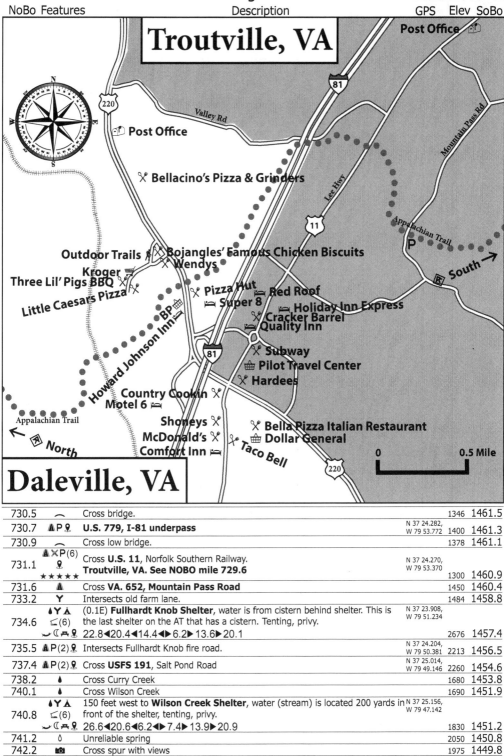

Troutville, VA

Daleville, VA

NoBo	Features	Description	GPS	Elev	SoBo
730.5	⌒	Cross bridge.		1346	1461.5
730.7	⚠P♀	**U.S. 779, I-81 underpass**	N 37 24.282, W 79 53.772	1400	1461.3
730.9	⌒	Cross low bridge.		1378	1461.1
731.1	⚠✗P(6)♀ ★★★★★	Cross **U.S. 11**, Norfolk Southern Railway. **Troutville, VA. See NOBO mile 729.6**	N 37 24.270, W 79 53.370	1300	1460.9
731.6	⚠	Cross **VA. 652, Mountain Pass Road**		1450	1460.4
733.2	Y	Intersects old farm lane.		1484	1458.8
734.6	♦Y⚠ ⊏(6) ⌣☾⇌♀	(0.1E) **Fullhardt Knob Shelter**, water is from cistern behind shelter. This is the last shelter on the AT that has a cistern. Tenting, privy. 22.8◀20.4◀14.4◀▶6.2▶13.6▶20.1	N 37 23.908, W 79 51.234	2676	1457.4
735.5	⚠P(2)♀	Intersects Fullhardt Knob fire road.	N 37 24.204, W 79 50.381	2213	1456.5
737.4	⚠P(2)♀	Cross **USFS 191**, Salt Pond Road	N 37 25.014, W 79 49.146	2260	1454.6
738.2	♦	Cross Curry Creek		1680	1453.8
740.1	♦	Cross Wilson Creek		1690	1451.9
740.8	♦Y⚠ ⊏(6) ⌣☾⇌♀	150 feet west to **Wilson Creek Shelter**, water (stream) is located 200 yards in front of the shelter, tenting, privy. 26.6◀20.6◀6.2◀▶7.4▶13.9▶20.9	N 37 25.156, W 79 47.142	1830	1451.2
741.2	◊	Unreliable spring		2050	1450.8
742.2	📷	Cross spur with views		1975	1449.8
743.0	📷	Narrow side trail with views.		1675	1449.0

NoBo	Features	Description	GPS	Elev	SoBo
743.3	Y▲P♀	Trail east to USFS 186; **BRP MP 97.7** Old Fincastle Road, Black Horse Gap	N 37 25.497, W 79 45.436	2402	1448.7
744.1	▲📷 P(12)♀	Cross **BRP MP 97.0** at Taylors Mountain Overlook	N 37 25.884, W 79 44.999	2350	1447.9
745.0	Y	Blue blazed Spec Mines Trail leads south to milepost 96.		2451	1447.0
745.2		Montvale Overlook; BRP MP 95.9		2400	1446.8
745.8	▲📷🚻 P(20)♀	Cross Harveys Knob Overlook; **BRP MP 95.3**	N 37 26.714, W 79 43.597	2550	1446.2
747.4	Y	Blue blazed Hammond Hollow Trail west.		2335	1444.6
748.2	♦Y⌐(6) ☾♀	(0.2W) **Bobblets Gap Shelter**, water (spring) is located to the left of the shelter but frequently goes dry but look farther downstream if dry, privy. 28.0◄13.6◄7.4◄►6.5►13.5►18.4	N 37 28.032, W 79 42.084	1920	1443.8
748.9	▲P♀	Cross Peaks of Otter Overlook; **BRP MP 92.5**	N 37 28.464, W 79 41.525	2350	1443.1
749.6	P(15)♀	Mills Gap Overlook; **BRP MP 91.8**, parking west.	N 37 28.773, W 79 40.931	2450	1442.4

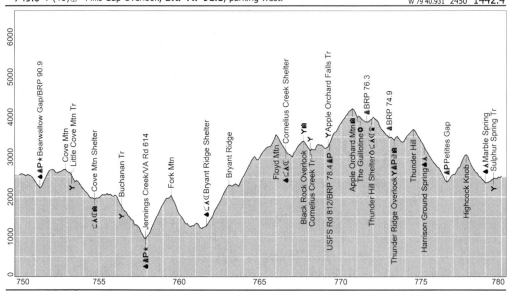

| 751.3 | ▲P(6)♀ ★★★★★ | Intersects with **VA. 43** for (0.1), Bearwallow Gap; **BRP MP 90.9**. | N 37 28.976, W 79 40.133 | 2228 | 1440.7 |

🛏▲✗🏪 **(5.5E) Peaks of Otter Lodge & Restaurant** 540-586-1081 (www.peaksofotter.com). (0.1) east on to the Blue Ridge Parkway overpass, then follow BRP to the left (5.0). 🛏 Motel rooms $126 weekdays, $169 weekends, higher in fall. ✗ Restaurant is open for breakfast, lunch and dinner. Sunday buffet brunch 11:30 am-3:30 pm. 🏪 Limited supplies in camp store. Off season operation Dec-Mar reduced to Th-Su and lower lodging pricing. ▲ Camping is managed separately, 540-586-7321, Open end of Apr - end of Oct, $16-19.

Buchanan, VA (downtown) (5.0W) see NOBO mile 756.3

📫♀	**PO** M & Th 9am-7pm; Tu, W, F 9am-5pm; Sa 9am-1pm, 540-254-2538. 19698 Main St. Buchanan, VA 24066 N 37 31.624, W 79 40.806
✗🍴	**Rasones Fountain & Grille** 540-254-1800, 🍴 Pharmacy 540-254-2904. located at 19771 Main St.
✗	**Burger King**, M-Sa 6am-12am, Su 7am-12am.
💻	**Library** 540-254-2538. M 9am-7pm, T-W 9am-5pm, Th 9am-7pm, F 9am-5pm, Sa 9am-1pm, Su closed.

Buchanan, VA

752.9	▲	Cove Mountain summit.		2707	1439.1
753.3	Y	Little Cove Mountain Trail		2600	1438.7
754.7	Y ▲ ⌐(6) ⦿ ⦿	East to **Cove Mountain Shelter**, water (stream) is located on a steep un-marked trail to left of the shelter leads (0.5) downhill, tenting, privy.	N 37 30.703, W 79 39.066		1437.3
		20.1◄13.9◄6.5◄► 7.0►11.9►17.2		1925	1437.3
754.8	📷	Pass rocky outlook to west.		1735	1437.2
756.4	Y	Buchanan Trail		1790	1435.6
757.2	◊	Intermittent stream.		1339	1434.8
757.9	◆ ◢ ▲ ▲ P(15)♀ ★★★★★	Intersects with **VA. 614** and crosses **Jennings Creek Road** on bridge, Jennings Creek. **See map of VA. 614.**	N 37 31.755, W 79 37.368	955	1434.1

    ▲ ⌂ ⌐ ◈ (1.2E) **Middle Creek Campground** 540-254-2550. (www.middlecreekcampground.com)
    ✗ ⌂ ▲ ♨ ◈ AT Passport location.
    ▲ ⊕ ▲ ⊡ If walking off AT go east on 614 for (0.2), and then left 1 mile on 618.
        Thru hiker rates, ▲ ↝ Camping/hammocking $15 per person, includes ♨ showers and ♨ pool or
        $5.00 for just shower and pool use. ⌂ Cabins begin at $60, A/C, rec room with couches, outlets, mov-
        ies. Night registration is available. Grill serves burgers, fries, milkshakes, nachos, wings, and more. ⊕
        Resupply, pouch meats, instant food, spices, oatmeal, tuna, ▲ denatured alcohol, fuel, beer. ⌁ Laundry.
        ⊕ Free WiFi. Call for free shuttle to and from trail head, phone signal strongest near parking area.
        ⊡ Mail drops: 1164 Middle Creek Rd, Buchanan, VA 24066.

Buchanan, VA (west side) (4.6W on VA 614) see NOBO mile 750.8
    ⌂ ✗ ⊕ **Wattstull Inn** 540-254-1551. (wattstullinn.com)
        ⌂ Hiker rates starting at $65, pets $15, includes continental breakfast, fridge, ⊕ free WiFi, ♨ outdoor
        pool. Free ride to and from trail head with stay.
        ✗ **Foot of the Mountain Café**, on site restaurant.

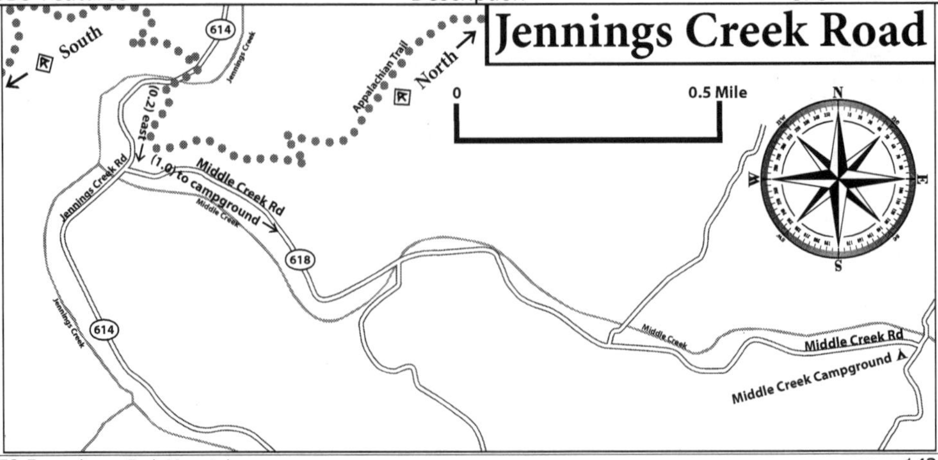

NoBo	Features	Description	GPS	Elev	SoBo
759.5	▲	Fork Mountain		2042	1432.5
760.1	Y P 📍	Blue blazed side trail leads (0.8) east to VA. 714 terminus.	N 37 31.806, W 79 35.381	1656	1431.9
760.6	💧	Cross creek on two large rocks		1350	1431.4
761.4	💧	Cross Hamps Branch.		1256	1430.6
761.7	💧 Y ⌂(16) ☾ 📍	Steps up to **Bryant Ridge Shelter**, water (stream) is located 25 yards in front of the shelter and also crossed on the trail to the shelter, privy. Blue blazed trail (0.1N) of shelter leads (0.5E) to VA 714. 20.9◀13.5◀7.0◀▶4.9▶10.2▶22.8	N 37 31.802, W 79 35.136	1330	1430.3
761.8	💧 Y ⛺ P 📍	Cross stream junction, campsite and blue blaze trail that leads (0.5) east to VA. 714 terminus.	N 37 31.806, W 79 35.381	1467	1430.2
762.0	Y	Intersects old road.		1543	1430.0
763.1	▲	Cryant Ridge crest.		2246	1428.9
766.0	▲	Floyd Mountain crest, wooded.		3560	1426.0
766.6	💧 Y ⛺ ⌂(6) ☾ 🪑 📍	(0.1E) **Cornelius Creek Shelter**, water is located on trail to shelter, tenting, privy. 18.4◀11.9◀4.9◀▶5.3▶17.9▶21.8	N 37 29.635, W 79 32.832	3145	1425.4
767.5	Y	Side trail leading west 200 feet to Black Rock.		3450	1424.5
767.8	💧	Cross stream.		3373	1424.2
768.1	Y	Intersects with Cornelius Creek Trail Recreation Trail west.		3246	1423.9
769.2	Y	Intersects with Apple Orchard Falls Trail (1.1W) to 200 foot waterfall		3250	1422.8
769.3	🛣 P 📍	Cross **USFS 812, Parkers Gap Road; BRP MP 78.4**	N 37 30.642, W 79 31.355	3410	1422.7
770.7	▲	Top of Apple Orchard Mountain, radar dome		4206	1421.3
771.0	⭘	The Guillotine, a large rock boulder suspended over the trail in a narrow rock cleft.		4090	1421.0
771.6	🛣 P(2) 📍	Cross Upper **BRP crossing MP 76.3**	N 37 31.315, W 79 30.237	3900	1420.4
771.7	🛣	Cross woods road.		3883	1420.3
771.9	💧 ⛺ ⌂(6) ☾ 🪑 🐻 📍	**Thunder Hill Shelter**, water is a walled in spring south on AT and unreliable during dry seasons, privy, tent sites north of shelter. Bear box. 17.2◀10.2◀5.3◀▶12.6▶16.5▶25.3	N 37 31.643, W 79 30.252	3960	1420.1
772.8	Y	Hunter Creek Trail east (2.0) to USFS 45.		3607	1419.2
772.9	🛣	Cross Lower **BRP crossing MP 74.9**		3650	1419.1
773.2	Y	Thunder Ridge loop trail leads east.		3518	1418.8
773.5	📷 🗑 🛣 P 📍	Unmarked trail leads east 85 feet to Thunder Hill Overlook; **BRP MP 74.7**	N 37 32.321, W 79 29.511	3525	1418.5
774.4	Y 📷	Path west leads to view of Arnold Valley and Devils Marblehead.		3672	1417.6
774.5	▲	Thunder Hill summit, wooded		3666	1417.5
775.2	💧 ⛺	Harrison Ground Spring, tenting.		3200	1416.8
775.5	📷	Ridgecrest with views.		3113	1416.5
775.7	💧	Intermittent spring.		2932	1416.3
776.2	🛣	Intersects old road to east.		2640	1415.8
776.6	🛣 P(6) 📍	Cross **Pettties Gap Road/SR 781**, Petties Gap; **BRP MP 71.0**	N 37 33.565, W 79 27.520	2369	1415.4
777.8	▲	Highcock Knob summit.		3054	1414.2
779.0	💧 ⛺	Marble Spring, campsite in sag.		2290	1413.0
779.3	📷	Pass area with open view.		2567	1412.7
779.5	Y	Sulphur Spring Trail to east (south crossing)		2400	1412.5

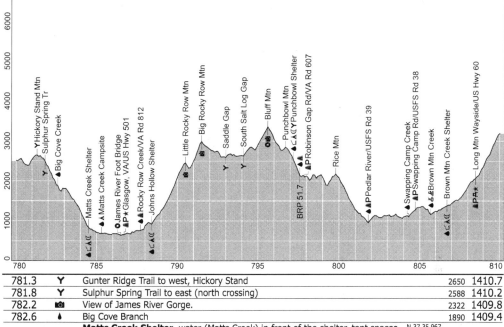

NoBo	Features	Description	GPS	Elev	SoBo
781.3	Y	Gunter Ridge Trail to west, Hickory Stand		2650	1410.7
781.8	Y	Sulphur Spring Trail to east (north crossing)		2588	1410.2
782.2	📷	View of James River Gorge.		2322	1409.8
782.6	♦	Big Cove Branch		1890	1409.4
784.5	♦Y▲ ⊏(6) ⌣((⛺⚲	**Matts Creek Shelter**, water (Matts Creek) in front of the shelter, tent spaces nearby, privy. Several small swimming holes are nearby. Matts Creek Trail (2.5E) to US 501 22.8◄17.9◄12.6◄▶ 3.9▶ 12.7▶22.2	N 37 35.967, W 79 24.810	835	1407.5
784.6	Y	Matts Creek Trail to east.		816	1407.4
785.3	♦▲	Campsite, water		700	1406.7
786.5	⌣●⚲⚲	Cross **James River Foot Bridge**, James River. This bridge is the longest foot bridge on the AT.	N 37 35.738, E 79 23.455	678	1405.5
786.7	▲P(25)⚲ ★★★★★	Cross **U.S. 501/VA. 130**. See map of Glasgow, VA.	N 37 35.818, E 79 23.477	680	1405.3
	🚌	**Ken Wallace** 434-609-2704 Shuttles from Buchanan to Waynesboro areas.			

Glasgow, VA 24555 (5.9W)

🏤⚲	**PO** M-F 8am-11:30am & 12:30pm-4:30pm, Sa 8:30am-10:30pm, 540-258-2852. 805 Blue Ridge Rd. Glasgow, VA 24555. N 37 37.889, W 79 26.963	
①	**Town Hall** 540-258-2246 Maintains shelter and Knick Field restrooms.	
🏠◈△ 🖥🍴🖂	**Stanimal's 328 Hostel & Shuttle Service Glasgow** 540-480-8325. AdamStanley06@gmail.com (www.stanimals328.com)	

◈ AT Passport location.

Guests enjoy complimentary pickup and drop off from 501 James River trailhead, 🖥 computer available for use, 📶 WiFi, △ complimentary laundry services, 🚿 shower, clean linens and bunks with mattresses. Property is ultra clean and features 55" flat screen with Netflix. Pizza, drinks & ice cream plus snacks available for purchase at reasonable prices. Caretaker provides breakfast for $6 and dinner for $10. Full house available to hikers plus kitchen privileges. $30/night plus private room options available for additional fee. 🚌 Paid shuttles available. for guests and non-guests at lowest rates. No cell service at 501 trailhead. Guests can call ahead from ridge to arrange for pickup at 501. Owned and operated by Adam Stanley "STANIMAL" AT '04 PCT '10

🖂 Mail drops free for guest, $5 for non guests: 1131 Rockbridge Road, Glasgow, VA 24555.

🛒🍴	**Glasgow Grocery Express** 540-258-1818.	

M-Sa 6am-11:30pm, Su 8am-1130pm. 🛒 Large selection of grocery and hiker foods. Hardware section, beer, dairy, frozen, ice cream. 🍴 Coleman and alcohol fuel by the ounce, heat in bottles, Isobutane fuel in two size cans. Hiker Friendly Store.

🐾	**Natural Bridge Animal Hospital** 540-291-1444.	

Located at 466 Buck Hill Rd, Natural Bridge Station Va 24579
M-F 8am-6pm, Sa 8am-12pm Sunday and all Major holidays Closed.

△	**Lew's Laundromat**, M-Su 24 hours.	
🖥	**Library** 540-258-2509. M 10am-6pm, Tu-W 10am-5:30pm, Th 10am-7pm, F-Sa 10am-2pm.	
🚗🍴	**Gary Serra** 757-681-2254. Pickups at Glasgow and Buena Vista trail heads. Shuttles along the AT, to Roanoke, Lynchburg, Charlottesville and Glasgow, airports, and to Amtrak station. Specialize in long distance shuttling. Sells fuel canisters.	

🚗 **Stanimal's Shuttle Service** 540-480-8325 covers all of Virginia.

Big Island, VA 24526 (5.6E)

📧 📍 **PO** M-F 8:15am-12pm & 1pm-4pm, Sa 8am-10am. 434-299-5072. 10830 Lee Jackson Hwy. Big Island, VA 24526. N 37 32.111, W 79 21.665

🏪 ✖ 🛏 **H&H Food Market** 434-299-5153.
🏪 M-Su 6am-9pm, 7 days a week, ✖ serves breakfast, lunch, and dinner 6:30am-8pm.
✉ Mail drops: 11619 Lee Jackson Hwy, Big Island, VA 24526.

☤ **Big Island Family Medical Center** 434-299-5951 M-Tu 8:30am-5pm, W closed, Th-F 8:30am-5pm, Sa-Su closed.

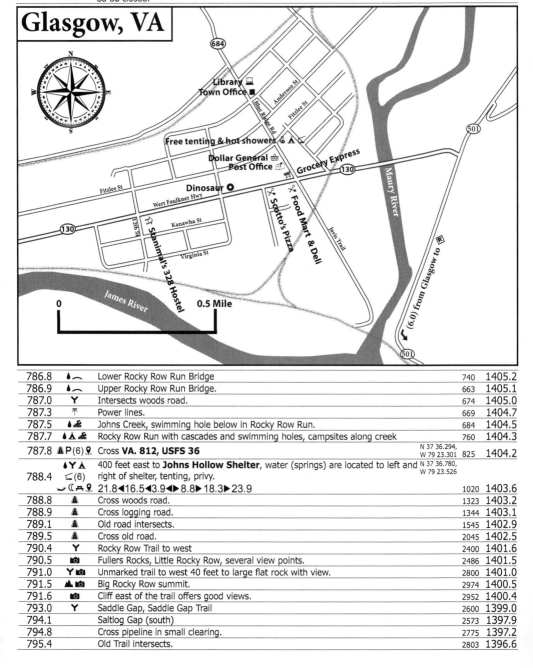

Glasgow, VA

NoBo		Feature	GPS	Elev	SoBo
786.8	⬥⌒	Lower Rocky Row Run Bridge		740	1405.2
786.9	⬥⌒	Upper Rocky Row Run Bridge.		663	1405.1
787.0	Y	Intersects woods road.		674	1405.0
787.3	⚡	Power lines.		669	1404.7
787.5	⬥⚓	Johns Creek, swimming hole below in Rocky Row Run.		684	1404.5
787.7	⬥🅰⚓	Rocky Row Run with cascades and swimming holes, campsites along creek		760	1404.3
787.8	🅰P(6)📍	Cross **VA. 812, USFS 36**	N 37 36.294, W 79 23.301	825	1404.2
788.4	⬥Y🅰 ⌂(6) 〰⦅🚗📍	400 feet east to **Johns Hollow Shelter**, water (springs) are located to left and right of shelter, tenting, privy. 21.8◀16.5◀3.9◀▶8.8▶18.3▶23.9	N 37 36.780, W 79 23.526	1020	1403.6
788.8	🅰	Cross woods road.		1323	1403.2
788.9	🅰	Cross logging road.		1344	1403.1
789.1	🅰	Old road intersects.		1545	1402.9
789.5	🅰	Cross old road.		2045	1402.5
790.4	Y	Rocky Row Trail to west		2400	1401.6
790.5	📷	Fullers Rocks, Little Rocky Row, several view points.		2486	1401.5
791.0	Y📷	Unmarked trail to west 40 feet to large flat rock with view.		2800	1401.0
791.5	▲📷	Big Rocky Row summit.		2974	1400.5
791.6	📷	Cliff east of the trail offers good views.		2952	1400.4
793.0	Y	Saddle Gap, Saddle Gap Trail		2600	1399.0
794.1		Saltlog Gap (south)		2573	1397.9
794.8		Cross pipeline in small clearing.		2775	1397.2
795.4		Old Trail intersects.		2803	1396.6

NoBo	Features	Description	GPS	Elev	SoBo
795.6	📷O♀	Bluff Mountain, **Ottie Cline Powell Memorial.** On 9 November 1891 at a school located 7 miles down the mountain from here, a teacher sent the kids out to collect kindling. Ottie Cline Powell who was going to turn five later that month, wandered off to help collect kindling but did not return. A search was organized later to find little Ottie with no luck. In April 1892, a hunter crossing over Bluff Mountain found Ottie's body. It has become somewhat of a little tradition for hikers that pass by this monument to leave a small toy or something at the monument.	N 37 39.597, W 79 20.785	3391	1396.4
796.1	▲	Intersects old road.		2933	1395.9
796.5	▲	Cross old road.		2770	1395.5
796.7	▲	Punchbowl Mountain summit, wooded.		2850	1395.3
797.2	♦Y▲ ⊏(6) ⌣⊂♀	(0.2W) **Punchbowl Shelter**, water (spring) is located by a tree next to the pond drainage in front and to the left of the shelter, tenting, privy. 25.3◄12.7◄8.8◄►9.5►15.1►25.3	N 37 40.665, W 79 20.328	2500	1394.8
797.6	♦▲P(8) 📷♀	Cross Punchbowl Mountain crossing; **BRP MP 51.7**, water north of road	N 37 40.428, W 79 20.082	2170	1394.4
797.7	♦	Trail to the east leads 150 feet to a reliable pipe spring.		2147	1394.3
797.9	▲P♀	Cross **VA. 607, Robinson Gap Road**	N 37 40.566, W 79 19.920	2100	1394.1
799.8	▲	Rice Mountain summit, wooded.		2169	1392.2
800.5	♦	Spring west sided of trail.		1602	1391.5
800.9	▲	**USFS 311A**, dirt road.		1235	1391.1
801.7	▲P(5)♀	**USFS 39/Reservoir Road**, possible camping (0.2) south on road.	N 37 40.257, W 79 16.988	990	1390.3
801.8	⌐	Pedlar River Bridge		970	1390.2
804.3	♦	Cross Swapping Camp Creek.		1088	1387.7
804.7	▲P♀	Cross USFS 38, Swapping Camp Road	N 37 41.134, W 79 16.281	1000	1387.3
805.3	▲	Cross old logging road.		1409	1386.7
805.7	♦⌐⅄≋	Cross footbridge over Brown Mountain Creek. Swimming hole and waterfalls upstream.		1249	1386.3
805.8	♦≋	Swimming hole on east side of trail.		1178	1386.2
806.7	♦▲⊏(6) ⊂♀	**Brown Mountain Creek Shelter**, water (spring) is located in front of and uphill from, the shelter, tenting across the creek, privy. 22.2◄18.3◄9.5◄►5.6►15.8►22.4	N 37 42.614, W 79 16.092	1395	1385.3
806.9	♦Y	Old walled spring 15 yards east of tail.		1484	1385.1
807.6	♦	Cross branch of Brown Mountain Creek.		1684	1384.4
808.4	▲	Intersects old road.		2049	1383.6
808.5	▲⅄⌐ P(15)♀ ★★★★★	Cross **U.S. 60, Lexington Turnpike**, Long Mountain Wayside, picnic table.	N 37 43.412, W 79 15.029	2060	1383.5
	🚗P	**Three Springs Shuttles** 434-922-7069 Shuttles year-round. Range Daleville-Waynesboro VA. P Parking available for section hikers.			

Buena Vista, VA 24416 (9.3W) See map of Buena Vista, VA.

✉♀	**PO** M-F 8:30am-4:30pm, 540-261-8959. 2071 Forest Ave. Buena Vista, VA 24416. N 37 44.043, W 79 21.213
▲≋≋	**Glen Maury Park Campground** 540-261-7321. (www.glenmaurypark.com) Open Apr-Oct. Located at south end of town across river. ▲ AT hiker special $5 tent site. ≋ Free shower, even without stay, ≋ pool. South end of town across river. Yearly Maury River Fiddlers Convention and Beach Music Festival takes place in mid-June.
🛏📶🚗	**Buena Vista Motel** 540-261-2138. (http://buenavistamotel.us) 🛏 $45 and up, microwave, fridge, free local calls. 📶 Free WiFi. 🚗 Shuttle to and from trail for a fee.
🛏⌂📶	**Budget Inn** 540-261-2156. (www.budgetinnbv.net) 🛏 $59.95 and up, microwave, fridge, ⌂ laundry, pets $10 and must use smoking room.
🍴✗	**Amish Cupboard** 540-264-0215 (www.theamishcupboard.com) 🍴 M-F 10am-7pm, Deli open till 6 pm, Sa 10 am-5:30 pm, Su closed. ✗ Deli, Ice Cream, jerky, and dried foods.
🍴✗	**Lewis Grocery** 540-261-6826. 🍴 M-F 10am-9pm, Sa-Su 11am-8:30pm, ✗ short order grill.
🍴	**Food Lion** 540-261-7672, M-Su 7am- 10pm.
🚌	**Maury Express** 800-964-5707, 540-343-1721. M-F 8am-6pm, Sa 10am-4pm, Su closed. Area bus makes hourly loops though Buena Vista and connects with a Lexington loop bus. Fee (small).
🐾	**Edgewater Animal Hospital** 540-261-4114 (www.edgewateranimalhospitalpc.com) M-F 8am-6pm, Sa 8am-1 pm.
ⓘ♦♦P♀	**Regional Visitor Center** 540-261-8004 Allows multi-day parking. N 37 44.645, W 79 20.332

Lexington, VA. (15.0W of Buena Vista, VA)

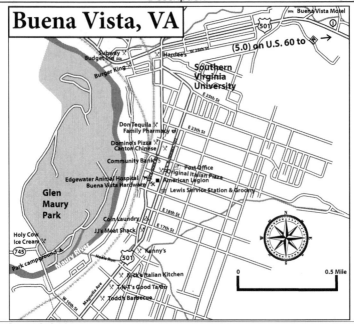

Buena Vista, VA

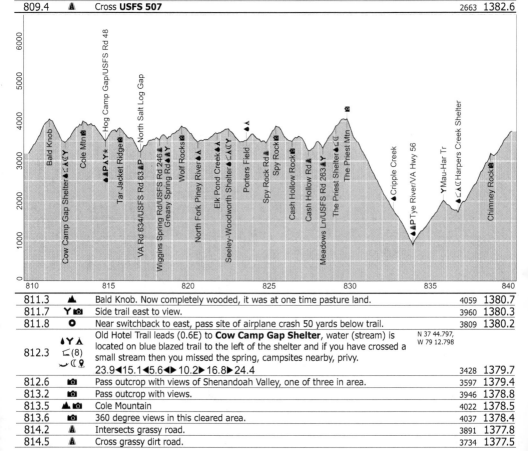

809.4	🏕	Cross **USFS 507**		2663	1382.6
811.3	🏔	Bald Knob. Now completely wooded, it was at one time pasture land.		4059	1380.7
811.7	Y 📷	Side trail east to view.		3960	1380.3
811.8	⊙	Near switchback to east, pass site of airplane crash 50 yards below trail.		3809	1380.2
812.3	⬤Y⅄ ⊏(8) ⌣⊂⊄⚲	Old Hotel Trail leads (0.6E) to **Cow Camp Gap Shelter**, water (stream) is located on blue blazed trail to the left of the shelter and if you have crossed a small stream then you missed the spring, campsites nearby, privy. 23.9◀15.1◀5.6◀▶ 10.2▶16.8▶24.4	N 37 44.797, W 79 12.798 3428	1379.7
812.6	📷	Pass outcrop with views of Shenandoah Valley, one of three in area.		3597	1379.4
813.2	📷	Pass outcrop with views.		3946	1378.8
813.5	🏔📷	Cole Mountain		4022	1378.5
813.6	📷	360 degree views in this cleared area.		4037	1378.4
814.2	🏕	Intersects grassy road.		3891	1377.8
814.5	🏕	Cross grassy dirt road.		3734	1377.5

NoBo	Features	Description	GPS	Elev	SoBo
814.8	♦▲◡▲P ♀ ★★★★★	Cross **USFS 48, Wiggins Spring Road**, Hog Camp Gap. Grassy meadow with lots of campsites. Water (spring) is located (0.3) north on road.	N 37 45.582, W 79 11.713	3485	1377.2
815.4	�foodP 🎥	**Three Springs Shuttles** See listing under Buena Vista, VA. Tar Jacket Ridge		3840	1376.6
817.0	▲P(6)♀	Cross **USFS 63, VA. 634**, Salt Log Gap (north)	N 37 46.797, W 79 10.918	3290	1375.0
818.2	▲	Cross **USFS 246**		3500	1373.8
818.7	Y▲	**Greasy Spring Road**, just north is blue blazed Lovingston Spring Trail.		3600	1373.3
818.9	♦	Unmarked spring 20 yards east.		4919	1373.1
819.7	Y🎥	Wolf Rocks 50 yards to the west.		3785	1372.3
820.6	♦▲	Cross two branches of the North Fork of Piney River.		3500	1371.4
821.8	♦▲	Cross Elk Pond Branch.		3750	1370.2
822.5	♦Y▲ ⊆(6) ◡《🚻♀	120 yards east to **Seeley–Woodworth Shelter**, water (pipe spring) is located (0.1) beyond shelter downhill to right, campsites nearby, privy. 25.3◄15.8◄10.2◄► 6.6► 14.2►20.4	N 37 49.136, W 79 09.306	3770	1369.5
823.6	♦▲	Porters Field, spring 100 feet down old road to the west. Camping both east and west of trail.		3650	1368.4
824.8	▲▲◡ P(15)♀ ★★★★★	Cross **Spy Rock Road, formerly Fish Hatchery Rd**, gravel. Parking (1.0W).	N 37 50.514, W 79 07.869	3454	1367.2

Montebello, VA. (2.0W) See map of Montebello, VA.

Location from AT; (1.0W) West downhill gravel road (Spy Rock Rd.) to parking area, (0.2E) from the parking lot (Fish Hatchery Rd.), (0.4W) at intersection of Crabtree Falls Hwy (VA 56), from here it is (0.4) miles.

✉♀ **PO** M-F 10am-2pm, Sa 10am-1pm, 540-377-9218. 15048 Cratree Falls Hwy. Montebello, VA 24464. N 37 51.153, W 79 07.877

▲🏪⌂ **Montebello Camping & General Store** 540-377-2650. (www.montebellova.com)
🏪 Store open year-round. Apr thru Oct 8am-6pm, Dec thru March 9am-5pm.
▲ Campground open Apr 1 - Oct 31. Thru-hiker rate on tent site $15 EAP, more for additional people.
⌂ Laundry.

🚗 **Earl Arnold** 540-377-6646. When available, shuttles from James River to Rockfish Gap.

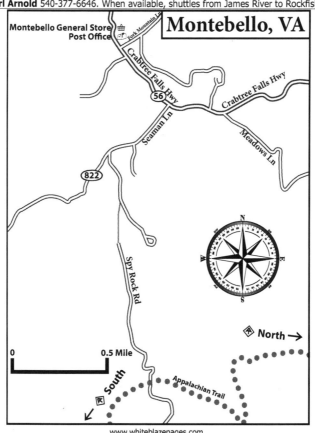

Montebello General Store 🏪
Post Office ✉

Montebello, VA

Fork Mountain Ln
Crabtree Falls Hwy
56
Crabtree Falls Hwy
Seaman Ln
Meadows Ln
822
Spy Rock Rd

N

★ North →

0   0.5 Mile

South

★

Appalachian Trail

NoBo	Features	Description	GPS	Elev	SoBo
825.3	📷	Spy Rock with 360 degree views from the top, wonderful camping area and has great views. Water needs to be carried in.		3680	1366.7
826.4	📷	Cash Hollow Rock		3550	1365.6
827.4	🏕	Cross **Cash Hollow Road**, dirt		3280	1364.6
828.2	◊🏕	Cross **VA. 826, Crabtree Farm Road**, Crabtree Falls Trail, water is located (0.5) west		3350	1363.8
829.1	◐⊑(6) ⌣℃💲	(0.1E) **The Priest Shelter**, water (spring) is located left of the shelter, privy. 22.4◀16.8◀6.6◀▶ 7.6▶13.8▶29.6	N 37 49.065, W 79 04.236	3840	1362.9
829.5	Y📷	Path west 150 feet to boulders with 180 degree view.		4088	1362.5
829.6	📷	The Priest summit, wooded. There are 36 switchbacks.		4063	1362.4
832.6	◊	Cripple Creek		1800	1359.4
833.9	P(20)💲	Cross **VA. 56, Crabtree Falls Highway**, River suspension bridge.	N 37 50.307, W 79 01.395	997	1358.1
834.0	◊🏕	Tye River		950	1358.0
835.5	🏕	Cross old logging road.		1323	1356.5
835.8	Y	Mau-Har Trail		2090	1356.2
836.7	◊🏕⊑(6) ⌣℃🍴💲	Cross the creek west to **Harpers Creek Shelter**, water (Harpers Creek) in front of shelter, tent sites, privy. 24.4◀14.2◀7.6◀▶ 6.2▶22.0▶34.7	N 37 51.385, W 79 00.072	1800	1355.3
838.3	📷	Flat-rock overlook to the east with view.		3188	1353.7
838.7	📷	Chimney Rocks, a faint unblazed trail ascends steeply for 25 yards, then passes around the left side of the summit to the Chimney Rock overlook.		3190	1353.3

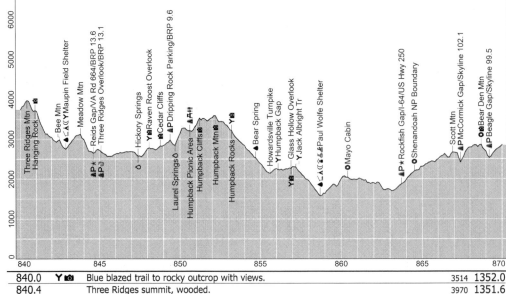

840.0	Y📷	Blue blazed trail to rocky outcrop with views.		3514	1352.0
840.4		Three Ridges summit, wooded.		3970	1351.6
840.9	📷	Hanging Rock, good views.		3750	1351.1
842.5	▲📷	Bee Mountain summit, limited views.		3077	1349.5
842.9	◊Y🏕(6) ⊑(6)℃💲 ★★★★★	The Mau-Har Trail leads 300 feet west to **Maupin Field Shelter**, water (spring) behind the shelter, tent sites, privy. Mau-Har Trail northern intersection. Jeep road leads (1.4) to BRP. 20.4◀13.8◀6.2◀▶ 15.8▶28.5▶41.5	N 37 53.093, W 78 59.634	2720	1349.1
	🚐🏕✕🏠 🚐	(1.7W) **Royal Oaks Cabins & Country Store** 540-943-7625 (www.vacabins.com) 🚐 Cabin $60D (M-Th), $85D (F-Su),up to 3 guests, 🏕 Tenting $20,up to two guests/tent. Cabin and tenting both include 🚐 WiFi and Shower. From Maupin Field Shelter, follow jeep road behind shelter (1.2) west to the Blue Ridge Parkway (first paved road). Turn left on BRP for (0.5) to Love Rd (814). Turn right for 75 feet to Royal Oaks Hikers/Bikers entrance. Call for shuttle from Reeds Gap - Free with Cabin Rental. Store open year-round M-Sa 10 am-6 pm, Su 11 am-4 pm. Have 🔥 Butane/Propane Blended Fuel Canisters, snacks, sodas, canned food and ✕ Seasonal Deli Subs & Panini's on-site.			
844.6	🏕P(20)💲 ★★★★★	Cross Reids Gap, **VA. 664; BRP MP 13.6**	N 37 54.098, W 78 59.121	2645	1347.4

⚠ ❖ ✕ (5.4E) on 664 to **Devils Backbone Basecamp Brewpub & Meadows** 434-361-1001. (www.dbbrew-ingcompany.com)

❖ AT Passport location.

⚠ Hikers can camping on site for free.

Brewpub, Open Daily 11:30am until last call. ✕ Full service restaurant and bar serving lunch & dinner.

The Summit, Open M-Sa 7am–12pm, Su 7am–2pm serving specialty coffees & breakfast. $5 breakfast offered to AT thru-hikers.

The Oak Grill, Open weekends 11:30am until last call, serving a fast casual menu, with the outdoor bar serving Devils Backbone beers, local cider, and wine.

NoBo	Features	Description	GPS	Elev	SoBo
845.1	⚐⚠P(10)	Cross **BRP MP 13.1**; Three Ridges Parking Overlook	N 37 54.425, W 78 58.784	2700	1346.9
847.4	◊	Cross stream, unreliable.		2640	1344.6
848.1	Y▣	Side trails to the west 400 feet to rocky outcrop with views.		2824	1343.9
848.9	▣	Cedar Cliffs, grassy top with views.		2800	1343.1
849.4	◊⚠P(5)♀	Cross **BRP MP 9.6**; Dripping Rock Parking Area, small spring behind overlook sign is unreliable.	N 37 56.474, W 78 56.202	2950	1342.6
849.7	◊	Laurel Springs to the east is unreliable.		2915	1342.3
850.3	Y▣	Side trail leads 25 yards to overlook with views.		3313	1341.7
850.6	Y⚏	Blue blaze trail leads (0.3) west to Humpback Rocks picnic area.		3260	1341.4
851.2	▣	Pass along top of cliff with views.		3550	1340.8
852.2	▣	Humpback Mountain		3606	1339.8
853.2	Y▣	Blue blazed trail to Humpback Rocks leads (0.2) west to view at the rocks		3250	1338.8
853.9	◊	Spring to the east is unreliable.		2871	1338.1
854.7	▲	Bear Spring is up hill west of trail.		3200	1337.3
855.6	⚠	Intersects **Howardsville Turnpike** (old road).		3317	1336.4
856.1	⚠P(15)♀	Intersects **Howardsville Turnpike** (old road).	N 37 58.083, W 78 53.950	3236	1335.9
856.9	▣	Side trail (0.2E) to Glass Hollow Overlook, view to the east		2750	1335.1
857.2	YP(10)♀	Side trail leads (0.2) west to Humpback Gap parking.	N 37 58.160, W 78 53.847	2150	1334.8
857.3	⚠Y	Old road, Jack Albright Trail, Humpback Gap parking area.		2385	1334.7
858.1	Y▣	Pass cleared overlook with views.		3296	1333.9
858.7	◖⌂(10)♀ ⏚☾☂⚏ ⚒♀	**Paul C. Wolfe Shelter,** water (Mill Creek) is located 50 yards in front of shelter, privy. Waterfall with pool 100 yards. Bear pole. Swimming hole with small waterfalls just downstream.	N 37 59.138, W 78 53.034		
		29.6◄22.0◄15.8◄► 12.7►25.7►38.9		1700	1333.3
860.4	◉	Pass remnants of Mayo cabin that dates back to the 1900's, chimney and hearth remain.		2085	1331.6
861.9	▲	Cross stream.		1992	1330.1
863.7	⚠P(15) ⊕⚏▐♀ ★★★★★	Cross **U.S. 250, I-64**, Rockfish Gap.	N 38 01.866, W 78 51.541	1902	1328.3

⊕❖ **Rockfish Gap Tourist Information Center** 540-943-5187.

⚏▐⊕⚠P ❖ AT Passport location.

Open most days 9 am-5 pm.

Info on town services. Maintains a listing of local trail angels. If the center is closed, the listing is displayed in the window. Some lodging facilities offer free pickup and return from here. Long-term parking is permitted here but not encouraged; it's a "park at your own risk" situation. It is recommended to park for free in Waynesboro at the police-monitored lot near Kroger's (fill out a waiver at the police department). Hikers that leave their car in town can then catch a ride to the AT with one of the trail angels.

🛏⚠⛺⊕ (0.5W on 250) **Colony House Motel** 540-942-4156.

🖥 $42-70, microwave and fridge. Ask about tenting. Pets $10. Laundry. Free WiFi.

Mail drops for guest: 494 Three Notched Mountain Hwy, Waynesboro, VA 22980.

Waynesboro, VA 22980 (3.7W) on route 250 (all major services) See Map of Waynesboro, VA.

🏣♀ **PO** M-F 9am-5pm, Sa pickup (only) 8am-12pm, 540-942-7320. 200 S Wayne Ave. Waynesboro, VA 22980. N 38 04.055, W 78 53.359

⚠⚒⊕ **YMCA** 540 943-YMCA(9622).

⚠ Free camping and ⚒ showers. Use of YMCA facilities for $10. ⊕ Free WiFi. Check-in at front desk, need photo ID.

It's not what you take, it's what you give

Stanimal's 328 Hostel Waynesboro 540-290-4002 AdamStanley06@gmail.com (www.stanimals328. com)
◈ AT Passport location.
⌂ $30 hiker only hostel includes pickup and return to trail, mattress with clean linens, shower with towel, soap, loaner clothes, △ laundry.
Private rooms available plus full kitchen privileges.
Private area including sunroom and finished basement, ▭ laptop, ◐ WiFi and DVDs. Fridge, freezer and microwave. Snacks, drinks, and ice cream for sale. ◑ Discounted slackpacking for multi-night guests. Large property located downtown near grocery, restaurants, and fastfood. Please respect noise level. Hikers are required to call ahead and speak with owner prior to staying.
Owned by Adam Stanley AT '04, PCT '10.
✉ Mail drops free for guest, $5 for non guests: 1333 West Main Street, Waynesboro, VA 22980.

Grace Hiker Hostel - Supervised Lutheran Church Hostel
◈ AT Passport location.
Open May 16-June 19, closed Su nights, 2-night limit. 20 hiker maximum. Please do not call the church office. ⊗ No pets, smoking, drugs, alcohol, firearms or foul language. Donations gratefully accepted. Check-in 5 pm-8pm, check-out 9 am; hikers staying over may leave packs. Cots in air-conditioned Fellowship Hall, showers, ▭ internet, big-screen TV and DVD, hiker lounge with kitchenette, snacks and breakfast foods. △ Laundry. ◐ Free WiFi. Congregation cooks free dinner Thursday nights followed by optional vespers service.

Tree Streets Inn 540-949-4484. (www.treestreetsinn.com)
No pets. $80 and ip, includes breakfast, microwave, fridge, free WiFi, pool, snacks. Free pickup and return from Rockfish Gap with stay.
Mail drops for pre-registered guests only: 421 Walnut Avenue, Waynesboro, VA 22980.

Belle Hearth B&B
540-943-1910. (www.bellehearth.com)
⊗ No pets, no smoking, no alcohol.
▭ $85S +tax, $99D +tax, higher on weekends, includes breakfast, pool, pickup and return. 10 day cancellation policy. ◐ WiFi.
✉ Mail drops guest only: 320 S. Wayne Ave, Waynesboro, VA 22980

Quality Inn 540-942-1171.
▭ Hiker rates $62S $67 up to 4 plus tax, pets $10. Includes continental breakfast, microwave, fridge, ☷ outdoor pool. ▭ Computer available for use, ◐ free WiFi.

Heritage on Main 540-946-6166. (www.heritageonmainstreet.com)
M-Th 11am-12am, F-Sa11 am 1am, Su 11am-12am. Hiker friendly sports bar, beer, burgers, salads.

Weasie's Kitchen
540-943-0500. M-F 5:30 am-8 pm, Sa 6 am- 2 pm, Su 7 am-2 pm.

Ming Garden 540-942-8800. (www.minggardenwbo.com)
◈ AT Passport location.
✗ M-F 10 am- 10pm, Sa-Su 10 am- 11 pm. **All you can eat meals**.

Ace Hardware 540-949-8229. M-F 7:30am-6pm, Sa 8am-5pm, Su closed. Coleman by the ounce.

Rockfish Gap Outfitters 540-943-1461.
◈ AT Passport location.
⚐ Full service outfitter, Coleman and alcohol by the ounce, other fuels, shuttle info. Freeze dried foods. Located between town and trail.

Stanimal's Shuttle Service 540-290-4002 covers all of Virginia.

DuBose Egleston "Yellow Truck" 540-487-6388 shuttles Roanoke to Harpers Ferry.

Scott McLellan based out of Harrisonburg, VA. 757-817-3901
Covers all of Shenandoah National Park. Based 25 minutes from Swift Run Gap. 15 Minutes from Madison Run Road and Furnace Mountain Trailhead. Quickest access for thru hikers is Furnace Mountain Rd. It's an easy hike down from Blackrock Hut. Shuttles also include Grottoes, Harrisonburg, Luray, Staunton, Waynesboro, Front Royal, Tyro, and Dayton.

NoBo Features | Description | GPS Elev SoBo

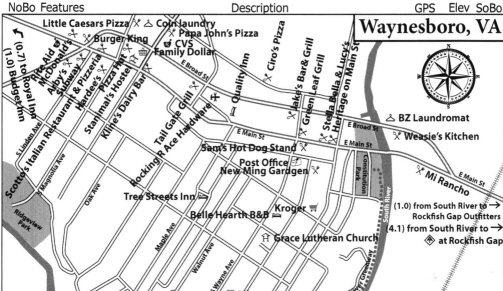

Waynesboro, VA

Little Caesars Pizza   Coin laundry
Burger King   Papa John's Pizza
McDonald's   CVS
Rite Aid   Family Dollar
Subway   Quality Inn
Arby's   Pizza Hut
Hardee's   Pizza & Pizzeria
Stanimal's Hostel
Scott's Italian Restaurant & Pizzeria
Kline's Dairy Bar
Tail Gate Grill
Rocking R Ace Hardware
Ridgeview Park
S. Linden Ave
S. Magnolia Ave
Oak Ave
Maple Ave
Walnut Ave
S Wayne Ave

E Broad St
E Main St
Ciro's Pizza
Jake's Bar & Grill
Green Leaf Grill
Stella Bella & Lucy's Heritage on Main St
Constitution Park
South River
South River Greenway

Sam's Hot Dog Stand
Post Office
New Ming Garden
Tree Streets Inn
Belle Hearth B&B   Kroger
Grace Lutheran Church
Library
Royal   YMCA

BZ Laundromat
Weasie's Kitchen
E Broad St
E Main St
Mi Rancho
E Main St

(1.0) from South River to →
Rockfish Gap Outfitters
(4.1) from South River to →
at Rockfish Gap

Hiker tenting and hammocking

0   0.2 Mile

				GPS	Elev	SoBo
863.8	⚑P☕	Cross **I-64 overpass**, Rockfish Gap		N 38 01.866, W 78 51.541	1902	1328.2
864.0	⚑P☕	**Skyline Drive MP 105.2**		N 38 01.912, W 78 51.502	1902	1328.0
864.5	★★★★★	SNP kiosk for self-registration; park entrance station			2200	1327.5

PERMITS
Shenandoah National Park (Virginia)
-**Backcountry Permit:** While there is no charge for permits, they are required of all backcountry travelers. The permit can be obtained at visitor contact stations during business hours. Permits for A.T. long-distance hikers are available by self-registration on the Trail at the park's north and south entry points. If you are planning your visit well in advance (allow two full weeks), permits are also available by mail from Park Headquarters. For more information, https://www.nps.gov/shen/planyourvisit/campbc.htm. Shenandoah National Park 540-999-3500 (www.nps.gov/shen) Emergency line: 1-800-732-0911.

-**Shelter and Hut Regulations:** Two types of structures are near the A.T.: day-use ("shelters") and over-night-use ("huts"). Camping at or near day-use shelters is prohibited. Huts are available to long-distance hikers (those spending at least three consecutive nights in SNP) as space is available. Tenting at huts is permitted in designated campsites; all huts within the park have campsites available.

-**Camping Regulations:** Only thru-hikers (defined as those "walking the Appalachian Trail from point of beginning to an exit, which is not the place of beginning) may camp on Pennsylvania Game Commission lands, and these hikers must camp within 200 ft of A.T., at least 500 ft from a stream or spring.

Groups are limited to 10 people. Campfires are only permitted at preconstructed fire rings at the huts. Pets must be leashed.
Concrete 4"x4" signposts are used to mark intersections thoughout the SNP. Information is stamped into an aluminum band around the top of the post.

Campgrounds information: 877-444-6777. (www.recreation.gov). Campsites allow for 2 tents and up to 6 people. All have All have coin operated laundry and showers except Mathews Arm. Most close November-May.

🚗   **Yellow Cab of the Shenandoah** 540-692-9200 serves all of SNP (24/7). Pet friendly, accepts Credit cards.

				GPS	Elev	SoBo
867.4	⚑P(20)☕	Cross **Skyline Drive MP 102.1**; McCormick Gap.		N 38 03.581, W 78 49.056	3450	1324.6
868.7	📷⚙☕	Bear Den Mountain. Larger TV tower. **Old tractor seats**, the tractor seats were put here because the family that owned this property used to have picnics and cookouts and bonfires, particularly to watch the fireworks on July fourth. Vista		N 38 04.016, W 78 47.923	2885	1323.3

NoBo Features	Description	GPS	Elev	SoBo
869.2 ▲P(12)🚰	Cross **Skyline Drive MP 99.5**; Beagle Gap	N 38 04.387, W 78 47.601	2550	1322.8

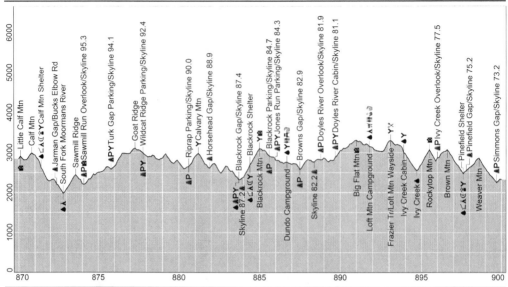

870.1	▲📷	Little Calf Mtn, open with great views. Calf Mtn is at 870.1 but it's just a pile of rocks in the woods.			1321.9
871.4	♦Y▲ ⊑(6) ☾☏🚰	(0.3W) **Calf Mountain Shelter**, water (piped spring) on the access trail, tenting, privy, bear pole. 34.7◄28.5◄12.7◄► 13.0►26.2►34.4	N 38 05.131, W 78 47.208	2700	1320.6
872.0	♦	Water (spring)		2200	1320.0
872.4	▲P(8)🚰	Jarman Gap; Skyline Drive MP 96.9 (0.1) east; SNP southern boundary. Sign on road said it was called Bucks Elbow Rd.	N 38 05.882, W 78 46.880	2173	1319.6
872.6	♦▲	Spring, trail crosses dirt South Fork Moormans River Road near spring.		2150	1319.4
872.8	▲	Trail follows Soth Fork Moormans River for a short disatnace, there are a couple of campsites near the stream.			1319.2
874.2	▲P(20)🚰	Cross **Skyline Drive MP 95.3**; Sawmill Run Overlook	N 38 06.803, W 78 47.009	2200	1317.8
875.5	Y	Junction with Turk Mountain Trail, west (1.0) to summit of Turk Mountain.			1316.5
875.8	▲P(11)🚰	Cross **Skyline Drive MP 94.1**; Turk Gap	N 38 07.751, W 78 47.089	2600	1316.2
877.8	▲P(4)🚰	Cross **Skyline Drive MP 92.4**	N 38 08.947, W 78 46.464	3100	1314.2
878.2	Y	Junction with Wildcat Ridge Trail, west (2.7) to Riprap Trail.			1313.8
880.7	P	Parking area for Riprap Trail at Skyline Drive MM 90.0.			1311.3
881.1	Y	Junction with Riprap Trail, west (4.6) to Wildcat Ridge Trail.			1310.9
881.9	▲	Cross **Skyline Drive MP 88.9**		2350	1310.1
883.7	▲P🚰	Blackrock Gap; Skyline Drive MP 87.4	N 38 12.410, W 78 44.969	2321	1308.3
883.9	▲	Cross **Skyline Drive MP 87.2**		2700	1308.1
884.4	♦Y▲ ⊑(6) ⌣☾🚰	(0.2E) **Blackrock Hut**, water (piped spring) is located 10 yards in front of the shelter, tenting, privy. 41.5◄25.7◄13.0◄► 13.2►21.4►33.8	N 38 12.845, W 78 44.562	2645	1307.6
885.0	📷	Blackrock, open rocky summit		3100	1307.0
886.0	▲P(11)🚰	Cross **Skyline Drive MP 84.3**, parking east	N 38 13.355, W 78 43.991	2800	1306.0
886.2	P(10)🚰	Intersection with Jones Run Trail leads east 100 feet to parking area.	N 38 13.811, W 78 43.587	2949	1305.8
886.7		(0.1W) Dundo Group campground, primitive, reserved for group use		2700	1305.3
887.5	▲P(10)🚰	Cross **Skyline Drive MP 82.9**; Browns Gap	N 38 14.430, W 78 42.637	2600	1304.5
888.4	▲	Cross **Skyline Drive MP 82.2**		2800	1303.6
888.8	▲🚰	Doyles River overlook. Skyline Drive MP 81.9, parking west	N 38 14.819, W 78 41.694	2800	1303.2
889.7	▲P(15)🚰	Parking Area; Trail leads (0.3) west to Doyles River Cabin (locked); **Skyline Drive MP 81.1** to the west and parking.	N 38 15.264, W 78 40.981	2900	1302.3
890.3	Y	First side trail to Loft Mountian campgrouond going NoBo, west (0.3) to camp store and showers.			1301.7
891.0		Trail reaches high point on Big Flat Mountain.			1301.0

NoBo		Description	GPS	Elev	SoBo
891.8	Y ★★★★	First side trail SoBo (0.2W) to Loft Mountain campground.		3300	1300.2
	🛠🏕️♨️⛺ ⛽	**Loft Mountain Campground Campsites** ⛺ $20. AT skirts the campground, several short side trails lead to campsites and the camp store. Open mid May-Oct. Camp store, M-Th 8am-7pm, F-Sa 8am-8pm, Su 8am-7pm. ♨️ Restroom, ♨️ Showers, ⛺ laundry and 🛠 long term resupply available from camp store.			
	✗	**Loft Mountain Wayside** 434-823-4515. (1.1) miles from camp store, serves Breakfast, lunch and dinner from a short order menu. Open mid Apr-early Nov, daily 9am-7pm.			
892.5	Y ⛺	Frazier Discovery Trail leads to (0.3) west to Loft Mountain Wayside		2950	1299.5
893.1		Loft Mountain		3200	1298.9
893.9	♦	Water, (spring) is located (0.1) west		2950	1298.1
896.0	⛽P(15)♨️	Ivy Creek Overlook; **Skyline Drive MP 77.5**, parking area.	N 38 17.047, W 78 39.542	2800	1296.0
897.6	♦Y⛺ ⛺(6) ⚓☾☂♨️	(0.1E) **Pinefield Hut**, water (spring) is located behind the shelter 50 yards and it is known to fail during dry seasons, tenting located past the privy, privy. Bear box. 38.9◀26.2◀13.2◀▶ 8.2▶20.6▶32.1	N 38 17.433, W 78 38.760	2430	1294.4
897.8	⛽P(5)♨️	Cross **Skyline Drive MP 75.2**; Pinefield Gap, parking 50 yards west.	N 38 17.468, W 78 38.515	2590	1294.2
899.7	⛽P(7)♨️	Cross **Skyline Drive MP 73.2**; Simmons Gap, Simmons Gap ranger station on paved road (0.2E) from where AT crosses Skyline. Water available at pump outside buildings.	N 38 18.105, W 78 37.361	2250	1292.3

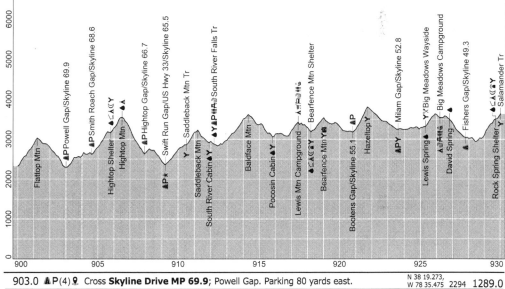

NoBo		Description	GPS	Elev	SoBo
903.0	⛽P(4)♨️	Cross **Skyline Drive MP 69.9**; Powell Gap. Parking 80 yards east.	N 38 19.273, W 78 35.475	2294	1289.0
903.4	📷	Little Roundtop Mountain		2700	1288.6
904.6	⛽P(8)♨️	Cross **Skyline Drive MP 68.6**; Smith Roach Gap	N 38 19.716, W 78 34.500	2600	1287.4
905.8	♦Y⛺(8) ⛺(6) ⚓☾♨️	(0.1W) **Hightop Hut**, water (piped spring) is located (0.1) from the shelter on a side trail, tenting, privy. 34.4◀21.4◀8.2◀▶ 12.4▶23.9▶34.8	N 38 19.982, W 78 33.516	3175	1286.2
906.3	♦	Water (box spring)		3450	1285.7
906.4	⛺(7)	Hightop Mountain, south on A.T. there are three tent sites, side trail to top of High Top has room for four more tents.		3587	1285.6
907.9	⛽P(6)	Cross **Skyline Drive MP 66.7**, parking west	N 38 20.688, W 78 33.191	2650	1284.1
909.2	♦Y⛺ ★★★★★	Cross **Skyline Drive MP 65.5 over U.S. 33** on overpass; Swift Run Gap; Spotswood Trail.		2367	1282.8
	�- ⛺🏪🚗 🖃	(2.9W) **Country View Motel** 540-298-0025 (www.countryviewlodging.com) 🚪 Room with 1 queen bed $75.11 including tax for single bed, two queen beds $91.20 including tax for double beds. All rooms have microwave and fridge. ⛺ No charge for laundry with stay, but you must have detergent which they sell. ⛽ Free WiFi. 🚗 Shuttle service from Swift Run Gap may be available for small fee 🖃 Mail drops for guests only: 19974 Spotswood Trail, Elkton, VA 22827.			

NoBo		Features	Description	GPS	Elev	SoBo
		(3.2W) **Swift Run Campround** 540-298-8086, 540-713-8292. (www.shenandoahvalleyweb.com/swiftrun)			
		Open year-round. $20 campsite, shower, and snack bar, game room, seasonal pool.			
		Bear Grocery & Deli 540-298-9826. M-F 5am-8pm, Sa 6am–8pm, Su 8am-7pm.			
Elkton, VA 22827 (6.5W)						
		PO M-F 8:30am-4:30pm, Sa 9am-11am, 540-298-7772. 102 W Rockingham St. Elkton, VA 22827. N 38 24.515, W 78 37.149			
		Food Lion M-Su 7am-11pm.			
		Pizza Hut 540-298-9439. M-F 11am-10pm, F-Sa 11am-11pm, Su 11am-10pm.			
		Rite Aid M-Sa 8am-8pm, Sun 10am-8pm. **Pharmacy**; M-F 8am-8pm, Sa 9am-6pm, Sun 10am-6pm.			
912.2		(0.1) west to South River Parking Area, Picnic Grounds. Falls Trail to east, parking west	N 38 22.902, W 78 31.152	3200	1279.8
915.5		Pocosin Cabin (locked), parking (0.15) west on Skyline Drive	N 38 24.816, W 78 29.382	3150	1276.5
915.8		Water (spring)		3100	1276.2
917.5		(0.1W) **Lewis Mountain Campground and Cabins, Skyline Drive MP 57.6**, parking west	N 38 26.232, W 78 28.740	3500	1274.5
		Lewis Mountain Campground & Cabins 540-999-2255. Reservations 877-247-9261. Open mid May-Oct. Campsites $20, small bunkhouse, cabin rates seasonal. Camp store open same dates, M-Th 9am-6pm, F-Sa 9am-7pm, Su 9am-6pm.			
918.2		(0.1E) **Bearfence Mountain Hut**, water (piped spring) is located in front of the shelter, tent sites, privy.	N 38 26.645, W 78 28.242		
		33.8◄20.6◄12.4◄►11.5►22.4►26.8		3110	1273.8
919.8		Campsite		3400	1272.2
920.8		Cross Conway River Fire Road; **Skyline Drive MP 55.1**, parking is 50 feet west; Bootens Gap		3243	1271.2
921.7		Hazeltop		3812	1270.3
923.6		Cross **Skyline Drive MP 52.8**; Milam Gap	N 38 29.994, W 78 26.744	3300	1268.4
924.5		Water (spring)		3380	1267.5
925.3		Lewis Spring; Big Meadows Wayside; Harry F. Byrd Sr. Visitor Center is located (0.2) east.	N 38 31.016, W 78 26.520	3390	1266.7
926.2		(0.1E) Big Meadows Lodge, Big Meadows campground		3500	1265.8
		Big Meadows Wayside			
		AT Passport location			
		Open late-March through Nov. M-Su 8am-8pm, daily. Resupply foods, breakfast, lunch, dinner from a short order menu, fuel by the ounce at gas station. Open Mar 24-Nov 13.			
		Big Meadows Lodge 877-847-1919. Open 11 May- 06 Nov. Lodge rooms, cabins and suites, reservations required. Some pet-friendly rooms. Breakfast 7:30am-10am, lunch 12pm-2pm, dinner 5:30pm-9p.m. ATM.			
926.8		David Spring		3490	1265.2
927.8		Fishers Gap; Skyline Drive MP 49.3		3050	1264.2
929.7		(0.2W) **Rock Spring Hut and (locked) Cabin**, water is located down a steep trail in front of the hut and flows from beneath a rock, tent sites, privy.	N 38 33.211, W 78 24.492		
		32.1◄23.9◄11.5◄►10.9►15.3►28.4		3465	1262.3

NoBo	Features	Description	GPS	Elev	SoBo
930.0	Y⚐🏕	Trail to Hawksbill Mountain (0.9E), Byrd's Nest #2 Picnic Shelter		3600	1262.0
931.0	▲P(15)🛗	Hawksbill Gap; Skyline Drive MP 45.6	N 38 33.701, W 78 22.983	3361	1261.0
931.4	Y	Trail to Crescent Rock Overlook; Skyline Drive MP 44.4		3450	1260.6
933.5	▲P(5)🛗	Cross **Skyland Service Road (south)**; horse stables	N 38 35.202, W 78 23.004	3550	1258.5
934.3	▲P(20)🛗 ★★★★★	Cross **Skyland Service Road (north)**, best access to Skyland leads (0.2) west	N 38 35.569, W 78 22.560	3790	1257.7
	🛏🍴📶🛗	**Skyland Resort and Restaurant** 540-999-2212. Open Mar 30-Dec. 🛏 Rates seasonal, reservations required. Snack foods and sodas sold at gift shop and vending machines. 🍴 Dining hours: Breakfast 7:30am-10:30am, Lunch 12pm-2:30pm, Dinner 5:30 pm-9:00pm. 📶 ATM, 🍴 restroom.			
934.7	Y⚐	Trail to Stony Man Mountain summit.		3837	1257.3
936.3	♦Y📷▲P 🛗	Hughes River Gap; Trail to Stony Man Mountain Overlook (0.2W), Skyline Drive MP 38.6. parking east.	N 38 36.617, W 78 21.829	3097	1255.7
938.5	♦🏕🍴🏞 ▲P(15)🛗	Pinnacles Picnic Ground; Skyline Drive MP 36.7	N 38 37.505, W 78 20.466	3390	1253.5
938.6	Y	Trail to Jewell Hollow Overlook; **Skyline Drive MP 36.4**		3350	1253.4
939.6	📷	The Pinnacle		3730	1252.4
940.6	♦Y⚐ ⊏(8)☾🛗	**Byrds Nest #3 Hut**, water (spring) is located (0.3) east and down the fire road, tenting, privy. 34.8◄22.4◄10.9◄|►4.4►17.5►28.0	N 38 38.066, W 78 19.423	3290	1251.4
941.3	♦	Water (Meadow Spring) is located (0.3) west		3100	1250.7
941.9	📷	Mary's Rock, vista		3514	1250.1
943.8	▲P(30)🛗 ★★★★★	Cross **U.S. 211**; Thornton Gap, Panorama Skyline Drive MP 31.5. Two parking options.	N 38 39.594, W 78 19.198 N 38 39.637, W 78 19.317	2307	1248.2
	🛏🍴📶	(4.5W on US 211) **Brookside Cabins & Restaurant** 540-743-5698 (www.brooksidecabins.com) 🛏 $85-$200 cabins open year-round, range in size (2-6 persons). 🍴 Restaurant AYCE M- Th closed, F 10 am-8 pm, Sa 9 am- 8pm, Su 9 am-5 pm. Closed Dec-Mar. 📶 Free WiFi.			
	🛏⛺🍴🛗 ⛺🚿🛗	(5.3W) **Yogi Bear's Jellystone Park** 540-743-4002. (www.campluray.com) Open late Mar to late Nov. Has some pet friendly sites. 🛏 Cabins $66-$552. ⛺ Tent sites $37-75, 2-night min. All stays include free water slide, paddle boat, mini golf. Snack Shop: Open Memorial to Labor Day, 🍴 serves hamburgers, hot dogs, pizza. 🏪 Camp store, ⛺ coin laundry, 🏊 pool. 🚿 Showers for guests only.			
	🛏⛺💻📶	(6.9W) **Days Inn** 540-743-4521. (www.daysinn-luray.com) 🛏 Rates: $79.00 - $140.00, $10 extra person, $10.00 for extra bed, pets under 50lbs $15.00. Includes continental breakfast. Microwave, fridge, ⛺ laundry, seasonal 🏊 outdoor pool, 💻 computer available for use, 📶 free WiFi.			

Luray, VA 22835 (9.0W) (all major services) See map of Luray, VA.

🏤🛗	**PO** M-F 8:30am-4:30pm, 540-743-2100. 102 S Broad St. Luray, VA 22835. N 38 39.884, W 78 27.621		

Open Arms Hostel & Inn 540-244-5652, www.OpenArmsLuray.com, OpenArmsLuray@gmail.com. Thru-hikers call or text for availability and pick up schedule. Section hikers please email dates of stays and shuttle requests.
◈ AT Passport location.
Open year round. Complimentary pick-up & drop-off at trail head and for resupply (Rt. 211/Thornton Gap) for guests. 🏠 Beds $30 cash/ $31 card PP, 🛆 camping $15PP cash/ $15.50 card with shower and kitchen privileges. Breakfast, soda and snacks for sale on-site. ⌂ Laundry $5 per load, shared loads permitted. 🖥 Computer for guests. 📶 Free WiFi.
✉ Free mail drop for guests ($2/ package for non-guests): 1260 E. Main St., Luray, VA 22835. On-site parking. Shuttles for a fee from DC airports, Harper's Ferry, SNP, and south to Waynesboro.

Budget Inn 540-743-5176. (www.hotelluray.com)
$69.95-$129.95, $10EAP, pets $10. 10% off if you mention that you saw the 10% discount on there web site. Microwave, fridge. Fre WiFi.
Mail drops (non-guests $10): 320 W. Main St, Luray, VA 22835.

Cardinal Inn 540-743-5010. (www.cardinalinn.com)
🛏 Hiker rate: winter $55, summer $75. Microwave, fridge. Free local calls. 📶 Free WiFi.

Best Western 540-743-6511
No smoking. 🛏 $80 and up, pet fee $20. Microwave, fridge. ♒ Outdoor pool. 🖥 Computer available for use, 📶 free WiFi.
✗ Restaurant onsite.

Appalachian Outfitters 540-743-7400 (www.appalachianoutfittersluray.com/)
🥾 M-Sat 10 am-6 pm, Su 1 pm-5 pm.
Full-service outfitter. ⛽ Coleman and alcohol fuel by the ounce, canisters, Dr. Bonner's by the ounce, freeze dried foods. 📶 Free WiFi. ① Have a brochure with information, places to stay, eat, trail angels, and shuttles.
✉ Mail drops: 2 West Main St, Luray, VA 22835.

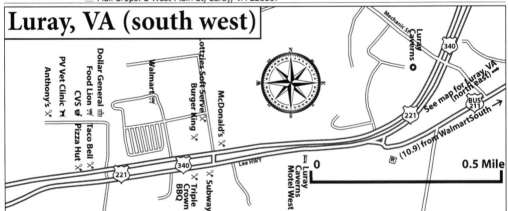

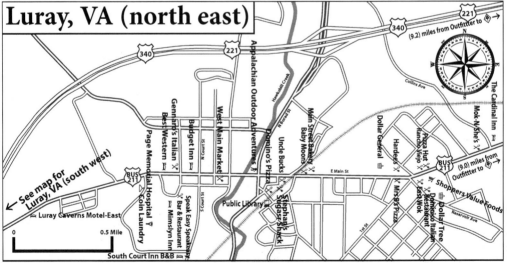

NoBo	Features	Description	GPS	Elev	SoBo
945.0	♦Y𝘈 ⊏(8) ℂ🐻♀	(0.2E) **Pass Mountain Hut**, water (piped spring) is located 15 yards behind shelter, privy, tenting, bear box and pole. 26.8◄15.3◄4.4◄► 13.1►23.6►31.7	N 38 40.600, W 78 19.137 2690		1247.0
945.8	▲	Pass Mountain, wooded summit.	3052		1246.2
946.9	𝘈	Cross **Skyline Drive MP 28.6**	2490		1245.1
947.2	📷𝘈 P(25)♀	Side trail leads (0.1) east to Skyline Drive MP 28.5; Beahms Gap.	N 38 41.949, W 78 19.235	2490	1244.8
947.3	𝘈(2)	Tenting, west side of trail. Space for 2 tents, maybe 3. 350 feet south of spring on AT.	N 38 41.795, W 78 19.299	2495	1244.7
947.4	♦♀	Formal piped Spring on the west side of trail, 150 feet off trail.	N 38 41.828, W 78 19.340	2457	1244.6
948.2	♦🛏♀	Neighbor Mtn, Trail to **Byrds Nest #4 Picnic Shelter** (0.6) east, water is located (0.5) east.	N 38 42.199, W 78 19.924	2600	1243.8
950.8	𝘈(2)♀	Tenting, east side of trail. Space for 2 tents.	N 38 43.906, W 78 19.288	2484	1241.2
951.1	𝘈(2)♀	Tenting, west side of trail. Space for 2 tents, maybe 3. 350 feet south of spring on AT.	N 38 44.170, W 78 19.211	2773	1240.9
951.9	♦♀	Small stream crossing, possibly from spring.	N 38 44.541, W 78 19.057	2600	1240.1
952.2	♦♀	Formal piped SNP spring on the east side of trail, 50 feet off trail.	N 38 44.571, W 78 18.832	2341	1239.8
952.4	🪑P♀	Elkwallow Gap picnic area.	N 38 44.288, W 78 18.566	2396	1239.6
952.7	🗙♦🛏▲ P(30)♀	Cross **Skyline Drive MP 23.9**; Elkwallow Gap, (0.1E) to Elkwallow Wayside and parking on Skyline Drive.	N 38 44.288, W 78 18.566	2480	1239.3
953.2	♦	(0.1E) Range View Cabin (locked)		2950	1238.8
953.9	📷𝘈P(8) ♀	Rattlesnake Point Overlook Skyline Drive MP 21.9, parking (0.1) east.	N 38 45.095, W 78 17.331	3100	1238.1
954.5	Y𝘈	Tuscarora Trail (southern terminus) to (0.7W) Matthews Arm campground. The Tuscarora Trail recoonects back to the AT in PA at Blue Mountain.		3400	1237.5
954.9	𝘈P(15)♀	Cross **Skyline Drive MP 21.1**, parking west.	N 38 45.681, W 78 16.913	3350	1237.1
955.1		Hogback Third Peak		3400	1236.9
955.2	📷𝘈 P(15)♀	Skyline Drive MP 20.8	N 38 45.772, W 78 16.789	3350	1236.8
955.4		Hogback Second Peak		3475	1236.6
955.6	♦𝘈(4)♀	Water (spring) is located (0.2) east at N38° 45.543' W78° 16.365'. 100 yards down the trail to the spring are a few tent sites on the left. There is room for 4 tents, coordinates N38° 45.664' W78° 16.328'		3250	1236.4
955.7		Hogback First Peak		3390	1236.3
956.4	Y𝘈 P(10)♀	Little Hogback Overlook; Skyline Drive MP 19.7, side trail leads 50 feet east to parking.	N 38 45.531, W 78 15.764	3000	1235.6
956.5	📷	Little Hogback Mountain, views 30 feet west.		3050	1235.5
957.0	𝘈	Cross **Skyline Drive MP 18.9**		2850	1235.0
958.1	♦Y𝘈 ⊏(8) ℂ🐻♀	Bluff Trail leads (0.2E) to **Gravel Springs Hut**, water (boxed spring) is located on side trail near the shelter, tent sites on a blue blazed trail, privy. A bear pole at the shelter and another up towards the tent sit, also a box. 28.4◄17.5◄13.1◄► 10.5►18.6►24.1	N 38 45.834, W 78 14.018 2480		1233.9
958.3	𝘈P(8)♀	Cross **Skyline Drive MP 17.7**; Gravel Springs Gap, parking.	N 38 46.074, W 78 14.014	2666	1233.7
959.4		South Marshall Mountain		3212	1232.6
959.9	𝘈P(12)♀	Cross **Skyline Drive MP 15.9**, parking west.	N 38 46.514, W 78 12.652	3050	1232.1

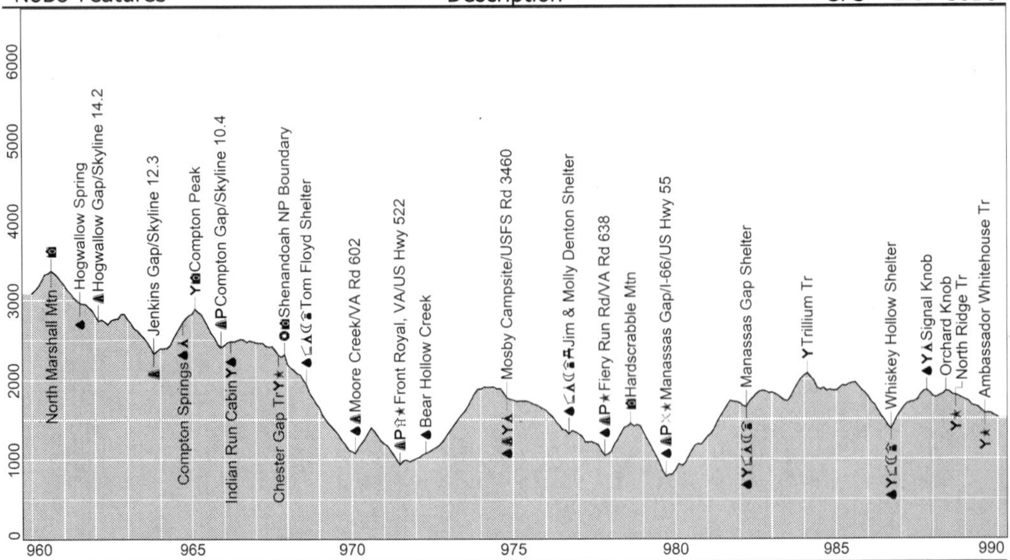

Elevation profile labels (left to right):
North Marshall Mtn · Hogwallow Spring · Hogwallow Gap/Skyline 14.2 · Jenkins Gap/Skyline 12.3 · Compton Springs · Compton Peak · Indian Run Cabin · Compton Gap/Skyline 10.4 · Chester Gap Tr · Shenandoah NP Boundary · Tom Floyd Shelter · Moore Creek/VA Rd 602 · Front Royal, VA/US Hwy 522 · Bear Hollow Creek · Mosby Campsite/USFS Rd 3460 · Jim & Molly Denton Shelter · Fiery Run Rd/VA Rd 638 · Hardscrabble Mtn · Manassas Gap/I-66/US Hwy 55 · Manassas Gap Shelter · Trillium Tr · Whiskey Hollow Shelter · Signal Knob · Orchard Knob · North Ridge Tr · Ambassador Whitehouse Tr

NoBo	Features	Description	GPS	Elev	SoBo
960.6		North Marshall Mountain		3368	1231.4
961.5	▲⚲	Hogwallow Spring	N38° 47.042' W78° 11.629	2950	1230.5
962.1	▲P⚲	Cross **Skyline Drive MP 14.2**; Hogwallow Gap, parking west.	N 38 47.388, W 78 11.322	2739	1229.9
963.8	▲P(14)⚲	Side trail leads east parking at Skyline Drive MP 12.3; Jenkins Gap.	N 38 48.395, W 78 10.842	2400	1228.2
964.7	▲⚲	Compton Springs	N38° 48.966' W78° 10.632	2700	1227.3
965.1	📷	Compton Peak, blue blaze trail (0.2) east to Columnar Jointing Geologic Feature and (0.2) west to views.		2909	1226.9
965.9	▲P(14)⚲	Cross **Skyline Drive MP 10.4**; Compton Gap	N 38 49.418, W 78 10.231	2550	1226.1
966.2	▲	Water (Indian Run Spring) is located (0.2) west		2350	1225.8
967.7	Y ★★★★★	Compton Gap Horse Trail, Trail to Chester Gap. **See Map of Terrapin Station Hostel.**		2350	1224.3

🛏 ◈ ⑧⚷ (0.5E) **Terrapin Station Hostel** 540-539-0509. Owned by Mike Evans
📶🍴�car✉ ◈ AT Passport location.
Open Apr 30-July 1, 2018.
⑧ No dogs. At concrete post in SNP the AT turns left. North bounders go straight and follow Compton Gap Trail (0.5) to paved road. On paved road the Hostel is first home on left. Enter in back through marked gate. Hikers only, picture ID required, 🛏 bunk only $25, shower with soap and shampoo $3, ⚷ laundry $3. One night hiker special $30 includes bunk, shower, laundry, pizza and soda. Two night hiker special $50 also includes slackpack and 2nd night but not 2nd dinner. 📶 Free WiFi, charging stations, TV, library, music, room to chill. All visits include free town shuttle. �car Other shuttles for a fee. Reservations recommended.
✉ Mail drops for guests only: 304 Chester Gap Rd, Chester Gap, VA 22623.
�car **Mobile Mike's** 540-539-0509 shuttles and more (Mike Evans)

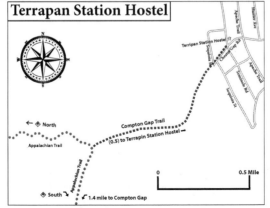

Terrapan Station Hostel

NoBo	Features	Description	GPS	Elev	SoBo
967.9	📷⭕	Possums Rest Overlook with 180 degree views, SNP kiosk for self-registration, SNP northern boundary		2300	1224.1
968.6	⬧🏕⛺(6) 🎒☾⚲	Path west to **Tom Floyd Wayside**, water is located (0.2) on a blue blazed trail to the right of the shelter and is not reliable, tent sties, privy, bear pole. 28.0◀23.6◀10.5◀▶8.1▶13.6▶18.1	N 38 51.023, W 78 09.834	1900	1223.4
968.7	⬧🏕	Blue blaze trail leads west (0.2) to Ginger Spring and tent site. Built for shelter overflow.		1956	1223.3
968.9	Y	Blue blaze trail leads west (0.3) VA. 601.		1762	1223.1
969.3	☂	Power line.		1480	1222.7
969.4	Y🚶 P(10) ★★★★★	Side trail leads (0.3) west to Northern Virginia 4-H Swimming Pool.		1350	1222.6
	✕🚶⛵🛁 P	**Northern VA 4H Center (0.4W)** 540-635-7171 (www.nova4h.com/appalachian-trail) Swimming pool open Memorial Day thru Labor Day, shower $1, concession stand. Free parking up to 30 days, register on-line or check in at office. Donations graciously accepted.			
970.0	◊	Cross stream, not reliable. **Do not use water from stream because of houses upstream.**		1280	1222.0
970.1	🅰	Cross **VA. 602**		1150	1221.9
971.5	🅰P(10)⚲ ★★★★★	Cross **U.S. 522. See note below under Vistors Center about trolley that runs from here to Front Royal.**	N 38 52.679, W 78 09.033	950	1220.5
	🚗	🚗 Trolley runs from trail head to the town of Front Royal Mid-May thru July, call for details. Fifty cents to ride the trolley. 540-635-5788.			
	🏠🛏◈ 🛁⛺⚲ P🚗📧	(0.4E) **Mountain Home "Cabbin"** 540-692-6198. MountainHomeAT@gmail.com. Lisa & Scott Jenkins ◈ AT Passport location. Open year round, call/email ahead recommended, drop-ins are OK. Located; 120 steps east of AT, where it bends north from Route 522. Look for long stone wall on left and red brick "Cabbin" on the hill. 🏠 Sleeps 6-8. $30PP includes bed, fresh linens, shower, breakfast, 📶 WiFi, some cell, hiker clothes, hiker box, boot dryers, town shuttle for meals and resupply. 🛁 $5 laundry onsite. 🐕 Max 1 dog per night for $5; outdoor kennel available for short day use. Pizza, ice cream, snacks & ⛽ fuel for sale on site. All are welcome to lemonade, cookies, water from faucet on southwest corner of Cabbin. P Parking $3 per day for non-guests. 🛏 Private rooms are offered in the historic Main House; call for rates and availability. 📧 Mail drops: 3471 Remount Rd., Front Royal, VA. 22630.			

Front Royal, VA. (4.0W) (all major services) See map of Front Royal, VA.

📪⚲	**PO** M-F 8:30am-5pm, Sa 8:30am-1pm, 540-635-8482. 120 E 3rd St. Front Royal, VA 22630. N 38 55.404, W 78 11.525	
ⓘ◈ 🚗🚻📶📧	**Visitors Center** 540-635-5788. (www.discoverfrontroyal.com) ◈ AT Passport location. ⓘ Open 7 days a week 9am-5pm, except Thanksgiving, Christmas, and New Years. Hiker goody bags, hiker box, pack storage. Cold drinks for sale. Sells stamps. 🚻 Restrooms, 📶 free WiFi. 📧 Mail drops: 414 East Main Street, Front Royal, VA, 22630	
🚶◈ 🛁🛒 🚻📶🚗📧	**Mountain Trails, Base Camp** 540-749-2470 ◈ AT Passport location. 🚶 Full service outfitter. M-Sa 9:30am-6PM, Su 12-5PM. 🛒 Hiker food resupplies. ⛽ Coleman and alcohol fuel by the ounce, canister fuel. 🛁 Coin laundry, 🚿 showers, 🚻 restrooms, lockers and boot dryer. 📶 Free WiFi. 🚗 Shuttles possible if staff is avaialble. 📧 Mail drops: 120 E Main St, Front Royal, VA 22630	
🛏✕🛁📶 📧	**Quality Inn** 540-635-3161. Recently Renovated. Call for rate, $10EAP (up to 4) includes hot continental breakfast. Pets $15. 🛁 Guests laundry, microwave, fridge, flat screen TV and HBO, 📶 free WiFi. 🏊 Outdoor pool. When you check in let them know if you need a ride back to the AT in the morning(free). ✕ Thai restaurant onsite 📧 Mail drops for guests only: 10 Commerce Avenue, Front Royal, VA 22630.	
🛏🛁📶	**Parkside Inn** 540-631-1153. (www.parksideinnfrontroyal.com) Clean, hiker friendly: 🛏 $50-75, microwave, fridge, 🛁 laundry, 📶 free WiFi. Trail pickup and drop off when available.	
🛏📶🖥	**Super 8** 540-636-4888. 🛏 $62.60 and up, 10% hiker discount. Pets $10. Microwave, fridge, 🖥 computer available for use, 📶 free WiFi.	
🛏📶	**Scottish Inn** 540-636-6168. 🛏 $50/up. Pets $10. Microwave, fridge, 📶 free WiFi.	
🛏📶	**Budget Inn** 540-635-2196. (www.budgetinnfrontroyal.com) 🛏 $49.95 and up, Pet fee. Microwave, 📶 fridge, free WiFi.	
🚗	**Patriot Travel** Corley "Pi" Puckett, 571-236-4161 Shuttle hikers, family members, and pets between Waynesboro VA and Waynesboro PA. Shuttle to regional airports and Washington DC attractions. Long distance shuttles available	

Front Royal, VA

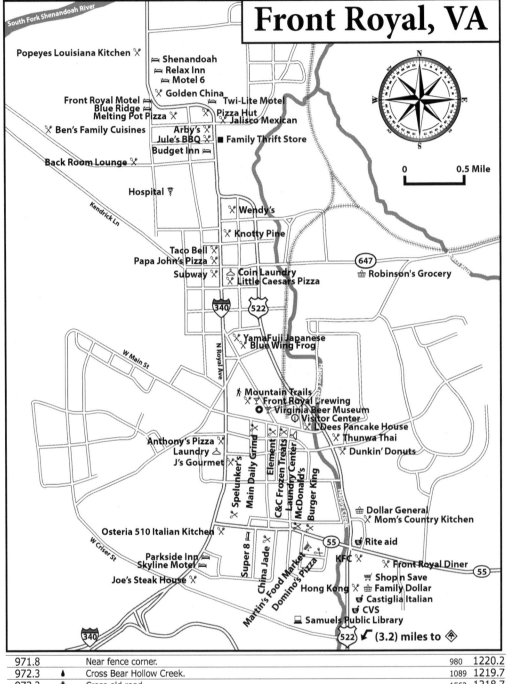

971.8		Near fence corner.		980	1220.2
972.3	♦	Cross Bear Hollow Creek.		1089	1219.7
973.3	▲	Cross old road.		1562	1218.7
973.4	▲	Cross road.		1575	1218.6
974.7	▲	Cross **Forest Road 3460**.		1808	1217.3
974.8	♦Y▲(4) ♀	Cross stream. Blue blaze east 100 yards to Mosby campground. Tom Sealock Spring is located 25 yards downhill from campsite, spring coordinates listed.	N38 52.767, W78 06.104	1800	1217.2
975.5	⌐	Power line.		1653	1216.5

NoBo	Features	Description	GPS	Elev	SoBo
976.7	♦Y▧⚠ ⊏(7)〜 《🏕▧🍴 ☕	50 yards west to **Jim and Molly Denton Shelter**, water (spring) is located on the AT, lots of tenting sites, privy, solar shower, bear pole, picnic table and pavilion, horseshoe pit. 31.7◀18.6◀8.1◀▶ 5.5▶ 10.0▶18.4	N 38 53.405, W 78 04.998	1310	1215.3
976.8	⛰	Old road intersects west.		1342	1215.2
977.5	Y	Intersection with another trail.		1164	1214.5
977.6	♦	Small stream.		1088	1214.4
977.8	⛰P☕ ★★★★★	Cross **VA. 638**	N 38 54.557, W 78 03.200	1150	1214.2
Linden, VA. (0.9W)					
	✉☕	**PO** M-F 8-am12pm & 1pm-5pm, Sa 8am-12pm, 540-636-9936, packages only held for 15 days. 13474 John Marshall Hwy. Linden, VA 22642. N 38 54.595, W 78 04.497			
	✗🚗	**Apple House Restaurant** 540-636-6329. (www.theapplehouse.net) ✗ Open M 7am-5pm, Tu-Su 7am-8 pm. Hiker specials, 🚗 supplies and rides sometimes available.			
	🏪	**Monterey Convenience Store**			
979.6	✗	Cross railroad tracks.		867	1212.4
979.7	⛰P(4)☕ ★★★★★	Junction of **VA. 55 and VA, 725**, Manassas Gap	N 38 54.557, W 78 03.198	800	1212.3
Linden, VA .(1.2W) See notes at NoBo mile 977.8					
980.7	Y	Blue blaze trail leads east to overgrown view.		1339	1211.3
982.2	♦Y▲ ⊏(6) 〜《🏕☕	70 yards east to **Manassas Gap Shelter**, water (spring) is located near the shelter on a side trail, tenting, privy, bear pole. Blue-blazed trail south of shelter leads (0.9W) to VA 638. 24.1◀13.6◀5.5◀▶ 4.5▶ 12.9▶19.8	N 38 55.844, W 78 01.962	1655	1209.8
983.4	◊	Stream, unreliable.		1789	1208.6
984.1	YP(10)	Trico Tower Trail (aka Trillium Trail) leads (0.3) west to Trico Road just short of Trillium parking area on VA. 638.		1900	1207.9
986.7	♦Y▲ ⊏(4)⊏(9) 〜《🏕☕	(0.2E) **Whiskey Hollow Shelter**, water TREAT WATER. (Whiskey Hollow Creek) is located in front of the shelter, tenting, hammocking, privy, bear pole. 18.1◀10.0◀4.5◀▶ 8.4▶ 15.3▶26.3	N 38 58.195, W 77 59.820	1230	1205.3
986.8	⛰P(8)☕	Cross dirt road.	N 38 59.127, W 77 59.985	1546	1205.2
987.7	♦▲	Water (spring)		1578	1204.3
987.8	YP(10)☕	Side trail (0.1) west AT parking area for 10 cars on Signal Knob.	N 38 59.127, W 77 59.983	1799	1204.2
988.4	YP(10)☕	Pass path to the west side leading (0.1) to Orchard parking area for 10 cars.	N 38 59.509, W 77 59.693	1821	1203.6
988.9	♦Y▲ P(6)🚗 ♦♦🏕	Blue blaze trail leads (1.3) to Sky Meadows campground or (1.7) to Sky Meadows State Park Side and parking.		1780	1203.1
989.0		Cross gas pipeline.		1761	1203.0

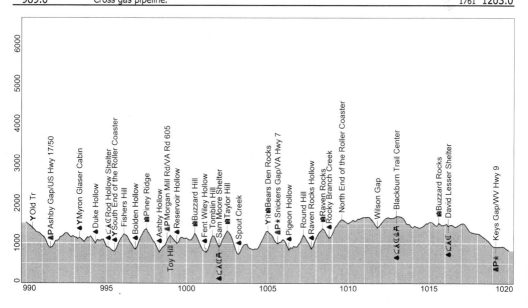

© WhiteBlaze Pages 2019

NoBo	Features	Description	GPS	Elev	SoBo
990.3	⚑	Cross old roadbed.		1372	1201.7
990.4	Y	Old Trail, purple blazed.		1380	1201.6
991.5		Cross U.S. 50, US. 17, Ashby Gap		900	1200.5
991.7	YP(6)⚲	Blue blaze trail leads 85 yards east to PATC trail head parking lot.	N 39 0.992, W 77 57.721	1084	1200.3
993.0	♦	Cross creek		1095	1199.0
993.3	Y	Blue blaze leads to Myron Glaser Cabin, reserved for PATC members only.		1100	1198.7
993.5	♦	Cross creek		1022	1198.5
993.8	Y	Blue blaze leads (0.2) to Myron Glaser Cabin, reserved for PATC members only.		1015	1198.2
995.1	◊YⒶ ⌂(7) ～℄⛺⚲	(0.1W) **Rod Hollow Shelter**, water (spring) is located in the streams just south of the shelter, tenting, privy. 18.4◀12.9◀8.4◀▶ 6.9▶ 17.9▶21.1	N 39 02.869, W 77 56.664	840	1196.9
995.4	Y	Fishers Hill Loop Trail to west.		800	1196.6
995.5	⌒	30 foot boardwalk.		826	1196.5
996.8	♦	Cross creek.		1189	1195.2
997.4	📷	Piney Ridge knoll, view.		1342	1194.6
998.3	♦⌒	Cross footbridge over Morgans Mill Stream.		772	1193.7
998.8	⚑P(6)⚲	Cross **VA. 605, Morgans Mill Road**	N 39 04.326, W 77 54.725	1140	1193.2
999.6	♦	Cross creek.		1096	1192.4
1000.0	♦	Old foundation, spring located 50 yards south		1016	1192.0
1000.6	Y📷	Trail west leads to summit of Buzzard Hill with nice views.		1183	1191.4
1001.2	♦	Cross creek.		775	1190.8
1001.4	⚑	Cross old road.		1028	1190.6
1001.6		Top of Tomblin Hill		1169	1190.4
1002.0	♦Ⓐ(2) ⌂(6) ～℄⛺🐻 ⚲	Cross branch of Spout Run. Blue blaze 35 yards south leads east to unreliable Sawmill Spring and to continue of 90 yards to **Sam Moore Shelter**, water (Sawmill Spring) is located in front of shelter or spring to left of shelter, tenting, privy. Bear pole. 19.8◀15.3◀6.9◀▶ 11.0▶ 14.2▶29.8	N 39 05.438, W 77 53.196	990	1190.0
1002.1	⚑	Cross old road.		932	1189.9
1003.2		Cross Spout Run		741	1188.8
1004.4	♦⌒	Cross creek on footbridge.		864	1187.6
1005.0	♦Y📷⌂ ★★★★★	Bears Den Rocks with good views, (0.2E) Bears Den Hostel, tap water available.	Bears Den Hostel N 39 06.666, W 77 51.255	1350	1187.0

⌂ Ⓐ ◈⛺ (0.2E) **Bears Den Hostel** 540-554-8708. (www.bearsdencenter.org)
△⚲🖥⛺⟶ ◈ AT Passport location.
📱P✉ Stone lodge, ATC owned and PATC operated.
⌂ Bunk $20PP, Ⓐ tenting $12PP includes full house privileges. Hiker Special: Bunk, laundry, pizza, soda and pint of Ben & Jerry's ice cream $30PP. All stays include shower and self serve pancake breakfast. △ Laundry, 🖥 computer available for use, ⟶ free WiFi. Hiker room with TV, shower, Internet and sodas, accessible all day by entering a mileage code at the hostel door. Upper lodge, kitchen, ⛺ camp store and office open 5 am-9 pm daily. Check-out 9am. 📱 Slackpacking and 🚌 shuttles may be available during summer months. P Parking $3 per day. Credit Cards accepted.
✉ Mail drops, picked up during office hours: Bears Den Hostel, 18393 Blue Ridge Mountain Rd, Bluemont, VA 20135

| 1005.4 | YP(10)⚲ | Blue blaze trail to parking lot. Same parking as Snikers Gap. | N 39 06.934, W 77 50.919 | 1139 | 1186.6 |
| 1005.6 | ⚑P(10)⚲ ★★★★★ | Cross **VA. 7, VA. 679**, Snickers Gap.
Caution against parking on the shoulders of VA 679 if the VA 679 parking lot is full - vehicles parked on either shoulder will be towed. Alternate parking is available nearby at the intersection of VA 7 and VA 601, where a rather large parking lot is located. If your car is towed, contact the Clarke County Communications Center at 540-955-1234. | N 39 06.934, W 77 50.919 | 1000 | 1186.4 |

Bluemont, VA 20135

	📱⚲	(1.7E) **PO** M-F 10am-1pm & 2pm-5pm, Sa 8:30am-12pm, 540-554-4537. 33775 Snickersville Tpke. Bluemont, VA 20135. N 39 06.601, W 77 49.933			
	✗	(0.3W) **Horseshoe Curve Restaurant** 540-554-8291 M Closed, Tu-W 5pm-9pm, Th-Su 12 pm-9pm.			
	✗⟶☎	(0.9W) **Pine Grove Restaurant** 540-554-8126. ✗ M-Sa 7am-8pm, Su 7am-2pm. Welcomes hikers, serves breakfast, lunch and dinner, breakfast served all day. ⟶ Free WiFi, ☎ ATM			
1006.4	♦	Pigeon Hollow, stream.		850	1185.6
1007.8	♦	Water (spring)		1083	1184.2
1008.1	📷 State Line	Virginia–West Virginia State Line. View to the west.		1140	1183.9

NoBo	Features	Description	GPS	Elev	SoBo
1008.2	📷	Crescent Rock		1252	1183.8
1008.8	◧▲Y	Old road leading west 70 yards to Sand Spring (seasonal), 20 yards further to a dependable spring and Ridge to River Trail..		1150	1183.2
1008.9	⌇	Power line. Devils Racecourse, boulder field.		1200	1183.1
1011.8		Wilson Gap		1380	1180.2
1012.7	Y▲	Side trail leads (0.2) east **Blackburn AT Center** see **notes below** (0.1) east to campground.		1651	1179.3
1013.0	◧Y▲ ⊑(8)☾ P(6)🚻 ★★★★★	Side trail leads (0.2) east to **Blackburn Trail Center**, water, tenting, privy. 26.3◀17.9◀11.0◀▶3.2▶18.8▶22.9	N 39 11.262, W 77 47.868	1650	1179.0
	Y⌂▲ ◈📱🍴⛺	(0.2E) **Blackburn Trail Center** 540-338-9028. ◈ AT Passport location. Open year round. The Center offers a hiker cabin with ⌂ four double bunks with a 🛏 picnic pavilion; ▲ six tent sites and a tent platform are located below the hiker cabin. ◧ Water is available from an outside spigot and a solar shower is located on the lower lawn. On porch of main building are logbook, donation box, 📱 pay phone, and electrical outlets. (0.1E) **Group campground** with tent sites, picnic tables, and a privy is located on the north blue blaze trail. The Trail Center is owned and operated by the Potomac Appalachian Trail Club and is used to house trail crews, hold meetings, training seminars and retreats. A caretaker lives on site.			
1013.1	📷	Path west to outcrop with views.		1666	1178.9
1015.1	▲	Clearing with campsites.		1527	1176.9
1015.6	Y	Blue blazed trail west (0.1) to Buzzard Rocks, left branch in trail has limited views, right branch of trail has no views.		1512	1176.4
1016.2	◧Y▲ ⊑(6) ⌇☾🛏🚻	115 yards east to **David Lesser Memorial Shelter**, water (spring) is located (0.4) downhill from the shelter, tenting, privy. 21.1◀14.2◀3.2◀▶15.6▶19.7▶24.7	N 39 13.635, W 77 46.746	1430	1175.8
1017.2	▲	Cross old road.		1516	1174.8
1018.1	▲	Primitive campsite.		1229	1173.9
1018.8		Cross polluted stream, **Do not drink water from stream**.		1048	1173.2
1019.2	▲P(12)🚻 ★★★★★	Cross **W.VA. 9**, Keys Gap	N 39 15.684, W 77 45.747	935	1172.8

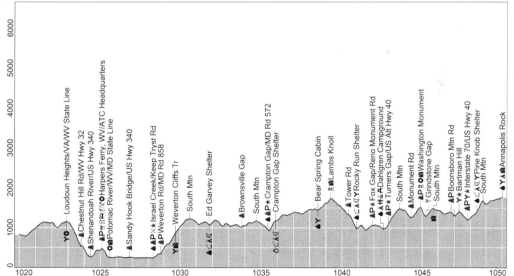

(0.3E)**Sweet Springs Country Store** 540-668-7200.

🛒✕♨🏧 Good selection of hiker foods. Fuel available. Full deli, sandwiches, hamburgers, subs and fried chicken.
🖥 M-Sa 4am-11pm, Su 7am-11pm.
Mail drops: 34357 Charles Town Pike, Purcellville, VA 20132.

🏧✕ (0.3) west at intersection) **Mini-Mart & Torlone's Pizza** 304-725-0916.
M-Th 11am-9pm, F-Sa 11am-10pm, Su 12pm-8pm. Restaurant and conveyance store.

(5.0W) Stoney Brook Organic Farm 540-668-9067, 540-668-7123

🛏🍴✕⚑ ⛺ Optional Work for stay, ✕ meals, 🚿 shower, ⚑ laundry. Rustic Cabin accommodations. Market hours M-Th 6 AM–8 PM, F6 am-3 pm, Sa closed, Su 9 am-8 pm. Pickup and return from Bears Den, Blackburn Trail Center, Keys Gap, Harpers Ferry.

✉ Mail drops for guest only: 37091 Charles Town Pike Hillsboro, VA 20132

Run by a twelve Tribes spiritual community

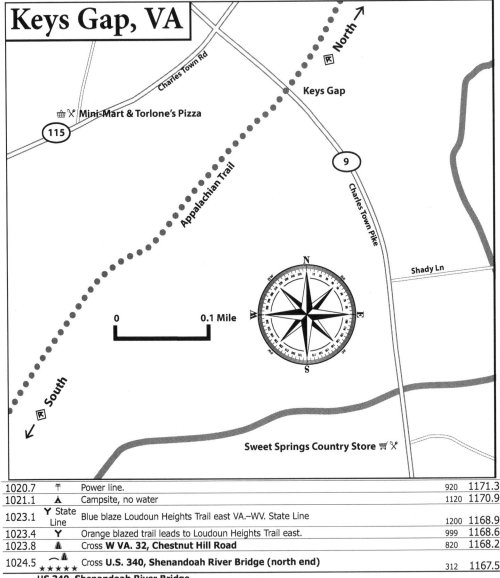

Keys Gap, VA

Charles Town Rd

🏪 ✕ **Mini-Mart & Torlone's Pizza**

115

Appalachian Trail

Keys Gap

North

9

Charles Town Pike

Shady Ln

0   0.1 Mile

South

Sweet Springs Country Store 🛒 ✕

NoBo		Feature		GPS Elev	SoBo
1020.7	🗲	Power line.		920	1171.3
1021.1	⚑	Campsite, no water		1120	1170.9
1023.1	Y State Line	Blue blaze Loudoun Heights Trail east VA.–WV. State Line		1200	1168.9
1023.4	Y	Orange blazed trail leads to Loudoun Heights Trail east.		999	1168.6
1023.8	🛤	Cross **W VA. 32, Chestnut Hill Road**		820	1168.2
1024.5	★★★★★	Cross **U.S. 340, Shenandoah River Bridge (north end)**		312	1167.5

US 340, Shenandoah River Bridge

🛏♿⚑💻 (0.1W) on 340 **Quality Inn/Econo Lodge** 304-535-6391.
🐾 ♿ No pets. 🛏 Rates $93–$119. 10% hiker discount, hot breakfast bar. ⚑ Laundry. 💻 Computer available for use, 🛜 free WiFi.

⚑🛏✕🏪 (0.8W) on 340 **Harpers Ferry KOA** 304-535-6895. (www.koa.com/campgrounds/harpers-ferry) ⚑
⚑🚿 Camping $40 and up, 🛏 cabins $85 and up, $8EAP. ⚑ Coin laundry on-site, 🚿 shower only $5, 🛜 WiFi. 🏪 Camp store.

🛏✕⚑💻 (1.2W) on 340 **Clarion Inn** 304-535-6302.
🛜🏊 Rates $123 and up, continental breakfast, ⚑ laundry, 🏊 indoor pool, Spa, 💻 computer available for use, 🛜 free WiFi. ✕ Restaurant onsite.

Charles Town, WV 25414 (6.0W) (All major services)

NoBo	Features	Description	GPS	Elev	SoBo

	🛒🦷	**Walmart with grocery and pharmacy** 304-728-2720. Open M-Su 24 hours. 🦷 Pharmacy M-F 9am-9pm, Sa 9am-7pm, Su 10am-6pm.			
	🏥	**Jefferson Urgent Care** 304-728-8533 (www.jeffersonurgentcare.com)M-F 8 am-8 pm, Sa-Su closed. Closed Thangsgiving and Christmas.			
	🏥	**Winchester Foot & Ankle** 304-725-5000 (www.footcarecenterva.com)			
	🐾	**Jefferson Animal Hospital** 304-725-0428			
	🐾	**Animal Care Associates, Inc** 304-344-2244. (www.acawv.com) M 7:30am-7:30pm, Tu-Th 7:30am-6:30pm, F 7:30am-7:30pm, Sa 8am-3pm, Su 12pm-3pm.			

Frederick, MD 21701 (20E) (All major services)

1024.8	Y○♀ ★★★★★	Blue blazed trail leads (0.2) west to **Appalachian Trail Conservancy**, coordinates to the ATC. **Harpers Ferry, WV.**	N 39 19.533, W 77 44.431	394	1167.2
	①◈○☎ ♨☑♀	**ATC Headquarters** 304-535-6331. (www.appalachiantrail.org) ◈ AT Passport location. Open year round; 7 days 9am–5pm, closed Thanksgiving, Christmas, New Year's Day. **If you're thru-hiking or section hiking this is where you need to stop and register.** Hiker lounge, register, scale, ☎ free WiFi, cold and hot drinks inside. ♨ Coleman and denatured alcohol by the ounce for a donation. Information board on the front porch. ☑ Mail drops: (USPS) PO Box 807 or (FedEx/UPS) 799 Washington St, Harpers Ferry, WV 25425. Coordinates; N 39 19.518, W 77 44.436			
	🚗	**Rhonda Adams** 304-596-1911 (cell), best to text message. Based in Harpers Ferry, will shuttle as far south as SNP Big Meadows and as far North as Pine Grove General Store			
1025.2	Y	Path to west leads a few yards to Harpers Cemetery.		471	1166.8
1025.3	Y○📷	Path to east leads to Jefferson Rock with good views.		425	1166.7
1025.4	▲P(15)♀ ★★★★★	**Shenandoah Street**; Harpers Ferry National Historical Park. Parking is available for up to two weeks at Harpers Ferry National Historical Park Visitor Center. You must register your vehicle with rangers at the visitors center or entrance station and pay a one-time $6.00 entrance fee. Gates are sometimes locked at night. For more information, call (304) 535-6298.	N 39 18.952, W 77 45.411	315	1166.6

Harpers Ferry, WV. See map of Harpers Ferry, WV.

	✉♀	**PO** M-F 8am-4pm, Sa 9am-12pm, 304-535-2479. 1010 Washington St. Harpers Ferry, WV 25425. N 39 19.597, W 77 44.702			
	🏠◈🅱⛺ 💻☎☑	**(0.5W) Teahorse Hostel & Backpacker Resupply** 304-535-6848. (www.teahorsehostel.com) ◈ AT Passport location. 🅱 No pets, alcohol or smoking. Open for check in and resupply 1pm-9pm. 🏠 $34 per bunk plus tax includes waffle breakfast. ⛺ Laundry $6. 💻 Computer available for use, ☎ WiFi. Visit their web site to reserve or check availability. ☑ Mail drops for guests: 1312 W. Washington St., Harpers Ferry, WV 25425.			
	🛏🏠◈✕ 🏪⛺🚗	**The Town's Inn** 304-702-1872 (mobile) or 932-0677. (www.thetownsinn.com) 🛏 Private room $110-$210 up to 6 persons, one pet room. 🏠 Hostel walk-in only $35PP. ✕ Dining available 6am-10pm daily year-round. 🏪 Shop stocked for hiker resupply. ⛺ Laundry $5. 🚗 Shuttles $1/mile.Visa/MC accepted. **No mail drops.**			
	🥾◈🏪	**The Outfitter at Harpers Ferry & Harpers Ferry General Store** 888-535-2087. (www.theoutfitteratharpersferry.com) ◈ AT Passport location. 🥾 Full service outfitter with good selection of shoes & 🏪 trail food. Shuttle referrals. M-Su 10am-6pm, later on F-Sa. Located just steps off the AT across the street from the train station at 161 Potomac St.			
	①◈P	**Harpers Ferry National Historical Park** 304-535-6029. ◈ AT Passport location. $10 entrance fee, P parking up to 2 weeks (must register). Free shuttle bus to lower town. Gates open 9am-dusk.			
	🚗	**HostelHiker Rideshare Shuttles** 304-885-9550, 202-670-6323. info@hostelhiker.com (www.HostelHiker.com) Shuttles throughout Maryland, north to Boiling Springs, Pennsylvania, south to Swift Run Gap, Virginia, and east to Washington, D.C., and Baltimore. Airport shuttles to IAD, DCA, and BWI. Dogs allowed to ride with human companion. A max of 11 people can ride together on van. Online booking is mobile friendly at (www.hostelhiker.com).			
	🚗	**Mark "Strings" Cusic** 304-433-0028. mdcusic@frontier.com. Based out of Harpers Ferry. Shuttle range Rockfish Gap to Duncannon.			
	🚗	**Chris "Trailboss" Brunton** based in Harpers Ferry. North to Boiling Springs, PA and South to Waynesboro, VA. Can also do some airport pickup ups and drops. Have Dodge Caravan and can take dogs. Contact 703-967-2226 voice or text. trailbossbtc@msn.com.			

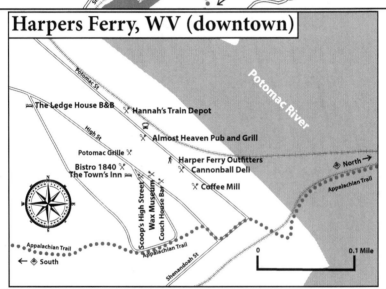

Harpers Ferry, WV

Harpers Ferry, WV (downtown)

1025.5	State Line	Cross Potomac River on Goodloe E. Bryon Memorial Footbridge, West Virginia–Maryland State Line		250	1166.5
1025.7	♦Y	C&O Canal Towpath MP 60.2 (AT west junction)		290	1166.3
1026.8	▲⌒	Cross **under US. 340 bridge**, Sandy Hook Bridge above, underpass.		290	1165.2
1028.3	Y	C&O Canal Towpath MP 58 (AT east junction) Lockhouse 38		290	1163.7
1028.4	✕▲P(8) ⚲ ★★★★★	Cross Railroad tracks; Intersects with **Keep Tryst Road**.	N 39 19.785, W 77 40.928	320	1163.6

Knoxville, MD. (1.0W)

⌂ ▲ ◈ ⌂ **Harpers Ferry Hoste**l 301-834-7652. (www.hiusa.org/hostels/maryland/knoxville/harpers-ferry)

⚸🖥🖥🚙 ◈ AT Passport location.

P🖃 Open April 15–Nov 15 for individuals, year-round for groups. Check-in 5-10pm, check-out 10am. ID required for any stay. Beer and wine okay. No liquor.

⌂ Thru-hiker rate $22.40 includes tax, shower, WiFi, linens, A/C and heat, free "make your own breakfast". ⌂ Laundry $4. ▲ Tenting $10PP, pay extra $5 for day use (inc. indoor access+ breakfast). 🖥 WiFi and phone charging on front porch. Porta-potty, ⌂ outdoor shower stalls, fire pits, outdoor brick oven, grill on lawn. Service dogs okay inside, otherwise dogs on leash allowed only if tenting. Store with hiker snacks inside and there is often free food indoors. Complimentary meals on Tu, Fr, & Sa. P Non-guest parking $5 per day.

🖃 Mail drops for guests: 19123 Sandy Hook Rd, Knoxville, MD 21758.

NoBo	Features	Description	GPS	Elev	SoBo
	🛏⚊☕	**Knights Inn** 301-660-3580 🛏 $69.99and up, fridge, microwave, continental breakfast, ☕ WiFi. ⚊ Hiker laundry $5.			
	🏠✗☎	**Hillside Station** 301-834-5300. 🏠 Convenience store with ✗ some hot food, pizza, ☎ ATM. M-Sa 6am-9pm, Sa 7am-9pm, Su 8am-8pm.			

Brunswick, MD 21716 (2.5E from Keep Tryst Rd)

	✉🚻	**PO** M-F 8am-4:30pm, Sa 9am-12pm, 301-834-9944. 315 Brunswick St. Brunswick, MD 21716. N 39 18.882, W 77 37.870			
	✗	**Wing n' Pizza Shack** 301-834-5555. (www.wingnpizzashack.com) Not just pizzas, they have other foods. Delivers to Harper Ferry Hostel. M-Th 11am-9pm, F-Sa 11am-10pm, Su 12pm-9pm.			
1028.6	▲	Cross under **U.S. 340**, underpass.		400	1163.4
1028.8	▲P(24)🚻	Intersects with **Weaverton Road**	N 39 19.992, W 77 41.002	420	1163.2
1029.7	Y📷	Weaverton Cliffs Trail. Potomac River view, Congressman Goodloe E. Bryon plaque		780	1162.3
1031.8	▲Y▲ ⊏(12) ☾🚻	100 yards east to **Ed Garvey Shelter**, water is located in reliable spring (0.4) at the end of a steep side trail in front of the shelter, tenting, privy. 29.8◄18.8◄15.6◄►4.1►9.1►16.6	N 39 21.591, W 77 39.723	1100	1160.2
1033.8	▲	Cross Brownsville Gap, dirt road		1140	1158.2
1034.1	●	Glenn R. Caveney Memorial Plaque		1150	1157.9
1035.5	▲▲P🚻 ★★★★★	Cross **Gapland Road, MD. 572**. Gathland State Park, Crampton Gap Monument. Frost-free spigot by restrooms.	N 39 24.341, W 77 38.386	650	1156.5
	🛏▲🏠⚊	**(0.4W) Maple Tree Campground** 301-432-5585 (www.thetreehousecamp.com) Open year round. ▲ $30 tent site for 1-3 people, $10EAP, ⚊ showers. Wooded tent sites are $10/person per night and there is a 3 person minimum. Field tent sites for $8/person per night, but they are usually intended for larger groups with a 10-person minimum. They do make exceptions for hikers when there is space available. 🛏 Treehouses/Tree Cottages, Non-insulated rustic Treehouses available for $43-$72/night, and insulated Tree Cottages with mattresses and wood stoves available for $65-$79/night. Also has a Hobbit House, for 140.00, and a deluxe tree house for 120.00. 🏠 Campstore has snacks, candy bars, sodas, batteries. Located: west of AT on Gapland Road, taker the right onto Townsend Road.			
1035.9	◊▲⊏(6) ⌇☾🚻	**(0.25E) Crampton Gap Shelter**, water intermittent (spring) is located (0.1) south on AT, tenting, privy. 22.9◄19.7◄4.1◄►5.0►12.5►20.7	N 39 24.752, W 77 38.256	1000	1156.1
1038.5	▲Y	Trail to Bear Spring Cabin (locked), water is located (0.5) west		1480	1153.5
1039.1	📷	White Rocks Cliff, quartzite cliff with good view		1500	1152.9
1039.3	Y📷	Lamb's Knoll, unmarked trail west leads 50 yards to antenna tower		1600	1152.7
1040.4	▲	Cross **Tower Road**		1300	1151.6
1040.9	▲Y▲ ⊏(5) ⌇☾🚻	**(0.2W) Rocky Run Shelter**, water (Rocky Run Spring) is located at old shelter a few hundred yards on blue blaze, tenting and hammocks sites, privy. 24.7◄9.1◄5.0◄►7.5►15.7►20.6	N 39 27.649, W 77 37.884	970	1151.1
1041.2	▲	Intersects with old road.		967	1150.8
1041.4	⏛📷	High tension power line clearing, view.		950	1150.6
1041.9	▲P✗🚻 ★★★★★	Cross **Reno Monument Road**, Fox Gap.	N 39 28.234, W 77 37.056	910	1150.1
	■	**(2.0E) to South Mountain Creamery** 301-371-8565. (www.southmountaincreamery.com). M-Sa 10 am-6 pm, Su 12-6 pm.			
1042.7	▲Y▲♯♯ ⚊🛏	Dahlgren Backpacker campground west of trail.		980	1149.3
1042.9	▲P(10)🚻 ★★★★★	Cross **U.S. Alt. 40**, Turners Gap.	N 39 29.045, W 77 37.195	1000	1149.1
	✗Y☕	**(0.1W) Old South Mountain Inn** 301-432-6155. (www.oldsouthmountaininn.com) Please shower first. Men, no sleeveless shirts.. Dining reservations preferred. Tu–F 5pm until close, Sa 4pm until close, Su 2pm until close. Brunch on Sundays 10:30am-1:30pm, except Easter and Mothers Day. Winter hours may differ. OUtdoor shower for hikers. Hiker friendly grocries.			

Boonsboro, MD (2.5W) See map of Boonsboro, MD.

	✉🚻	**(2.5W) PO** M-F 9am-1pm & 2pm-5pm Sa 9am-12pm, 301-432-6861. 5 Patomac St. Boonsboro, MD 21713. N 39 30.383, W 77 39.161			
	✗	**Vesta Pizzeria** 301-432-6166. (www.vestapizza.com) M-Tu 11am-9pm, W-Su 11am-10pm.			
	✗	**Mountainside Deli** 301-432-6700. M-Sa 11am-7pm, Su 11am-5pm. Accepts Credit Cards.			
	🏠	**Cronise Market Place** 301-432-7377. (www.cronisemarket.com) Fruits and vegetables, limited. M-F 9am-7pm, Sa 9am-6pm, Su 12pm-6pm.			
	☕✗	**Turn the Page Book Store Café** 301-432-4588. (www.ttpbooks.com) M-Sa 10am-6pm, Su 11am-4pm.			
	✗🏠	**Crawfords** 301-432-2903. M-F 7am-5pm, Sa 7am-3pm. Limited.			

Boonsboro, MD

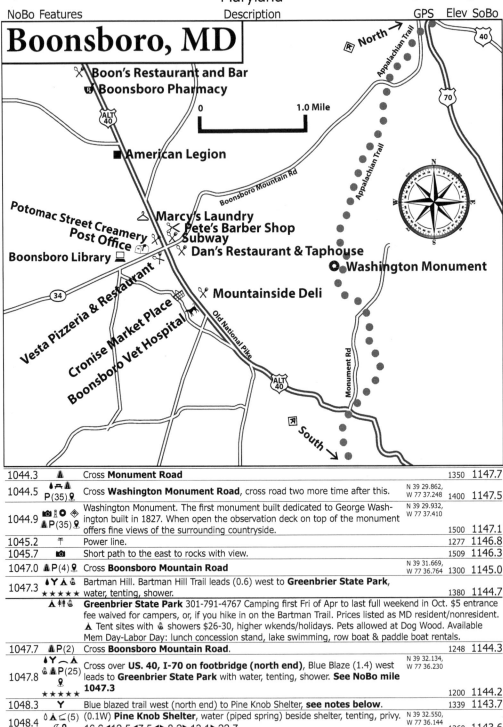

⚔ Boon's Restaurant and Bar
🏪 Boonsboro Pharmacy

0   1.0 Mile

⬛ American Legion

Boonsboro Mountain Rd

Potomac Street Creamery   ☖ Marcy's Laundry
Post Office   ⚔ Pete's Barber Shop
                          ⚔ Subway
Boonsboro Library 💻   ⚔ Dan's Restaurant & Taphouse
                          ◉ Washington Monument

34

Vesta Pizzeria & Restaurant   ⚔ Mountainside Deli

Cronise Market Place
Boonsboro Vet Hospital
Old National Pike

Appalachian Trail

North →

South ↓

Monument Rd

40

70

40

1044.3	⛺	Cross **Monument Road**		1350	1147.7
1044.5	🅿(35)	Cross **Washington Monument Road**, cross road two more time after this.	N 39 29.862, W 77 37.248	1400	1147.5
1044.9	📷 ⛺ 🅿(35)	Washington Monument. The first monument built dedicated to George Washington built in 1827. When open the observation deck on top of the monument offers fine views of the surrounding countryside.	N 39 29.932, W 77 37.410	1500	1147.1
1045.2	🗼	Power line.		1277	1146.8
1045.7	📷	Short path to the east to rocks with view.		1509	1146.3
1047.0	⛺🅿(4)	Cross **Boonsboro Mountain Road**	N 39 31.669, W 77 36.764	1300	1145.0
1047.3	◆Y⛺ ★★★★★	Bartman Hill. Bartman Hill Trail leads (0.6) west to **Greenbrier State Park**, water, tenting, shower.		1380	1144.7
	⛺♦	**Greenbrier State Park** 301-791-4767 Camping first Fri of Apr to last full weekend in Oct. $5 entrance fee waived for campers, or, if you hike in on the Bartman Trail. Prices listed as MD resident/nonresident. ⛺ Tent sites with 🚿 showers $26-30, higher wkends/holidays. Pets allowed at Dog Wood. Available Mem Day-Labor Day: lunch concession stand, lake swimming, row boat & paddle boat rentals.			
1047.7	⛺🅿(2)	Cross **Boonsboro Mountain Road**.		1248	1144.3
1047.8	◆Y⌒⛺ 🚿⛺🅿(25) ★★★★★	Cross over **US. 40, I-70 on footbridge (north end)**, Blue Blaze (1.4) west leads to **Greenbrier State Park** with water, tenting, shower. **See NoBo mile 1047.3**	N 39 32.134, W 77 36.230	1200	1144.2
1048.3	Y	Blue blazed trail west (north end) to Pine Knob Shelter, **see notes below**.		1339	1143.7
1048.4	◊⛺⌐(5) ☾	(0.1W) **Pine Knob Shelter**, water (piped spring) beside shelter, tenting, privy. 16.6◄12.5◄7.5◄►8.2►13.1►22.7	N 39 32.550, W 77 36.144	1360	1143.6

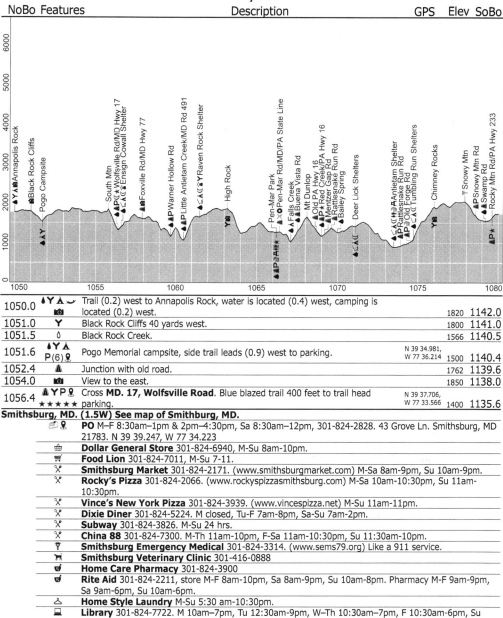

1050.0	◆Y▲☞ 📷	Trail (0.2) west to Annapolis Rock, water is located (0.4) west, camping is located (0.2) west.		1820	1142.0
1051.0	Y	Black Rock Cliffs 40 yards west.		1800	1141.0
1051.5	◊	Black Rock Creek.		1566	1140.5
1051.6	◆Y▲ P(6)⚲	Pogo Memorial campsite, side trail leads (0.9) west to parking.	N 39 34.981, W 77 36.214	1500	1140.4
1052.4	▲	Junction with old road.		1762	1139.6
1054.0	📷	View to the east.		1850	1138.0
1056.4	▲YP⚲ ★★★★★	Cross **MD. 17, Wolfsville Road**. Blue blazed trail 400 feet to trail head parking.	N 39 37.706, W 77 33.566	1400	1135.6

Smithsburg, MD. (1.5W) See map of Smithsburg, MD.

✉⚲	**PO** M–F 8:30am–1pm & 2pm–4:30pm, Sa 8:30am–12pm, 301-824-2828. 43 Grove Ln. Smithsburg, MD 21783. N 39 39.247, W 77 34.223
🏬	**Dollar General Store** 301-824-6940, M-Su 8am-10pm.
🛒	**Food Lion** 301-824-7011, M-Su 7-11.
✗	**Smithsburg Market** 301-824-2171. (www.smithsburgmarket.com) M-Sa 8am-9pm, Su 10am-9pm.
✗	**Rocky's Pizza** 301-824-2066. (www.rockyspizzasmithsburg.com) M-Sa 10am-10:30pm, Su 11am-10:30pm.
✗	**Vince's New York Pizza** 301-824-3939. (www.vincespizza.net) M-Su 11am-11pm.
✗	**Dixie Diner** 301-824-5224. M closed, Tu-F 7am-8pm, Sa-Su 7am-2pm.
✗	**Subway** 301-824-3826. M-Su 24 hrs.
✗	**China 88** 301-824-7300. M-Th 11am-10pm, F-Sa 11am-10:30pm, Su 11:30am-10pm.
☤	**Smithsburg Emergency Medical** 301-824-3314. (www.sems79.org) Like a 911 service.
🐾	**Smithsburg Veterinary Clinic** 301-416-0888
♥	**Home Care Pharmacy** 301-824-3900
♥	**Rite Aid** 301-824-2211, store M-F 8am-10pm, Sa 8am-9pm, Su 10am-8pm. Pharmacy M-F 9am-9pm, Sa 9am-6pm, Su 10am-6pm.
🧺	**Home Style Laundry** M-Su 5:30 am-10:30pm.
💻	**Library** 301-824-7722. M 10am–7pm, Tu 12:30am-9pm, W–Th 10:30am–7pm, F 10:30am-6pm, Su closed.
✗	**Ace Hardware** 301-733-7940. M 7am-6pm, Tu-W 7a,-5pm, Th 7am-6pm, F 7am-5pm, Sa 7am-3pm, Su closed.

The world is changed
by your example,
not your opinion

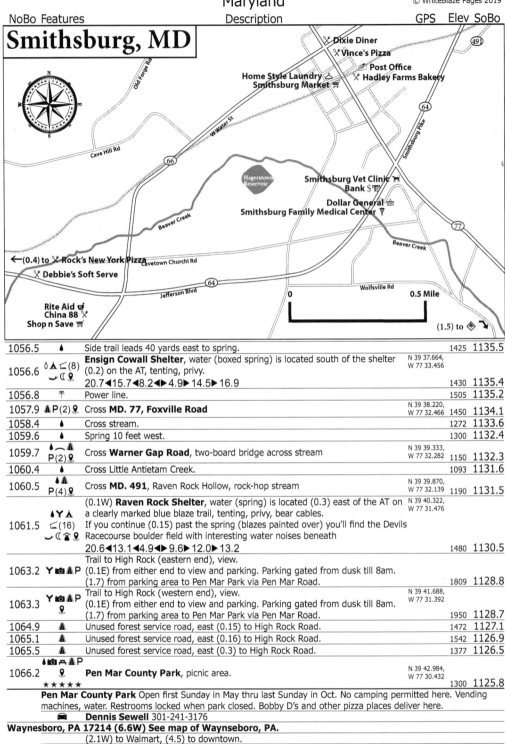

Smithsburg, MD

Dixie Diner
Vince's Pizza
Post Office
Home Style Laundry — Hadley Farms Bakery
Smithsburg Market

Old Forge Rd
W Water St
Cave Hill Rd
66
Smithsburg Pike
64

Hagerstown Reservoir
Smithsburg Vet Clinic
Bank $
Dollar General
Smithsburg Family Medical Center
Beaver Creek
77
Beaver Creek

←(0.4) to Rock's New York Pizza
Cavetown Church Rd
Debbie's Soft Serve
Jefferson Blvd
64
Wolfsville Rd
491

Rite Aid
China 88
Shop n Save
0   0.5 Mile
(1.5) to

1056.5	♦	Side trail leads 40 yards east to spring.		1425	1135.5
1056.6	◊▲⌐(8) ⌣((♀	**Ensign Cowall Shelter**, water (boxed spring) is located south of the shelter (0.2) on the AT, tenting, privy.	N 39 37.664, W 77 33.456	1430	1135.4
		20.7◄15.7◄8.2◄▶4.9▶14.5▶16.9			
1056.8	⊤	Power line.		1505	1135.2
1057.9	▲P(2)♀	Cross **MD. 77, Foxville Road**	N 39 38.220, W 77 32.466	1450	1134.1
1058.4	♦	Cross stream.		1272	1133.6
1059.6	♦	Spring 10 feet west.		1300	1132.4
1059.7	♦⌐▲ P(2)♀	Cross **Warner Gap Road**, two-board bridge across stream	N 39 39.333, W 77 32.282	1150	1132.3
1060.4	♦	Cross Little Antietam Creek.		1093	1131.6
1060.5	♦▲ P(4)♀	Cross **MD. 491**, Raven Rock Hollow, rock-hop stream	N 39 39.870, W 77 32.139	1190	1131.5
1061.5	♦Y▲ ⌐(16) ⌣((♠♀	(0.1W) **Raven Rock Shelter**, water (spring) is located (0.3) east of the AT on a clearly marked blue blaze trail, tenting, privy, bear cables. If you continue (0.15) past the spring (blazes painted over) you'll find the Devils Racecourse boulder field with interesting water noises beneath	N 39 40.322, W 77 31.476		
		20.6◄13.1◄4.9◄▶9.6▶12.0▶13.2		1480	1130.5
		Trail to High Rock (eastern end).			
1063.2	Y◎▲P	(0.1E) from either end to view and parking. Parking gated from dusk till 8am. (1.7) from parking area to Pen Mar Park via Pen Mar Road.		1809	1128.8
1063.3	Y◎▲P ♀	Trail to High Rock (western end), view. (0.1E) from either end to view and parking. Parking gated from dusk till 8am. (1.7) from parking area to Pen Mar Park via Pen Mar Road.	N 39 41.688, W 77 31.392	1950	1128.8
1064.9	▲	Unused forest service road, east (0.15) to High Rock Road.		1472	1127.1
1065.1	▲	Unused forest service road, east (0.16) to High Rock Road.		1542	1126.9
1065.5	▲	Unused forest service road, east (0.3) to High Rock Road.		1377	1126.5
1066.2	♦◎⌐▲P ♀ ★★★★★	**Pen Mar County Park**, picnic area.	N 39 42.984, W 77 30.432	1300	1125.8

Pen Mar County Park Open first Sunday in May thru last Sunday in Oct. No camping permitted here. Vending machines, water. Restrooms locked when park closed. Bobby D's and other pizza places deliver here.
🚗 **Dennis Sewell** 301-241-3176

Waynesboro, PA 17214 (6.6W) See map of Waynesboro, PA.
(2.1W) to Walmart, (4.5) to downtown.
🏤♀ **PO** M-Fi 8:30am - 5:00pm, SA 9:00am - 12:00pm, Su Closed. 717-762-1513. 118 E Main St. Waynesboro PA 17268. N 39 45.237, W 77 34.504

NoBo Features — Description — GPS Elev SoBo

Cobblestone Hotel 717-765-0034. $90/up +tax, includes hot breakfast, microwave, fridge, laundry, computer available for use, free WiFi, indoor pool, outdoor grill for use, convenience Store.

Bobby D's Pizza 717-762-0388. (www.bobbydsonline.com) M-Th: 11am-9pm, F-Sa 11am-10pm, Su 11am-9pm.

Burgundy Lane B&B 717-762-8112. (hwww.burgundylane.biz)
AT Passport location.
$90-110, includes full breakfast, free laundry, computer available for use, WiFi, and shuttle to trail head or town stop. Longer shuttles for fee.
Mail drops for guests: 128 W Main St, Waynesboro, PA 17268.

Days Inn 717-762-9113. $59.99 and up, $5EAP, $10 pet fee. Continental breakfast, microwave, fridge, free WiFi, laundry close by.

Laundry Station 717-762-7203

Waynesboro Hospital 717-765-4000. Location 501 E Main St.

Waynesboro Walk-in Clinic 717-265-1154. (www.waynesborowalkin.com) M-F 8am-7pm, Sa-Su 9am-5pm.

Wayne Heights Animal Hospital 717-765-9636. (www.whahvet.com) M-F 8am-12pm & 2pm-6pm.

(2.1W) **Walmart** 540-943-4087. M-Su 24 hours; **Pharmacy** 540-943-4637 M-F 9am-9pm, Sa 9am-7pm, Su 10am-6pm.

Cascade, MD (1.4E on Pen Mar/High Rock Rd)

PO M-F 10am-1pm & 2pm-5pm, Sa 8am-12pm, 301-241-3403. 25208 Military Rd. Cascade, MD 21719. N 39 42.526, W 77 29.350

Sanders Market M 8:30am-9pm, 8:30-8pm, W-F 8:30am-9pm, Sa 8:30-8pm, Su closed.

Fort Ritchie Community Center 301-241-5085. (www.thefrcc.org) Showers, computer avaialble for use, free WiFi. M-Th 6am-9pm, F 6am-6pm, Sa 9am-5pm, Su 10am-4pm.

Rouzerville, PA 17250 (1.8W) most major services.

PO M-F 8:30am-1pm & 2am-4:30pm, Sa 8:30am-11:30pm 717-762-7050. 11738 Pen Mar Rd. Rouzerville, PA 17250. N 39 44.221, W 77 31.481

Cobblestone Hotel & Suits 717-765-0034, ask for hiker discount.

Waynesboro, PA

Laundry Station
Days Inn
Waynesburger
Don Carlos Tienda Y Restaurante
Dollar General
Franks Pizza
Sapporo Japanese
Nu-Way
Post Office
Pizza Hut
McDonald's
Northeast Ave
Subway
Waynesboro Hospital
Velvet Cafe
CVS
Bank
China King
Domino'a Pizza
Montezuma Mexican
Martin's Foods
W 5th St
YMCA
State Hill Rd
Rite Aid
Hardee's
Burger King
Dairy Queen
Old Forge Rd
Cobblestone Hotel
Walmart
Subway
Applebee's
Keystone Family Restaurant
China Maple
Cafe Del Sol
KFC
(6.6) Miles to →
0   0.5 Mile
Red Run Grill
Blondies
Brother's Pizza
Old Rte 16

				GPS	Elev	
1066.4	State Line	Mason–Dixon Line Maryland–Pennsylvania State Line			1250	1125.6
1066.5	P ★★★★★	Cross **Pen Mar Road**.		N 39 43.249, W 77 30.425	1240	1125.5

© WhiteBlaze Pages 2019

NoBo	Features	Description	GPS	Elev	SoBo
	P	An advance parking pass is now available for overnight parking at Pen Mar (across the street from the county park). While the pass is not required, it is strongly recommended for those leaving their vehicle for an extended period. Here's how to get the pass: Email Christine Casey ccasey@washco-md.net at the Washington County Parks and Facilities Dept. the following information: (1) The make and model of your vehicle (2) Registered owners name (3) Tag information (4) Dates the vehicle will parked Ms. Casey will respond with a "do not tow" pass, as an attachment, that is to be printed and posted in your vehicle so local police will know that the vehicle has been registered. The phone number to call to reach Ms. Casey is 240-313-2700 Tue-Fri. 6am - 4:30pm (reduced hours in winter and more information here.)			
		Rouzerville, PA.(1.5W), See Notes at mile 1066.2.			
1067.1	♦⌂Å	Falls Creek Footbridge		1100	1124.9
1067.5	Å♦	Cross **Buena Vista Road**, roadside spring on the west		1290	1124.5
1068.7	Å	Cross **Old PA. 16**. Limited parking.		1350	1123.3
1069.0	ÅP(5)♀ ★★★★★	Cross **PA. 16**.	N 39 44.484, W 77 29.430	1200	1123.0
		Blue Ridge Summit, PA (1.2E)			
	■	**Synergy Massage Wellness Center** 877-372-6617 (www.synergymassage.com) Massage, hiker discount. Free outdoor shower, hot tub and pool.			
	✗	**Unique Bar and Grill** 717-794-2565. (www.uniquebarandgrill.com)			
1069.2	ÅP(2)	Cross **Mentzer Gap Road**, Mackie Run		1250	1122.8
1069.6	Å	Cross **Rattlesnake Run Road**		1370	1122.4
1069.8	♦	Bailey Spring, box spring 15 yards west.		1300	1122.2
1071.1	♦Å⊏(8) ⌣℃♀	**Deer Lick Shelters** (two shelters hold four hikers each), water (spring) (0.25) on a blue blazed trail to the east of the shelter, tenting, privy. 22.7◄14.5◄9.6◄►2.4►3.6►10.2	N 39 45.971, W 77 29.112	1420	1120.9
1072.0	Å	Woods road, Rattlesnake Run Road is (0.17) east.		1408	1120.0
1073.5	◊⌂Å ⊏(6) ⌣℃♀	Old Forge Park, cross two foot bridges. **Antietam Shelter**, water is located (0.2) north on the AT at a springhouse with spigot by the ballfield in Old Forge Park, tenting, privy. 16.9◄12.0◄2.4◄►1.2►7.8►13.4	N 39 47.629, W 77 28.980	890	1118.5
1073.6	♦♥♠	Old Forge Picnic Grounds, restroom, frost-free water tap. Water source for Antietam Shelter.		900	1118.4
1073.9	ÅP	Cross **Rattlesnake Run Road**.		900	1118.1
1074.5	♂ÅP(20)♀	Cross **Old Forge Road**	N 39 48.196, W 77 28.520	1000	1117.5
1074.7	♦Å⊏(8) ⌣℃♀	30 yards west to **Tumbling Run Shelters** (two shelters hold four hikers each), water is located 100 yards to the west of the shelter, tenting, privy. 13.2◄3.6◄1.2◄►6.6►12.2►19.6	N 39 48.300, W 77 28.698	1120	1117.3
1076.0	Y📷	Blue blaze trail east to Chimney Rocks or west to PATC Hermitage Cabin (locked)		1900	1116.0
1076.8		Pipe line.		1603	1115.2
1078.0	⟙	Power line.		1901	1114.0
1078.6	ÅP(3)♀	Cross **Snowy Mountain Road**. Parking pull-off on the west side of the road just north of the trail crossing.	N 39 50.247, W 77 30.254	1680	1113.4
1078.9	Å	Cross dirt road.		1648	1113.1
1079.2	Å	Junction with **Swamp Road (south)**.		1560	1112.8
1079.3	Å	Junction with **Swamp Road (north)**.		1560	1112.7
1079.4	Y	Raccoon Run Trail east goes to Caledonia State Park.		1624	1112.6
1079.6	ÅP(4)♀ ★★★★★	Cross **PA. 233**.	N 39 50.982, W 77 30.529	1600	1112.4
		South Mountain, PA. (1.3E)			
	⌂♀	**PO** M-F 12pm-4pm, Sa 8:30am-11:30am. 717-749-5833. 10444 S Mountain Rd. South Mountain, PA 17261. N 39 50.898, W 77 29.384			
	✗Å⌗	**South Mountain Tavern** 717-749-3845 ✗ Historic Bar & Grill, serves lunch and dinner. Å Ask about tenting M-Sa 9am-2am, Su 12pm-2am.			
		Waynesboro, PA. (5.2W) see NOBO mile 1066.2.			
1079.8	Å	Gravel road.		1751	1112.2

Elevation profile labels (left to right): Rocky Mtn Shelters · Caledonia State Park/US Hwy 30 · Quarry Gap Rd · Quarry Gap Shelters · Stillhouse Rd · Middle Ridge Rd · Means Hollow Rd · Milesburn Rd · Ridge Rd · Rocky Knob Tr · Birch Run Shelter · Shippensburg Rd · AT Midpoint · Michener Cabin · Woodrow Rd · Toms Run Shelters · Michaux Rd · Toms Creek · Pine Grove Rd/PA Hwy 233 · Pine Grove Furnace State Park · Mountain Creek · Pole Steeple Tr · Piney Mtn

NoBo	Features	Description	GPS	Elev	SoBo
1081.3	⬥Y⚲ ⌐(8)☾⚲	(0.2E) **Rocky Mountain Shelters**, (two shelters hold four hikers each), water (pipe spring) is located (0.5) on trail to road and then right 75 yards, tenting, privy. 10.2◀7.8◀6.6◀▶5.6▶13.0▶19.2	N 39 52.114, W 77 30.054	1520	1110.7
1084.2		Cross pipe line.		1501	1107.8
1084.3	⬥⚲⬥✗ ⚲⚲ P(12)⚲ ★★★★★	Cross U.S. 30, **Caledonia State Park, Snack Bar, Thaddeus Stevens Museum** ⬥ AT Passport location, at snack bar. Parking (0.6E), Overnight parking SW corner of US 30 & Pine Grove Rd, check-in at park HQ. Caledonia State Park now requests that those parking overnight at the parking area on Rt. 30 register at the park office. For more information, contact the park at 717-352-2161. AT Passport is located at the Snack Bar.	N 39 54.354, W 77 28.716	960	1107.7
	✗⬥⬥⚲ ⬥	(0.7W) **Timbers Restaurant & Ice Cream** 717-401-0605. ⬥ AT Passport location. ⬥ Snacks, ⚲ fuels, charging station, ⬥ WiFi, hiker friendly. M-Su 7 am-9 pm. ✉ Maildrop: 8228 Lincoln Way, Fayetteville, PA 17222			
	⌂⚲⚲ ⚲⬥⬥✉	(0.9W) **Trail of Hope Outreach Ministries Hostel** 717-360-1481, 717-352-2513. ⬥ AT Passport location. ⌂ $22 bunk or ⚲ $12 camping. ⬥ Coin laundry, use of kitchen, resupply, ⚲ white gas, denatured alcohol by the ounce, canister fuel. ⬥ Call for shuttles from Timbers. ✉ Mail drops: 7798 Lincoln Way East Fayetteville, PA 17222.			
Fayetteville, PA (3.5W)					
	✉⚲	(3.2 W) PO M-F 8-4:30; Sa 8:30-12, 717-352-2022. 4025 Lincon Way E. Fayetteville, PA 17222. N 39 54.648, W 77 33.595			
	⬥✗⬥⬥ ✉	**Scottish Inn and Suites** 717-352-2144, 800-251-1962. ⬥ $62.99 and up, $15 pets. $5PP for pickup or return to trail. $10 for ride to Walmart. ⬥ Coin laundry, ⬥ free WiFi. ✗ Restaurant on site. ✉ Mail drops for guests only: 5651 Lincoln Way East, Fayetteville, PA 17222.			
	⬥✗⬥	**Rutters Convenience store** 717-401-0626. ⬥ M-Su 24 hours. ✗ Deli, ⬥ free WiFi.			
	✗	**Flamingo Restaurant** 717-352-8755. (www.flamingofamilyrestaurantllc.com) Breakfast, lunch and dinner.M-Th 5:30am-8pm, F-Sa 5:30am-9pm, Su 6:30am-2pm.			
	✗	**Vince's Pizza** 717-401-0096.			
	⬥⬥	**Freeman's Shuttle Service** 717-352-2513 or 717-360-1481. ⬥ Front Royal to DWG. ⬥ Slackpacking Pen Mar to Duncannon.			
	⬥⬥	(6.5W) **Walmart** 717-264-2300 with 24 hours grocery. ⬥ Pharmacy M-F 9 am-9 pm, Sa 9 am-7 pm, Su 10 am-6 pm.			
1086.2	⬥	Cross **Quarry Gap Road**		1250	1105.8
1086.9	⬥⚲⌐(8) ⌣☾⚲	**Quarry Gap Shelters**, (two shelters hold four hikers each), water is located 10 yards in front of the shelter, tenting, privy. 13.4◀12.2◀5.6◀▶7.4▶13.6▶24.5	N 39 55.918, W 77 29.188	1455	1105.1
1088.4	⬥P(5)⚲	Junction with **Stillhouse Road**, Sandy Sod Junction	N 39 56.825, W 77 29.476	1980	1103.6
1089.2	⊤	Power line cut.		1861	1102.8
1089.6	⬥	Cross old woods road.		1990	1102.4
1091.0	⬥	Cross **Middle Ridge Road**		2050	1101.0

NoBo	Features	Description	GPS	Elev	SoBo
1091.1	Y	Dughill Trail.		2073	1100.9
1091.5	▲P(5)✇	Junction with **Ridge Road, Means Hollow Road**	N 39 58.563, W 77 27.548	1800	1100.5
1091.9	♦▲	Cross **Milesburn Road**, (0.2) east to Milesburn Cabin (locked)		1600	1100.1
1092.3	▲	Cross **Ridge Road**.		1909	1099.7
1093.0	Y	Cross Rocky Knob Trail.		1905	1099.0
1094.3	♦▲⊑(8) ⌣ℂ✇	**Birch Run Shelter**, water (spring) is located 30 yards in front of the shelter, tenting, privy. 19.6◄13.0◄7.4◄► 6.2► 17.1►25.2	N 39 59.106, W 77 25.169	1795	1097.7
1095.6	▲P(12)✇	Cross **Shippensburg Road**, Big Flat parking area	N 39 59.857, W 77 24.326	2040	1096.4
1096.2	⊙	2016 Midpoint		2000	1095.8
1097.5	♦	PATC Michener Cabin (locked), (0.2E) to water		1850	1094.5
1099.4	▲P(4)✇	Cross **Woodrow Road**	N 40 01.765, W 77 22.088	1850	1092.6
1100.5	♦▲⊑(4) ⌣ℂ✇	**Toms Run Shelter**, water (spring) is located near old chimney, dining pavilion, numerous tent pads, privy. 19.2◄13.6◄6.2◄► 10.9► 19.0►37.2	N 40 02.020, W 77 21.407	1300	1091.5
1100.8	⊙	2011 Midpoint Sign		1300	1091.2
1101.7	▲✇	Intersects with **Michaux Road**	N 0 02.346, W 77 20.549	1320	1090.3
1102.4	♦	Halfway Spring		1100	1089.6
1103.9	▲P	Cross **PA. 233**		900	1088.1
1104.2	♦⊙▲♨ P(20)✇ ★★★★★	**Pine Grove Furnace State Park.** Pine Grove Furnace State Park requires that hikers check in with the park office before leaving a vehicle in the park and that vehicles be left for no more than one week.	N 40 01.902, W 77 18.324	850	1087.8

Pine Grove Furnace State Park

⌂ ◈ ⛺🖳☏🖳	**Ironmasters Mansion Hostel** 717-486-4108. ironmasterspinegrove@gmail.com (www.ironmasters-mansion.com) ◈ AT Passport location. Open Apr 1-Oct 31; sometimes closed for special events. Check-in, 5pm -9pm; closed 9am–5pm. Closed on Tuesdays. Call or email for reservations. ⌂ $25PP; Dinner and breakfast are $5 each. 🖳 Computer available for use, ☏ free WiFi, ⛺ laundry $3. 🖳 Mail drops: Ironmasters Hostel, 1212 Pine Grove Rd, Gardners, PA 17324.	
🏪 ◈ ✗🖳☏	**Pine Grove General Store** 717-486-4920. ◈ AT Passport location. M-Su 8am-7pm mid-May thru Labor Day; weekends only mid-Apr thru mid-May and Labor Day thru Oct. 🏪 Selection of hiking food, cold drinks, ⛽ canister fuel, fuel by the ounce. ✗ Short order grill. Soda machine outside. ☏ Free WiFi and phone charging. ☏ ATM **"Home of the Half-Gallon Challenge!"**.	
ⓘ ◈	**A.T. Museum** 717-486-8126. (www.atmuseum.org) ◈ AT Passport location. Hikers welcome. Artifacts and photos of past hikers, signs from Springer & Katahdin. Sells halfway patch and bandana. Open; Mar 25-April 30, Weekends only 12pm to 4pm. May 6-July 16, Every day 9am to 4pm. July 17-Aug 20, Every day 12pm to 4pm. Aug 23-Oct 29, Wed-Sun, 12pm to 4pm. (open Labor day and Columbus day)	
▲⌣♨P	**Pine Grove Furnace State Park** 717-486-7174 From end of Dec to end of Mar open weekdays only; open 7 days rest of year. ▲⌣ Campsites start at $17 weekdays, weekends are a little more, $2 off for PA residents. Dogs allowed in some sites. ♨ Restrooms. P Check with park office before parking overnight.	

| 1104.4 | ✗♨⛴ | Fuller Lake, beach, ⛴ swimming, ♨ Showers. | | 850 | 1087.6 |
| 1106.7 | Y | Pole Steeple side trail | | 1300 | 1085.3 |

OK, don't think about your aching feet. Don't think about your feet. Don't think about... DANG IT!!!

BootsMcfarland.com
© Geolym Carvin
Boots Mcfarland

NoBo	Features	Description	GPS	Elev	SoBo
1110.0	▲	Old roadbed		1080	1082.0
1110.2	♦Y▲ P(4)♀ ★★★★★	Trail to **Mountain Creek Campground**, on Pine Grove Road, (0.7W) to tenting, long term resupply, water, shower, swimming. See below.	N 40 03.626, W 77 13.529	1050	1081.8
	⮞▲⛺⛄ ✗⚒	**Mountain Creek Campground** 717-486-7681. (www.mtncreekcg.com) Open Apr-Nov, ⮞ cabins $52+ tax, ▲ tentsites $27. ⛺ Camp store has sodas and ice cream, ⛄ laundry, ✗ short-order grill on weekends. ⚒ Swimming.			
1111.0	♦	Side trail leads (0.1) west to spring, signed.		750	1081.0
1111.4	♦▲⌂(9) ℂ♀	Tagg Run. (0.2E) **James Fry (Tagg Run) Shelter**, water is located (0.4) east of the AT on a blue blazed, tenting, privy. 24.5◀17.1◀10.9◀▶ 8.1▶26.3▶33.6	N 40 03.778, W 77 12.384	805	1080.6
1112.0	▲✗▲	Cross **Pine Grove Road. Camping (0.4W)**		750	1080.0
	▲⚄⮞⚒	(0.4W) **Cherokee Family Campground** 717-486-8000 (www.cherokeecampgroundpa.com) cherokeecamp@aol.com ▲ Tent sites $25, ⚄ showers, ⮞ WiFi, ⚒ swimming pool, ⮞ store.			
	✗♀	(0.6E) **The Twirly Top** 717-486-3424 (www.thetwirlytop.com) Serves lunch and dinner. April-May: Tu-Sa 11am-9pm, Su/M Closed. May-Sept: M-Sa 11am-10pm, Su Closed. Sept-End of Season: M-Sa 11am-9pm, Su Closed. Accept credit cards. Coordinates: N 40 04.147, W 77 11.640.			
1113.0	▲P(18)♀ ★★★★★	Cross **PA. 34, Hunters Run Road**, parking (0.1E) **Gardners, PA.**	N 40 04.666, W 77 11.61	670	1079.0
Gardners, PA. (0.2E)					
	⮞✗⛺♦♦	(0.2E) **Green Mountain Store & Deli** 717-486-4558 M-F 7am-8pm, Sa 8am-8pm, Su 9am-6pm. Hiker foods, prepared foods, ice cream, canister fuel, Heet. Restroom.			
1114.6	▲P ★★★★★	Cross **PA. 94.**		880	1077.4
Mt. Holly Springs, PA. (2.5W)					
	⌂♀	**PO** M–F 8am-1pm & 2pm-4:30pm, Sa 9am-12pm. 717-486-3468. 16 W Pine St. Mt Holly Springs, PA 17065. N 40 06.858, W 77 11.416			
	⮞✗⌂⮞	**Holly Inn Lodging and Dinning** 717-486-3823. (www.hollyinn.com) ⮞ $65-150, $10EAP, ⌂ computer avaiaible for use, ⮞ free WiFi, continental breakfast, free ride to and from AT with stay, $5 round trip from Pine Grove Furnace State Park. ✗ Restaurant open Su-Th 11:30am-9pm, F-Sa 11:30am-10pm.pm. ⅄ Tavern open M-Th 11:30-10pm, F-Sa 11:3-12am, Sun 11:30am-11pm.			
	⮞	**Sheetz** M-Su 24 hours, **Dollar General** M-Su 8am-10pm, **Family Dollar** M-Su 8am-10pm.			
	✗	**Subway** 717-486-8655. M-Th 7am-9pm, F 7am-10pm, Sa 8am-10pm, Su 8am-9pm.			
	✗	**Sicilia Pizza** 717-486-4011. M-Th a1am-9pm, F-Sa 11am-10pm, Su 11am-9pm.			
	⚕	**Holly Pharmacy** 717-486-5321. M-Sa 8:30am-7pm, Sun Closed.			
1114.8	▲P(4)♀ ★★★★★	Cross **Sheet Iron Roof Road**, (0.4W) to tenting, restaurant, lodging, short term resupply, shower, laundry, swimming	N 40 05.581, W 77 09.873	680	1077.2
	⮞▲✗⛄ ⚄⛄⚒	(0.4W)**Deer Run Campground** 717-486-8168. (www.deerruncampingresort.com) Tent with shower $10, cabin $75.			

NoBo	Features	Description	GPS	Elev	SoBo
1115.9	▲	Cross old road.		734	1076.1
1116.0	▲	Cross **old town road**.		794	1076.0
1117.4	◑▲P(4)♀	Cross **Whiskey Spring Road**, Whiskey Spring. Beware of parking here, vehicles have been vandalized here.	N 40 05.879, W 77 07.719	830	1074.6
1119.4	▲	Cross woods road with orange blazes, leads (1.7) to Boy Scout Camp Tuckahoe.		905	1072.6
1119.5	◐Y⌐(7) ↲☾♀	580 feet east to **Alec Kennedy Shelter**, water (spring) is located on a side trail behind the shelter but is known to go dry, privy. 25.2◀19.0◀8.1◀▶18.2▶25.5▶33.8	N 40 06.708, W 77 06.254	850	1072.5
1120.4	Y🎦	Center Point Knob which at one time was mid point for the AT, White Rocks Trail		1060	1071.6
1121.7	●	Pass evidence of mining operations.		558	1070.3
1122.3	▲P♀	Intersects with **Leidigh Drive**. Very limited parking.	N 40 08.482, W 77 06.929	560	1069.7
1123.0	◑☾▲✕	Backpackers campsite, near railroad tracks to east. Privy after Memorial Day.		500	1069.0
1123.1	▲⌐💧▲	Intersects with **Mountain Road**, Yellow Breeches Creek, (1.5W) to shelter, tenting, shower		500	1068.9
1123.2	☾▲P♀	Cross **Bucher Hill Road**	N 40 08.871, W 77 07.450	500	1068.8
1123.4	◑▲P♀ ★★★★★	Intersects with **PA. 174**, ATC Mid-Atlantic Office, limited use parking. **Boiling Springs, PA.** Limited parking.	N 40 09.004, W 77 07.630	500	1068.6

Boiling Springs, PA. See map of Boiling Springs, PA.

🏤♀	**PO** M-F 9am-12pm & 1pm-4:30pm, Sa 9am-12pm. 717-258-6668. 3 E 1st St. Boiling Springs, PA 17007. N 40 09.031, W 77 07.619
🛏⊛♿	**Red Cardinal B&B** 717-245-0823. (www.redcardinalbedandbreakfast.com) ⊛ No pets, no smoking. 🛏 $125 and up, queen bed room includes full breakfast and pickup and return from Boiling Springs, ⊛ free WiFi.
🛒	**Karn's Quality Foods** 717-258-1458. M-Su 7am–10pm.
🏬☎	**Gettys Food Mart** 717-241-6163. ☎ ATM inside.
🐾	**Boiling Springs Animal Hospital** 717-258-4575. (www.bsahvets2.com) M 9am-7:30pm, Tu 9a,-6pm, W 9am-7:30pm, Th-F 9am-6pm, Sa 9am-1pm.
✕	**Anile's Ristorante & Pizzeria** 717-258-5070. M-Th 11am-10pm, F-Sa 11am-11pm, Su 11am-10pm.
✕	**Boiling Springs Tavern** 717-258-3614. (www.boilingspringstavern.com) Serves lunch and dinner. M closed, Tu-Sa 11:30-9pm, Su closed.
🏊♿	**Boiling Springs Pool** 717-258-4121.(www.bspool.com) Memorial Day-Labor Day, M-Su 11am-7pm, $2 hot shower. If you want to swim, visit ATC Regional Office for $3 off the $12 admission.
🔧⊛♿	**TCO Fly Shop** 610-678-1899. (www.tcoflyfishing.com) ⊛ AT Passport location. ♿ Canister fuel and some hiking items. M-F 9am-7pm, Sa 9am-5pm, Su 9am-3pm.
🚗	**Mike's Shuttle Service** 717-497-6022. As far north or south as hikers need.
⊛♿🛒	**ATC Mid-Atlantic Regional Office** 717-258-5771. ⊛ AT Passport location. M-F 8am-5pm, Sa-Su closed. Spigot on south side of building, may be off in winter. Ask staff about trail conditions and check bulletin board. Small shop with maps. ♿ Fuel by the ounce for donation. Hiker box. ⊛ WiFi.

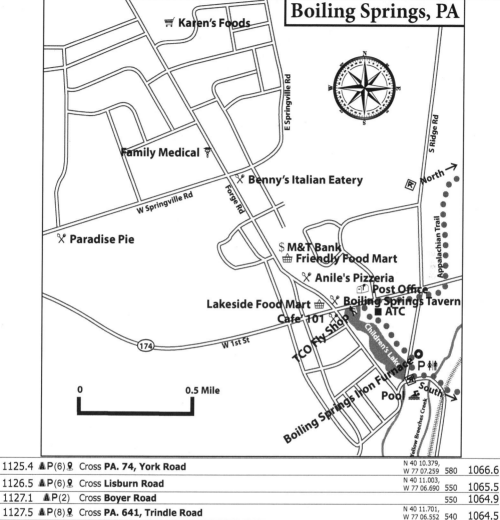

Boiling Springs, PA

				GPS	Elev	
1125.4	▲P(6)♀	Cross **PA. 74, York Road**		N 40 10.379, W 77 07.259	580	1066.6
1126.5	▲P(6)♀	Cross **Lisburn Road**		N 40 11.003, W 77 06.690	550	1065.5
1127.1	▲P(2)	Cross **Boyer Road**			550	1064.9
1127.5	▲P(8)♀	Cross **PA. 641, Trindle Road**		N 40 11.701, W 77 06.552	540	1064.5
1128.6	▲ ★★★★★	Cross **Ridge Drive**.			460	1063.4

🛏 ◈ ⚠ ⊚ (0.5W) **Pheasant Field B&B** 717-258-0717.
◈ AT Passport location.
(www.pheasantfield.com) 🛏 $135 and up, free pickup and return to trail head with stay, big breakfast, microwave, fridge, ⚠ laundry for fee, ⊚ free WiFi, behaved pets ok. NOBO's call from Trindle Rd at **mile 1125.7,** or from Ridge Rd, go (0.25W) to Hickory Town Rd, turn left on road, they are located on right.

1129.2	▲	Cross **Old Stonehouse Road**			470	1062.8
1129.9	▲	Cross **Appalachian Drive**			510	1062.1
1130.2	▲	Cross over **I-76 Pennsylvania Turnpike,** overpass			495	1061.8
1130.8	✕	Cross **Norfolk Southern Railroad Tracks**			470	1061.2
1131.4	⌒▲ ★★★★★	Cross over **U.S. 11, pedestrian footbridge.**			490	1060.6

New Kingston, PA. 17073 (1.9W)
⌂♀ (1.7W) **PO** M-F 8:30am - 4pm, Sa 10am - 12pm, Su Closed. 31 E Main St, New Kingstown, PA 17072. N 40 14.060, W 77 04.643.

Carlisle, PA 17013 (0.5W) Post office further into Carlisle.
⌂♀ (5.1W) **PO** M-F 9am - 6pm, Sa 9am - 1pm, Sun Closed. 717-243-3531. 66 W Louther St, Carlisle, PA 17013. N 40 12.167, W 77 11.426.
✕ **Middlesex Dinner** 717-241-2021, 24 hours.
🛏⚠⊚ **Days Inn** 717-245-2242 🛏 Hiker rate $55.95, continental breakfast, pets $20. ⊚ WiFi.

NoBo	Features	Description	GPS	Elev	SoBo
	🛏⛺📶📧	**Super 8 Motel** 717-249-7000. 🛏 $65 and up, continental breakfast, ⛺ laundry, 📶 free WiFi, $10 pet fee. 📧 Mail drops for Guests: 1800 Harrisburg Pike, Carlisle, PA 17013.			
	🛏	**Red Roof Inn** 717-245-2400. Call for pricing.			
	🛏📶	**Americas Best Value Inn** 717-249-7775. 🛏 $43.95 and up + tax, continental breakfast, $15 pet fee, microwave, fridge, 📶 free WiFi.			
	✗🏪🚿⛺	**Flying J Truck stop** 717-243-6659, M-Su 24hrs. 🏪 Convenience store, ✗ diner, 🚿 showers $12 includes towel, ⛺ laundry.			
Mechanicsburg, PA 17050 (5.0E)					
	🛒	(3.0E) **CVS** 717-697-1645. M-Sa 8am-9pm, Su 9am-7pm; Pharmacy M-F 9am-9pm, Sa 9am-6pm, Su 9am-5pm.			
	🛒	(4.3E) **Giant Food** 717-796-6555. M-Su 24 hours			
	🛒	(4.6E) **Walmart** 717-691-3150. M-Su 24 hours.			
1132.3	⌒🅿(5)🔦	Cross over I-81, overpass on Bernhisel Bridge Road.	N 40 14.566, W 77 06.048	485	1059.7
1133.7	⚠⌒☾ 🚗🅿🔦	Cross Conodoguinet Creek Bridge, **ATC Scott Farm Trail Work Center**, AT work center. P Parking is limited; users must contact the Appalachian Trail Conservancy to determine parking availability, driving and parking on the grass are strictly prohibited. See next entry north for Sherwood Drive for alternate parking.	N 40 15.594, W 77 06.250	480	1058.3
1134.8	⚠🅿(6)🔦	Intersects with **Sherwood Drive**	N 40 16.440, W 77 05.970	420	1057.2
1135.7	⚠	Cross **PA. 944**, pedestrian tunnel Donnellytown, PA.	N 40 17.063, W 77 05.627	480	1056.3
1136.7	◆Y	Spring at Wolf Trail Junction, spring is west 50 feet follow blue blaze. **NoBo's Get Water Here.**		650	1055.3
1137.6	Y	Tuscarora Trail (northern terminus), Darlington Trail		1390	1054.4
1137.7	◊Y⚠ ⊏(5) 🍳☾🔦	(0.1E) **Darlington Shelter**, water (spring) is located (0.2) on a blue blazed trail in front of the shelter but is unreliable, lots of tenting, privy. 37.2◄26.3◄18.2◄►7.3►15.6►22.3	N 40 18.122, W 77 05.212	1250	1054.3
1138.8	▲	Crest of Little Mountain		910	1053.2
1139.6	⚠	Cross **Millers Gap Road**, paved		700	1052.4

1140.0	⚠🅿(6)🔦	Cross **PA. 850, Valley Road**	N 40 19.309, W 77 04.689	650	1052.0
1141.4	◆	Cross stream.		761	1050.6
1142.5	Y📷	Pipe line clearing with views. Unmarked trail leads west down to State Game lands parking.		1315	1049.5
1144.1	Y	Blue blaze trail leads west steeply down to service road for Duncannon Water Company.		1246	1047.9
1145.0	◆Y⊏(8) 🍳☾🔦	(0.2E) **Cove Mountain Shelter**, water (spring) is located 125 yards away on a steeply graded trail near the shelter, privy. 33.6◄25.5◄7.3◄►8.3►15.0►33.0	N 40 21.819, W 77 04.042	1200	1047.0
1146.9	📷	Hawk Rock, view of Duncannon		1140	1045.1

NoBo	Features	Description	GPS	Elev	SoBo
1148.1	▲	Intersects with **Inn Road**		360	1043.9
1148.2	⌒▲	Cross over **Sherman Creek Bridge**		360	1043.8
1148.6	⊨▲P	Intersection with **PA. 274, U.S. 11 & 15**, underpass, (0.5W) to long term resupply		385	1043.4
1149.1	▲ ★★★★★	Intersection of **Market and Cumberland Street**. **Duncannon, PA. See map of Duncannon, PA.**		385	1042.9

PO ID required, M-F 8am-11am & 12pm-4:30pm, Sa 8:30am-12:30pm. 717-834-3332. 203 N Market St. Duncannon, PA 17020. N 40 23.553, W 77 01.757

Doyle Hotel 717-834-6789.
◈ AT Passport location.
⊨ $25S, $35D, $10EAP + tax, ✗ resturaunt serves lunch, dinner, homemade meals and vegan choices.
⚗ Coleman, alcohol by the ounce and canister fuel. Recharging station. Pool Table. Credit cards Visa, MC, Discovery.
✉ Mail drops: Real names only as they require ID to pick up any mail drop. (USPS/UPS/FedEx) 7 North Market Street, Duncannon, PA 17020.

Stardust Motel 717-834-3191. No pets. $45S, $55D, laundry. Sometimes pickup and return rides available.

Red Carpet Inn 717-834-3320. ⊨ $55S, $60D + tax. ⚗ Laundry, ⚭ free WiFi. Pickup and return from Duncannon for $10.

Riverfront Campground 717-834-5252. (www.riverfrontcampground.com)
▲ Site and ⚗ shower $5PP, check-in daylight until dark. 🚐 Shuttles available Take note of the railroad tracks.

Sorrento Pizza 717-834-5167. (www.sorrentosduncannon.com) M-Th 11am-10:30pm, F-Sa 11am-11:30pm, Su 11am-10:30pm. Bar and Lounge; every day 4pm- last call. Dinner service ends 10pm.

Goodies Breakfast 717-834-6300. M closed, Tu-Su 6am-11am.

Ranch House Restaurant 717-834-4710. (www.ranchhouseperryco.com)
M-Fr 5:30am-9pm, Sa 6am-9pm, & Su 7am-9pm. Serves breakfast, lunch and dinner. Soup & Salad Bar is available everyday for lunch & dinner (11AM to 7PM). Breakfast bar on Sa-Su.

Lumberjack's Kitchen 717-834-9099. (www.lumberjackskitchen.weebly.com)
Seasonal hours, open in the summer and spring M-Th 9am-9pm, F-Sa 8am-9pm, Su 8am-8pm. In the Fall and Winter open M-Th 10am- 8pm, F-Sa 8am-9pm, Su 8am-7pm. Located near Red Carpet Inn

Mutzabaugh's Market 717-834-3121. (www.www.mutzabaughsmarket.com) 🚐 Hiker friendly, M-Su 6am-10pm. Will pickup and return to Doyle at 4pm daily.

Rite Aid 717-834-6303. M-F 8am-9pm, Sa 8am-7pm, Su 8am-8pm. Pharmacy M-F 9am-9pm, Sa 9am-6pm, Su 10am-6pm.

Pilot Travel Plaza 717-834-3156, M-Su 24 hours, ⚗ $12 showers.

Cove Mountain Animal Hospital 717-834-5534. (www.covemountainanimalhospital.vetstreet.com)
M-W 9am-8pm, Th 9am-5pm, F 9am-6pm, Sa 9am-12pm, Su closed.

Christ Lutheran Church 717-834-3140. (www.clcduncannon.org)Free hiker dinner Wednesdays in June & July 5pm-7pm at 115 Church St., the corner of Plum St and Church St. Sunday service 10am.

Trailangelmary 717-834-4706.
◈ AT Passport location.
2 Ann St, Duncannon, PA 17020

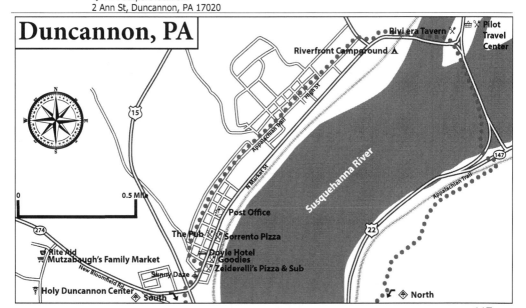

NoBo	Features	Description	GPS	Elev	SoBo
1149.2	⛺	Intersects with **High Street**.		260	1042.8
1150.1	🏕🏕	Intersects with **PA. 849, Newport Road**, Juniata River		380	1041.9
1150.9	～⛺P🅿	Susquehanna River on Clarks Ferry Bridge (west end). Cross **U.S. 22 & 322, Norfolk Southern Railway**	N 40 23.756, W 77 00.510 N 40 23.774, W 77 00.465	400	1041.1
1151.0	Y	Blue blazed Susquehanna Trail, rejoins A.T. north		650	1041.0
1151.4	⛺	Old logging road.		1169	1040.6
1151.5	📷	Views of Duncannon and Susquehanna River.		1177	1040.5
1152.0	Y	Blue blazed Susquehanna Trail, rejoins A.T. south		1150	1040.0
1153.1	♦Y🏕(3)	Side trail to campsite, spring		1160	1038.9
1153.3	♦Y🏕 ⛺(8) ～(🅿	300 feet east to **Clarks Ferry Shelter**, water (pipe spring) 0.1 beyond shelter, tenting, privy. 33.8◀15.6◀8.3◀▶6.7▶24.7▶38.1	N 40 23.536, W 76 59.630	1260	1038.7
1153.9	⊤	Power line.		1314	1038.1
1154.8		Cross pipeline.		1374	1037.2
1157.2	⌒⛺ P(10)🅿	Cross **PA. 225** on footbridge.	N 40 24.698, W 76 55.816	1250	1034.8
1157.4	📷	View.		1278	1034.6
1157.8	⊤	Power line.		1275	1034.2
1159.2	Y📷	Blue blaze east 33 yards to Table Rock View		1200	1032.8
1160.0	◊⛺(16) ～(🅿	**Peters Mountain Shelter**, water is located (0.3) down a steep blue blazed trail of almost 300 rock steps in front of shelter, privy. 22.3◀15.0◀6.7◀▶18.0▶31.4▶35.5	N 40 25.543, W 76 52.765	970	1032.0
1161.0	Y	Blue blazed Victoria Trail to east.		1300	1031.0
1161.6	Y	Pink blazed Whitetail Trail		1310	1030.4
1162.7	📷	Blue blazed trail to east 60 yards to Kinter View.		1320	1029.3
1164.1	Y🅿	Blue blazed Shikellimy Trail east leads (0.9) to parking area.	N 40 26.171, W 76 49.471	1250	1027.9
1166.4	♦	Blue blaze 136 yards to spring.		700	1025.6
1166.7	♦⛺(30)🅿	Cross **PA. 325**, Clark's Valley, Clark Creek	N 40 27.174, W 76 46.603	550	1025.3
1166.8	Y	Blue blazed Water Tank Trail to east.		570	1025.2
1167.1	♦	Spring		620	1024.9
1167.2	♦Y	Red blazed Henry Knauber Trail to east		680	1024.8
1167.7	◊	Cross stream, unreliable.		1052	1024.3
1168.9	◊	Spring, unreliable.		1453	1023.1
1169.4	◊	Spring, unreliable.		1486	1022.6
1169.9	Y	Horse-Shoe Trail (northern end). Horse-Shoe Trail leads to Valley Forge, PA, it is a total of 140 miles. See (www.hstrail.org).		1638	1022.1

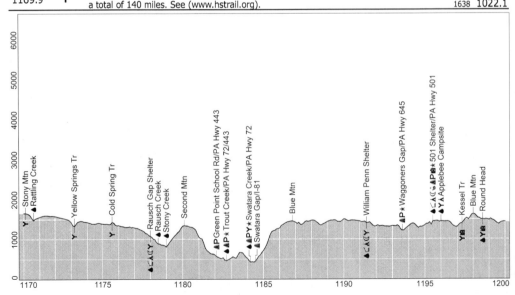

Pennsylvania

NoBo	Features	Description	GPS	Elev	SoBo
1170.0	Y▲	Stony Mountain summit.		1650	1022.0
1170.6	♦	Cross Rattling Run.		1547	1021.4
1173.2	Y	Yellow Springs Trail		1380	1018.8
1173.4	Y	Yellow Springs Village Site, trail register		1450	1018.6
1175.4	Y	Sand Spring Trail		1380	1016.6
1175.6	Y	Cold Spring Trail		1400	1016.4
1178.0	♦Y▲ ⌐(6) ⌣(☾♀	(0.2E) **Rausch Gap Shelter**, water (spring) next to the shelter, tenting, privy. 33.0◄24.7◄18.0◄► 13.4► 17.5►32.6	N 40 29.918, W 76 36.010	980	1014.0
1178.5	♦⌐	Rausch Creek, stone arch bridge		920	1013.5
1178.6	⌐	Raush Gap Village, sign		920	1013.4
1178.9	♦⌐	Haystack Creek, wooden bridge		840	1013.1
1179.7		Second Mountain		1350	1012.3
1182.1	▲P(3)♀	Cross **Greenpoint Schoolhouse Road** then **150 feet to cross PA. 443**	N 40 29.402, W 76 33.062	570	1009.9
1182.7	▲✗▲ ☵▲P♀	Cross **PA. 443**, underpass Green Point, PA., (2.6W) to tenting, restaurant, laundry, shower.	N 40 28.946, W 76 33.012	550	1009.3
1184.1	▲P(5)♀ ★★★★★	Cross **PA. 72**, Swatara Gap.	N 40 28.850, W 76 32.019	480	1007.9

Lickdale, PA (2.1E) See map of Lickdale, PA. Establishments are listed as Jonestown but that is because they have no post office box for Lickdale.

⊨☖⌨⊕ **Days Inn** 717-865-4064. ⊨ $85.15 and up (goes up in summer months), includes continental breakfast, pets $10. Microwave, fridge, ☖ laundry, ⌨ computer available for use, ⊕ free WiFi.

⊨☖⌨⊕ **Fairfield Inn & Suites by Marriott** 717-865-4234. Call for pricing.

⊨☖⌨⊕ **Comfort Inn** 717-865-8080. ⊨ $127 and up, includes breakfast, microwave, fridge, ☖ laundry, ⌨ computer available for use, ⊕ free WiFi, ⚓ pool. Pets $25

⊨▲✗⛺ **Jonestown KOA** 877-865-6411. (www.koa.com/campgrounds/jonestown) M-Su 7 days. Summer 5am-
☖⊕ 9pm. ▲ Tent site $38 and up, ⊨ cabin also available. Pets on leash okay. ☖ Laundry, ⛺ camp store, ✗ snack bar, ⊕ free WiFi.

⛺✗⛽ **Love's Travel Stop with** ✗ **McDonalds, Chesters** 717-861-7390. $10 ♨ showers, ☎ ATM, ⊕ WiFi,
⊕☎▤ all M-Su 24 hrs.

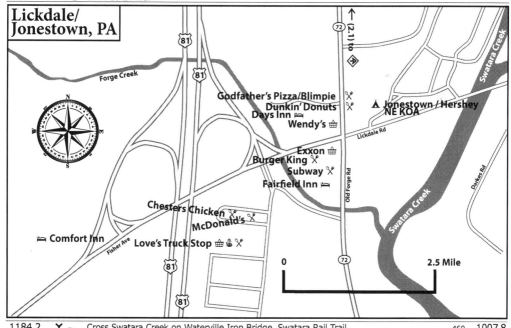

Lickdale/ Jonestown, PA

1184.2	Y⌐	Cross Swatara Creek on Waterville Iron Bridge, Swatara Rail Trail.		460	1007.8
1184.5	▲	Cross **I-81**, underpass		450	1007.5
1184.8	▲	Cross woods road.		710	1007.2
1185.4		Circle of old hearth.		1187	1006.6
1188.7	📷	View of Monroe Valley to east.		1383	1003.3
1190.2		Cross pipe line.		1442	1001.8

NoBo	Features	Description	GPS	Elev	SoBo
1191.4	♦Y((▲ ⊏(16) ⌣♀	Blue Mountain Spring. Water is located 200 yards west on a blue blazed trail off the AT. (0.12E) William Penn Shelter, privy, tenting across AT from shelter. 38.1◄31.4◄13.4◄►4.1►19.2►33.9	N 40 29.736, W 76 24.864	1300	1000.6
1193.6	▲P(10)♀ ★★★★★	Cross PA. 645.	N 40 30.396, W 76 22.608	1250	998.4

Pine Grove, PA. (3.4W) See map of Pine Grove, PA.

⌂♀	**PO** M-F 8:30am-4:30pm, Sa 9am-1pm. 570-345-4955. 103 Snyder Ave. Pine Grove, PA 17963. N 40 33.022, W 76 23.017	
✗	**Original Italian Pizza** 570-345-5432. M closed, Tu-Th 11am-10pm, F 11am-11pm, Sa-Su 11am-10pm. Delivers to 501 shelter.	
✗⌂♙▲	**Pilot Travel Center** 570-345-8800, ♙ laundry, ♙ $12 shower, ☎ ATM. M-Su 24 hours. ✗ **Subway**,	
☎	**Dairy Queen**	
✗	**Pizza Town** 570-345-4041. M 11am-9pm, Tu closed, W-Th 11am-9pm, F-Sa 11am-10pm, Su closed.	
✗	**New China** 570-345-8666. M-Th 11am-10pm, F-Sa 11am-11pm, Sun 11am-10pm.	
🛒	**Bergers Market** 570-345-3663. M-F 8am-9pm, Sa-Su 8am-6pm.	
✗	**Original Italian Pizza, Do's Pizza, Turkey Hill Minit Market**	
♙	**Tri-Valley Pharmacy** 570-345-4966. (www.trivalleypharmacy.com) M-F 9am-7pm, Sa 9am-1pm, Su closed.	
♙	**Action Laundry**	
🚗	**Carlin's AT Shuttle Service** 570-345-0474, 570-516-3447 Commercially insured for your safety. All of PA (MD line to Delaware Water Gap and beyond). Please call between 8 am and 10 pm unless it is an emergency situation. Pickups earlier than 8 am, please call the night before.	

Pine Grove, PA

✗ Buddy's Log Cabin Restaurant

New China ✗

Sweet Arrow Lake Rd

✗ Dunkin' Donuts

Dominick's Pizzeria ✗

443

Swatara Creek

N Tulpehocken St

Upper Swatara Creek

Outwood Rd

Oak Grove Rd

Do's Pizza ✗

Post Office

Tri Valley Pharmacy

Turkey Hill Mini Mart ☎

Action Laundry

VFW ■

E Pottsville St

E MH St

Mill St

Community Pool

Pine Grove Theatre

Swatara Creek

Lower Swatara Creek

81

895

✗ Arby's

443

Suedberg Rd

501

✗ Knights's Inn Pine Grove

McDonald's ✗

General Dollar

(3.5) to 🏕

Comfort Inn

Econo Lodge

Pilot Travel

0   0.5 Mile

Hampton Inn Pine Grove

1195.4	📷	Kimmel Lookout		1330	996.6
1195.5	♦Y▲⊏ ⌣((♙▲ P♀ ★★★★★	Cross PA. 501 (0.1W) **501 Shelter**, water is located at faucet adjacent to house. Tenting, privy, solar shower. No smoking no alcoholic beverages allowed in shelter. Pets allowed but must be leashed. Some Pine Grove restaurants might deliver here. 35.5◄17.5◄4.1◄►15.1►29.8►38.9	Shelter N 40 30.792, W 76 20.784 Parking N 40 30.753, W 76 20.678	1460	996.5

NoBo	Features	Description	GPS	Elev	SoBo

Bethel, PA (4.1E)

	✉🧍	**PO** M-F 8am-12pm & 1:15am-4:30pm, Sa 8:30am-10:30am. 717-933-8305. 10 Legion Dr. Bethel, PA 19507. N 40 28.483, W 76 17.543			
	🏪	Several small convenience stores in the area.			
	💻	**Bethel Library** 717-933-4060. (www.berks.lib.pa.us/sbe) M-TH 10am-8pm, F 8am-6pm, Sa 10am-2pm, Su closed.			
	🐎	**Bethel Animal Hospital** 717-933-4916			
1196.0	♦Y⛺	Blue blazed Pilger Ruh Spring Trail to east to spring which is a water spot dated back to colonial days. Applebee campsite to west.		1450	996.0
1197.4		Kessel Trail to the east.		1486	994.6
1198.5	📷	Unmarked trail to east leads 100 feet to unnamed lookout.		1483	993.5
1198.6	♦Y📷	Blue blaze trail to Round Head and Shower Steps with view.		1500	993.4

1200.7	▲📷	Shikellamy summit and overlook		1390	991.3
1201.1	♦▲🏕	Hertlein campsite, stream south of campsite.		1200	990.9
1201.2		Shuberts Gap		1200	990.8
1201.9		Cross pipe line.		1212	990.1
1204.5	♦	Fort Dietrich Snyder Marker, (0.2W) to spring		1440	987.5
1204.8	▲P(6)🧍 ★★★★★	Cross **PA. 183**, Rentschler Marker.	N 40 31.618, W 76 13.413	1440	987.2
	🏠	(1.6W) **Rock 'n Sole Hostel** Owners Craig and Jody Stine. **Closed for the 2019 season**			

Pine Grove, PA. (4.2W) See Notes at mile 1193.6.

1205.3	P🧍	Cross **Service Road to PA. 183**	N 40 31.516, W 76 13.000	1490	986.7
1206.1	◊	Blazed trail 30 yards east to Black Swatara Spring, unreliable. **No Camping.**		1510	985.9
1207.2	♦	Cross spring.		1536	984.8
1209.9	♦Y	Sand Spring Trail, (0.14E) to walled spring. **No Camping near spring.**		1510	982.1
1210.4	▲	Cross **Game Lands Road**		1592	981.6
1210.6	♦Y▲ ⊏(8) ⌣☾🧍	Blue blaze trail leads (0.2) east to water (Yeich Spring), continue on for another (0.1) to **Eagle's Nest Shelter**, spring on trail to shelter, tenting, privy. 32.6◄19.2◄15.1◄►14.7►23.8►31.2	N 40 32.963, W 76 09.146	1510	981.4
1212.5	▲	Cross **Shartlesville Cross–Mountain Road**		1450	979.5
1214.0	▲	Intersects with **State Game Lands Road** for about 100 yards.		1492	978.0
1215.2	◊	Unmarked Phillip's Canyon Spring trail is located east down a steep descent 135 yards in a stone enclosure, unreliable.		1500	976.8
1215.9	▲	Diagonally cross **State Game Lands Road**.		1330	976.1
1216.1	Y	Marshall's Path		1370	975.9
1216.7	Y📷	Auburn Lookout on trail to the east.		1400	975.3
1217.0	▲	Cross **State Game Lands Road**.		1415	975.0
1217.8		Cross pine line.		1359	974.2
1218.2		Cross pipe line.		1275	973.8
1219.0	Y✕〰	Intersection of Broad Street, Cross Schuylkill River on bridge.		420	973.0

NoBo	Features	Description	GPS	Elev	SoBo
1219.1	⌒P⚲	Cross Schuylkill River on bridge.	N 40 34.762, W 76 01.655	400	972.9
1219.2	▲P(4)⚲ ★★★★★	Intersection with **Penn Street**. **Port Clinton, PA. See map of Port Clinton, PA.**	N 40 34.703, W 76 01.436	400	972.8

⌂⚲   **PO** M-F 12:30am-4:30pm, Sa 8am-11pm. 610-562-3787. 6 Broad St. PA. Port Clinton, 19549. N 40 34.824, W 76 01.464

🛏✗◈⛺   **Port Clinton Hotel** 610-562-3354. (www.portclintonhotel.net)
◈ AT Passport.
🛏 Limited room, call for prices. $10 deposit for room key and towel. ⛺ Laundry. ✗ Dining M- closed, Tu-Th 11am-9om, F-Sa 11am-10pm, Su 11am-9pm. Please shower before dine. Credit cards accepted.

🛏⛺   **Union House B&B** 610-562-3155. 610-562-4076. $65 and up. Open F-Su.

✗📶   **3C's Family Restaurant** 610-562-5925. 📶 Free WiFi. M-F 5am-2pm, Sa-Su 6am-2pm.

🛒◈🏧   **The Peanut Shop** 610-562-0610.
◈ AT Passport location.
Su-F 10am-6pm, Sa 10am-8pm, Su 10am-6pm. 🛒 Sodas, candy, dried fruit, trail mixes, 🏧 ATM.

🔥▲☾   (0.2W) on Penn Street to **Pavilion** No alcohol or drugs. ▲ Tenting max 2 nights, no car camping. 🔥 Water can be obtained from a spigot outside the Port Clinton Hotel. Permission required for more than two nights, call LaVerne Sterner 570-366-0489.

✗◈🚐   **Port Clinton Barber** Shop 484-336-8516.
◈ AT Passport location.
Hikers are welcome to hang out. Coffee, cookies, and phone charging available. Dog friendly. 🚐 Shuttle available. Lots of music. M-F 8-5, Sa 8am-2 pm, Su closed.

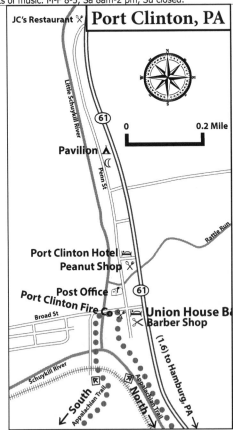

| 1219.9 | ▲P(10) ★★★★★ | Cross **PA. 61, Port Clinton Avenue** , underpass. | | 490 | 972.1 |

Hamburg, PA 19526 (1.6E) See map of Hamburg, PA.

⌂⚲   **PO** M-F 9am-5pm, Sa 9am-12pm. 610-562-7812. 50 N 3rd St. Hamburg, PA 19526. N 40 33.363, W 75 59.077

🛏✗⛺📶   **Microtel Inn** 610-562-4234. Includes contintental breakfast.
✉   ✉ Mail for guest only with: 100 Industrial Drive, Hamburg, PA 19526

🚶   **Cabela's** 610-929-7000, M-F 9am-10pm, Sa 8am-10pm, Su 9am-9pm. Lots of hiking items, canister fuel. They will pickup from trail head if staff is available.

NoBo Features		Description	GPS	Elev SoBo

Walmart Superstore 484-668-4001. M-Su 24 hours, with grocery and ✗ Subway M-Su 7am-9pm.

Many restaurants in area, **Pizza Hut, Red Robin, Logan's Steakhouse, Five Guys Burgers, Taco Bell/Long John Silver, Cracker Barrel.**

Rite Aid 610-562-9454, M-Su am-10pm. Pharmacy M-F 8am-9pm, Sa 8am-6pm, Su 9am-5pm.

Hamburg Coin Laundry 610-562-4890

Hamburg Animal Hospital 610-562-5000 (www.hamburganimalhospital.com) M-Th 9am-7pm, F 9am-5pm, Sa 9am-11am, Su closed.

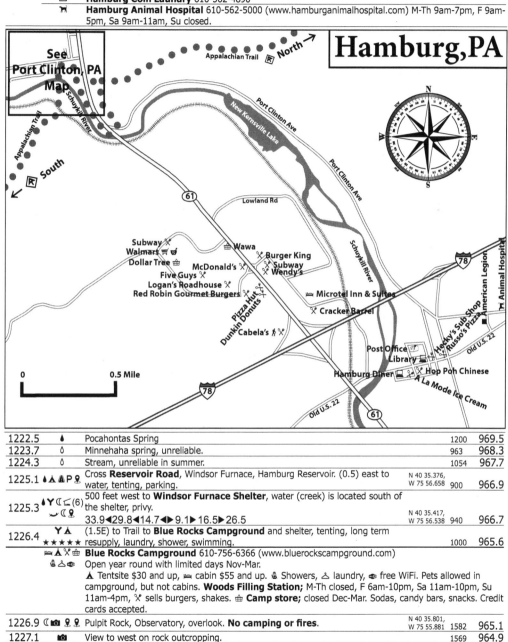

Hamburg, PA

1222.5	◆	Pocahontas Spring		1200	969.5
1223.7	◊	Minnehaha spring, unreliable.		963	968.3
1224.3	◊	Stream, unreliable in summer.		1054	967.7
1225.1	◆▲⚑P⚐	Cross **Reservoir Road**, Windsor Furnace, Hamburg Reservoir. (0.5) east to water, tenting, parking.	N 40 35.376, W 75 56.658	900	966.9
1225.3	◆Y℄(6) ⌣℄	500 feet west to **Windsor Furnace Shelter**, water (creek) is located south of the shelter, privy. 33.9◄29.8◄14.7◄▶9.1▶16.5▶26.5	N 40 35.417, W 75 56.538	940	966.7
1226.4	Y▲ ★★★★★	(1.5E) to Trail to **Blue Rocks Campground** and shelter, tenting, long term resupply, laundry, shower, swimming.		1000	965.6
	⌂▲✗⌂ 🛁⌂🛜	**Blue Rocks Campground** 610-756-6366 (www.bluerockscampground.com) Open year round with limited days Nov-Mar. ▲ Tentsite $30 and up, ⌂ cabin $55 and up. 🛁 Showers, ⌂ laundry, 🛜 free WiFi. Pets allowed in campground, but not cabins. **Woods Filling Station;** M-Th closed, F 6am-10pm, Sa 11am-10pm, Su 11am-4pm, ✗ sells burgers, shakes. ⌂ **Camp store;** closed Dec-Mar. Sodas, candy bars, snacks. Credit cards accepted.			
1226.9	℄📷⚐⚐	Pulpit Rock, Observatory, overlook. **No camping or fires.**	N 40 35.801, W 75 55.881	1582	965.1
1227.1	📷	View to west on rock outcropping.		1569	964.9
1228.7	Y▲ ★★★★★	Side trail leads (1.5) east to **Blue Rocks Campground** and shelter, tenting, long term resupply, laundry, shower, swimming. **See Notes at mile 1226.4.**		1150	963.3
1229.1	Y📷	Trail to east 80 yards leads to The Pinnacle, overlook		1615	962.9

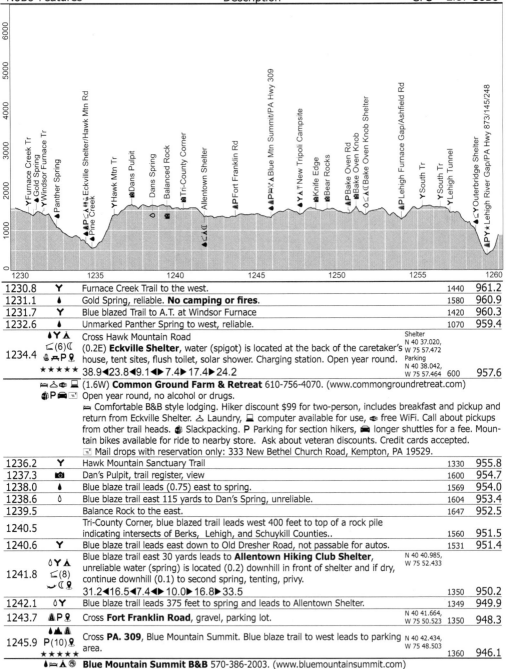

1230.8	Y	Furnace Creek Trail to the west.		1440	961.2
1231.1	♦	Gold Spring, reliable. **No camping or fires**.		1580	960.9
1231.7	Y	Blue blazed Trail to A.T. at Windsor Furnace		1420	960.3
1232.6	♦	Unmarked Panther Spring to west, reliable.		1070	959.4
1234.4	♦Y⚑ ⊏(6)☾ ⬟♦P⚲ ★★★★★	Cross Hawk Mountain Road (0.2E) **Eckville Shelter**, water (spigot) is located at the back of the caretaker's house, tent sites, flush toilet, solar shower. Charging station. Open year round. 38.9◄23.8◄9.1◄▶ 7.4▶ 17.4▶ 24.2	Shelter N 40 37.020, W 75 57.472 Parking N 40 38.042, W 75 57.464	600	957.6
	🛏⛺☕🖥 🍴P🚗🖃	(1.6W) **Common Ground Farm & Retreat** 610-756-4070. (www.commongroundretreat.com) Open year round, no alcohol or drugs. 🛏 Comfortable B&B style lodging. Hiker discount $99 for two-person, includes breakfast and pickup and return from Eckville Shelter. ⛺ Laundry, 🖥 computer available for use, ☕ free WiFi. Call about pickups from other trail heads. 🍴 Slackpacking. P Parking for section hikers, 🚗 longer shuttles for a fee. Mountain bikes available for ride to nearby store. Ask about veteran discounts. Credit cards accepted. 🖃 Mail drops with reservation only: 333 New Bethel Church Road, Kempton, PA 19529.			
1236.2	Y	Hawk Mountain Sanctuary Trail		1330	955.8
1237.3	📷	Dan's Pulpit, trail register, view		1600	954.7
1238.0	♦	Blue blaze trail leads (0.75) east to spring.		1569	954.0
1238.6	◊	Blue blaze trail east 115 yards to Dan's Spring, unreliable.		1604	953.4
1239.5		Balance Rock to the east.		1647	952.5
1240.5		Tri-County Corner, blue blazed trail leads west 400 feet to top of a rock pile indicating intersects of Berks, Lehigh, and Schuykill Counties..		1560	951.5
1240.6	Y	Blue blaze trail leads east down to Old Dresher Road, not passable for autos.		1531	951.4
1241.8	◊Y⚑ ⊏(8) ⌣☾⚲	Blue blaze trail east 30 yards leads to **Allentown Hiking Club Shelter**, unreliable water (spring) is located (0.2) downhill in front of shelter and if dry, continue downhill (0.1) to second spring, tenting, privy. 31.2◄16.5◄7.4◄▶ 10.0▶ 16.8▶ 33.5	N 40 40.985, W 75 52.433	1350	950.2
1242.1	◊Y	Blue blaze trail leads 375 feet to spring and leads to Allentown Shelter.		1349	949.9
1243.7	▲P⚲	Cross **Fort Franklin Road**, gravel, parking lot.	N 40 41.664, W 75 50.523	1350	948.3
1245.9	♦▲▲ P(10)⚲ ★★★★★	Cross **PA. 309**, Blue Mountain Summit. Blue blaze trail to west leads to parking area.	N 40 42.434, W 75 48.503	1360	946.1
	♦🛏⚑⊛ 🍴🚗🖃	**Blue Mountain Summit B&B** 570-386-2003. (www.bluemountainsummit.com) Pending new owners in 2018. Stay tuned data may change. Open 7 days by appointment. ⊛ No pets. 🛏 $95–$125D, includes breakfast. ♦ Water from outside spigot at southwest corner. Please be respectful of non-hiking guests at the B&B and restaurant. Please don't loiter in front or hang clothes out to dry. ▲ Camping with permission, no fires. 🚗 Ask about parking and shuttles. 🍴 **Restaurant;** M-W closed, Th 12pm-9pm, F 12pm-10pm, Sa 12pm-9pm, Su 12pm-8pm. All major credit cards accepted. 🖃 Mail drops for guests only (call first): 2520 W Penn Pike, Andreas, PA 18211.			

NoBo	Features	Description	GPS	Elev	SoBo
1247.7	♦Y▲⊤	Blue blaze trail west (0.2) leads to New Tripoli campsite, spring, power line.		1400	944.3
1248.7	📷	Knife Edge " The Cliffs", view		1525	943.3
1249.4	📷	Blue blaze west to Bear Rocks with a little difficulty but 360 degree view.		1525	942.6
1250.8	▲P(30)⚲	Cross State Game Lands parking lot and **Bake Oven Knob Road**, dirt road.	N 40 44.681, W 75 44.306	1450	941.2
1251.2		Bake Oven Knob		1560	940.8
1251.8	◊▲(3) ⌐(6) ⌣(⚲	**Bake Oven Knob Shelter**, water is located at trail in front of shelter leads downhill to multiple water sources and more reliable farther down but all sources are unreliable in dry weather, privy. Campsites are located south side below the AT. 26.5◄17.4◄10.0◄►6.8►23.5►37.2	N 40 45.247, W 75 43.644	1380	940.2
1254.2	♦▲P⚲	Cross **Ashfield Road** in Lehigh Furnace Gap, Ashfield, PA., radio tower, (0.7E) to spring. Parking is under the power lines.	N 40 46.170, W 75 41.656	1320	937.8
1255.3	Y	South Trail (southern jct.)		1596	936.7
1256.4	Y	South Trail (northern jct.)		1571	935.6
1257.0	Y	North Trail (southern jct.), Lehigh Valley Tunnel of PA. Turnpike is underneath A.T.		1570	935.0
1258.5	Y	North Trail		1550	933.5
1258.6	◄⌐(6) ⌣⚲	**George W. Outerbridge Shelter**, water (piped spring) is located north 150 yards on the AT north of the shelter. **The surrounding area suffers from heavy-metal contamination from the zinc plant at Palmerton.** 24.2◄16.8◄6.8◄► 16.7►30.4►61.6	N 40 46.951, W 75 37.079	1000	933.4
1259.0	⊤📷	Power lines with view.		557	933.0
1259.2	⌐▲P(8)⚲	Intersection with **PA. 873, Lehigh River Bridge (west end)**, Lehigh Gap	N 40 46.873, W 75 36.521	380	932.8

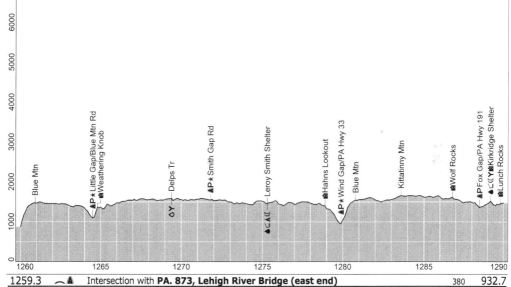

| 1259.3 | ⌐▲ | Intersection with **PA. 873, Lehigh River Bridge (east end)** | | 380 | 932.7 |

Slatington, PA. (2.0E) See map of Slatington, PA.

	🏪⚲	**PO** M-F 8:30am - 11:00am, 1:30pm - 4:00pm, Sat 8:30am - 11:30am, Sun Closed. 610-767-2182. 605 Main St. Slatington, PA 18080. N 40 45.088, W 75 36.755
	✚	**Bechtel's Pharmacy** 610-767-4121. (www.bechtelspharmacyinc.com) Open M-F 9am-8pm, Su 9am-2pm, Su closed.
	💻	**Slatington Library** 610-767-6461. (www.slatelibrary.com) M 9am-7pm, Tu 9am-3pm, W 9am-7-m, Th closed, F 9am-5pm, Sa 8am-2pm, Su closed.

| 1259.5 | ▲YP(3) ⚲ ★★★★★ | Cross **PA. 145/248**. | N 40 46.873, W 75 36.521 | 380 | 932.5 |

Walnutport, PA (2.0E) See map of Walnutport, PA.

	🏪⚲	**PO** M-F 8:30am-5pm, Sa 8:30am-12pm. 610-767-2182. 249 Lehigh Gap St. Walnutport, PA 18088. N 40 45.240, W 75 35.518
	🏬✚	**Kmart** 610-767-1812, M-Su 8am-10pm. ✚ **Pharmacy** 610-767-2541. M-F 9am-9pm, Sa 9am-5pm, Su 10am-4pm.
	✗	**Pizza Hut, Subway, Ritas, Burger King, Great Wall, Mamma's, Pizza**
	⛨	**St Luke's Family Practice Center** 610-628-8922.

Rite Aid 610-767-9595. M-Su 8am-10pm, Su 9am-8pm. **Pharmacy** M-F 9am-9pm, Sa 9am-6pm, Su 9am-5pm.

Blue Ridge Veterinary Clinic 610-767-4896. (www.blueridgeveterinary.com) M-W 9am-7pm, Th 9am-6pm, F 8:30am-5:30pm, Sa 9am-12pm, Su closed. Call first.

Palmerton, PA 18071 (1.5W) See map of Palmerton, PA.

PO M-F 8:30am-5pm, Sa 8:30am-12pm. 610-826-2286. 128 Delaware Ave Frnt. Palmerton, 18071. N 40 47.959, W 75 36.891

Bert's Restaurant 610-826-9921.
◈ AT Passport location.
M-T 7am-2pm, W-Th 7am-8pm, F-Sa 7am-8:30pm, Su 8am-8pm. ☏ WiFi in restaurant, ⛺ ask about overnight stay, ⚿ shower $5.

Palmerton Hotel Restaurant 610-826-5454. (www.palmertonhotel.com) Dining M-Sa 11am-10pm, Su closed.

Country Harvest 610-824-3663. (www.countryharvestmarkets.com) M-Su 8am-9pm. ☎ ATM.

Tony's Pizzeria 610-826-6161. M-Su 11am-10:30pm. Serves lunch and dinner.

Joe's Place 610-826-3730. Serves luch and dinner, deli sandwiches. M-Su 11am-8pm.

(3.5W) Little Gap Animal Hospital 610-826-2793. (www.littlegapanimalhospital.com)

24/7 Laundry 484-547-9307. Coin, 24 hours.

Blue Mountain Family Medicine 610-826-5110.

Jason "SoulFlute" 484-341-3356 Palmertonarea shuttles. ⏚ Slackpacks Port Clinton to DWG. If you call and can not reach please send text message.

Brenda 484-725-9396 Call for pricing. Shuttles ranging from local to bus terminals and airports.

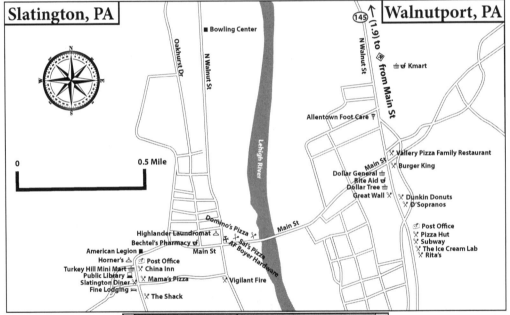

Palmerton, PA

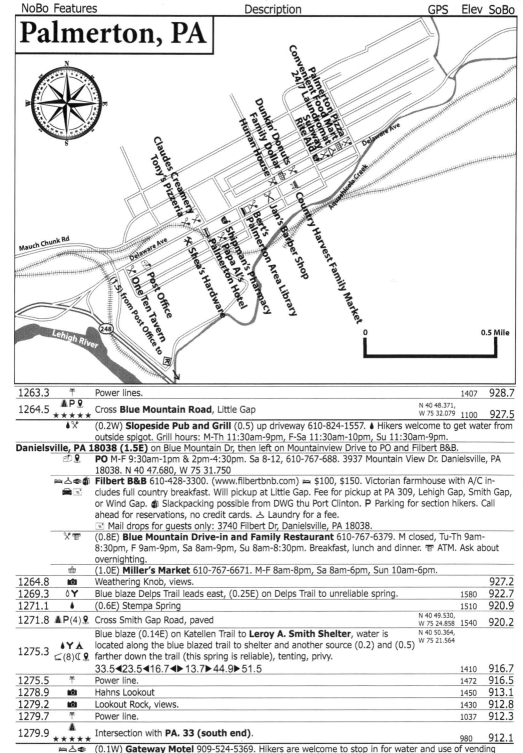

NoBo		Description	GPS	Elev	SoBo
1263.3	⊤	Power lines.		1407	928.7
1264.5	▲P⚲ ★★★★★	Cross **Blue Mountain Road**, Little Gap	N 40 48.371, W 75 32.079	1100	927.5
	♦✕	(0.2W) **Slopeside Pub and Grill** (0.5) up driveway 610-824-1557. ♦ Hikers welcome to get water from outside spigot. Grill hours: M-Th 11:30am-9pm, F-Sa 11:30am-10pm, Su 11:30am-9pm.			

Danielsville, PA 18038 (1.5E) on Blue Mountain Dr, then left on Mountainview Drive to PO and Filbert B&B.

	⊡⚲	**PO** M-F 9:30am-1pm & 2pm-4:30pm. Sa 8-12, 610-767-688. 3937 Mountain View Dr. Danielsville, PA 18038. N 40 47.680, W 75 31.750			
	⇎⚲⊜⏚ ⇌⊡	**Filbert B&B** 610-428-3300. (www.filbertbnb.com) ⇌ $100, $150. Victorian farmhouse with A/C includes full country breakfast. Will pickup at Little Gap. Fee for pickup at PA 309, Lehigh Gap, Smith Gap, or Wind Gap. ⏚ Slackpacking possible from DWG thu Port Clinton. **P** Parking for section hikers. Call ahead for reservations, no credit cards. ⚹ Laundry for a fee. ⊡ Mail drops for guests only: 3740 Filbert Dr, Danielsville, PA 18038.			
	✕⏚	(0.8E) **Blue Mountain Drive-in and Family Restaurant** 610-767-6379. M closed, Tu-Th 9am-8:30pm, F 9am-9pm, Sa 8am-9pm, Su 8am-8:30pm. Breakfast, lunch and dinner. ⏚ ATM. Ask about overnighting.			
	⌂	(1.0E) **Miller's Market** 610-767-6671. M-F 8am-8pm, Sa 8am-6pm, Sun 10am-6pm.			
1264.8	◙	Weathering Knob, views.			927.2
1269.3	◊Y	Blue blaze Delps Trail leads east, (0.25E) on Delps Trail to unreliable spring.		1580	922.7
1271.1	♦	(0.6E) Stempa Spring		1510	920.9
1271.8	▲P(4)⚲	Cross Smith Gap Road, paved	N 40 49.530, W 75 24.858	1540	920.2
1275.3	♦Y⚠ ⊏(8)☾⚲	Blue blaze (0.14E) on Katellen Trail to **Leroy A. Smith Shelter**, water is located along the blue blazed trail to shelter and another source (0.2) and (0.5) farther down the trail (this spring is reliable), tenting, privy. 33.5◀23.5◀16.7◀▶13.7▶44.9▶51.5	N 40 50.364, W 75 21.564	1410	916.7
1275.5	⊤	Power line.		1472	916.5
1278.9	◙	Hahns Lookout		1450	913.1
1279.2	◙	Lookout Rock, views.		1430	912.8
1279.7	⊤	Power line.		1037	912.3
1279.9	▲ ★★★★★	Intersection with **PA. 33 (south end)**.		980	912.1
	⇎⚹⊜	(0.1W) **Gateway Motel** 909-524-5369. Hikers are welcome to stop in for water and use of vending machine.			
	🐾	(4W) **Creature Comforts** 570-992-0400. (www.creaturecomfortsvet.net) M-Su 24 hours.			

Wind Gap, PA 18091 (1.0E) See map of Wind Gap, PA.

⊡ 🏕 **PO** M–F 8:30am–5pm, Sa 8:30am–12pm, 610-863-6206. 138 N Broadway. Wind Gap, PA 18091. N 40 51.053, W 75 17.512

🛏🛎🚗 **Travel Inn** 717-885-3101 $59.99D weekdays, $69.99D weekends. Room for 4 $69.99 weekdays, $79.99 weekends.

🛏🚗 **Red Carpet Inn** 610-863-7782 Stay includes continental breakfast.

🛒 **Giant Food Store** M-Su 24 hours. Offers deli and salad bar.

🛒🛍 **K-Mart** M-Sa 8am-10pm, Su 8am-9pm. 🛍 **Pharmacy** M-F 8am-8pm, Sa 9am-5pm, Su closed.

✕ **Beer Stein** 610-863-8338. (www.thebeerstein.net) M-Tu 3pm-2am, W-Su 11am-2am. Serves lunch and dinner.

✕ **J&R's Smokehouse** 610-863-6162. Serves lunch and dinner. M-4pm-9:30pm, Tu-Th 11am-9:30pm, F-Sa 12pm-10pm, Su 9am-9pm.

✕ **Sal's Pizza** 610-863-7565, delivers. M-W 11am-10pm, Sa 11am-11pm, Su 11am-10pm.

✕ **Hong Kong Chinese** 610-863-9309. Lunch and dinner buffet. M-Su 11am-10:30pm.

🛍 **CVS** 610-863-5341. M-Su 8am-9m. **Pharmacy** M-F 8am-8pm, Sa 9am-6pm, Su pam-5pm.

⚕ **Priority Care** 610-654-5454. Walk- n clinic M-F 8am-8pm, Sa 10am-5pm, Su 10am-4pm.

⚕ **Slate Belt Family Practice** 610-863-3019. (www.slatebeltfamilypractice.com) M-Tu 8am-8pm, W 8am-1pm & 4pm-7pm, Th 8am-8pm, F 8am-1pm & 4pm-7pm, Sa 9am-12pm, Su closed.

🚗 **WGM Taxi** 570-223-9289

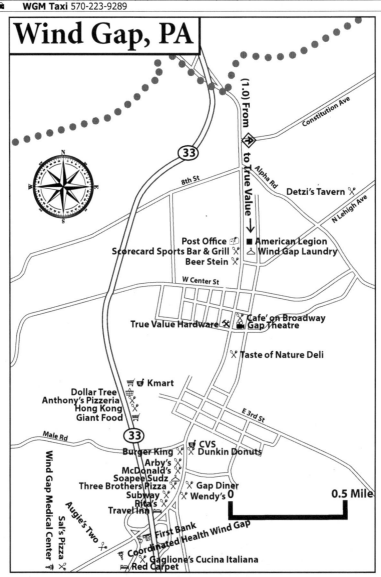

Pennsylvania

NoBo	Features	Description	GPS	Elev	SoBo
1280.0	▲P♀	Intersection with **PA. 33 (north end)**.	N 40 51.642, W 75 17.561	1571	912.0
1282.0	▲	Cross Private road to Blue Mountain Water Company.		1571	910.0
1286.3	♦Y	Wolf Rocks Bypass Trail (south end), signed spring		1550	905.7
1286.8	📷	Wolf Rocks		1620	905.2
1287.0	Y🕆	Wolf Rocks Bypass Trail (north end). Power line.		1510	905.0
1288.4	▲P(6)♀	Cross **PA. 191**, Fox Gap, small parking lot.	N 40 56.125, W 75 11.819	1400	903.6
1288.8	Y	Orange blazed The Great Wall Trail descends (0.8) down the mountain.		1419	903.2
1289.0	♦Y⊏(8) ⌣((📷♀	Blue blazed trail (south end) to **Kirkridge Shelter**, water is located on outside tap to rear of shelter before the Kirkridge Retreat facility parking lot, privy. Views. 37.2◄30.4◄13.7◄►31.2►37.8►43.6	N 40 56.205, W 75 11.186	1500	903.0
1289.1	Y	Blue blazed trail (North end) to Kirkridge Shelter, **see notes above**.		1495	902.9
1289.2	📷	Nelson's Overlook, good views.		1527	902.8
1289.8	📷	Lunch Rock located 50 feet east, view.		1482	902.2

NoBo	Features	Description	GPS	Elev	SoBo
1290.7	🕆	Power line.		1349	901.3
1290.9	▲	Cross Totts Gap, gravel road		1300	901.1
1292.9	▲	Mt. Minsi, summit		1461	899.1
1293.2	📷	Panoramic view of Delaware Water Gap.		1339	898.8
1293.9	Y📷	Side trail east to Lookout Rock, view of Delaware River and Delaware Water Gap.		800	898.1
1294.1	♦	Cross Eureka Creek.		733	897.9
1294.7	📷	Council Rock, view		600	897.3
1295.0	♦	Pass Lake Lenape. A blue blaze side trail east reconnects to the AT at (0.8) and (15.0).		492	897.0
1295.2	P♀	Pass hiker parking lot.	N 40 58.789, W 75 08.524	510	896.8
1295.3	▲	Intersection of **Lake Road and Mountain Road**.		457	896.7
1295.4	▲ ★★★★★	Intersection with **PA. 611 and Delaware Ave**. **See map of Delaware Water Gap, PA**.		400	896.6

⌂♀ **PO** M-F 8:30am-12pm, & 1pm-4:45pm, Sa 8:30am-11:30pm. 570-476-0304. 12 Shepard Ave. Delaware Water Gap, PA 18327. N 40 59.014, W 75 08.565

⌂ ◈♿ **Church of the Mountain Hiker Center** 862-268-1120, 570-476-0345, 570-992-3934. (www.churchofthemountain.org)
◈ AT Passport location.
⌂ Bunkroom, ♨ showers, ▲ overflow tenting. Donations encouraged. 2 night maximum. No laundry. There is a phone listing of people who can help posted in the hostel. Cars may not be parked on the property at any time. Mail drops are not accepted but the post office is next door.

🛏◉♨⛟ **Pocono Inn** 570-476-0000. (www.poconoinnwg.com)
◉ No pets. 🛏 $75 and up, higher on weekends. ♨ Coin laundry, ⛟ free WiFi.

🛏◉✗ **Deer Head Inn** 570-424-2000. (www.deerheadinn.com)
◉ No pets. 🛏 $120 and up. ✗ Restaurant and lounge.

NoBo	Features	Description	GPS	Elev	SoBo

| | ✗ 🏪 | **Village Farmer & Bakery** 570-476-9440. (www.villagefarmerbakery.com) M-SU 8am-8pm. ✗ Serves a hot dog and slice of pie $2.95. Breakfast sandwiches, salads, sandwiches. Credit card minimum $10. | | | |
| | ✗ | **Doughboy's Pizza** 570-421-1900. (www.doughboysofthepoconos.com) M-Th 11am-11pm, F-Sa 11am-11pm, Su 11am-9pm. | | | |
| | 🏃�
🚗 | **Edge of the Woods Outfitters** 570-421-6681. (www.edgeofthewoodsoutfitters.com/theshop.html) Full line of gear, 🏪 carries a large selection of hiker trail food, backpacking meals, ultralight back pack gear, and footwear. 🔥 Alcohol and Coleman by the ounce. 🚐 Shuttles from Little Gap to Bear Mtn by advance reservation only. Open 7 days, Memorial - Labor Day.
✉ Mail drops: (FedEx/UPS only) 110 Main St, Delaware Water Gap, PA 18327. USPS will be held at the post office. | | | |
| | 🏃🚗 | **Water Gap Adventures** 570-424-8533. (www.adventuresport.com) Apr-Oct. | | | |

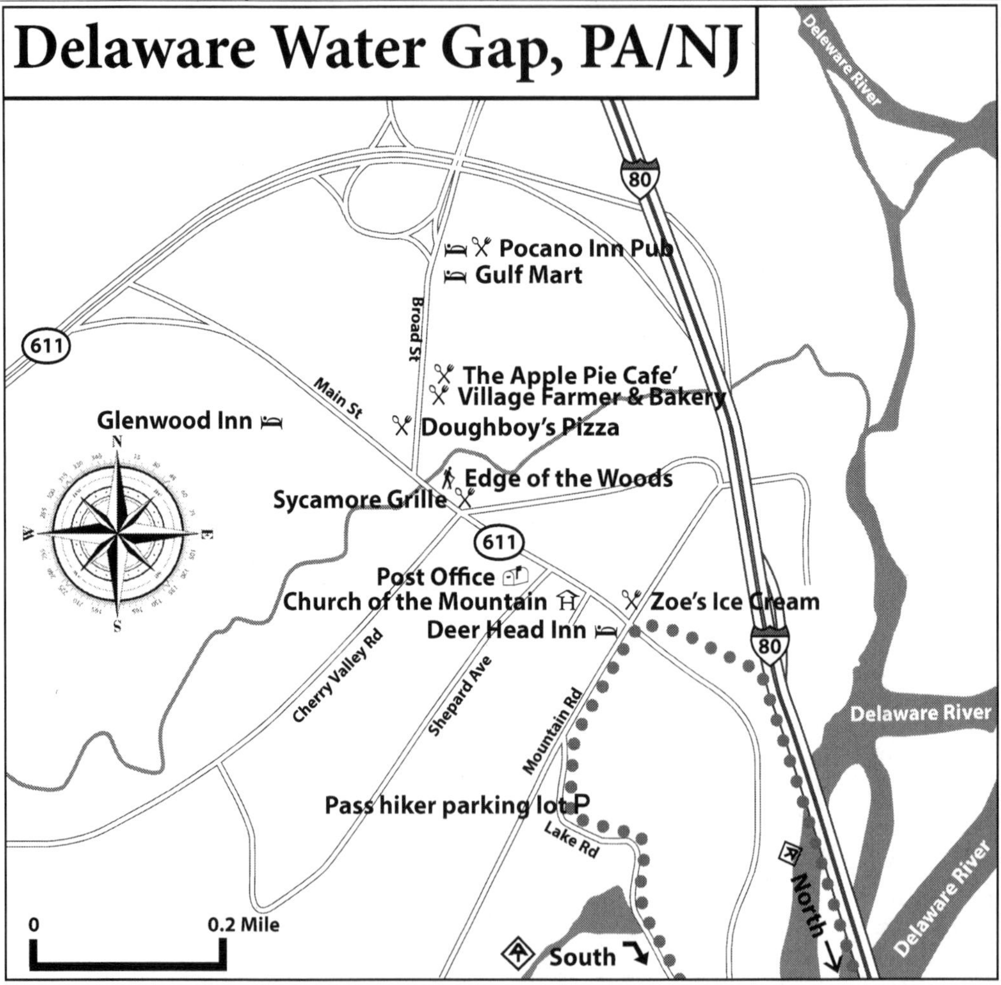

Delaware Water Gap, PA/NJ

| 1295.6 | ⌢ State Line | Cross Delaware River Bridge (west end), Pennsylvania–New Jersey State Line | | 350 | 896.4 |
| 1295.7 | ⌢ State Line | Cross Delaware River Bridge (east end), Pennsylvania–New Jersey State Line | | 350 | 896.3 |
| 1296.6 | 💧🕐◈🏃🏻
🍴🚐🅿🍴 | Delaware Water Gap National Recreation Area Kittatinny Point Visitors Center. ◈ AT Passport location. | N 40 58.215, W 75 07.712 | 350 | 895.4 |
1297.0	▲	Cross **under I-80**, underpass		350	895.0
1297.1	💧▲🅿🍴	Dunnfield Creek Natural Area, water pump at northern end of parking area	N 40 58.288, W 75 07.532	350	894.9
1297.5	💧Y	Blue blazed Blue Dot Trail leads (1.8) east to the summit of Mt. Tammany overlooking Delaware Water Gap. Green blazed Dunnfield Hollow Trail to Dunnfield, Creek Falls, (0.25E) to water.		350	894.5
1298.6	💧Y	Red blazed Holly Springs Trail (0.2E) to water. Yellow blazed Beulah Trail west.		950	893.4

NoBo	Features	Description	GPS	Elev	SoBo
1299.6	♦Y▲🛁	Blue blazed Douglas Trail to Backpacker campsite. (1.7) west to tenting, water and shower		1300	892.4
1300.2	▲	Pass Backpacker Site, no water. Blue blaze Douglas Trail west.		1353	891.8
1300.8	♦	Sunfish Pond, glacial pond, **NO CAMPING**		1382	891.2
1301.1	♦	Outlet stream of Sunfish Pond. Unmarked Sunfish Drainage Trail to the west.		1387	890.9
1301.5	Y	Turquoise Trail to the east.		1445	890.5
1301.6	♦Y	Orange blazed Garvey Spring Trail west and leads 600 feet to spring.		1400	890.4
1302.5	♦	Cross brook.		1454	889.5
1303.2	⅂	Power line.		1568	888.8
1303.3	📷	Large pile of rocks, views on both sides of trail.		1579	888.7
1303.7	♦Y	Blue on White, Kaiser Road Trail leads east (0.3) to spring.		1445	888.3
1304.0	YP	Blue on White, Kaiser Road Trail leads west (1.5) to Old Mine Road and parking lot.		1419	888.0
1304.4	📷	Open rocks, view.		1480	887.6
1305.3	▲	Open area to east can be used for camping.		1325	886.7
1305.9	♦▲P ★★★★★	Cross **Camp Road**. Just south of road crossing trail crosses Yards Creek water source and red blazed Coppermines Trail on west side of AT. **AMC Mohican Outdoor Center**		1150	886.1
	♦Y⌂▲ ◈✕🍴📶 📧	(0.3W) **Mohican Outdoor Center** 908-362-5670. (www.outdoors.org/lodging/mohican) ◈ AT Passport location. ⌂ Thru-hiker rates $30 PP bunk room includes electricity, showers, full kitchen and access to WiFi typically. ▲ Tenting with access to showers, bear boxes, and 📶 WiFi, $10 PP, price subject to change, call ahead and inquire. Towel rental is $3. 🛁 Shower for non-guests are $5 PP. Sheets and blankets available for rent at varying rates. 🐕 If you are hiking with a dog, please call ahead. Thru-hiker's dogs only allowed overnight. All legitimate ADA-compliant Service Dogs welcome anytime. Campfires only in designated areas. ♦ Water available at the lodge or at spigot near the garage across the street. ⚗ IsoPro fuel canisters, Coleman and Alcohol fuel by the ounce as well as camp supplies, 🏪 Good-To-Go Dried Meals, trekking poles, rain gear, etc. ✕ The Mohican Outdoor Center Deli is open and we are ready to satiate your Hiker Hunger! We have sandwiches, ice cream, breakfast all day AND an exclusive Hiker Hunger menu with high calorie meal options, simply ask at the front desk. Welcome center and camp store hours April- October Su-Th 8am-7pm, F 8am-9pm, Sa 8am-8pm.Our off-season hours are Nov-Apr Su-Th 9am-5pm, F 9am-7pm, Sa 9am-6pm. After hours arrivals, please call ahead for lodging. 📧 Mail drops: c/o AMC Mohican Outdoor Center 50 Camp Mohican Rd, Blairstown, NJ 07825. Please include approximate date of arrival.			
1308.3	▲⌘♀	Catfish Fire Tower, 360 degree views.	N 41 02.855, W 74 58.347	1565	883.7
1308.6	▲	Intersects with fire tower road.		1485	883.4
1308.9	♦▲	Rattlesnake Spring 50 feet west, dirt road.		1260	883.1
1309.3	▲♦▲ P(6)♀	Cross **Millbrook–Blairstown Road/County Road 602**, (1.1W) to water, park overnight at your own risk.	N 41 03.564, W 74 57.808	1260	882.7
1309.8	⌒	Cross bridge over outlet of beaver pond.		1258	882.2
1310.1	⅂📷	Powerline, view.		1451	881.9
1310.2	Y📷	Side trail east leads to viewpoint.		1463	881.8
1311.0	Y	Red and white blaze trail descends east over private property to Camp No-Bo-Bo-Sco (boy scout camp).		1458	881.0
1311.6	▲	Intersects with dirt road.		1486	880.4
1312.9	▲📷	Unmarked woods road leads east 125 feet to view.		1457	879.1
1313.2	▲P(8)♀	Blue **Mountain Lakes Road (Flatbrookville-Stillwater Road)**	N 41 05.387, W 74 54.689	1350	878.8
1314.5		Pass swamp to east of trail.		1407	877.5
1315.0	♦Y📷P♀	Crater Lake Trail leads east 150 feet to view overlooking Crater Lake, (0.3E) to water	N 41 06.563, W 74 53.514	1560	877.0
1315.3	Y	Hemlock Pond Trail west (0.4) to Hemlock Pond.		1470	876.7
1316.1	♦Y⚒	Buttermilk Falls Trail leads west descending to Buttermilk Falls, (1.5) west on trail to water, dependable.		1560	875.9
1317.1	Y	Unmarked trail to west leads to view from slanted rock slabs.		1499	874.9
1317.6	♦⌒Y	Cross stream on logs. Just north of stream is a blue blazed trail east to water.		1291	874.4
1318.0	▲▲📷	Rattlesnake Mountain summit, open ledges		1492	874.0
1318.3	♦	Cross stream on rocks.		1405	873.7
1318.8	▲	Intersects with dirt road.		1483	873.2
1319.5	📷	Reach crest of ridge with good views.		1441	872.5

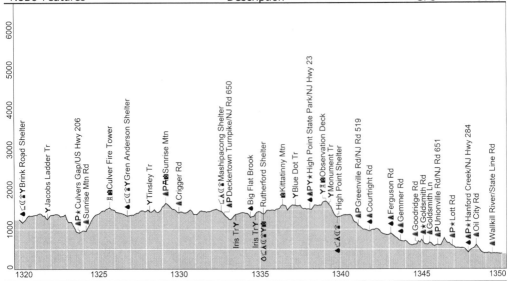

1320.2	♦Y⊏(8) ⊏☎♀	900 feet west to **Brink Shelter**, water (spring) is located across the road 100 yards northeast of the shelter, privy, bear box.	N 41 09.192, W 74 50.292		
		61.6◀44.9◀31.2◀▶6.6▶12.4▶15.0		1110	871.8
1321.7	Y	Unmarked side trail leads east to overlook of Lake Owassa.		1343	870.3
1321.9	Y	Jacobs Ladder is a blue and gray blazed trail descending to the west.		1365	870.1
1322.6	📷	View point.		1360	869.4
1323.3	☂📷	Power line, views.		1245	868.7
1323.8	♠P(30)♀ ★★★★★	Cross **U.S. 206**, Culvers Gap. **See map of Culvers Gap, NJ.**	N 41 10.621, W 74 47.468 935		868.2

🚍🛖♿✗ **Stokes State Park** 973-948-3820 🛖 Tentsites are located (2.0) away from State Park office near Rte 206. Tent site 1-6 persons $25 an up. ✗ Snack bar and ♿ free showers at Stony Lake . Open Memorial Day thru Columbus Day. Accessiblew from (1.0) Stony Lake Trail.

✗☎ **Mountain House Tavern and Grill** 973-250-3300. (www.mountainhousenj.com) ☎ free WiFi available. M 11:30am-8pm, Tu Closed, W-Th 11:20pm-8pm, F-Sa 11:30-9PM, Su 11:30pm-8pm. Open seven days a week in Spring and Summer.

✗ **Gyps Tavern** 973-948-5013. Serves lunch and dinner. Inside and lakeside seating for hikers, charging outlets. Outdoor seating on the lake with a pergola, (arched trellis), and fire pits. Sells beer & wine to go. M Closed,Tu-Th 11am-1am, F-Sa 11am-2am, 11am-1am.

🚍🛌☎🖥 (1.9W) **Forest Motel** 973-948-5456.
🚍 $60 and up, pets $20, 🛌 laundry for a fee, ☎ free WiFi.
🖥 Mail drops for guests: 104 Rte 206 N, Branchville, NJ 07826.

✗ (1.1E) **Jumboland Diner** 973-948-6802. Serves breakfast, lunch and dinner. Thursday dinner buffet. M-Sa 4am-11pm, Su 5am-11pm.

🏪 (1.6E) **Dale's Market** 973-948-3078. (www.www.dalesmarket.com) M-F 6am-9pm, Sa-Su 7am-9pm

🛏 (2.5E) **Cobmin Ridge Motel** 973-948-3459, 973-652-0780 $50 and up.

Branchville, NJ 07826 (3.4E) See map of Branchville, NJ.

📫♀ **PO** M–F 8:30am–5pm, Sa 8:30am–1pm. 973-948-3580. 1 Broad Rd. Branchville, NJ 07826. N 41 08.802, W 74 45.102

🛏 (2.5 from AT) **Cobmin Ridge Motel** 973-948-3459. Call for prices.

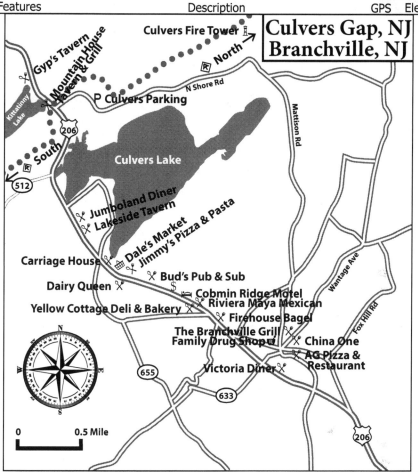

Culvers Gap, NJ
Branchville, NJ

NoBo	Features	Description	GPS	Elev	SoBo
1324.0	⚑	Unmarked trail to parking area.		987	868.0
1324.2	⚑P	Cross **Sunrise Mountain Road**. Limited parking.		970	867.8
1324.7	📷	View point to the west.		1260	867.3
1325.6	Y	Unmarked trail intersects west, leads 75 feet to good view.		1534	866.4
1325.7	📷🗼	Culver Fire Tower, good views.		1550	866.3
1325.8	Y	Green blaze Tower Trail intersects west.		1535	866.2
1326.7	♦	Cross Stony Brook.		1512	865.3
1326.8	♦Y⌂(8) ⌇🌙(☂🐻⚲	(0.1W) **Gren Anderson Shelter**, water (spring) is located downhill and to the left of shelter 70 yards, privy. Stony Brook trail is brown blazed west (0.3) to Sunrise Mountain Road and continues on (1.0) to Stony Lake.	N 41 11.963, W 74 45.186		865.2
		51.5◄37.8◄6.6◄▶ 5.8▶8.4▶ 13.0		1320	
1328.1	📷	View point west.		1450	863.9
1328.2	Y	Intersects with yellow blazed Tinsley Trail.		1476	863.8
1329.2	🚗⚑📷 P(25)⚲	Sunrise Mountain, picnic pavilion, panoramic views.	N 41 13.090, W 74 43.224 parking N 41 13.165, W 74 43.105 1653		862.8
1329.3	Y	Path leading to parking lot.		1617	862.7
1330.0	⚑	Cross **Crigger Road, dirt**		1400	862.0
1330.9	♦	Cross swamp outlet.		1407	861.1
1331.9	⚑	Trail joins woods road for 225 feet.		1484	860.1
1332.6	⚑⌂(8) ⌇🌙(☂🐻⚲	**Mashipacong Shelter**, NO WATER here, bear box.	N 41 15.130, W 74 41.183 1425		859.4
		43.6◄12.4◄5.8◄▶ 2.6▶7.2▶ 19.6			
1332.8	⚑P(10)⚲	Cross **Deckertown Turnpike**, paved	N 41 15.138, W 74 41.362 1320		859.2
1333.5	Y	Intersects with red on white blazes of Iris Trail.		1414	858.5
1333.9	Y📷	Clear strip of land, a buried pipeline. A trail east leads to view.		1417	858.1

NoBo	Features	Description	GPS	Elev	SoBo
1334.3	⬤⌒	Cross stream on logs. Just north of stream is a blue blazed trail east to water.		1334	857.7
1334.7	▲Y	Intersects with woods road and the red and white blazes of Iris Trail.		1370	857.3
1335.2	⬤Y▲ ⊂(6) ⌣《🏕📷	Dutch Rock with views. **(0.4E) Rutherford Shelter**, Spring 100 yards before shelter on connecting trail. Slow stream. Tenting, privy, bear box.	N 41 16.651, W 74 40.689		
	♀	15.0◀8.4◀2.6◀▶4.6▶17.0▶28.5		1345	856.8
1336.5	📷	View east.		1614	855.5
1336.9	📷	View west over Sawmill Lake.		1590	855.1
1337.0	⬤Y▲	Blue Dot Trail, (0.4W) to tenting and water		1600	855.0
1338.0	Y	Trail intersection. Yellow blaze; Mashipacong Trail west. Red and white blaze; Iris Trail east.		1552	854.0
1338.1	⬤▲⚹ ★★★★★	Cross **N.J. 23; High Point State Park HQ**	N 41 18.156, W 74 40.068	1500	853.9
	⬤▲ ◈♦♦	**High Point State Park Headquarters** 973-875-4800.			
	P(20)⊡	◈ AT Passport location. Office is open year round M-Su 9am-4pm. ♦♦ Bathrooms inside, ⬤ water spigot outside. P Overnight parking (0.25E). ⊡ Mail drops: 1480 State Rte 23, Sussex, NJ 07461.			
	🛏⛺🛒⊕ ⊡	**(1.5E) High Point Country Inn** 973-702-1860 🛏 $90 and up, pets $10. ⛺ Laundry $7, ⊕ free WiFi. Free pickup and return to trail from NJ 23, �car longer shuttles for a fee. ⊡ Mail drops for guests: 1328 NJ 23, Wantage, NJ 07461.			
Port Jervis, NY 12785 (4.4W)					
	🛏⊕🖥⊡	**Days Inn** 845-856-6611 🛏 $80 and up, $10EAP, pets $25. Free continental breakfast. 🖥 Computer available for use, ⊕ free WiFi. ⊡ Mail drops for guests: 2247 Greenville Turnpike, Port Jervis, NY 12771.			
	✗	**Village Pizza** 973-293-3364. (www.villagepizzaitalianrestaurant.com) M-Sa 11am-11pm, Su 12-11pm.			
	🛒⊘	**Shop Rite Market** M-Su 6am-12am.			
	⊘	**Rite Aid** 845-856-8342. M-Sa 7am-10pm, Su 9am-8pm, Pharmacy M-F 8am-9pm, Sa 9am-6pm, Su 9am-5pm.			
		Medicine Shoppe 845-856-6681. M-F 9am-6pm, Sa 9am-1pm, Su closed.			
	☤	**Bon Secours Community Hospital** 845-858-7000. (www.bonsecourscommunityhosp.org)			
	🐾	**Tri-States Veterinary Medical** 845-856-1914. M-Tu 8am-5pm, W-Th 8am-7pm, F 8am-5pm, Sa 8am-2pm, Su closed.			
1339.1	Y📷🍴 ♦♦🍴	Observation Platform		1680	852.9
1339.3	Y📷🍴	Side Trail to High Point Monument intersects with red and green blazed Monument Trail.		1600	852.7
1339.8	⬤Y⊂(8) 《🏕♀	**(0.1E) High Point Shelter**, streams on both sides of shelter are known to dry up at times, privy, bear box.	N 41 19.665, W 74 38.628		
		13.0◀7.2◀4.6◀▶12.4▶23.9▶36.0		1280	852.2
1340.1	⬤	Cross brook at head of ravine, unreliable.		1233	851.9
1341.1	🛏▲P(5) ♀	Cross **County Road 519**, paved, (2.5E) to lodging	N 41 19.759, W 74 38.595	1100	850.9
1341.8	⬤	Cross two streams in area.		951	850.2
1341.9	▲	Cross **Courtwright Road**, gravel		1000	850.1
1342.1		Follow blazes carefully in area along stone walls.		994	849.9
1342.6	⬤	Pass pond to the west.		916	849.4
1342.9		Intersection of stone walls.		864	849.1
1343.0	⬤⌒	Cross steam on bridge.		861	849.0
1343.1	▲♀	Cross **Ferguson Road also known as Mt. Salem Road**.	N 41 19.292, W 74 36.991	900	848.9
1343.7	▲P(2)♀	Cross **Gemmer Road**, paved.	N 41 18.982, W 74 36.473	740	848.3
1343.8	⬤⌒	Cross wooden bridge over brook.		727	848.2
1344.0	⬤⌒	Cross stream over wooden bridge.		741	848.0
1344.4	⬤	Cross two wooden brides over streams.		710	847.6
1344.7	▲P(2)♀	Cross **Goodrich Road**, paved	N 41 18.895, W 74 36.148	610	847.3
1344.9	⬤	Cross over concrete dam (outlet of pond).		700	847.1
1345.0		Reach crest of Wolf Pit Hill, open field.		741	847.0
1345.1	⬤Y▲⊂ 《🏕▲ ★★★★★	Cross **Goldsmith Road**, road leads (0.2) west to Jim Murray property, water, shelter, tenting, privy, shower.		660	846.9
	⬤《⊂▲ 🏕▲	**Private cabin** open for the use of long distance hikers as it has been for nearly 20 years, tenting, well water, shower and privy. If you feel the need to change your brain chemistry this is probably not your stop but serious hikers welcome. No groups please.			
1345.2	▲	Cross **Goldsmith Lane**, gravel. Vernie Swamp (southern end)		600	846.8

NoBo	Features	Description	GPS	Elev	SoBo
1345.4		Vernie Swamp (northern end).		590	846.6
1345.5	🔺	Cross **Goldsmith Lane**.		674	846.5
1345.8		Reach hilltop, overgrown fields with abandon apple orchards.		654	846.2
1346.0	🔺P(3)♀	Cross **Unionville Road, county Road 651.** **See map of Unionville, NY (0.8W).**	N 41 18.136, W 74 34.549	610	846.0
1346.1		Pass old quarry pit.		638	845.9
1346.2	🔺P(5)♀	Cross **Quarry Road, paved.** **See map of Unionville, NY (0.7W).**	N 41 18.018, W 74 34.308	678	845.8
1346.9	🔺P(2) ♀ ★★★★★	Cross **Lott Road, also known as Jersey Avenue. See map of Unionville, NY (0.4W).**	N 41 17.792, W 74 33.758	590	845.1

Unionville, NY. (0.7W)

📫♀	**PO** M-F 8am-11:30am & 1pm-5pm, Sa 9am-12pm. 845-726-3535. 1 Main St. Unionville, NY 10988. N 41 18.091, W 74 33.726	
♦🔺🛉	**Village Office** 845-726-3681. 🔺 Check-in at office or at Horler's Store for overnight tenting.	
✗🕾	**Wit's End Tavern** 845-726-3956. (www.witsendtavern.com) ✗ Serves ribs, burgers, wings and more. 🕾 ATM. M-Th 12pm-2am, F-Sa 12pm-4am, Su 12pm-2am.	
🛒✗🕾	**Horler's Store** 845-726-3210. 🛒 M–Sa 6am–8pm, Su 7am–7pm. ✗ Has a short order grill open M-F 6:30am-3pm, Sa-Su 7am-1pm. 🕾 ATM.	
🏧🕾	**End of the Line Grocery** 845-726-3228. Deli, ATM. M-Su 7am-7pm.	
✗	**Annabel's Pizza** 845-726-9992 (www.annabelspizza.com) M-Sa 11am-10pm, Su 11am-9pm.	

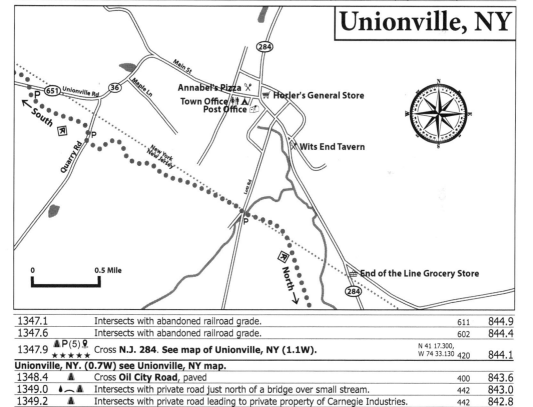

1347.1		Intersects with abandoned railroad grade.		611	844.9
1347.6		Intersects with abandoned railroad grade.		602	844.4
1347.9	🔺P(5)♀ ★★★★★	Cross **N.J. 284. See map of Unionville, NY (1.1W).**	N 41 17.300, W 74 33.130	420	844.1

Unionville, NY. (0.7W) see Unionville, NY map.

1348.4	🔺	Cross **Oil City Road**, paved		400	843.6
1349.0	♦🔺	Intersects with private road just north of a bridge over small stream.		442	843.0
1349.2	🔺	Intersects with private road leading to private property of Carnegie Industries.		442	842.8
1349.4	🔺♀	Cross bridge over Wallkill River on **Oil City Road.**	N 41 17.264, W 74 32.053	410	842.6
1349.7	🔺♀	Intersects with **Oil City Road**, Wallkill National Wildlife Preserve	N 41 17.119, W 74 31.853	410	842.3

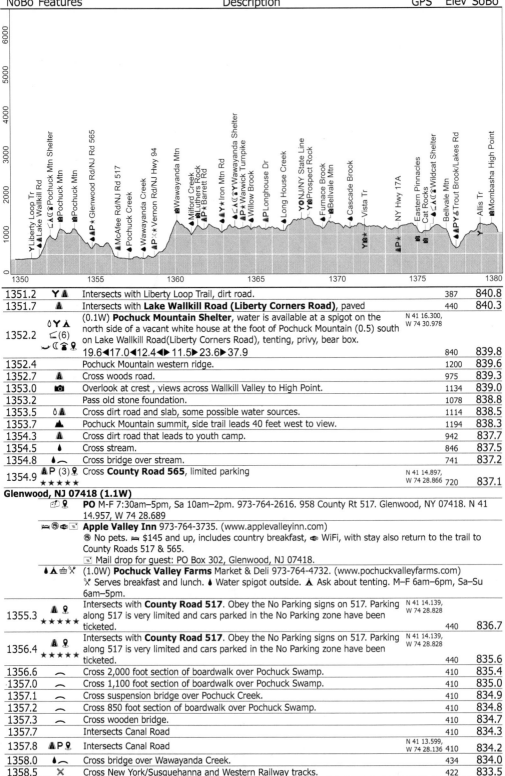

NoBo	Features	Description	GPS	Elev	SoBo
1351.2	Y▲	Intersects with Liberty Loop Trail, dirt road.		387	840.8
1351.7	▲	Intersects with **Lake Wallkill Road (Liberty Corners Road)**, paved		440	840.3
1352.2	◊Y▲ ⊏(6) ⌣《🚿🐻⚲	(0.1W) **Pochuck Mountain Shelter**, water is available at a spigot on the north side of a vacant white house at the foot of Pochuck Mountain (0.5) south on Lake Wallkill Road(Liberty Corners Road), tenting, privy, bear box.	N 41 16.300, W 74 30.978		839.8
		19.6◀17.0◀12.4◀▶11.5▶23.6▶37.9		840	
1352.4		Pochuck Mountain western ridge.		1200	839.6
1352.7	▲	Cross woods road.		975	839.3
1353.0	📷	Overlook at crest , views across Wallkill Valley to High Point.		1134	839.0
1353.2		Pass old stone foundation.		1078	838.8
1353.5	◊▲	Cross dirt road and slab, some possible water sources.		1114	838.5
1353.7	▲▲	Pochuck Mountain summit, side trail leads 40 feet west to view.		1194	838.3
1354.3	▲	Cross dirt road that leads to youth camp.		942	837.7
1354.5	◊	Cross stream.		846	837.5
1354.8	◊⌢	Cross bridge over stream.		741	837.2
1354.9	▲P (3)⚲ ★★★★★	Cross **County Road 565**, limited parking	N 41 14.897, W 74 28.866	720	837.1

Glenwood, NJ 07418 (1.1W)

🏤⚲	**PO** M-F 7:30am–5pm, Sa 10am–2pm. 973-764-2616. 958 County Rt 517. Glenwood, NY 07418. N 41 14.957, W 74 28.689			
🛏🚿🍴💻	**Apple Valley Inn** 973-764-3735. (www.applevalleyinn.com) 🚫 No pets. 🛏 $145 and up, includes country breakfast, 💻 WiFi, with stay also return to the trail to County Roads 517 & 565. 📧 Mail drop for guest: PO Box 302, Glenwood, NJ 07418.			
◊▲🏠✕	(1.0W) **Pochuck Valley Farms** Market & Deli 973-764-4732. (www.pochuckvalleyfarms.com) ✕ Serves breakfast and lunch. ◊ Water spigot outside. ▲ Ask about tenting. M–F 6am–6pm, Sa–Su 6am–5pm.			
1355.3	▲ ⚲ ★★★★★	Intersects with **County Road 517**. Obey the No Parking signs on 517. Parking along 517 is very limited and cars parked in the No Parking zone have been ticketed.	N 41 14.139, W 74 28.828	440	836.7
1356.4	▲ ⚲ ★★★★★	Intersects with **County Road 517**. Obey the No Parking signs on 517. Parking along 517 is very limited and cars parked in the No Parking zone have been ticketed.	N 41 14.139, W 74 28.828	440	835.6
1356.6	⌢	Cross 2,000 foot section of boardwalk over Pochuck Swamp.		410	835.4
1357.0	⌢	Cross 1,100 foot section of boardwalk over Pochuck Swamp.		410	835.0
1357.1	⌢	Cross suspension bridge over Pochuck Creek.		410	834.9
1357.2	⌢	Cross 850 foot section of boardwalk over Pochuck Swamp.		410	834.8
1357.3	⌢	Cross wooden bridge.		410	834.7
1357.7		Intersects Canal Road		410	834.3
1357.8	▲P⚲	Intersects Canal Road	N 41 13.599, W 74 28.136	410	834.2
1358.0	◊⌢	Cross bridge over Wawayanda Creek.		434	834.0
1358.5	✕	Cross New York/Susquehanna and Western Railway tracks.		422	833.5

NoBo	Features	Description	GPS	Elev	SoBo

1358.7 ⓐ P(8) ⓨ ★★★★★ Cross **N.J. 94. See map of Vernon, NJ.** — N 41 13.162, W 74 27.311 450 — **833.3**

🏠👥🚻🍴 **(0.1W) Heaven Hill Farm** 973-764-5144. (www.heavenhillfarm.com) Has bakery items, vegetables, ice cream, 🍴 picnic tables, 🏧 ATM. M-F 9am–7pm, Su 9am-6pm.

✕🍴 **(0.2E) Mitch's Roadside Grill Hot dog Stand** 973-715-2608. M-Su 11am-3pm Hot dogs, sodas, Italian Ice and potato knish, picnic tables.

🛏⛺♨🖥 **(1.2E) Appalachian Motel** 973-764-6070. (www.appalachianmotel.com) 🛏 $70 and up $10EAP. Call for ride. Pets $20. Microwave, fridge, ⛺ laundry $10, 📶 Wifi.
🖥 Mail drops for guests: 367 Route 94, Vernon, NJ 07462.

Vernon, NJ 07462 (2.4E) See map of Vernon, NJ.

📫ⓨ **PO** M-F 8:30am-5pm, Sa 9:30am-12:30pm. 973-764-9056. 530 County Route 515 Unit 13. Vernon, NJ 07462N 41 11.705, W 74 28.991

🛒🚻🏧 **Acme Market** 973-764-5350. 🚻 Pharmacy, 🏧 ATM. M-Sa 6am-12am, Su 6am-10pm.

✕ **China Star, Dairy Queen, Burger King, Paesano Pizza, Ming's Asian Bistro**

🍷 **Vernon Urgent Care** 973-209-2260. (1.0) mile beyond hostel, M–F 8am–8pm, Sa–Su 9am–5pm.

🐾 **Vernon Vet Clinic** 973-764-3630. (www.vernonvet.com) M-Su by appointment.

New Milford, NY (2.7W) See Mile 1361.8

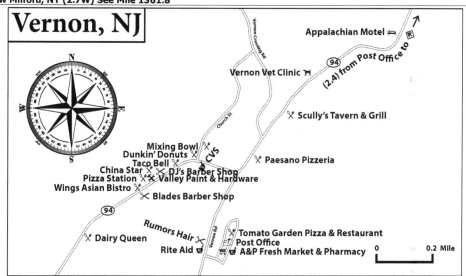

1359.1	📷	Cross old stone wall above overgrown field with views.		562	832.9
1359.7		Reach the south most point of Wawayanda Mountain.		1244	832.3
1360.0	Y📷	Blue blaze trail west (0.1) to Pinwheel's Vista along the cliffs of Wawayanda Mountain.		1345	832.0
1360.1	📷	Wawayanda Mountain, trail register.		1340	831.9
1360.6	⚠	Cross woods road.		1143	831.4
1361.0	💧	Cross stream on footbridge.		989	831.0
1361.4	📷	Luthers Rock, limited views through trees.		1206	830.6
1361.8	ⓐP(2)ⓨ ★★★★★	Cross **Barrett Road**, New Milford, NY.	N 41 12.881, W 74 25.247	1140	830.2

New Milford, NY 10959 (1.8W)

📫ⓨ **(1.4W)** on Barret Rd, then right (0.6) on NJ 94 to shoe store and
Post Office. M-F 8:30am-12:30pm, Sa 9am-11:30am. 845-986-3557. 3 Jockey Hollow Rd Ste 2. New Milford, NY 10959. N 41 14.067, W 74 24.987

✕ **Mom's Home Style Deli** 845-988-9089. M-F 6am-3pm, Sa 7am-3pm, Su 8:30am-3pm.

■ **Sneakers to Boots** 845-986-0333 (www.sneakerstoboots.com) Carries brand name footwear from Merrell, Keen, Oboz, Salomon, and Hi-Tec. M-F 10am-6pm, Sat 10am-5pm, Su 11am-2pm

1362.0		Cross drain.		1145	830.0
1362.1	⚠	Intersects with woods road.		1203	829.9
1362.5	💧	Stream, unreliable.		1185	829.5

© WhiteBlaze Pages 2019

NoBo	Features	Description	GPS	Elev	SoBo
1362.9	♦︎⁀	Cross iron bridge over Double Kill, 1890's era bridge.		1046	829.1
1363.1	▲ X	Intersects with **Iron Mountain Road**. At intersection blue trail east (1.6) to restaurant and water at Wawayanda Lake. Follow blue blaze trail (1.2) and cross a paved road, continue (0.4) to Lake. From Memorial Weekend to Labor Day, visitors can swim 10–6. Restrooms, first-aid station, food concession (ice cream, burgers, soda), and boat rental.		1060	828.9
1363.2	▲	Cross woods road.		1195	828.8
1363.5	▲	Intersects with **Wawayanda Road**, dirt.		1150	828.5
1363.7	▲⊑(6) ⊂☂♀	275 feet to **Wawayanda Shelter**, privy, water is available at the park office which can be reached by going north on the AT (0.1) and east (0.2) on Hoeferlin Trail. Privy, bear box. 28.5◀23.9◀11.5◀▶12.1▶26.4▶31.7	N 41 12.131, W 74 23.910	1200	828.3
1363.9	♦Y▲P ♦♦⊟♦♀	Cross woods road, Hoeferlin Trail leads (0.2) east to quarters of Wawayanda State Park.	N 41 11.886, W 74 23.850	1200	828.1
1364.0	⁀	Cross plank bridge over swamp outlet.		1114	828.0
1364.2	▲P(8)♀ ★★★★★	Cross **Warwick Turnpike**, (2.7W) to long term resupply and restaurant.	N 41 12.094, W 74 23.483	1140	827.8

Warwick, NY (2.7W)

	🛒🛍	**Price Chopper** 845-987-6333. M-Su 24 hours; Pharmacy M-F 8am-8pm, Sa 9am-5pm, Su 9am-3pm.			
1364.4		South end of farm road on edge of field.		1194	827.6
1364.5		North end of edge of farm road along field.		1197	827.5
1364.7	♦	Cross brook.		1152	827.3
1364.9	▲	Cross old woods road.		1183	827.1
1365.5	◊	Cross logs on stream, unreliable.		1136	826.5
1365.6	▲P(4)♀	Intersects with **Long House Road (Brady Road)** for short distance.	N 41 11.736, W 74 22.292	1080	826.4
1365.9		Follow grassy woods road.		1154	826.1
1366.1	▲	Follow woods road for a short distance.		1155	825.9
1366.3	♦⁀	Cross wooden bridge over stream.		1160	825.7
1366.7	♦⁀	Cross log bridge over Long House Creek.		1085	825.3
1366.8	▲	Follows dirt road for a short distance.		1087	825.2
1367.0	▲	Cross two woods roads in a short distance.		1193	825.0
1367.1	♦	Cross stream on rocks.		1365	824.9
1367.3	📷	Rock ledge with view west.		1379	824.7
1367.5	Y	Yellow blazed Ernest Walter Trail leads east.		1368	824.5
1367.6	📷	View overlooking Surprise Lake and Sterling Ridge.		1393	824.4
1367.8	Y State Line	New Jersey–New York State Line State Line Trail; Hewitt, N.J.		1385	824.2
1367.9		Pass trail register.		1364	824.1
1368.2	📷	Prospect Rock, views over Greenwood Lake and south.		1433	823.8
1368.3	Y	Zig Zag trail leads west to Cascade Lake Park.		1402	823.7
1368.4	📷	Rock promontory west of trail.		1379	823.6
1369.2	♦	Cross Furnace Brook.		1135	822.8
1369.4	♦	Cross stream, seasonal.		1224	822.6
1369.5	📷	Rock outcrop with panoramic view south.		1328	822.5
1370.3	📷	Exposed rock outcrop, limited views.		1273	821.7
1370.4	♦	Cross several small streams in the area.		1268	821.6
1370.8	♦	Cross Cascade Brook.		1246	821.2
1371.2	♦	Cross brook.		1173	820.8
1371.5	📷	Exposed rock outcrops with views of Greenwood Lake.		1280	820.5
1371.7	📷 ★★★★★	Vista Trail leads (0.8) east to the village of **Greenwood Lake, NY (0.8E)**.		1180	820.3

Greenwood Lake, NY (0.8E) See note at NOBO mile 1373.8

1372.9	♦	Cross brook.		1199	819.1
1373.3	⊤	Power line.		1159	818.7
1373.8	▲P(12)♀ ★★★★★	Cross **N.Y. 17A**	N 41 14.657, W 74 17.230	1180	818.2

	X	**Hot Dog Plus** Korean War Army Veteran Bernard "Bud" Whitt is open seasonally Tu-Sa 10:30-3:30.			
	♦X	(0.3W) **Bellvale Farms Creamery** 845-988-1818. (www.bellvalefarms.com) X Ice cream. ♦ Water/electric charging station available outside.			

Bellvale, NY 10912 (1.6W)

	X	**Bellvale Market** 845-544-7700. (www.bellvalemarket.com) M-F 8am-7pm, Sa 8am-6pm, Su 8am-4pm.			

Greenwood Lake, NY 10925 (2.0E) See map of Greenwood Lake, NY.

	✉♀	**PO** M–F 8am–5pm, Sa 9am–12pm. 845-477-7328. 123 Windermere Ave. Greenwood Lake, NY 10925. N 41 13.585, W 74 17.505			

Anton's on the Lake 845-477-0010. (www.antonsonthelake.com)
Open year round.
⊗ No pets or smoking. ⇆ Thru hiker rate, 2-night min, price per night: Su-Th $80S/D, F-Sa $125/up. Credit cards are accepted, rooms with whirlpool available, △ small laundry loads only, ⚓ swimming, paddle boats and canoe. ⌨ Computer available for use, ⊕ Wifi. ⛟ Free shuttles and slackpacking with stay, longer shuttles for fee. ✗ Restaurant on site.
🖃 Mail for guests: (USPS) PO Box 1505 or (FedEx/UPS) 7 Waterstone Rd, Greenwood Lake, NY 10925.

Lake Lodging 845-477-0700, 845-705-2005.
⊗ No Pets. ⇆ Hiker rates, ⊕ free WiFi, **no credit cards.**

Breezy Point Inn 845-477-8100. (www.breezypointinn.com)
⊗ No pets, no smoking. ⇆ $185 and up. ⊕ Free WiFi, ☎ ATM. ✗ Serves lunch and dinner M-Su. Closed month of January.
🖃 Mail drops for guests: (UPS/FedEx) 620 Jersey Ave, Greenwood Lake, NY 10925.

✗	**Country Kitchen, Ashley's Pizza, Sing Loong Kitchen, Subway**
🛒	**Country Grocery** 845-477-0100. M-F 8am-8pm, Sa 10am-7pm, Su 10am-6pm.
✚	**CVS** M-Su 8am-9pm, **Pharmacy** M-F 8am-8pm, Sa 9am-6pm, Su 9am-5pm.
✗	**True Value Hardware** 845-477-3327. M-Sa 8am-6pm, Su 9am-2pm.
🚗	**Greenwood Lake Taxi** 845-477-0314. (www.greenwoodlaketaxi.com)

Greenwood Lake, NJ

1374.4		Clearing for gas pipe line.	1216	817.6
1375.0	📷	Eastern Pinnacles, views to the east and south.	1294	817.0
1375.3	♦	Cross brook.	1026	816.7
1375.5	📷	Cat Rocks, 360 degree views. Blue blaze trail to the east bypasses this.	1080	816.5
1375.8	♦Y⅄(3) ⌂(8) ⌇(☎⚡	600 feet west to **Wildcat Shelter**, water (spring) is located 75 yards downhill and left from the shelter, tenting, privy, bear box. 36.0◀23.6◀12.1◀▶14.3▶19.6▶22.8	N 41 16.101, W 74 16.098 1180	816.2
1376.0		Cross old stone wall and pass foundation to the west.	1201	816.0
1376.7	Y	Highlands Trail, teal diamond blazed leads west but runs with the AT north for (2.1) miles.	1127	815.3
1377.3	⚠P(2)⚡	Cross **Lakes Road**, paved	N 41 16.420, W 74 15.252 680	814.7

NoBo	Features	Description	GPS	Elev	SoBo
1377.4	◑⌒	Cross wooden bridge over Trout Brook.		643	814.6
1377.5	Y	Blue blaze trail leads east, avoiding two more crossings of Trout Brook during high water seasons, rejoining at Fitzgerald Falls.		662	814.5
1377.6	◊Y⚒	Fitzgerald Falls. Blue blaze bypass trail leads east after crossing the brook avoids two more crossings of Trout Brook during high water seasons.		800	814.4
1377.7	◑	Cross Trout Brook and tributary.		666	814.3
1378.0		Pass old stone walls and remains of abandoned settlement.		965	814.0
1378.8	Y	Allis Trail leads (2.5) east and descends over One Cedar Mountain to N.Y. 17A.		1198	813.2
1379.6	📷	Mombasha High Point		1280	812.4

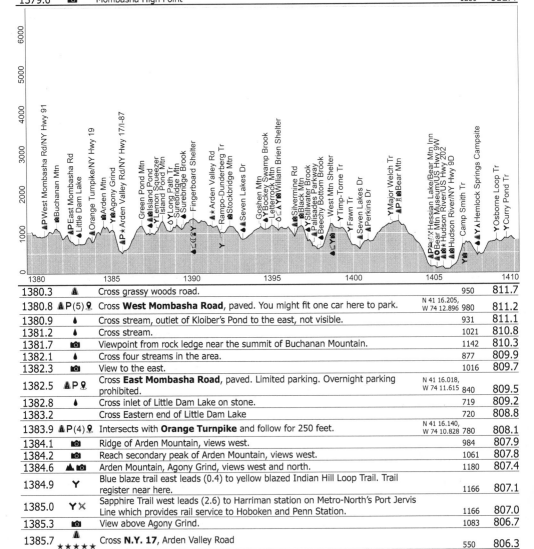

NoBo	Features	Description	GPS	Elev	SoBo
1380.3	⛺	Cross grassy woods road.		950	811.7
1380.8	⛺P(5)⚑	Cross **West Mombasha Road**, paved. You might fit one car here to park.	N 41 16.205, W 74 12.896	980	811.2
1380.9	◑	Cross stream, outlet of Kloiber's Pond to the east, not visible.		931	811.1
1381.2	◑	Cross stream.		1021	810.8
1381.7	📷	Viewpoint from rock ledge near the summit of Buchanan Mountain.		1142	810.3
1382.1	◑	Cross four streams in the area.		877	809.9
1382.3	📷	View to the east.		1016	809.7
1382.5	⛺P⚑	Cross **East Mombasha Road**, paved. Limited parking. Overnight parking prohibited.	N 41 16.018, W 74 11.615	840	809.5
1382.8	◑	Cross inlet of Little Dam Lake on stone.		719	809.2
1383.2		Cross Eastern end of Little Dam Lake		720	808.8
1383.9	⛺P(4)⚑	Intersects with **Orange Turnpike** and follow for 250 feet.	N 41 16.140, W 74 10.828	780	808.1
1384.1	📷	Ridge of Arden Mountain, views west.		984	807.9
1384.2	📷	Reach secondary peak of Arden Mountain, views west.		1061	807.8
1384.6	▲📷	Arden Mountain, Agony Grind, views west and north.		1180	807.4
1384.9	Y	Blue blaze trail east leads (0.4) to yellow blazed Indian Hill Loop Trail. Trail register near here.		1166	807.1
1385.0	Y✕	Sapphire Trail west leads (2.6) to Harriman station on Metro-North's Port Jervis Line which provides rail service to Hoboken and Penn Station.		1166	807.0
1385.3	📷	View above Agony Grind.		1083	806.7
1385.7	⛺ ★★★★★	Cross **N.Y. 17**, Arden Valley Road		550	806.3

NY 17 Southfields, NY (2.1E)

✉⚑	**PO** M–F 10am–12pm & 1pm–5pm, Sa 8:30am–11:30am. 845-351-2628. 996 Route 17, Southfields, NY 10975. N 41 14.534, W 74 10.558
🛏⊛⛺✉	**Tuxedo Motel** 845-351-4747. (www.tuxedomotelinc.com) ⊛ No pets, no cooking. 🛏 $54.50S, $59.50D, $10EAP. ⛺ Laundry. Accepts Visa, MC. ✉ Mail drops: 985 Route 17 South, Southfields, NY, 10975.
🏪	**Valero** (0.1W) of Post Office.
🚗	**Suffern's Deborah Taxi** 845-300-0332. Text is best or deborahtaxi@gmail.com Based out of Suffern, NY/Mahwah, NJ. Deborah Tapp. Shuttles from NJ to CT. (from Delaware Water Gap, Pa. to Hoyt Rd.)

Harriman, NY. (3.7W) Lodging, restaurants.

NoBo	Features	Description	GPS	Elev	SoBo
1385.9	▲	Cross over **I-87 N.Y. State Thruway**, overpass		560	806.1
1386.0	▲P(30)♀ ★★★★★	Pass entrance to Elk Pen parking area.	N 41 15.921, W 74 09.210	587	806.0
1386.1	▲ ★★★★★	Intersects with **Arden Valley Road**.		680	805.9
	🚗P	**Harriman Shuttle** Runs Sa, Su and holidays will pickup here at 11:43 and Tiorati circle at 11:40. Connects to town of Southfields and Tuxedo Train Station. $5 per ride.			
1386.2	▲	Intersects with **Old Arden Road.**		628	805.8
1387.0	▲	Green Pond Mountain summit		1180	805.0
1387.2	▲	**Island Pond Road** briefly joins the AT.		988	804.8
1387.3	▲	Cross gravel road.		1006	804.7
1387.4	♦	Cross Island Pond Outlet		1350	804.6
1387.5	▲ 📷	Reach crest with view of Island Pond.		1309	804.5
1387.7	▲	**Crooked Pond Road**, and old woods road briefly joins the AT and crosses the inlet of Island Pond.		1073	804.3
1388.0	Y	Lemon Squeezer. Arden-Surebridge Trail (A-SB) leads east.		1150	804.0
1388.2	▲	Island Pond summit.		1303	803.8
1388.6	Y	Cross the Aqua-blazed Long Path Trail.		1160	803.4
1388.8	◊	Stream, unreliable.		1130	803.2
1389.1	▲	Surebridge Mountain		1200	802.9
1389.4	♦	Cross Surebridge Brook..		1103	802.6
1389.5	▲	**Surebridge Mine Road** joins the AT.		1197	802.5
1390.0	Y	Rampo-Dunderberg Trail (R-D) leads east, marked with red on white blazes.		1354	802.0
1390.1	♦Y⊏(8) 〰((☂♀	350 feet east to **Fingerboard Shelter**, water (spring) is located downhill to left but is unreliable. 37.9◄26.4◄14.3◄▶5.3▶8.5▶40.7	N 41 15.799, W 74 06.243	1300	801.9
1390.7	▲	Fingerboard Mountain summit.		1374	801.3
1391.1		Pass round water tank.		1204	800.9
1391.2	♦▲⚏ ★★★★★	Cross **Arden Valley Road**, to Lake Tiorati Circle, (0.3W) to water and shower.		1196	800.8
	♦✕⚏♦♦ 🍴🚗🚉	(0.3E) **Lake Tiorati Beach** 845-429-8257. M-Su 9am-7pm, mid Jun thru mid Aug, Only open on weekends in spring and fall. ⚏ Free showers, ♦♦ restrooms, 🗑 trash cans, 🛋 picnic tables, vending machine, 🏊 swimming.			
1391.9	▲Y	Cross wide woods road diagonally to the left. Ramapo-Dunderberg Trail (R-D) east marked with red on white blazes.		1026	800.1
1392.4	📷	Reach high point with view through trees.		1182	799.6
1393.2	♦	Cross stream.		862	798.8
1393.4	▲	Cross **Seven Lakes Drive** diagonally to the left.		850	798.6
1394.6	Y	Cross over Bockey Swamp Brook between Goshen and Letterock Mountains. Ramapo-Dunderberg Trail (R-D) marked with red on white blazes.		1105	797.4
1395.4	◊▲⊏(8) 〰📷♀	**William Brien Memorial Shelter**, Water is located at a unreliable spring-fed well 80 yards down blue blazed trail to right of shelter. Tenting. 31.7◄19.6◄5.3◄▶3.2▶35.4▶44.4	N 41 16.782, W 74 03.594	1070	796.6
1395.5		Cross rocky high point of Letterrock Mountain.		1143	796.5
1396.3	▲	Cross **Silvermine Road**, fire road.		913	795.7
1396.4	📷	Overlook with view of Silvermine Lake.		1060	795.6
1396.8	📷	South side of Black Mountain, views of Hudson River and Bew York City.		1175	795.2
1397.2	Y	Cross the 1779 Trail east.		822	794.8
1397.5	♦♦♦🚻⊕🏛	Cross Palisade Interstate Parkway, divided highway, (0.4W) to water		680	794.5
1397.6	Y	Rampo-Dunderberg Trail (R-D) leads east, marked with red on white blazes.		685	794.4
1397.7	♦〰	Cross Beechy Bottom Brook on wooden bridge.		660	794.3
1397.8	♦	Cross stream.		606	794.2
1398.0	▲	Cross **Beechy Bottom Road**, marked with blue on white plastic blazes as a bike path.		665	794.0
1398.6	Y⊏(8) 📷♀	(0.6E) on Timp-Torne Trail to **West Mountain Shelter**. Views of Hudson River and NYC. 22.8◄8.5◄3.2◄▶32.2▶41.2▶49.0	N 41 17.944, W 74 00.553	1240	793.4
1398.9	📷	Flat rock on West Mountain near ledges with views.		1120	793.1
1399.2	Y	Timp-Torne Trail (T-T) west.			792.8
1399.3	📷	View on West Mountain looking at Bear Mountain and Hudson River.			792.7
1399.8	Y	Fawn Trail west, red blazed.			792.2
1400.0	▲	Follows woods road which is not a cross country ski trail.			792.0
1400.4	▲	Cross **Seven Lakes Drive**		610	791.6
1400.9	▲	Intersects with **Perkins Drive**, paved.		950	791.1
1401.4	▲	Intersects with wide road, now an abandoned section of Perkins Memorial Drive.			790.6
1401.5	📷	View over West Mountain.			790.5

NoBo	Features	Description	GPS	Elev	SoBo
1401.8	Y 📷	Panoramic view west. Blue blaze trail leads (0.2) to another viewpoint.			790.2
1401.9	Y	Blue blaze (0.2) east to the summit of Bear Mountain.			790.1
1402.4	Y	Intersects with Major Welch Trail, red ring on white blazed.		1151	789.6
1402.8	📷 ⓘ P(99) ⛾	Bear Mountain, Perkins Tower	N 41 18.689, W 74 00.411	1305	789.2
1403.4	▲	Intersects with paved **scenic drive**.		1206	788.6
1403.6	▲	Intersects with paved **scenic drive**.		1152	788.4
1404.6	⌒📷	Cross 28 foot wooden bridge, view of Hudson River.		456	787.4
1404.8	♦P🚗⛾	Passes by Bear Mountain Inn, Hessian Lake. See notes for Bear Mountain Inn under Fort Montgomery, NY.	N 41 18.781, W 73 59.339	155	787.2
1405.5	ⓧ ★★★★★	Cross under U.S. 9W in tunnel, **Bear Mountain Museum and Zoo.**		124	786.5
	📫⛾	**PO** 9am-11am, Sat-Sun Closed, 845-786-3747. 30 Service Rd. Bear Mountain, NY 10911. N 41 18.664, W 73 59.247			
	ⓧ ◈	**Bear Mountain Museum and Zoo** ◈ AT Passport location. ⓧ No pets allowed. If closed, or if you have a dog, use bypass. 845-786-2701 Open 10 am-4:30 pm; no charge for hiking through.			
1405.6	▲ ⌒📷 ★★★★★	Intersects with **U.S. 9W**, Bear Mountain Circle, Bear Mountain Bridge (south end), Hudson River **Bear Mountain, NY. See map of Bear Mountain/Fort Montgomery, NY.**		150	786.4

Fort Montgomery, NY 10922 (1.8W) See map of Bear Mountain/Fort Montgomery, NY.

	📫⛾	**PO** M-F 8am-1pm & 2:30pm-5pm, Sa 9am-12pm, 845-446-8459. 130 Firefighters Memorial Dr. Fort Montgomery, NY 10922. N 41 19.878, W 73 59.256
	🛏✗🖥📶 ☎	**Bear Mountain Inn** 845-786-2731 🛏 $149 and up, includes continental breakfast, ✗ restaurant, 🖥 computer available for use, 📶 free WiFi, ☎ ATM.
	🛏📶	**Overlook Lodge** 845-786-2731 🛏 $149 and up, continental breakfast, pet rooms 📶 free WiFi.
	🛏ⓧ📶✉	**Bear Mountain Bridge Motel** 845-446-2472. ⓧ No pets. 🛏 $75D, pickup and return to trail at park, zoo or bridge with stay, 📶 free WiFi. Accepts Visa, MC. ✉ Mail drops for guests: PO Box 554, Fort Montgomery, NY 10922.
	🛏⛺🖥📶 ✉	**Holiday Inn Express** 845-446-4277. To make reservations, please call for rates and availability, walk-ins welcome also. Free Express Start Breakfast with stay. ⛺ Coin laundry, 🏊 indoor pool and sauna. 📶 Complimentary Wi-Fi and business center includes 🖥 computer and printer for use. ✉ Mail drops for guests: 1106 Route 9 W, Fort Montgomery, NY 10922-0620.
	✗	**Foodies Pizza** 845-839-0383. M-Sa 11am-9pm, Su 12pm-9pm. Serves breakfast, lunch and dinner.

Highland Falls, NY (3.8W)

	🛏📶	**Fairbridge Inn & Suites** 845-446-9400. $75 and up, includes continental breakfast. Pets $10.
	🛒	**My Town Marketplace** 845-446-3663. M-Sa 8am-9pm, Su 8am-6pm.
	✚	**Rite Aid** 845-446-3170. M-Su 8am-10pm, Pharmacy M-F 9am-9pm, Sa 9am-6pm, Su 9am-5pm.
	🖥	**Highland Falls Library** 845-446-3113. (www.highlandfallslibrary.org) M 10am-5pm, Tu 10am-7pm, W 10am-5pm, Th-F 10am-5pm, Sa 10am-2pm, Su closed.

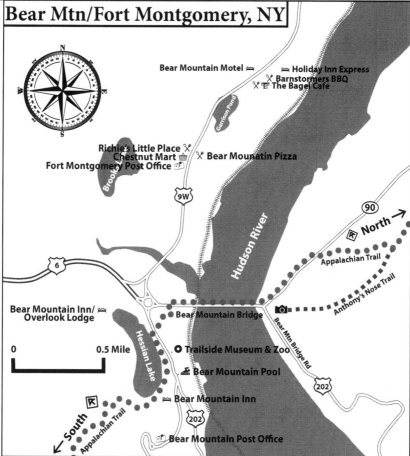

Bear Mtn/Fort Montgomery, NY

Bear Mountain Motel

Holiday Inn Express
Barnstormers BBQ
The Bagel Cafe

Gärison Pond

Richie's Little Place
Chestnut Mart
Fort Montgomery Post Office

Bear Mounatin Pizza

Brooks

9W

Hudson River

90

North

Appalachian Trail

Anthony's Nose Trail

6

Bear Mountain Inn/
Overlook Lodge

Bear Mountain Bridge

Bear Mtn Bridge Rd

Hessian Lake

0   0.5 Mile

Trailside Museum & Zoo

Bear Mountain Pool

202

South

Appalachian Trail

Bear Mountain Inn

202

Bear Mountain Post Office

NoBo	Features	Description	GPS	Elev	SoBo
1406.1		Intersects with U.S. 9W, Bear Mountain Bridge (south end), Hudson River		150	785.9
1406.3	P(3)	Cross **NY. 9D**.	N 41 19.352, W 73 58.549	230	785.7
1406.8	Y	Camp Smith Trail to Anthony's Nose (0.5E) with view of Hudson River.		700	785.2
1407.0		Intersects with rocky dirt road.		786	785.0
1407.7		Cross brook.		551	784.3
1407.8	YAA	Intersects with dirt road ay a "Y" intersection. Blue blaze trail leads 100 feet east to Hemlock Springs Campsite, nearby spring. Do not camp in the area where blue blaze trail leaves the AT.		550	784.2
1408.0	P(4)	Intersects **South Mountain Pass Road** and follows the road for 250 feet.	N 41 19.786, W 73 57.141	460	784.0
1408.1		Trail register.		667	783.9
1408.9		High point near Canada Hill summit.		832	783.1
1409.0	Y	Osborn Loop Trail west.		787	783.0
1409.1		Unmarked woods road east.		864	782.9
1409.5	Y	Curry Pond Trail west, yellow blazed.		821	782.5

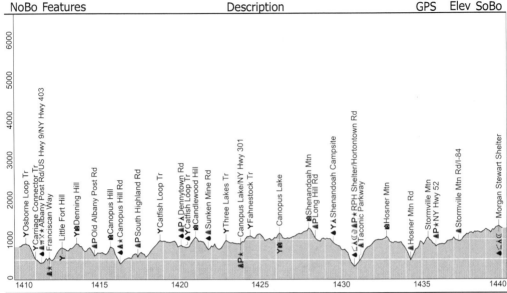

NoBo	Features	Description	GPS	Elev	SoBo
1410.3	Y	Blue blaze trail leads 100 feet to view over Hudson River and Bear Mountain Bridge.	931		781.7
1410.4	Y	Osborn Loop Trail west.	872		781.6
1410.9	Y	Carriage Connector Trail west leads to Hudson Highlands State Park.	708		781.1
1411.4 ★★★★★		Cross U.S. 9, NY. 403	400		780.6

Appalachian Market at trail head. 845-424-6241. Hiker-friendly, open 24hrs, ✕ deli serves breakfast, lunch and dinner. ☎ ATM. ♦ Water spigot on north side of building. M-Su 24 hours.

✕   (0.8E) **Stadium Sports Bar** 845-734-4000. (www.stadiumbarrest.com) M-Su 11:30am-10pm. Closed the months of Jan-Feb.

Peekskill, NY 10566 (4.5E) All major services.

PO M–F 9am–5pm, Sa 9am-4pm. 914-737-6437. 738 South St. NY. Peekskill, 10566. N 41 17.375, W 73 55.383

| 1411.6 | | Cross Old Highland Turnpike, paved | | | 780.4 |
| 1411.9 ★★★★★ | Y♦ | Graymoor Spiritual Life Center Franciscan Way, blue blazes lead to ballfield. See map of Graymoor, NY. | N 41 21.138, W 73 55.204 520 | | 780.1 |

  (0.4E) **Graymoor Spiritual Life Center** 845-424-2111.

Follow signs and blue blazes; stay to the left at both forks in the road. Hikers are permitted to sleep free at monastery's ball field and picnic shelter Mar-Nov. ♦ Water, privy and ☂ shower. Dogs are allowed but please keep them leashed and pick up after them. Please call ahead of arrival to insure space is available.

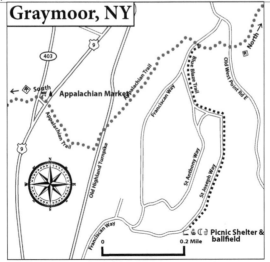

Graymoor, NY

NoBo	Features	Description	GPS	Elev	SoBo
1412.0	⛺	Cross Old West Point Road		550	780.0
1412.1	⛺	Pass private gravel road.		576	779.9
1412.7	Y	Short side trail marked with orange blazes leads east to a shrine on Graymoor Spiritual Life Center.		863	779.3
1413.5	⛺	Intersects with woods road.		889	778.5
1413.6	⛺Y📷	Follows woods road. Blue blaze side trail leads 650 feet west to good view of Hudson River.		960	778.4
1413.9	📷	(0.1W) Denning Hill, panoramic view south.		900	778.1
1414.7	⛺P(3)⚲	Cross **Old Albany Post Road–Chapman Road**	N 41 22.741, W 73 53.753	607	777.3
1415.7	📷	View on top of Canompus Hill		820	776.3
1416.3	♦	Cross brook.		350	775.7
1416.4	⛺⚲ ★★★★★	Cross **Canopus Hill Road**.	N 41 23.181, W 73 52.635	420	775.6
	✗☰☎	(1.6E) **Putnam Valley Market** 845-528-8626. (www.theputnamvalleymarket.com) (0.3E) on Campus Hill Road, (0.1E) on Canopus Hollow Road, (1.2W) on Sunset Hill Road. ☰✗ Pizza, hot food off the grill, ☎ ATM, open M-Sa 6am–9pm, Su 9am-7pm.			
1417.4	⛺P(2)⚲	Cross **South Highland Road**	N 41 23.976, W 73 52.590	570	774.6
1417.8	📷	Rocky knob with limited views.		715	774.2
1418.0	⛺	Intersects with old woods road.		665	774.0
1418.2	⛺	Intersects with old woods road.		836	773.8
1418.5	⛺	Intersects with old woods road.		980	773.5
1418.6	♦	Cross stream.		998	773.4
1418.9	Y	Catfish Loop Trail east, red blazed.		976	773.1
1419.6	📷	View east, limited.		1019	772.4
1420.1	♦⛺⛺⚲ P(12)	Cross **Dennytown Road**, water faucet on building	N 41 25.244, W 73 52.132	860	771.9
1420.3	Y	Catfish Loop Trail east , red blazed.		862	771.7
1420.4	♦	Cross stream.		838	771.6
1421.0	📷	High point on ridge, views west.		1073	771.0
1421.7	⛺⚲	Cross **Sunk Mine Road**, leads west to blue blazed Three Lakes Trail.	N 41 25.842, W 73 50.993	800	770.3
1421.8	♦⌒	Cross bridge over stream.		823	770.2
1422.9	Y	Cross Three Lakes Trail.		1019	769.1
1423.1		Intersects with old mine-railway bed (south end).		1000	768.9
1423.8	⛺P(9)⚲ ★★★★★	**NY. 301** (south side), old mine-railway bed (north end), Canopus Lake.	N 41 27.179, W 73 50.216	920	768.2
	⛺✗⛺⚑	(1.0E) **Clarence Fahnestock State Park** 845-225-7207, 800-456-2267 Open mid-Apr to mid-Dec. ⛺ Thru-hikers get one free night of camping. ⛺ Restrooms. Concession at beach open weekends only Memorial Day - June; open daily July - Labor Day. Hours M-Sa 9-5, Su 9-6.			
1423.9	⛺	Intersects with **NY. 301 (north side)**		1009	768.1
1424.1		Trail register.		1092	767.9
1424.4	Y	Fahnestock Trail west.		1118	767.6
1424.7	♦	Cross rocky stream.		1111	767.3
1425.8	♦	Cross stream.		1197	766.2
1426.1	📷	View south of Canopus Lake. Blue blazed trail leads east around lake and (0.5) to park campground.		1038	765.9
1426.2	Y	Side trails lead west to views of Catskills.		1149	765.8
1426.6	♦	Cross small stream.		1061	765.4
1426.8	⛺	Intersects with woods road.		1055	765.2
1426.9		Ruins of stone building.		1086	765.1
1427.6	⛺	Trail follows woods road, stone wall to east.		1185	764.4
1428.0	⛺📷	Shenandoah Mountain summit, good views.		1282	764.0
1428.1	📷	Views to west.		1266	763.9
1428.4	⛺P(5)⚲	Cross **Long Hill Road**	N 41 30.017, W 73 48.821	1100	763.6
1428.7	◊	Cross stream, unreliable.		991	763.3
1429.0	⚡	Power line.		993	763.0
1429.5	♦Y⛺	Blue blaze trail leads (0.1) west to Shenandoah Tenting Area, water from pump.		900	762.5
1429.8	📷	Shenandoah Mountain high point with views through trees.		1060	762.2
1429.9	♦	Cross stream.		907	762.1
1430.5	♦	Cross stream.		875	761.5
1430.6	♦⌒	Cross bridge over brook.		837	761.4
1430.8	♦Y⛺ ⌂(6)☾ ⛺P(3)⚲ ★★★★★	Side trail to **RPH Shelter**, water is a hand pump, tenting, privy, trash can. 40.7◄35.4◄32.2◄► 9.0► 16.8►25.6 300 feet north to Hortontown Road.	Shelter N 41 30.869, W 73 47.548 Parking N 41 30.854, W 73 47.473	350	761.2

NoBo	Features	Description	GPS	Elev	SoBo
	✕	**Carlo's Pizza Express** 845-896-6500. (www.carlospizzaexpress.com) Pizza delivered after 4pm only.			
	✕	**Gian Bruno's** 845-227-9276. (www.gianbrunorestaurant.com) M closed, Tu-Su 12pm-3pm.			
1431.0	◢⌒	Cross bridge over brook.		480	761.0
1431.1	▲	Cross under **Taconic State Parkway**, underpass		650	760.9
1431.2	▲	Intersects with **Rockledge Road**.		540	760.8
1432.1	📷	Rocky viewpoint.		968	759.9
1432.4	◢	Cross small brook.		1077	759.6
1432.5	Y	Hosner Mountain Side Trail west.		1020	759.5
1432.7	📷	View, panoramic view of Hudson Highlands, Shawangunks, and Catskills at top of rocks.		1075	759.3
1433.0	Y	Hosner Mountain Side Trail west.		1074	759.0
1433.5	📷	Rocky area with views of Hudson River Valley and Fishkill Plains.		1000	758.5
1434.3	▲	Cross **Hosner Mountain Road**		500	757.7
1434.9	📷	Views of Hudson Valley.		1026	757.1
1435.1	Y	Old trail west.		989	756.9
1435.4	▲	Stormville Mountain summit.		1056	756.6
1435.9	▲P(4)♀ ★★★★★	Cross **NY. 52**	N 41 32.469, W 73 43.963	800	756.1
	◢🏠✕▲ 📞🏧✕	(0.4E) **Mountaintop Market Deli** 845-221-0928. 📞 ATM, 🖥 pay phone inside, ◢ water from faucet on side of building and electric outlets for charging. ▲ Camping allowed. M-F 6am–8pm. **Danny's Pizzeria** 845-223-5888. pizza by the slice.			
Stormville, NY 12582 (1.9W)					
	📧♀	**PO** M–F 8:30am–5pm, Sa 9am–12pm. 845.226.2627. 7 Old Route 52. Stormville, NY 12582. N 41 33.830, W 73 44.468			
1436.9	♀Y	Blue blaze trail to parking area on NY. 52	N 41 32.469, W 73 43.963	893	755.1
1437.1	▲P(4)♀	Intersects with **Stormville Mountain Road (south end)**	N 41 32.694, W 73 43.051	999	754.9
1437.3	▲	Intersects with **Stormville Mountain Road (north end), Mountain Top Road, and crosses over I-84**, overpass		950	754.7
1437.5	▲	Cross **Graplow Road**.		982	754.5
1439.2	◢	Cross brook.		1222	752.8
1439.5	📷	Ridgecrest with good views.		1278	752.5
1439.7	▲	Mt. Egbert summit		1329	752.3
1439.8	◢Y ▲⌂(6) ☾♀	75 feet east to **Morgan Stewart Shelter**, water is a well with a pump located downhill and in front of the shelter, tenting, privy. 44.4◄41.2◄9.0◄►7.8►16.6►20.6	N 41 33.874, W 73 41.506	1285	752.2

1440.1	Y📷	Side trail to view.		1327	751.9
1440.4	◊	Seasonal pond.		1313	751.6
1440.9	▲P(6)♀	Cross **Depot Hill Road**, near radio tower.	N 41 34.357, W 73 40.856	1230	751.1
1442.7	✕	Railroad tracks.		719	749.3
1442.8	▲P(3)♀	Cross **Old Route 55**, paved	N 41 35.271, W 73 39.690	750	749.2

NoBo	Features	Description	GPS	Elev	SoBo

1443.1 ⓐP(5)♀ ★★★★★ Cross **N.Y. 55**, parking (0.1W) — N 41 35.384, W 73 39.551 — 720 — **748.9**

✗ (1.5W) **Pleasant Ridge Pizza** 845-724-3444. (www.pleasantridgepizzarestaurant.com) Serves lunch and dinner. Accepts major credit cards. M-Sa 10:30am-10pm, Su 11am-9pm.

✗ (1.5W) **A&A Italian Deli** 845-724-3400. M-F 6am-7pm, Sa 7am-6pm, Su 8am-3:30pm.

✪ (1.5W) **Total Care Pharmacy** 845-724-5757. M-F 9am-8pm, Sa 9am-3pm.

✗ (1.6W) **Great Wall** 845-724-5387.

Poughquag, NY 12570 (3.1W)

🖂♀ **PO** M–F 8:30am–1pm & 2pm-5pm, Sa 8:30am–12:30pm. 845-724-4763. 2546 Route 55. Poughquag, NY 12570. N 41 37.487, W 73 41.281

🛏⊛🖭 **Pine Grove Motel** 845-724-5151. ⊛ No pets. 🛏 $70S $75D. 🖭 Free WiFi. Accepts Visa/MC/Disc.

✗ **Clove Valley Deli & Café** 845-227-1585.

✪ **Beekman Pharmacy** 845-724-3200. M-F 9am-8pm, Sa 9am-4pm, Su 10am-2pm.

🐾 **Beekman Animal Hospital** 845-724-8387. M-Tu closed, W 12pm-6pm, Th closed, F 8am-1pm, Sa-Su closed.

1443.3 ♈P♀ Blue blaze west to parking area on NY. 55. — N 41 35.384, W 73 39.551 — **748.7**

1443.4 ♈ Beekman Uplands Trail west. — **748.6**

1444.1 ♦ Cross stream. — **747.9**

1444.5 ♦ Cross stream, outlet of Nuclear Lake. Nuclear Lake between 1958-72 was a facility licensed by the government to experiment with bomb-grade uranium and plutonium. It was cleaned up in 1972 and purchased by the National Park Service in 1979. — 750 — **747.5**

1444.6 ♈ Nuclear Loop Trail east, yellow blazed. — **747.4**

1445.4 ♈ Nuclear Loop Trail east, yellow blazed. — **746.6**

1445.7 ◊ Cross stream, unreliable. — **746.3**

1445.8 ♈ Beekman Uplands Trail west. — **746.2**

1446.8 ⚠ Cross **Penny Road**, dirt. — **745.2**

1447.3 📷 West Mountain, views — 1200 — **744.7**

1447.4 📷 Side trail leads 100 feet to rocky ledge with views. — 1153 — **744.6**

1447.6 ◊⚠⊏(6)ℂ♀ (0.1E) **Telephone Pioneers Shelter** trail crosses stream, if dry go (0.7) north at the Champion residence, tenting, privy. N 41 36.256, W 73 37.158
49.0◄16.8◄7.8◄►8.8►12.8►21.2 — 910 — **744.4**

1448.0 ♦ Cross stream. — 520 — **744.0**

1448.3 ◉⚠P(5)♀ ★★★★★ Cross **County Road 20, West Dover Road, Dover Oak. See map of Pawling, NY.** N 41 36.175, W 73 36.686 — 650 — **743.7**

Pawling, NY 12564 (3.1E) See map of Pawling, NY.

🖂♀ **PO** M-F 8:30am-5pm. Sa 9am-12pm. 845-855-2669. 10 Broad St. Pawling, NY 12564. N 41 33.829, W 73 36.125

⚠⊛♥⚊ **Edward R. Murrow Memorial Park** ⊛ No pets. ⚠ Town allows hikers to camp in the park for one night only. Located one mile from the center of town, ♥ restrooms, ⚊ swimming.

✗ **Vinny's Deli & Pasta** 845-855-1922. (www.vinnysdeliandcatering.com) M-Sa 8am-6pm, Su 9am-2pm.

✗ **Gaudino's Italian Kitchen** 845-855-3200. M-Sa 11am-10pm, Su 12pm-8pm.

✗ **Great Wall** 845-855-9750. M-F 11am-10:30pm, Sa-Su 11am-11:30pm.

✗ **McGrath Tavern** 845-855-0800. (www.mcgrathstavern.com) Serves lunch and dinner. M 11:30am-9pm, Tu 4pm-9pm, W-Th 11:30am-9pm, F-Sa 11:30am-10pm, Su 11:30am-9pm.

🖥 **Pawling Free Library** M-12pm-5pm, Tu-TH 10am-8pm, F 12pm-5pm, Sa 10am-4pm, Su 12pm-4pm. Closed Sundays in July and August.

🚗 **Martin and Donna** 845-505-1671, 845-546-1832. Nights and weekends only. Shuttle range RPH Shelter to Kent, CT.

Pawling, NY

Map features:
- Pawling House B&B
- Old Rte 55
- (3.6) to / from downtown Pawling
- Charles Coleman Blvd
- (3.0) to / from downtown Pawling
- (2.5) to / from downtown Pawling
- Clouter Ave
- 55
- Post Office
- Great Wall II Take out Chinese
- Pawling Public Library
- Cleanery
- W Main St
- Book Covey
- Station Inn Pawling
- Corner Bakery
- Vinny's Deli & Pasta
- McKinney & Doyle Fine Foods Cafe
- CVS
- The Bakeria
- Gaudino's Italian Kitchen
- Freshcuts Barber Shop
- (2.1) mile from downtown to Hannafords
- 3 Guys
- KFC
- E Main St
- 0   0.2 Mile

NoBo	Features	Description	GPS	Elev	SoBo
1450.3	♦	Cross Swamp River.		415	741.7
1450.6	⛰	Intersects with dirt road west.		430	741.4
1450.7	⛰ 🅿(15) 🚻	Cross **NY. 22**, Appalachian Trail Metro–North Train Platform ★★★★★	N 41 35.564, W 73 35.255	480	741.3

Native Landscapes & Garden Center 845-855-7050. (www.nativelandscaping.net)
⬥ AT Passport location.
M-Su 9-5, please do not loiter after hours. Owner Pete Muroski is hiker friendly. 🚿 Free outside cold shower, $5 for indoor hot shower, charging outlet, 🚻 use of restrooms. No loitering inside please, hikers please leave your packs outside in the outdoor gazebo when going inside. Drinks, snacks, freeze-dried meals and ⛽ canister fuel sold at the garden center.
✉ Mail drops: 991 Route 22, Pawling, NY 12564.

(0.6E) **Tony's Deli** 845-855-9540. (www.tonysdeli22.com)
✗ Short order grill, sandwiches, salads, soda machine outside. 📶 WiFi. ⛺ Ask about camping. M-F 3:30 am-12am, Sa 4am-12am, Su 5am-12am.

Pawling, NY 12564 (2.5E) see mile 1448.3
Wingdale, NY 12594 (4W)

PO M-F 8:30am-12:30pm & 1:30pm-5pm, Sa 8am-12:30pm. 845-832-6147. 1809 route 22. Wingdale, NY 12594. N 41 38.894, W 73 33.829

Dutchess Motor Lodge 845-832-6400, 914-525-9276. (www.dutchessmotorlodge.com)
🛏 $73 for single, A/C, Fridge, 🧺 Guest laundry $7, 📶 Free WiFi. One pet room available. Ride for a fee when available.
✉ Mail drops for guests: 1512 Route 22, Wingdale, NY 12594.

Wingdale Supermarket 845-832-9361

Cousins Pizza 845-832-6510. (www.cousinspizzawingdale.com) Acceptss Visa, Master Card & Discover. M-Sa 11am-10pm, Su 1pm-9pm.

Peking Kitchen 845-832-9500. M-Th 10:30am-10pm, F-Sa 10:30am-10:30pm, Su 10:30am-10pm.

Dunkin Donuts 845-832-6118. M-Su 24 hours.

Ben's Deli 845-832-9460. M-Su 3am-9pm.

Big W BBQ 845-832-6200. (www.theforkingpig.com) M-Tu closed, W-Th 12pm-8pm, F-Sa 12pm-9pm, Su 12pm-8pm.

Dover Plains Library 845-832-6605. M-F 10am-8pm, Sa closed, Su 10am-8pm.

NoBo	Features	Description	GPS	Elev	SoBo
1450.9	⛰	Cross **Hurds Corners Road**, paved		480	741.1
1451.1	♦	Cross stream.		473	740.9
1451.5	Y	Pawling Nature Preserve, blue blaze trail west, trail register		675	740.5
1452.5	Y	Pass terminus of Red Trail.		1010	739.5
1452.7	♦	Cross stream.		934	739.3
1453.0	♦Y	Cross stream. Yellow Trail in the area.		921	739.0
1453.4	Y	Intersection of Red Trail east and Green Trail west.		968	738.6
1454.3	Y	Yellow Trail east.		900	737.7
1456.0	⛰	Cross **Leather Hill Road**, dirt road		750	736.0

NoBo	Features	Description	GPS	Elev	SoBo
1456.3	🅰	Cross logging road, dirt		829	735.7
1456.4	♦🅰⌂(6) ⌒(🛈♀	**Wiley Shelter**, water is located at pump on trail (0.1) north of the shelter on the AT beyond tent platform, tenting, privy. 25.6◄16.6◄8.8◄►4.0►12.4►19.7	N 41 38.272, W 73 31.944	740	735.6
1456.5	♦	Pump, water source.		593	735.5
1456.6	🅰P(5)♀	Cross **Duell Hollow Road**, paved	N 41 38.190, W 73 31.794	620	735.4
1456.9	♦⌒	Cross wooden bridge over Duell Hollow Brook.		567	735.1
1457.4	🅰	Trail briefly follows old woods road.		417	734.6
1457.6	🅰P(4)♀ State Line	Cross **Hoyt Road**, New York–Connecticut State Line	N 41 38.463, W 73 31.211	400	734.4
1457.9	Y P(12)♀	Side trail west leads to CT. 55 and large parking area.	N 41 38.683, W 73 31.153	424	734.1
1458.1	♦	Cross brook, reliable.		445	733.9
1458.3	🅰P(12)♀ ★★★★★	Cross **CT. 55**, Gaylordsville, CT. 06755, (2.5E) Post Office, long term resupply, restaurant.	N 41 38.683, W 73 31.153	580	733.7

Gaylordsville, CT (2.9E)
(2.4E) across bridge on route 55, (0.5) further on route 7 south to PO and diner.

	✉♀	**PO** M-F 8am-1pm & 2pm-5pm, Sa 8am-12pm. 9am. 860-354-9727. 3 Geo. Washington Plz Unit 8. Gaylordsville, CT 06755. N 41 38.362, W 73 28.925			
	✗	**Gaylordsville Diner** 860-210-1622. Servers breakfast, lunch and dinner.			

1459.4	📷	Top of Ten Mile Hill, views of Housatonic Valley		1000	732.6
1459.5	Y	Herrick Trail east.		948	732.5
1459.9	◊	Spring west, unreliable.		761	732.1
1460.1	🅰	Cross dirt road.		584	731.9
1460.4	♦Y🅰 ⌐(6) ⌒(🛈♀	(0.1E) **Ten Mile River Shelter**, water is a hand pump 100 feet south and west of the shelter, tenting, privy, bear box. 20.6◄12.8◄4.0◄►8.4►15.7►25.7	N 41 39.912, W 73 30.583	290	731.6
1460.6	♦⌐⌒	Cross Ten Mile River on footbridge. Camping at **10 Mile River Campsite**, is in field south of the bridge.		280	731.4
1461.3	🅰P(14)♀ ★★★★★	Cross **Bulls Bridge Road**, Trail to Bulls Bridge Parking Area (0.2E)	N 41 40.522, W 73 30.624	450	730.7
	🏠☎	(0.5E) **Country Market** 860-619-8199. (www.cornwallcountrymarket.com) ✗ Deli, bakery, breakfast, fruit, ice cream, soda, ☎ ATM. M-F 7am-5pm Sa-Su 8-5pm.			
	✗	(0.5E) **Bulls Bridge Inn** 860-927-1000. (www.bullsbridge.com) M-Th 5am-9pm, F 5am-9:30pm, Sa-Su 12pm-9:30, Su 12-9pm. American foods, meals reasonable, bar.			
1462.0	🅰	Intersects with **Schaghticoke Road**.		320	730.0
1462.3	♦	Cross stream.		524	729.7
1463.5	📷	View.		1190	728.5
1463.7		Skirts the west of Schaghticoke Mountain.		1331	728.3
1464.0	◊	Two seasonal springs in the area.		1282	728.0
1464.9 State Line		Connecticut–New York State Line		1250	727.1
1465.0	♦	Cross stream.		1193	727.0
1465.3	📷	Indian Rocks		1290	726.7
1465.7	📷	Open ledge with good views of Housatonic River.		1285	726.3
1465.9	♦(🛈🅰	Blue blaze west to Schaghticoke Mountain campsite, **NO FIRES**.		950	726.1
1467.3	📷	Reach high point with good views.		1403	724.7
1467.8	♦	Cross Thayer Brook		900	724.2
1468.2	⛰	Reach height of land on Mt. Algo.		1190	723.8
1468.8	♦Y🅰 ⌐(6) ⌒(🛈♀	200 feet west to **Mt. Algo Shelter**, water is located on the blue blaze trail leading to shelter, 15 yards in front of shelter, tenting, privy. 21.2◄12.4◄8.4◄►7.3►17.3►28.6	N 41 43.899, W 73 29.802	655	723.2
1469.1	🅰P(10)♀ ★★★★★	Cross **CT. 341, Schaghticoke Road**.	N 41 43.863, W 73 29.439	350	722.9

Kent, CT 06757 (0.8E) See map of Kent, CT.

	✉♀	**PO** M-F 8am-1pm & 2pm-5pm, Sa 8:30am-12:30pm. 860-927-3435. 31 Kent Green Blvd. Kent, CT 06757. N 41 40.720, W 73 28.244			
	🛏☎✗🍴	**Fife 'n Drum Restaurant & Inn** 860-927-3509. (www.fifendrum.com)			
	✉	🛏 No pets. 🛏 Hiker room rates $140D +tax weekdays, $170D +tax weekends, $25EAP +tax. Front desk closed Tu, so make prior arrangements for Tu night stays. ✉ Mail drops for guests: (USPS) PO Box 188 or (FedEx/UPS) 53 N Main Street, Kent, CT 06757. ✗ Restaurant hours: Lunch; M 11:30am-3pm, Tu closed, W-Sa 11:30am – 3pm, Su Brunch 11:30am-3pm Dinner; M 5:30pm-9:30pm, Tu closed, W-Th 5:30pm-9:30pm, Fr-Sa 5:30pm-10pm, Su 3pm-8:30pm			

Cooper Creek B&B 860-927-4334.
(2.5) north of town on US 7.
🛏 Hiker rate Sunday thru Thursday $110 plus 11% CT Lodging tax. Weekend rates $145-200 +tax. 💻
Free WiFi. Shuttles to and from Kent with stay, 🎒 slackpacking and 🚗 longer shuttles for a fee.

Starbuck Inn 860-927-1788. (www.starbuckinn.com)
🚫 No pets.
🛏 $220D/up + tax, includes full breakfast and afternoon tea. Includes healthy breakfast made with local ingredients, it's different every day.
💻 Free WiFi. Sometimes discounted mid-week, accepts credit cards.

🛒 **Davis IGA** (860) 927-4093. (www.davisiga.com) M-Sa 8am-7pm, Su 8am-6pm.

🚶 **Annie Bananie General Store (Closed their doors Dec 2018)**

⚼ **Laundromat** 860-927-1144. (www.kentgreenlaundromat.com) M-Su 6am-11pm.

🏧✗ **JP Gifford** 860-592-0200. (www.jpgifford.com/kent)
✗ Breakfast sandwiches, salads, bakery, coffee and supplies. M-Sa 6:30am-6pm, Su 7am-3pm.

✗ **Kent Pizza Garden** 860-927-3733. (www.kentpizzagarden.com) M-Th 11am-1am, F-Sa 11am-2am, Su 11am-1am.

✗ **Panini Cafe & Gelateria** 860-927-5083. M-Su 9:30am-5pm.

✗ **Shanghai** 860-927-4809. M-Sa 11:30pm-10pm, Su 12pm-9pm.

✗ **Chris's Hot Dog Cart**

🐾 **Kent Animal Clinic** 8600927-1200.

💻 **Library** 860.927.3761. (www.kentmemoriallibrary.org) M-F 10am-5:30pm, Sa 10am-4pm.

🚗 **Dave the Driver** 203-788-7926(cell)
Based in Kent, CT. Will drive from NY/NJ line to VT/MA line.

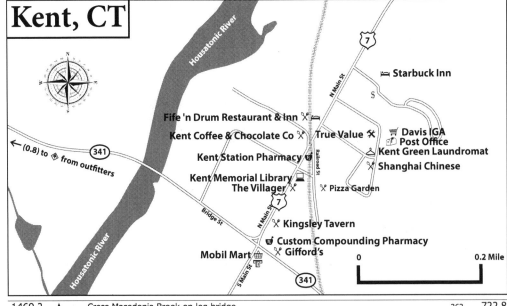

1469.2	🔥	Cross Macedonia Brook on log bridge.	363	722.8
1469.9	📷	Ledge with view of Kent and Housatonic Valley.	799	722.1

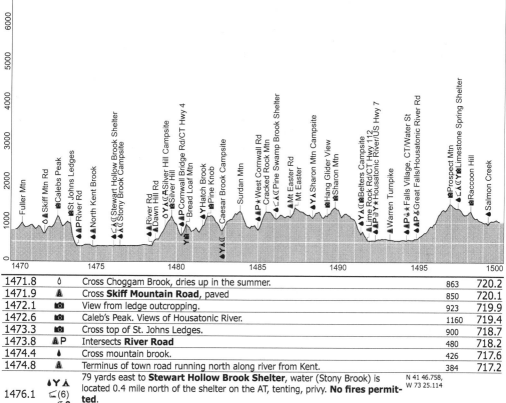

NoBo	Features	Description	GPS	Elev	SoBo
1471.8	◊	Cross Choggam Brook, dries up in the summer.		863	720.2
1471.9	▲	Cross **Skiff Mountain Road**, paved		850	720.1
1472.1	📷	View from ledge outcropping.		923	719.9
1472.6	📷	Caleb's Peak. Views of Housatonic River.		1160	719.4
1473.3	📷	Cross top of St. Johns Ledges.		900	718.7
1473.8	▲P	Intersects **River Road**		480	718.2
1474.4	♦	Cross mountain brook.		426	717.6
1474.8	▲	Terminus of town road running north along river from Kent.		384	717.2
1476.1	♦Y▲ ⊂(6) ⤳((♀	79 yards east to **Stewart Hollow Brook Shelter**, water (Stony Brook) is located 0.4 mile north of the shelter on the AT, tenting, privy. **No fires permitted.** 19.7◄15.7◄7.3◄► 10.0►21.3►28.7	N 41 46.758, W 73 25.114	400	715.9
1476.5	♦▲(	Cross Stony Brook, campsites nearby, privy. **No fires permitted**.		440	715.5
1478.5	♦▲P(5)♀	Cross dirt **River Road** that parallels Housatonic River. Seasonal spring a few feet north of trail crossing.	N 41 48.342, W 73 23.700	460	713.5
1478.7	▲	Cross Dawn Hill Road, paved.		541	713.3
1479.3	◊Y▲⤳ ((🛏	Side trail 160 feet to Silver Hill Campsite, water pump, privy. **No fires permitted.**		1000	712.7
1480.1	📷	Lookout at north side of Sliver Hill.		1142	711.9
1480.2	◊▲P(12) ★★★★★	Cross **CT. 4**		700	711.8

Cornwall Bridge, CT (0.9E) See map of Cornwall Bridge, CT.

🏤♀   **PO** M-F 8:30am-1pm & 2pm-5pm, Sa 9am-12pm. 860-672-6710. 18A Kent Rd S. Cornwall, CT 06754. N 41 49.092, W 73 22.263

🛏⛺🍴🚗   **Hitching Post Motel** 860-672-6219. (www.cthitchingpostmotel.us)
🖥️   🛏 $65/up weekdays, $85/up weekends. Pets $10, ⚞ laundry $5, ⚛ WiFi, 🚗 shuttles $2 per mile.
     📧 Mail drops for guests: 45 Kent Road, Cornwall Bridge, CT 06754.

🛏◈⛺⚛   **The Amselhaus** 860-248-3155. (www.theamselhaus.com)
🖥️   ◈ AT Passport location.
     Located behind carpet store, check-in at grey house next door to apartments. 🛏 $85S, $100 for couple, $50 EAP. 2-3 bedroom apartments, ⛺ includes laundry, satelite TV, local and long-distance phone, ⚛ WiFi. Rides available.
     📧 Mail drops for guests: C/O Tyler, 6 Rug Road South, Cornwall Bridge, CT 06754.

🛏▲⚓   **Housatonic Meadows State Park** 860-672-6772.
     Camping and Cabins 1.3 miles north of town on US 7.
     No hammocks. No alcohol.
     Open mid-May to Oct, registration at main cabin by gate. ▲ Campsite $17 for CT residents, $27 nonresidents, $3 walk-in fee for first night. 🛏 Cabins $60 with 2 nights minimum, CT resident fees for cabins is $50 plus tax.
     Reservations can be made Memorial Day Through Labor Day by contacting ReserveAmerica.com or by calling 1-877-668-2267

Cornwall Inn 860-672-6884. (www.cornwallinn.com)
(2.2) miles south on US 7.
Su-Th $129D +tax, includes cont. breakfast. Weekends 10% hiker discount. Seasonal pool and hot tub. Free WiFi. Pet fee. Pickup and return to trail head and other shuttles for a fee. Mail drops with reservation.

Cornwall Country Market 860-619-8199. (www.cornwallcountrymarket.com)
AT Passport location.
Hiker friendly, hot meals, breakfast, groceries, charging stations, WiFi, Restrooms. M-F 6am-5pm, Sa-Su 7am-5pm.

Citgo 860-672-6786. M 6am-11pm, Tu-Sa 6am-10pm, Su 6am-9pm.

Cornwall Package Store 860-672-6645. (www.cornwallpackagestore.com)
AT Passport location.
Water available from spigot outside. Stop in to sign their register. M-Th 10am-7pm, F 10am-8pm Sa 11am-3pm, Su closed.

Housatonic Veterinary Care 860-672-4948. (www.housatonicveterinarycare.com) M-Tu 9am-5:30pm, W closed, Th-F 9am-5:30pm, Sa 9am-1pm, Su closed.

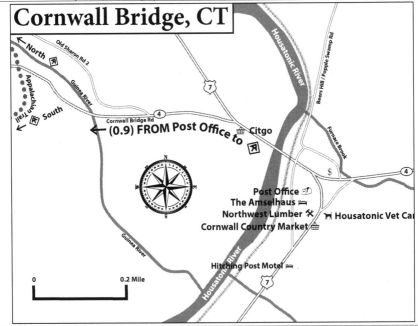

Cornwall Bridge, CT

1480.3	Y	Cross Guinea Brook, **camping and fires not permitted**. During times of high water hikers can detour on Old Sharon Road and CT. 4.	650	711.7
1480.4		Cross Old Sharon Road, dirt.	750	711.6
1480.5	YP(10)	Side trail leads (0.1) to summit of Bread Loaf Mountain and (0.7) to US. 7 trail head parking. N 41 49.990, W 73 23.000	744	711.5
1481.6		Cross Hatch Brook	880	710.4
1481.7	YA	Pine Knob Loop Trail, (0.62E) to parking and another (0.35) to Housatonic Meadows State Park with tenting and shower.	1150	710.3
1481.9		Pine Knob, view of Housatonic Valley.	1097	710.1
1482.3	YA	Pine Knob Loop Trail, (0.7E) to Housatonic Meadows State Park with tenting and shower.	794	709.7
1482.7	AC	Cross abandoned Caesar Road, Caesar Brook campsite is on a knob south of Caesar Brook, privy.	760	709.3
1484.1		Cross abandoned Surdam Road.	874	707.9
1484.9		Cross Carse Brook on log bridge.	810	707.1
1485.0	P (3) ★★★★★	Cross **West Cornwall Road**, paved. **See map of Falls Village, CT for US 7/ CT 112.** N 41 52.406, W 73 23.467	800	707.0
		Bearded Woods B&D One of a Kind Bunk & Dine, will pickup at trail heads between West Cornwall Road to Salisbury with stay. **See Notes at mile 1492.3**		

West Cornwall, CT 06796 (2.2E)

PO M-F 8:30am-12pm & 2pm-4:30pm, Sa 9am-12pm. 860-672-6791. 408 Sharon Goshen Tpke. West Cornwall, CT 06796. N 41 52.304, W 73 21.663

Sharon, CT 06069 (4.7W)

☎♀	**PO** M–F 9:30am–4:30pm, Sa 9:30am–12:30pm. 860-364-5306. 2 Low Rd. Sharon, CT 06069. N 41 53.057, W 73 28.214			
🛒	**Sharon Farm Market** 860-397-5161. M-Sa 8am-8pm, Su 8am-7pm.			
⚕	**Sharon Hospital** 860-364-4141. (www.sharonhospital.com)			
⚕	**Sharon Pharmacy** 860-364-5272. M-F 8am-6pm, Sa 8am-3pm, Su 8am-12pm.			
1486.1 ♦Y⅄ ⚓(6) ⌁(♀	95 yards west to **Pine Swamp Brook Shelter**, water is located on the blue-blazed trail, tenting, privy. 25.7◀17.3◀10.0◀▶11.3▶18.7▶19.9	N 41 52.898, W 73 23.526 1075		705.9
1487.0 ⛺	Cross **Mt. Easter Road**	1150		705.0
1487.3	Skirt the summit of Mt. Easter	1350		704.7
1488.4 ♦	Cross brook, source of water for Sharon Mountain Campsite.	1271		703.6
1488.5 Y⅄	Side trail to Sharon Mountain campsite.	1200		703.5
1489.3 📷	Hang Glider View	1150		702.7
1490.1 📷	Several viewpoints along the ridge area.	1137		701.9
1491.3 ♦Y⅄⚓(📷	Side trail to Belter's campsite, privy.	770		700.7
1491.4 📷	Belter's Bump, scenic look.	721		700.6
1491.7 ⛺P♀	Cross **U.S. 7 (south end)**, CT. 112	N 41 55.855, W 73 21.859 520		700.3
1492.3 ♦⌁⛺🅿 P(12)♀ ★★★★★	Cross **U.S. 7 (north end)**, Warren Turnpike, Housatonic River Bridge. **See map of Falls Village, CT.**	N 41 55.957, W 73 21.806 500		699.7
✗	(0.2E) **Mountainside Café Restaurant** 860-824-1397. (www.mountainside.com/café) 860-824-7876, M–Su 7am-3pm. After crossing Housatonic River on US. 7 and just before the Trail turns left onto Warren Turnpike, cross bridge over railroad tracks, then continue (0.2) mile.			
🏠◈⑂⑤ ⛺🍴⑆⚖ 🚗	(3.6E) **Bearded Woods Bunk & Dine** 860-480-2966. (www.beardedwoods.com) Hudson & Big Lu ◈ AT Passport location ⑤ No Pets. Call/text Hudson for reservations, no walk-ins. ID required. Check-in between 1 & 6pm. Not a party place, no mail drops & no pets. Open 7 days a week in May. Weekends only (Friday-Sunday) June 1st - Sept 1st. Limited services may be available outside of those dates. Pickup at: W Cornwall Rd, Falls Village or Salisbury. 🏠 $50pp Includes: Shuttle to and from trail and local Post Office, clean bunk with linens, shower with amenities, ⛺ communal laundry, loaner clothes and Hearty Breakfast. Dinner $10pp for 5 or more guest. ⑆ WiFi. Cash or Paypal. ⑂ Free slackpacking between those locations with 2nd night stay. 🚗 Longer shuttles for fee any distance. ⚖ Stove fuel, pizza, drinks, snacks and ice cream available for purchase. **See Map**			
1492.4 Y✗	Mohawk Trail Junction. (0.16E) on Mohawk Trail to US 7 then left on US 7 for (0.3) to Mountainside Café restaurant.	500		699.6
1493.2 ⛺	Cross **Warren Turnpike.**	564		698.8
1494.1 ♦⛺⚖ P(20)♀ ★★★★★	Intersects with **Water Street**, Hydroelectric Plant **Falls Village, CT.** There is a shower available for use by hikers that is located on the side of the hydro-plant. It is overgrown with ivy.	N 41 57.348, W 73 22.050 530		697.9
☎♀	**PO** M-F 8:20-1pm &2pm-5pm, Sa 8:30am-12pm. 860-824-7781. 5 Miner St. Falls Village, CT 06031. N 41 57.280, W 73 21.689			
✗⅄	**Toymakers Café** 860-824-8168. ✗ Serves breakfast and lunch. ⅄ Ask about free tent sites, hiker friendly, knock on upstairs door if closed. Cash only. M-W closed, Th-F 7am-2pm, Sa-Su 7am-4pm.			
🛏◈✗	**Falls Village Inn** 860-824-0033. (www.thefallsvillageinn.com) ◈ AT Passport location. 🛏 $239 and up, ✗ restaurant and bar.			
🏠	**Bearded Woods B&D**, will pickup at trail heads between West Cornwwall Road to Salisbury with stay. **See Notes at mile 1492.3**			

Falls Village, CT

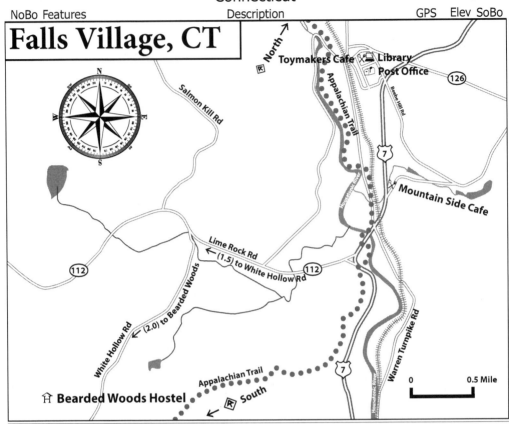

NoBo		Features	GPS	Elev	SoBo
1494.2	⌒ ▲P🍴♀	Cross Iron Bridge, Housatonic River, picnic area	N 41 57.430, W 73 22.253	510	697.8
1494.6	▲🅿♀	Cross Housatonic River Road, Great Falls	N 41 57.738, W 73 22.440	650	697.4
1495.4	◊	Spring, seasonal		750	696.6
1496.7	▲	Prospect Mountain summit		1475	695.3
1497.4	♦Υ▲ ⊑(6) ◡⊄♀	(0.5W) **Limestone Spring Shelter**, water is behind shelter, tenting, privy. 28.6◀21.3◀11.3◀▶ 7.4▶8.6▶17.4	N 41 58.508, W 73 23.538	980	694.6
1497.5	📷	Rand's View, some say it's one of the best views on the AT.		1250	694.5
1498.0	⦿	Cross Giant's Thumb, rock formation on Raccoon Hill.		1220	694.0
1498.3	📷	Billy's View, views over the Salmon Kill Valley.		1150	693.7

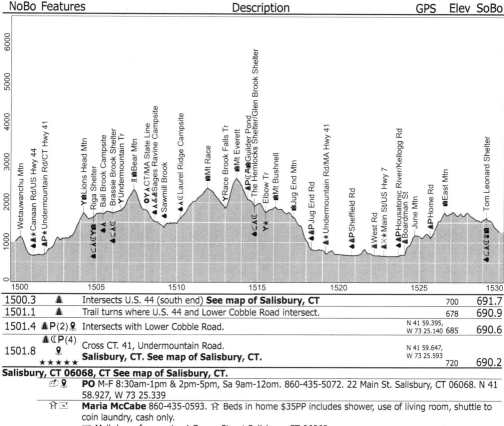

NoBo	Features	Description	GPS	Elev	SoBo
1500.3	▲	Intersects U.S. 44 (south end) **See map of Salisbury, CT**		700	691.7
1501.1	▲	Trail turns where U.S. 44 and Lower Cobble Road intersect.		678	690.9
1501.4	▲P(2)⚲	Intersects with Lower Cobble Road.	N 41 59.395, W 73 25.140	685	690.6
1501.8	▲ℂP(4) ⚲ ★★★★★	Cross CT. 41, Undermountain Road. **Salisbury, CT. See map of Salisbury, CT.**	N 41 59.647, W 73 25.593	720	690.2

Salisbury, CT 06068, CT See map of Salisbury, CT.

✉⚲	**PO** M-F 8:30am-1pm & 2pm-5pm, Sa 9am-12om. 860-435-5072. 22 Main St. Salisbury, CT 06068. N 41 58.927, W 73 25.339
⌂ ▣	**Maria McCabe** 860-435-0593. ⌂ Beds in home $35PP includes shower, use of living room, shuttle to coin laundry, cash only. ▣ Mail drops for guests: 4 Grove, Street Salisbury, CT 06068.
⌂ ⛺ �car ▣	**Vanessa Breton** 860-435-9577, 860-671-9832. ⌂ Beds in home $40PP, pets $5, ⛺ laundry $5. �car Shuttle range 100 miles. ▣ Mail drops for guests (fee for non-guests $5). Street address is 7 The Lock Up Rd, but send mail drops to PO Box: PO Box 131, Salisbury, CT 06068.
🛒✗	**LaBonne's Market** (www.labonnes.com) Grocery, deli, bakery, pizza. M–Sa 8am–7pm, Su 8am-6pm.
ⓘ ♦♦ ☏	**Town Hall** 860-435-5182. M-F 8:30-4 ⓘ Hikers welcome to use ♦♦ bathrooms and ☏ phone (local calls only, ☏ WiFi.
💻	**Scoville Memorial Library** 860-435-2838. (www.scovillelibrary.org) M closed, Tu-W 10am-5pm, Th 10am-7pm, F 10am-5pm, Sa 10am-4pm, Su 1pm-4pm.

Lakeville, CT (2.0 mi. south of Salisbury)

✗	**Boathouse** 860-435-2111. (www.theboathouseatlakeville.com) Sports bar and restaurant. M-Th 11am-9pm, F-Sa 11am-11pm, Su 11am-9pm.
✗	**Mizza's Pizza** 860-435-6266. (www.mizzas.com) M-Sa 11am-10:30pm Su 12pm-10:30pm.
⛺	**Washboard Laundromat** Located behind Mizza's Pizza.
⌂	**Bearded Woods B&D**, will pickup at trail heads between West Cornwwall Road to Salisbury with stay. **See Notes at mile 1492.3**

Connecticut

© WhiteBlaze Pages 2019

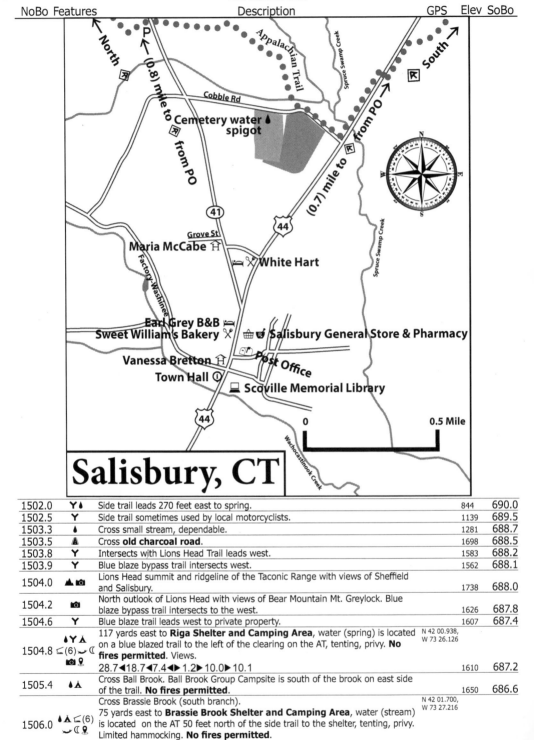

NoBo	Features	Description	GPS	Elev	SoBo
1502.0	Y♦	Side trail leads 270 feet east to spring.		844	690.0
1502.5	Y	Side trail sometimes used by local motorcyclists.		1139	689.5
1503.3	♦	Cross small stream, dependable.		1281	688.7
1503.5	⚠	Cross **old charcoal road**.		1698	688.5
1503.8	Y	Intersects with Lions Head Trail leads west.		1583	688.2
1503.9	Y	Blue blaze bypass trail intersects west.		1562	688.1
1504.0	▲📷	Lions Head summit and ridgeline of the Taconic Range with views of Sheffield and Salisbury.		1738	688.0
1504.2	📷	North outlook of Lions Head with views of Bear Mountain Mt. Greylock. Blue blaze bypass trail intersects to the west.		1626	687.8
1504.6	Y	Blue blaze trail leads west to private property.		1607	687.4
1504.8	♦Y▲ ⊏(6)⌣℄ 📷♀	117 yards east to **Riga Shelter and Camping Area**, water (spring) is located on a blue blazed trail to the left of the clearing on the AT, tenting, privy. **No fires permitted**. Views. 28.7◄18.7◄7.4◄►1.2►10.0►10.1	N 42 00.938, W 73 26.126	1610	687.2
1505.4	♦▲	Cross Ball Brook. Ball Brook Group Campsite is south of the brook on east side of the trail. **No fires permitted**.		1650	686.6
1506.0	♦▲⊏(6) ⌣℄♀	Cross Brassie Brook (south branch). 75 yards east to **Brassie Brook Shelter and Camping Area**, water (stream) is located on the AT 50 feet north of the side trail to the shelter, tenting, privy. Limited hammocking. **No fires permitted**. 19.9◄8.6◄1.2◄►8.8►8.9►23.2	N 42 01.700, W 73 27.216	1705	686.0
1506.5	Y	Riga Junction, Trail intersects with Undermountain Trail leading east (1.1) to Paradise Lane Trail and group camping area, and (1.9) to CT. 91 which is one of the most popular trail heads in CT.		1820	685.5

NoBo	Features	Description	GPS	Elev	SoBo
1506.7	▲P(3)	Intersects with **Bear Mountain Road**, old charcoal road.		1920	685.3
1507.0	▲ 📷 ⌷	Cross Bear Mountain summit, rock observation tower		2316	685.0
1508.1	Y ⚠ State Line	Connecticut–Massachusetts State Line. Paradise Lane Trail intersects above the ravine to the east. A good camping area is east the intersection of the AT.		1800	683.9
1508.2	♦▲⚒⚓	Sages Ravine Brook campsite, water falls.		1360	683.8
1508.8	♦	Sawmill Branch (Sages Ravine).		1340	683.2
1510.0	♦▲☾	Laurel Ridge campsite (0.1) west, privy.		1750	682.0
1511.8	♦	Cross Bear Rock Stream		1548	680.2
1511.9	▲📷	Race Mountain summit, open ledges, views.		2365	680.1
1513.0	♦Y▲☾🐻	Race Brook Falls Trail, (0.2E) to tenting, (0.4W) to water. Privy, bear box.		1950	679.0
1513.7	📷	Mt. Everett		2602	678.3
1514.3	▲	Cross summit road, **Mt. Evertt Road**.		2189	677.7
1514.4	♨☾▲ P(20)⚐	Guilder Pond Picnic Area, day use only, privy.	N 42 06.420, W 73 26.151	2050	677.6
1514.5	Y	Side trail west to Guilder Pond, highest fresh water pond in MA.		2042	677.5
1514.8	♦Y⊏(10) ☾⚐	(0.1E) **The Hemlocks Shelter**, water is located on the blue blazed access trail, privy. 17.4◄10.0◄8.8◄► 0.1► 14.4► 19.7	N 42 06.594, W 73 25.740	1880	677.2
1514.9	♦Y▲(2) ⊏(4) ⌣☾⚐	(0.1E) **Glen Brook Shelter**, water (stream) is located in front of and downhill from the shelter, 2 tent platforms and extensive tenting area, privy. 10.1◄8.9◄0.1◄► 14.3► 19.6►21.4	N 42 06.668, W 73 25.698	1885	677.1
1515.5	Y ★★★★★	Elbow Trail leads (1.5E) to **MA. 41**.		1750	676.5
	⌂✗🍴	**Racebrook Lodge** 413-229-2916. (www.rblodge.com) Open year round. ⌂ Call for rates, lowest during off season (Nov-May). M-Th $85-$160, F-Su $115-170. ⊕ Free WiFi. Stay includes breakfast. Pets $25 per night. Accepts Visa, MC, Disc.			
1517.2	📷	Jug End summit, rocky with good views.		1750	674.8
1518.3	♦▲P(3)⚐	Cross **Jug End Road (Curtiss Road)**, (0.25E) to spring.	N 42 08.664, W 73 25.896	890	673.7
1519.2	▲ ★★★★★	Cross **MA. 41, Undermountain Road**, ATC Kellogg Conservation Center		810	672.8

South Egremont, MA (1.2W)

	🏤⚐	**PO** M–F 8:15am–12pm & 12:30pm–4pm, Sa 9am–11:30am. 413-528-1571. 64 Main St. South Egremont, MA 01258. N 42 09.644, W 73 25.177			
	♦🛏⊕	(0.1W) **ATC New England Regional Office** 413-528-8002. Located in Kellogg Conservation Center. ♦ Water from hose, ♨ picnic table, 2 charging outlets, ⊕ free WiFi, no camping or parking.			
	✗🍴	**Egremont Market** 413-528-0075 Market & deli, ice cream, trail mix, sodas. M-Su 6:30am-7pm.(6pm in winter)			
	✗	**Mom's Country Cafe** 413-528-2414. Servers breakfast and lunch, breakfast all day, free coffee refills, outdoor water spigot available, hikers welcome. M-Su 6:30am-3pm.			
1519.4	⌒	Cross bog bridges.		707	672.6
1519.6	▲	Trail follows old woods road along a narrow ridge.		791	672.4
1520.0	⌒	Cross bog bridges.		722	672.0
1520.8	♦⌒	Cross Hubbard Brook on boardwalk and bridge.		675	671.2
1521.0	▲P(6)⚐	Cross Sheffield–Egremont Road Shay's Rebellion Monument	N 42 08.826, W 73 23.202	700	671.0
1521.5	▲O	Lime Kiln Road is 100 yards east, where **two historical lime kilns** can be seen on the north side of the road.		814	670.5
1522.2	▲	Cross **West Road**.		694	669.8
1522.6	⌒	Cross long boardwalk across swamp.		664	669.4
1522.7	✗	Cross active railroad tracks of the Housatonic Railroad.		668	669.3
1522.8	▲ ★★★★★	Cross U.S. 7		700	669.2

Sheffield, MA (3.0E)

	🏤⚐	**PO** M–F 9am–4:30pm, Sa 9am–12pm. 413-229-8772. 99 Main St. Sheffield, MA 01257. N 42 06.588, W 73 21.253			
	⌂▲△⊕	**Jess Treat** 860-248-5710. jesstrea@gmail.com			
	🚗	⌂ $40PP or $55 shared bed, cash or paypal only. ▲ $15PP tenting includes shower. Stay includes pickup and return; ask about resupply stop and mail drops. ⚒ Shower, breakfast, ⊕ free WiFi. Clean private home, not a party place, reservations needed. △ $5 laundry, pets outside only. Convenience store and cafe and BBQ/Pizza restaurant in walking distance. 🚗 Fee for shuttles.			

Moon in the Pond Farm
413-229-3092(home) 413-446-3320(text/cell) dom@mooninthepond.org (www.mooninthepond.org)
816 Barnum St., Sheffield, MA 01257
Dominic Palumbo offers exchange for farm work (minimum full day's work): organic farm meals, tent site, shower, $2 laundry, insight into farming, farm work and food justice issues. Call ahead to reserve. Plan to arrive late afternoon for following work day. Pick up and drop off from: Salisbury, CT, Jug End Rd, MA 41, Shay's Rebellion, US Rte. 7, Home Rd. or Great Barrington.

Great Barrington, MA 01230 (3.0W) (all major services) See map of Great Barrington, MA.

PO M-F 8:30am-4:30pm, Sa 8:30am-12:30pm. 413-528-3670. 222 Main St. Great Barrington, MA 01230. N 42 11.781, W 73 21.685

Days Inn 413-528-3150. ⊗ No pets. Rates $89 and UP, includes continental breakfast, free WiFi, nonsmoking rooms.

Mountain View Motel 413-528-0250. (www.themountainviewmotel.com) ⊗ No pets. Week days $69S $89D, $20EAP +tax. Microwave, fridge, free WiFi. Rides sometimes available.

Monument Mtn Motel 413-528-3272. (www.monumentmountainmotel.com) Weekdays $65S $75D. Free WiFi, outdoor pool.
Mail drops for guests with reservations: 247 Stockbridge Rd, Rt 7, Great Barrington, MA 01230.

Fairfield Inn & Suites 413-644-3200. ⊗ No pets. Prices seasonal, call for pricing. Full breakfast, heated pool and hot tub.
Mail drops for guests with advance reservations: 249 Stockbridge Rd, Rt 7, Great Barrington, MA 01230.

Travel Lodge 413-528-2340 Su-Th $59-89D + tax, $10EAP, continental breakfast, coin laundry, free WiFi.

Berkshire South Regional Community Center 413-528-2810. (www.berkshiresouth.org) 15 Crissey Rd at north end of town.
⊗ No Pets. No smoking, drugs, alcohol. Free tenting, check-in at front desk. $5PP for use of facilities, showers, saunas, pool. Free dinner M 5pm-6pm, donations accepted.

Guido's Organic produce, 413-528-9255. (www.guidosfreshmarketplace.com) Cold juices, and more.
Berkshire Co-op 413-528-9697. (www.berkshire.coop). M-Su 8am-8pm.

Price Chopper 413-528-8415. M-Sa 6am-12am, Su 7am-12am; **Pharmacy** M-F 8am-8pm, Sa 9am-7pm, Su 9am-3pm.
Big Y Foods 413-528-1314. M-F 7am-10pm, Sa 7am-10pm, Su 7am-9pm; **Pharmacy** 413-528-5460 M-F 9am-8pm, Sa 9am-5pm.

Aroma Bar & Grill 413-528-3116, 413-528-3992. (www.aromabarandgrill.com) Lunch M-closed, Tu-Su 11:30am-3pm. Dinner M-Th 4:30pm-10pm, F-Su 4:30pm-10:30pm.
Manhattan Pizza 413-528-2550. M-Th 11am-10pm, F-Sa 11am-11pm, Su 12pm-10pm.
528 Café 413-528-2233. M-W 7am-4pm, Th-Su 7am-9pm.
Four Brothers Pizza 413-528-9684. M-Su 10am-10pm.
McDonalds 413-528-0434. M-Su 5am-11pm.

Fairview Hospital 413-528-0790. (www.berkshirehealthsystems.org/fairview) M-Su 24 hours.

All Points Driving Service 413-429-7397 Range from Salisbury to Dalton.

Great Barrington, MA

NoBo	Features	Description	GPS	Elev	SoBo
1522.9		Cross footbridge over drainage in middle of agricultural fields.		661	669.1
1523.7	P(6)	Cross **Housatonic River Bridge, Kellogg Road**	N 42 08.659, W 73 21.644	720	668.3
1524.1		Cross **Boardman Street** near it's intersection with Kellogg Road.		694	667.9
1524.7		Cross rim of June Mountain.		1206	667.3
1525.4		Cross intermittent brook.		1184	666.6
1525.7	P(5)	Cross **Home Road also known as Brush Hill Road. (2.3W) to Geat Barraington.**	N 42 09.290, W 73 20.473	1150	666.3
1527.1		Ridge at southern end of East Mountain, offers good views.		1800	664.9
1528.2		Cross overgorwn woodland road.		1681	663.8
1528.7	Y	Pass obscure trail junction.		1541	663.3
1529.2	(10)	47 yards east to **Tom Leonard Shelter**, water (stream) is located (0.2) down a ravine on a blue blazed trail to the left of the shelter, campsite overlooking ravine north of shelter, privy, bear box, view.	N 42 09.893, W 73 18.351		
		23.2◀14.4◀14.3◀▶5.3▶7.1▶21.1		1540	662.8
1529.3		Steep cliffs, view.		1616	662.7

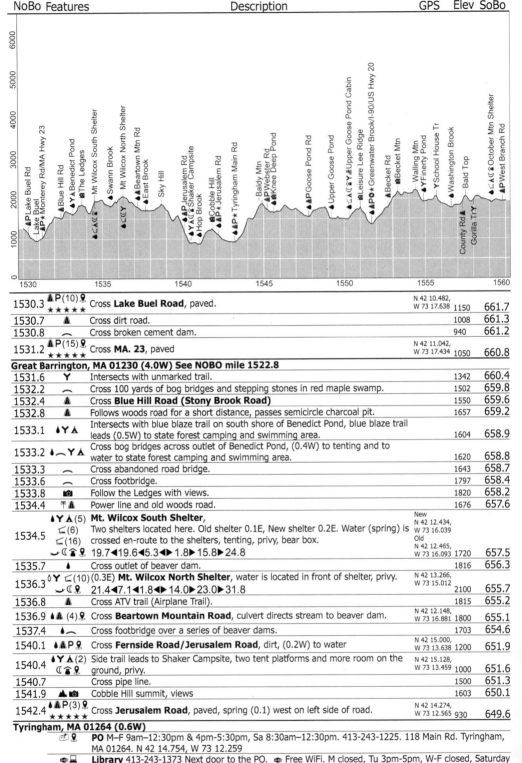

NoBo	Features	Description	GPS	Elev	SoBo
1530.3	▲P(10)⚲ ★★★★★	Cross **Lake Buel Road**, paved.	N 42 10.482, W 73 17.638	1150	661.7
1530.7	▲	Cross dirt road.		1008	661.3
1530.8	⌒	Cross broken cement dam.		940	661.2
1531.2	▲P(15)⚲ ★★★★★	Cross **MA. 23**, paved	N 42 11.042, W 73 17.434	1050	660.8
Great Barrington, MA 01230 (4.0W) See NOBO mile 1522.8					
1531.6	Y	Intersects with unmarked trail.		1342	660.4
1532.2	⌒	Cross 100 yards of bog bridges and stepping stones in red maple swamp.		1502	659.8
1532.4	▲	Cross **Blue Hill Road (Stony Brook Road)**		1550	659.6
1532.8	▲	Follows woods road for a short distance, passes semicircle charcoal pit.		1657	659.2
1533.1	♦Y▲	Intersects with blue blaze trail on south shore of Benedict Pond, blue blaze trail leads (0.5W) to state forest camping and swimming area.		1604	658.9
1533.2	♦⌒Y▲	Cross bog bridges across outlet of Benedict Pond, (0.4W) to tenting and to water to state forest camping and swimming area.		1620	658.8
1533.3	⌒	Cross abandoned road bridge.		1643	658.7
1533.6	⌒	Cross footbridge.		1797	658.4
1533.8	📷	Follow the Ledges with views.		1820	658.2
1534.4	⊤▲	Power line and old woods road.		1676	657.6
1534.5	♦Y▲(5) ⌐(6) ⌐(16) ⌣⟨☂⚲	**Mt. Wilcox South Shelter**, Two shelters located here. Old shelter 0.1E, New shelter 0.2E. Water (spring) is crossed en-route to the shelters, tenting, privy, bear box. 19.7◄19.6◄5.3◄► 1.8► 15.8►24.8	New N 42 12.434, W 73 16.039 Old N 42 12.465, W 73 16.093	1720	657.5
1535.7	♦	Cross outlet of beaver dam.		1816	656.3
1536.3	◊Y⌐(10)(0.3E) ⌣⟨⚲	**Mt. Wilcox North Shelter**, water is located in front of shelter, privy. 21.4◄7.1◄1.8◄► 14.0►23.0►31.8	N 42 13.266, W 73 15.012	2100	655.7
1536.8	▲	Cross ATV trail (Airplane Trail).		1815	655.2
1536.9	♦▲(4)⚲	Cross **Beartown Mountain Road**, culvert directs stream to beaver dam.	N 42 12.148, W 73 16.881	1800	655.1
1537.4	♦⌒	Cross footbridge over a series of beaver dams.		1703	654.6
1540.1	♦▲P⚲	Cross **Fernside Road/Jerusalem Road**, dirt, (0.2W) to water	N 42 15.000, W 73 13.638	1200	651.9
1540.4	♦Y▲(2) ⟨☂⚲	Side trail leads to Shaker Campsite, two tent platforms and more room on the ground, privy.	N 42 15.128, W 73 13.459	1000	651.6
1540.7		Cross pipe line.		1500	651.3
1541.9	▲📷	Cobble Hill summit, views		1603	650.1
1542.4	♦▲P(3)⚲ ★★★★★	Cross **Jerusalem Road**, paved, spring (0.1) west on left side of road.	N 42 14.274, W 73 12.565	930	649.6
Tyringham, MA 01264 (0.6W)					
	⊠⚲	**PO** M–F 9am–12:30pm & 4pm-5:30pm, Sa 8:30am–12:30pm. 413-243-1225. 118 Main Rd. Tyringham, MA 01264. N 42 14.754, W 73 12.259			
	⊞🖥	**Library** 413-243-1373 Next door to the PO. ⊞ Free WiFi. M closed, Tu 3pm-5pm, W-F closed, Saturday 10am-12pm, Su closed.			

NoBo	Features	Description	GPS	Elev	SoBo
Lee , MA 01238 (5.0W) See Notes at mile 1552.1					
1542.5		Cross active cow pasture.		889	649.5
1542.7	◊	Cross intermitted brooks.		891	649.3
1542.8		Cross buried pipe line.		903	649.2
1543.4	⌒	Cross extensive boardwalk over wet fields.		956	648.6
1543.5	◊▲P(5)⚲ ★★★★★	Cross **Tyringham Main Road**	N 42 14.118, W 73 11.664	930	648.5
Tyringham, MA 01264 (0.9W) See Notes at mile 1542.4					
Lee , MA 01238 (5.3W) See Notes at mile 1552.1					
1545.4	◊▲P(2)	Cross **Webster Road**	N 42 15.153, W 73 10.737	1800	646.6
1546.0	Y📷	Unmarked trail gives view to Knee Deep Pond west.		1654	646.0
1546.9	◊Y	Unmarked side trail (0.1) leads west to spring.		1762	645.1
1547.8	▲P(10)⚲	Cross **Goose Pond Road**, gravel, parking (0.1E)	N 42 16.464, W 73 11.016	1650	644.2
1548.0	⌒	Telephone pole bridge over marsh of Cooper Brook beaver pond.		1570	644.0
1549.7	◊	Cross outlet of Upper Goose Pond.		1500	642.3
1550.2		Pass old Chimney and Plaque		1520	641.8
1550.3	◊Y ◈▲ ⊏(14) ☾☂⛺🛶	(0.5W) **Upper Goose Pond Cabin** Open daily mid May - mid Oct. ◈ AT Passport location. Cabin offers bunks, fireplace, covered porch, tenting platforms, privy, bear box, swimming and canoeing. During the summer, the resident volunteer caretaker brings water by canoe from a spring across the pond; otherwise, the pond is the water source. No fee is charged for staying at this site but donations are appreciated. **No Alcohol.** Campsites open year round. 21.1◀15.8◀14.0◀▶8.8▶17.6▶34.5	N 42 17.319, W 73 10.878	1480	641.7
1550.5	📷	Ridge overlooking I-90 and Upper Goose Pond Natural Area, register box. **No camping or fires allowed.**		1752	641.5
1551.7	⌒▲	Cross **I-90 MA**. Turnpike, pedestrian bridge		1400	640.3
1551.8	◊⌒○	Cross Greenwater Brook on high bridge over historical mill site on outlet stream.		1400	640.2
1552.1	▲P(20)⚲ ★★★★★	Cross **U.S. 20**	N 42 17.576, W 73 09.684	1400	639.9
	◊🛏⊛🚲⚲	(0.1E) **Berkshire Lakeside Lodge** 413-243-9907. (www.berkshirelakesidelodge.com) ⊛ No pets. 🛏 Weekdays $60-90, Weekends 94-160, which includes $5 hiker discount. Weekly rates available at 230 to 400 depending on time of year and style of room. Includes continental breakfast, fridge. Soda available for purchase by guests and passers through. ◊ Hikers may get water. ✉ Mail drops (call ahead to arrange pickup): 3949 Jacob's Ladder Rd, Rt 10, Becket, MA 01223			
Lee, MA 01238 (5.0W) (all major services)					
	✉⚲	**PO** M–F 8:30am–4:30pm, Sa 9am–12pm. 413-243-1392. 35 Frank P Consolati Way. Lee, MA 01238. N 42 18.313, W 73 15.043			
	🛏	Several hotels and motels but very expensive.			
	🏪	**Rite Aid** M-F 7am-9pm, Sa 7am-8pm, Su 8am-6pm; **Pharmacy** M-F 8am-8pm, Sa 9am-6pm, Su 9am-5pm.			
	🐾	**Valley Veterinary Clinic** 413-243-2414. (www.valleyveterinaryservice.com) M-F 8am-5pm, Sa 8am-12pm, Su closed.			
	⚲	**Lee Coin-Op Laundry** 413-243-0480.			
1552.2	YP⚲	Trail leads west to parking area.	N 42 17.576, W 73 09.684	1407	639.8
1552.3	⚡	Power line.		1574	639.7
1552.9	▲P⚲	Cross **Tyne Road also known as Becket Road**. US. 20 is (0.9) west. MA 8 is (3.5) east. Very limited parking.	N 42 17.808, W 73 09.029	1750	639.1
1553.4	▲📷	Becket Mountain summit, concrete footing mark the location of the old fire tower, register box.		2180	638.6
1554.4		Overgrown Walling Mountain.		2220	637.6
1555.0	◊Y	South side of Finerty Pond, crosses an ATV trail.		1900	637.0
1555.2	◊	Skirt west side of Finerty Pond.		1928	636.8
1555.3	◊	Northwest side of Finerty Pond.		1947	636.7
1555.9		High point north of Finerty Pond		2070	636.1
1556.1	Y	School House Trail, ATV trail.		1991	635.9
1556.8	◊	Cross some streams in the area.		1799	635.2
1557.5	▲P	Cross **County Road**, road leads (4.0) east to MA. 8.		1850	634.5
1557.7	⌒	Bald Top summit, overgrown		2040	634.3
1558.2	Y	Gorilla Trail, motorcycle/ATV trail.		1933	633.8

| 1559.3 ◊▲⊑(12) ⌣🛏☂♦ | 15 yards west to **October Mountain Shelter**, water (stream) is located south of the shelter on the AT, tenting, privy, bear cables.
24.8◄23.0◄9.0◄▶ 8.8▶25.5▶32.1 | N 42 21.292,
W 73 09.270

1950 | 632.7 |

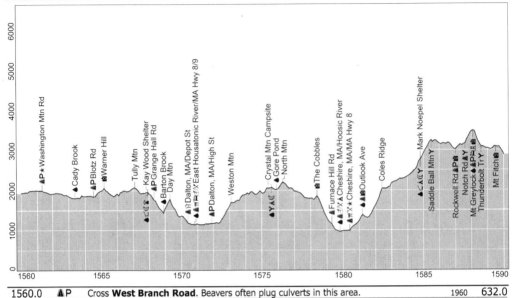

1560.0	▲P	Cross **West Branch Road**. Beavers often plug culverts in this area.	1960	632.0
1561.4	▲	Intersects with service road leading west.	1978	630.6
1561.5	▲P(6)♀ ★★★★★	Cross **Washington Mountain Road, Pittsfield Road**.	N 42 22.629, W 73 09.039 2000	630.5
	♦▲🚗✉	Home of the "**Cookie Lady**" 100 yards east. 413-623-5859. ♦ Water spigot near the garage door, please sign register on the steps. Homemade cookies often available. Soda, ice cream, boiled eggs and pick your own blueberries. ▲ Camping allowed, ask permission first. 🚗 Shuttle range from Kent, CT to Manchester Center, VT. Please notify before you send a ✉ Mail drops: Roy & Marilyn Wiley, 47 Washington Mountain Road, Becket, MA 01223.		

Becket, MA 01223 (5E)

	🖂♀	**PO** M–F 8am–4pm, Sa 9am–11:30pm. 413-623-8845. 623 Main St. Becket, MA 01223. N 42 16.731, W 73 03.617		
	🛏⌂🚗 ✉	**Becket Motel** 413-623-8888. (www.thebecketmotel.com) 🛏 $95-156 +tax, 🚗 includes shuttle from and to US 20 or Washington Mountain Rd. Tavern next door. ⌂ coin laundry, 📶 WiFi. ✉ Mail drops for guests: 29 Chester Road, Becket, MA 01223.		
1563.5	♦	Cady brook.	1950	628.5
1564.7	▲P(4)♀	Cross **Blotz Road** through small parking lot.	N 42 24.568, W 73 08.985 1850	627.3
1565.4	▲📷	Warner Hill summit just off the trail to east, view of Mt. Greylock.	2050	626.6
1568.0	🕆	Power line.	1936	624.0
1568.1	♦⊑(10) ☂♀	(0.2E) **Kay Wood Shelter** , water is located on a blue blazed trail to the left of the shelter, privy, bear box. 31.8◄17.8◄8.8◄▶ 16.7▶23.3▶33.2	N 42 27.128, W 73 09.698 1860	623.9
1568.4	▲P♀	Cross **Grange Hall Road**	N 42 27.396, W 73 09.712 1650	623.6
1570.5	✗	Cross CSX Railroad crossing.	1250	621.5
1570.6	▲	Cross intersection of **Housatonic Street and Depot Street**.	1245	621.4
1571.0	♦▲ ★★★★★	Intersects with **Depot St.**, water at 83 Depot St.	1240	621.0
	🏠	Thomas Levardi's hostel, **see notes under Dalton, MA listing.**		
1571.1	▲	Junction of **Depot Street and MA. 8.**	1200	620.9
1571.2	▲ ★★★★★	Junction of High Street with MA. 8 and MA. 9. **Dalton, MA. See map of Dalton, MA.**	1200	620.8
	🖂♀	**PO** M-F 8:30am-4:30pm, Sa 9am-1pm. 413-684-0364. 609 Main St. Dalton, MA 01226. N 42 33.709, W 73 09.472		
	🏠◈	**Thomas Levardi**, 83 Depot St., 413-684-3359, cell 413-212-9691. ◈ AT Passport location. ♦ Allows hikers to use a water spigot outside his home and provides the hospitality of his front porch and back yard for tenting (limited space, get permission first)		

	🛏 ⬦	**Shamrock Village Inn** 413-684-0860. (www.shamrockvillage.webs.com)			
	⛺🖥📶	⬦ AT Passport location.			
		🛏 Hiker rates Su-Th are $70.60S, $75D, $85 king bed. F-Sa prices $85.50/$93.60/$99 respectively. Add tax to all prices. Well behaved pets allowed with $75 deposit. ⛺ Coin laundry, 🖥 free use of computer and 📶 WiFi.			
	🛒🗡	**Walmart** 413-442-1971. M-Su 7am-12am; 🗡 **Pharmacy** M-F 8am-8pm, Sa 9am-7pm, Su 10am-6pm.			
	🛒🗡	**Price Chopper** 413-443-5449. M-Su 7am-12am.			
	🍴	**Angelina's Subs** 413-443-9875. (www.angelinassubshop.com) M-Su 8:30am-11pm.			
	🍴	**Dalton Restaurant** 413-684-0414. Serves breakfast, lunch and dinner. M-Th 6am-8pm, F-Sa 6am-8:30pm, Su 6am-12:30pm.			
	🍴	**SweetPea's Ice Cream Shop** 413-684-9799. Serving 32 flavors of Hershey's ice cream, 🍴 Hot Dogs, Pulled Pork and Chicken Sandwich, and a daily Lunch Special. Summer hours; M-Th 12pm-9pm, F-Sa 12pm-10pm, Su 1pm-8pm.			
	⛺	**Dalton Laundry** 413-684-9702. M-F 9am-5:30pm, Sa 8am-4:15pm, Su 10am-2pm.			
	🚿	(0.7 from AT) **Dalton CRA** (www.daltoncra.org) 413-684-0260. Free Showers M-F 5am-8pm, Sa 7am-3:30pm, Su 9am-1pm.			
	🗡	**O'Laughlin's Pharmacy** 413-684-0023.			
	🍴	**LP Adams** 413-684-0025. (www.lpadams.com) Coleman fuel and denatured alcohol available. M-F 6am-5pm, Sa 6am-1pm, Su closed.			

Pittsfield, MA Many stores and restaurants approx. (2.0W) from Dalton.

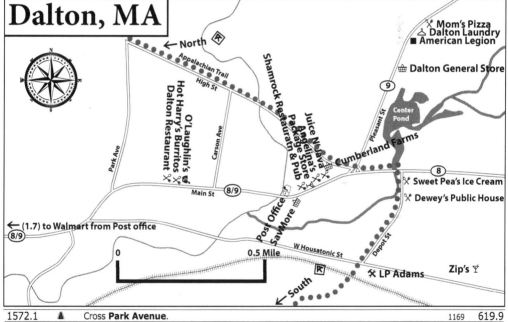

1572.1	⛰	Cross **Park Avenue**.		1169	619.9
1572.2	⛰P(6)🅿	Cross parking lot on Gulf Road which becomes High Street, hiker kiosk.	N 42 28.903, W 73 10.693	1180	619.8
1575.5	🌲	Power line. **Beware!** Bears are around when the berries abound!.		1920	616.5
1575.9	🔹Y⛺(5)☾	(0.2E) Crystal Mountain campsite, privy.		2100	616.1
1576.3	🔹	Cross outlet of Gore Pond.		2050	615.7
1578.7	📷	Blue blaze side tail to The Cobbles, series of white quartz ledges, good views.		1850	613.3
1579.5	⛰	Intersection of **Furnace Hill Road and East Main Street.**		964	612.5
1579.7	Y🚻⛰	Intersects with **Church St.**, Hoosic River, Ashuwillticook Rail Trail		950	612.3
1579.9	🔹⛰ ★★★★★	Intersects with Church St., School St., hiker kiosk. Post office across the street. **Cheshire, MA. See map of Cheshire, MA.**		970	612.1
	📫🅿	**PO** M-F 7:30am-1pm & 2pm-4:30pm, Sa 8:30am-11:30am. 413-743-3184. 214 Church St. Cheshire, MA 01225. N 42 33.709, W 73 09.472			
	🍴	**Diane's Twist** 413-743-9776. Limited hours, deli sandwiches, soda, ice cream.			
	🏬	**HD Reynolds** 413-743-9512. (www.reynoldslawnmower.com) General store, hiker snacks, Coleman fuel by the ounce. M-W 8a,-5pm, Th 8am-7pm, F 8am-5pm, Sa 8am-3pm, Su closed.			

A ♦♦ ◈ **St Mary of the Assumption Church**

◈ AT Passport location. Located one block west from the Post Office at corner of Church and School Street. St. Mary of the Assumption in Cheshire will be offering limited services to hikers. ♦♦ Restroom facilities will be open from May 1st to October 1st from 9:00 a.m. until 7:00 p.m. each day. A Tent camping on the east lawn is available. No indoor sleeping. No showers.

💻 **Cheshire Public Library** 413-743-4746. M 9am-3pm, Tu 10am-2pm & 5pm-8pm, W closed, Th 3pm-6pm, F-Su closed.

1580.4	A ★★★★★	Cross **MA. 8.** See map of Cheshire, MA.	1000	611.6
	🏛	**Shell** 413-743-1535. M-Su 9am-5pm.		
	✗	**Dunkin' Donuts** 413-749-7007. M-Su 5am -11pm.		
	🖈	(2.2E) **Berkshire Outfitters** 413-743-5900. (www.berkshireoutfitters.com) Full-service outfitter. Coleman fuel and alcohol by the ounce, canister fuel, freeze-dried foods. Often provides return ride to Cheshire. M-F 10am-6pm, Sa 10am-5pm, Su 11am-4pm.		
Adams, MA 01220 (4.2E)				
	📪🦮	**PO** M-F 8:30am-4:30pm, Sa 10am-12pm. 413-743-5177. 1 Center St. Adams, MA 01220. N 42 37.210, W 73 07.234		
	🛒	**Big Y Foods Supermarket** 413-743-1941. M-Su 7am-9pm; **Pharmacy** 413-743-5702. M-F 8am-7pm, Sa 8am-5pm, Su closed.		
	💊	**Rite Aid** 413-743-4659. M-Sa 8am-8pm, Su 9am-5pm; **Pharmacy** M-F 8am-8pm, Sa 9am-6pm, Su 8am-5pm.		
	🐾	**Adams Veterinary Clinic** 413-743-4000. (www.adamsveterinary.com) M, Closed, Tu 8:30am-12pm, W 8:30am-12pm & 1:30pm-5pm, Thu 1:30pm-5:30pm, F 8:30am-12pm & 1:30pm-5pm, Sa-Su closed.		
	🧺🎽	**Thrifty Bundle Laundromat** 413-664-9007. Coin laundry. **Waterworks Laundromat**		
1581.1	♦Y	Spring west on footpath on edge of woods.	1373	610.9
1581.2	A 📷	Cross **Outlook Ave**, between hayfields. There is a curious rock and tree formation called Reynolds Rock on side of road crossing.	1350	610.8
1581.4	⟊	Power lines.	1353	610.6
1582.9	📷	Views from open ledges.	2217	609.1
1583.9	AP(15)	Cross **Old Adams Road**	2350	608.1

NoBo	Features	Description	GPS	Elev	SoBo
1584.8	▲Y▲(2) ⊏(10) ☾♀	(0.2E) **Mark Noepel Shelter**, water (stream) is located on a blue blazed trail to the right of the shelter, tenting platforms, privy, fire pit.	N 42 36.518, W 73 11.052	2750	607.2
		34.5◄25.5◄16.7◄►6.6►16.5►23.7			
1585.4	Y	Side trail to Jones Nose Trail intersects along the southern end of Saddle Ball Mountain.		3150	606.6
1587.0	⌒📷	View of Mt. Greylock just north of bog bridges.		3254	605.0
1587.6	▲P♀	Meet **Rockwell Road** at hairpin turn in road. Gravel parking lot.	N 42 37.860, W 73 10.690	3290	604.4
1587.8	▲Y	Intersection of **Rockwell Road** and Cheshire Harbor Trail, which descends east.		3119	604.2
1587.9	Y	Intersection with Hopper Trail, descends west to Sperry Campground.		3132	604.1
1588.0	▲P♀	Crosses the junction of **Notch, Rockwell, and Summits Roads**. Old water supply and pump house are on AT south of this junction. East of this junction is a gravel parking lot.	N 42 38.034, W 73 09.250	3177	604.0
1588.1	▲▲℩📷 ▲P♀ ★★★★★	Mt. Greylock summit, **Summit Road**, Bascom Lodge, War Memorial. Many parking spots.	N 42 38.235, W 73 09.956	3491	603.9
	⍾⛺✕♨ ☞	**Bascom Lodge** on summit of Mt Greylock, 413-743-1591. (www.bascomlodge.net) No smoking. ☞ Private rooms $125 and up, bunkroom $40PP. ⛺ Bunkroom includes use of shower and continental breakfast. ♨ Shower and towel without stay $5, some snacks, ✕ restaurant serves breakfast, lunch and dinner, ☞ free WiFi. Open May 20-mid Oct 2017.			
1588.6	Y	Intersects with Thunderbolt Trail and Bellows Pipe Trail to the east and a shorter connecting trail to the Robinson Point Trail and Notch Road to the west, all within 100 yards of each.		3095	603.4
1589.4	📷	Unusual outcropping of milky quartz atop of Mt. Fitch.		3096	602.6

1590.2	Y	Four way junction with Bernard Farm Trail east.		2772	601.8
1590.4	▲📷	Mt. Williams summit, register box.		2951	601.6
1591.3	▲▲P(4)♀	Intersects with **Notch Road**, water (0.25E)	N 42 40.160, W 73 10.066	2400	600.7
1591.4	◊Y▲ ⊏(8) ⌣☾☂♀	(0.3W) on Money Brook Trail to **Wilbur Clearing Shelter**, water (stream) is located to the right of the shelter but is unreliable at times, tenting, bear box, privy.	N 42 40.069, W 73 10.208		600.6
		32.1◄23.3◄6.6◄►9.9►17.1►23.0		2300	
1591.6	Y	Intersects with Mt. Prospect Trail to the west. When the wind is right hang gliders will launch on the summit ledge.		2502	600.4
1593.5	▲▲P(5)♀	Cross **Pattison Road**	N 42 41.258, W 73 09.586	900	598.5
1593.7	▲	Local off road trail for ATV's cross the trail here.		854	598.3
1593.9	▲	Intersects with a steep driveway called **Phelps Avenue Extension**.		746	598.1
1594.0	▲	Catherine Street-Phelps Road		670	598.0
1594.4	▲P♀ ★★★★★	Cross intersection of **Phelps Avenue and MA. 2**	N 42 41.940, W 73 09.210	650	597.6
	P	**Greylock Community Center** 413-664-9020. Park on grass, west side of building. Leave a note with name and vehicle registration number in mailbox. Donations accepted.			

NoBo Features	Description	GPS Elev SoBo

Williamstown, MA 01267 (2.6W) See map of Williamstown (downtown and mid-town).

📫🚰 **PO** M-F 8:30am-4:30pm, Sa 9am-12pm. 413-458-3707. 56 Spring St. Williamstown, MA 01267. N 42 42.630, W 73 12.247

🛏🛁🖥 **Willows Motel** 413-458-5768. (www.willowsmotel.com) 🚭 No pets, no smoking. 🛏 $79-149, includes 🖥🛜 continental breakfast, free pick-up and return to trail with stay. Microwave, fridge. 🛁 Laundry $6, 🏊 outdoor pool, 🖥 computer available for use, 🛜 free WiFi.

🖂 Mail drops for guests: 480 Main Street, Williamstown, MA 01267.

🛏🛁🖥🛜 **Williamstown Motel** 413-458-5202. (www.williamstownmotel.com) 🛏 $68 to 109 weekdays, $89 🖂 $169 weekends, includes continental breakfast, microwave, fridge. 🛁 Laundry $8, (they do it for you). 🖥 Computer available for use, 🛜 free WiFi. Will pickup at Route MA 2. All major credit cards accepted.

🖂 Mail drops for guests: 295 Main Street, Williamstown, MA 01267.

🛏🖥🛜🖂 **Howard Johnson** 413-458-8158, 🛏 Rates seasonal, continental breakfast, 🏊 outdoor pool, BBQ grills, 🖥 Computer available for use, 🛜 free WiFi.

🖂 Mail drops free for guests (fee for non guests): 213 Main Street, Williamstown, MA 01267.

🛏🏊🛜 **Maple Terrace** 413-458-9677. (www.mapleterrace.com) 🛏 Prices seasonal, call for rates. 🏊 Heated pool, 🛜 WiFi, all rooms non smoking.

🛏P **River Bend Farm** 413-458-3121. (www.riverbendfarmbb.com) 🛏 $120 includes breakfast. Free pickup and return to trail when available, P short term parking for guests.

🛏🍽- **Williams Inn** 413-458-9371. (www.williamsinn.com) 🛏 $155 and up, includes continental breakfast, 🚿🍸🏊P 🏊 pool, hot tub, sauna. 🚿 Non-guests can pay $8 for use of shower, pool and sauna. 🍸 ATM. 🍽 Restaurant M-Su 5am-10pm. Short term parking $2 per day.

🛒🥤 **Stop & Shop** 413-664-8100. M0Sa 6am-12am, Su 7am-9pm; 🥤 **Pharmacy** 413-664-8550. M-F 9am-9pm, Sa 9am-8pm, Su 9am-6pm.

🛒 **Wild Oats** 413-458-8060. (www.wildoats.coop) M-Sa 7am-8pm, Su 9am-8pm.

🍽 **Desperado's** 4130458-2100. (www.mydesperados.net) M-Th 4pm-9pm, F-Sa 4pm,-10pm, Su 3pm-9pm.

🍽 **Spice Root Indian Cuisine** 413-458-5200. (www.spiceroot.com)Weekday Lunch Buffet - Served Tu-F 11:30pm 2:30pm ~ $10.95; Weekend Maharaja Brunch Buffet Served Sa: 11:30pm 2:30pm; Sunday: 12pm 3pm ~ $12.95. 10% hiker discount.

🍽 **Water Street Grill** 413-458-2175. (www.waterstgrill.com) Serves lunch and dinner. M-Su 11:30am-11pm.

🛶🖂 **Nature's Closet** 413-458-7909. (www.naturescloset.net) Clothing, footwear, 🛶 canister fuel. M-Th 10am-6pm, F-Sa 10am-7pm, Su 10am-6pm.

🖂 Mail drops: 61 Spring St, Williamstown, MA 01267.

🖥 **Milne Public Library** 413-458-5369. (wwwmilnelibrary.org) M-Tu 10am-5:30pm, W 10-8, Th-F 10am-5:30pm, Sa 10am-4pm, Su closed.

North Adams, MA 01247 (2.5E) See map of North Adams, MA.

📫🚰 **PO** M-F 8:30am-4:30pm, Sa 10am-12pm. 413-664-4554. 67 Summer St. North Adams, MA 01247. N 42 41.889, W 73 06.642

🛏🍽🛁🖥 **Holiday Inn** 413-663-6500. 🛏 Summer rates $170 and up, 🏊 pool, hot tub, 🖥 computer available for 🏊🛒 use. 🍽 **Richmond Grill** on location.

🛒 **Big Y** 413-663-6549. M-F 7am-9pm, Sa-Su 7am-9pm.

🏬 **Family Dollar** M-Su 9am-9pm.

🍽 **Subway, Brewhaha, McDonalds, Dunkin Donuts**

🍽◈ **Papa John's Pizza** 413-663-7272. ◈ AT Passport.

🥤 **Rite aid** 413-663-5270. m-Sa 8am-8pm, Su 9am-6pm; **Pharmacy** M-F 8am-8pm, Sa 9am-6pm, Su 9am-5pm.

CVS 413-664-8712. M-Su 8am-9pm; **Pharmacy** M-F 8am-8pm, Sa 9am-6pm, Su 9am-5pm.

🐕 **Greylock Animal Hospital** 413-663-5365. (www.greylockanimalhospital.com) M-F 8am-8pm, Sa-Su 8am-4pm.

🚗 **David Ackerson** 413-346-1033, 413-652-9573. daveackerson@yahoo.com. Shuttles range from Bear Mtn Bridge to Hanover NH, and to and from area airports.

Williamstown, MA (downtown)

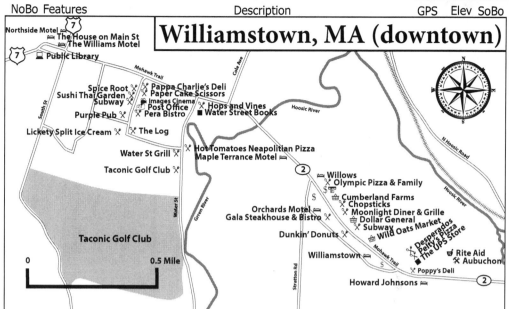

Northside Motel 🏨 7
🏨 The House on Main St
🏨 The Williams Motel
7
💻 Public Library

Mohawk Trail

Gale Ave

Spice Root ✕   ✕ Pappa Charlie's Deli
Sushi Thai Garden ✕   ✕ Paper Cake Scissors
Subway ✕   🎞 Images Cinema
Post Office   ✕ Hops and Vines
Purple Pub ✕   ✕ Pera Bistro   ■ Water Street Books

South St

Lickety Split Ice Cream ✕   ✕ The Log

Hoosic River

Water St Grill ✕   ✕ Hot Tomatoes Neapolitian Pizza
Maple Terrance Motel 🏨

Taconic Golf Club ✕

Water St

Green River

2   🍺 Willows
✕ Olympic Pizza & Family
$ 🛒 Cumberland Farms
✕ Chopsticks
Orchards Motel 🏨   ✕ Moonlight Diner & Grille
Gala Steakhouse & Bistro ✕   🛒 Dollar General
✕ Subway   Wild Oats Market
Dunkin' Donuts ✕   Desperados
Petty's Pizza
The UPS Store

Taconic Golf Club

Williamstown 🏨   🏪 Rite Aid
✕ Aubuchon

N Hoosic Road

Hoosic River

Mohawk Trail

Stratton Rd

✕ Poppy's Deli

Howard Johnsons 🏨   2

0   0.5 Mile

North Adams, MA

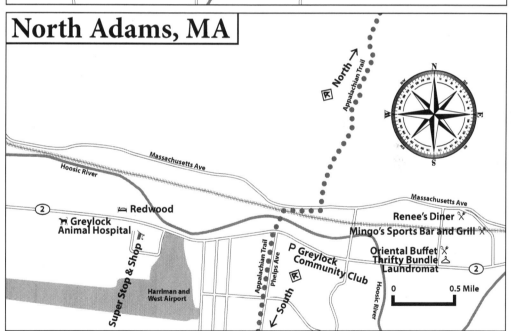

🚉 North →

Appalachian Trail

Massachusetts Ave

Hoosic River

2   🏨 Redwood   Massachusetts Ave

Renee's Diner ✕

🐾 Greylock
Animal Hospital   Mingo's Sports Bar and Grill ✕

Appalachian Trail

Phelps Ave

P Greylock
Community Club   Oriental Buffet ✕
Thrifty Bundle △
Laundromat   2

Super Stop & Shop

Harriman and
West Airport

Hoosic River

🚉 South ↙

0   0.5 Mile

North Adams, MA (downtown)

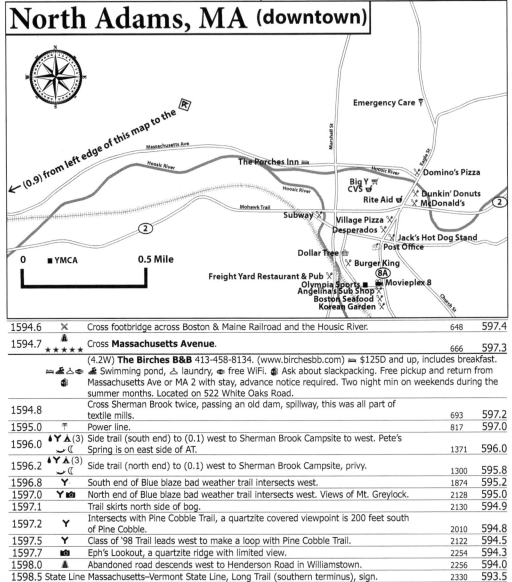

		Description	GPS	Elev	SoBo
1594.6	✕	Cross footbridge across Boston & Maine Railroad and the Housic River.		648	597.4
1594.7	▲ ★★★★★	Cross **Massachusetts Avenue**.		666	597.3
	🛏🍴⚕⛺ 🛶 🛁 🛜 📱	(4.2W) **The Birches B&B** 413-458-8134. (www.birchesbb.com) 🛏 $125D and up, includes breakfast. 🛥 Swimming pond, ⛺ laundry, 🛜 free WiFi. 📱 Ask about slackpacking. Free pickup and return from Massachusetts Ave or MA 2 with stay, advance notice required. Two night min on weekends during the summer months. Located on 522 White Oaks Road.			
1594.8		Cross Sherman Brook twice, passing an old dam, spillway, this was all part of textile mills.		693	597.2
1595.0	ⵜ	Power line.		817	597.0
1596.0	💧Y🏕(3) 🛶☾	Side trail (south end) to (0.1) west to Sherman Brook Campsite to west. Pete's Spring is on east side of AT.		1371	596.0
1596.2	💧Y🏕(3) 🛶☾	Side trail (north end) to (0.1) west to Sherman Brook Campsite, privy.		1300	595.8
1596.8	Y	South end of Blue blaze bad weather trail intersects west.		1874	595.2
1597.0	Y📷	North end of Blue blaze bad weather trail intersects west. Views of Mt. Greylock.		2128	595.0
1597.1		Trail skirts north side of bog.		2130	594.9
1597.2	Y	Intersects with Pine Cobble Trail, a quartzite covered viewpoint is 200 feet south of Pine Cobble.		2010	594.8
1597.5	Y	Class of '98 Trail leads west to make a loop with Pine Cobble Trail.		2122	594.5
1597.7	📷	Eph's Lookout, a quartzite ridge with limited view.		2254	594.3
1598.0	▲	Abandoned road descends west to Henderson Road in Williamstown.		2256	594.0
1598.5 State Line		Massachusetts–Vermont State Line, Long Trail (southern terminus), sign.		2330	593.5
1598.9	💧	Brook		2300	593.1
1601.3	💧Y🏕 ⊏(8) 🛶☾🚰	(0.2W) **Seth Warner Shelter**, water (brook) is located 150 yards to the left of the shelter but is known to go dry, tenting, privy. 33.2◀16.5◀9.9◀▶ 7.2▶13.1▶21.6	N 42 46.310, W 73 08.256	2180	590.7
1601.6	▲P(4)🚰	Cross **County Road.** Getting to this road can be iffy in wet weather if you don't have a 4WD vehicle.	N 42 46.505, W 73 07.994	2290	590.4
1602.5	💧	Side trail east 100 feet to Ed's Spring.		2890	589.5
1602.8	📷	View of Mt. Greylock.			589.2
1603.0	📷	Ridgeline with views.		3025	589.0
1603.4	ⵜ	Power line.		2906	588.6
1604.1	💧📷	Follow along eastern shore of old beaver pond, view of Scrub Hill.		1516	587.9
1604.3	💧	Cross Roaring Branch at base of beaver dam.		2470	587.7
1604.5		Pass over knob.		2615	587.5
1604.8		Pass over knob.		2773	587.2
1605.5	▲	Consultation Peak summit, wooded.		2840	586.5

NoBo	Features	Description	GPS	Elev	SoBo
1606.5	⛰	Cross woods road, leads (0.2) west to clearing on eastern shore of Sucker Pond.		2232	585.5
1606.9		Cross Sucker Pond outlet brook.		2180	585.1
1607.4		Pass old foundation, nineteenth century tavern.		2209	584.6
1607.6	⛰	Cross woods road.		2162	584.4
1607.9	⬦	Stamford Stream		2040	584.1
1608.5	⬦⛰⊏(8) ⌣☾⚲	**Congdon Shelter**, water (brook) is located in front of the shelter, tenting, privy. 23.7◀17.1◀7.2◀▶5.9▶14.4▶18.7	N 42 50.883, W 73 06.624	2060	583.5
1609.1	⛰	Cross **Old Bennington-Heartwellville Road**, also known as **Burgess/Old Stage Road**.		2220	582.9
1609.2	⬦	Cross small stream.		2268	582.8
1610.7	⬦	Cross brook.		2262	581.3
1611.0	⛰📷	Harmon Hill summit, views of Bennington		2325	581.0
1612.8	⬦⌢⛰ P(1) ⚲ ★★★★★	Cross stream on bridge. Cross **VT. 9**, City Stream.	N 42 53.105, W 73 06.947	1360	579.2

VT 9 Bennington, VT (5.1W) See map of Bennington, VA.

🏤⚲ **PO** M-F 8am-5pm, Sa 9am-2pm. 802-442-2421. 108 Elm St. Bennington, MA 05201. N 42 52.584, W 73 11.906

🛏⛺🍴🚗 **Catamount Motel** 802-442-5977. (www.catamountmotel.com)
🛏 1 Hiker $54 plus tax, 2 Hikers $65 plus tax. each extra person $5, ⛺ laundry $4, $5 dog fee. ✆ Free WiFi. 🚗 Free shuttle service. Credit cards accepted.
✉ Mail drops for guests: 500 South St. Route 7 Bennington VT 05201

🛏⛺🖥🍴 **Autumn Inn Motel** 802-447-7625. (www.theautumninn.com) 🛏 $60-99, microwave, fridge, ⛺ laun-
🚗✉ dry, 🖥 computer available for use, ✆ free WiFi. Pickup or return to trail for $10 each way. Pets $10.
✉ Mail drops for guests: 924 Main Street, Bennington, VT 05201.

🛏🖥✆🏊 **Knotty Pine Motel** 802-442-5487. (www.knottypinemotel.com) 6.5 miles from the AT on VT 9, 🛏
✉ $89D and up, $8EAP up to 4. Includes continental breakfast, pets free, microwave, fridge, 🏊 pool, 🖥
computer available to use, ✆ free WiFi.
✉ Mail drops for guests: 130 Northside Drive, Bennington, VT 05201.

🛏⛺🖥✆ **Best Western** 802-442-6311. $99 and up.
🛏⛺🖥✆ **Hampton Inn** 802-440-9862. call for prices, seasonal rates, includes hot breakfast.
🛒 **Spice & Nice Natural Foods** 802-442-8365. (www.spicennice.net) M-Sa 9am-5:30pm, Su 1am-4pm.

🛒 **Price Chopper** M-Su 24 hours; ⚕ **Pharmacy** M-F 8am-8pm, Sa 9am-6pm, Su 9am-3pm.
Walmart 802-447-1614. M-Su 6am-12am; **Pharmacy** M-F 8am-8pm, Sa 9am-8pm, Su 10am-6pm.
🍴 **Lil' Britain** 802-442-2447. Fish & chips. M closed, Tu-Sa 11:30am-8pm, Su closed.
⚕ **Express Care Walk-in Clinic** 802-440-4077. (www.svhealthcare.org) M-Su 8am to 6pm.
🎦 **Cinema 7** 802-442-8170.

BootsMcfarland.com

© Geolym Carvin

Boots Mcfarland

Hiker's Blog
Stardate 2012.7.28

Hiked 17 miles, made a burrito, ate it, and went to bed.

Bennington, VT

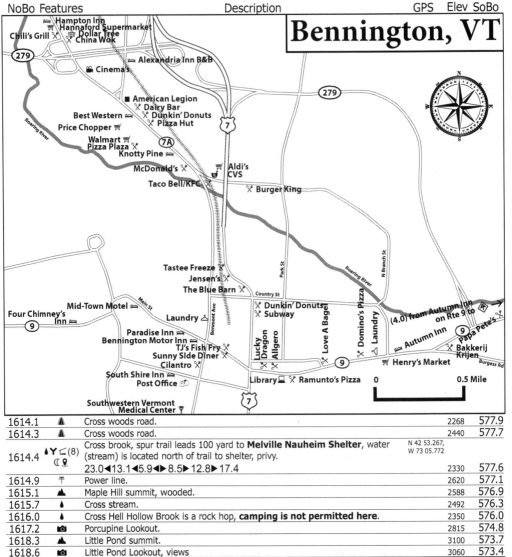

Hampton Inn
Hannaford Supermarket
Dollar Tree
China Wok
Chili's Grill
279
Alexandria Inn B&B
Cinema's
American Legion
Dairy Bar
Best Western
Dunkin' Donuts
Price Chopper
Pizza Hut
7
Walmart
Pizza Plaza
7A
Knotty Pine
McDonald's
Aldi's
CVS
Taco Bell/KFC
Burger King
Roaring River
279
Park St
Roaring River
N Branch St
Tastee Freeze
Jensen's
The Blue Barn
Country St
Dunkin' Donuts
Subway
Mid-Town Motel
Main St
Four Chimney's Inn
9
Laundry
Bennont Ave
Lucky Dragon
Allgero
Love A Bagel
Domino's Pizza
Laundry
(4.0) from Autumn Inn on Rte 9 to
Autumn Inn
9
Papa Pete's
Paradise Inn
Bennington Motor Inn
TJ's Fish Fry
Sunny Side Diner
Cilantro
Bakkerij Krijen
Burgess Rd
South Shire Inn
Post Office
Henry's Market
9
Southwestern Vermont Medical Center
Library
Ramunto's Pizza
7
0   0.5 Mile

NoBo		Features	GPS	Elev	SoBo
1614.1		Cross woods road.		2268	577.9
1614.3		Cross woods road.		2440	577.7
1614.4		Cross brook, spur trail leads 100 yard to **Melville Nauheim Shelter**, water (stream) is located north of trail to shelter, privy.	N 42 53.267, W 73 05.772		577.6
		23.0◄13.1◄5.9◄▶ 8.5▶ 12.8▶ 17.4		2330	
1614.9		Power line.		2620	577.1
1615.1		Maple Hill summit, wooded.		2588	576.9
1615.7		Cross stream.		2492	576.3
1616.0		Cross Hell Hollow Brook is a rock hop, **camping is not permitted here**.		2350	576.0
1617.2		Porcupine Lookout.		2815	574.8
1618.3		Little Pond summit.		3100	573.7
1618.6		Little Pond Lookout, views		3060	573.4

DAY 1

We brought way too much food!

DAY 4

We didn't bring enough food!

BootsMcfarland.com
© Geolym Carvin
Boots McFarland

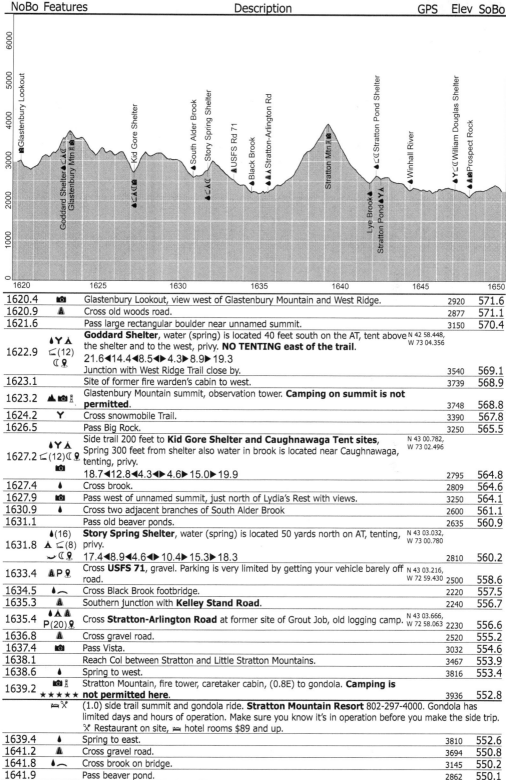

NoBo	Features	Description	GPS	Elev	SoBo
1620.4	📷	Glastenbury Lookout, view west of Glastenbury Mountain and West Ridge.		2920	571.6
1620.9	▲	Cross old woods road.		2877	571.1
1621.6		Pass large rectangular boulder near unnamed summit.		3150	570.4
1622.9	♦Y▲ ⊏(12) ☾♀	**Goddard Shelter**, water (spring) is located 40 feet south on the AT, tent above the shelter and to the west, privy. **NO TENTING east of the trail.** 21.6◄14.4◄8.5◄►4.3►8.9►19.3 Junction with West Ridge Trail close by.	N 42 58.448, W 73 04.356	3540	569.1
1623.1		Site of former fire warden's cabin to west.		3739	568.9
1623.2	▲📷🅸	Glastenbury Mountain summit, observation tower. **Camping on summit is not permitted.**		3748	568.8
1624.2	Y	Cross snowmobile Trail.		3390	567.8
1626.5		Pass Big Rock.		3250	565.5
1627.2	♦Y▲ ⊏(12)☾♀ 📷	Side trail 200 feet to **Kid Gore Shelter and Caughnawaga Tent sites**, Spring 300 feet from shelter also water in brook is located near Caughnawaga, tenting, privy. 18.7◄12.8◄4.3◄►4.6►15.0►19.9	N 43 00.782, W 73 02.496	2795	564.8
1627.4	♦	Cross brook.		2809	564.6
1627.9	📷	Pass west of unnamed summit, just north of Lydia's Rest with views.		3250	564.1
1630.9	♦	Cross two adjacent branches of South Alder Brook		2600	561.1
1631.1		Pass old beaver ponds.		2635	560.9
1631.8	♦(16) ▲⊏(8) ⌣☾♀	**Story Spring Shelter**, water (spring) is located 50 yards north on AT, tenting, privy. 17.4◄8.9◄4.6◄►10.4►15.3►18.3	N 43 03.032, W 73 00.780	2810	560.2
1633.4	▲P♀	Cross **USFS 71**, gravel. Parking is very limited by getting your vehicle barely off road.	N 43 03.216, W 72 59.430	2500	558.6
1634.5	♦⌒	Cross Black Brook footbridge.		2220	557.5
1635.3	▲	Southern junction with **Kelley Stand Road**.		2240	556.7
1635.4	♦▲▲ P(20)♀	Cross **Stratton-Arlington Road** at former site of Grout Job, old logging camp.	N 43 03.666, W 72 58.063	2230	556.6
1636.8	▲	Cross gravel road.		2520	555.2
1637.4	📷	Pass Vista.		3032	554.6
1638.1		Reach Col between Stratton and Little Stratton Mountains.		3467	553.9
1638.6	♦	Spring to west.		3816	553.4
1639.2	📷🅸 ★★★★★	Stratton Mountain, fire tower, caretaker cabin, (0.8E) to gondola. **Camping is not permitted here.**		3936	552.8
	🛏✗	(1.0) side trail summit and gondola ride. **Stratton Mountain Resort** 802-297-4000. Gondola has limited days and hours of operation. Make sure you know it's in operation before you make the side trip. ✗ Restaurant on site, 🛏 hotel rooms $89 and up.			
1639.4	♦	Spring to east.		3810	552.6
1641.2	▲	Cross gravel road.		3694	550.8
1641.8	♦⌒	Cross brook on bridge.		3145	550.2
1641.9		Pass beaver pond.		2862	550.1

NoBo	Features	Description	GPS	Elev	SoBo
1642.2	◊ Y ⊑(16) ⚠ Ⓒ$⚑	Stratton Pond Trail leads 100 yards west to **Stratton Pond Shelter**, plenty of tenting, water, privy. Overnight/caretaker fee. **Camping is not permitted here at shelter, NO FIRES.**	N 43 06.085, W 72 58.128		549.8
		19.3◄15.0◄10.4◄►4.9►7.9►12.7		2565	
1642.4	◊ Y	Willis Ross Clearing at Stratton Pond and intermittent spring 25 feet north on trail, unreliable. Lye Brook Trail leads west to Bigelow Spring Pond Trail.		2583	549.6
1642.5	◊ Y ⚠	Stratton Pond. North Shore Trail leads (0.5) west to North Shore Tenting Area.		2555	549.5
1644.3	◊ ⌒	Cross Winhall River, footbridge.		2175	547.7
1647.1	◊ Y ⊑(10) ⌣ Ⓒ⚑	Branch Pond Trail (0.5W) to **William B. Douglas Shelter**, water (spring) is located south of the shelter, privy.	N 43 08.670, W 72 59.484		544.9
		19.9◄15.3◄4.9◄►3.0►7.8►15.9			
		100 feet after the side trail to the shelter you Cross brook on AT.		2210	
1648.0	◊ 📷 ⚠	Junction with side trail to Prospect Rock and Old Rootville Road. 50 yards to Prospect Rock, views of Manchester and Mt. Equinox. Water is 150 feet west. No parking is permitted here.		2079	544.0
1649.7		Pass west of summit.		2300	542.3

NoBo	Features	Description	GPS	Elev	SoBo
1650.1	◊ Y ⚠(10) ⊑(16) Ⓒ⚑	(0.1W) **Spruce Peak Shelter**, water (piped boxed spring) is located 100 feet to the right of the shelter, tenting, privy.	N 43 10.716, W 72 59.742		541.9
		18.3◄7.9◄3.0◄►4.8►12.9►17.6		2180	
1650.5	📷	Side trail 100 yards west to Spruce Peak, views of Taconic Range and valley below.		2040	541.5
1652.4	◊	Cross small brook.		1770	539.6
1652.5	⚠	Cross **abandoned Old VT. 30** and bridge over stream.		1760	539.5
1652.9	◊⚠ P(26)⚑ ★★★★★	Cross **VT. 11 & 30**	N 43 12.414, W 72 58.242	1840	539.1

Manchester Center, VT (5.4W) See map of Manchester, VT.

🛏◊⛺🏊 ✉	**Red Sled Motel** 802-362-2161. (www.redsledmotel.com) Hiker friendly. 🛏 $78. ⛺ Laundry for a fee, 🏊 swimming pool, trout pond. Ride to trail when available. Located (1.5E) of town.	(3.6W)
	✉ Mail drops for guests: 2066 Depot Street, Manchester Center, VT, 05255.	
🛏🍴🏊✉	**Econo Lodge** 802-362-3333, 🛏 $88 and up, includes continental breakfast, microwave, fridge, 🏊 outdoor pool. Pets $15, 📶 WiFi.	(3.4W)
	✉ Mail drop for guests: 2187 Depot St, Manchester Center, VT 05255.	
📫⚑	**PO** M-F 8:30am-4:30pm, Sa 9am-12pm. 802-362-3070. 3452 Richville Rd. Manchester, VT 05255. N 43 10.073, W 73 02.846	
💻	**Manchester Library** 802-362-2607 Open M-Th 10am-6pm, F-Sat 10am to 4pm.	
🍴	**Cilantro Restaurant** 802-768-8141. (www.cilantrorestaurantvt.com) Burritos, ice cream, sodas. Summer hours; M-Sa 11am-9pm, Su 11:30am-3pm. Winter hours; M-Sa 11:30am-8pm, Su closed.	
🍴	**Starbucks**	

Green Mountain House 330-388-6478. (www.greenmountainhouse.net)
AT Passport location.
◈ Jeff & Regina Taussig host hikers at their home.
Open Jun 7 - Sep 15. Not a party place, no alcohol. ⌂ Space is limited so reservations are essential.
$35+tax per person. Clean bed with linens, ⚿ shower, △ free laundry, ☐ computer available for use, ⊷
free WiFi, well equipped hiker kitchen. Private room for couples. Free breakfast supplies; make your own
pancakes, eggs, cereal, coffee. Hikers with reservations get a ride to town, resupply, then call for pickup. Check-in from 1pm to 7pm. Free morning shuttle back to the trail for guests. Credit cards accepted.
$35+tax per person.

Sutton's Place 802-362-1165. (www.suttonsplacevermont.com) ⊷ $75and up, pets okay on porch, ⊷
WiFi. Accepts MC/Visa.
☑ USPS Mail drops for guests: (USPS) PO Box 142 or (UPS) 50 School St, Manchester Center, VT 05255.

Palmer House 802-362-3600. (www.palmerhouse.com) ⊛ No pets, ⊷ Call for pricing, ask for hiker
discount, stay includes continental breakfast, indoor and ⚓ outdoor pool (not heated), ⊷ WiFi. golf
course, tennis courts and trout pond (all equipment provided).

Carriage House 802-362-1706. (www.carriagehousemotel.com) ⊛ No pets. ⊷ $58 and up for sum-
mer, ⊷ WiFi.

Price Chopper 802-362-9896. M-Su 7am-8pm.

Up For Breakfast 802-362-4204.
◈ AT Passport location. Casual breakfast and brunch.
M-F 7am-13:30 pm, Sa-Su 7am-1:30pm.

Thai Basil, Gringo Jack's, Manchester Pizza, Subway, China City, McDonalds

Mountain Goat Outfitter 802-362-5159. (www.mountaingoat.com)
◈ AT Passport location.
⚶ Full service outfitter, ⚒ white gas, alcohol, by the ounce. canister fuel, footwear. M-Sa 10am-6pm, Su
10am-5pm.
☑ Mail drops: 4886 Main St, Manchester, VT 05255.

Rite aid 802-362-2230. M-Sa 8am-9pm, Su 8am-6pm. **Pharmacy**; M-F 9am-9pm, Sa 9am-6pm, Su
9am-5pm.

Peru, VT (4.3E)

(2.1E) **The Lodge at Bromley** 802-824-6941. (www.lodgeatbromley.com) ⊛ No pets. ⊷ Call for
pricing, $100 hiker rate, ⊷ WiFi, tavern with light menu, game room, ride to and from trail with stay. ☑
Mail for guests: (non-guests $5) 4216 VT 11, Peru, VT 05152.

(2.5E) **Bromley Market** 802-824-4444. (www.bromleymarket.com) M-Su 7am-7pm.

(3.6E) **Bromley View Inn** on VA 30, 802-297-1459. (www.bromleyviewinn.com) ⊷ $99 and up, ⊷
WiFi, includes hot breakfast, shuttle to and from trail head at VT 11/30 with stay.
☑ Mail drops for guests: 522 VT 30, Bondville, VT 05340.

(4.2E) **JJ Hapgood General Store & Eatery** 802-824-4800. (www.jjhapgood.com) Located in Peru,
next to PO. ✕ Restaurant serves breakfast, lunch and dinner, ☏ ATM, ⊷ WiFi. M-Su 7am-7pm, hours
may differ on weekends.

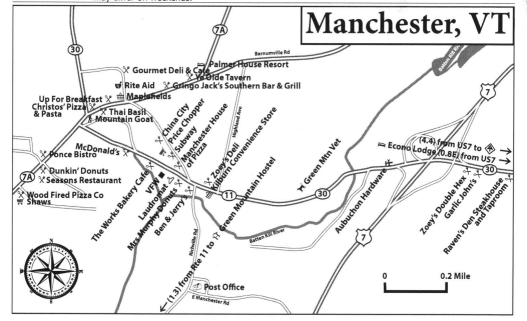

NoBo	Features	Description	GPS	Elev	SoBo
1653.0	⛺	Cross gravel road.		1856	539.0
1653.1	▲〰	Cross brook on I-beam bridge.		1852	538.9
1653.2	⟙	Power line.		1859	538.8
1653.6	▲〰	Cross Bromly Brook on bridge.		1043	538.4
1654.9	▲Y⛺(4) ⊆(12) ☾♀	100 yards east to **Bromley Shelter**, water (brook) is located at the terminus of the spur trail, privy, tenting is (0.1) north on the AT see next entry. 12.7◀7.8◀4.8◀▶8.1▶12.8▶14.3	N 43 14.370, W 72 56.232 2560		537.1
1655.0	⛺(4)	Bromley Shelter tent platforms.		2685	537.0
1655.9	☾📷	Bromley Mountain, ski patrol hut, **no tenting or fires** but it is okay to over-night in ski warming hut, **no smoking**, please keep hut clean so hikers can continue to use it.		3260	536.1
1658.4	⛺P(10)♀	Cross **USFS 21**, Mad Tom Notch, gravel.	N 43 15.462, W 72 56.317 2446		533.6
1660.0	⛺📷	Rock outcrop on Styles Peak summit, views of Bromley Mountain.		3394	532.0
1661.7	⛺	Peru Peak summit, wooded.		3429	530.3
1663.0	▲⛺⊆(10) ☾$♀	**Peru Peak Shelter**, water (brook) is located near the shelter, tenting, privy. Overnight/caretaker fee. 15.9◀12.9◀8.1◀▶4.7▶6.2▶6.4	N 43 18.079, W 72 57.174 2605		529.0
1663.1	〰	Cross wooden bridge.		2619	528.9
1663.2	〰	Cross wooden bridge.		2602	528.8
1663.3	▲	Eastern shore of Griffith Lake.		2600	528.7
1663.5	▲⛺	Pass west of Griffith Lake Tenting Area on slab. Griffith Lake.		2600	528.5
1663.7	▲Y	Griffith Lake (north end), junction with Old Job Trail. Griffith Lake Trail leads (2.0) west to USFS 58.		2600	528.3
1663.8	Y	Junction with Lake Trail.		2620	528.2
1664.6	⛺	Cross old woods road.		2627	527.4
1664.7	⛺	Cross old woods road.		2655	527.3
1665.6	Y	Baker Peak Trail west.		2760	526.4
1665.7	⛺📷	Baker Peak summit.		2850	526.3
1666.2		Reach height of land.		2664	525.8
1667.5	⛺	Intersection with wide grassy fire road.		2278	524.5
1667.7	▲Y⛺(10) ⊆(6) 〰☾♀	100 feet west to **Lost Pond Shelter**, water is Stare Brook in a ravine below site, tenting, privy. 17.6◀12.8◀4.7◀▶1.5▶1.7▶5.0	N 43 20.726, W 72 57.186 2150		524.3
1669.2	▲Y⛺(12) ⊆(8)☾♀	(1.0E) on Old Job Trail to **Old Job Shelter**, water (Lake Brook) is source, tenting, privy. 14.3◀6.2◀1.5◀▶0.2▶3.5▶8.3	N 43 21.244, W 72 55.734 1525		522.8
1669.4	▲⛺(12) ⊆(8)☾♀	**Big Branch Shelter**, water (Big Branch) is located in front of the shelter, tent-ing, privy. This shelter is close to road and heavily used on weekends. 6.4◀1.7◀0.2◀▶3.3▶8.1▶13.2	N 43 21.844, W 72 56.814 1460		522.6
1670.6	▲⛺	Intersects with **USFS 10, Danby–Landgrove Road (southern junction)**		1598	521.4
1670.7	▲〰☾♀ P(25)♀ ★★★★★	Intersects with **USFS 10, Danby–Landgrove Road (northern junction)**, bridge over Black Branch.	N 43 22.362, W 72 57.762 1521		521.3
	🏠♀	(3.2W) **PO** M–F 7:15am–10:15am & 11:15am-2:15pm, Sa 7am–10:30am. 802-293-5105. 214 N Main St. Danby, VT 05739. N 43 20.991, W 72 59.781			
	🏪	(3.2W) **Mt. Tabor Country Store** 802-293-5641. M-Sa 5am-8pm, Su 6am-7pm.			
	🏪	(3.3W) **Nichols Store & Deli** 802-293-5154. M-Su 6am-8pm.			
	💻	(3.4W) **Silas Griffith Library** 802-293-5106. (www.slgriffithlibrary.wordpress.com) W 2pm-7pm, Sa 9am-12pm, one computer.			
1671.3	▲〰	Cross Little Black Branch on I-beam bridge.		1686	520.7
1671.5	▲	Rock hop across Little Black Branch.		1740	520.5
1672.6	▲Y	Little Rock Pond (southern end), junction with Little Rock Pond Loop Trail which rejoins the AT mile 1673.0.		1880	519.4
1672.7	▲⛺(28) ⊆(8)☾$♀	100 feet east to **Little Rock Pond Shelter and Tenting Area**, Overnight fee. Water is located at the caretaker's platform, tenting, privy. Overnight/caretaker fee. 5.0◀3.5◀3.3◀▶4.8▶9.9▶13.6	N 43 24.253, W 72 57.216 1920		519.3
1672.8	▲	Spring, water for LRP Shelter		1854	519.2
1673.0	▲Y	Little Rock Pond (northern end), rejoins the AT at mile 1672.6. Junctions with Green Mountain Trail to Homer Stone Brook Trail.		1854	519.0
1673.1	⛺	Side trail leads east to camping with tent platforms.		1878	518.9
1673.8		Aldrichville clearing.		1914	518.2
1674.0	▲〰	Cross Homer Stone Brook on footbridge.		1900	518.0
1674.2	⛺	Cross **South Wallingford-Wallingford Pond Road**, snowmobile trail.		1983	517.8
1676.2		West of White Rocks Mountain summit.		2680	515.8

Vermont

NoBo	Features	Description	GPS	Elev	SoBo
1677.0	Y 📷	Side trail to White Rocks Cliffs, (0.2W) vista		2400	515.0
1677.5	◊ Y ⊏(8) ☾ ♀	(0.2E) **Greenwall Shelter**, water (spring) is located 200 yards along a trail behind the shelter and is known to go dry, privy.	N 43 26.425, W 72 55.746		514.5
		8.3◄8.1◄4.8◄►5.1►8.8►14.9		2025	
1678.2	Y	Junction with Keewaydin Trail.		1380	513.8
1678.3	♦	Cross Bully Brook.		1760	513.7
1678.9	▲	Cross **Sugar Hill Road**, gravel, descends (0.5) west to VT. 140, passing White Rocks Road USFS 52.		1260	513.1
	♦▲⌒				
1679.0	P(25)♀ ★★★★★	Cross **VT. 140, Wallingford Gulf Road**, Roaring Brook, parking (0.2E)	N 43 27.414, W 72 55.962	1160	513.0

Wallingford, VT (2.8W)

	✉♀	**PO** M–F 8am–4:30pm, Sa 9am–12pm. 802-446-2140. 137 N Main St Unit A. Wallingford, CT 05773. N 43 28.421, W 72 58.639			
	🏪	**Wallingford Country Store & Deli** 802-446-2352. Country store, deli and snack bar food. **Cumberland Farms**			
	🔧	**Nail It Down Hardware** 802-446-2133			
	💻📶	**Gilbert Library** 802-446-2685. (www.ghlib.wordpress.com) 🖥 Computer avaiable to use, 📶 free WiFi. M 10am-5pm, Tu closed, W 10am-8pm, Th-F 10am-5pm, Sa 9am-12pm, Su closed.			
1679.1	P ♀	Pass trail head parking lot.	N 43 27.407, W 72 55.937	1195	512.9
1679.6	▲	Cross abandon **Bear Mountain Road**.		1441	512.4

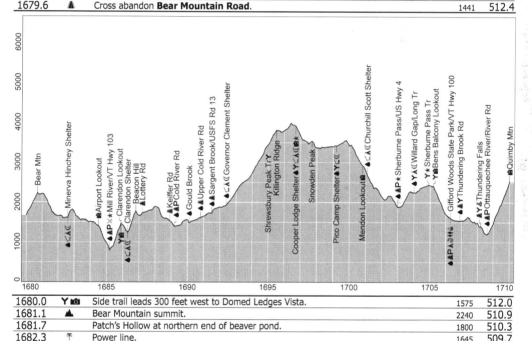

1680.0	Y 📷	Side trail leads 300 feet west to Domed Ledges Vista.		1575	512.0
1681.1	▲	Bear Mountain summit.		2240	510.9
1681.7		Patch's Hollow at northern end of beaver pond.		1800	510.3
1682.3	⊤	Power line.		1645	509.7
1682.6	♦Y▲(10) ⊏(8) ⌣☾♀	200 feet east to **Minerva Hinchey Shelter**, water (spring) is located 150 feet south of shelter and follow "Wada" signs, tenting, privy.	N 43 29.267, W 72 55.500		509.4
		13.2◄9.9◄5.1◄►3.7►9.8►14.1		1605	
1683.2		Spring Lake Clearing.		1620	508.8
1683.3	⊤	Power line with airport beacons.		1658	508.7
1684.2	📷	Overlook.		1291	507.8
1684.3	📷	Overlook.		1516	507.7
1684.5	📷	Rutland Airport Lookout, views west of Taconic Range.		1478	507.5
1684.9	▲	Cross **Knipes Road**, gravel, gated.		1108	507.1
1685.2	♦⌒ ✕▲	Cross high suspension bridge over Mill River in Clarendon Gorge.		800	506.8
1685.3	P(14)♀ ★★★★★	Cross **VT. 103, railroad tracks**	N 43 31.289, W 72 55.550	860	506.7
	🏪	(1.0W) **Loretta's Deli** 802-772-7638. Full Service Deli and meals to go. Fuel by the ounce, water filters. M–F 6am-7pm, Sa-Su 10am-5pm.			

North Clarendon, VT 05759 (4.2W)

NoBo	Features	Description	GPS	Elev	SoBo
	🏤📞	**PO** M–F 8am–1pm & 2pm–4:30pm, Sa 8am–10am. 802-773-7893. 47 Moulton Ave. North Clarendon CT 05759. N 43 33.881, W 72 58.010			
	🏬	**Mike's Country Store** 802-773-7100. M-F 10am-5pm, Sa 10am-2pm, Su closed.			
Rutland, VT (8W of VT 103) see NOBO mile 1703.0. See map of Rutland, VT (north/south)					
1685.4	🕱	Power line.		976	506.6
1685.6		Pass though boulder filled ravine.		1380	506.4
1685.7	Y📷	Side trail 400 feet east to Clarendon Lookout, rock outcrop with views of VT. 103 and Rutland Airport.		1516	506.3
1686.3	♦Y⛺(20) ⌐(12) ⌣☾📞	(0.1E) **Clarendon Shelter**, water (stream) is located 50 feet east from the shelter, tenting, privy. 13.6◄8.8◄3.7◄►6.1►10.4►12.9	N 43 31.412, W 72 54.786	1190	505.7
1686.4	♦	Cross brook.		1566	505.6
1686.8		Beacon Hill, airport beacon.		1740	505.2
1687.2	⚠	Cross **Lottery Road**, unpaved.		1720	504.8
1687.6	◊	Hermit Spring to east, unreliable.		1864	504.4
1687.9		Ridgecrest.		1947	504.1
1688.9	⚠P📞	Cross **Keiffer Road**, unpaved. Limited parking.	N 43 32.036, W 72 52.405	1533	503.1
1689.1	♦	Western bank of Cold River.		1403	502.9
1689.2	⚠P📞 ★★★★★	Cross **Cold River Road**, paved. Limited parking.	N 43 32.262, W 72 52.335	1400	502.8
	🍴✗	(2.4E) W.E. **Pierce Groceries** 802-492-3326. (www.piercesstorevt.com). ✗ Bakery & Deli. M-Sa 7am-7pm, Su 8am-5pm.			
1690.0	♦	Cross Gould Brook, ford, can be **hazardous in high water.**		1480	502.0
1690.8	♦⚠ P(2)📞	Cross **Upper Cold River Road**, gravel road.	N 43 33.012, W 72 51.415	1630	501.2
1691.5	♦⌒⚠	Junction with **Clement Shelter Road**, Sargent Brook Bridge, gravel road.		1730	500.5
1691.9		Overgrown clearing and stone wall.		1802	500.1
1692.2	♦⌒	Cross Robinson Brook on bridge.		1919	499.8
1692.4	♦⛺⌐(10) ⌣☾📞	**Governor Clement Shelter**, water (stream) is located across the road and north of the shelter, tenting, privy. Shelter is located close to road. 14.9◄9.8◄6.1◄►4.3►6.8►8.7	N 43 33.874, W 72 50.928	1900	499.6
1694.6	♦	Cross two small brooks in the area.		2040	497.4
1695.0	Y	Junction with Shrewsbury Peak Trail.		3500	497.0
1695.5		High point on Killington Ridge.		3719	496.5
1696.7	♦Y⛺(2) ⌐(12) ⌣☾📷📞 ★★★★★	**Cooper Lodge**, water, (spring) is located north of shelter on AT, privy, two tent platforms, privy. 14.1◄10.4◄4.3◄►2.5►4.4►16.3	N 43 36.363, W 72 49.347	3900	495.3
	Y✗	(0.2E) **Killington Peak Lodge** 800-621-6867. ✗ Food service at the summit lodge, gondola ride ($25 round trip) to the ski resort below. Summer hours 10am-5pm. There is a new, safe, easy, and short trail to get from Cooper Lodge on Mount Killington and the gondola and cafe on the other side of the mountain. There is no signage, yet at the trailhead, or signage at the summit, directing you to the gondola. The new trail starts just beyond the privy. You pass the top of a ski run take a set of stairs to the gondola area.			
1696.9	Y	Junction with Bucklin Trail.		3770	495.1
1697.7		Height of land on Snowden Peak.		3449	494.3
1699.2	♦Y⌐(12) $📞	Jungle Junction. Sherburne Pass Trail (southern junction) leads (0.5) east to **Pico Camp**, water is located 45 yards north on the Sherburne Pass Trail, privy. If caretaker is present, there is an overnight/caretaker fee. Pico Link trail leads (0.4) to Pico Peak summit and rejoins the AT north of Sheburne Pass (in VT). 12.9◄6.8◄2.5◄►1.9►13.8►23.7	N 43 38.347, W 72 49.832	3480	492.8
1700.8	📷	Mendon Lookout.		2890	491.2
1701.1	◊Y☾ ⛺(1) ⌐(8)📞	(0.1W) **Churchill Scott Shelter**, water is located on spur trail downhill behind shelter, privy, tent sites. **NO FIRES.** 8.7◄4.4◄1.9◄►11.9►21.8►34.1	N 43 38.693, W 72 51.203	2560	490.9
1701.2	♦	Cross brook.		2530	490.8
1703.0	♦⚠P(24) 📞 ★★★★★	Cross **U.S. 4. See map of Killington, VT.**	N 43 39.969, W 72 50.920	1880	489.0

NoBo Features	Description	GPS	Elev SoBo

(0.8E) **The Inn at Long Trail** 802-775-7181, 800-325-2540. (www.innatlongtrail.com)
◈ AT Passport location.
Ask about hiker rates, rooms include full breakfast. Limited pet rooms, reservations recommended on weekends. ▲ Overflow camping across street but there are no facilities. ☒ Coin laundry, ♦ outside water spigot. ☞ WiFi. Closed mid-April through Memorial Day. ✗ **McGrath's Irish Pub**; serves lunch and dinner from 11:30am-9pm.
☞ Mail drops for guests: (Packages FedEx/UPS only) 709 US 4, Killington, VT 05751.

(1.4W) **Mendon Mountain View Lodge** 802-773-4311. (www.mendonmountainviewlodge.com)
⊗ No pets. ☞ Hiker rate $70 and up, $15EAP. Breakfast $10. ☒ Heated pool, hot tub, sauna.
☞ Mail drops for guests: 5654 Route 4, Mendon, VT 05701.

Rutland, VT (8.5W from US 4 trail head) See map of Rutland, VT (north/south)

PO M-F 10am-2pm, Sa 8:30am-11:30pm. 802-773-0223. 151 West St. Ste JJ. Rutland VT 05701. N 43 36.484, W 72 58.894

Hikers Hostel at theYellow Deli 802-683-9378, 802-775-9800.or 773-0160 or 747-0407(www.hikershostel.org)
◈ AT Passport location. No alcohol, no smoking.
Run by a Twelve Tribes spiritual community. Donation or ♦ WFS. itchenette, ☒ laundry. ☒ Free showers even without stay. ☒ Shuttles sometimes available by donation. ☒ Hostel open 24 hours 7 days a week ✗ (Deli open sunday at noon through fiday 3pm) Stay includes breakfast and 15% off at deli. Friday night special. Sabbath Meal all are welcome.
Mail drops: Hiker Hostel, 23 Center Street, Rutland, VT 05701.

Mountain Travelers Outdoor Shop 802-775-0814. (www.mtntravelers.com) All gear, Coleman, alcohol by the ounce. M-Tu 10am-6pm, W closed, 10am-6pm, Su 12pm-5pm.

Walmart 802-773-0200. M-Su 7am-10pm; ☒ **Pharmacy** M-F 8am-8pm, Sa 9am-7pm, Su 10am-6pm. **Price Chopper** 802-438-6119. M-Su 6am-12am.

Rutland Food Co-op 802-773-0737. (www.rutlandcoop.com) M-Sa 9am-7pm, Su 10am-6pm.

Subway, Applebee's, Little Caesars

Beauchamps & O'Rourke Pharmacy 802-775-4321. (www.beauchamppharmacy.com) M-F 8am-6pm, Sa 9am-12pm, Su closed.

Rutland Veterinary 802-773-2779. (www.rutlandvet.com) M-F 7am-8pm, Sa-Su 7am-5pm.

Killington, VT 05751 (1.8E) from US 4, See **NOBO mile 1706.3**

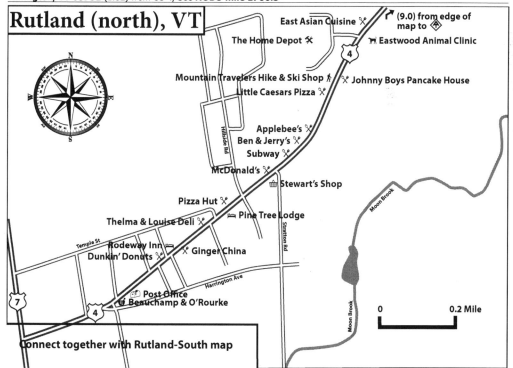

Rutland (north), VT

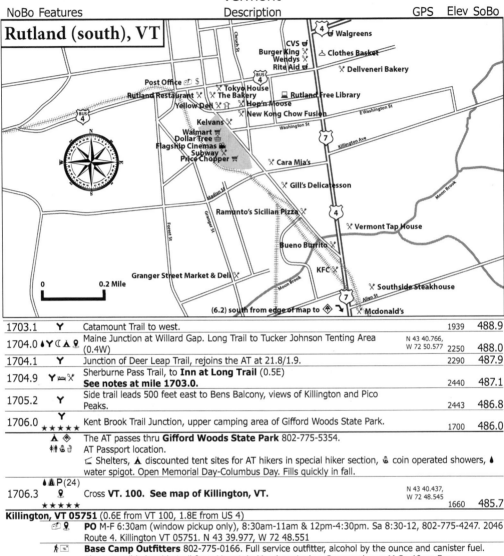

Rutland (south), VT

Map features: Walgreens, CVS, Burger King, Wendys, Rite Aid, Clothes Basket, Dellveneri Bakery, Post Office, Tokyo House, The Bakery, Rutland Restaurant, Yellow Deli, Hop'n Moose, Rutland Free Library, New Kong Chow Fusion, Kelvans, Walmart, Dollar Tree, Flagship Cinemas, Subway, Price Chopper, Cara Mia's, Gill's Delicatesson, Ramunto's Sicilian Pizza, Vermont Tap House, Bueno Burrito, KFC, Granger Street Market & Deli, Southside Steakhouse, Mcdonald's

0.2 Mile

(6.2) south from edge of map to

NoBo	Features	Description	GPS	Elev	SoBo
1703.1	Y	Catamount Trail to west.		1939	488.9
1704.0	♦Y☾▲♀	Maine Junction at Willard Gap. Long Trail to Tucker Johnson Tenting Area (0.4W)	N 43 40.766, W 72 50.577	2250	488.0
1704.1	Y	Junction of Deer Leap Trail, rejoins the AT at 21.8/1.9.		2290	487.9
1704.9	Y⇌✗	Sherburne Pass Trail, to **Inn at Long Trail** (0.5E) **See notes at mile 1703.0.**		2440	487.1
1705.2	Y	Side trail leads 500 feet east to Bens Balcony, views of Killington and Pico Peaks.		2443	486.8
1706.0	Y ★★★★★	Kent Brook Trail Junction, upper camping area of Gifford Woods State Park.		1700	486.0
	▲ ◈ ♦♦♿♂	The AT passes thru **Gifford Woods State Park** 802-775-5354. AT Passport location. ⊏ Shelters, ▲ discounted tent sites for AT hikers in special hiker section, ♨ coin operated showers, ♦ water spigot. Open Memorial Day-Columbus Day. Fills quickly in fall.			
1706.3	♦▲P(24) ♀ ★★★★★	Cross **VT. 100. See map of Killington, VT.**	N 43 40.437, W 72 48.545	1660	485.7

Killington, VT 05751 (0.6E from VT 100, 1.8E from US 4)

⌂♀   **PO** M-F 6:30am (window pickup only), 8:30am-11am & 12pm-4:30pm. Sa 8:30-12, 802-775-4247. 2046 Route 4. Killington VT 05751. N 43 39.977, W 72 48.551

🚶▭   **Base Camp Outfitters** 802-775-0166. Full service outfitter, alcohol by the ounce and canister fuel. Also accessible by side trail from Mountain Meadows Lodge. Summer hours M-Su 10am-5pm.
     ▭ Mail drops: 2363 Route 4, Killington VT 05751.

🛏   **Killington Deli & Marketplace** 802-775-1599. (www.killingtondeli.com)

⇌⊗☎   **Greenbrier Inn** 802-775-1575. (www.greenbriervt.com)
     ⊗ No pets. ⇌ Ask about the 15% hiker discount. Fridge, ☎ free WiFi.

⇌▱☎♨   **Killington Motel** 802-773-9535. (www.killingtonmotel.com) No smoking rooms. ⇌ Call for pricing and ask for hiker rate, includes continental breakfast, ♨ pool, fridge, ☎ free WiFi.

✗♨   **JAX Food & Games** 802-422-5334. (www.jaxfoodandgames.com) ✗ Eat, have a drink, while your doing your ♨ laundry. M-Su 3pm-2am. Located (0.8) south on US 4 on Killington Rd.

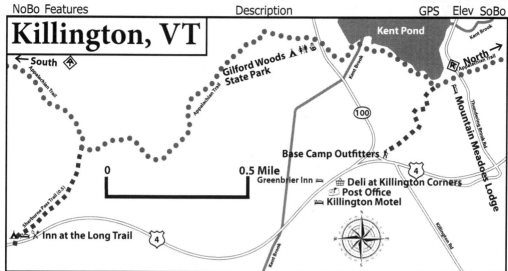

Killington, VT

← South

Kent Pond

Gilford Woods State Park

Kent Brook

North →
Appalachian Trail

Kent Brook

Appalachian Trail

100

Mountain Meadows Lodge

Base Camp Outfitters

Thundering Brook Rd.

0   0.5 Mile

Greenbrier Inn

4

Deli at Killington Corners

Post Office

Killington Motel

Sherburne Pass Trail (0.5)

Inn at the Long Trail

4

Kent Brook

Killington Rd

NoBo	Features	Description	GPS	Elev	SoBo
1706.4		Cross Kent Brook on footbridge.		1580	485.6
1706.5	★★★★★	Kent Pond, shore. Trail to Base camp Outfitters.		1621	485.5
		Mountain Meadows Lodge 802-775-1010. (www.mountainmeadowslodge.com)			
		AT Passport location.			
	P	No pets inside. Rooms $69D, single room sometimes available for $59. Meals and lodging are not available most weekends & during events. Okay to charge phones, but please do not loiter when events are being held at the lodge. Occasional work for stay. Lunch or dinner $10. Hot tub, sauna, game room, laundry, computer available to use, free WiFi, and canoe for guests. P Parking for section hiking guests. Ask about tenting.			
		Mail drops free, even for non-guests: 285 Thundering Brook Rd, Killington, VT 05751.			
1707.0	Y	Junction with **Thundering Brook Road (southern junction)**.		1450	485.0
1708.2		Junction with **Thunderinging Brook Road (northern junction)**, gravel road.		1280	483.8
1708.4	Y	Side trail leads 200 feet west on boardwalk to Thundering Falls.		1226	483.6
1708.6		Views from boardwalk of Ottauquechee floodplain.		1224	483.4
1708.7	P(6)	Cross **River Road**.	N 43 40.840, W 72 46.935	1214	483.3
1709.5		Vista of Ottauquechee River Valley.		2136	482.5

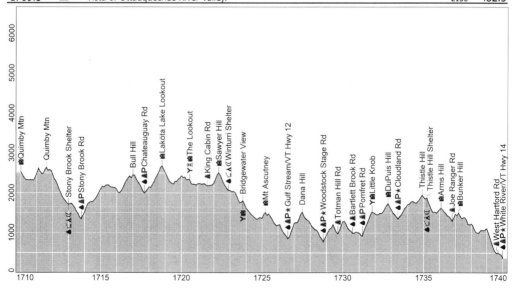

NoBo	Features	Description	GPS	Elev	SoBo
1710.0		Summit of unnamed hill.		2523	482.0
1710.5	⊤	Power line.		2334	481.5
1710.8	▲	Cross woods road.		2374	481.2
1711.1	▲	Cross unnamed summit.		2600	480.9
1711.9		Northern shoulder of Quimby Mountain.		2550	480.1
1713.0	◑Y▲ ⊆(6) ⌣☾♀	(0.1E) **Stony Brook Shelter**, water (brook) is located 100 yards north of shelter on AT, tenting, privy. 16.3◀13.8◀11.9◀▶9.9▶22.2▶31.0	N 43 41.507, W 72 43.836 1760		479.0
1713.2		Aluminum ladder on steep ledge.		1793	478.8
1713.8	◑▲P(4)♀	Cross Mink Brook or Stony Brook a few times, **Stony Brook Road**.	N 43 41.476, W 72 43.211	2000	478.2
1715.2		Reach height of land.		2260	476.8
1715.7		Small pond in sag known locally as the Continental Divide.		2198	476.3
1716.1	▲	Cross logging road.		2176	475.9
1716.2	◊	Cross intermittent brook.		2073	475.8
1717.0		West of Bull Hill.		2445	475.0
1717.2	▲	Cross logging road.		2464	474.8
1717.7	▲P(8)♀	Cross **Chateauguay Road**, gravel.	N 43 41.368, W 72 40.429	2000	474.3
1718.1	◑	Cross brook.		2248	473.9
1718.6	◊	Cross intermittent brook.		2670	473.4
1718.8	📷	Lakota Lake Lookout, view of Lakota Lake below and White Mountains. This lookout is now overgrown.		2640	473.2
1720.5	Y📷 ﹗	(0.2W) to private cabin and observation deck, owners permit its use as a viewpoint for hikers, **no fires**.		2320	471.5
1721.3	▲	Junction with **Lookout Farm Road**.		2297	470.7
1721.4	▲♀	Junction with **King Cabin Road (southern junction)**.	N 43 40.126, W 72 38.150	2262	470.6
1721.6	▲P(6)♀	Junction with **King Cabin Road (northern junction)**.	N 43 40.904, W 72 39.377	2249	470.4
1722.2	📷	Don's Rock on The Pinnacle, view of Killington and Pico Peaks.		2494	469.8
1722.3		Reach height of land on Sawyer Hill.		2537	469.7
1722.9	◑Y▲ ⊆(6)☾♀	(0.2W) **Winturri Shelter**, water (spring) is located to the right of the shelter, tenting, privy. 23.7◀21.8◀9.9◀▶12.3▶21.1▶28.4	N 43 39.731, W 72 37.356 1910		469.1
1723.7	▲	Cross old woods road.		1794	468.3
1723.9	Y📷	On crest of ridge side trail leads east view of North Bridgewater.		1805	468.1
1724.5	▲	Cross old woods road.		1630	467.5
1725.3	📷	Ridge with views of Mt. Ascutney.		1525	466.7
1725.5	📷	Bald hilltop with panoramic views.		1488	466.5
1726.5		Clearing with wooden stile that crosses electric fence.		967	465.5
1726.7	◑⌒▲ P(10) ♀ ★★★★★	Cross **VT. 12**, Gulf Stream Bridge **Woodstock, VT. (4.2E)**	N 43 39.313, W 72 33.974 882		465.3
	🏛	(0.2W) **On The Edge Farm** 802-457-4510. (www.ontheedgefarm.com) Mid-May to Labor Day M-Su 10am-5:30pm otherwise off season M 10am-5pm, Tu-W closed, Th-Su 10am-5pm. Local goods, pies, fruit, ice cream, smoked meats and cheese, cold drinks.			

Woodstock, VT 05091 (4.2E)

	✉♀	**PO** M-F 8:30am-5pm, Sa 9am-12pm. 802-457-1323. 22 Central St. Woodstock VT 05091. N 43 37.540, W 72 31.054			
	🛏⊞	**Shire Woodstock** 802-457-2211. (www.shirewoodstock.com) 🛏 Call for pricing, 🖧 free WiFi. This is a tourist town.			
	🛏⊞	**Braeside Motel** 802-457-1366. (www.braesidemotel.com) 🛏 $98-$168, fridge, 🖧 free WiFi.			
	✗	**Pizza Che** 508-765-5979. (www.pizzachefsouthbridge.com) M-W 11am-10pm, Th-Sa 11am-11pm, Su 12pm-10pm.			
	🏛	**Cumberland Farms, Gillingham & Sons** 802-457-2100. (www.gillinghams.com) M-Sa 8:30am-6:30pm Su 10am-5pm.			
	✇	**Woodstock Pharmacy** 770-926-6478. M-F 9am-6pm, Sa 9:30am-1:30pm, Su closed.			
	🐾	**Woodstock Veterinary Hospital** 860) 974-1802. M-9am-7pm, Tu-W 9am-6pm, Th 9am-7pm, F 9am-6pm, Sa-Su 9am-2pm.			
	💻	**Norman Williams Public Library** 802-457-2295. (www.normanwilliams.org) M-F 10am-6pm, Sa 10am-4pm, Su closed.			
1727.4		Cross corner of hilltop field.		1265	464.6
1727.8		Dana Hill, tree covered.		1530	464.2
1728.9	◑⌒▲ P(3) ♀ ★★★★★	Cross **Woodstock Stage Road** and Barnard Brook on footbridge.	N 43 40.313, W 72 33.226 820		463.1

South Pomfret, VT 05067 (1.0E)

NoBo		Features / Description	GPS	Elev	SoBo
	📧🍴	**PO** M-F 10am-2pm, Sa 8:30am-11:30am. 802-457-1147, located inside of Teago's General Store. 2035 Ponfret Rd Unit B. Aouth Promfret VT 05067. N 43 39.893, W 72 32.327			
	🏪	**Teago's General Store** 802-457-1626. Homemade soups, salads, sandwiches, ice cream. M-Sa 7am-6pm, Su 8am-4pm.			
1729.4		Cross notch between Totman Hill and Breakneck Hill.		1192	462.6
1729.6	♦	Cross brook.		1285	462.4
1729.7	⚠	Cross **Totman Hill Road**, dirt road.		1010	462.3
1730.4	♦⌒⚠🍴	Cross **Bartlett Brook Road**, gravel, footbridge, brook.	N 43 40.815, W 72 31.630	1050	461.6
1731.1	♦⚠P(4)	Cross **Pomfret–South Pomfret Road**, Pomfret Brook		980	460.9
1731.6	📷	Hilltop field with view.		1515	460.4
1731.8	Y	Four way junction with old AT.		1544	460.2
1731.9	⚠	Follow old town road.		1525	460.1
1732.0	Y◊	Side trail leads 50 feet east uphill to spring, unreliable.		1503	460.0
1732.4	▲	DuPuis Hill summit.		1630	459.6
1732.9	⚠P🏪🍴 ★★★★★	Cross **Cloudland Road**. Limited parking.	N 43 41.203, W 72 30.010	1370	459.1
	♦🏪	**(0.2W) Cloudland Farm Market** 802-457-2599. (www.cloudlandfarm.com) Family run farm. Mid-June-mid-Oct: Closed Sun thru Tues., Open We'd. 10-3 & Thurs. - Sat. 10-5. Rest of the year: Closed Sun. thru Wed., Open Thurs. 10-3 and Fri. & Sat. 10-5. ♦ Hikers are always welcome to fill up on tap water via an outdoor spigot. Soda, ice cream, cheeses and crackers, their own beef jerky, pickles, t-shirts, hats, soaps and balms. Occasionally have granola and sandwiches. Family run farm.			
1733.7	⏚	Power line.		1485	458.3
1734.9	⚠	Cross woods road on top of Thistle Hill, wooded.		1800	457.1
1735.2	♦Y⚠ ⌐(8)⌣☾	**(0.1E) Thistle Hill Shelter**, water (stream) is located near the shelter, tenting, privy.	N 43 41.710, W 72 28.548		456.8
	🍴	34.1◄22.2◄12.3◄►8.8►16.1►25.6		1480	
1735.9	♦	Cross brook.		1596	456.1
1736.0	📷	Open field called Arms Hill, views.		1609	456.0
1736.5	📷	Open field with views.		1416	455.5
1736.7	⚠P(3)🍴	Cross **Joe Ranger Road**, gravel, by small pond with stone dam.	N 43 42.318, W 72 27.748	1280	455.3
1737.3	▲	Bunker Hill summit, wooded.		1466	454.7
1737.4	⚠	Cross old town road by a cemetery.		1412	454.6
1737.6	📷	Hilltop pastures with views.		1418	454.4
1737.7	⚠	Cross old farm road.		1161	454.3
1739.0	📷	Hilltop field with views of White River Valley.		1005	453.0
1739.7	⚠	Cross **Quechee - West Hartford Road**.		461	452.3
1739.9	⚠	Junition with **Promfret Road** on west bank of White River.		474	452.1

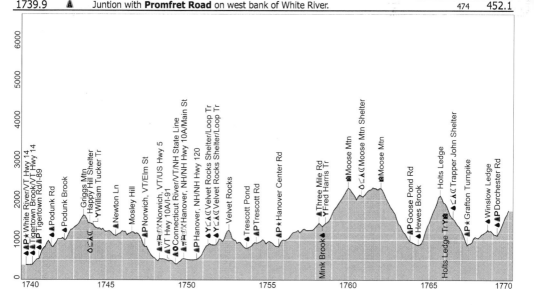

NoBo	Features	Description	GPS	Elev	SoBo
	♦⌒▲▲P				
1740.0	♀ ★★★★★	Junction with **VT. 14 (eastern end)**, Patriots Bridge over White River.	N 43 42.743, W 72 25.055	390	452.0
	🚗	**Big Yellow Taxi** 802-281-8294. Covers Woodstock, Norwich, Hanover, Lebanon and White River Junction.			
1740.4	▲	Junction with **VT. 14 (western end)**.		390	451.6
1740.5	▲	Stetson Road joins to the east.		430	451.5
1740.6	▲P(3)♀	Junction with **Podunk Road at Tigertown Road**.	N 43 43.244, W 72 24.793	540	451.4
1741.4	▲P(3)♀	Cross **Podunk Road (northern junction)**	N 43 43.104, W 72 24.012	860	450.6
1741.5	♦	Cross Podunk Brook.		860	450.5
1741.7	▲	Cross logging road.		897	450.3
1742.0	▲	Cross logging road.		994	450.0
1742.3	♦	Cross East Fork of Podunk Brook and a logging road.		1100	449.7
1742.4	▲	Cross logging road.		1109	449.6
1743.5		Wooded shoulder of Griggs Mountain.		1570	448.5
1743.8	◊	Cross small stream, seasonal.		1572	448.2
1744.0	◊Y▲(10) ⌂(8) ⌐♺(♀	(0.1E) **Happy Hill Shelter**, water (brook) is located near the shelter but known to go dry, tenting privy. 31.0◀21.1◀8.8◀▶7.3▶16.8▶22.5	N 43 43.432, W 72 21.942	1460	448.0
1744.2	Y	Junction with William Tucker Trail.		1320	447.8
1745.6	▲	Cross **Newton Lane**.		1145	446.4
1746.5		Skirt east side of Mosley Hill.		1180	445.5
1746.9	⊤	Power line.		1166	445.1
1747.0	♦	Cross stream.		1195	445.0
1747.5	▲	Intersects with Elm Street Trail head.		750	444.5
1747.8	▲	Cross **Hopson Road**.		606	444.2
1748.0	♦	Cross Bloody Brook.		567	444.0
1748.3	▲ ★★★★★	Junction of **Elm Street and U.S. 5**. **Norwich, VT.**		537	443.7
	⊨✗💻⌐ 🖳	**Norwich Inn** 802-649-1143. (www.norwichinn.com) ⊨ $189 and up, 2 pet rooms available, no smoking, reservations recommended. 🖳 Computer available to use, ⌐ free WiFi.			
		🖃 Mail drops for guests: PO Box 908, Norwich, VT 04055, or FedEx to 325 Main St. ✗ **Murdocks Ale House** Located in the Norwich Inn. Serves diiner M-Su, serves breakfast and lunch W-Su.			
	🛒⌇	(0.1W) on Main St. **Dan & Whits General Store** 802-649-1602. (www.danandwhitsonline.com) M-Su 7am-9pm. Hikers get free day-old sandwiches, when available. Small gear items, ⌇ canister fuel, batteries, ponchos, hardware and grocery.			
	🖳⌐	**Norwich Library** 802-649-1184. (www.norwichlibrary.org) M 1am-8pm, Tu-W-F 10am-5:30pm, Th 10am-8pm, F 10am-5:30pm, Sa 10am-3pm, Su 12pm-4pm.			
1748.9	▲	**I-91 passes over VT. 10A**, AT on sidewalk.		450	443.1
1749.3	▲ State Line	Connecticut River, Vermont-New Hampshire State Line		380	442.7
1749.8	▲P(24) ♀ ★★★★★	**NH. 10, Intersection of North Main and East Wheelock streets**. Dartmouth College. **See map of Hanover, NH.**	N 43 42.242, W 72 17.907	520	442.2
	🖃♀	**PO** M-F 8:30am-5pm, Sa 8:30am-12pm, Sat pick-up available until 3pm. 603-643-4544. 50 S Main St. Hanover NH 03755. N 43 42.040, W 72 17.354			
	①	**Hanover Friends of the AT** produce a brochure with complete list of hiker services. Brochures can be found at the DOC, PO, libraries, Co-op.			
	①🖳⌐	**Dartmouth Outing Club (DOC)** 603-646-2428. (www.outdoors.dartmouth.edu) Offers room for pack storage in Robinson Hall and Howe Library, but packs cannot be left overnight as both areas are unsecured. Not available during Dartmouth orientation (mid Aug - mid Sept). Both places have computers for free internet use.			
	P	Overnight parking on Wheelock Street Lot A, see map. No parking near Connecticut River Bridge.			
	⊨⌂⌐🖃	**Sunset Motor Inn** 603-298-8721. (www.sunsetinnnh.com) M-Su 8-11. ⊨ Call ahead for availability, Ask for hiker discount. Will shuttle when bus is not running, ⌂ free laundry before 6pm, ⌐ free WiFi, quiet after 10pm, $15 pet fee.			
		🖃 Mail drops for guest only: 305 N Main Street, West Lebanon, NH 03874.			
	⊨✗	**Hanover Inn** 603-643-4300. (www.hanoverinn.com) ⊨ $249 and up, discount sometimes available. Very pricey.			
	✗	**Everything But Anchovies** 603-643-6135. (www.ebas.com) full menu and beer, daily specials. Pizza buffet Tuesday night $7.95. M-Su 11am-2:10am.			
	✗	**Allen St. Deli** 603-643-2245. M-Su 7am-4om. One free bagel for thru-hikers.			
	✗	**Jewel of India Buffet** 603-643-2217. (www.jewelofindiahanover.com) M-Sa Lunch 11:30am-2:30pm, Dinner 4:30pm-10pm. Sunday brunch 11:30am-2:30pm, dinner 2:20pm-10pm.			
	✗	**C&C Pizza** 603643-2966. (www.candapizza.net) M-Th 11am-11pm, F-Sa 11am-12pm, Sun 11am-11pm.			

NoBo	Features	Description	GPS	Elev SoBo

Stinson's Village Store Deli & Catering 603-643-6086. ✗ Deli sandwich, soda & small bag of chips. $5 hiker lunch special. M-Su 8am-12am.

Hanover Food Co-op 603-643-2667. Deli and food bar. Please use member #7000 at check out to help fund AT related initiatives. ☎ WiFi. M-Su 7am-8pm.

Richard W. Black Recreation Center 603-643-5315. M 9am-5pm, Tu-F 9am-6pm, Sa 10am-6pm, Su closed. 🚿 Shower with towel and soap $3, 🧺 laundry with soap $2, must finish before 4:30pm. ☎ WiFi.

Zimmerman's 603-643-6863. Canister fuel, Aquamira, outdoor clothing. ✉ Mail drops: 63 Main St, Hanover, NH 03756.

Howe Library 603-643-4120. (www.howelibrary.org) M-Th 10am-8pm, F 10am-6pm, Sa 10am-5pm, Su 1pm-5pm.

Hanover Hardware 603-643-2308. 🔥 Coleman fuel and alcohol fuel by the ounce. M-F 8am-5:30pm, Sa 9am-5pm, Su 9:30am-2:30pm.

Hanover Veterinary 603-643-3313. (www.hvcvets.com) M-F 8am-5:30pm, Sa 8am-12pm, Su closed.

Lebanon & West Lebanon, NH (5.0E)

Days Inn 603-448-5070, 4 mi. south of the Co-op on Route 120 on free bus route. ☎ Call for pricing, includes continental breakfast, 🖥 computer avaialbel for use, ☎ free WiFi, pets $20.

EMS 603-298-7716. M-F 8am-8pm, Sa 8am-5pm, Su closed.

LL Bean 603-298-6975. M-F 9am-8pm, Sa 9am-5pm, Sun closed.

Shaw's 603-298-0388. M-Sa 7am-10pm, Su 7am-9pm.

Hanover, NH

← South

The Dartmouth Green

E Wheelock St

10

W Wheelock St 10A

N

Tuk Tuk Thai Cuisine ✗
Murphy's on the Green ✗
Canoe Club ✗
Dartmouth Bookstore 🖥
Kata Thai Kitchen ✗
Mollys ✗

🛏 Hanover Inn Dartmouth

✗ Lou's Restaurant & Bakery
✗ Market Table

West St

Orient ✗ ✗ | ✗ C&A Pizza

S Park St

120

Nugget Theater 🎬
Post Office ✉
$

Maple St

Irving ⛽
Sushiya ✗

Umpleby's Bakery Cafe
True Value
Noodle Station

Lebanon St

Summer St

🖥 Howe Library

CVS 💊

S Main St

0   0.2 Mile

Community Center ✈ Hanover Co-op

10

Connecticut River

North →

NoBo		Description	GPS	Elev	SoBo
1750.5	⛺	Intersects with **NH. 120** at a service station in Hanover.		490	441.5
1750.7	⛺Y	Juntion with DOC Chase Field and Trail, soccer field.		504	441.3
1751.0	◊	Spring to east, unreliable.		746	441.0
1751.3	⚡Y⛺ ⌐(4) ⌣ℂ♀	Junction of loop trail (southern end) leading (0.2W) to **Velvet Rocks Shelter**, water (Ledyard Spring) is located along the northern access trail on northern access to shelter, tenting, privy. 28.4◄16.1◄7.3◄►9.5►15.2►21.9	N 43 42.154, W 72 15.881 1040		440.7
1751.8	Y◊	Junction of loop trail (northern end) leading (0.4) west to Velvet Rocks Shelter. Ledyard Spring Trail is (0.2) west on the loop trail.		1200	440.2
1752.4	Y	Unsigned junction with Trescott Road Spur Trail, blue blazed.		1001	439.6
1752.6		High point on Velvet Rocks		1243	439.4
1753.7	◊⌐	Cross bridge over cattail marsh and beaver pond.		864	438.3
1754.3	⛺P(8)♀	Cross **Trescott Road**.	N 43 42.323, W 72 13.786 915		437.7
1755.4	◊	Cross brook.		960	436.6
1755.5	◊	Cross brook.		892	436.5
1755.6		Cemetery to west.		839	436.4
1755.7	⛺P♀ ★★★★★	Cross **Etna–Hanover Center Road**, Etna, NH.	N 43 42.229, W 72 12.717 845		436.3

NoBo	Features	Description	GPS	Elev	SoBo
	⌂ ◈ ⛺ ⛄	**Tiggers Tree House** 603-643-9213.			
	◈	AT Passport location.			
	⌂	Private home; not a party place. No drive-ins. Advance notice ensures a place to stay. Call from trail head, Etna General Store (will let you use phone) or Dartmouth Outing Club for pickup. Pets allowed, donations accepted or buy laundry soap or ⛄ work for stay. Rides to grocery store, Walmart, EMS.			
	⌂ ✗	(0.8E) **Etna General Store** 603-643-1655. Deli, hot meals. M-F 6am-7pm, Sa 8am-7pm, Su closed.			
1756.3	📷	Cross large field with view.		1092	435.7
1757.7	▲	Cross Cory Road, woods road.		1245	434.4
1758.2	▲P(4)⚲	Cross **Three Mile Road**	N 43 43.080, W 72 10.560	1350	433.8
1758.4	◊	Cross Mink Brook.		1320	433.6
1758.6	▲Y	Cross road at junction with Fred Harris Trail.		1804	433.4
1760.0	▲📷	South peak of Moose Mountain.		2290	432.0
1760.6	▲	Cross **Old Wolfeboro Road (woods road)** at junction of abandon DOC Clark Pond Loop.		2000	431.4
1760.8	◊Y⛺(8) ⛢(8) ◡⛺⚲	Loop trail (southern junction) leads 75 yards to **Moose Mountain Shelter**, water is located on the AT north of the shelter follow loop trail to end, tenting, privy. 25.6◄16.8◄9.5◄►5.7►12.4►17.7	N 43 43.669, W 72 08.850	1850	431.2
1760.9	Y	Loop trail (northern junction) leads 100 yards to Moose Mountain Shelter.		2113	431.1
1762.0	▲📷	North peak of Moose Mountain, views from quartzite ledges.		2300	430.0
1763.6	◊	Cross South Fork, Hewes Brook.		1100	428.4
1764.0	▲P(6)⚲	Cross **Goose Pond Road**, paved.	N 43 45.168, W 72 07.398	952	428.0
1764.3	◊〜	Cross beaver pond on dam.		918	427.7
1764.9	▲	Cross snowmobile trail.		1160	427.1
1765.7		Reach height of land on Holts Ledge.		2100	426.3
1766.0	📷	Side trail (0.1) east to Holts Ledge, view, Peregrine Falcon rookery		1930	426.0
1766.3	◊	Cross small intermittent brook.		1586	425.7
1766.5	◊Y⛺ ⛢(8) ◡⛺⚲	(0.2W) **Trapper John Shelter**, water (brook) is located 15 yards to the left of the shelter, tenting, privy. 22.5◄15.2◄5.7◄►6.7►12.0►27.5	N 43 46.982, W 72 06.720	1345	425.5
1766.7	▲	Cross ski area access road.		1508	425.3
1767.4	▲P(5)⚲ ★★★★	Cross **Dartmouth Skiway, Lyme–Dorchester Road**.	Area 1 N 43 47.550, W 72 06.167 Area 2 N 43 47.437, W 72 06.073	880	424.6

Lyme Center, NH 03769 (1.3W)

	⌖⚲	**PO** M–F 8am–10am, Sa 8am–11:30am. 603-795-4037. 181 Dorchester RD Unit 3. Lyme Center NH 03769. N 43 47.974, E 43 47.974			

Lyme, NH 03768 (3.2W)

	⌖⚲	**PO** M–F 7:45am–12pm & 1:30am–5:15pm, Sa 7:45am–12pm. 603-795-4421. 5 Main St. Unit 5. Lyme NH 03768. N 43 48.688, W 72 09.490			
	🛏🖥📺	**Dowd's Country Inn B&B** 603-795-4712 (www.dowdscountryinn.com) 🛏 Call in advance and let them know you are a hiker. Pickup and return to trail head is available. Rates change depending on the season mid week starting at $100 and up. Includes full breakfast and afternoon tea. Pets $15, allowed in some rooms. 🖥 Computer available to use, 📶 free WiFi. 📺 Mail drops for guests: 9 Main Street, Lyme, NH 03768.			
	⌂✗📺📠	(3.3W) **Lyme Country Store** 603-795-2213. (www.lymecountrystore.com) Local products, fresh cut meats, ✗ deli salads, homemade baked goods, ice cream, produce, deli. M-Su 6am-8pm. They do not take mail drop but they do offer shipping Shipping UPS and FEDEX. 📺 Mail drops: 13 Main St, Lyme, NH 03768			
	🐾	(2.8W) **Lyme Veterinary Hospital** 603-795-2747. (www.lymevethospital.com) Loated on High St, hospital is 50 yards on the left. M-F 8am-5pm, Sa 8am-12pm, Su closed.			
	🚗	**Vtrips LLC** 781-762-6998, go@ridevtrips.com Covers Appalachian trail heads from VT and New Hampshire and areas in between. Major bus stations and airports.			
1768.7	◊	Northwest side of Winslow Ledge, cross stream is shallow gorge.		1232	423.3
1769.1	▲	Junction of old road at granite AT marker.		1216	422.9
1769.3	◊	Cross Grant Brook		1090	422.7
1769.4	◊▲P(5)⚲	Cross **Lyme–Dorchester Road**	N 43 47.822, W 72 06.295	1100	422.6

NoBo	Features	Description	GPS	Elev	SoBo
1770.2	📷	Pass numerous quartzite ledge outcrops in this area along Lambert Ridge while passing in and out of the woods.		2039	421.8
1771.2	📷	North end of Lamberts Ridge, view of summit.		2252	420.8
1771.7	◊	Cross stream.		2392	420.3
1772.6	Y	Smarts Mountain Ranger Trail leads east.		2848	419.4
1773.1	◊ 🛆 (4) 🍴	Side trail leads 500 feet east to Smarts Mountain Tent site. Intermittent spring north on trail, unreliable.		3200	418.9
1773.2	◊ ⌒ (12) ☾ 📷 ♀	50 yards west to **Smarts Mountain Fire Warden's Cabin**, water (Mike Murphy Spring) is located (0.2) north of cabin on blue blazed Daniel Doan Trail, privy. Abandoned fire tower with panoramic views. Southern end of J Trail. 21.9◄12.4◄6.7◄▶ 5.3▶20.8▶27.9	N 43 49.517, W 72 02.268	3230	418.8
1773.4	Y	Junction to the east with abandon DOC Clark Pond Loop.		3237	418.6
1777.0	◊	Cross South Jacob's Brook on rocks.		1450	415.0
1777.1	◊	Cross South Jacob's Brooks.		1538	414.9
1777.7	📷	Eastman Ledges, rocky		2010	414.3
1778.2	🛆 ◊	Cross old logging road and North Branch of Jacob's Brook.		1900	413.8
1778.5	◊ Y 🛆 (2) ⌒ (8) ⌣ ☾ ♀	Cross a branch of North Jacob's Brook. Just south is a side trail that leads (0.3E) to **Hexacuba Shelter**, water (stream) is located at the blue blaze junction to the shelter, tenting, privy. 17.7◄12.0◄5.3◄▶ 15.5▶22.6▶31.6	N 43 52.438, W 72 01.740	1980	413.5
1779.9	Y 📷	Mt. Cube (south summit), Cross Rivendell Trail Junction.		2909	412.1
1780.1	Y 📷	Side trail leads (0.3) west to Mt. Cube (north summit).		2911	411.9
1780.9		Stone chair west.		2276	411.1
1781.6	◊	Ford Brackett Brook, ford		1400	410.4
1782.9	🛆	Cross logging road, gravel.		1287	409.1
1783.4	🛆 P (8) ♀ ★★★★★	Cross **N.H. 25A**.	N 43 54.082, W 71 59.033	900	408.6
	🛆	(1.9W) **Mount Cube Farm** 603-353-4111. Open year-round, pets welcome. Maple syrup products. Store is not manned, but caretaker makes frequent stops. Hikers may tent outside or may be allowed to stay in the sugar house. Sometimes more is offered.			
	◊ 🛆 ☾	**Camping on private property by permission only** Only allowed when owners are at location, call ahead. 603-801-9261 Owners have running water as well as an outhouse with a flush toilet. Brook flows through the center of the property. Owners have invested a lot into a substantial Wi-Fi grid which allows access from any location on the property. This offers connectivity with loved ones as well as making cellular phone calls.. Additional GPS updates can be made and any other internet browsing.			

Wentworth, NH 03282 (4.5E) on NH 25A, then right (0.2) on NH 25

	✉ ♀	(4.7E) **PO** M–F 7am–11am & 2:45pm–4:45pm, Sa 7:15am–12pm. 603-764-9444. 12 Wentworth Village RD Unit B. Wentworth NH 03282. N 43 52.172, W 71 54.657			
	🛒 🍴	(4.9E) **Shawnee's General Store** 603-764-5553. M-Su 5am-8pm.			
1783.5		Edge of swampy area.		1043	408.5

NoBo	Features	Description	GPS	Elev	SoBo
1785.0	⚠ P (3) ♀ ★★★★★	Cross **Cape Moonshine Road**	N 43 54.960, W 71 57.869	1400	407.0
	🏠 ⚑ ◈ 👤⚑	(1.4E) **Dancing Bones Intentional Community** 802-440-1612. (www.dancingbones.net) ◈ AT Passport location. Welcome Hikers!! ⚑ Free tenting & clean water. ⚑ WIFI. Charging station for devices, 🏠 We offer rooms for $50.00 per night (cash), which includes washing machine, shower, and use of kitchen space. This is a family community, please be respectful when using shared facilities. Smoking is permitted in designated areas. 🐕 Pets are welcome with responsible dog owners, we have dogs & a gargoyle. 🚗 Need a ride, just ask.			
1785.6	◊ Y ⚑ (2) ☾	Side trail 100 yards east to Ore Hill campsite, water is 150 yards south of campsite, privy.		1720	406.4
1785.9		Height of land on Sentinel Mountain.		1925	406.1
1786.2	◊	Spring on side trail to east.		1800	405.8
1786.5	⚑	Cross woods road.		1525	405.5
1786.9	◊	Cross small stream.		1686	405.1
1787.2		Beaver pond to east.		1650	404.8
1787.9		High point on Ore Hill.		1850	404.1
1788.2	⚠ P (10) ♀ ★★★★★	Cross **N.H. 25C**, Ore Hill Brook.	N 43 57.225, W 71 56.687	1550	403.8
	✗ Y ⚑	(0.7W) **Green House Food & Spirits** 603-764-5708. M-W closed, Th-F 3pm-11pm, Sa 12pm-12pm, Su 12pm-9pm. Bands on Saturdays 7pm-10pm, karaoke on Sundays 4pm-7pm. ⚑ Hiker friendly, hikers can stay in our field out back.			

Warren, NH 03279 (4.0E)

	📪 ♀	PO M-F 7:30am-9:30am & 3pm-5pm, Sa 7:30am-12pm. 603-764-5733. 18 Lake Tarleton RD Unit 1. Warren NH 03279. N 43 55.373, W 71 53.440
	✗	**Calamity Jane's Restaurant** 603-764-5288. Serves breakfast, lunch and dinner. M 6am-2pm, Tu & Wed closed, Th 6am-2pm, F 6am-8pm, Sa 6am-8pm, Su 8am-2pm. Serves breakfast and lunch M, Thurs-Su. Serves dinner F-Sa.
	✗ ◈ ⚑	**Moose Scoops** 603-764-9134. (www.moosescoopsicecream.com) ◈ AT Passport location. Open seasonally, see web site for hours. Hard & soft ice cream, soda, coffee, t-shirts and souvenirs. ⚑ Free WiFi.
	🛒	**Tedeschi Food Shop** 603-764-9002. Grocery with produce, deli with sandwiches & pizza, deli closes 7pm Su-Th, 8pm F-Sa. Store hours M-Su 5am-11pm.
	⚑	**Laundry** M-Su 8:30am-8:30pm.
	💻⚑	**Joseph Patch Library** 603-764-9072. M 9am-1pm, Tu 1pm-5pm, W 3pm-7pm, Sa 10am-1pm, Su closed.

1790.7	⚑ 📷	Mt. Mist summit.		2200	401.3
1790.8	📷	Vista east overlooking Wachipauka Pond.		2000	401.2
1790.9	◊ Y	Junction with Webster Slide Trail.		1650	401.1
1791.1	◊	Hairy Root Spring.		1600	400.9
1791.2	◊	Wachipauka Pond.		1493	400.8
1792.0	⚑	North summit of Wyatt Hill.		1700	400.0
1793.1	◊⚑ P (20) ♀ ★★★★★	**NH. 25**, Ford Oliverian Brook, ford, road bypass if high water.	N 43 59.392, W 71 53.959	1000	398.9

NH 25 Glencliff, NH (0.25E)

	📪 ♀	PO M-F 12pm-2pm, Sa 7am-1pm. 603-989-5154. 1385 NH Route 25 Unit 1. Glencliff NH 03238. N 43 59.131, W 71 53.784
	🏠 ⚑ ◈ ⚑🚗💻	**Hikers Welcome Hostel** 603-989-0040. Hikerswelcome@yahoo.com (www.hikerswelcome.com) Owned by Alyson, and John "Packrat" Robblee (AT'94, PCT'99, CDT'06) ◈ AT Passport location. Opens mid May to Oct 1. 🏠 Bunk ($30) and ⚑ camping ($18.50) includes shower. ⚑ Shower only with towel $3, ⚑ laundry: $3 wash, $3 dry. Snacks, sodas, pizza, breakfast sandwiches, ice cream. All hikers (even non-guests) are welcome to hang out and enjoy huge DVD and music library, 💻 computer available for use, ⚑ free WiFi. ⚑ Coleman and alcohol fuel by the ounce. Tools to help with gear repair, and selection of used gear available, particularly winter wear. ⚑ Slackpacking over Mt. Moosilauke, and other shuttles available based on mileage. 🚗 Town shuttle free with stay (6 miles to resupply in Warren). 🐕 Pet Friendly. ✉ Both guests and non-guests are welcome to send mail drops (USPS/FedEx/UPS): C/O Hikers Welcome Hostel, 1396 NH Rt 25, PO Box 25, Glencliff, NH 03238.

Warren, NH (5.0E) See NOBO mile 1788.2

1794.0	◊ 🏕 (8) ☾ ♀	Loop trail leads (0.1W) to **Jeffers Brook Shelter**, water (Jeffers Brook) is located in front of the shelter, privy.	N 43 59.793, W 71 53.364		398.0
		27.5◀20.8◀15.5◀▶7.1▶16.1▶20.1		1393	398.0
1794.1	◊ Y	Side trail leads 40 yards to cascades on Jeffers Brook in Oliverian Notch.		1383	397.9
1794.2	Y	Junction of loop trail leading 70 yards west to Jeffers Brook Shelter.		1350	397.8

NoBo	Features	Description	GPS	Elev	SoBo
1794.4	▲ Y	Junction of **Long Pond Road** and Town Line Trail.		1330	397.6
1794.6	▲	Cross **USFS 19, Long Pond Road**		1330	397.4
1794.9	▲ P ♀ ★★★★★	Cross **High Street**.	N 43 59.888, W 71 52.939	1480	397.1
1795.2	♦	Cross brook.		1634	396.8
1795.3	Y	Junction with Hurricane Trail.		1680	396.7
1795.9	♦	Cross stream.		2322	396.1
1797.9	▲ Y	Junction with Glencliff Trail and spur trail to Mt. Moosilauke (south peak)		4460	394.1
1798.2	📷	Middle peak of Mt. Moosilauke, side trail leads 50 feet with views of ravine.		4500	393.8
1798.6		Tree line on Mt. Moosilauke.		4600	393.4
1798.8	Y 📷	Mt. Moosilauke (north peak), Gorge Brook Trail descends (2.6) east to DOT Ravine Lodge.		4802	393.2
1799.2	Y	Junction with Benton Trail		4550	392.8

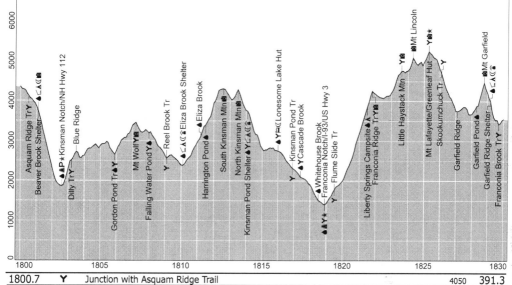

1800.7	Y	Junction with Asquam Ridge Trail		4050	391.3
1801.1	♦ ▲(2) ⊆(8) ☾📷♀	80 yards west to **Beaver Brook Shelter and campsite**, water (Beaver Brook) is located on the spur trail leading to the shelter, tenting, privy. Nice view of Franconia Ridge 27.9◀22.6◀7.1◀▶9.0▶13.0▶28.1	N 44 01.978, W 71 48.708	3750	390.9
1801.5	♦	Beaver Brook Cascades		3000	390.5
1802.4	♦〰	Cross Beaver Brook on bridge.		1890	389.6
1802.5	♦〰	Cross Beaver Brook on bridge.		1880	389.5
1802.6	▲ P(25) ♀ ★★★★★	Cross **NH. 112**; Kinsman Notch.	N 44 02.396, W 71 47.518	1870	389.4

🏠 (0.5E) **Lost River Gorge & Boulder Caves** 603-745-8031. (www.lostrivergorge.com) Open early May-late Oct. Tourist attraction. Gift store with microwave and microwavable food, snacks, coffee, soda.

▲ ⛺ 🛁 🚿 (3.0E) **Lost River Valley Campground** 603-745-8321, 800-370-5678. (www.lostriver.com) ▲ Primitive camp sites $22, pets allowed but not in cabins, cabin $65 and up. 🚿 Showers, △ coin laundry, ◑ WiFi, 🏧 ATM, open mid-May to Columbus Day, quiet hours 10pm-8am.

✉ Mail drops for guests: 951 Lost River Rd, North Woodstock, NH 03262.

🚗 Ⓢ 🛏 🏊 (16E) **Wise Way Wellness Center** 603-726-7600.
(16E) Wise Way Wellness Center 603-726-7600.
Open May- Oct.
◈ No smoking or pets. 🛏 $89 for 1-2 persons, includes a.m. coffee and muffins. Cabin is 10 miles south of Lincoln in Thornton NH. Rustic cabin with no TV or phone but does have ◑ wifi, 🏊 pool, mini-fridge and camp stove. Bathroom and shower inside adjacent building. Licensed Massage Therapist on-site. Additional services: sauna and outdoor Epsom salt bath. No pick up / drop off service. Cash, checks or PayPal.

North Woodstock, NH (5E), Lincoln, NH (6E) See Notes at miles 1818.9

1803.2	Y	Junction with Dilly Trail descends over rough terrain (0.5) to Lost River Gorge and Boulder Caves on NH. 112.		2650	388.8
1803.5		Cross summit of knob, wooded.		2750	388.5
1805.9	Y	Junction with Gordon Pond Trail.		2700	386.1

NoBo	Features	Description	GPS	Elev	SoBo
1806.5	⬥	Cross small brook, reliable.		3100	385.5
1807.1	▲	Mt. Wolf (western summit).		3360	384.9
1807.2	▲ Y ◉	Mt. Wolf (East Peak), Side trail leads 60 yards east to outlook.		3478	384.8
1808.0	Y	Side trail descends 20 yards east to edge of bog, known as Falling Water Pond with views of South Kinsman Mountains.		3200	384.0
1809.1	Y	Junction with Reel Brook Trail.		2600	382.9
1809.6	⌇	Power line.		2625	382.4
1810.1	⬥▲(4) ⌐(8) ⌣(☎⚲	75 feet west to **Eliza Brook Shelter and campsite**, water (Eliza Brook), 3 single tent pads and one double, privy, bear box. 31.6◄16.1◄9.0◄►4.0►19.1►24.6	N 44 06.047, W 71 44.544	2400	381.9
1810.4	▲	Junction with logging road, grass cover.		2650	381.6
1810.6	⬥	Cascades west of trail.		2760	381.4
1811.2	⬥	Cross headwaters to Eliza Brook.		2880	380.8
1811.5	⌒	East of Harrington Pond, bog bridges.		3400	380.5
1811.6	⬥	Cross brook.		3425	380.4
1812.5		An exposed knob on South Kinsman Mountain		4300	379.5
1812.6	◉	15 yards west of north knob of South Kinsman Mountain		4358	379.4
1813.1		Col between South and North Kinsman Mountains.		4050	378.9
1813.5	▲	North Kinsman Mountain summit.		4293	378.5
1813.9	Y	Junction with Mt. Kinsman Trail.		3900	378.1
1814.1	⬥▲(4) ⌐(12) ⌣(☎⚲$ ⚲ ★★★★★	Kinsman Pond Trail loop trail (south) leads (0.1) east to **AMC Kinsman Pond Shelter and campsite**, water, (Kinsman Pond) treat pond water, 2 single and 2 double tent platforms, privy, bear box. Overnight/caretaker fee. Kinsman Pond Trail loop trail rejoins AT 2.0/14.3. 20.1◄13.0◄4.0◄►15.1►20.6►29.6	N 44 08.215, W 71 43.944	3750	377.9

The **Appalachian Mountain Club** (AMC) 603-466-2727 operates huts in the Whites, with bunk space for 30-90 people. There is no road access, no heat, and no showers. They use alternative energy sources and composting toilets. Overnight stays vary in price during the weekday and more on weekends, discounts for AMC members. Reservations recommended. Includes a bunk, dinner and breakfast. Work for stay is available to the first 2 thru-hikers; 4 at Lakes of the Clouds Hut and more at the croo's discretion. Work for stay hikers get floor space for sleeping and feast on leftovers. Do not count on hut stays without reservations, and camping is not allowed near most of the huts.

�car **AMC Hiker Shuttle** 603-466-2727 Schedule of stops and time are on line at (www.outdoors.org/lodging/lodging-shuttle.cfm) Operates June-mid Sept daily, and weekends and holidays through mid Oct. Stops in Lincoln, at Franconia Notch, Crawford Notch, Highland Center, Pinkham Notch, and in Gorham; $23 for non AMC members, $19 for AMC members. Walk-ins on a space-available basis ONLY! **Reservations are strongly recommended!**

NoBo	Features	Description	GPS	Elev	SoBo
1816.0	⬥Y ❖ ⌣⇥⚲	**AMC Lonesome Lake Hut**, junction of Around-Lonesome Lake Trail. **Lonesome Lake Hut** is a AT Passport location.	N 44 08.308, W 71 42.222	2760	376.0
1816.1	⬥Y	Southern edge of Lonesome Lake, junction with Fishin' Jimmy Trail, **No Camping permitted here.**		2740	375.9
1816.9	Y	Junction with Kinsman Pond Trail (north)		2294	375.1
1817.4	⬥Y	Junction with Basin–Cascade Trail, Cross Cascade Brook, ford		2084	374.6
1818.5	⬥	Cross Whitehouse Brook		1610	373.5
1818.7	Y	Junction with Pemi Trail.		1520	373.3
1818.8	▲	Pass under **I-93, US. 3 (south side)**.		1450	373.2
1818.9	▲ Y⚲ ★★★★★	Pass under **I-93, U.S. 3 (north side)**, Franconia Notch, Pemigawasset River, Franconia Notch paved bike path east to Liberty Springs hiker parking and shuttle; and beyond to The Flume Visitor center; west to Lafayette Place campground.	N 44 05.992, W 71 40.938	1450	373.1
	✗🍴⇥🖃 🖃	(0.7E) **Flume Visitor Center** 603-745-8391. ✗ Has a cafeteria, serves pastries, hamburgers, hot dogs, pizza remainder of the day. ⇥ Restrooms, ☎ payphone. May–late Oct, M-Su 9am–5pm. 🖃 Mail drops: Flume Gorge, 850 Daniel Webster Hwy, Lincoln, NH 03251.			
	▲⊛⇥⚲🖃 🖃	(2.1W) **Lafayette Place Campground** 603-823-9513. Open mid May-Columbus Day. ⊛ No pets. ▲ Tent sites $25, ⇥ limited store, quiet time 10pm. 🖃 Mail drops: 2 Franconia Notch State Park, Franconia, NH 03580			
	⇥⊜🖃 🖃	(1.2E) **Profile Motel & Cottages** 603-745-2759. (www.profilemotel.com) ⇥ Call for prices. Microwave, fridge, ⊜ free WiFi, A/C. 🖃 Mail drops to 391 US-3, Lincoln, NH 03251.			
	⇥⊛⊜ 🖃	(3.0E) **Mt. Liberty Lodging** 603-745-3600. (www.mtlibertylodging.com) Open May-Oct. ⊛ No pets or smoking. Prices increase during tourist season. ⇥ $69 and up for off season, microwave, fridge, ⊜ free WiFi, includes pickup and return from Kinsman, and Franconia Notch. Fee for town shuttle. ⚖ Laundry $5. CC accepted. 🖃 Mail drops for guests: 10 Liberty Road, Lincoln, NH 03251.			

🚍   **AMC Hiker Shuttle, See Notes at mile 1814.1**

North Woodstock, NH (4.8E) of Franconia Notch. See map of North Woodstock/Lincoln, NH.

📫 ♨   **PO** M-F 9:30am-12:30pm & 1:30pm-4:30pm, Sa 9am-12pm. 603-745-8134. 159a Main St North. North Woodstock NH 03262. N 44 02.010, W 71 41.215

🏠 ◈ ⚠   **The Notch Hostel** 603-348-1483 (www.notchhostel.com) Reserve by website, text, or call.
🖥◈🚍🖃 ◈   AT Passport location.
Ideally situated for slackpack between Kinsman & Franconia Notch. Bunk in large, white farmhouse on NH 112 (Lost River Rd). 1.0 W of North Woodstock, 2.0 W of Lincoln. 🏠 $33PP includes bunk, linens, towel, shower, ⚠ group laundry service, coffee/tea, make-ur-own pancakes, 🌐 WiFi, 🖥 computer, guest kitchen, fridge & large yard. Check-in 4-9p, (earlier ok with text/call: follow welcome sheet if no one home). 🚍 Shuttles run June 1 - Oct. 1, Su - Th for guests with reservations. Beer & wine OK in moderation. **No liquor.** Small store: ice cream, pizza, soda. Rental bikes $5/day. 🚍 Town and Trailhead shuttles depart from hostel 7AM and 6PM. Kinsman Notch (NH 112) Pickup +5min, Flume Visitors Center Pickup +25min, Town +40min. Additional mid-day shuttles are offered during busy season; guests with reservations may text for current schedule and to sign up for a shuttle.
🖃 Maildrops: C/O The Notch Hostel, 324 Lost River Rd. North Woodstock, NH 03262.

🚍✗🌐   **Woodstock Inn** 603-745-3951, 800-321-3985. (www.woodstockinnnh.com) Ask about 10% thru-hikers discount, prices are seasonal, includes full breakfast, free WiFi. Pet rooms available. Woodstock Station restaurant, outdoor bar, and a micro-brewery.

🚍⚠🌐   **Autumn Breeze** 603-745-8549. (www.autumnbreezemotel.com) Open year round. 🚍 $60 hiker rate includes kitchenette, ⚠ laundry, 🌐 free WiFi, shuttle to and from trail head. One pet room. 🚍 Shuttle to town if available. Credit cards accepted.

🚍⊛🌐⚓   **Inn32** 603-745-2416. (www.inn32.com)
🖃   ⊛ No pets. $69 and up, game room, ⚓ pool, grills, 🌐 free WiFi.
🖃 Mail drops: PO Box 198, 180 Main St, North Woodstock, NH 03262.

🛒✗🍴   **Wayne's Market** 603-745-8819. (www.lincolnwoodstockmarket.com) Open year round. ✗ Deli, meats, cheap sandwiches, 🏧 ATM. M-Su 5am-10pm.

🏪   **Fadden's General Store & Maple Sugarhouse** 603-745-8371. (www.nhmaplesyrup.com) Open year-round. Maple sugar products, ice cream, fudge and more. M-Su 9am-5pm.

Lincoln, NH (5.8S of Franconia Notch) See map of North Woodstock/Lincoln, NH.

📫 ♨   **PO** M-F 8am-5pm, Sa 8am-12pm. 603-745-8133. 10 Lumber Yard Dr Unit 9 03251. N 44 02.488, W 71 40.272

🏠 ◈   **Chet's One Step at a Time** 603-745-8196.
⚠🖥🖃 ◈ AT Passport location.

🛒🍴   **Price Chopper** M-Su 24 hours.

🥾   **Lahout's Summit Shop** 603-745-2882. (www.lahouts.com) Full service outfitter, packs, Coleman and alcohol fuel by the ounce, canister fuel, freeze dried foods. Located at 165 Main St. in the plaza next to Subway. M-F 9:30am-5:30pm, Sa 9am-5:30pm, Su 9am-5pm.

🖥   **Chat Room Coffee House & Books** 603-745-2626. (www.chatroomcoffeehouse.com) M-Sa 10-6, Su closed.

⚠   **Homerun Laundromat** 603-620-8497. Coin operated. M-Su 24 hours.

🚍   **AMC Hiker Shuttle, See Notes at mile 1814.1**

Franconia, NH 03580 (11W of Franconia notch)

📫 ♨   **PO** M-F 8:30am-1pm & 2pm-5pm, Sa 9am-12pm. 603-823-5611. 308 Main St. Franconia NH 03580. N 44 13.678, W 71 44.992

🚍⚠🖥🖃   **Gale River Motel** 603-823-5655, 800-255-7989. (www.galerivermotel.com) Open year round. 🚍
🚍🖃 $50–$200, pets with approval, ⚠ laundry wash $1, dry $1, ⚓ Coleman by the ounce. Free pickup and return to Franconia Notch trail heads with stay, 🚍 longer shuttles for a fee. Credit cards accepted.
🖃 Mail drops (fee for non-guest): 1 Main Street, Franconia, NH 03580.

🛒   **Mac's Market** 603-823-7795. M-Su 7am-8pm.

🏪✗   **Franconia Village Store** 603-823-7782. 🏪 Convenience store and ✗ deli. M-Sa 6am-9pm, Su 6:30am-7pm.

🖥🌐   **Abbie Greenleaf Library** 603-823-8424. (www.abbielibrary.org) Free WiFi. M-Tu 2pm-6pm, W 10am-12pm & 2pm-6pm, Th-F 2pm-5pm, Sa 10am-1pm, Su closed.

North Woodstock, NH

White Mountain
Motel & Cottages

The Common Man
The Kancamagus Lodge
Kancamagus Hwy
Pub32

93

Pullman's Lunch
Clark's Trading Post

Nachos Mexican Grille
Pollard Rd
Enzos Pizzeria

Black Mtn Burger
Gordi's Fish & Steakhouse

Sunny Day Diner

Lahout's
Subway
Thai 9
Flapjacks
El Greco's Pizza

Texas Toast Eatery

Connector Rd

Main st

3

Rite Aid
Dunkin' Donuts

PO
Family Dollar
Cinemas 4
Prop Chopper

Holiday Inn Express

112

Home Run
Autumn Breeze Inn
Wayne's Market
Post Office

Inn32

0   0.5 Mile

Lost River Rd

112

Fadden's General Store
Peg's
Imperial Palace

Landmark II
Nancy's Hairstyles
Homemade Ice Cream
Truants Taverne

93

Lincoln, NH

NoBo	Features	Description	GPS	Elev	SoBo
1819.5	Y	Side trail to Flume Side Trail		1800	372.5
1820.0	♦	Cross brook.		2050	372.0
1820.3	⚠	Junction of old logging road (northern).		1350	371.7
1821.5	♦⚑(10) ↵	10 yards east to AMC Liberty Springs Tent site, 7 single and 3 double tent platforms, accommodates 44.		3870	370.5
1821.8	Y📷	Junction of Liberty Spring Trail and Franconia Ridge Trail, (0.3) to Mt. Liberty summit.		4260	370.2
1823.6	▲Y📷	Little Haystack Mountain summit, Falling Waters Trail, above tree line for next 2.5 miles north on Franconia Ridge		4800	368.4
1824.3	▲📷	Mt. Lincoln summit		5089	367.7
1824.8		Unnamed hump.		5020	367.2
1825.3	♦Y▲⚑ ❋☾📷♀	Mt. Lafayette summit, Greenleaf Trail. (1.0W) on Greenleaf Trail to **AMC Greenleaf Hut** AT Passport location.	N 44 09.624, W 71 39.620	5260	366.7
1825.7	▲	North peak of Mt. Lafayette.		5000	366.3
1826.1	Y	Tree line and junction with Skookumchuck Trail, above tree line for the next 2.5 miles south on Franconia Ridge.		4680	365.9
1828.3	♦	Garfield Pond east.		3860	363.7
1828.8	▲	Side trail leads 50 yards east to Mt. Garfield summit		4500	363.2
1829.0	Y	Garfield Trail		4180	363.0
1829.2	♦Y⚑(7) ⊏(12) ↵☾🏠$♀	(0.1W) **AMC Garfield Ridge Shelter and campsite**, water (spring) at the junction to the campsite, two single and five double tent platforms, privy, bear box. Overnight/caretaker fee. 28.1◄19.1◄15.1◄►5.5►14.5►56.5	N 44 11.441, W 71 36.502	3900	362.8
1829.7	Y	Franconia Brook Trail leads (2.2) east to 13 Falls Tent site with nine tent pads, accommodates 36, bear box, water on site.		3420	362.3

NoBo	Features	Description	GPS	Elev	SoBo
1831.0	📷	Ledge knob with view.		3420	361.0
1831.3	Y	Gale River Trail		3390	360.7
1831.9	♦Y🏠 ℂ♀	Joins the Garfield Trail. Frost Trail leads 40 yards east to **AMC Galehead Hut.** Twin Brook Trail. AT Passport location.	N 44 11.278, W 71 34.134	3780	360.1
1832.7	▲Y	South Twin Mountain summit and junction with North Twin Spur.		4902	359.3
1833.6	📷	Ledgy hump with views of South Twin Mountain and Guyot and Carrigain Mountains.		4550	358.4
1834.7	♦Y⚠(6) ⊏(12) ⏝ℂ☎$♀	Mt. Guyot summit. 100 yards south of summit is junction with Bondcliff Trail leading (0.8) east to **AMC Guyot Shelter and campsite**, water (spring) is located at the campsite, four single and two double tent platforms will accommodate 18, privy, bear box. Overnight/caretaker fee. 24.6◀20.6◀5.5◀▶ 9.0▶51.0▶ 57.1	N 44 09.658, W 71 32.136	4580	357.3
1836.0	▲	Side trail leads (0.1) west to Zealand Mountain summit		4250	356.0
1837.2	♦Y	Side trail leads (0.1) east to Zeacliff Pond.		3800	354.8
1837.6	Y	Junction with Zeacliff Trail (south), rejoins the AT again (2.8) north.		3700	354.4
1837.7	Y📷	100 yard side loop trail east to spectacular lookout edge of Zeacliff.		3700	354.3
1838.8	♦ Y	Junction with Lend-a-Hand Trail. Whitewall Brook is crossed twice in this area.		2750	353.2
1838.9	♦🍴🏠 ℂ📷♀	**AMC Zealand Falls Hut** AT Passport location.	N 44 11.748, W 71 29.667	2630	353.1
1839.0	Y⚓	Side trail east leads to Zealand Falls.		2600	353.0
1839.1	Y	Junction with Zealand Trail (south), former railroad bed.		2460	352.9
1840.4	Y	Junction with Zeacliff Trail (north)		2448	351.6
1840.7	Y	East side of trail shows slide and scarred slopes of Whitewall Mountain.		2450	351.3
1841.2	Y	Junction with Thoreau Falls Trail. **Camping is not permitted here.**		2460	350.8
1841.4	♦〰	Cross North Fork on wooden bridge.		2490	350.6
1841.7	Y	Shoal Pond Tr. (0.8) east to water		2500	350.3
1841.9	♦	Cross brook.		2520	350.1
1843.7	♦⚠(5) ⊏(10) ⏝ℂ☎$♀	250 yards west to **AMC Ethan Pond Shelter and campsite**, Caretaker on site. Overnight fee. Water (brook) is inlet brook to the pond, three single and two double tent platforms, privy, bear box. Overnight/caretaker fee. 29.6◀14.5◀9.0◀▶42.0▶48.1▶61.8	N 44 10.631, W 71 25.607	2860	348.3
1844.2		Height of land.		2900	347.8
1844.7	Y	Willey Range Trail		2680	347.3
1845.0	Y	Kedron Flume Trail		2450	347.0
1846.1	Y	Junction with Arethusa–Ripley Falls Trail.		1600	345.9
1846.3	✕▲ P(10)♀	Cross Railroad Tracks, Junction with Willey House Station Road. For parking go all the way up Willey House Station Road.	N 44 10.251, W 71 23.283	1440	345.7
1846.6	▲🏠 P(10) ★★★★★	Cross **U.S. 302**, Crawford Notch, Presidential Range. See previous entry for parking.		1275	345.4
	✕🏨	(1.0W) **Willey House** 603-271-3556. Memorial Day-Columbus Day. Snack bar. M-Su 9:30am-5pm.			

NoBo	Features	Description	GPS	Elev	SoBo
	▲⚲⚐	**(1.8E) Dry River Campground** 603-374-2272. (www.nhstateparks.com/crawford.html) Open May-late Oct. ▲ Tent sites $25. Pets allowed, ⚐ coin laundry and ⚱ showers. Quiet time 10pm-8am.			
	⛺⛩⊛ ✗	**(3.5W) AMC Highland Center** 603-278-4453. (www.outdoors.org)			
	⛻⛗☒	⊛ No pets, no smoking. Rates in summer during tourist season and during holidays. ⛩ Call ahead for prices. AMC members get a discount. AMC Shuttle stops daily mid-Jun thru Columbus Day, after this time it only stops on weekends and holidays. ✗ Restaurant serves breakfast, lunch and dinner. ⛗ Store carries snacks, sodas, ⚱ canister fuel and some clothing, ⛛ WiFi. ☒ Mail drops (include ETA): Route 302, Bretton Woods, NH 03574.			
	⛺▲⛗	**(3.3E) Crawford Notch General Store & Campground** 603-374-2779 (www.crawfordnotch.com) Open mid May-mid Oct. ⛺ Cabins $75-95, ▲ tent sites, space for two tents $30. 9% lodging tax. ⛗ Store carries hiker foods, ice cream and beer.			
	🚗	**AMC Hiker Shuttle, See Notes at mile 1814.1**			
1846.7	⌒	Cross Saco River, footbridge	1350		345.3
1846.8	♦Y	Junction with Saco River Trail (southern)	1350		345.2
1846.9	Y	Junction Saco River Trail (northern)	1400		345.1
1848.4	📷	Webster Cliffs, view.	3025		343.6
1849.0	📷	View from ledge looks down at state park buildings.	3506		343.0
1849.9	▲📷	Mt. Webster summit	3910		342.1
1850.0	Y	Junction with Webster Branch and Webster Jackson Trail.	3820		342.0
1851.3	▲📷	Mt. Jackson summit.	4052		340.7
1852.9	Y	Mizpah Cutoff to the west.	3816		339.1
1853.0	♦Y◈ ▲(7) ⌣⛩ ⛺✗⚲	Junction with Mt. Clinton Trail. **AMC Mizpah Spring Hut, AMC Nauman Tent site**, 5 single and 2 double tent platforms accommodate 30, privy, bear box, water from stream. **Mizpah Hut** is a AT Passport location.	N 44 13.160, W 71 22.206 3800		339.0
1853.8	▲📷	Mt. Pierce (Mt. Clinton) summit, above tree line for the next 12.7 miles north	4312		338.2
1853.9	♦	Spring. Join or leave Webster Cliff Trail or the Crawford Path.	4350		338.1
1854.7	♦	Cross small stream in Col.	4226		337.3
1855.0	Y	Junction of Mt. Eisenhower Loop (south) which leads (0.4) west to Mt. Eisenhower summit and rejoins the AT (0.5) north.	4425		337.0
1855.6	Y📷	Mt. Eisenhower Loop (north), Edmonds Path	4475		336.4
1855.7	Y	Junction with Mt. Eisenhower Trail.	4423		336.3
1856.0	♦	Spring	4480		336.0
1856.6	📷	West of summit of Mt. Franklin	5004		335.4
1856.7	Y	Unmarked path leads 130 yards east to summit of Mt. Franklin.	4972		335.3
1856.9		Junction with Mt. Monroe Loop Trail (southern), leads (0.4) west to Mt. Monroe summit.	5077		335.1
1857.6	Y📷	Junction with Mt. Monroe Loop Trail (northern), leads (0.4) west to Mt. Monroe summit.	5075		334.4
1857.7	♦◈ ⌣⛺⚲ ★★★★★ ⛺⛩♦⛱⛴	**AMC Lakes of the Clouds Hut**, "**The Dungeon**". AT Passport location. Paid lodging and work-for-stay. Also, "**The Dungeon**," a bunkroom available for 6 thru-hikers for $10PP with access to hut restroom and the common area. When the hut is closed, The Dungeon serves as an emergency shelter.	N 44 15.528, W 71 19.137 5125		334.3
1857.8	Y	Junction with Tuckerman Crossover and Camel Trail, which leads (0.7) east to Davis Path.	5125		334.2
1858.5	Y	Junction with Davis Path is 35 yards south on the AT. Junction with Westside Trail which rejoins the AT (1.5) north. Westside Trail (south).	5625		333.5
1858.9	Y	Gulfside Trail to the west.	6150		333.1
1859.1	▲⛰✗ ⛻📷▲P ⚲ ★★★★★	Mt. Washington Summit, Mt. Washington Auto Road, Cog Railroad. Junction with Tuckerman Ravine Trail leads (2.0) east to **AMC Hermit Lake Shelter**, Pinkham Notch at NH. 16. Many parking spots at the top. **Mt. Washington, NH.**	N 44 16.180, W 71 18.124 6288		332.9
	⛵	**PO** M-S 10am-4pm. For outgoing mail only. Do not send mail drops here.			
	✗⛗⛻▲	**Sherman Adams Building** 603-466-3347. M-Su 8am-6pm mid-May thru Columbus Day. Snack bar M-Su 9am-6pm.			
1859.3	Y	Junction with Trinity Heights Connector.	6100		332.7
1859.4	✗	Cross Cog Railroad Tracks.	6090		332.6
1859.5	Y	Great Gulf Trail leads east.	5925		332.5

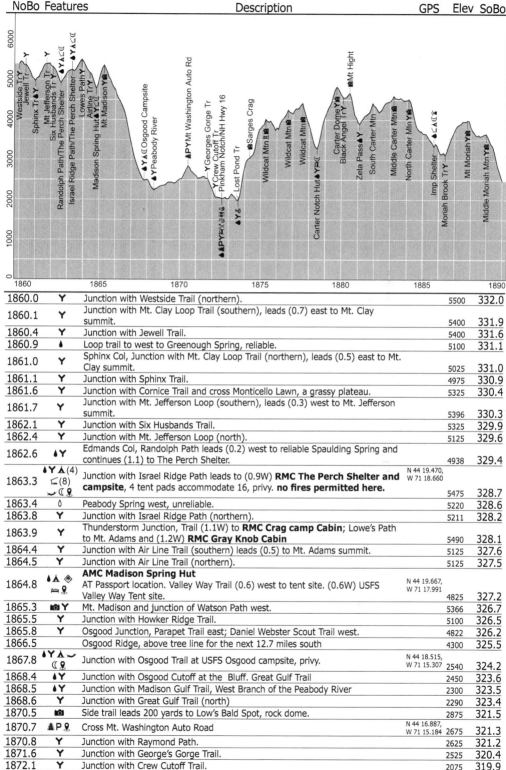

NoBo	Features	Description	GPS	Elev	SoBo
1860.0	Y	Junction with Westside Trail (northern).		5500	332.0
1860.1	Y	Junction with Mt. Clay Loop Trail (southern), leads (0.7) east to Mt. Clay summit.		5400	331.9
1860.4	Y	Junction with Jewell Trail.		5400	331.6
1860.9	♦	Loop trail to west to Greenough Spring, reliable.		5100	331.1
1861.0	Y	Sphinx Col, Junction with Mt. Clay Loop Trail (northern), leads (0.5) east to Mt. Clay summit.		5025	331.0
1861.1	Y	Junction with Sphinx Trail.		4975	330.9
1861.6	Y	Junction with Cornice Trail and cross Monticello Lawn, a grassy plateau.		5325	330.4
1861.7	Y	Junction with Mt. Jefferson Loop (southern), leads (0.3) west to Mt. Jefferson summit.		5396	330.3
1862.1	Y	Junction with Six Husbands Trail.		5325	329.9
1862.4	Y	Junction with Mt. Jefferson Loop (north).		5125	329.6
1862.6	♦Y	Edmands Col, Randolph Path leads (0.2) west to reliable Spaulding Spring and continues (1.1) to The Perch Shelter.		4938	329.4
1863.3	♦Y⅄(4) ⊏(8) ⌇((⚲	Junction with Israel Ridge Path leads to (0.9W) **RMC The Perch Shelter and campsite**, 4 tent pads accommodate 16, privy. **no fires permitted here.**	N 44 19.470, W 71 18.660	5475	328.7
1863.4	◊	Peabody Spring west, unreliable.		5220	328.6
1863.8	Y	Junction with Israel Ridge Path (northern).		5211	328.2
1863.9	Y	Thunderstorm Junction, Trail (1.1W) to **RMC Crag camp Cabin**; Lowe's Path to Mt. Adams and (1.2W) **RMC Gray Knob Cabin**		5490	328.1
1864.4	Y	Junction with Air Line Trail (southern) leads (0.5) to Mt. Adams summit.		5125	327.6
1864.5	Y	Junction with Air Line Trail (northern).		5125	327.5
1864.8	♦▲◈ ⛺⚲	**AMC Madison Spring Hut** AT Passport location. Valley Way Trail (0.6) west to tent site. (0.6W) USFS Valley Way Tent site.	N 44 19.667, W 71 17.991	4825	327.2
1865.3	📷Y	Mt. Madison and junction of Watson Path west.		5366	326.7
1865.5	Y	Junction with Howker Ridge Trail.		5100	326.5
1865.8	Y	Osgood Junction, Parapet Trail east; Daniel Webster Scout Trail west.		4822	326.2
1866.5		Osgood Ridge, above tree line for the next 12.7 miles south		4300	325.5
1867.8	♦Y⅄⌣ ((⚲	Junction with Osgood Trail at USFS Osgood campsite, privy.	N 44 18.515, W 71 15.307	2540	324.2
1868.4	♦Y	Junction with Osgood Cutoff at the Bluff. Great Gulf Trail		2450	323.6
1868.5	♦Y	Junction with Madison Gulf Trail, West Branch of the Peabody River		2300	323.5
1868.6	Y	Junction with Great Gulf Trail (north)		2290	323.4
1870.5	📷	Side trail leads 200 yards to Low's Bald Spot, rock dome.		2875	321.5
1870.7	▲P⚲	Cross Mt. Washington Auto Road	N 44 16.887, W 71 15.184	2675	321.3
1870.8		Junction with Raymond Path.		2625	321.2
1871.6	Y	Junction with George's Gorge Trail.		2525	320.4
1872.1	Y	Junction with Crew Cutoff Trail.		2075	319.9

NoBo	Features	Description	GPS	Elev	SoBo
1872.6	▲P♀ ★★★★★	Cross **N.H. 16**, Pinkham Notch, Pinkham Notch Visitor center, AMC Joe Dodge Lodge. Many parking spots.	N 44 15.425, W 71 15.147	2050	319.4
	⌂✕♥♥ ⚎⛺♿⚏ ☎⛏	**Pinkham Notch Visitor Center & Joe Dodge Lodge** 603-466-2721. (www.outdoors.org) Open year-round. ⊗ No pets. Rates in summer during tourist season and during holidays. Check ahead for pricing and availability. Rates very according to season. AMC members get a discount. ♥♥ Restrooms. ✕ Meals available to non guests; AYCE breakfast 6:30am-9am daily, food to order for lunch, family style dinner Sat-Thurs 6pm, Friday dinner buffet. ⚎ Coin-op shower available 24 hours, ⛺ coin laundry, $2 towel rental. Vending machines. ⚏ Coleman fuel and alcohol fuel by the ounce, canister fuel, ⊚ free WiFi. Shuttle 7:30am daily. Accepts credit cards. ✉ Mail drops: AMC Visitor Center, C/O Front Desk, 361 Rte. 16, Gorham, NH 03581.			
	🚍	AMC Hiker Shuttle, See Notes at mile 1814.1			
Gorham, NH (10.7W from Pinkham Notch) See map of Gorham, NH.					
1872.7	Y	Junction with Square Ledge Trail.		2020	319.3
1873.5	Y⚎	Junction with Lost Pond Trail. Glen Ellis Falls (0.1) east on Whitecat Ridge Trail.		1990	318.5
1874.3	📷	Open Ledge, Sarge's Crag, views.		3000	317.7
1874.6	♦	Side path west to signed spring.		3250	317.4
1874.9	📷	Steep ledge with views of ravine and Mt. Washington.		3500	317.1
1875.3	▲	Cross just yards west of Wildcat Mountain Peak E.		4046	316.7
1875.5		Wildcat Mountain Ski Area Gondola.		4020	316.5
1875.6	📷⛽	Wildcat Mountain, Peak D		4020	316.4
1875.9		Wildcat Col.		3770	316.1
1876.7	📷	Wildcat Mountain, Peak C		4298	315.3
1877.1		Wildcat Mountain, Peak B		4330	314.9
1877.6	📷	Wildcat Mountain, Peak A, views down into Carter Notch.		4442	314.4
1878.3	Y	Junction with Wildcat Ridge Trail.		3388	313.7
1878.5	♦Y🚐◈ ☾♀	Junction with Nineteen Mile Brook Trail which leads (0.2) east to (0.2E) **AMC Carter Notch Hut** into Carter Notch. AT Passport location.	N 44 15.558, W 71 11.725	3350	313.5
1878.9	📷	View into Carter Notch.		4000	313.1
1879.2	♦Y	60 yards west to good spring.		4300	312.8
1879.7	▲Y📷	Carter Dome summit and junction with Rainbow Trail.		4832	312.3
1880.1	Y	Black Angel Trail		4600	311.9
1880.5	▲📷	Mt. Hight summit.		4675	311.5
1881.1	♦Y	Zeta Pass and junction with Carter Dome Trail junction. **No camping permitted here.**		3890	310.9
1881.9	▲	South Carter Mountain summit, wooded.		4458	310.1
1883.2	▲	Middle Carter Mountain summit, wooded.		4610	308.8
1883.5	📷	Open ledges of Mt. Lethe.		4584	308.5
1883.8	Y	Junction with North Carter Trail.		4500	308.2
1884.0	▲📷	North Carter Mountain summit, wooded.		4539	308.0
1885.7	♦Y⛺(5) ⛺(12) ⌣☾⛺$♀	(0.2W) **AMC Imp Shelter and campsite**, water (stream) is located near shelter, four single and one double tent pads, privy. Overnight/caretaker fee. tent platform, bear box. 56.5◄51.0◄42.0◄▶6.1▶19.8▶25.0	N 44 19.739, W 71 09.007	3250	306.3
1886.4	Y	Junction with Stony Brook Trail which descends (3.6) west to NH. 16, Moriah Brook Trail.		3127	305.6
1887.8	Y	Junction with Carter Moriah Trail to Mt. Moriah Mountain summit.		4000	304.2
1889.0	📷	East of Middle Moriah summit.		3640	303.0
1889.2	Y	Junction with Kenduskeag Trail.		3300	302.8

NoBo	Features	Description	GPS	Elev	SoBo
1890.3	◆	Cross Rattle River		1700	301.7
1891.4		Cross East Rattle River, **difficult in high water.**		1500	300.6
1891.8	◆▲⊏(8) ⌇◖⚲	**Rattle River Shelter and campsite**, water (Rattle River), tenting, privy. 57.1◀48.1◀6.1◀▶ 13.7▶18.9▶23.3	N 44 22.802, W 71 06.449	1260	300.2
1893.5	◆▲P(12) ⚲ ★★★★★	Cross **U.S. 2 (southern end). See Map of Gorham, NH.**	N 44 24.064, W 71 06.561	780	298.5

⇌⛺✕⛺ **Rattle River Lodge & Hostel** 603-466-5049 (rattleriverhostel.com)
⛺⛺⛺P   Open year round. Online booking available. Located on the AT.
⌐   ⇌ Clean B&B style rooms, some private rooms starting at $75 with fresh linens & towels. ⛺ Thru hiker bunk rate $37PP includes breakfast, ⛺ laundry, loaner clothes, showers, ⛺ fast WiFi, free resupply shuttle to Walmart. Sodas, ice cream, Mr. Pizza delivery available for guests & non-guests. ⛺ Town shuttles for guests $2. Free morning shuttle to Post Office and gas station at 8:30am. Bus pickup and drop off available. Late bus pickup fees may apply. ⛺ Long distance shuttles avail $2 mile one way. Section hike planning assistance. ⛺ 21 Mile slackpack free with 2 night stay (Pinkham Notch to US 2). Pickup at Pinkham Notch available at 8am, noon, and 5pm for $5PP, ($20 for unscheduled pickup) based on availability. P Parking available for section hikers. Authorized Sierra Madre Research hammock outfitter.
⌐   Mail drops free for guests and $5 for nonguests. Label side of box with last name and eta. Mail: 592 State Route 2, Shelburne, NH 03581.

⛺▲◈   (1.7W) **White Birches Camping Park** 603-466-2022. (www.whitebirchescamping.com)
⛺⛺⛺⛺   ◈ AT Passport location.
⌐   Open May-Oct. ⛺ Bunks $15, ▲ tent sites $13PP, ⛺ laundry, ⛺ pool, air hockey, pool table, pets allowed, ⚲ coleman, alcohol by the ounce and canister fuel, ⛺ free WiFi. Free shuttle to and from trail head and town with stay. Credit cards accepted.
⌐   Mail drops for guests ($5 fee for nonguest): 218 US 2, Shelburne, NH 03581.

⇌✕⛺⛺   (2.6W) **Town & Country Inn and Resort** 603-466-3315. (www.townandcountryinn.com)
Open year round. $68.00 to $155.00 plus tax, seasonal, pets $25.00 daily fee, complimentary WiFi, microwave oven and fridge.
Breakfast and dinner served daily, lounge with entertainment. Indoor heated pool, Jacuzzi, Sauna, steam room and fully equipped health club.

Gorham, NH 03581 (3.5W from U.S. 2 Trail head). See map of Gorham, NH.
⌐⚲   **PO** M-F 8:30am-5pm, Sa 8:30am-12pm. 603-466-2182. ID required; all packages should include your legal name. 165 Main St. Gorham NH 03581. N 44 23.411, W 71 10.947

⇌⛺▲◆   **Libby House Inn & The Barn Hikers Hostel** 603-466-2271. (www.libbyhouseinn.webs.com)
⛺⛺⛺   ◈ AT Passport location.
⛺⛺⛺⌐   Open year-round. Serving the AT hikers for 36 years.
⛺ No pets. ⛺ Full and twin beds $25, ▲ tenting $15PP, ⇌ B&B rooms available. Hot country breakfast available. Fast, free pickup and return to Route 2 trail head for guests. Fast pickup and return to Rte 2 with for guests. Shuttle from Pinkham Notch free with 2 night stay to facilitate ⛺ slackpacking and ⛺ Shuttle to Walmart can be arranged. Clean beds with linens, full kitchen with cookware and refrigerator, lounge with big screen TV, ⛺ free WiFi. ⛺ Laundry $5. Visa MC accepted.
⌐   Mail drops free for guests, $15 fee for non-guests: 55 Main Street, Gorham, NH 03581.

NoBo	Features	Description	GPS	Elev SoBo

Hiker's Paradise at Colonial Fort Inn 603-466-2732. (www.hikersparadise.com) AT Passport location.
No pets. Bunks $24 (includes tax) with linen, tub and shower, kitchen, free WiFi. Private rooms available. Coin laundry for guests.
Coleman fuel and alcohol fuel by the ounce., WiFi. Free shuttle with stay to and from Route 2, other limited shuttles. Credit cards accepted. Smoking only on outside porch. No mail drops.

Royalty Inn 603-466-3312. (www.royaltyinn.com) Hiker rate $89 weekday, $99 weekend depending on the season. Pet fee $20. Indoor and outdoor pool, jucuzzi, sauna, A/C, laundry, free WiFi. Vending machines.

Top Notch Inn 603-466-5496. (www.topnotchinn.com)
Open May-mid Oct. Call for pricing. Guest laundry, limited shuttles, pool, hot tub, laundry, free WiFi, well behaved dogs under 50 lbs okay, no smoking. Credit cards accepted. 10% local restaurant discount.
Mail drops for guests and non guests: 265 Main St, Gorham, NH 03581.

Northern Peaks Motor Inn 603-466-2288. (www.northernpeaksmotorinn.com)
$70/up + tax, pets $5, A/C, free WiFi, no smoking. Hikers welcome. Accepts Master, Visa, Discover and American express card.

Gorham Motor Inn 603-466-3381 $58-$158 Open May-Oct.

Gorham Hardware & Sports 603-466-2312. (www.nhhockeyshop.com) Clothing, hiking poles, water treatment, hiking food, cold weather clothes, white gas, alcohol fuel by the ounce and canisters. Accepts Visa MC Disc. M-F 8am-5:30pm, Sa 8am-4pm, Su 8am-1pm. Close Su after Columbus Day.

AMC Hiker Shuttle, See Notes at mile 1811.9

(6.7W) **Walmart** 603-752-4621. M-Su 7am-10pm; **Pharmacy** M-F 8am-8pm, Sa 9am-7pm, Su 10am-6pm.

Berlin, NH (10.1W) from U.S. 2 trail head)

Androscoggin Valley Hospital 603-752-2200.

Gorham, NH

1893.7		Cross **U.S. 2 (northern end)**.		780	298.3
1893.8		Intersects with **North Road, Cross railroad tracks**.		755	298.2
1894.0		Cross Androscoggin River on Leadmine Bridge at power plant, North Road.	N 44 24.384, W 71 07.008	750	298.0
1894.2		Junction with **North Road**		760	297.8
1894.5	P(4)	Junction with **Hogan Road**, unpaved	N 44 24.245, W 71 07.213	800	297.5
1895.2		Cross Brook.		1350	296.8
1897.3		Mt. Hayes, Mahoosuc Trail		2555	294.7
1897.6		Junction with Centennial Trail and Mahoosuc Trail below Mt. Hayes.		2550	294.4
1898.3		Water in Col between Cascade Mountain and Mt. Hayes.		1960	293.7
1898.7		Good views on large steep open rock slabs and ledges.		2631	293.3
1899.5		Cascade Mountain summit, wooded.		2631	292.5
1900.6	(4)	Side tail leads (0.1) west to Trident Col Tent site, water at spring 50 yards from campsite, 4 tent sites accommodates 16, privy, bear box.		2020	291.4
1901.6		Trident Pass, pass south of Page Pond over outlet.		2240	290.4
1902.2		View 50 yards west on Wockett Ledge, shoulder of Bald Cap.		2780	289.8

NoBo	Features	Description	GPS	Elev	SoBo
1902.9		Cross Upper Branch of Peabody Brook.		2750	289.1
1903.3		Cross Dream Lake inlet brook, Junction with Peabody Brook Trail leads to Dryad Falls Trail.		2610	288.7
1904.8		Northwestern shore of Moss Pond.		2630	287.2
1905.1		Southwest shore of Upper Gentian Pond.		2530	286.9
1905.5		Junction of Austin Brook Trail leads (0.2E) **Gentian Pond Shelter and campsite**, water is the inlet brook of Gentian Pond, three single and one double tent platforms accommodate 18, privy, bear box. 61.8◀19.8◀13.7◀▶5.2▶9.6▶14.7	N 44 27.110, W 71 04.163	2166	286.5
1906.9		Cross small brook.		2500	285.1
1908.3	▲	Mt. Success summit, alpine meadows on north side.		3565	283.7
1908.9	Y	Junction with Success Trail.		3170	283.1
1910.2	State Line	New Hampshire–Maine State Line		2972	281.8
1910.7		Junction with Carlo Col Trail leads to (0.3W) **Carlo Col Shelter and campsite**, water (spring) is located left of the lean-to, two single and one double tent platforms, privy, bear box. 25.0◀18.9◀5.2◀▶4.4▶9.5▶16.4	N 44 29.321, W 71 00.970	2945	281.3
1911.1		Mt. Carlo summit, 360 degree views.		3565	280.9
1911.7		Sag between Mt. Carlo and West Peak of Goose Eye Mtn.		3165	280.3
1912.5		Goose Eye Trail to Goose Eye Mountain (West Peak), (0.1W) to summit		3854	279.5
1912.8	Y	Junction with south fork of Wright Trail.		3659	279.2
1912.9	▲	Goose Eye Mountain summit (East Peak)		3794	279.1
1913.0	Y	Junction of north fork of Wright Trail.		3466	279.0
1914.1		Goose Eye Mountain (North Peak)		3675	277.9
1914.5		Tree line on North Peak of Goose Eye Mtn.		3320	277.5
1915.1		300 feet east to **Full Goose Shelter and camps**, water (stream) is located behind shelter, three single and one double tent platforms, privy, bear box. 23.3◀9.6◀4.4◀▶5.1▶12.0▶15.5	N 44 31.506, W 70 58.884	3030	276.9
1915.6	▲	Fulling Mill Mountain (South Peak)		3395	276.4
1915.7		Tree line of South Peak of Goose Eye Mtn.		3400	276.3
1916.6	Y	Mahoosuc Notch Trail, Mahoosuc Notch (west end)		2400	275.4
1917.7		Mahoosuc Notch (east end), Bull Branch		2150	274.3
1918.2		Cross brook, Mahoosuc Notch Two.		2593	273.8
1919.3	Y	Mahoosuc Arm Summit, Joe May Cut-off Trail Jct		3765	272.7
1919.9		Cross Speck Pond Brook, outlet of Speck Pond		3430	272.1

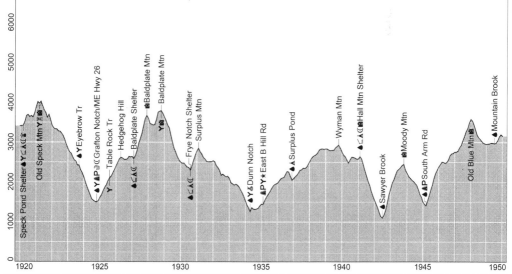

| 1920.2 | | Junction with Speck Pond Trail.
AMC Speck Pond Shelter and campsite, NO FIRES. Water (spring) is located (0.1) west on the blue blazed trail behind the caretaker's yurt, three single and three double tent platforms, bear box. Overnight/caretaker fee. Speck Pond is the highest body of water in Maine.
14.7◀9.5◀5.1◀▶6.9▶10.4▶20.9 | N 44 33.879,
W 70 58.416 | 3500 | 271.8 |

NoBo	Features	Description	GPS	Elev	SoBo
1920.8	◊	Sag with intermittent spring.		3855	271.2
1920.9	Y ≬ 🔲	Junction with Old Speck Trail and Grafton Loop Trail, (0.3E) to observation tower		3985	271.1
1921.1		Top of an old slide now overgrown with brush.		4017	270.9
1923.3	🔲	Several knobs on the north shoulder of Old Speck.		3718	268.7
1923.6	Y	Junction with Eyebrow Trail, upper junction		2480	268.4
1923.7	♦	Cross brook, last water for the next 3.5 miles south		2500	268.3
1924.5	♦	Cross small brook		1760	267.5
1924.7	Y	Junction with Eyebrow Trail, lower junction		1530	267.3
1924.8	☾ ⎔ ▲ P(50) ⚲ ★★★★★	Cross **ME. 26**, Grafton Notch.	N 44 35.388, W 70 56.806	1495	267.2

▲ ✗ ⏚ ⌂ (12.8E) **Stony Brook Camping** 207-824-2836. (www.stonybrookrec.com) ▲ tent site $30, ⌂ lean-to
⚲ ⊕ ⚄ 🔲 $35. Will shuttle from Grafton Notch for a fee. ⚓ Pool, miniature golf, zip line, rec room, ⏚ campstore,
⚲ shower, ⌂ laundry, ⊕ free WiFi, swimming. Store with groceries and supplies; ✗ eat in or take out
prepared foods; beer and wine. Location: (12.2E) on Hwy 26, then left (0.6) miles on Route 2.
🔲 Mail drops for guests: 42 Powell Place, Hanover, ME 04237.

Bethel, ME 04217 (17.9E) Directions: (12.2E) to Rt 2, right (5.7) miles on Rt 2.

⌂ ⚲ **PO** M-F 9am-4pm, Sa 10am-12:30pm. 207-824-2668. 82 Main St. Bethel ME 04217. N 44 24.432, W 70 47.366

⇔ ⌂ ⌂ ⊕ **Chapman Inn** 207-824-2657. (www.chapmaninn.com) ⌂ Bunk space $35 includes ⚲ shower and full
🔲 breakfast, $25 without breakfast. ⇔ Rooms $69 and up, include breakfast. Kitchen privileges, ⌂ $6
laundry, ⊕ free WiFi.
🔲 Mail drops for guests: PO Box 1067, Bethel, ME 04217.

▲ ⌂ ⊕ 🚌 **Bethel Outdoor Adventure** 207-824-4224. (www.betheloutdooradventure.com) ▲ campsites $24/
night, walking distance of Bethel. ⚲ Laundry, ⊕ free WiFi. 🚌 Will shuttle to and from Grafton Notch
trail head $45 group each way (one way).

✗ **Sudbury Inn Restaurant & Pub**, 207-824-2174. (www.thesudburyinn.com) $89 and up, higher
depending on the season, includes a full country breakfast. Restaurant is Thurs-Sat 5:30-9 and Pub is
Daily 11:30am-9:30pm.

🛒 **Bethel Foodliner** 207-824-2121. (www.bethelfoodliner.com) M-Th 8am-8pm, F-Sa 8am-9pm, Su 8am-
7pm.

🔦 ◈ **True North Adventureware** 207-824-2201. (www.truenorthadventureware.com)
◈ AT Passport location.
M-Th 10am-6pm, F-Sa 9am-6pm, Su 10am-5pm.
🔦 Full service outdoor store, clothing, gear and footwear.
Trekking pole repair, warranty sock replacement, Coleman fuel and alcohol fuel by the ounce and canis-
ters, freeze dried foods, WiFi.

🐾 **Bethel Animal Hospital** 207-824-2212. (www.bethelanimalhospital.com) M-Th 8am-6pm, F 8am-5pm,
Sa 8am-12pm, Su closed.

NoBo	Features	Description	GPS	Elev	SoBo
1924.9	Y	Junction with Table Rock Trail (lower junction).		1556	267.1
1925.2		Bottom of steep slope.		1841	266.8
1925.6	Y 🔲	Junction with Table Rock Trail, upper junction, views at Table Rock.		2125	266.4
1927.1	♦ Y ▲(4) ⌂(8) ⌇ ☾ ⚲	(0.1E) **Baldpate Lean-to**, water (stream) next to lean-to, 4 tent sites, privy. 16.4◄12.0◄6.9◄▶3.5▶14.0▶26.8	N 44 35.907, W 70 54.697	2645	264.9
1927.9	🔲	Baldpate Mountain (West Peak)		3662	264.1
1928.5		Bottom of sag between East and West Peaks of Baldpate Mountain.		3471	263.5
1928.8	Y 🔲	Baldpate Mountain (East Peak), Grafton Loop Trail Junction		3812	263.2
1929.3		Little Baldpate Mountain		3442	262.7
1929.4		Tree line on north side of Little Baldpate Mountain.		3303	262.6
1930.6	♦ ▲(5) ⌂(6) ⌇ ☾ ⚲	**Frye Notch Lean-to**, water (Frye Brook) is located in front of the lean-to, 5 tent sites, privy. 15.5◄10.4◄3.5◄▶10.5▶23.3▶31.6	N 44 37.663, W 70 54.048	2280	261.4
1931.1		Surplus Mountain, highpoint on NE ridge		2875	260.9
1932.5		Sharp turn in trail on north east ridge of Surplus Mountain.		2554	259.5
1934.1		South rim of Dunn Notch.		1615	257.9
1934.3	♦ Y ⚷	Dunn Notch and Falls on side trail (0.2) west. West Branch Ellis River, ford.		1350	257.7
1935.0	♦	Cross small brook.		1435	257.0
1935.1	Y ▲ ▲ P(6) ⚲ ★★★★★	Junction with Cascade Trail. Cross **East B Hill Road**, not an ATC approved camping spot.	N 44 40.103, W 70 53.589	1485	256.9

East B Hill Rd Andover, ME 04216 (8.0E). See map of Andover, ME.

PO M-F 9:15am-12pm & 1pm-4:15pm, Sa 9am-12pm. 207-392-4571. 6 Church St. Andover ME 04216. N 44 37.946, W 70 44.982

Pine Ellis Lodging 207-392-4161. (www.pineellislodging.com)

AT Passport location. Host Ilene Trainor.

No pets. private rooms $45S, $60D, $75 triple, $25EAP. Bunks $25PP. Stays include kitchen privileges, laundry and morning coffee, free WiFi. Trail head pickup for a fee, call in advance, slackpack Grafton Notch to Rangeley, and shuttles to nearby towns, airport and bus station. Multi-day slackpacking packages for groups. Resupply of trail snacks And meals, coleman fuel and denatured fuel by the ounce, canister fuel.

Mail drops for guests: (USPS) PO Box 12 or (UPS) 20 Pine Street, Andover ME 04216.

Paul's AT Camp for Hikers Stay in a rustic cabin for $60 for 4. Located 3 miles from Andover. Stay includes, water, electricty in the cabin and shower house, one round trip shuttle from the hostel. "Great for families and friends meeting up with hikers". Contact Pine Ellis for more information.

Andover General Store 207-392-4172. Food to order off grill, pizza, ice cream. ATM. M-Sa 5am-8pm, Su 6am-8pm, in summer month they close at 9pm.

Mills Market 207-392-3062. groceries, deli meats and cheese. Friday Pizza Special 16" one topping pizza and any 2 liter soda for $9.99. M-Th 5am-9pm, F-Sa 5am-10pm, Su 5am-9pm.

Little Red Hen 207-392-2253. (www.littleredhendiner.com)

AT Passport location.

Mexican buffet Thursday night, prime rib & baby back ribs and other specials Friday night, Italian buffet Saturday night. Ask about tenting. Laundry & shower facility available $5 each, free WiFi. M closed, Tu 6:30am-2pm, W 6:30am-2pm, Th 6:30am-2pm & 5pm-8pm, F 6:30am-8pm, Sa - 6:30am-8pm, Su - 7am-2pm.

Mail drops: 28 south Main Street, Andover ME 04216.

Andover Public Library 207-392-4841. (www.andover.lib.me.us) M closed, Tu-W 1pm-4:30pm, Th 1pm-4:30pm & 6pm-8pm, Sa 1pm-4:30pm, Su closed.

Donna Gifford massage therapist, 207-357-5686. Call for rates. Free pickup at Hostel and return to Hostels in Andover.

(10.0E) **The Cabin** 207-392-1333. (www.thecabininmaine.com)

Located (2.8) from Andover.

AT Passport location.

Alumni hikers welcome; by reservation only. Hiker kitchen, laundry, computer available for use, free WiFi.

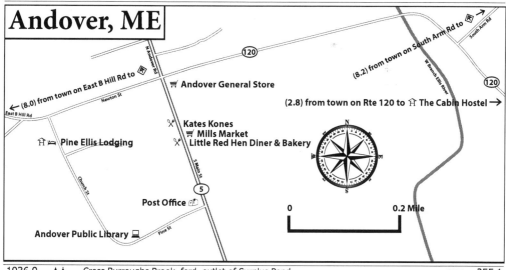

Andover, ME

(8.0) from town on East B Hill Rd to
East B Hill Rd

(8.2) from town on South Arm Rd to → South Arm Rd
W Branch Ellis River

120

Andover General Store

(2.8) from town on Rte 120 to The Cabin Hostel →

Newton St
N Andover Rd

Kates Kones
Mills Market
Little Red Hen Diner & Bakery

Pine Ellis Lodging

Church St
S Main St

5

Post Office

0   0.2 Mile

Andover Public Library   Pine St

NoBo		Features	GPS	Elev	SoBo
1936.9		Cross Burroughs Brook, ford, outlet of Surplus Pond.		2050	255.1
1937.0		Cross gravel logging road		2050	255.0
1938.9		Southern shoulder of Wyman Mountain.		2381	253.1
1939.8		Wyman Mountain (north peak)		2945	252.2
1940.7		Cross small brook.		2869	251.3
1941.1	(6)	**Hall Mountain Lean-to**, water (spring) is located south of the lean-to on the AT, tent sites available, privy. Trail to view behind shelter. 20.9◀14.0◀10.5◀▶12.8▶21.1▶32.3	N 44 42.050, W 70 49.506	2635	250.9
1942.4		Cross small brook just below cascade.		1196	249.6
1942.5		Sawyer Notch, cross Sawyer Brook, ford		1095	249.5

NoBo	Features	Description	GPS	Elev	SoBo
1943.4		Moody Mountain		2440	248.6
1944.1		Saddle between Sawyer and Moody Mountain.		2229	247.9
1944.5	♦	Cross small brook.		2266	247.5
1944.7		North shoulder of Sawyer Mountain.		2136	247.3
1945.2	♦▲P(6)♀ ★★★★★	Cross Black Brook and **South Arm Road**, ford, campsite.	N 44 43.291, W 70 47.148	1410	246.8

Andover, ME. (8.2E) See NOBO mile 1935.1 See map of Andover, ME.

NoBo	Features	Description	GPS	Elev	SoBo
1945.8	📷	Views of Black Brook Notch below.		2401	246.2
1947.5		Base of western slope of Sawyer Mountain.		2742	244.5
1948.0	▲📷	Old Blue Mountain summit		3600	244.0
1948.4		Base of northern slope of Old Blue Mountain.		3215	243.6
1949.5		Reach Col. with old growth.		3051	242.5

NoBo	Features	Description	GPS	Elev	SoBo
1951.2	♦Y	Junction with Bemis Stream Trail.		3350	240.8
1952.2		Bemis Mountain (West Peak)		3592	239.8
1952.3	▲	Bemis Mountain East Peak		3532	239.7
1953.5	▲	Bemis Mountain Third Peak.		3115	238.5
1953.9	◊▲(4) ⊑(8) ⌣⊂♀	(0.1E) **Bemis Mountain Lean-to**, water small (spring) is located to left of lean-to, 4 tent sites, privy. 26.8◄23.3◄12.8◄▶8.3▶19.5▶28.4	N 44 48.615, W 70 45.354	2790	238.1
1955.4		Bemis Range (Second Peak), open ledges		2915	236.6
1956.3	▲	Bemis Mountain First Peak.		2604	235.7
1956.8	📷	Knob on east ends of Bemis Range.		2608	235.2
1957.0		Tree line at north end of series of knobs.		2358	235.0
1957.4	♦	Small spring.		1747	234.6
1957.5	♦▲▲ P(3)♀	Cross gravel road, former rail bed, not an ATC approved camping spot.	N 44 50.080, W 70 43.454	1550	234.5
1957.7	♦	Cross Bemis Stream, ford		1495	234.3
1958.5	📷▲ P(30) ♀ ★★★★★	Cross **ME. 17**, view of Mooselookmeguntic Lake. Parking at the scenic overlook.	N 44 50.259, W 70 42.610	2200	233.5

Oquossoc, ME (10.8W)

☏♀	**PO** M–F 8am–10am & 2:15pm–4:15pm, Sa 9am–12pm. 207-864-3685. 92 Carry Rd. Oquoccoc ME 04964. N 44 57.951, W 70 46.498	
🏪✗🍴⛽	**Oquossoc Grocery** (207-864-3662. (www.oquossocgrocery.com) ✗ Deli, bakery, ⛽ Coleman fuel. M-Th 6am-8pm, F-Sa 6am-9pm, Su 6am-8pm.	
✗	**Gingerbread House** (207-864-3602. (www.gingerbreadhouserestaurant.net) Breakfast 7am-11am, lunch 11:30am-3pm, dinner 5pm-9pm. Pub menu available 3pm-9pm. Sunday Breakfast until 11:30am. Ice cream available all day.	

NoBo	Features	Description	GPS	Elev	SoBo
1959.3		Spruce Mountain		2530	232.7
1960.1	♦	North shore of Moxie Pond		2400	231.9

NoBo	Features	Description	GPS	Elev	SoBo
1961.2	📷	Bates Ledge. View south over Long Pond.		2713	230.8
1961.9	◢⛺	Northeastern shore of Long Pond, sandy beach		2330	230.1
1962.2	◊▲(1) ⌐(8) ⌣⊂⛺⚲	78 yards west to **Sabbath Day Pond Lean-to**, water (piped spring) is located near pond in front of lean-to, 1 tent platform and tent sites available, privy. Sandy beach (0.3) south on AT, swimming.	N 44 50.457, W 70 39.723		
		31.6◄21.1◄8.3◄► 11.2► 20.1► 28.1		2390	229.8
1962.7		Cross Houghton Fire Road		2300	229.3
1963.9	⟙	Power line.		2788	228.1
1964.4		Unnamed high point.		2938	227.6
1966.8	◢▲⌣⊂	Little Swift River Pond, tent sites available, privy.		2460	225.2
1968.0	◊	Cross Chandler Mill Stream, outlet of boreal bog		2150	224.0
1969.5	◊	Skirt western shore of South Pond.		2174	222.5
1970.5	📷	View at top of steep slope.		1986	221.5
1971.6	◢P(20)⚲ ★★★★★	Cross **ME. Route 4**.	N 44 53.228, W 70 32.465	1700	220.4

⌂▲⌂🍴 (0.3W) **The Hiker Hut** 207-897-8984, 207-670-8095. hikerhut@gmail.com.
🚗✉ ⌂ $25PP includes bunk with mattress, pillows, shuttles into Rangeley. Extra meals $7, ⌂ laundry $3. Private couples hut $50. Quiet, restful sanctuary along the Sandy River. Massage therapist on hand. 🚗 Shuttles and 🎒 slackpacking available, 🏪 small resupply shop with snacks and ⛽ fuel.
✉ Mail drops: ($5 non-guest fee): C/O Steve Lynch 2 Pine Rd. Sandy River Plantation, ME 04970.

Rangeley, ME (9.0W) See map of Rangeley, ME.
✉⚲ **PO** M-F 9:30am-12:30pm & 1:30pm-4:15pm, Sa 9:30am-12pm. 207-864-2233. 2517 Main St. Rangeley ME 04970. N 44 57.951, W 70 46.498

🚗⌂◈⑤ **Fieldstone Cottages** 207-670-5507
🛏🎒P✉ ◈ AT Passport location.
⑤ No pets. New Location and name, same owners as the Farmhouse Inn. Located on the edge of town. Not a party location. Low density. Reservations requested. Catering to 🎒 Slackpackers and Section hikers. ⌂ Features Bunks in cabins for $40PP, includes shower with towel and return to Route 4 trail head with stay. Nice new clean facility. 📶 Free Wifi. 🛏 Private Cabin rentals available. 🚗 Rides back to trail head without stay $10PP depending on availability. P Parking available.
✉ Mail drops accepted for reservation guests only: 2342 Main St. Rangeley, Maine, 04970. $5 per package for non staying guests.

🛏◈🚗⛵ **Town & Lake Motel** 207-864-3755. (www.rangeleytownandlake.com)
✉ 🛏 Ask about hiker rate. Plus, $10.00 a person over two people. Pets $10. ⛵ Canoes for guest use.
✉ Mail drops for guests: PO Box 47, Rangeley, ME 04970.

🛏◈ **Rangeley Inn & Tavern** 207-864-3341. (www.therangeleyinn.com)
🍴⛵📶 ◈ AT Passport location.
🛏 Rates start at $150 in summer, $125 in fall (after Oct 20). Complimentary breakfast. Direct booking discount, ⛵ kayaks/canoe, 📶 free wifi, free calls to US and Canada.

🛏🍴📶 **Rangeley Saddleback Inn** 207-864-3434. (www.rangeleysaddlebackinn.com) 🛏 $120 and up, prices vary depending on the season, includes continental breakfast, pets $10 includes . 📶 WiFi. Ride to and from trail head are sometimes available.

🛏📶 **North Country Inn B&B** 207-864-2440 (www.northcountrybb.com) info@northcountrybb.com 🛏 $99-149 includes full breakfast, specials mid-week and off-season. 📶 WiFi. Multi-night discount.

🏪🍴 **Moose Loop Cafe** 207-864-3000. (www.rangeleysmooseloop.com) Café, Deli, bakery and rental. M-Su 9am-5pm.

🍴 **Sarge's Sports Pub & Grub** 207-864-5616. Serves lunch and dinner also has a bar. M-Su 11am-1pm. Entertainment on weekends, outdoor deck. 2454 Main St.

🍴 **Moose Alley** 207-864-9955. (www.moosealleymaine.com) Bowling, billiards, darts, dance floor, food.

🛒🍴 **IGA Supermarket** 207-864-5089. (www.rangeleyiga.com) ATM. Summer hours M-Su 7am-9pm. Winter hours M-Su 7am-8pm.

🚶◈ **Ecopelagicon** 207-864-2771. (www.ecopelagicon.com)
🏪◊🚗✉ ◈ AT Passport location.
Good selection of hiking gear & accessories. ⛽ Fuel (canister, alcohol & white gas by the oz.) 🏪 freeze dried foods, snacks, water purification, Leki poles & warranty work, Darn Tough, Superfeet, Osprey & Big Agnes gear, first aid, rain gear and lots more. Free charging station, 📶 WIFI, ◊ water fill-up. 🚗 Ask about shuttles. Trail Town Festival Sat. of Labor Day weekend. www.rangeleytrailtown.com.
✉ Mail drops: USPS- PO Box 899, UPS/FedEx- 7 Pond Street, Rangeley, ME 04970.

🚶⛽ **Alpine Shop** 207-864-3741. (www.alpineshoprangeley.com) Clothing and some hiking gear, ⛽ fuel by the ounce. M-Th 9am-5pm, F-Sa 9am-6pm, Su 10am-5pm.

🚶 **Back Woods** 207-864-2335 Clothing, some gear. M-Sa 9am-5pm, Su 10am-4pm.

🚿⛽ **Rangeley Family Medicine** 207-864-3303. (www.rangeleychc.org) Location: 42 Dallas Hill Road. 🚿 $5 shower, towel provided. M-Th 5am-8pm, F 5am-7:30pm, Sa-Su 8-2.

Rangeley, ME

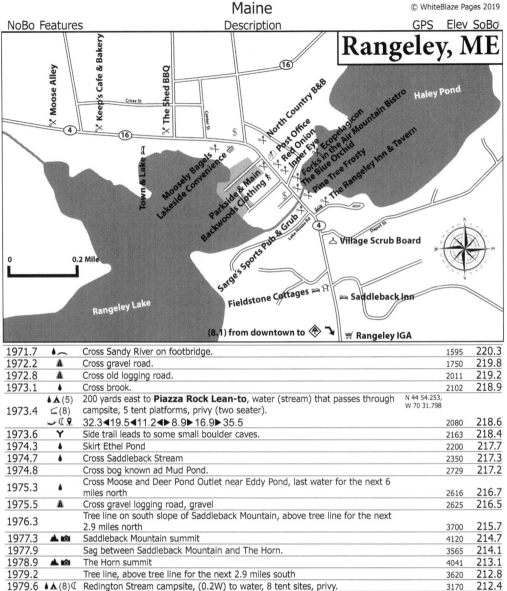

Moose Alley
Keep's Cafe & Bakery
Cross St
The Shed BBQ
Center St
North Country B&B
Post Office
Red Onion
Inner Eye
Ecopelagicon
Forks in the Air Mountain Bistro
Haley Pond
The Blue Orchid
Pine Tree Frosty
The Rangeley Inn & Tavern
Moosely Bagels
Lakeside Convenience
Town & Lake
Parkside & Main
Backwoods Clothing
Sarge's Sports Pub & Grub
Lake House Rd
Depot St
Village Scrub Board
Fieldstone Cottages
Saddleback Inn
Rangeley Lake

0   0.2 Mile

(8.1) from downtown to   Rangeley IGA

NoBo	Features	Description	GPS	Elev	SoBo
1971.7	⬥⌒	Cross Sandy River on footbridge.		1595	220.3
1972.2	⚠	Cross gravel road.		1750	219.8
1972.8	⚠	Cross old logging road.		2011	219.2
1973.1	⬥	Cross brook.		2102	218.9
1973.4	⬥▲(5) ⌂(8) ⌒☾♀	200 yards east to **Piazza Rock Lean-to**, water (stream) that passes through campsite, 5 tent platforms, privy (two seater). 32.3◄19.5◄11.2◄►8.9►16.9►35.5	N 44 54.253, W 70 31.798	2080	218.6
1973.6	⅄	Side trail leads to some small boulder caves.		2163	218.4
1974.3	⬥	Skirt Ethel Pond		2200	217.7
1974.7	⬥	Cross Saddleback Stream		2350	217.3
1974.8		Cross bog known ad Mud Pond.		2729	217.2
1975.3	⬥	Cross Moose and Deer Pond Outlet near Eddy Pond, last water for the next 6 miles north		2616	216.7
1975.5	⚠	Cross gravel logging road, gravel		2625	216.5
1976.3		Tree line on south slope of Saddleback Mountain, above tree line for the next 2.9 miles north		3700	215.7
1977.3	▲📷	Saddleback Mountain summit		4120	214.7
1977.9		Sag between Saddleback Mountain and The Horn.		3565	214.1
1978.9	▲📷	The Horn summit		4041	213.1
1979.2		Tree line, above tree line for the next 2.9 miles south		3620	212.8
1979.6	⬥▲(8)☾	Redington Stream campsite, (0.2W) to water, 8 tent sites, privy.		3170	212.4

Almost there!

False promises.

BootsMcfarland.com
© Geodym Carvin
Boots Mcfarland

ME

NoBo	Features	Description	GPS	Elev	SoBo

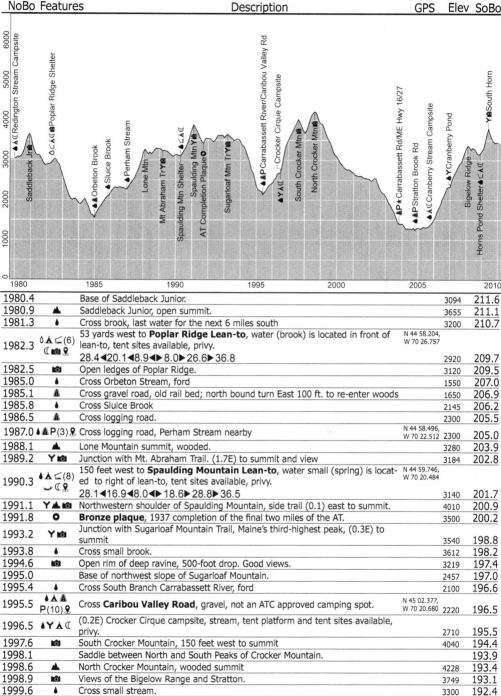

NoBo	Features	Description	GPS	Elev	SoBo
1980.4		Base of Saddleback Junior.		3094	211.6
1980.9	▲	Saddleback Junior, open summit.		3655	211.1
1981.3	♦	Cross brook, last water for the next 6 miles south		3200	210.7
1982.3	♦▲⌐(6) ℂ📷♨	53 yards west to **Poplar Ridge Lean-to**, water (brook) is located in front of lean-to, tent sites available, privy.	N 44 58.204, W 70 26.757		209.7
		28.4◄20.1◄8.9◄►8.0►26.6►36.8		2920	209.7
1982.5	📷	Open ledges of Poplar Ridge.		3120	209.5
1985.0	♦	Cross Orbeton Stream, ford		1550	207.0
1985.1	▲	Cross gravel road, old rail bed; north bound turn East 100 ft. to re-enter woods		1650	206.9
1985.8	♦	Cross Sluice Brook		2145	206.2
1986.5	▲	Cross logging road.		2300	205.5
1987.0	♦▲P(3)♨	Cross logging road, Perham Stream nearby	N 44 58.496, W 70 22.512	2300	205.0
1988.1	▲	Lone Mountain summit, wooded.		3280	203.9
1989.2	Y📷	Junction with Mt. Abraham Trail. (1.7E) to summit and view		3184	202.8
1990.3	♦▲⌐(8) ⌣ℂ♨	150 feet west to **Spaulding Mountain Lean-to**, water small (spring) is located to right of lean-to, tent sites available, privy.	N 44 59.746, W 70 20.484		201.7
		28.1◄16.9◄8.0◄►18.6►28.8►36.5		3140	201.7
1991.1	Y▲📷	Northwestern shoulder of Spaulding Mountain, side trail (0.1) east to summit.		4010	200.9
1991.8	●	**Bronze plaque**, 1937 completion of the final two miles of the AT.		3500	200.2
1993.2	Y📷	Junction with Sugarloaf Mountain Trail, Maine's third-highest peak, (0.3E) to summit		3540	198.8
1993.8	♦	Cross small brook.		3612	198.2
1994.6	📷	Open rim of deep ravine, 500-foot drop. Good views.		3219	197.4
1995.0		Base of northwest slope of Sugarloaf Mountain.		2457	197.0
1995.4	♦	Cross South Branch Carrabassett River, ford		2100	196.6
1995.5	♦▲▲ P(10)♨	Cross **Caribou Valley Road**, gravel, not an ATC approved camping spot.	N 45 02.377, W 70 20.680	2220	196.5
1996.5	♦Y▲ℂ	(0.2E) Crocker Cirque campsite, stream, tent platform and tent sites available, privy.		2710	195.5
1997.6	📷	South Crocker Mountain, 150 feet west to summit		4040	194.4
1998.1		Saddle between North and South Peaks of Crocker Mountain.			193.9
1998.6	▲	North Crocker Mountain, wooded summit		4228	193.4
1998.9	📷	Views of the Bigelow Range and Stratton.		3749	193.1
1999.6	♦	Cross small stream.		3300	192.4
2001.7	♦	Cross small stream, in stand of large white birch trees.		2500	190.3

NoBo	Features	Description	GPS	Elev	SoBo

2003.8 ▲P(20) ⚲ ★★★★★ Cross **ME. 27**. — N 45 06.137, W 70 21.351 — 1450 — **188.2**

🛒 (2.7E) **Mountainside Grocers** 207-237-2248. M-Su 7:30am–8pm.

Stratton, ME 04982 (5.0W)

☎⚲ **PO** M-F 8:30am-1pm & 1:30pm-4pm, Sa 8:30am-11am. 207-246-6461. 95 Main St. Stratton ME 04982. N 45 08.425, W 70 26.274

🛏⌂◈ ☎🚗P 🖥 **Stratton Motel** 207-246-4171 (www.strattonmotel.com)
◈ AT Passport location
⌂ $35 bunk. 🛏 $80 private room. Shuttle from trail head $5PP (when available). Same owners as the former Farmhouse Inn of Rangeley (now known as FieldStone Cottages). ☎ Free Wifi. P Parking available. 🚗 Shuttle range Gorham NH to Monson and to airports, train, bus, and rental car hubs in Portland, Bangor, Farmington, Augusta, and Waterville.
🖥 Mail Drops: PO Box 284, Stratton, ME, 04982; Fedex & UPS 162 Main St. Stratton, ME, 04982.

🛏◈✕ ☎🍴🖥 **White Wolf Inn & Restaurant** 207-246-2922. (www.thewhitewolfinn.com)
◈ AT Passport location.
🛏 Hiker rate $69 mid-week, $79 weekends and holidays, $10EAP. Pets $15, ☎ free WiFi, 🍴 ATM.
✕ **Restaurant:** M 11am-8:30pm, Tu closed, W closed, Th-Su 11am-8:30pm. Serves lunch and dinner, . Home of the 8oz Wolf Burger; Fish Fry Friday. Visa, M/C accepted $20 min.
🖥 Mail drops for guests (non-guest fee): 146 Main St, PO Box 590, Stratton, ME 04982.

🛏☎🖥 **Spillover Motel** 207-246-6571. (www.spillovermaine.com)
🛏 $89 and up, pets $15, includes continental breakfast. Full kitchen for use by guests, gas grill, ☎ free WiFi.
🖥 Mail drops for guests: PO Box 427, Stratton, ME 04982.

🛏✕ **Stratton Plaza Hotel** 207-246-2000. (www.strattonplazahotel.com) ✕ Dining, some rooms. Tuesday: Pitcher and Pizza $10. M closed, Tu-Sa 11am-1am, Su closed.

🛒♨🍴 **Fotter's Market** 207-246-2401. (www.fottersmarket.com) M-Th 8am-7pm, F-Sa 8am-8pm, Su 9am-5pm. ♨ Coleman and alcohol fuel by the ounce, 🍴 ATM.

🏪✕♨☎ 🍴 **Flagstaff General Store** 207-246-2300. ✕ Deli, hot coffee, snacks, subs, pizza, salads, fried foods, ♨ canister fuel, ☎ free WiFi, 🍴 ATM. M-F 6am-9pm, Sa 7am-9pm, Su 7am-7pm.

🖥☎ **Stratton Public Library** 207-246-4401. (www.stratton.lib.me.us) M 10am-5pm Tu 1pm-5pm, W 10am-5pm Th 1pm-5pm, F 10am-5pm, Sa 9am-1pm, Su closed. WiFi.

2004.6 ▲P(10)⚲ Cross **Stratton Brook Pond Road**. — N 45 06.708, W 70 20.962 — 1250 — **187.4**

2004.7 ▲ Cross logging road, gravel. — 1290 — **187.3**

2004.8 ▲⌒ Cross Stratton Brook on footbridge — 1230 — **187.2**

2005.4 ▲ Cross tote road. — 1356 — **186.6**

2005.7 ▲🅰(3)⌣☾ Cranberry Stream campsite, 3 tent sites available, privy. — 1350 — **186.3**

2007.0 ▲Y Junction with Bigelow Range Trail, Cranberry Pond (0.2W) — 2400 — **185.0**

2007.1 Slab cave system. — 2246 — **184.9**

2007.9 Y Side trail to views of Sugarloaf and Crooker Mountains. — 2957 — **184.1**

2008.1 📷 Views of Bigelow, Sugarloaf, Horns, and Crooker Mountains. — 3278 — **183.9**

2008.6 Y Side trail to overlook of Horns Pond. — 3278 — **183.4**

2008.7 Y Junction with Horns Pond Trail leads (3.9) to Stratton Brook Pond Road. — 3200 — **183.3**

2008.9 ▲🅰⌐(16)⌣☾⚲ 52 yards east to **Horns Pond Lean-to's**, two lean-to's, water is located north of the lean-tos or Horns Pond, tent sites available, privy. Caretaker, no fee. — N 45 08.633, W 70 19.783
35.5◄26.6◄18.6◄►10.2►17.9►27.9 — 3160 — **183.1**

2009.2 ▲ Box spring — 3400 — **182.8**

2009.3 Y Side Trail to North Horn, (0.2W) to summit — 3792 — **182.7**

2009.4 ▲📷 South Horn summit — 3831 — **182.6**

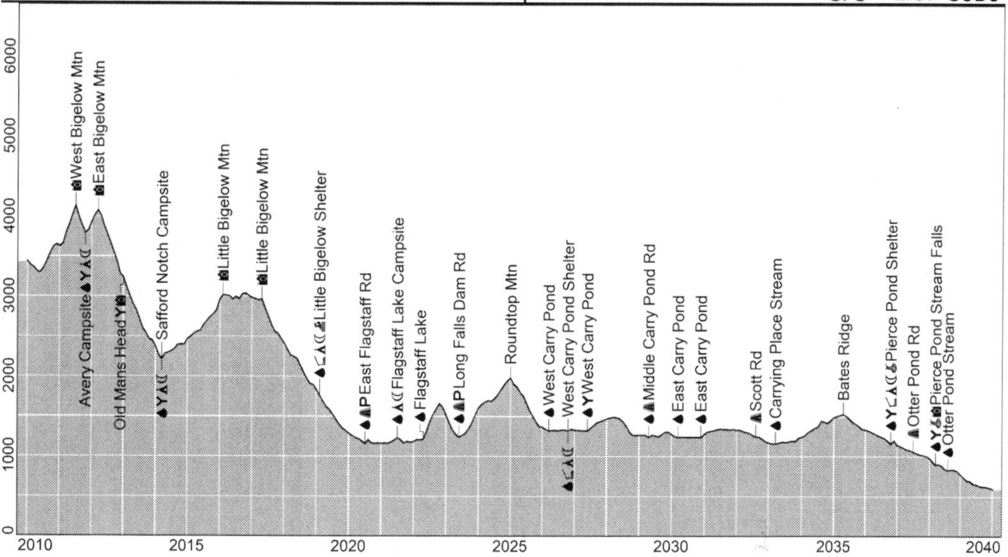

NoBo	Features	Description	GPS	Elev	SoBo

NoBo	Features	Description	GPS	Elev	SoBo
2011.5	▲ 📷	Bigelow Mountain (West Peak), 260 degree views.		4145	180.5
2011.8	◊ Y ▲ (6) ✈ ℂ	Bigelow Col, Fire Warden's Trail, Avery Memorial campsite, 6 tent platforms available, privy.		3850	180.2
2012.0	◊	Spring		3900	180.0
2012.2	▲ 📷	Bigelow Mountain, Avery Peak		4090	179.8
2013.0	Y 📷	Side trail to Old Man's Head.		3187	179.0
2014.1	Y	Junction with Safford Brook Trail leading (2.2) to East Flagstaff Road and (0.3) more to Flagstaff Lake.		2260	177.9
2014.2	◊ ▲ (2) ℂ	(0.3E) Safford Notch and campsite, 2 tent platforms and tent sites available, privy.		2230	177.8
2016.0		Little Bigelow Mountain (west end)		3035	176.0
2017.4		Little Bigelow Mountain (east end)		3040	174.6
2019.1	◊ ▲ (2) ⊑ (8) ✈ ℂ ♨ ♀	(0.1W) **Little Bigelow Lean-to**, water (spring) is located 50 yards in front of the lean-to, 2 tent platforms and tent sites available, privy. Swimming in "the Tubs" along the side trail. 36.8◄28.8◄10.2◄▶7.7▶17.7▶27.4	N 45 08.347, W 70 11.496 1760		172.9
2020.5	▲ P ♀	Cross **East Flagstaff Road**, 80 yards east to parking	N 45 08.077, W 70 10.282	1200	171.5
	�foodbed📶🍴 🚗🚙✉	(15.3E) **Mountain Village Farm B&B** 207-265-2030. (www.mountainvillageinn.com) �foodbed Room rates range from $99 to $140 double occupancy with private bath and full breakfast included. 📶 Free WiFi. 🚗 Round trip shuttle $50 for up to four hikers. Pets welcome. Bed & Breakfast on an organic farm; ask about work for stay. Town center within walking distance has grocery, laundry and restaurants. 🚙 Slackpack the Bigelows (Stratton to East Flagstaff Rd, either direction) $50 per car load. ✉ Mail drops: PO Box 216, Kingfield, ME 04947.			
2020.6	◊▲ ★★★★★	Cross **Bog Brook Road**, Flagstaff Lake, inlet. (0.2W) to Lake		1150	171.4
Kingfield, ME (25.7E) see NOBO mile 2020.5					
2021.6	◊ ▲ (9) ✈ ℂ	Campsites, privy.		1210	170.4
2023.3	▲ P (10) ♀ ★★★★★	Cross **Long Falls Dam Road**.	N 45 09.363, W 70 09.264	1225	168.7
Kingfield, ME (27.0E) see NOBO mile 2020.5					
2023.4	◊	Cross Jerome Brook.		1300	168.6
2023.7	▲	Cross logging road, gravel		1400	168.3
2025.0		Northern side of Roundtop Mountain		1760	167.0
2025.8	◊	Cross brook.		1604	166.2
2026.1	◊	South west corner of West Carry Pond (west side)		1320	165.9
2026.8	◊ ▲ (2) ⊑ (8) ✈ ℂ ♨ ♀	72 yards east to **West Carry Pond Lean-to**, water (spring house) is located to the left of the lean-to or West Carry Pond, tent sites available, privy. Swimming in pond. 36.5◄17.9◄7.7◄▶ 10.0▶ 19.7▶28.7	N 45 09.478, W 70 05.984 1340		165.2

NoBo	Features	Description	GPS	Elev	SoBo
2027.5	♦ Y	West Carry Pond (east side), side trail west to Arnold Point Beach on Arnold Trail		1320	164.5
2029.0	⌒	Arnold Swamp, many bog bridges		1255	163.0
2029.2	⛰	Intersection with **Long Pond Road**.		1250	162.8
2029.4	♦⌒⛰	Cross Sandy Stream and **Middle Carry Pond Road**, bridge		1229	162.6
2030.2	⛰	Cross East Carry Pond Logging Road, gravel		1250	161.8
2030.4	♦	Western shore of East Carry Pond.		1237	161.6
2030.9	♦	Northeast shore of East Carry Pond.		1256	161.1
2032.6	⛰	Cross **Scott Road**, main logging road		1300	159.4
2033.3	♦	North Branch of Carrying Place Stream, ford		1200	158.7
2033.8	♦	Spring.		1220	158.2
2035.3		Saddle in Bates Ridge.		1526	156.7
2036.8	♦⛺⌂(6) ⌒◖⛺	67 yards west to **Pierce Pond Lean-to**, water (Pierce Pond), tenting, privy. 27.9◄17.7◄10.0◄►9.7►18.7►22.8	N 45 14.420, W 70 03.360 1150		155.2
2036.9	Y ★★★★★	Side trail leads (0.3) to Harrison's Camps.		1162	155.1
	⇌ ✗	**Harrison's Pierce Pond Camps** 207-672-3625, 207-612-8184. (www.harrisonspiercepondcamps.com) May-Nov, 7 days. ⇌ Bed, shower, and 12- pancake breakfast $40. ✗ For breakfast only, ($9-12 served 7am), **reserve a seat the day before.** $ Cash only, no reservations for overnight stay. Okay to get water at camp and dispose of trash. Shortest route to camp is west from the north end of blue-blaze shelter loop trail.			
2037.0	♦⌒	Cross Wooden Dam, outlet of Pierce Pond		1120	155.0
2037.1	Y⚓	Side trail at top of waterfall.		1145	154.9
2037.2	Y	Trail to Harrison's Pierce Pond camps (0.1E)		1100	154.8
2037.5	⛰P⚓	Cross **Otter Pond Road**, gravel	N 45 14.331, W 70 02.780 1080		154.5
2038.0	Y⚓	Side trail leads (0.1) east to top of waterfall.		1042	154.0
2038.2	♦Y⚓	Side trail leads (0.1) east to pool at base of waterfalls, Pierce Pond Stream.		850	153.8
2038.6	♦⌒	Cross Otter Pond Stream, bridge		900	153.4
2039.2	📷⚓	Ledge overlooking several high waterfalls.		785	152.8

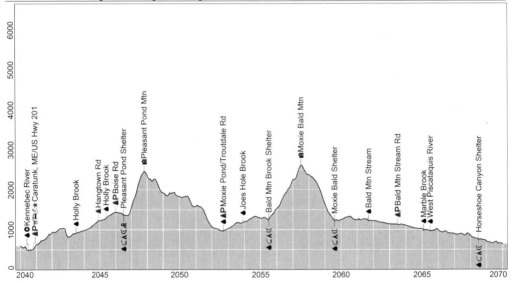

| 2040.5 | ♦ | Cross Kennebec River, ferry | | | |
| | ★★★★★ | **See Schedule below** | | 490 | 151.5 |

The ferry is free for hikers during open hours. Management of the ferry is by ATC and MATC with additional support by ALDHA and the dam operator. Operated by Greg Caruso of Maine Guide Service, LLC. His contact is 207-858-3627, gcaruso@myfairpoint.net.

The Kennebec Ferry schedule for 2019 is:
24 May - 30 June, 9 am–11 am
1 July - 30 September, 9 am–2 pm
1 October - 14 October, 9:00 am – 11:00 am
Off hours, hikers can schedule a crossing for $50, 207-858-3627.
Off hours crossings are possible only at the operator's discretion and availability.
No service will be provided 1 November - 30 April.
Hikers have drowned while attempting to ford the Kennebec Rever.

Do not attempt to ford the river!!!

	■	**Cheryl Anderson** 207-672-3997 Pivately run for fee ferry service.			
2040.8	▲P(20)⚑	Cross **U.S. 201.**	N 45 14.301,		
	★★★★★		W 69 59.769 520		151.2

US 201 Caratunk, ME (0.3E)

	⌂⚑	**PO** M-F 2pm-4pm, Sa 7:30am-11:15am, 207-672-3416 Post office accepts debit cards with limited cash. 172 Main St. Caratunk ME 04925. N 45 14.038, W 69 59.511
	⌂🛏◈ 🏪🚗🖂	**Caratunk House** (150 yds from AT) 207-672-4349. ◈ AT Passport location. Open 1 June and closed 30 Sept. 🛏 A full service hiker B&B with a 🏪 resupply store, "One Braid's" family style breakfasts. 🚗 Ask about shuttles. 🖂 Mail drops: 218 Main St Caratunk Maine 04925 or PO Box 98.
	🛏⌂◈ 🍴♨⚑ 💻🖂⚑	(1.4E) **The Sterling Inn** 207-672-3333. maineskeptsecret@yahoo.com (www.mainesterlinginn.com/AT-hikers) Open year-round. ◈ AT Passport location. ♨ Free laundry, 🚿 shower, 💻 Wi-Fi, recharge, telephone & mail drops for guests and non-guests. 🍴 Complete resupply, shuttle to/from the trail and PO (call from courtesy phone for pick-up). ⌂ Rooms and bunks from $25 per person include breakfast, free shuttle to nearby restaurants and convenience store (alcohol; tobacco). 🚗 Shuttle to locations throughout Maine can be arranged. Multi-night discount, pets welcome. **Caratunk Country Store**, located inside the Sterling House. resupply has everything a hiker needs, including ⛽ fuel by the ounce, canister fuel, batteries, candy bars, ice cream, cold drinks, cook yourself options and more. Free shuttle to and from trail head, Post Office and nearby restaurants with stay. Credit and debit cards accepted. Physical address: 1041 Route 201. 🖂 Mail drops: PO Box 129, Caratunk Maine 04925. Coordinates: N 45 13.146, W 69 59.253

The Forks, ME (2.0W)

	🛏⌂⛺⊛ ✗🍴⚑ 💻🚲🖂	(2.0W) **Northern Outdoors** 207-663-4466. (www.northernoutdoors.com) ⊛ No pets in campground, lodge rooms, logdominiums or the main lodge. Pets are only allowed in free standing cabins. Hikers welcome, 🚗 free shuttle, use of resort facilities with or without stay; hikers receive 30% lodging discount; prices vary, call for rates. ♨ Coin laundry, giant hot tub, 🏊 wimming pool, 💻 free WiFi, ☎ ATM, ✗ food & craft beer in Kennebec River Brewpub. 🖂 Mail drops: C/O Northern Outdoors, 1771 Route 201, The Forks, ME 04985. Please provide date of anticipated arrival
	⌂⛺◈ ✗🏪💻☎ 🖂	(4.0W) **Three Rivers Trading Post** 207-663-2104. (www.threeriverswhitewater.com) Bunks, tenting and ✗ restaurant open May-Oct. 🏪 Store open year-round, carries variety of packaged food, beer & wine. ⌂ Bunk $27PP, ⛺ tenting $12PP, 💻 free WiFi, ☎ ATM. Rafting trips by reservation. Boatman's Bar & Grill open M-Su 4pm-1am. Mail drops: 2265 US Route 201, The Forks, ME 04985.
	🏪	(7.6W) **Berry's General Store** 207-663-4461. Open year round. M-Su 5am-7pm, open till 8pm in summer.

2042.9	▲	Sharp turn in trail at tote road.		848	149.1
2043.5	♦	Cross Holly Brook		900	148.5
2044.2	♦	Cross Holly Brook tributary.		1076	147.8
2044.9	▲	Cross **Hangtown Road**, gravel logging road. (1.0) east to Pleasant Pond settlement and (3.2) further to Caratunk.		1240	147.1
2045.4	♦	Cross Holly Brook.		1339	146.6

NoBo	Features	Description	GPS	Elev	SoBo
2046.1	⚑	Cross **Boise–Cascade Logging Road**. (1.4) east to Pleasant Pond settlement and (3.2) further to Caratunk.		1400	145.9
2046.2	⚑P(10)⚲	Trail head parking area on logging road.	N 45 16.295, W 69 55.411	1462	145.8
2046.5	◔⚑▲⊏(6) ⌣☾♨⚲	100 yards east to **Pleasant Pond Lean-to**, water small (brook) is located on the path to the lean-to or pond, tent sites available, privy. Beach (0.2) on side trail beyond lean-to.	N 45 16.274, W 69 55.004		145.5
		27.4◀19.7◀9.7◀▶9.0▶13.1▶22.0		1320	
2046.7	◔Y♨	Side trail leads (0.2) east to Pleasant Pond Beach, sand beach.		1360	145.3
2047.8	▲📷	Pleasant Pond Mountain summit. Signs of old fire tower still visible on summit.		2477	144.2
2052.2	◔	Cross brook.		1098	139.8
2052.6	🕆	Power line.		1010	139.4
2052.7	⚑P(4)⚲	Junction with road near **Moxie Pond (south end), Joe's Hole, Troutdale Road**.	N 45 14.979, W 69 49.860	970	139.3
2052.8	◔	Cross Baker Stream, ford.		1010	139.2
2053.2	🕆	Power line.		1027	138.8
2053.9	◔	Cross Joe's Hole Brook.		1240	138.1
2055.3	◔▲⌣	Cross Bald Mountain Brook, Bald Mountain Brook campsite, tent sites available.		1200	136.7
2055.5	◔▲⊏(8) ⌣☾⚲	(0.1E) **Bald Mountain Brook Lean-to**, water (Bald Mountain Brook) is located in front of lean-to, tent sites available, privy.	N 45 15.516, W 69 47.967		136.5
		28.7◀18.7◀9.0◀▶4.1▶13.0▶25.0		1280	
2055.6	⚑P(4)⚲	Cross gravel road.	N 45 15.548, W 69 47.911	1367	136.4
2056.9	Y	Summit bypass trail, recommended in bad weather.		2250	135.1
2057.5	▲📷	Moxie Bald Mountain summit, 360 degree views.		2629	134.5
2057.8	Y	Summit bypass trail, recommended in bad weather.		2490	134.2
2058.5	Y📷	Side trail leads (0.7) west to Moxie Bald Mountain summit.		2320	133.5
2059.6	◔▲⊏(6) ⌣☾⚲	100 feet east to **Moxie Bald Lean-to**, water (stream) is located near by or Moxie Bald Pond, tent sites available, privy.	N 45 16.241, W 69 44.723		132.4
		22.8◀13.1◀4.1◀▶8.9▶20.9▶28.3		1220	
2061.1	⚑	Cross gravel road.		1290	130.9
2061.7	◔	Cross Bald Mountain Stream, outlet of Bald Mountain Pond, ford.		1213	130.3
2063.6	⚑P(6)⚲	Cross **Bald Mountain Stream Road**, gravel.	N 45 16.580, W 69 41.394	1100	128.4
2065.1	⚑	Cross Marble Brook and "Jeep Road".		990	126.9
2065.4	◔	Ford confluence of West Branch Piscataquis River.		900	126.6
2068.5	◔▲⊏(8) ⌣☾⚲	(0.1E) **Horseshoe Canyon Lean-to**, water (spring) is located at the AT junction or the river in front of and below the lean-to, tent sites available, privy.	N 45 16.968, W 69 37.657		123.5
		22.0◀13.0◀8.9◀▶12.0▶19.4▶24.1		880	
2068.6	◔Y	(0.1E) Horseshoe Canyon Lean-to, see notes above. Spring at trail junction.		859	123.4

| 2070.8 | ◔ | Ford East Branch Piscataquis River, 50-feet wide, and usually knee-deep. Difficult to cross during high water. | | 650 | 121.2 |
| 2071.1 | | Cross Old Bangor and Aroostook Railroad bed, bed no longer has rails. | | 800 | 120.9 |

NoBo	Features	Description	GPS	Elev	SoBo
2071.2	▲P(6)👤	Cross **Shirley–Blanchard Road**, paved.	N 45 17.087, W 69 35.206	880	120.8
2072.7	▲	Cross logging road.		970	119.3
2074.2	Y▲P(6) 👤 ★★★★★	Side trail leads (0.3) east to parking area on north side of Lake Hebron. Not an ATC approved camping spot	N 45 17.412, W 69 31.083	900	117.8
Monson ME (1.7W) to the left when coming off blue blaze trail. **See NOBO mileage 2077.5.**					
2075.3		East side of Buck Hill.		1390	116.7
2076.1	Y	Side trail leads (0.1) west to Doughty Ponds, two ponds.		1240	115.9
2077.5	▲P(20) 👤 ★★★★★	Cross **ME. 15**.	N 45 19.866, W 69 32.125	1215	114.5

Monson, ME (3.6E). See map of Monson, ME.

📬👤 **PO** M-F 9:15am-12:15pm & 1:15pm-4:15pm, Sa 7:30am-11am. 207-997-3975. 2 Greenville Rd. Monson ME 04464. N 45 17.167, W 69 30.026

🛏🏠🏕 **Shaw's Lodging** 207-997-3597. shawshikerhostel@gmail.com (www.shawshikerhostel.com)
◈✕🍴⛟ ◈ AT Passport location.
💻🏪🍴🚿 Open Mid-May through Oct.
🏠🚐📧 🏠 Bunks $25, 🛏 private room $50S $60D, 🏕 $12 tenting. Free pickup and return at Pleasant Street and Route 6 trail heads with stay. $9 breakfast, 🧺 $5 laundry, 🚿 $5 shower without stay and towel, 💻 computer available for use, 📶 free WiFi. Food drops.
Licensed and insured 🚐 slackpacking and 🚌 shuttles for all over Maine. Gear supplies include 🔥 Coleman and alcohol fuel by the ounce, canister fuel, Aquamira, 🍱 freeze dried and packaged food. Gear repair and shakedowns available. Credit cards accepted.
✉ Mail drops for guests (nonguests $5): PO Box 72 or 17 Pleasant St, Monson, ME 04464.

🛏🏠◈🍴 **Lakeshore House Lodging & Pub** 207-997-7069, 207-343-5033. (www.thelakeshorehouse.com)
✕🏕🚿💻 ◈ AT Passport location.
🏪📺🛶🏊 🏠 Bunkroom $25PP cash or $32.40PP with credit card. 🛏 Private rooms $45S/$60D w/shared bath.
🚐P📧 Microwaves, fridge, coffee maker available for hiker. 🍴 Ask about work for stay. Well behaved dogs okay. Reservations appreciated, packs out by 10:30am; full check-out/vacate by noon please, unless otherwise arranged. Free pickup and return from route 6 trail head for guests only, only till 11am for return, loaner clothing, 💻 loaner laptop available for use, 📶 free WiFi, 🛶 kayaks, paddleboat, 🏊 swimming, 📺 ATM. 🧺 Laundry $5 and 🚿 shower $5 available to non-guests. Pub hours: M closed, Tu-Sa 12pm-9pm, Su 12pm-9pm, bar open later. House quiet by 10pm and NO BINGE DRINKING, social drinking okay. Shaw's guests welcome for breakfast. Accepts credit cards. 🅿 Parking $1 per day.
✉ Mail drops for guests (non-guests $5): PO Box 215, C/O Lakeshore House, Monson, ME 04464 or UPS/FedEx (no Sat delivery): 9 Tenney Hill Rd.

🚗🚐 **Charlie Anderson** 207-965-5678, 207-997-7069 Statewide shuttles, slackpack, food drops, call for prices.

🍱✕ **Monson General Store** Deli & Grocery 207-997-3800. Features foods grown locally and local artisan products. ✕ DELI offers delicious freshly made items to eat in or take out. In addition to sandwiches, choose from a daily selection of salads, baked goods and other treats.

✕🍱📺 **A.E. Robinson's Convenience Store** 207-997-3700. ✕ **Country Cafe Deli** inside serves burgers, pizza, breakfast. 📺 ATM. M-Su 4am-10pm.

✕ **Spring Creek Bar-B-Q** 207-997-7025. (www.springcreekbar-b-qmaine.com) M-W closed, Th-Sa 11am-8pm, Sunday 11am-6pm.

■◈ **The Monson Appalachian Trail Visitor Center** monsonvisitorcenter@appalachiantrail.org(www. facebook.com/monsonatvisitorcenter).
◈ AT Passport location.
Open 7 days a week, early June 6 through mid October, from 8am-11am and 1pm-5pm. The Visitor Center is a critical source of information for long distance hikers, short term backpackers and day hikers on the trail in Maine. Northbound long distance hikers should stop in to make plans for entering and staying in Baxter State Park, climbing Katahdin and leaving the Trail. There will also be a small retail operation with souvenirs, maps and t-shirts available.

Greenville, ME 04485 (10.4W from ME 15)

🛏📶 **Kineo View Motor Lodge** 207-695-4470. (www.kineoview.com) 🛏 $79 and up-$99D, $10EAP includes continental breakfast, microwave, fridge, 📶 WiFi. From trail head (7.6) north on route 5 and right turn on Overlook Drive (0.4) up drive to Lodge.

✕ **Kelly's Landing** 207-695-4438. (www.kellysatmoosehead.com) M-Su 7am-9pm, Su offers AYCE breakfast.

✕ **Dairy Bar** ice cream

💊✕ **Harris Drug Store** 207-695-2921. Family owned and operated pharmacy serving the Moosehead Lake region since 1896. ✕ Also featuring an old fashioned soda fountain ,dining counter inside. M-Sa 8am-5:30pm, Su 9am-1pm.

🥾🛒 **Indian Hill Trading Post & Supermarket** 207-695-2104. (www.indianhill.com) M-Su 8am-8pm.

🍱 **Jamos Pizza** 207-695-2201. Pizza, sandwiches, take out, breakfast sandwiches, ice, groceries, Ben & Jerry's Ice Cream, beer and wine, local information. M-Th 5am-9pm, F-Sa 5am-10pm, Su 6am-9pm.

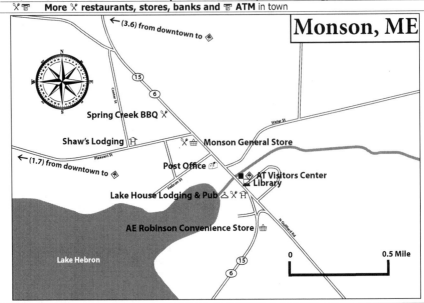

Northwoods Outfitters 207-695-3288. (www.maineoutfitter.com) Full service Gear supplier with pack's, Poles, Clothing and Footwear. Osprey, Thermarest, MSR, Leki, Patagonia, The Northface and many more. Cafe' inside- Espresso bar, pastries & free WiFi. M-Su 8am-5pm.

Charles Dean Memorial Hospital 207-695-5200. (www.cadean.org)
More restaurants, stores, banks and ATM in town

Monson, ME

← (3.6) from downtown to

Spring Creek BBQ

Shaw's Lodging

Monson General Store

← (1.7) from downtown to

Post Office

AT Visitors Center
Library

Lake House Lodging & Pub

AE Robinson Convenience Store

Lake Hebron

0   0.5 Mile

NoBo		Description	GPS	Elev	SoBo
2077.6	♦	Cross Goodell Brook, Spectacle Pond Outlet		1163	114.4
2078.4	▲	Cross **Old Stage Road**. Was once a stagecoach road to Greenville in the 1800's.		1295	113.6
2078.7	♦	South shore of Bell Pond .		1278	113.3
2078.8	⌐	Power line.		1337	113.2
2079.1	📷	Open ledges on ridge.		1438	112.9
2079.4	♦	Side trail leads to Lily Pond.		1130	112.6
2080.5	♦▲⊏(6) ⌣ℂ♀	**Leeman Brook Lean-to**, water (stream) is located in front of lean-to, tenting, privy.	N 45 21.096, W 69 29.921		111.5
		25.0◄20.9◄12.0◄►7.4►12.1►16.1		1060	
2081.3	♦	Cross stream from North Pond		1000	110.7
2081.7	▲	Cross **North Pond Tote Road**		1100	110.3
2082.7		Skirt Mud Pond.		1057	109.3
2083.0		Rim of Bear Pond Ledges		1200	109.0
2083.8	♦	Cross James Brook.		950	108.2
2084.0	▲	Cross gravel haul road.		1000	108.0
2084.1	♦📷	Little Wilson Falls, 60 ft. high. One of the highest falls on the AT.		850	107.9
2084.3	♦▲⌣	Ford Little Wilson Stream, ford, not an ATC approved camping spot.		750	107.7
2084.6		Cross 200 yard beaver dam.		929	107.4
2084.7	▲	Follow gravel road for 100 yds.		900	107.3
2085.2	📷	High point along (0.5) long slate ridge.		1152	106.8
2086.2		Deep rock gully.		806	105.8
2086.6	▲	Cross **Big Wilson Tote Road**.		620	105.4
2086.7	♦	Cross Thompson Brook.		620	105.3
2087.2	♦	Ford Big Wilson Stream.		600	104.8
2087.5	✕	Cross Montreal, Maine & Atlantic Railroad Tracks		850	104.5
2087.9	♦▲⊏(6) ⌣ℂ♀	42 yards west to **Wilson Valley Lean-to**, water small (spring) is located in front of the lean-to on the opposite side of the AT, tenting, privy.	N 45 23.878, W 69 27.606		104.1
		28.3◄19.4◄7.4◄►4.7►8.7►15.6		1000	
2088.5		Cross old winter logging road.		1190	103.5
2089.1	📷	Open ledges with views east and of Barren Mountain.		1278	102.9
2089.4	📷	Cross 150 yard rocky slope.		967	102.6
2090.7		Base of ridge.		681	101.3
2091.1	♦	Cross Wilber Brook.		660	100.9

NoBo	Features	Description	GPS	Elev	SoBo
2091.2	♦⌇	Cross Vaughn Stream, top of 20 ft. waterfall		670	100.8
2091.7	▲	Bodfish Farm–Long Pond tote road.		650	100.3
2091.8	♦	Ford Long Pond Stream, usually knee deep.		620	100.2
2092.5	♦Y⌇	Side Trail to Slugundy Gorge and Falls		870	99.5
2092.6	♦▲⌐(8) ⌣(♀	67 yards east to **Long Pond Stream Lean-to**, water from small spring, tenting, privy.	N 45 25.269, W 69 24.612	930	99.4
		24.1◄12.1◄4.7◄►4.0►10.9►20.8			
2092.7	YP(6)♀	Side trail east leads to parking area off Bodfish Valley Road.	N 45 24.818, W 69 25.014	1006	99.3
2093.7	Y☐	Side trail leads 250 feet to top of Barren Slide with good views.		2024	98.3
2093.9	☐	Barren Ledges with very good views of Bodfish Intervale, Lake Onawa and Borestone Mountain.		2022	98.1
2094.9		Base of Barren Mountain.		1942	97.1
2095.7	▲☐	Barren Mountain summit, remnants of old fire tower		2670	96.3
2096.6	♦Y▲ ⌐(6) ⌣(♀	(0.4E) **Cloud Pond Lean-to**, water small (stream) is located to the left of the lean-to, tenting, privy.	N 45 25.088, W 69 21.229		95.4
		16.1◄8.7◄4.0◄►6.9►16.8►24.0		2420	
2098.0	♦	Cross small stream.		1981	94.0
2098.3		Bog between Fourth and Barren Mountain.		2188	93.7
2098.7	▲☐	Fourth Mountain summit, wooded.		2383	93.3
2099.5	◊	Cross stream at bottom of sag, unreliable.		1844	92.5

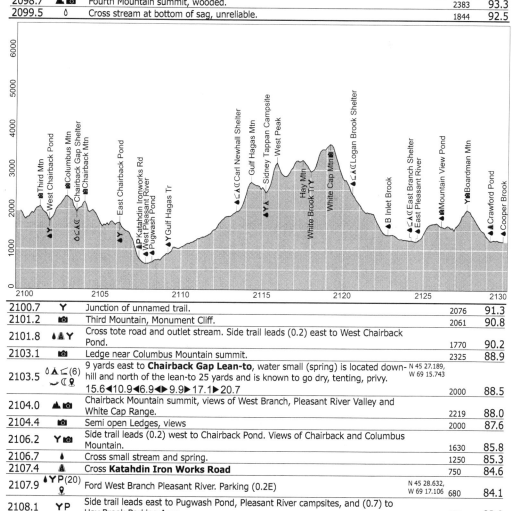

2100.7	Y	Junction of unnamed trail.		2076	91.3
2101.2	☐	Third Mountain, Monument Cliff.		2061	90.8
2101.8	♦▲Y	Cross tote road and outlet stream. Side trail leads (0.2) east to West Chairback Pond.		1770	90.2
2103.1	☐	Ledge near Columbus Mountain summit.		2325	88.9
2103.5	◊▲⌐(6) ⌣(♀	9 yards east to **Chairback Gap Lean-to**, water small (spring) is located downhill and north of the lean-to 25 yards and is known to go dry, tenting, privy.	N 45 27.189, W 69 15.743		88.5
		15.6◄10.9◄6.9◄►9.9►17.1►20.7		2000	
2104.0	▲☐	Chairback Mountain summit, views of West Branch, Pleasant River Valley and White Cap Range.		2219	88.0
2104.4	☐	Semi open Ledges, views		2000	87.6
2106.2	Y☐	Side trail leads (0.2) west to Chairback Pond. Views of Chairback and Columbus Mountain.		1630	85.8
2106.7	♦	Cross small stream and spring.		1250	85.3
2107.4	▲	Cross **Katahdin Iron Works Road**		750	84.6
2107.9	♦YP(20)♀	Ford West Branch Pleasant River. Parking (0.2E)	N 45 28.632, W 69 17.106	680	84.1
2108.1	YP	Side trail leads east to Pugwash Pond, Pleasant River campsites, and (0.7) to Hay Brook Parking Area.		680	83.9
2108.2		Side trail leads 200 feet to The Hermitage. **No camping permitted here.**		695	83.8
2109.2	♦Y	Junction with Gulf Hagas Loop Trail.		950	82.8

NoBo	Features	Description	GPS	Elev	SoBo
2109.9	♦Y	Junction with Gulf Hagas Cut-off Loop Trail leads (1.0) west joining up with Gulf Hagas Loop Trail.		1050	82.1
2113.4	◊▲⊏(6) ⊂♀	Cross Gulf Hagas Brook. 30 yards west to **Carl A. Newhall Lean-to**, water (Gulf Hagas Brook) is located south of shelter, tenting, privy.	N 45 31.866, W 69 18.907		
		20.8◄16.8◄9.9◄►7.2►10.8►18.9		1860	78.6
2114.3	▲	Gulf Hagas Mountain summit.		2683	77.7
2115.2	♦▲	Sidney Tappan campsite, (0.2) east to spring, tent sites available.		2425	76.8
2115.9	▲	West Peak summit		3178	76.1
2117.5	▲	Hay Mountain summit, wooded.		3244	74.5
2118.1	Y	Junction with White Brook Trail.		3125	73.9
2119.2	▲◙	White Cap Mountain summit, view of Katahdin.		3654	72.8
2120.2	◙	Side trail with lookout of Logon Brook Ravine.			71.8
2120.6	♦▲⊏(6) ⊂♀	**Logan Brook Lean-to**, water (Logan Brook) is located behind the lean-to and cascades are farther upstream, tenting, privy.	N 45 33.668, W 69 14.124		
		24.0◄17.1◄7.2◄►3.6►11.7►23.1		2480	71.4
2122.2	▲P	Cross **West Branch Ponds Road**, gravel	N 45 34.726, W 69 13.488	1650	69.8
2122.7	♦	Cross B Inlet Brook.		1438	69.3
2124.2	♦▲⊏(6) ⊂♀	**East Branch Lean-to**, water (Pleasant River) is located in front of lean-to, tenting, privy.	N 45 35.805, W 69 11.894		
		20.7◄10.8◄3.6◄►8.1►19.5►23.8		1225	67.8
2124.5	♦	Ford East Branch Pleasant River.		1200	67.5
2125.1	◙	View of White Cap Range.		1625	66.9
2126.1	♦	Cross Mountain View Pond outlet stream.		1597	65.9
2126.4	♦	Side trail east to spring.		1580	65.6
2126.9		Saddle between Big and Little Boardman Mountain.		1405	65.1
2127.7	Y◙	Little Boardman Mountain, 300 feet to summit		2017	64.3
2129.1	▲P(4)♀	Cross **Kokadjo-B Pond Road**, gravel	N 45 36.993, W 69 7.835	1380	62.9
2129.3	♦	Between two sand beaches on south shore of Crawford Pond. **No camping permitted here**.		1230	62.7

2130.0	♦	Cross Crawford Pond outlet. **No camping permitted here**.		1240	62.0
2132.3	♦▲⊏(6) ⌣⊂ ⚒♨♀	42 yards east to **Cooper Brook Falls Lean-to**, water (Cooper Brook) is located in front of lean-to, tenting, privy across trail and up hill. Water Falls in front of lean-to. Swimming hole in front of lean-to.	N 45 38.427, W 69 05.246		
		18.9◄11.7◄8.1◄►11.4►15.7►21.5		880	59.7
2132.5	♦	Cross Cooper Brook tributary.		833	59.5
2135.3	◙	Views of Church Pond can bee seen through trees.		681	56.7
2136.0	♦▲▲ P(10)♀ ★★★★★	Cross **Jo-Mary Road**, gravel.	N 45 39.040, W 69 01.841	625	56.0

Maine

NoBo	Features	Description	GPS	Elev	SoBo
	⚑⌇⚑⚐	(9.0E) **Jo-Mary Campground** 207-723-8117. Open mid May - Mid Sep. Two person minimun, ⚑ campsites $7 per person. ME residents $12. Pets welcome, ⚐ coin operated ♨ showers and laundry.			
2137.3	♦Y	Side trail leads (0.2) east to Cooper Pond.		600	54.7
2138.6	▲	Cross gravel logging road, snowmobile bridge over Cooper Brook nearby.		520	53.4
2138.9	♦⌇	Cross over east end of Mud Brook, Mud Pond Outlet on bridge		508	53.1
2139.5	▲	Cross logging road.		565	52.4
2140.2	♦▲⌇(	Side trail leads 100 yards to Antlers campsite, tent sites available, privy.		500	51.8
2141.4	♦	Cross brook. Treat water due to beaver activity.		574	50.6
2141.7	📷	Side trail leads (0.75) west to Potaywadjo Ridge with good views.		588	50.3
2141.9	♦⚒	Side trail leads 100 feet to Lower Jo-Mary Lake, sand beach, good swimming.		580	50.1
2143.7	♦▲⊏(8) ⌇(♨	31 yards west to **Potaywadjo Spring Lean-to**, water (Potaywadjo Spring) is located to the right of the lean-to, tent sites available, privy.	N 45 42.390, W 69 00.450		
		23.1◄19.5◄11.4◄►4.3►10.1►18.2		710	48.3
2144.2	♦⌇	Cross Twitchell Brook, bridge		590	47.8
2144.3	♦📷	Side trail leads 75 feet to shore of Pemadumcook Lake, views of Katahdin.		580	47.7
2145.5	♦	Cross Deer Brook.		588	46.5
2146.4	▲	Cross gravel logging road.		580	45.6
2146.5	Y ★★★★★	Cross Mahar Tote Logging Road, Blue-blazed trail 0.2E **White House Landing** pickup.		580	45.5
	⌂⛺◈ 🍴♨⚓⌇	**White House Landing** 207-745-5116. Open May 15. ◈ AT Passport location. Reservation recommended but not required. 1 night minimum for pickup and return to trail head area, arrival dates flexible. ⛺ Bunk $35PP, semi-private $45S, $85D. ♨ Shower, towel, pillow case included; linens extra. AYCE breakfast. 🍴 Dinner menu includes burgers, pizza and more. Can charge cell phones for a fee. ⚓ Free use of canoes. Credit cards accepted. NoBo's and SoBo's, consider staying here, enjoy all the amenities we offer, and receive your 100-Mile Wilderness supplies here as a free, (for guests only, secured, mail drop. Cached drops in the 100-Mile Wilderness are expensive, sometimes difficult to arrange and are prone to theft. Call with your cell, or use the 2-way radio at the dock, for a free pickup. ⌇ Mail drops for guests only: PO Box 1, Millinocket, ME 04462. Allow 10 days for drop to PO box.			
2146.6	♦	Cross branch of Nahmakanta Stream.		580	45.4
2147.5	♦	Cross Tumbledown Dick Stream.		590	44.5
2148.0	♦▲(6) ⊏(8)⌇(	400 feet west to **Nahmakanta Stream Lean-to**, water from the stream, 6 tent sites available.	N 45 43.974, W 69 05.755		
		23.8◄15.7◄4.3◄►5.8►13.9►25.4		600	44.0
2149.5	Y	Junction with Tumble Down Dick Trail.		625	42.5
2150.6	♦	Wood Rat's Spring		740	41.4
2150.9	▲	Cross gravel road.		749	41.1
2151.2	♦▲ P(6)♀	Cross gravel road. Nahmakanta Lake (south end).	N 45 44.155, W 69 06.218	650	40.8
2152.1	♦	Cross Prentiss Brook.		590	39.9
2152.7	♦	Gravel beach on lake shore.		668	39.3
2153.4	♦Y	Side trail leads 50 feet west to Sand Beach, east to spring		595	38.6
2153.7	♦	Cross Wadleigh Stream.		680	38.3
2153.8	◊▲⊏(6) ⌇(♀	40 yards west to **Wadleigh Stream Lean-to**, water (spring) is located on the beach, tenting, privy.	N 45 44.840, W 69 08.712		
		21.5◄10.1◄5.8◄►8.1►19.6►33.0		685	38.2
2154.5		Unusual rock formation with rock roof.		964	37.5
2155.7	▲Y📷	Nesuntabunt Mountain summit, side trail leads 250 feet to ledge overlooking Nesuntabunt Lake and views of Katahdin.		1520	36.3
2156.9	▲	Cross logging road.		1010	35.1
2157.5	♦	Crescent Pond (east end)		1014	34.5
2158.1	♦	Crescent Pond (west end)		980	33.9
2158.2	Y	Side trail leads to bottom of Pollywog Gorge.		1021	33.8
2158.5	📷	Side trail leads 150 feet to Pollywog Gorge, good view of gorge.		1050	33.5
2159.5	♦⌇▲ P(6)♀	Cross Pollywog Stream on logging road bridge.	N 45 46.775, W 69 10.336	682	32.5

Elevation profile chart with features labeled including: Murphy Stream, Rainbow Stream Shelter, Rainbow Lake, Rainbow Spring Campsite, Rainbow Mtn Tr, Rainbow Lake, Rainbow Ledges, Hurd Brook Shelter, Penobscot River/Golden Rd, Abol Stream Tr, Katahdin Stream, Foss & Knowlton Brook, Nesowadnehunk Stream, Big Niagara Falls, Little Niagara Falls, Daicey Pond Campground, Elbow Pond, Tracy Pond, Park Tote Rd, The Birches Shelter/Katahdin Stream Campground, Katahdin Stream Falls, Thoreau Spring, The Gateway, Mt Katahdin/AT Northern Terminus

Elevation markers: 2160, 2165, 2170, 2175, 2180, 2185, 2190

NoBo	Features	Description	GPS	Elev	SoBo
2160.2	📷	Flume in gorge, remains of old logging dam		1000	31.8
2161.5	⬧	Cross Murphy Pond Outlet Stream.		1020	30.5
2161.9	⬧▲⊑(6) ⌣℄♀	**Rainbow Stream Lean-to**, water (Rainbow Stream) is located in front of lean-to, tenting and hammocking, privy. 18.2◄13.9◄8.1◄► 11.5►24.9	N 45 47.945, W 69 10.260	1020	30.1
2162.1	⬧	Cross stream, Rainbow Deadwaters (south end).		1060	29.9
2163.7	⬧	Cross stream, Rainbow Deadwaters (north end).		1086	28.3
2163.9	⬧📷	Rainbow Lake (west end), dam on side trail with Katahdin view		1080	28.1
2165.7	⬧▲(2)℄	Rainbow Spring campsite, spring west 150 feet, 2 tent sites available, privy.		1100	26.3
2167.2	Y	Unmarked side trail.		1140	24.8
2167.4	Y	Side trail leads (0.75) east to Rainbow Mountain summit.		1100	24.6
2169.1	⬧	Rainbow Lake (east end)		980	22.9
2169.2	Y	Side trail leads (0.1) east to Little Beaver and (0.4) further to Big Beaver Ponds.		1100	22.8
2170.9	📷	Rainbow Ledges, open ledges with views of Katahdin.		1517	21.1
2173.4	⬧▲⊑(6) ℄♀	**Hurd Brook Lean-to**, water (Hurd Brook), tenting, privy. 25.4◄19.6◄11.5◄► 13.4	N 45 49.112, W 69 01.140	710	18.6
2174.1	⬧	Small spring.		740	17.9
2176.3		Pass through extensive cedar bog.		625	15.7
2176.7	▲	Junction with **Golden Road (Greenville-Millinocket Road)**		600	15.3
2176.9	⌢📷▲P ♀ ★★★★★	Parking area located between Abol Bridge and trail head. Many many parking spots. Cross Abol Bridge over West Branch of Penobscot River, junction with International A.T., Abol Bridge campground and Store **Millinocket, ME. (19.6E).**	N 45 50.112, W 68 58.158	588	15.1

PERMITS
Baxter State Park (Maine)
2019 Appalachian Trail Long Distance Hiker Permit: A free A.T. long distance hiker permit will be required of all long distance A.T. hikers: Northbound Thru-Hikers (Nobos), Southbound Thru-Hikers (Sobos), Flip-Flop Thru-Hikers and Section-hikers.

Long distance A.T. hikers must obtain a permit card in person at Katahdin Stream Campground when the A.T. (Hunt Trail) opens for hiking. Once hikers obtain a permit card they will need to have it stamped at the Katahdin Stream Ranger Station.

The number of AT-Hiker Permit Cards for 2018 are limited by a Baxter State Park quota: 3150 A.T. hikers. If all available permit cards have been issued for 2018, "The Birches" long distance hiker camp will close for the year. Hikers may complete their hike by obtaining a Day Use Parking Reservation (DUPR) (www.baxterstatepark.org/general-info/#reserve) or campground reservation (www.baxterstatepark.org/camp-summer/#reserve) and enter the Park through the Togue Pond Gate.

For more information, please visit the Baxter State Park webpage and ATC's Baxter FAQs, which can be found at www.appalachiantrail.org/updates.

-Thru-Hiker Campsite Fees: Those hiking the A.T. and walking more than 100 miles continuously on foot before entering the park are eligible to stay at The Birches site, but must still pay a camping fee. If the site is full, hikers must wait for space to become available.
-Non-Long Distance Hiker Campsite Fees: To camp overnight, a reservation is required and a fee is charged.
-Car Parking Reservation: To access Baxter State Park by vehicle for a day-hike, a day use parking reservation is strongly recommended, as there are a finite number of parking spots. Once all parking spots are full, you cannot enter the park.
-To make parking or camping reservations, (www.baxterstatepark.org/)

Abol Bridge Campground & Store 207-447-5803. (www.mainewoodsresorts.com
Open summer (May-Sept),
Campsites $25pp includes breakfast buffet. Bunk cabin $75 for 2, $25 each additional sleeps up to 6. Store hours M-Su 7am-7pm.
Full store with subs, sodas, ice cream, long-term resupply.
Coin laundry. Free showers, non-guests $5. Satellite Pay phone available.
Visa/MC accepted.

The Northern Restaurant, full service restaurant with full bar onsite open mid-June to end of Sept 11am-7pm.
Mail drops: $10 mail drop fee, and call before sending, and send well in advance: P.O. Box 536 Millinocket, ME 04462.

Abol Pines $8 ME residents $4, self register tent sites and shelters. Located across the street from Abol Bridge Store.

Connie McManus 207-723-6795, 207-731-3111 Privately run kennel service; pickup and drop off at Abol Bridge.

Millinocket, ME 04462 (19.6E) from Abol Bridge. See map of Millinocket, ME.
PO M-F 9am - 4pm, Sa 9am - 11:30am, Sun Closed. 207-723-5921. 113 Penobscot Ave. Millinocket ME 04462. N 45 39.303, W 68 42.524

The Appalachian Trail Lodge 207-723-4321. (www.appalachiantraillodge.com)
AT Passport location.
No pets. Bunkroom $25, private room $55, family suite $95D $10EAP. Showers for non-guests $5. Coin laundry. Computer available for use, free WiFi. Free daily shuttle from Baxter State Park from Sept 1-Oct 24, between 3:30pm–4:30pm. Licensed and insured shuttle service for hire to and from bus in Medway, into 100-Mile Wilderness or Monson, food drops. Slackpack in 100-Mile Wilderness, other shuttles by arrangement, P free parking. Southbound special: pickup in Medway, bed in bunkroom, breakfast at AT Cafe, and shuttle to Katahdin Stream Campground. $70 per person, by reservation.
Mail drops for guests only: 33 Penobscot Avenue, Millinocket, ME 04462.
Ole Man's Gear Shop Full line of gear; ULA & Hyperlite packs, bags, fuel, stoves, poles. No clothing or shoes.

The Appalachian Trail Café 207-723-6720.
AT Passport location.
Serves breakfast and lunch. M-Su 5am-2pm.

Katahdin Cabins 207-723-6305. (www.katahdincabins.com)
No Pets.
Skip & Nicole Mohoff run eco-friendly cabins with continental breakfast, TV, DVD, microwave, fridge. $65 up to 3 persons, $85 up to 5.
Cafe' on site with coffee and baked goods. No smoking. Gas grill, bikes free for use, community room. WiFi. Accepts Credit cards cash and checks.
Mail drops for guests: 181 Medway Rd, Millinocket, ME 04462.

Parks Edge Inn 207-447-4321, 207-227-2692. Rooms for guests ranging from $65 to $150. Large capacity rooms sleep 6-8. All rooms have kitchen, bath, TV, DVD players, free WiFi. Mail drops for guests with reservations: 19 Central St, Millinocket, ME 04462.

Pamola Motor Lodge 800-575-9746. (http://www.pamolalodge.com) $69 and up $10EAP up to 4, prices vary depending on season, includes continental breakfast, A/C, free WiFi. Pets $10. Restaurant on site.

Baxter Park Inn 207-723-9777. (www.baxterparkinn.com) $99 and up, prices vary depending on season, $10EAP, pets $25, sauna, pool, free WiFi.

Ice Fish Inn 207-723-9999. (www.icefishinn.com) $115 and up, prices vary dependingon season, includes full hot breakfast ($15 off with out breakfast). WiFi. Mail drops for guests: PO Box 136, Millinocket, ME 04462.

Hotel Terrace & Ruthie's Restaurant 207-723-4545. $64.95S, $74.95D, free WiFi. Ruthie's; serves breakfast, lunch and dinner.

Katahdin Inn 207-723-4555. (www.katahdininnandsuites.com) Room rates starting from $94.99/night for two people, includes continental breakfast, indoor heated pool, hot tub, computer available to use, free WiFi, coin laundry, pool tables.

Wilderness Edge Campground 207-447-8485. (www.wildernessedgecampground.com) Open May 15-Oct 15 (weather permitting) Tent sites $12pp,with free hot showers for thru hikers. Pool (Memorial Day thru Labor Day). Fuel canisters. Shuttle Service available for a fee. Coin operated laundry, soap available at store for $1.00. Free Wifi . Camp Store with bug repellant, soap, toothbrushes, drinks, candy, ice cream, map, souvenirs, etc. RV sites $39.95 for 2 adults. RV sites have water & electric hookups. Dump station on site. Dump station privilege for non-campers $10. Arrangements can be made ahead of time to meet hikers when they exit the 100 mile wilderness or summit Katahdin or to get them to the bus depot in East Millinocket.

Sawmill Grill 207-447-6996. (www.sawmillbargrill.com) M closed, Open Tu-Sun 11am-11pm in summer. Pizza, spaghetti sandwiches, burgers.

LanMan's Lounge AT Passport location. 28 Hill St. Lounge with TV, restroom; pack storage $5.

Maine Quest Adventures 207-447-5011. (www.mainequestadventures.com) Will shuttle and pick up anywhere, Medway bus station, Katahdin Stream, Abol Bridge, 100 Mile Wilderness, he means anywhere. Also does Food Drops for by arrangement.

Bull Moose Taxi 207-447-8079. Medway to Millinocket $18, Millinocket to KSC $57. Fares are per ride, $1 EAP up to 4 persons. Covers all of Maine. M-Su 6am-2am.

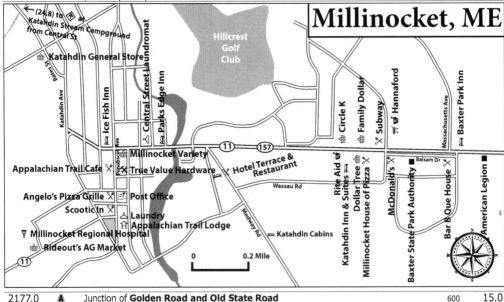

2177.0		Junction of **Golden Road and Old State Road**	600	15.0
2177.3		Junction of gravel and paved roads.	600	14.7
2177.5		Ski trail leads (1.0) east to Abol Pond on old road.	611	14.5
2177.6		Abol Stream Trail, Abol Stream, Baxter Park Boundary, bridge, ski trail	620	14.4
2177.8		BSP Hiker Kiosk, registration for "The Birches campsite"; Abol Pond & Blueberry Ledges trails	620	14.2
2178.0		Katahdin Stream, bridge	620	14.0

NoBo	Features	Description	GPS	Elev	SoBo
2178.1	Y	Foss and Knowlton Ponds Trail		630	13.9
2178.5	⬩	Cross small brook.		618	13.5
2178.8	⬩⌒	Cross Foss and Knowlton Brook on bog bridge.		625	13.2
2181.0	⬩Y	Pine Point. Side trail east is high water bypass trail.		640	11.0
2181.4	⬩	Ford Lower Fork Nesowadnehunk Stream.		630	10.6
2182.4	⬩	Ford Upper Fork Nesowadnehunk Stream.		800	9.6
2182.5		Upstream ledges.		778	9.5
2182.8	⬩	Big ledge above Rocky Rips		850	9.2
2183.2	⬩Y♿📷	Side trail leads west 150 feet to Big Niagara Falls.		850	8.8
2183.4	⬩	Side trail leads 150 feet east to spring.		990	8.6
2183.5	Y♿	Side trail leads 150 feet west to Toll Dam and Little Niagara Falls.		1030	8.5
2184.3	Y☾	Junction with Daicey Pond Nature Trail.		1090	7.7
2184.4		Daicey Pond Campground and Ranger Station.		1114	7.6
2184.5	⛺P⚇	Daicey Pond campground Road, side trail leads to Sentinel Mountain.	N 45 52.945, W 68 1.904	1100	7.5
2185.0	Y	Junction with Tracy and Elbow Ponds Trail.		1100	7.0
2185.5	⬩	Junction with Grassy Pond Trail.		800	6.5
2185.7	⬩⌒	Cross Elbow Pond on bridge.		1103	6.3
2185.8	⬩⌒	Cross Tracy Pond on bridge, views of O-J-I and Doubletop Mountains.		1092	6.2
2186.0	⛺P⚇	**Perimeter Road** (south end), tote road.	N 45 53.446, W 68 0.566	1101	6.0
2186.7	⛺	**Perimeter Road** (north end), tote road.		1070	5.3
2186.8	⬩⛺ ⌂(12) ⛺P⚇ ★★★★★	Katahdin Stream campground, Ranger Station; (0.24E) **The Birches campsite**, Overnight fee. Advance reservations 33.0◀24.9◀13.4◀	N 45 53.231, W 68 59.991	1070	5.2

Millinocket, ME 04462 (24.8E) from Katahdin Stream Campground. See NoBo mile 2176.9. See map of Millinocket, ME.

NoBo	Features	Description	GPS	Elev	SoBo
2187.8	Y	Junction with The Owl Trail.		1570	4.2
2187.9	⬩⌒	Cross Katahdin Stream on footbridge.		1500	4.1
2188.0	⬩♿📷	Side trail leads 50 feet west to Katahdin Stream Falls.		1550	4.0
2188.9	◊	Cross small brook, unreliable.		2721	3.1
2189.5		"The Cave", small slab cave		4500	2.5
2189.6	📷	Hunt Spur, tree line at base of "The Boulders"		3400	2.4
2190.4	📷	Gateway to Tablelands		4600	1.6
2191.0	⬩	Thoreau Spring		4627	1.0
2192.0	📷	Katahdin, Baxter Peak, sign, plaque, cairn.		5268	0.0

AntiGravity Gear	910-794-3308	www.antigravitygear.com
Arc 'Teryx	866-458-BIRD	www.arcteryx.com
Asics	800-678-9435	www.asicsamerica.com/footwear/
Asolo/Lowe Alpine	603-448-8827, ext. 105	www.asolo.com
	800-490-4502	
Backcountry	800-953-5499	www.backcountry.com/
Big Agnes	877-554-8975	www.bigagnes.com
Black Diamond Equipment	877-554-8975	www.blackdiamondequipme nt.com/
Camelbak	877-404-7673	www.camelbak.com
Campmor	800-226-7667	www.campmor.com
Camp Trails	800-345-7622	www.camptrails.eu/
Cascade Designs/		
MSR/Therm-a-Rest/Platypus	800-531-9531	www.cascadedesigns.com
Cedar Tree (packa)	276-780-2354	www.thepacka.com
Cnoc Outdoors	503-446-6000	www.cnocoutdoors.com/
Columbia	800-622-6953	www.columbia.com
Danner	877-432-6637	www.danner.com
	802-444-1800	
Darn Tuff Socks	877-327-6883 - toll free	www.darntough.com/
Dutch Ware gear	717-947-7849	www.dutchwaregear.com
Eastern Mountain		
Sports(EMS)	888-463-6367	www.ems.com
Elemental horizons	919-280-5402	www.elementalhorizons.com/
Elightened Equipment	507-474-6225	www.enlightenedequipment.com
Etowah Outfitters	770-975-7829	www.etowahoutfittersultralightbackpackinggear.com/
Eureka	888-6EUREKA	www.eurekacampingctr.com
Ex Officio	800-644-7303	www.exofficio.com
Farm to Feet	336-783-6043	www.injinji.com/
Feathered Friends	206-292-2210	www.featheredfriends.com
Frogg Toggs	800-349-1835	www.froggtoggs.com
Garmin	800-800-1020	ww.garmin.com
Garmont	800-943-4453	www.garmont.com/en
Gossamer Gear	512-374-0133	www.gossamergear.com
Golite	888-546-5483	www.golite.com/
Gossamer gear	512-374-0133	www.gossamergear.com/
Granite Gear	218-834-6157	www.granitegear.com
Gregory Mountain		
Products	877-477-4292	www.gregorypacks.com
	800-521-1698	
Hi-Tec US	209-545-1111	www.hi-tec.com/us/
Hyperlite Mountain		
Gear	800-464-9208	www.hyperlitemountaingear.com
Inoveight	508-480-8856	www.inov-8.com/
Jacks 'R' Better	757-643-8908	www.jacksrbetter.com
Jansport	800-552-6776	www.jansport.com/
Katadyn/PUR	800-755-6701	www.katadyn.com
Keen	866-676-5336	www.keenfootwear.com/
	866-349-7225	
Kelty Pack, Inc.	800-535-3589	www.kelty.com
Lawson Equipment		www.lawsonequipment.com/
Leki	800-255-9982, ext 150	www.leki.com
Lightheart Gear		www.lightheartgear.com/
L.L.Bean	800-441-5713	www.llbean.com
Lowe Alpine		
Systems	303-926-7228	www.lowealpine.com
Marmot	888-357-3262	www.marmot.com
Merrell	800-288-3124	www.merrell.com
Mont-bell	303-449-5331	www.montbell.com
Montrail	855-698-7245	www.montrail.com
Moonbow Gear	603-744-2264	www.moonbowgear.com
Mountain		
Hardwear	877-927-5649	www.mountainhardwear.com
Mountain Laurel	540-588-1721	www.mountainlaureldesigns.com/
Mountainsmith	800-426-4075, ext. 2	www.mountainsmith.com
MSR	800-531-9531	www.cascadedesigns.com/msr
Mystery Ranch	406-585-1428	www.mysteryranch.com/
NEMO Equipment	800-997-9301	www.nemoequipment.com/
New Balance	800-595-9138	www.newbalance.com/
The North Face	855-500-8639	www.thenorthface.com
Oboz tail shoes	406-522-0319	www.obozfootwear.com
Osprey	866-284-7830	www.osprey.com
Outdoor Research	888-467-4327	www.outdoorresearch.com

Manufacturers

Patagonia	800-638-6464	www.patagonia.com
Peak 1/Coleman	800-835-3278	www.coleman.com/
Petzl	877-807-3805	www.petzl.com
Photon	877-584-6898	www.photonlight.com
Platypus	800-531-9531	www.platy.com/
Primus	888-546-2267	www.primusstoves.com
Princeton Tec	609-298-9331	www.princetontec.com
REI	800-426-4840	www.rei.com
Royal Robbins	800-587-9044	www.royalrobbins.com
Salomon	800-654-2668	www.salomonsports.com
Sea to Summit		www.seatosummitusa.com/
Sierra Designs	800-736-8592	www.sierradesigns.com
Sierra Trading Post	800-713-4534	www.sierratradingpost.com
Six Moon Designs	503-430-2303	www.sixmoondesigns.com
Slumberjack	800-233-6283	www.slumberjack.com
Speer Hammocks	252-619-8292	www.tttrailgear.com
SOTO Outdoors	503-314-5119	www.sotooutdoors.com
Speer Hammocks	252-619-8292	www.tttrailgear.com/
Spot	866-651-7768	www.findmespot.com/en/
	855-258-0900	
Suunto	800-543-9124	www.suunto.com
Tarptent by Henry Shires	650-587-1548	www.tarptent.com
Teva/Deckers Corporation	800-367-8382	www.teva.com
The Underwear Guys/Warm Stuff	570-573-0209	www.theunderwearguys.com/www.warmstuff.com
Toaks	805-300-7685	www.toaksoutdoor.com/
ULA-Equipment	435-753-5191	www.ula-equipment.com
Vasque	800-224-4453	www.vasque.com
Western Mountaineering	408-287-8944	www.westernmountaineering.com
Zpacks		www.zpacks.com
ZZManufacturing (Zipztove)	800-594-9046	www.zzstove.com

Planning

Planning and preparing for hiking the Appalachian Trail curtails a lot. Every person is different. Some want to hike with the lightest gear they can find. Some are warm weather people and want to carry gear that will keep them warmer than others. Other want to dehydrate their own food, others will mail drop food to themselves or buy food along the way. Then there is the dilemma of what tent should you take or should you take a hammock. There is a lot to planning and hiking on the Appalachian Trail. I could go on and on and on about this but each person is different. You can ask and research some of this on web sites like www.whiteblaze.net.

I think the most important part of hiking on the Appalachian Trail is the mental preparation which is discussed next.

Mental Preparation

I have offered my opinion to prospective thru hikers for years, explaining that the trail is more mental than physical. Kyle Rohrig talks about mental preparedness in his book titled "Hear the Challenge... Hike the Appalachian Trail". I have paraphrased a portion of it and I believe his explanation is real good.

Completing an Appalachian Trail thru-hike is a major undertaking.

For completing a thru-hike (completing the whole trail in a calendar year) it is usually about 10% physical and 90% mental. You've got the gear, you've got the money, but do you have the mental toughness/strength and tenacity needed to achieve your goal? Once you get out there you can be sure to expect pain, misery, discomfort, and suffering within a wide range of varying degrees (do not let this scare or intimidate you). Some of your gear, as well as how much money you brought will sometimes play a part in how little or how much of this you endure (in some areas). In other areas, nothing will save you from some of the more unpleasant experiences of the Appalachian Trail. When these unpleasant experiences occur, what will you do? Will you break and quit? Or will you rise to the occasion, bend with your circumstances and adapt accordingly to any and all obstacles as you encounter them? Yes, your mind, attitude, and outlook will be the deciding factor on whether you complete your epic endeavor or not.

Mental Toughness "Mental Toughness:" is something you're going to need a great deal of when it comes to completing your thru-hike. In its most basic definition, mental toughness is the voice in the back of your head that tells you "keep going, don't give up, you can't quit now." While out on the trail, you're going to have A LOT of internal dialogue with yourself, possibly more than you've ever had in your entire life. The big question is... what will the tone of that internal dialogue be? Will it be mostly negative or positive? Will you be trying to talk yourself "into quitting" or "out of quitting?" Will you be counting the reasons to "stay on" trail, or reasons to "get off" trail? Your internal dialogue while on the trail will play a huge part in your mental state; in turn, directly influencing your chances of victory.

Besides the internal dialogue that you will be having with yourself nearly every solitary second spent out there, you will have a large amount of other factors that will evoke responses from your mental/emotional state. One of the greatest markers of mental toughness is the ability to control your emotions. Not "control" so much in the sense of repressing them, but in understanding them. If you're not in control of your emotions, then they're in control of you. Being able to realize and understand why you feel a certain way, but still be able to make rational decisions despite how you may feel is HUGE. I cannot emphasize that point enough. So many people make snap/impulse decisions based on how they feel at the present moment; they seldom stop to think, "Why do I really feel this way?" or "Is this really the best thing to do at this exact moment?"

This sort of mental toughness comes into play when you're thinking about quitting. There are many things that will make you question your decision to thru-hike and possibly consider quitting; things like physical pain, misery, suffering brought on by the elements, missing home, missing loved ones, missed expectations, becoming bored, or thoughts of, "I'll never make it." Thoughts are strong, but feelings are stronger. Your feelings of discomfort, boredom, or pain in the present moment can mislead your thoughts into making irrational decisions that have long term consequences/effects. You can lie to yourself with your thoughts, but your feelings will always be true, yet less in your control. This is why being able to understand and control your feelings to a certain extent is so important. You need to be able to use your thoughts clearly when your temporary feelings of the present moment may be clouding your judgment. To put it in better perspective; pain, misery, depression, discomfort, etc. are all "feelings" that can very rapidly lead to low morale and the decision to quit. There's no getting around the fact that you will experience these feelings at some point during your journey, if not many times throughout. Once these feelings arise, they're going to be accompanied by thoughts - the voice inside your head that interprets those feelings. Are your thoughts going to feed into the negative aspects of your feelings, subsequently initiating a downward spiral? Or will you keep a focused, level headed handle on your thoughts... understand and accept your feelings for whatever they may be, then use them to get through whatever outward or inward obstacle you may be facing? Don't let your thoughts defeat you on account of your feelings. Pain, misery, bad weather, tough terrain; none of it lasts forever - so don't make a decision that does. Remember, "This too shall pass."

When you've gone out there to attempt a thru-hike, it's safe to say that you "wanted it" pretty badly. At some point in your life you decided you wanted to hike over 2,000 miles and accomplish one of the great feats and adventures our planet has to offer. However, in order to seize that goal, you'll have to want it more than anything else in the world, before and during the endeavor. You know that deep inside yourself, completing the Appalachian Trail is what you want. So, what is the only thing (besides injury and running out of money) that can possibly stop you from achieving your desire of a completed thru-hike? The answer is YOU. You are the only one who can stop yourself from reaching your goal. Completing an Appalachian Trail thru-hike is as simple as not quitting. Don't quit, no matter what, and your dream is as good as realized.

So, let us delve deeper into things that make people quit, as well as why someone would make the decision to quit. The most blatant explanation for quitting in almost any circumstance would undoubtedly be "rationalization." We humans are rational creatures, and we can rationalize just about anything in order to make it make sense to us, or seem like the right thing to do. You can rationalize positive things, as well as negative things. If you put your mind to it, you can rationalize pretty much any decision you could ever make to seem like the right or wrong decision. It all depends on whichever one you "feel" is more beneficial to you at the present moment. Pain and suffering (feelings!) do funny things to the human brain. It can cause you to rationalize decisions you "think" you really want to make, when in fact you really don't. Rationalization is so powerful that when you're under stress and pain, you can actually convince yourself that finishing your Appalachian thru-hike is something you never truly wanted. Maybe this is true, but more often than not, you're only fooling yourself. You don't decide to hike over 2,000 miles and not have really wanted it at some point. When do most people realize they rationalized a lie to themselves when they decided quitting was the best decision to make (at whatever time they decided to make it)? That moment of regret is when they realize they deceived themselves. They made a decision in the heat of the moment that they didn't actually believe in, and then regretted it very shortly afterward. Once they're away from the pain and suffering of the moment, and able to think clearly, they realize, "What was I thinking? I really did want to complete this adventure! Why did I talk myself out of it and quit!?" Mental toughness will help you to avoid rationalizing "heat of the moment" decisions you will later regret. It is the ability to look past your present suffering to realize you will most likely regret any decisions to quit, thus deterring you from quitting; this ability is part of what demonstrates an aspect of your mental toughness.

Portions taken from - Hear the Challenge, Hike the Appalachian Trail

By

Kyle S. Rohrig

Keeping a journal during your hike or thru hike

If you are thinking about keeping a journal during your hike, I highly recommend it. Keeping a journal is something that you will never regret and will greatly appreciate later on in life. As the days and years go by after the conclusion of your hike your memories get a little vague and fuzzy on how events happened and what took place during your hike. Time has a way of making us forget things. Keeping a journal of some type will allow you to go back and recapture all those memories and feelings that you experienced. Your journal is a souvenir to your future self. You will be able to look back and smile and laugh when you reread it, a truly priceless gift. It will also anchor you to where you were at a given point in time, on and off the trail during your hike.

I find myself going back and looking at my journals to see where I was on a certain date during my hike and end up reading through the entire day's entry. It brings my mind back to the places I was and sometimes just reading that journal entry reminds me of things I forgot to include. The journal was such a great gift to myself.

Getting into the habit of writing it down

Start your journal before your hike. Try to get yourself in the habit before you start your hike by doing a journal entry daily. This will help you get into the routine of keeping a journal. During your hike, you can write in it any time you want, as the thought or the occurrence happens or whenever the moment strikes you. Remember this is your journal; write in it when you want or as much as you want. (I did mine at the end of the day before I went to bed, that was what worked best for me.). I also stopped at times during my hike and wrote notes in it to remind me of things to write.

Finding the time during your hike

Find the time to write in your journal is the most important tip of all. If you do not get into the routine of writing in your journal regularly, you will find yourself skipping a day here and a day there. Next thing you know you will be skipping a whole week. Try to commit or program yourself to write to it daily, or do some form of regular writing. You should not make writing in your journal a chore; rather make it something you want to do. Find a way to make it enjoyable. A journal can be a helpful way to wind down at the day's end, especially if it's a comfortable place for you. Use your camera to take lots of pictures of something to help you remember what went on during the day or what your thoughts were at that time.

Don't fuss about grammar, spelling, or other imperfections. You need to write it down while it is still fresh in your memory. You can always go back and fix the grammar and spelling later. Wanting to erase errors while working through the day's events and your thoughts and ideas can hamper your flow. Pretend you are with a group of friends that were not with you during the day and you are telling them all the details and events of what went on during that day. Write in your journal anything you want. Doodles are totally acceptable. Lyrics to songs, poems, book excerpts, anything goes. Remember this is your journal, write whatever you want.

Always remember to date your entries and your location!

Notes for using any cell phone

I know hikers that used cell phones for their journals. They worked well for them but the biggest complaint from them was their batteries were always going dead. When you're not using your phone either turn off the phone or place it into airplane mode. Putting it into airplane mode will turn your phone off from trying to find cell phone towers. That is the biggest battery drain your phone will experience when you are hiking. When your phone is on it is constantly looking for a cell phone tower to lock onto and if it is not locked onto a tower it will continue to look for one until it finds one. Roaming is the biggest battery drain your phone will most likely experience. This is the reason to either turn it off or place it in airplane mode when not using it. Off is most likely better.

Date:

Date:

Date:

Date:

Date:

Date:

Date:

Date:

About the author:

Rick "Attroll" Towle

Rick's love for the Appalachian Trail began in the early 1980's. It became a focus of attention for him, filling his dreams, both day and night, prompting him to acquire, moderate, and improve, two web sites: www.whiteblaze.net and www.hammockforums. net, successfully developing them into two of the worlds's most-visited and informative backpacking and hiking websites. Rick achieved his goal of thru-hiking the entire Appalachian Trail in 2010.

A good friend once told him that he was a good example of what Mark Twain said:

"...I never let my schooling get in the way of my education..."

Rick has combined his hiking skills, website development knowledge, and computer expertise, with extensive research and data collection, to compile, and incorporate, accurate, up-to-date trail information, reliable GPS data, and detailed maps, into White-Blaze Pages, the most informative and user-friendly Appalachian Trail guidebook ever published!!!